April 1977

Stephen Chambers

THE
ATHENIAN EMPIRE

THE
ATHENIAN
EMPIRE

——

RUSSELL MEIGGS

OXFORD
AT THE CLARENDON PRESS

Oxford University Press, Ely House, London W. 1

GLASGOW NEW YORK TORONTO MELBOURNE WELLINGTON
CAPE TOWN IBADAN NAIROBI DAR ES SALAAM LUSAKA ADDIS ABABA
DELHI BOMBAY CALCUTTA MADRAS KARACHI LAHORE DACCA
KUALA LUMPUR SINGAPORE HONG KONG TOKYO

ISBN 0 19 814296 x

© *Oxford University Press 1972*

First published 1972
Reprinted with corrections 1973, 1975

Printed in Great Britain
at the University Press, Oxford
by Vivian Ridler
Printer to the University

To my pupils
V S L M

PREFACE

WHEN I studied Greek history as an undergraduate at Oxford nearly fifty years ago it was reasonable to think that nothing significantly new could be written about the Athenian Empire. Thucydides' dark picture of the character of Athenian control was generally accepted, and what little could be gleaned from the sources about the methods employed by Athens had been exhausted. There seemed little prospect of important new evidence being found and, though nothing would put a stop to articles on the Peace of Callias, and though military campaigns could always be rewritten, the nineteenth century had apparently said all that could be said about the central issues.

The first signs of new life came with the masterly work of Meritt and West, who in a series of brilliant studies succeeded in determining the relative positions of all the fragments of the pre-war tribute lists, without which their use by the historian had been hazardous in the extreme. Their reconstruction of the first two stelai marked the beginning of an epoch and became even more fruitful when the American excavations in the Agora yielded an unexpected crop of inscriptions, many of which threw new light on Athenian imperialism. The fruits of their work were garnered in the four volumes of *The Athenian Tribute Lists*, in which Meritt was joined by Wade-Gery and by McGregor, who had worked closely with West and became his successor when West was tragically killed in a road accident. The title of their work is too modest, for they included in their province a wide range of evidence, especially epigraphic, which was only very indirectly related to the tribute lists. Their third volume, indeed, will remain the basic foundation for any comprehensive study of the empire.

The first draft of this book was begun in February 1961, the completed text was delivered in March 1970. In the long interval the text had to face strong competition from a full teaching programme, much enjoyed, and the dubious charms of essential administration, stoically endured. The sixties, however, were years of fertile controversy and I probably gained rather than lost by the delay. Since parting with my manuscript, however, there has been an embarrassing outpouring of books and articles that bear directly on the topics I have discussed. As there is too much substance in them for piecemeal patching I have left my text unaltered and added a supplementary bibliography of contributions that I have read since March 1970, with a note to outline their effects on some of my views.

During the ten years of incubation I have had much help from many people. Tony Andrewes read through an untidy manuscript in its penultimate stage, and his judicious admixture of criticism and comfort was psychologically invaluable. I have also profited considerably from discussions with David Lewis, and have to thank them both for two books which have made a major contribution to my study. The revised edition of Hill's *Sources for Greek History*, in spite of occasional carelessness, is a most useful collection of evidence, and the recent publication of *Greek Historical Inscriptions* has saved me from holding up the narrative with indigestible discussions of individual documents. Colin Kraay has been my main adviser on numismatic problems, and such use as I have made of the evidence from coins is largely due to his generous help; I am, however, particularly anxious that he should feel free to disown anything that I have written about coins.

My debt to my pupils of many generations is of a different kind, but very real. They have stifled many wild heresies before they could grow wings, and have been my keenest critics, without damping my enthusiasm. Indirectly at least they will be responsible for some of my mistakes. A few names must serve for many. Kenneth Dover has always found time to answer my questions patiently and authoritatively, and John Barron has been my liaison with the world of archaeology. Kenneth Cavander has contributed two lively translations. Glen Bowersock, Alan Hall, Jonathan Barnes, and Robin Law gave useful advice on form and substance in the middle years and at the end Thomas Braun helped in the correction of proofs and improved my text at many points. In the first year of my retirement it is appropriate that I should dedicate this book to these and my other pupils of many years.

Towards the end of my work it was necessary for me to make

the Epigraphic Museum in Athens a second home. I am very grateful to the Craven Committee who made it easier for me to settle in Athens during two summers, and to M. Mitsos and D. Peppa Delmousou, successive directors, whose kindness in the Museum enabled me to make the best use of my time. These visits to Athens also enabled me to discuss my problems with a wider range of scholars of different background. Homer Thompson did his generous best to modify my ignorance of building techniques, and stimulating sessions with Sterling Dow, Kendrick Pritchett, Eugene Vanderpool, and Alexander Fuks also helped to offset the rigours of the search for three-barred sigmas.

My wife has throughout been my production manager, sheltering me from unnecessary interruptions, releasing me from all but a minimum of domestic duties, and sending me off alone to Greece. In the last phase particularly she combined encouragement with discipline most astutely. Without her this would never have become a book, and we both have a special debt to Rosamund Broadley, who struggled heroically with handwriting that even its author finds challenging. For my helpers in the Clarendon Press my movements through 1970 and 1971 have been a tiresome complication, but their letters to Greece, America, and Mexico have been unfailingly polite and helpful.

The authors of *The Athenian Tribute Lists* have generously allowed me to use their map to illustrate the tribute districts of the empire, and for this I am very grateful. I am even more grateful for the material and incentive which their work provided for mine.

R. M.

Garsington
July 1971

CONTENTS

MAPS

(at end of book)

ABBREVIATIONS

AFD	B. D. Meritt, *Athenian Financial Documents of the Fifth Century*, Ann Arbor, 1932.
AJA	*American Journal of Archaeology.*
AJP	*American Journal of Philology.*
AM	*Mitteilungen des deutschen archäologischen Instituts: Athenische Abteilung.*
Ant. Class.	*L'Antiquité classique.*
Arch. Anz.	*Archäologischer Anzeiger: Beiblatt zum Jahrbuch des archäologischen Instituts.*
ATL	*The Athenian Tribute Lists*, by B. D. Meritt, H. T. Wade-Gery, and M. F. McGregor, 4 vols., Cambridge (Mass.), i, Princeton, ii–iv, 1939–53.
BCH	*Bulletin de correspondance hellénique.*
BSA	*Annual of the British School at Athens.*
CAH	*The Cambridge Ancient History*, Cambridge, 1923– .
Class. Journ.	*Classical Journal.*
CP	*Classical Philology.*
CQ	*Classical Quarterly.*
CR	*Classical Review.*
DAA	A. E. Raubitschek, *Dedications from the Athenian Akropolis*, Cambridge (Mass.), 1949.
DAT	B. D. Meritt, *Documents on Athenian Tribute*, Cambridge (Mass.), 1937.
Ehrenberg Studies	*Ancient Society and Institutions*: Studies presented to Victor Ehrenberg on his seventy-fifth birthday, Oxford, 1966.
FGH	F. Jacoby, *Die Fragmente der griechischen Historiker*, Berlin and Leyden, 1923– .
Gk. Rom. Byz. Stud.	*Greek, Roman, and Byzantine Studies.*
Gomme, *HCT*	A. W. Gomme, *A Historical Commentary on Thucydides*, 3 vols. (to v. 24), Oxford, 1945–56.
Harv. Stud.	*Harvard Studies in Classical Philology.*
Hesp.	*Hesperia.*
Hill, *Sources²*	G. F. Hill, *Sources for Greek History* (revised edition), 1951.
Hist.	*Historia, Zeitschrift für Alte Geschichte*, 1950–
IG	*Inscriptiones Graecae*, Berlin, 1873– .

JHS	*Journal of Hellenic Studies.*
Judeich, *Topographie*²	*Topographie von Athen* (2nd edition), Munich, 1931.
ML	R. Meiggs and D. M. Lewis, *A Selection of Greek Historical Inscriptions to the end of the Fifth Century* B.C., Oxford, 1969.
Num. Chron.	*Numismatic Chronicle.*
Proc. Afr. Class. Ass.	*Proceedings of the African Classical Associations.*
Proc. Camb. Phil. Soc.	*Proceedings of the Cambridge Philological Society.*
RE	Pauly–Wissowa–Kroll, *Real-Encyclopädie der classischen Altertumswissenschaft*, Stuttgart, 1894– .
REG	*Revue des Études grecques.*
Rev. Num.	*Revue numismatique.*
Rev. Phil.	*Revue de philologie, de littérature et d'histoire anciennes.*
RF	*Rivista di Filologia e di Istruzione classica.*
Rh. Mus.	*Rheinisches Museum für Philologie.*
Robinson Essays	Essays in Greek Coinage presented to Stanley Robinson (ed. C. M. Kraay and G. K. Jenkins), Oxford, 1968.
Robinson Studies	Studies presented to D. M. Robinson on his seventieth birthday, 2 vols., St. Louis, 1951 and 1953.
SEG	*Supplementum Epigraphicum Graecum.*
SIG	Dittenberger, *Sylloge Inscriptionum Graecarum* (3rd edition), Leipzig, 1915–24.
Staatsverträge	H. Bengtson, *Die Verträge der griechisch-römischen Welt*, vol. II, Munich and Berlin, 1962.
TAPA	*Transactions of the American Philological Association.*
Tod, *GHI* II	M. N. Tod, *A Selection of Greek Historical Inscriptions*, vol. II, from 403 to 323 B.C., Oxford, 1948.
Wade-Gery, *Essays*	H. T. Wade-Gery, *Essays in Greek History*, Oxford, 1958.

I

THE NATURE OF THE EVIDENCE

In the late summer or autumn of 478 Athens accepted the leadership of an offensive and defensive alliance of Greek states against Persia. Thirty years later this alliance of independent states, the Delian League, had become an empire whose resources were no longer directed against Persia but to the furtherance of Athenian policies at home and abroad. Sparta had led the Greek forces to victory in 480 and 479 when Xerxes invaded Greece, but she had not been prepared to carry the war into the east and had surrendered active leadership to Athens without a struggle. The growth of Athenian power, however, led to increasing restlessness among the more aggressive elements in Sparta and for ten years in the middle of the century the Spartan and Athenian alliances were at war; but operations were indecisive and, after a five years' truce in 451, it suited both sides to make a thirty years' peace in 446–445. It was soon clear that this peace could not be a final settlement. The Athenian democracy and its leaders did not at heart accept a dual leadership in Greece; an ambitious and expanding Athens was bound to provoke Sparta. Through the thirties it became increasingly clear that war was inevitable; war broke out in 431 and lasted twenty-seven years. It ended in the decisive defeat of Athens and the loss of her empire.

For most of this last phase of the story we have the unrivalled authority of Thucydides. He realized from the outset the significance of the war and followed its course with scrupulous attention to detail. He consulted original documents and was fully alive to the need for sifting the reports of his witnesses. His war narrative, particularly in the recording of revolts, throws invaluable light on the internal political conflicts within the cities of the empire and in a carefully designed series of speeches he provides a sharp-edged analysis of Athenian imperialism. Thucydides breaks off in 411. The events of the

last seven years of the war can be recovered from a collation
of Xenophon's *Hellenica* with what survives of a more accurate
historian whose original work is preserved only in papyrus
fragments, but is reflected also in Diodorus.[1]

The plays of Aristophanes provide an admirable complement to the historians. His primary purpose was to please his
audience and win the prize, but his audience expected topical
comment and were not disappointed. A gay scene from Cloudcuckoobury in the *Birds* tells us more about the actual methods
by which Athens controlled the allies than any other literary
source that has survived,[2] and the important part played by
the people's law-courts as an instrument of empire is vividly
illustrated, especially in the *Wasps*; Athens' relations with her
allies are the subject of repeated reference, sometimes light-
hearted, sometimes serious. Normally Aristophanes speaks in
character and his targets are generously diversified; but he
sometimes makes his own personal comment. He wished to
persuade as well as to amuse.[3] Thucydides and Aristophanes
together give us a realistic picture of Athens and her allies at
war, but when the Peloponnesian War broke out the conversion
of League to Empire had been completed. The achievements
of the early years of the League and the period of transition
are considerably less well documented.

In his digression on the growth of Athenian power Thucydides tells us that the writers who preceded him had taken the
archaic period or the Persian wars as their theme. Only
Hellanicus, in his chronicle of Athens, had covered the period
between the Persian and the Peloponnesian wars, and his
account was brief and his chronology incompetent.[4] Had
Hellanicus lived longer he might have had his own sharp comment to make on his successor's performance, and not without
reason; for Thucydides' brief summary of this period is one of
the least satisfactory parts of his work. He has reviewed these
fifty years, he tells us, partly in order to explain the growth of
Athenian power which in turn explains the greatness of the
war which he has chosen to relate. We should not therefore
criticize him for omitting events which seem important to us

---

[1] *Hellenica Oxyrhynchia*, ed. V. Bartoletti (Teubner, 1959).
[2] Ar. *Birds* 1021–55. See App. 17, p. 583.   [3] See pp. 391 ff.
[4] Thuc. i. 97. 2: βραχέως τε καὶ τοῖς χρόνοις οὐκ ἀκριβῶς ἐπεμνήσθη.

but are of little relevance to his theme, but we can expect him to give due weight to the main developments in the Delian League. The excursus begins promisingly with a brief description of the original structure of the League. Thucydides then proceeds to select those events in its history which in retrospect seemed to be significant in paving the way to empire; as a result we hear little of the fighting against Persians except the major engagements, the emphasis is rather on Athens' relations with her allies. The basic reasons for the allies' failure to maintain their independence are briefly sketched, but with few chronological signposts, and some of the most vital turning-points are ignored. Though adequate reasons are given for allied revolts and for their failure, Thucydides makes no mention of the transference of the League treasury from Delos to Athens. Yet it was the bringing of the League reserve to the Athenian Acropolis, as later writers saw, that gave Athens the complete control of League funds which would have been more difficult to impose at Delos.

More important, Thucydides tells us nothing of relations with Persia following the death of Cimon in Cyprus. We shall later argue that a definite peace was made, but this is a notoriously controversial issue. It is, however, beyond doubt that, even if no peace was formally made, Athenian policy was radically changed after Cimon's death. Fighting against Persia which had lasted for nearly thirty years, never for long discontinued, was now abandoned. This was a new situation and the combined evidence of literary sources and inscriptions suggests that there followed a period of fiercely contested political struggle in Athens and probably of widespread disturbance among the allies until the Thirty Years' Peace with Sparta in 446–445 and the ostracism in 443 of Thucydides, son of Melesias. These brought political peace to Athens and stability in what was becoming, if it had not already become, the empire. In Thucydides' condensed narrative these years have no special significance.

Thucydides maintained that the true cause of the Peloponnesian War was the growth of Athenian power which forced Sparta to fight. We should expect his account of the fifty years to become more detailed as he approached the outbreak of war; instead he breaks off his narrative at the crucial point. What we need to know is why the Athenian Empire seemed to Sparta and her allies more dangerous in 433 than in the late forties. In what ways had Athenian power and aggressiveness developed in the thirties? Thucydides ends his account with the crushing of the Samian revolt, in 439.[1]

The other fifth-century historians add little to Thucydides. The silence of Herodotus is our greatest disappointment, for he reached his maturity in the most vital phase of the League's development. Herodotus knew his Aegean world well and travelled widely in and beyond it. Born in Halicarnassus, for long an exile, living for some time in Samos, and familiar with Athens, he was uniquely fitted to take a detached view of the change from Delian League to Athenian Empire; a page of serious comment from Herodotus would be worth nearly all that remains of our secondary sources. But Herodotus was deliberately silent. It is true that his chosen subject ended with the capture of Sestus in 479–478 but elsewhere he does not restrict his narrative to what is directly relevant; and he does refer to isolated events after his closing date. He notes that Sophanes, a hero of Plataea, died with the Athenians who had established a colony at Ennea Hodoi at the time of the Thasian revolt; he tells us of the heroic resistance of the Persian garrisons of Eion and Doriscus in the seventies, and makes passing reference to the war against Carystus.[2] But there is no significant comment. He sees the Persian corpses from the battle of Papremis when Egypt revolted under the Libyan prince Inaros, but he says nothing of the Athenian-led expedition to support Inaros and its disastrous end.[3] He visits Thasos and describes her economic resources both on her own island and on the mainland, but not a word about the bitter fighting to defend those resources against Athens and the crippling of Thasos in the terms dictated by Athens.[4] One of the main topics of serious discussion when Herodotus travelled in the Aegean must have been the changing relations of Athens with

[1] A fuller discussion of Thucydides' account of the period 478–433, App. 1, p. 444.

[2] Hdt. ix. 75; vii. 107; ix. 105.

[3] Hdt. iii. 12. 4. Further reference to Inaros, iii. 15. 3, vii. 7. We might expect a reference to the last stages of the expedition when he briefly describes the island of Prosopitis (ii. 41. 5) where the Greeks made their last stand.

[4] Hdt. vi. 46–7.

her allies. It would have been impossible for a man so clearly fascinated by the instability of prosperity and the danger of greatness not to have wondered what would follow Athens' spectacular rise to dominance. But Herodotus never reveals his feelings on these big issues.

The historian of the empire, however, has much to gain from Herodotus. The months immediately following the victory of Mycale in the late summer of 479 were important in the shaping of the future, and Herodotus continues his detailed narrative to the fall of Sestus in the winter. There are significant differences between his account and that of Thucydides and his account is perhaps the more convincing. According to Thucydides the relations between Athens and Sparta were friendly when Athens established the Delian League; there are hints in Herodotus of a different and more realistic tradition.[1] But more important than questions of detail is the wider perspective that Herodotus encourages. Thucydides focuses intensely on the Peloponnesian War and particularly on the effect of that war on Athenian moods and politics: we tend to forget that there were people beyond the Aegean who are also part of the Greek story. Herodotus' journeys had taken him beyond the boundaries of the Greek world to Babylon, Egypt, and Scythia when the Delian League was changing into an Athenian Empire, and he was well equipped to see the Persian as well as the Greek viewpoint. Reading between his lines we can form a much fuller understanding of Greek attitudes to the Persians, for Herodotus was not a narrow nationalist regarding all non-Greeks as potential slaves. Though he probably did not go to Persia himself, he took the trouble to find out about Persian customs and character and he learnt to admire the bravery and truthfulness of Persian nobles.[2] He could not himself speak Persian but it was easy for him to make contact in Asia Minor with Persians who were interested in Greece and Greeks who owed their comfortable estates to the Persian king.

Herodotus' history, after a brief preface, begins with the mythical roots of the struggle between East and West as interpreted by Persians who were concerned with history. This story of rape and counter-rape, as Herodotus well knows, has nothing to do with history, but it reveals that there were

[1] See pp. 40 f. [2] Hdt. i. 131–9.

Persians sufficiently Hellenized to adapt Greek mythology to their own ends. It is from such men perhaps that Herodotus was able to transmit a catalogue of Persian satrapies and other information that seems to derive from Persian sources. But there were also Greeks in Asia Minor who are likely to have assimilated Persian ways. In the valley of the Caicus the towns of Pergamum, Teuthrania, and Halisarna had been granted to Demaratus, the Spartan king who shortly before Xerxes' invasion went over to the Medes and accompanied Xerxes to Greece. He must have been an acute embarrassment to Sparta, but in Herodotus' account he remains a dignified figure, faithful at heart to Sparta, but loyal to Xerxes. Near him was settled Gongylus 'the only Eretrian who Medized'. Descendants of both families were still living on these estates in the early fourth century.[1] Metiochus, the eldest son of Miltiades, victor of Marathon, failed to escape when his father, after the collapse of the Ionian Revolt, was forced to abandon his principality in the Chersonese. The Phoenicians took him to the king 'who did no harm to him but much good; for he gave him a house and property, and a Persian wife by whom he had children who are counted as Persians'.[2] Herodotus could respect such men and would have understood Alexander's later attempt to make Macedonians and Persians partners in his empire. Nor should we believe Herodotus to have been alone in his sympathy with Persian qualities; after him Xenophon could write an idealized and very long treatise on the upbringing of Cyrus.

This attitude towards Persia is not irrelevant to the politics of the Ionian cities in the middle of the century. From an inscription we know that Erythrae was for a time controlled by tyrants or a very narrow oligarchy, and that when Athens intervened they took refuge with the Medes.[3] The influence of Athenian democracy probably became more pervasive and insistent after the radical reforms of Ephialtes in 462 and it is not surprising that oligarchs should look towards the Persian satrap of Sardis. It would be extremely interesting to know what Herodotus thought of such oligarchs. From his writing one could imagine that he felt some sympathy for them. The

---

[1] Xen. *Hell.* iii. 1. 6. [2] Hdt. vi. 41. 2–4.
[3] Meiggs and Lewis (henceforward ML) *Greek Historical Inscriptions*, 40. See p. 113.

Ionian Revolt was to Herodotus a bad mistake, instigated by bad men for their own selfish ends. The help sent by Athens to the rebels was not the first chapter in the glorious story of Greece's triumphs over the barbarian hordes; it was 'the beginning of troubles'.[1] For the Ionians of Asia he has little respect:

> While the whole Greek race was weak, the Ionians were by far the weakest and of least account, for with the exception of Athens no city was noteworthy. The rest of the Ionians including the Athenians avoided the name, not wishing to be called Ionians, and even now most of them seem ashamed of the name. But these twelve cities were proud of the name and built a sanctuary for themselves which they named the Panionium.[2]

Did Herodotus think that the Ionians' proper course was to remain within the Persian Empire?

Herodotus also adds a little to our meagre evidence for the economic history of the Aegean during this period. He writes of the agricultural riches of Ionia and Cyrene, as well as the mineral wealth of Thasos, and he gives us a glimpse of the corn trade from the Euxine. But his most valuable contribution comes unexpectedly in his explanation of the water-supply along the desert routes into Egypt:

> I am going to tell you something which few of those who have sailed down to Egypt have noticed. There come each year to Egypt from all parts of Greece and from Phoenicia jars full of wine, yet not a single empty wine-jar, it might almost be said, is to be seen . . . Each demarch has to collect from his own city all the jars and bring them to Memphis, and from Memphis after filling them with water they bring them to these waterless parts of Syria.

This is good evidence of a brisk Greek trade with Egypt when Herodotus visited the country and a nice reminder that Athens did not monopolize the trade of the Aegean. The further implications of the passage, and particularly the relations of Greeks and Phoenicians, will be considered later.[3]

Hellanicus was the only contemporary who wrote a continuous history of fifth-century Athens but, even if his work was more impressive than Thucydides' harsh criticism would suggest, its

---

[1] Hdt. v. 97. 3: αὗται δὲ αἱ νέες ἀρχὴ κακῶν ἐγένοντο Ἕλλησί τε καὶ βαρβάροισι.
[2] Hdt. i. 143. 2–3.   [3] Hdt. iii. 6. 1. See p. 267.

survival would probably not have added much to our understanding of the League and Empire. His 'History of Athens from
the mythological period to the end of the Peloponnesian War'
was almost certainly compressed within two books and from the
few fragments that survive the narrative seems to have been
primarily factual. He is likely to have recorded major battles
and constitutional reforms, but it is doubtful whether he commented on administrative measures in the empire or the
changing temper of Athenian leadership.[1]

Though contemporary literary evidence for the growth and
development of the Delian League was always meagre,
Alexandrian scholars who needed to explain topical references
in Old Comedy and historians who wanted to rewrite Greek
history had ample material from the fourth century to draw
on. It would, however, have needed the critical power of a
Thucydides to sift fourth-century evidence competently and
the intellectual climate no longer produced a Thucydides.
Historical tradition in the fourth century became the victim
of two dangerous patrons, philosophy and rhetoric. In the fifth
century several of the leading philosophers had lived close to
the political scene and had accepted and justified the principles
and practice of Athenian democracy. Anaxagoras and Protagoras were associates of Pericles and may have influenced
his thinking; but the oligarchic revolutions at the end of the
century, the capitulation of Athens, and the condemnation of
Socrates introduced a sharp change. The early years of the
fourth century saw a series of bitter attacks on the fifth-century
politicians who were held responsible for corrupting the people
and leading Athens to ruin. Most of this literature is lost but
we can see its reflection in many of Plato's early dialogues. In
the funeral oration recorded by Thucydides Pericles emphasized
the energy, resilience, and sound judgement of the common man;
according to Plato's *Gorgias* Pericles had made the Athenians
a race of 'idlers, cowards, talkers and money-grubbers'.[2]

The influence of this oligarchic reaction can be traced far
into the Roman period; democracy's defence was left to the
orators whose picture of the fifth century is no less distorted
than that of their opponents. Both sides in the debate had lost
sight of history. This sharp decline in critical judgement is in

---

[1] *FGH* 323a.   [2] Plato, *Gorgias* 515e.

large part due to the influence of rhetoric for which Isocrates must take much of the blame. The fifth century had been more interested in substance than in form. Herodotus and Thucydides were not uninterested in style; each in his own way tried to make his writing match his thinking. But their main concern was to tell the truth as they saw it, without unnecessary adornment. Rhetoric was more concerned with persuasion than with truth and developed an unhealthy interest in ornament; the historian's function was extended to include that of the moral teacher. History must show what was right and what was wrong.[1]

The damaging effects of rhetoric are barely traceable in the two most important historians of the early years of the century, Xenophon and the unknown author of the Oxyrhynchus *Hellenica*, but they considerably affected the two historians who did most to fill the gaps left by Thucydides. Theopompus of Chios began his historical writing with a continuation of Thucydides and an epitome of Herodotus. His main work which followed was a history of the Greek world focused on Macedon from the beginning of the reign of Philip II to his death. Though Philip was the central character of this history Theopompus spread his net wide and devoted a complete book to a vicious attack on Athenian popular leaders of the fifth and fourth centuries. Like many other ancient historians he has suffered from the coincidences of survival. Had we no more than the scattered quotations of his work to guide us we could not regard him as a serious historian: it is his misfortune that a large proportion of his 'fragments' that survive come from Athenaeus who was more concerned with women and wine than with serious political issues. Theopompus' reputation in the Hellenistic period and later suggests that he was a considerable figure and it is certain that he exercised a considerable influence on later writers; but it is probable that his reputation rested more on his sensationalism than on the accuracy of what he wrote. He was a vigorous and colourful writer and a large part of the reading public will have shared his political prejudices. For it is clear that Theopompus was no lover of democracy. His father had been exiled from Chios for Spartan sympathies; the son

---

[1] Ephorus' views are probably reflected in Diodorus' preface (especially 1. 3); cf. *FGH* 70 F 191 (Ephorus or an epitome), F 2–5.

took his revenge in his writing. In losing Theopompus the historian of the Athenian Empire has lost a prejudiced attack on Athenian democracy which would have thrown little light on the questions that most interest him.[1]

Theopompus had studied with Isocrates; Ephorus from Aeolian Cumae was his contemporary and shared his apprenticeship. His chosen field was universal history and two of his books were devoted to Greek history in the fifth century. From the criticisms of Polybius and other writers we can form a general impression of his qualities as a historian. Unlike Theopompus Ephorus was an admirer of Athens and this admiration seems to have coloured his narrative. Battles that are evenly fought in Thucydides become Athenian victories: Sparta tends to be the villain of the story. His battle descriptions, according to Polybius, were completely unmilitary, and he used historical characters as pegs on which to hang his own moral reflections. In the arrangement of his material he broke sharply with the annalistic tradition established by Thucydides and instead of recording events as they happened year by year he arranged them by subject and completed one theme before beginning another. Ephorus clearly had serious weaknesses, but he too has been unfortunate in the evidence by which we have to judge him. For our main key to Ephorus' account of the fifth century lies in the use made of him by the Sicilian Diodorus in the age of Caesar.[2]

Diodorus, who was rightly modest of his own achievement, set out to provide in easily digestible form a world history which would provide an opportunity to study both Greek and Roman history in the same book against their backgrounds. In his attempt to cover such an enormous field he consulted a wide range of authors, but he lacked the mental energy and critical ability to assess his authorities and sift rival accounts. His natural tendency was to rely on one main source at a time with an occasional reference to one or more other sources. In his account of the fifth century there are several widely spaced passages which can be shown to derive from Ephorus. It is

[1] *FGH* 115. See especially T21 (Quintilian): oratori magis similis; 25 (a) (Lucian): φιλαπεχθημόνως κατηγοροῦντι τῶν πλείστων . . . ὡς κατηγορεῖν μᾶλλον ἢ ἱστορεῖν τὰ πεπραγμένα. For a more detailed evaluation see W. R. Connor, in *Theopompus and Fifth-century History.*

[2] Ephorus, *FGH* 70 (see especially T20) F 189–200.

generally assumed that Ephorus was his main source for Persian and mainland Greek history throughout the century.[1]

Many of Diodorus' mistakes, however, cannot be attributed to his source. We cannot believe that Ephorus, like Diodorus, recorded the death of King Archidamus of Sparta three years before the outbreak of the war which took his name and in whose opening years he led the Spartan invasions of Attica.[2] Nor is it likely that Ephorus followed the notice of a five years' truce between Athens and Sparta by a detailed account in the next year of a ravaging expedition round the Peloponnese, without comment.[3] Nor should Ephorus be blamed for Diodorus' chronology. Diodorus was imposing an annalistic framework on a narrative that deliberately rejected the annalistic pattern. We do not know what reference if any Ephorus made to absolute dates, but he certainly did not, like Diodorus, divide his narrative into annual instalments. His pattern we can sometimes recover from Diodorus. Under the archon year of 471–470 he records the ostracism of Themistocles, his stay at Argos, his condemnation in absence at Athens, his flight to Persia and death; the next year's entry includes Cimon's operations from the capture of Eion to the victory of the Eurymedon.[4] In each case he has compressed the events of more than five years into a single year, and it is virtually certain that he is imposing his own dates on Ephorus' narrative. Ephorus sometimes, as in these cases, groups his events round prominent characters, sometimes his sequence is confined to a geographic area: that is why Diodorus completes his record of the Egyptian revolt in 460–459 before the opening of the first Peloponnesian war in 459–458, in flagrant contradiction of Thucydides and other reliable evidence.[5] In cases such as these we can be virtually certain that Diodorus' dates are wrong and we think we can understand the reason for his mistake. The embarrassment begins when we consider the dates Diodorus has got right. In addition to Ephorus Diodorus has used a chronological source, from which he has taken the dates of kings and eponymous magistrates, which are generally accurate. He also seems to have dated accurately the foundations of cities such

[1] For Diodorus see App. 2, p. 447.
[2] Diod. xii. 35. 4.
[3] Diod. xi. 86. 1, 88. 1–2.
[4] Diod. xi. 54–9; 60–2.
[5] Diod. xi. 77–8; Thuc. i. 104–10.

as Amphipolis. The greater difficulty is to decide how much else he has taken from his chronological source and how reliable such a source would be for the dates of battles and constitutional measures. This difficult problem must be examined more closely in an appendix; our conclusion will be that Diodorus is more often wrong than right, and that apart from the dates of kings and magistrates and of the foundations of cities no clear principle can be established of distinguishing right from wrong dates.[1] We can at least hope to avoid the dangerous tendency of accepting him when he suits our own views while rejecting him when his evidence is inconvenient.

We must also attribute to Diodorus rather than Ephorus a strange tendency to create two episodes from what in Thucydides is only one. In Thucydides Pericles leads only one expedition round the Peloponnese during the fifties; in Diodorus he leads two, in 455–454 and 453–452, but they are suspiciously alike.[2] Thucydides records only one battle in Boeotia after Tanagra; on the sixty-second day after that battle the Athenians under Myronides won a great victory at Oenophyta. Diodorus first recounts a great victory near Tanagra which in its significance seems to correspond exactly with Thucydides' battle, but then adds a second battle at Oenophyta.[3] We may suspect other doublets in his accounts.

But most of the facts in Diodorus seem to come from Ephorus and many of them do not inspire confidence. Sometimes the accounts of Thucydides and Diodorus will closely correspond. It is clear for instance that Diodorus' account of the Samian revolt is derived ultimately, through Ephorus, from Thucydides. The number of ships on both sides is the same in the two accounts as is the main sequence of events; the only differences to be noted are slight changes in emphasis and the addition by Diodorus of comparatively unimportant details that are not in Thucydides.[4] On other occasions, however, we find a difference in figures and other details. If such instances were rare we might believe that in certain instances Ephorus had access to evidence which Thucydides did not use and might be justifiably correcting his predecessor; but the instances are too

[1] See App. 2, p. 456.   [2] Thuc. i. 111. 2–3; Diod. xi. 85, 88. 1–2.
[3] Thuc. i. 108. 2–3; Diod. xi. 81. 4–5, 82–3. 1.
[4] Thuc. i. 115. 2–117; Diod. xii. 27–8.

common. Where we can control Thucydides' detail from documents he survives the test, as his own insistence on accuracy would lead us to expect. We are left to believe that Ephorus, working on a Thucydidean basis, tended to modify numbers in order to give an air of independence to his narrative.[1] It is wrong in principle to accept any figure in Diodorus against Thucydides unless it is independently confirmed.

In spite of all the weaknesses of himself and of his sources Diodorus cannot be ignored. His is the only continuous surviving narrative of the fifth century, apart from some brief and unimpressive epitomes. He records some events that Thucydides passed over, and he sometimes provides at least plausible explanations of policy where Thucydides offers none. But of our literary sources incomparably the most useful as well as the most entertaining complement to Thucydides is Plutarch. Though he is not a historian Plutarch had read much history and enjoyed it. His primary concern was a moral evaluation of his character serving as a running commentary on the facts he could collect, and naturally the facts that most interested him were those which gave point and colour to the characters he was portraying. How much of the collecting Plutarch did himself and how much he relied on previous compilers is here irrelevant; Plutarch's importance to us is that he preserves tantalizing echoes of contemporary sources, which would otherwise have been totally lost. Sometimes he names his sources; more often he follows the common practice of Greek and Roman writers, quoting without acknowledgement, and herein lies the main difficulty in using Plutarch. Some of his stories are shown by internal inconsistency or external control to be fiction, but others which at first sight seem to be confused or misplaced echoes have been found to be genuine history. Plutarch's value is the value of his sources and in using any passage from his *Lives* we should at least satisfy ourselves that it could have a respectable pedigree.

Of the sources quoted by Plutarch two would have been of particular interest to us, because they were written not by Athenians but by members of allied states. Ion of Chios was a versatile writer who appreciated and profited from the development of Athens as the cultural centre of the Aegean

[1] See App. 2, p. 447.

world.[1] He wrote tragedies, comedies, dithyrambs, elegies, and other forms of verse but he also cultivated prose. Among his writings was the story of the foundation of Chios, a philosophical treatise, and a work entitled *Presbeutikos*, the record of an embassy on which perhaps he had served himself, or, less probably, a disquisition on embassies. Of these works we know virtually nothing, but he also published a collection of anecdotes variously entitled *Memoirs* or *A Traveller's Diary*, and from this work we have a few authenticated fragments and can guess at more. Ion was rich and well connected in Chios and moved in influential circles at Athens. When he was little more than a lad he went to a dinner party attended by Cimon and he records one of the great man's stories. From the story we get a brief but realistic glimpse of Athenian social life of the period and hints of a military campaign which we should not have anticipated.[2] Ion was also probably in Athens when the Spartans appealed in 462 for help against their helots in revolt; he records the famous phrase with which Cimon defended his policy: the Athenians 'must not suffer Hellas to be crippled nor their city to be robbed of her yoke-fellow'.[3] Later he was in Chios when Athens sent for reinforcements from Lesbos and Chios to crush the Samian revolt; from him we know that the tragedian Sophocles, general for the year, served on this mission.[4] Ion's first tragedy was performed in the eighty-second Olympiad (452–448) and he died in the late twenties. He seems clearly to have admired Cimon who will have made a great impression on him when he was young, and it may be partly for that reason that the allusions to Pericles which survive are unfavourable. They cannot, however, be used as evidence for Ion's hostility to Athenian democracy; he retained his association with Athens long after the reforms of Ephialtes and the death of Cimon. On one occasion he distributed Chian wine to the Athenian people to celebrate a tragic victory, and he was still competing on the Athenian stage in the Archidamian war; shortly after Ion's death Aristophanes could expect his audience to take the point of a playful allusion to his verse.[5]

[1] *FGH* 392; *RE* ix (1916), 1861 ff.; Jacoby, *CQ* xli (1947), 1–15; G. Huxley, *Gk. Rom. Byz. Stud.* vi (1965), 129–46.

[2] Plut. *Cim.* 9. 1 (F 13). See App. 4, p. 465.

[3] Plut. *Cim.* 16. 10 (F 14).

[4] Athenaeus xii. 603c–604d (F 6).   [5] Ar. *Peace* 835–7.

While Ion of Chios was a friend of Athens and was probably favourable to her in his writings Stesimbrotus of Thasos wrote with venom.[1] Like Ion he was a learned man and later generations remembered him best for his work on Homeric problems and on initiation ceremonies; but he also wrote a political pamphlet. Very little of this survives and that little may give an unfair impression of Stesimbrotus' work. He apparently attributed the leadership of the opposition to Themistocles' naval policy to Miltiades, who had died some seven years previously.[2] He made Themistocles sail in flight from Greece to Hiero, tyrant of Syracuse, and ask for his daughter in marriage before leaving for Asia: we can share Plutarch's doubts on this tradition though it is not unlikely that when Themistocles fled from Argos to Corcyra he was intending to sail to Sicily.[3] We can also, with Plutarch, dismiss Stesimbrotus' statement that during the blockade of Samos in 440 Pericles sailed to Cyprus to forestall the threat of Persian intervention; Thucydides more credibly takes Pericles no further than Caunus and Caria.[4] Other fragments retail scandal. Pericles' relations with women may have been less austere than the nineteenth century would have hoped but Stesimbrotus' story that he took the wife of his son Xanthippus looks like political malice.[5] Yet the title of the pamphlet from which these miserable scraps survive suggests that our loss may be serious. Stesimbrotus wrote *On Themistocles, Thucydides, and Pericles.* The conjunction of names is curious. Why Themistocles and why not Cimon?

Stesimbrotus was not writing a constitutional history of Athens. He was writing as a fifth-century Thasian concerned with the contemporary scene. Pericles was the main target for his abuse because Pericles more than anyone else had devised and controlled the policy that converted a league into an empire. Themistocles had lost his dominance before the League was established, but he remained the spiritual founder of the Athenian Empire. For the empire rested on the secure control of the Aegean by the strongest fleet in Greece and it was Themistocles' decisive intervention that created the Athenian

[1] *FGH* 107.
[2] Plut. *Them.* 4. 5 (F 2). But it is formally possible that Stesimbrotus was referring to Miltiades' opposition to Themistocles' naval policies when archon in 493–492. [3] Plut. *Them.* 24. 6 (F 3). See p. 81.
[4] Plut. *Per.* 26. 1 (F 8); Thuc. i. 116. 3. [5] Plut. *Per.* 36. 3 (F 11).

navy when a sudden influx of silver from a new vein in the Laurium area provided the necessary resources. Themistocles remained a controversial figure long after his death, and not only for his Medism. His place in Athenian democratic development was hotly disputed and Cleon was not thinking only of the creation of a fleet when, at the height of his power in 425, he compared himself to Themistocles.[1] It was not difficult for a member of an allied state who resisted Athenian control to remember Themistocles with bitterness. Themistocles' successful rival Cimon was, it seems, more generously treated. He lacked, according to Stesimbrotus, Attic cleverness and fluency, but there was a noble sincerity in his bearing; at heart he was more Lacedaemonian than Athenian.[2] But it is doubtful whether Stesimbrotus made the same schematic contrast as later writers between a generous-hearted anti-Persian crusader and later demagogic tyrants who persecuted allies rather than Persians. He reported and perhaps further coloured contemporary scandal about Cimon's half-sister Elpinice and he was unflattering about Cimon's marriage.[3] He is not likely to have appreciated Cimon's military leadership of the League for it was Cimon who, after a long and bitter siege, crushed the Thasian revolt.[4]

What would seem to be Cimon's natural place in the succession of Athenian leaders is taken by his kinsman, probably brother-in-law, Thucydides son of Melesias.[5] Had Plutarch's *Pericles* not survived we should know very little indeed of this Thucydides. His ostracism is recorded in literary sources and reflected on a large number of sherds from the Ceramicus; his memory was kept alive in Plato's circle, and scholiasts commenting on Aristophanes could add a little; but only Plutarch gives us the outline of a full-length portrait. Thucydides was Pericles' main opponent in the early forties, who organized and maintained opposition in the Assembly until he was ostracized in 443. The first great issue in Plutarch's brief account is the use of the accumulated reserve of the Delian League for the rebuilding of Athenian temples which Thucydides fought on principle.[6] It is possible that Thucydides was the hero of Stesimbrotus' tract, the man who stood for fair play for the

---

[1] Ar. *Knights* 813.
[2] Plut. *Cim.* 4. 5 (F 4).
[3] Plut. *Cim.* 14. 5 (F 5), 16. 1 (F 6).
[4] Plut. *Cim.* 14.
[5] E. Cavaignac, *Rev. Phil.* v (1929), 281–5.
[6] Plut. *Per.* 12.

allies against Athenian exploitation; Plato recalls that he had many friends among the allies.[1]

It is probably significant that Plutarch is the first author known to us to make any considerable use of Ion and Stesimbrotus. They had material which was not available in the standard histories and which appealed to Plutarch's interest in colour and character. He also recognized the importance of contemporary records and he takes a dilettante's delight in referring to inscriptions at first or second hand. An interest in official documents was one of the symptoms of the development from mythology to history, in the fifth century. Herodotus realized their importance; he noted dedicatory inscriptions as well as monuments in the course of his travels and recorded inscribed epigrams from Thermopylae. Thucydides copied texts of specially important documents such as the Peace of Nicias. The successors of Hellanicus who wrote histories of Athens made liberal use of Athenian archives. It must, for instance, have been from a contemporary official list that Androtion was able to name the ten generals of 441–440 when the Samian revolt broke out, and Philochorus' date for the dedication of the chryselephantine cult statue of Athena must also have come ultimately from a contemporary record.[2] An interest in monuments and inscriptions remained part of the essential equipment of men of learning.

Plutarch refers explicitly to the collection of decrees made by the Macedonian Craterus in the early third century, and by commenting on Craterus' methods Plutarch shows that he had more than a nodding acquaintance with this important source.[3] More often he cites or reflects decrees without any explanation. Sometimes they have come to him from literary predecessors, not always in correct form; by consulting Craterus he could, for example, have found that Cimon, not Themistocles, proposed the decree condemning Arthmius of Zelea, the *proxenos* of Athens who brought Persian money to the Peloponnese.[4] Sometimes perhaps his language implying an epigraphic source may be misleading. One suspects that in some Hellenistic wording 'The Athenians *decreed* an expedition'

---

[1] Plato, *Meno* 94d: οὐκ ἦσαν αὐτῷ πλεῖστοι φίλοι Ἀθηναίων καὶ τῶν συμμάχων;
[2] Androtion, *FGH* 324 F 38; Philochorus, *FGH* 328 F 121 = Schol. Ar. *Peace* 605.
[3] Plut. *Ar.* 26. [4] See App. 10 (c), p. 508.

is no more than a circumstantial periphrasis for 'The Athenians *sent* an expedition'; in the same way following a fashion of our times we are apt to use such words as 'statistics' and 'statistically' somewhat irresponsibly. But there are occasions when Plutarch seems to follow original documents without acknowledging his source. He knows that no writings of Pericles survived except his decrees and he probably looked through these either in a separate publication or in Craterus' collection.[1] We have to thank his curiosity for the only record we possess of a remarkable initiative taken in the mid century by the Athenians on Pericles' proposal, when they invited the Greeks of the mainland and eastern Aegean to send representatives to Athens to discuss the rebuilding of temples burnt by the Persians, the policing of the seas, and religious obligations remaining from the Persian War.[2] This record survives because the decree struck Plutarch as a very significant demonstration of Pericles' magnificence, and in places he keeps very close to the language of the decree. Unfortunately there are suspect elements in his paraphrase and we cannot feel sufficiently confident of the authenticity of the decree to make it our corner-stone for the reconstruction of Athenian policies in the early forties.[3]

Of the epigraphic evidence that could have been available to Plutarch much has been irretrievably lost, but more fifth-century inscriptions have been recovered in Athens than in all the other cities of Greece combined and this is no accident; it derives from the character of Athenian democracy and the prosperity of fifth-century Athens. Though the reforms of Ephialtes were regarded as a decisive turning-point in the development of Athenian democracy, the ancient sources are singularly vague in describing them and we are almost left to guess what powers were taken from the Areopagus and to what democratic bodies they were transferred. But it is clear that the reforms gave stronger emphasis to the sovereignty of the demos through Boule, Assembly, and law-courts and in particular to the control of the executive by the people. One aspect of this control was the publication on stone, where all could see them, of public decisions and public accounts. Before 462 the great majority of surviving Athenian inscriptions are dedications;

[1] Plut. *Per.* 8. 7.   [2] Plut. *Per.* 17.
[3] More fully discussed, App. 10 (D), p. 512.

fragments of only four decrees of the period survive and of these the earliest probably records the first Athenian cleruchy on the island of Salamis, towards the end of the sixth century, and the three others concern religious matters;[1] of decrees recording political decisions, public expenditure, administrative reforms we have nothing. Important public buildings were put up between the expulsion of the Pisistratids in 510 and the invasion of Xerxes. Had the accounts of these buildings been publicly displayed on stone, some fragments would have survived; we have none. By contrast, between 462 and 445 we have fragments of at least ten decrees and of the accounts of the Athena Promachos, the Parthenon, the Parthenos, and another unknown public work.[2] Inscriptions surviving from the fifties and early forties are a most important complement to the literary sources. Even if all the literature of the fifth and fourth centuries were preserved we should probably learn from it very little of the administrative regulations by which Athens controlled her empire. We should perhaps have a more complete list of revolts, but of the political settlements that followed the crushing of revolts we should know only the barest outline. Moreover, only in the preserved fragments of decrees can we catch the contemporary language and tone of Athenian imperialism. Thucydides in his speeches has left us a vivid analysis of Athens' relations with her allies, but it is still a matter of keen controversy whether he is in these speeches expressing the arguments and attitudes of his speakers or his own analysis of the situation.[3] The language of decrees shows at least that Athenian public statements could be strong and straight. There is very little sign of the velvet glove in the decree imposing Athenian currency, weights, and measures on the allies, or in the decree moved by Clinias which attempts to check evasions in the payment of tribute.[4]

The decrees are the most important of the inscriptions that survive. They tell us of revolts of which we should otherwise know nothing; they reflect the methods used by Athens to secure and maintain political control; they give some precision

---

[1] ML 14 (Salamis); *IG* i². 3–4, 5, 6. The Phaselis decree (ML 31) would be an exception if before 460.
[2] See tables, Meiggs, *JHS* lxxxvi (1966), 92, 94.
[3] See pp. 376–90. [4] ML 45, 46. See pp. 165–72.

to the more general statements of the literary sources. Casualty lists add a little to the military record. It was the Athenian custom each year at the end of the fighting season to accord a public funeral to those who had died fighting in the course of the year. An orator was elected to commemorate them and their ashes were publicly committed to burial in the Ceramicus. Above the grave the names of the dead were inscribed on a marble stele. A steadily increasing number of fragments from such lists have been found and three lists from this period are of particular interest. Of the first only fragments survive but they are sufficient to confirm a passage in Plutarch's *Cimon* which might otherwise be lightly discredited. Plutarch briefly describes a campaign in which Cimon with a very small fleet drove the remaining Persians from the Chersonese and he places the campaign between the battle of the Eurymedon (not earlier than 469) and the revolt of Thasos (465).[1] The implication that there were still Persians in the Chersonese some ten years after the capture of Sestus and Byzantium in 478 is very unexpected and we should be tempted to reject the story or relegate it to the seventies. But the casualty list shows that in the same year Athenians died at various points in or near the Hellespont and also in Thasos.[2] The campaign in the Hellespont can be firmly dated to the spring or early summer of 465.

The two other lists are completely preserved and add rather more to the literary record. One gives the members of the Erechtheid tribe who died in the same year on widely separated battlefields: Cyprus, Egypt, Phoenicia, Halieis, Aegina, Megara.[3] The most natural interpretation is that the Egyptian expedition and the First Peloponnesian War were both begun in the same year, 460 or 459, and the inclusion of Phoenicia raises questions that the literary sources do not answer.[4] The other list covers the casualties of all ten tribes and the losses occur in the Chersonese, at Byzantium, and 'in the other wars'. The total number of casualties in this list (58) is less than the casualties of Erechtheis alone in the earlier list (177); the 'other wars' will be scattered police-actions involving little serious

---

[1] Plut. *Cim.* 14. 1.
[2] *IG* i². 928 with *Hesp.* xxxvi (1967), 321–8, and? xxv (1956), 375. See also Endnote 3, p. 416.
[3] ML 33.   [4] See p. 105.

fighting. We shall see that the early forties provide a convincing context.[1] But the main advance in the last generation has been in the reconstruction and study of the fragments of the lists of *aparchai*, the mina in the talent paid to Athena each year from the allies' tribute, and of the changing tribute assessments drawn up and publicly displayed at Athens. These two series of documents together throw considerable light on both the economic and political aspects of empire, but though much has been added to what was known forty years ago, many of the most important inferences that can be drawn from this evidence still remain controversial.[2] In most years, for example, we know approximately the number of cities paying tribute, but no list is complete and the names of the absentees are more important than their number. In some years some states are recorded twice, implying payment in two instalments; we cannot yet be certain that this is politically significant.[3] The assessment of 425 shows a very sharp increase from pre-war figures, but since we know almost nothing of the assessment that immediately preceded, probably in 428, and have an incomplete picture of the assessment of 430, the focus of our judgement is blurred. But amidst the uncertainties some important conclusions are certain, others highly probable. From them we can confirm and expand our narrative at many points, though we learn more from the decrees even in their present fragmentary form.

With the approaching completion of the Agora excavations the discovery of new inscriptions will almost certainly slow down, but there are still important fragments to be found on the slopes of the Acropolis. We should also learn more about the economic aspects of empire when more sites in and round the Aegean have been excavated, and when more fifth-century coinages have been studied in detail. May's work on Aenus and Abdera and Barron's on the silver coinages of Samos are good illustrations of what can be gained.[4] Without such detailed

---

[1] ML 48. See pp. 160f.
[2] The foundation of discussion will always be *The Athenian Tribute Lists* (4 vols.), by B. D. Meritt, H. T. Wade-Gery, M. F. McGregor (Princeton, 1939–53), henceforward *ATL*. The evidence of the tribute lists is more fully discussed in Chapter 13.
[3] See p. 164.
[4] J. M. F. May, *The Coinage of Aenos* (1950), *The Coinage of Abdera* (1966), and J. P. Barron, *The Silver Coins of Samos* (1966).

study conclusions are hazardous, for there are few coin hoards to provide firm dates, and when dating depends only on design the margin of error is wide. It is doubtful whether we shall ever be able to reconstruct more than a tentative outline of economic developments in the Aegean but literary sources combined with inscriptions provide a credible picture in outline of the history of the Delian League. Serious gaps remain in both the military and political record and the most difficult problem is to trace the development in mood, language, and institutions chronologically. In the forties and thirties the Athenians seem to have been restless and aggressive, and there is little doubt that their control of the allies hardened between the Thirty Years' Peace and the outbreak of the Peloponnesian War; but how far and how fast the road to empire had been travelled in the first thirty years is a much more elusive question.

2

THE HISTORICAL BACKGROUND

THE history of the Athenian Empire has to be built up from a wide variety of sources. For the introduction to the narrative we rely almost exclusively on Herodotus, but he serves us well. When Herodotus came to write the history of the Persian wars he might have begun his story with the Ionian revolt of 499, for it was the help given by Athens and Eretria to the Ionians that provoked the punitive expedition which was crushed at Marathon, and Marathon led inevitably to Xerxes' great invasion ten years later. But Herodotus, though he draws no explicit distinctions between immediate and ultimate causes, had a surer instinct than to begin his story with the revolt. His starting-point is the fall of Croesus. Earlier Lydian kings had attacked Ionian towns, but Croesus was the first to reduce systematically the whole of Ionia and incorporate it in his empire.[1] When Croesus, much to the Greeks' surprise, was swiftly crushed by the newly risen power of Persia, Ionia was part of the prize that fell to Cyrus. And mainland Greece was already concerned, for Sparta, proud to partner Babylon and Egypt, had made alliance with Croesus.[2] Sardis fell before the Spartan force could leave the Peloponnese and no attempt was made by the allies to fight on together. But Sparta recognized a moral obligation; she sent envoys to warn Cyrus not to attack Greeks. Within months those few cities that resisted Persian attack were crushed; only Miletus who had been on special terms with Lydia, was allowed to retain her independence. Sparta had protested but no more.[3]

Under Croesus the Ionian cities, and with them their Aeolian and Dorian neighbours to the north and south, had paid

[1] Hdt. i. 5. 3–6. 2.
[2] Hdt. i. 69. 3 (Lydia's alliance with Sparta). Herodotus later refers to Lydia's alliance with Egypt and Babylon, i. 77. 2. That Sparta was also allied to these powers is suggested by the Egyptian king's gift of a splendid breast-plate to Sparta, iii. 47. 1–2.   [3] Hdt. i. 152.

annual tribute. This they now paid to Persia as parts of two
satrapies governed from Dascylium and Sardis. But whereas
Lydia by her long association with the coastal cities had become
superficially at least Hellenized and could understand Greek
political behaviour, the Persians were a completely alien power
in language, religion, and politics. The only form of rule that
they had known was monarchy; it was beyond their thinking
that power should be held by any but a restricted circle of
nobles under the king.[1] The natural sequel of Persia's incorporation of the eastern Greeks was the institution or encouragement of local rulers who could be relied on to maintain good
order and the appropriate subservience to Persia in the cities.

For nearly half a century there was no striking sign of unrest,
but in 499 Ionia revolted and it was nearly six years before
Persian control was fully restored.[2] Thucydides must have
thought very poorly of Herodotus' account of this revolt.
A strong prejudice against Ionians which is elsewhere made
explicit pervades the story. Individual personalities dominate
the foreground, Aristagoras and Histiaeus, and their portraits
are barely credible; the background lacks definition. A firm
chronological backbone is given, but the real history of the
revolt is missing. Personalities no doubt played their part, but
the selfish ambition of two Milesians cannot explain why, when
the military odds must have seemed overwhelming, the Ionians
acted with such unusual solidarity. Economic analysis was
once a popular solution. The Persian conquest, it was assumed,
had crippled the trade of the east Greeks and growing economic
distress led to the desperate attempt to recover freedom. Such
a view may now be regarded as old-fashioned; it is fairer to
admit that we have not enough evidence to pass judgement.

There is no evidence and little probability that the Persian
annexation of Egypt and the shores of the Euxine seriously
affected Greek trade. Perhaps a satrap's court at Sardis proved
a less lucrative market than the accumulated wealth of the
Lydian kingdom, but the Persians who required tribute had

---

[1] At the time of Darius' accession Herodotus records a Persian debate on the
rival merits of monarchy, oligarchy, and democracy, iii. 80–2; and later he insists
that this was a genuine record, vi. 43. 3. His source is probably a philhellenic
Persian or a Greek in close touch with Persians. In transmission the debate has
become considerably more Greek than Persian.

[2] Hdt. v. 28–vi. 21.

nothing to gain by discouraging trade. It is not unrealistically romantic to minimize the material factors and place the greater emphasis on the political issues. It is significant that the revolt opened with the overthrow of the pro-Persian tyrants who ruled the cities. Tyranny in its time had served as a useful solvent in the Greek states, breaking the power of exclusive aristocracies and paving the way for more flexible societies, but when their purpose had been fulfilled tyrants were no longer tolerated. They represented arbitrary rule without free discussion and division of responsibility, and though oligarchs and democrats were long to quarrel about how far the freedom of discussion should extend and how widely responsibility should be shared they were agreed that the suppression of constitutional government was unnatural and intolerable. When Persia chose to rule through tyrants tyranny was an anachronism. The cities were probably more concerned to become free than to become rich.

The full story of the revolt does not concern us but some points are significant for the future. The initiative came from Miletus and spread rapidly through the Ionian cities. Later many of the Aeolian and Hellespontine cities joined the movement but there is no mention of Dorians in Herodotus' account. In the full muster of the Greek fleet at Lade there are no ships from Cos, Cnidus, or the three cities of Rhodes;[1] it is at least possible that they did not follow the Ionian lead. Caria, however, was certainly involved, though not the whole of Caria. After a raid on Sardis with which the offensive had opened, the revolt had spread from Ionia to the Hellespont. The Greeks then, so Herodotus tells us, won over 'the greater part of Caria, for even Caunus which had not previously wanted to join the alliance joined them after the burning of Sardis'.[2] Of the Carian communities Herodotus mentions only Caunus, Mylasa, and Kindya, but they are sufficient to show that the revolt was not confined to the coastal area. When the Persians moved south from the Hellespont to crush the rebels before the revolt spread further the Carians took up a defensive position behind the line of the Maeander and were heavily defeated after a long and stubborn battle; Herodotus gives the casualties as 2,000 Persians and no less than 10,000 Carians. The survivors fell back on the sanctuary of Zeus, god of battles, at Labraunda

---

[1] Hdt. vi. 8.   [2] Hdt. v. 103. 2.

where they were encouraged by a contingent from Miletus to remain in the field. A second engagement, however, ended in decisive defeat and the Milesians suffered particularly heavy casualties. But the Carians fought back and succeeded in trapping the Persians in an ambush on the road to Pedasus.[1] From Herodotus' silence we assume that there was no more serious fighting in Caria. The cities of the Hellespont and Propontis offered considerably less resistance. Dardanus, Abydus, Percote, Lampsacus, and Paesus were taken in quick succession; a day for each sufficed.[2] The core of the resistance came from the coastal cities and islands of Ionia.

It is customary to disparage the organization and determination of the rebels; they deserve a more sympathetic hearing. Never before had so many Greek cities of the east combined against a common enemy. When the Lydian kings attacked the coastal cities each was normally left to fend for itself; Miletus, the largest and strongest of them, was helped by Chios alone when holding out stubbornly against Alyattes.[3] The pattern was repeated after the fall of Sardis when Cyrus detached a Persian force to reduce the Greeks. There were discussions at the Panionium and it was even proposed, by Bias according to Herodotus, that the Ionians should emigrate *en masse* and win for themselves the rich island of Sardinia: 'so they could be rid of slavery and would enjoy prosperity, occupying the largest of the islands and ruling over others. If they remained in Ionia he could see no hope of freedom for them.'[4] Thales advocated a closer union in Ionia: Teos should become their political capital and the other cities should be related to her as Attic demes to Athens.[5] No action was taken; the cities fell again one by one, most of them without fighting, though Phocaea and Teos chose to evacuate to Corsica and Abdera. Miletus alone was unaffected; she had made her terms with Persia as with Lydia before.[6] The lesson that their only hope lay in joint action had been learnt by the time of the revolt, and a surprising degree of unity was at first achieved. It was natural that the Ionians should appeal to Greece from which

---

[1] Hdt. v. 121. [2] Hdt. v. 117.
[3] Hdt. i. 18. 3. [4] Hdt. i. 170. 1–2.
[5] Hdt. i. 170. 3. The attribution of these two policies to Bias and Thales is probably arbitrary.
[6] Hdt. i. 143. 1.

they had originally come; it was their misfortune that the assistance they received should be so miserably inadequate. Sparta, who had at least shown concern for the east Greeks when Sardis fell, was no longer prepared to interfere; but Athens, to whom Aristagoras also appealed, was won over. Twenty ships were sent and they were joined by five from Eretria. Herodotus cynically remarks that it proved easier to persuade 30,000 men than one, and the implication has point.[1] The Athenian decision was taken in the emotional atmosphere of a packed Assembly, and the appeal to the leadership of Athens in the colonization of Ionia had strong emotional force; it is unlikely that the speeches analysed the military prospect realistically. There is no need therefore to assume a delicate balance of political parties in Athens to account for the withdrawal of the Athenian force after the first reverse. The rebels had boldly attacked Sardis, possibly to relieve pressure on Miletus.[2] They met with little resistance though the citadel held out, but on their return they were roughly handled by a Persian force. This setback and the more realistic appreciation of the military odds are sufficient to account for the withdrawal.

In the second year of the revolt the Ionians sailed east to stiffen revolt in Cyprus. Herodotus says that the fleet was sent by the common Council of the Ionians, τὸ κοινὸν τῶν Ἰώνων, confirming that there was central direction behind the strategy.[3] The Panionium which had begun as a meeting of representatives from the twelve Ionian cities to carry on a common cult had developed into an Ionian consultative council earlier, but this was the first occasion known to us that it had functioned effectively to execute as well as discuss policy. We can also attribute to this council an agreement by the cities to mint coins that could be interchangeable from city to city. This is the natural explanation, first suggested in 1908 by P. Gardner, of a series of electrum coins of a common weight and with a common reverse.[4] Among the obverses are city heraldic types such as the sphinx of Chios and the forepart of a winged horse from Lampsacus; but some of the coins cannot be so easily

---

[1] Hdt. v. 97. 2.
[2] So Plut. De mal. Herodoti 24 (861B). The account of Herodotus (v. 100–1) does not suggest it.
[3] Hdt. v. 109. 3. [4] See Endnote 25, p. 441.

identified, and no coins have yet been found which can be attributed to Miletus or Mytilene. The choice of type may have rested with the magistrates in charge of the mints. The main practical purpose of this monetary agreement was to provide a convenient coinage for paying troops; but it was also a 'nationalistic' gesture. Electrum recalled the earliest coinages of free Ionia; an electrum coinage was a reaction against the gold and silver of the Persians.

The part played by Cyprus needs brief consideration, for the significance of Cyprus is a controversial issue in the story of the Delian League. The island had been settled from Greece in the Mycenaean period but, as in Sicily, the Greeks had to face increasing competition from Phoenician settlements. In the dark ages that followed the destruction of the Mycenaean palaces in Greece and the Dorian invasion Cyprus had little contact with the Greek world, but when in the eighth century the Greeks opened up again the sea routes of their Mycenaean predecessors Cyprus renewed the links with her Greek past. The island occupied a key strategic position in the eastern Mediterranean, watching the coast of Cilicia and Syria and offering natural ports of call on the trade route to Syria and Egypt; but she was too far removed from the rest of the Greek world to maintain her independence and fell successively to the dominant empires of the near east, first Assyria, then Egypt, and finally Persia. Intermarriage and the increasing cosmopolitanism of trading ports tended to merge the sharp distinction between Greek and Phoenician in a common Cypriot stock, but the distinction was maintained at the higher levels and the rulers of the more Hellenized towns of Cyprus liked to emphasize their Hellenism. This is reflected in the fine series of Cypriot sculptures of the late archaic period which were produced in Cyprus, but are much closer to Greek than to Syrian, Phoenician, or Egyptian work.[1]

Onesilus, younger brother of the king of Salamis, was the leader of the Hellenists at the time of the revolt. According to Herodotus he had urged revolt from Persia earlier, but had failed to persuade his brother. He now seized power and succeeded in bringing over the whole island with the exception of Amathus. But the issue shows that the support he had won so

[1] See p. 477 n. 1.

rapidly was largely superficial. In the decisive battle the ruler of Curium withdrew his substantial contingent and the war chariots of Salamis followed their lead. Onesilus of Salamis and the king of Soli were both killed in the fighting; resistance in the field collapsed. A series of sieges followed by which the rebel cities were quickly reduced, with one exception. Soli, Herodotus tells us, resisted for four months; its ruler had once entertained the Athenian Solon and had been gracefully flattered by him in elegant verses.[1] The Ionian fleet meanwhile had won a victory off shore, but the Persian supremacy on land was decisive.[2] The short-lived Cyprian campaign, however, shows that the Ionians regarded the Greek cities of the island as partners in the revolt, sufficiently important to risk their navy more than 400 miles from their main bases.

The failure in Cyprus was a severe blow to Greek morale. Central direction of strategy weakened and the initiative passed to the Persians whose land forces were directed against the coastal cities on three fronts. They met with little serious resistance, but Miletus could not be taken by assault and the strong islands of Chios, Samos, and Lesbos were not likely to surrender without fighting. The final blow had therefore to be delivered by a naval expedition. In 494 the Persian fleet, assembled from Phoenicia, Cilicia, Cyprus, and Egypt sailed into the Aegean and overwhelmed a large Greek fleet at the battle of Lade. This Persian victory was primarily due to the failure of Greek morale. The Persians had been using the deposed tyrants to work on their people, and the growing hopelessness of the military situation had considerably eased their task. Some of the contingents as a result were completely undermined before the action began. Of the large Samian fleet of sixty triremes only eleven remained to fight it out. The Samian deserters were followed by the Lesbians. Only the Chians, who had manned 100 ships, fought fiercely to the end. This military and political collapse was less than a generation old when the Delian League was formed.[3]

The failure of the revolt had clearly demonstrated that the resources of the east Greeks in manpower and money were

---

[1] Plut. *Solon* 26. 3 (F 4). Archaeological evidence suggests that the resistance at Paphus may have been more determined than Herodotus implies, App. 7, p. 481.
[2] Hdt. v. 108–15.   [3] Hdt. vi. 6–17.

inadequate to secure and maintain independence; only if they had strong and continuous help from mainland Greece could they hope to hold their own. The Persians also had learnt a political lesson. The deposition of tyrants with which the revolt opened had been too widespread and popular to be ignored; a policy of concessions was now wisely adopted. To prevent the outbreak of wars between neighbours that could spread dangerously Artaphernes, satrap of Sardis, insisted that all disputes between states must be submitted to arbitration.[1] He also initiated a survey of the cities' territories and laid down a new assessment of tribute based on land measurement. A little later when a punitive force was about to sail against Greece and it was important to avoid any hostile reactions in Ionia, all remaining tyrants were deposed and the Persian general Mardonius was authorized to restore democracies.[2] Had there been no provocation from outside the Ionians would probably have accepted their lot and even been content with it. The Persian failure in Greece, however, created a new situation.

The invasion of Greece was at first regarded by the Persians as little more than police action. The first plan was to advance along the north coast of the Aegean and move south through Thessaly, but a severe storm wrecked Mardonius' fleet off the Athos promontory and the expedition was abandoned. Instead it was decided, two years later in 490, to sail across the Aegean. The force was entirely sea-borne and cannot have been very large, possibly some 20,000 fighting men;[3] but Persian confidence was high and with them on the expedition was Hippias, expelled from his tyranny twenty years earlier but still confident that he could attract support within Athens. The objectives were restricted, to destroy Eretria and Athens and to bring back their populations as slaves; and the campaign opened well. The Eretrians shut themselves up behind their walls and the gates were opened by traitors; those who did not escape

[1] Hdt. vi. 42. 1. A good example of the policy in practice in the early fourth century, *SIG* 134.

[2] Hdt. vi. 43. 3.

[3] The figure is no more than a reasonable inference from Herodotus' figure for the number of Persian dead, 6,400. In the battle the Persian centre was virtually wiped out; the two wings seem only to have been lightly engaged. But see Labarbe, *La Loi navale de Thémistocle*, 162–6, where it is noted that 6,000 is the same proportion of 300,000 (a figure commonly attributed to the Persians) as 192 (Athenian casualties) of 9,000 (Athenian total).

were rounded up to be shipped back to Persia when the second half of the operation was completed. The common expectation in Greece must have been that Athens would suffer the same fate. The Athenians, however, decided not to risk the hazards of a siege and marched out to meet the Persians where they had landed, at Marathon. Only the Plataeans were with them when the battle was fought, but the Spartans, who had promised help, arrived the next day.

The Spartans saw some 6,000 Persian dead on the battlefield and learnt that the Athenian losses had been negligible: the scene made a deep impression and was not forgotten when the Persians came again. On the Persian side the losses had been serious but not crippling. They still thought after the battle that by sailing at full speed to Phalerum they might take and hold Athens, but when they arrived off shore they found the Athenian army back from Marathon. They could not attempt a landing against troops made confident by victory. The Persians sailed back across the Aegean.

It would be interesting to know what was the reaction in the Persian Empire to this unexpected defeat. East of Sardis, apart from Persian court circles, Marathon probably raised barely a ripple. Only very limited resources had been committed; most of the satrapies had had no part in the affair. West of Sardis, in Miletus and the other coastal cities, there must have been excitement and interest. The Persian force had been mainly recruited in the east but, according to Herodotus, Ionians and Aeolians had also sailed with Datis.[1] They had seen the full measure of the defeat, but it is significant that there are no traces in the record of revolts in the Ionian cities. They knew too well that Marathon could not be the end, and they had learnt the lesson of the Ionian revolt; it is the last battle that counts. Egypt, however, not yet completely resigned to provincial status, tried to break away in 486 and it was not until 484 that the revolt was crushed. Darius had now been succeeded by Xerxes, a king of lesser stature in character and capacity. But there was nothing irresponsible in his decision to conquer Greece. Herodotus, strongly influenced by tragedy which was the dominant literary form as he grew to maturity, depicts Xerxes as vain and impatient, overriding the wise

[1] Hdt. vi. 98. 1.

counsels of experienced advisers. Hybris is the motive force, and Nemesis the inevitable issue. This picture is not historical; the incorporation of Greece within the Persian Empire was a logical objective. The northern command had already extended Persian control along the north Aegean shore through Macedon to the borders of Thessaly, and in Thessaly and other states there were powerful elements ready to welcome the Persians. The Ionian revolt had shown the close links between mainland and east Greeks; if Marathon were not avenged the Athenians might return to their meddling. The objective was no longer only the destruction of Athens and Eretria; Xerxes intended the complete conquest of Greece. For this more ambitious aim he decided to commit his main imperial levy, and it is doubtful if any of his military advisers seriously opposed him.[1]

In urging Sparta to war in 432 the Corinthians, according to Thucydides, claimed that in the great invasion the Persians failed primarily through their own mistakes.[2] His continuous disparagement of earlier history in comparison with the war which he was to relate is pitched rather too high, but this judgement on Xerxes' failure is fundamentally right. The Persian army was too large and cumbersome; the fleet was used without imagination; Xerxes was too confident to consider delay and made inadequate use of his political opportunities. Had he not decided to enter the straits at Salamis to force on a battle, the Greek fleet would have been powerless and the brittleness of Greek unity would soon have been exposed. Medism would have become a serious issue in most of the Peloponnesian states and it is doubtful whether an effective Greek army could have been put in the field in 479. But Xerxes, deceived by Themistocles' message, sent his fleet into the narrows by Salamis expecting the disintegration of Lade to be repeated. The Greek victory was complete but the war was not ended. Xerxes himself returned to Asia with much loss of dignity and what was left of the fleet withdrew; but Mardonius was left with a picked army that could have been more effective than the unwieldy masses that Xerxes had led the previous year.

---

[1] In Herodotus (vii. 10) Artabanus, uncle to the king, advises against the expedition, but the warner is too common as a literary device in Herodotus to inspire confidence.   [2] Thuc. i. 69. 5.

In 480 the Greeks had divided their effort between land and sea; in 479 the main emphasis was concentrated on the army. The Athenians, who in 480 had used all their available manpower in their fleet, now sent 8,000 hoplites to the Greek army under the Spartan regent Pausanias; the Spartan king Leotychidas, supported by the Athenian Xanthippus, commanded a fleet of only 110 ships. What part the strategic command assigned to the much-reduced Greek fleet is uncertain but its main commission was probably to ensure that the Persian fleet did not return to the offensive. In August Pausanias won a crushing victory at Plataea for which the Spartan hoplites were primarily responsible; soon afterwards news came that the Greek fleet had won a double victory at Mycale.

The first appeal to Leotychidas to take the offensive had come from a small group of Chian conspirators and had been rejected; Leotychidas escorted them to Delos but was not yet prepared to go further. Herodotus overdramatizes the situation: 'Beyond Delos all spelt danger to the Greeks; they did not know those areas and they thought that enemy forces were everywhere'.[1] We can be reasonably certain that this was not the Greek mood. They were more probably maintaining a defensive attitude until they saw the pattern of operations on land and had more reliable news of the situation in Ionia. The news that came to them at Delos was encouraging. Samian loyalists reported that Ionia was ready to revolt, and that the Persian fleet was in no shape to fight. They gave their pledge that Samos would join the alliance, and their leader, Hegesistratus, name of good omen, sailed with Leotychidas.[2] The Greek fleet made ready for action by the temple of Hera on Samos, but the Persians refused battle and withdrew to the mainland where they beached their ships under the protection of their army. The fortifications of the Persian camp had been rapidly improvised and did not long hold out. The Athenians broke through and were followed by the contingents from Corinth, Sicyon, and Troezen. The Persians themselves at first continued to fight and two of their commanders were killed in action, but soon resistance collapsed, the Persians fled, and their suspicions of the Ionian contingents proved fully justified. Before the battle they had disarmed the Samians and had detached the Milesians

---

[1] Hdt. viii. 132. 3.   [2] Hdt. ix. 91.

to guard the routes. Now the Samians did what they could to help the Greeks and the rest of the Ionians followed their example; the Milesians made good use of their position to cut down stragglers. 'So for the second time Ionia revolted from Persia.'[1]

From this victory the Greek fleet returned to Samos where a council of war was held. The situation which faced Leotychidas was one he had not anticipated and for which he was not fitted. The Ionians were deserting in embarrassing numbers; what was to be done with them? The Spartans proposed that those east Greeks who wished to throw off the Persian yoke should be conveyed back to Greece and settled in coastal towns to be taken from states which had Medized. This proposal was not as short-sighted as has generally been held. The Ionian revolt had shown that the east Greeks could not maintain their independence without substantial and continuous assistance. It was reasonable to believe that such continuous assistance was not militarily practicable and in a sense the Ionians would be returning to their home. But the Ionians were in no mood for such caution. The Persians had been decisively defeated by land and sea and strong Greek forces were now with them. As Herodotus elsewhere emphasizes, the Ionian cities enjoyed a splendid climate; they had no intention to leave their lands unless compelled. The Athenians supported them: Leotychidas had to follow, with a good grace.[2]

The outcome of the debate was that the Greeks brought into their alliance the Samians, Chians, and Lesbians and the other islanders who were with them. They bound them by pledge and oaths 'that they would remain loyal and not leave the Greek alliance'.[3] This is less than we should have expected. If Herodotus' report is correct the expansion of the Greek alliance was confined to islanders; Miletus and the other mainlanders were not yet admitted. The decision represents not a complete victory for Athens but a compromise, possibly reached after the issue had been referred to the Greeks on the mainland. The oaths, however, administered to the islanders

[1] Hdt. ix. 104.
[2] Hdt. ix. 106. 3. The Ionian climate, i. 142. 1. For the conflict between sources for the Council at Samos see Endnote 1, p. 413.
[3] Hdt. ix. 106. 4: πίστι τε καταλαβόντες καὶ ὁρκίοισι ἐμμενέειν τε καὶ μὴ ἀποστήσεσθαι.

implied that the war against Persia would be continued indefinitely under Spartan leadership. The first step was to sail to the Hellespont to break up the Persian bridges.

When the Greek fleet reached Abydus they found that the Persian bridges had already disintegrated. Leotychidas with the Peloponnesians thereupon decided to sail back to Greece, but the Athenians under Xanthippus remained. The Chersonese was a tempting objective, for it had been occupied by Athens in the time of Pisistratus and had been retained by the Philaids until the end of the Ionian revolt; local support could be expected. The Athenian fleet crossed from Abydus to besiege Sestus, the main focus of Persian resistance, and with them were the islanders who had been accepted into the Greek alliance by Leotychidas.[1] Thucydides' account is different: 'The Athenians and the allies from Ionia and the Hellespont, who had now revolted from the King, remained and besieged Sestus which was held by the Medes.'[2] The versions of Herodotus and Thucydides cannot lightly be reconciled by assuming that, after the Athenians had settled down to the siege, they were joined by contingents from Ionia and the Hellespont, because Thucydides in saying that they remained with the Athenians clearly implies that they were with the fleet that sailed to break down the Persian bridges.[3] Herodotus' account is the more convincing. Though the Athenians may have been joined by near neighbours of Sestus it is very doubtful whether the mainland Ionians, who had not yet been admitted into the alliance, took part in the reduction of Sestus.[4]

The Persian commander of the district had not expected a Greek attack. His food supplies were inadequate and before the winter was over the garrison was reduced to eating bedding. When even these emergency supplies were finished the commander and his Persian troops escaped through the Greek

[1] Hdt. ix. 114. 2. Herodotus does not say that the islanders remained with the Athenians, but the point that concerns him is the contrast between the Spartans and the Athenians; he had temporarily forgotten the islanders who in his account neither stay nor return home. Their interests will have led them to follow Athens.

[2] Thuc. i. 89. 2.

[3] Gomme, HCT i. 257 and ATL iii. 190f. minimize the difference between the two sources. See also H. D. Meyer, Hist. xii (1963), 405–46.

[4] There may possibly be confusion behind Thucydides' account. The Ionian and Hellespontine contingents should possibly be associated with the capture of Byzantium by Pausanias in 478.

lines; in the morning the inhabitants opened the gates. The Persian fugitives were quickly rounded up and their commander against whom the Greeks of the peninsula had old scores to settle was crucified after watching the stoning to death of his son. The Athenians and islanders sailed home and with them took the cables of the Persian bridges to be dedicated in their temples.[1] It has been suggested that the Athenian portico built along the side of the temple of Apollo at Delphi was designed to display some of them.[2] If this is right the Spartans may have wondered whether Delphi was the right place for such a dedication in the name of Athens alone.

When Herodotus writes of the sequel to the battle of Mycale 'so for the second time Ionia revolted from Persia' he is deliberately recalling the earlier revolt led by Aristagoras. There were indeed similarities, but the differences were more important. The Ionian cities were again the leaders in the movement, but they were considerably weaker than in 499. Miletus in particular had been crippled when the city had fallen in 494 and, though the impression given by Herodotus that the whole population was transplanted to the Persian Gulf is manifestly exaggerated, Miletus could not hope to recover within a generation. The losses in ships and men at the battle of Lade had been heavy, especially in the large fleet from Chios. But while Ionia was weaker, the prospect of help from the mainland was improved beyond measure. By accepting east Greeks into their alliance the Greeks of the mainland had virtually committed themselves to support Ionia and, however reluctant Leotychidas may have been, the sequel in 478 shows that the Greek alliance did not regard its work as completed. But the most revolutionary change was the growth in stature of Athens. Both politically and militarily she was now in a much stronger position than when she withdrew her twenty ships from the Ionian revolt. The quick succession of ostracisms in the ten years after Marathon points to sharp political antagonisms, but when Xerxes crossed into Europe the ranks closed; the ostracized were recalled and, thanks largely to the inspiring leadership of Themistocles, Athens presented a united front. There were Athenian refugees with Xerxes, Pisistratids and

---

[1] Hdt. ix. 114–21.

[2] P. Amandry, *Fouilles de Delphes*, ii. 37–121. Reservations, ML 25.

others, but they seem to have made no impression on Athenian morale. At the time of Marathon a fifth column at Athens had been prepared to admit the Persians;[1] when in 479 Mardonius sent a Hellespontine Greek to offer terms, a councillor who proposed that the terms should be put before the people was stoned to death.[2]

Athens was also much stronger militarily. In 483–482 a new and richer vein of silver had been struck in the Laurium area and the state, which normally could barely cover state expenditure from income, now suddenly had a large surplus available. It was first intended, Herodotus tells us, that this windfall should be distributed to citizens at 10 drachmas a head, but Themistocles was able to persuade the Assembly to divert the silver to the construction of triremes.[3] As a result the Athenians, who at the time of the Ionian revolt had probably less than 100 ships, including penteconters, had by 480 added 200 new triremes. No Greek state could match this fleet and it proved the backbone of the combined navy in 480 at Artemisium and Salamis; and the naval victory of Salamis had been the turning-point in the war. Herodotus goes out of his way to express his personal judgement which he knows will be unpopular in many parts of Greece:

If the Athenians had been overawed by the approaching danger and had abandoned their country, or if, without abandoning it, they had remained and surrendered to Xerxes, no one would have attempted to oppose the king by sea. And if no one had opposed Xerxes by sea this is what would have happened on land. Even if several lines of wall had been built by the Peloponnesians across the Isthmus the Lacedaemonians would have been betrayed by their allies, not willingly but inevitably; for the allied cities would have been captured one by one by the naval arm of the barbarians and the Lacedaemonians would have been isolated. Isolated, performing deeds of great valour, they would have died a noble death. Either they would have suffered this fate or seeing first that the rest of Greece was Medizing they would have made their terms with Xerxes. So in either case Greece would have come under Persian rule.[4]

In this declaration of faith Herodotus has often been thought to be speaking as a partisan of an Athenian empire that had

---

[1] Hdt. vi. 109. 5, 124. 2.   [2] Hdt. ix. 4–5.
[3] Hdt. vii. 144.   [4] Hdt. vii. 139. 1–4.

grown increasingly unpopular in the Greek world rather than as a historian making an independent judgement on the evidence available to him. It is easier to believe that his conclusion represents his own considered view. It was the right view, and the arguments he uses are militarily sound.

Unless Herodotus' account is misleading, Leotychidas had no wish to continue the offensive in the east. He was virtually forced to follow the Athenian lead but when he returned to Greece in the autumn he is likely to have called for a reconsideration of policy. Sparta, however, accepted the new development and in the next year Pausanias sailed east with a Greek fleet drawn from the Peloponnese, Athens, and other states.[1] This implies a meeting of states' representatives after the battle of Plataea, but possibly not before spring 478, at which it was decided to continue the war conjointly against Persia.[2] The fleet that sailed in the summer from Greece was less than 100 strong and Athens sent no more than thirty ships, but on the other side of the Aegean they would be joined by their island allies.

The first objective is interesting and somewhat puzzling. Why did the Greeks begin their new offensive against Persia by sailing as far east as Cyprus? Thucydides sums up the campaign very briefly: 'they reduced the greater part of the island'.[3] This suggests hostile action against a hostile island, but militarily this would seem positively irresponsible, for the Greeks could not expect to occupy and hold a hostile island so far from the Aegean. Diodorus gives a more intelligible account, though it may be no more than sensible rationalization, with which Thucydides can be reconciled. According to Diodorus 'the Greeks freed those cities which still had Persian garrisons'.[4] This looks more like an attempt to gain control of the island for the Greeks and it recalls at once the attempt of the Ionians in their earlier revolt to support the movement against Persia within the island. The main points of attack were probably the chief Phoenician cities; it is significant that a hoard of coins

---

[1] Thuc. i. 94. 1 gives 20 Peloponnesian, 30 Athenian ships καὶ τῶν ἄλλων ξυμμάχων πλῆθος. Diod. xi. 44. 2 has 50 Peloponnesian and 30 Athenian ships; the other allies are ignored. It is very doubtful whether Diodorus had good evidence for his figures. See App. 2, p. 447.

[2] For the so-called Covenant of Plataea see App. 10 (B), p. 507.

[3] Thuc. i. 94. 2: καὶ αὐτῆς τὰ πολλὰ κατεστρέψαντο.   [4] Diod. xi. 44. 2.

found at Citium seems to have been hidden at about this time.[1]
In his *Persae*, performed six years later, Aeschylus gives a stirring
catalogue of states that were won by Darius and under the
impact of the defeat at Salamis lost to the Persians. Included
are the Cyprian cities of Paphus, Soli, and Salamis.[2] Salamis
had led the revolt in 498 and throughout most of the fifth and
fourth centuries was to champion Hellenism in the island; Soli
had resisted longest after the decisive battle, and Paphus had
not given in without a struggle.[3] The result of Pausanias'
expedition of 478 was to end temporarily Persian control of
the island, to intimidate the Phoenicians, and to encourage the
Greek cities to pursue a Greek policy.

The second objective of the summer was Byzantium—a more
natural choice: it controlled one of the two shortest passages
between Asia and Europe and the attack was a logical sequel
to the capture in the previous winter of Sestus which controlled
the other. Byzantium also controlled the entry to the Euxine
from which came vitally needed supplies of corn to mainland
Greece. The Persians had little hope of holding the town against
a hostile population and the very brief record in the sources
implies that no serious opposition was offered; the young
Pausanias entered a rich inheritance in triumph. The brilliant
successes of 478 should have increased the solidarity of the
Greeks and convinced the Spartans that their decision to continue the war was right; but there were always elements at
Sparta opposed to overseas commitments and the behaviour
of Pausanias played into the hands of this opposition. The true
portrait of Pausanias is not recoverable. Ultimately he was
found guilty of intriguing with the Persian king and starved to
death when he took refuge in a temple at Sparta. But the evidence quoted by Thucydides looks suspicious and Herodotus
seems to imply that he at least did not believe that Pausanias
was as black as he was painted.[4] We cannot, however, completely rewrite the story. Pausanias was recalled to Sparta
towards the end of 478 and, though acquitted, was not replaced
in command. In his place, Dorcis was sent out with a small
force, but the allies made it clear that a Spartan commander

[1] P. Dikaios and E. S. G. Robinson, *Num. Chron.* 1935, 165–90.
[2] Aesch. *Persae* 891–2.   [3] See App. 7, p. 477.
[4] See App. 4, p. 465.

was no longer acceptable, and Sparta took no further action. The other Peloponnesians may have returned to Greece when Pausanias was recalled; it is virtually certain that they did not remain when Spartan leadership was finally rejected.

Thucydides says that the Spartans 'were anxious to be rid of the war against the Medes. They thought that the Athenians were capable of undertaking the leadership and that at the time they were well disposed towards them'.[1] The same tradition is reflected in the Athenian speech at the Spartan Assembly in the summer of 432, and later in Xenophon, the Aristotelian *Athenian Constitution*, and Plutarch.[2] It is difficult to believe that the transition was quite as smooth as this, and Herodotus suggests that it was not. After relating how the Greek allies refused to serve under an Athenian commander at Salamis and how Athens withdrew rather than cause divisions, he proceeds: 'They no longer advanced their claim against Sparta but gave way for as long as they urgently needed the allies. This they made plain, for when they had driven the Persian back and carried the fighting into his own country they made the arrogance of Pausanias their excuse and took the command from the Lacedaemonians.'[3] Diodorus is more explicit. He says that the Spartans resented losing the command and were angry with the allies. The Gerousia was called and presumably there followed a meeting of the Spartan Assembly. 'The younger generation and many others wanted to recover the command, thinking that it would bring wealth and power. It seemed that there was general support for this view and no opposition was expected until one of the Councillors, Hetoemaridas, persuaded them that it was not in Sparta's interest to compete for the sea.'[4] This debate Diodorus puts in 475–474, but it follows Sparta's abdication of the command and is separated from it by two years of exclusively western history. If there was such a debate it was most probably in 478 or 477, but the credentials are not very good.[5] However, though the

---

[1] Thuc. i. 95. 7: ἀπαλλαξείοντες δὲ καὶ τοῦ Μηδικοῦ πολέμου καὶ τοὺς Ἀθηναίους νομίζοντες ἱκανοὺς ἐξηγεῖσθαι καὶ σφίσιν ἐν τῷ τότε παρόντι ἐπιτηδείους.

[2] Thuc. i. 75. 2; Xen. *Hell.* vi. 5. 34; Arist. *Ἀθ. Πολ.* 23. 2: συνέβη ... τὴν τῆς θαλάττης ἡγεμονίαν λαβεῖν ἀκόντων Λακεδαιμονίων, with Gomme, *HCT* i. 262, n. on 1. 96. 1; Plut. *Ar.* 23. 7.

[3] Hdt. viii. 3. 2.   [4] Diod. xi. 50.

[5] For Diodoran chronology, see App. 2, p. 452.

debate may not be genuine, we believe that it is nearer to the atmosphere of the time than Thucydides' version. The Spartans had been humiliated by Athens in the years following the expulsion of the Pisistratids; they had been too late for Marathon; during Xerxes' invasion there had been considerable friction below the surface and, even more recently, the Spartans had seen Athens ignoring their protests and outwitting them to rebuild their walls. It is more likely that opinion was divided at Sparta, as it was to be so often later, between those who found Sparta's conservatism too restrictive and wanted a more dynamic foreign policy and those who remained satisfied with predominance in the Peloponnese. In 478 there may well have seemed to be a serious danger that Sparta would attempt to force her way back into the command. But it was not long before new factors eased relations between Athens and Sparta and made coexistence more acceptable to both. Sparta was soon preoccupied within the Peloponnese, where Argos again seemed dangerous and the Arcadians restless. At Athens Themistocles, who had little sympathy with Sparta, lost favour, and was eclipsed by Cimon who never concealed his Spartan sympathies. We hear no more of strained relations until Sparta, according to Thucydides, undertook to help Thasos in her revolt from Athens by invading Attica.

3

THE FOUNDATION OF THE DELIAN LEAGUE

Aｃｃｏｒｄｉｎｇ to Plutarch it was under pressure, particularly from Chians, Samians, and Lesbians, that Aristides on behalf of the Athenians took over the leadership of the allies. He adds the picturesque embroidery that, when Aristides asked for some more solid evidence that they meant what they said, Ouliades of Samos and Antagoras of Chios plotted at Byzantium and rammed Pausanias' vessel amidships.[1] They may indeed have been the commanders of their contingents in 478, whose names were preserved in local tradition, but the story, though not impossible, is more probably a later invention.[2] Nor should we put much faith in the later moralizing stories about Aristides. In Greek historical tradition Aristides became the perfect man of justice, preferring right to expediency, generous to friends and enemies.[3] It is salutary to remember that a contemporary, Callaeschrus, had very different views; for him Aristides was ἀλώπηξ Ἀλωπεκῆθεν, 'fox by deme and fox by nature'.[4] We can believe that Aristides had a shrewd idea of the benefits that a league under Athenian leadership could bring to Athens, but we should not be too

---

[1] Plut. *Ar.* 23. 4–5.

[2] Ouliades, a Samian name, Chr. Habicht. *AM* lxxii (1957), p. 183, no. 19, l. 1 (? late fourth cent.) ; *SIG* 619. 36. (second cent.)

[3] Already in Herodotus (viii. 79. 1) he is ἄριστον ἄνδρα γενέσθαι ἐν Ἀθήνῃσι καὶ δικαιότατον, but the preface τὸν ἐγὼ νενόμικα, πυνθανόμενος αὐτοῦ τὸν τρόπον suggests to me that Herodotus may be taking sides in a controversy; cf. the repetition in viii. 95. 1.

[4] *Epistolographi Graeci* (Hercher, 1873), p. 743, Letter IV: ἀλλ' ἐκεῖνος μὲν ἐρρώσθω ἐπίκοτος ὢν ἀεὶ καὶ δυσμένης καὶ φθονερὸς καί, ὥσπερ ποτε ἔφη Κάλλαισχρος ἐπ' αὐτόν, μᾶλλον τῷ τρόπῳ Ἀλωπεκῆθεν ἢ τῷ δήμῳ. The *Letters of Themistocles*, though merely literary exercises, were based on sources good as well as bad. This witticism, running so strongly against the main tradition, is likely to be genuine. Callaeschrus was presumably the father of Critias, one of the main leaders of the Thirty. He probably thought that Aristides was thinking too little of his own social class.

cynical. Fear was one of the motives for the Athenian decision to accept the responsibilities of leadership, because Athens knew that she more than any other Greek state might have to face renewed attack from Persia; but there was also pride and generosity in the Athenian mood in 478. Later conditions should not be read back into the early years. It was the allies who had most to gain from Athenian leadership and from the start it was freely recognized by all that Athens was to lead and not merely join the alliance.

The vital talks presumably took place on Aristides' flagship in the late summer or autumn of 478 at Byzantium. When in 377 Athens once again undertook the leadership of a maritime league for mutual defence, the structure of the league was the outcome of consultations with a small group of allies.[1] The same procedure is likely to have been adopted in 478; we can believe that principles and procedure were agreed after discussion between Aristides and the commanders from Chios, Samos, and Lesbos. The next stage was to advertise the proposals and win as many adherents as possible as soon as possible. We may accept the general assumption that heralds were sent out to the Greek cities of the Aegean islands and coastlands inviting them to send representatives to Delos in the early summer of 477 to inaugurate solemnly the new alliance.[2] Had military considerations alone been relevant Samos might have seemed the most appropriate headquarters as it had been in 479, but Delos had the strong advantage of its religious associations. It had in the archaic period been the scene of an Ionian festival shared by the islands, Athens and Ionia.[3] In the seventh century Naxos seems to have had the dominating influence and her dedications were probably still the most conspicuous in 477;[4] but in the sixth century Athenian and Samian tyrants in turn had championed Delian Apollo to demonstrate their piety and extend their influence.[5] Delos had also practical advantages to offer. It was well situated in the centre of the Aegean, it had a good harbour, and, like Delphi, it had always been too weak to have independent political ambitions.

---

[1] Diod. xv. 28; Tod, *GHI* ii. 123 with p. 66; Accame, *La Lega Ateniese*, 33–7.
[2] *ATL* iii. 225.   [3] Thuc. iii. 104.
[4] H. Gallet de Santerre, *Délos primitive et archaïque*, 290–6.
[5] Hdt. i. 64. 2; Thuc. iii. 104. 2; Gallet de Santerre, op. cit., pp. 300 ff.

Thucydides outlines the original organization with characteristic economy:

The Athenians determined which states were to contribute money against the barbarian and which ships. For the declared purpose was to take revenge for what they had suffered by ravaging the king's territory. *Hellenotamiai* were then first instituted as an Athenian office and they received the *phoros*, this being the name given to the money contributions. And the first assessment was 460 talents. Delos was their treasury, and the meetings were held in the sanctuary. At first the allies whom they led were autonomous and took counsel at meetings which Athens and allies alike attended.[1]

We are told later that each state had an equal vote, so that the stronger members had no formal advantage in council.[2] There is much that we should like Thucydides to have added, and what he does say needs filling out, but he was not intending to write a detailed history of the Delian League. In a compressed paragraph he has given us the essence of the matter.

In this brief account Thucydides' reliability has been widely questioned on two points. His figure for the first assessment has often been rejected; it does indeed raise serious difficulties, but these will be discussed later. Some have also thought that Thucydides was wrong in assigning the office of *hellenotamiai* from the outset to Athenians; they believe that this was a change closely related to the transference of the treasury from Delos to Athens in 454 and that originally the treasurers were drawn from the whole alliance, or were at least subject to the approval of the allies.[3] We need less hesitation here. There is no sign of a variant tradition in any of the other sources and Thucydides' account corresponds with what we should expect. There was no question of the allies in 478 safeguarding themselves against Athenian encroachment or believing that they were equal partners with Athens; they knew that without continued help

---

[1] Thuc. i. 96–7. 1. For a different meaning of the last sentence, see p. 460.

[2] Thuc. iii. 11. 4, but see also p. 460.

[3] E. M. Walker (*CAH* v. 46) inferred from the fact that the tribute quota lists from 454–453 are numbered by the annual boards of *hellenotamiai* that this office did not become Athenian until the transfer of the treasury from Delos. The number, however, only indicates the number of years in which the total procedure set out in the heading of the first list has been followed. A. G. Woodhead (*JHS* lxxix (1959), 149–52) argued on general grounds that the *hellenotamiai*, even if Athenian, must have been formally elected by the League synod. The natural interpretation of the evidence makes, I think, better sense.

from Athens they would soon again be the fringe of a Persian satrapy. It was natural that Athens should supply the treasurers as well as the commanders-in-chief. The relationship is reflected in the form of the oath sworn by each of the allies to Aristides as representative of the Athenian people.

Oath-taking was a normal accompaniment of the making of treaties and in the fifth century oaths still carried a strong religious sanction; to solemnize this occasion lumps of metal were sunk in the sea.[1] The main content of the oath can be recovered from evidence direct and indirect. Herodotus, as we have seen, briefly records the nature of the oaths taken by the islanders after Mycale, 'that they would remain loyal to the alliance and not desert';[2] we should expect a similar form to be used a year later. We have also several inscriptions recording oaths imposed by Athens on allies after revolt. The terms change with the changing mood of Athenian imperialism, but the earliest example preserved, in the settlement with Erythrae from near the middle of the century, has as its main clause: 'I will not desert the *plethos* (common people) of Athens nor the allies of the Athenians.'[3] The phrase probably reflects the language of the original oaths.[4] The Aristotelian *Athenian Constitution* has a different formulation, requiring the allies 'to have the same enemies and friends'.[5] This formula occurs in Thucydides, in two surviving texts of treaties of the second half of the fifth century, and is common in the fourth century, and later;[6] but had it been used in 478 it is more likely to have continued in use for the allies through the century. The issue, however, is of more literary than historical importance, for there is no substantive difference in meaning. But the formula we prefer brings out more clearly the relationship; the Delian League was essentially 'Athens and the allies', not just 'the allies'.

Thucydides says that the allies were at first autonomous; he does not, however, say that this was stipulated in the oath nor

---

[1] Ἀθ. Πολ. 23. 5; Plut. Ar. 25. 1.

[2] Hdt. ix. 106. 4: ἐμμενέειν τε καὶ μὴ ἀποστήσεσθαι.

[3] ML 40. 23–4: [κ]αὶ οὐκ [ἀποσ]τέσομαι Ἀθεναίον τὸ π[λ]έθος οὐδὲ [τ|ὸν] χσυνμάχον τὸν Ἀθεναίον. The texts of these oaths are collected in App. 16, p. 377.

[4] See also F. R. Wust, *Hist.* iii (1954–5), 149 f.

[5] Ἀθ. Πολ. 23. 5.

[6] Thuc. i. 44. 1; *IG* i². 71 (= *SEG* x. 86). 20; ML 87. 17.

in any other formal record, and it almost certainly was not. The allies were not in a suspicious mood. Autonomy was taken for granted; there was no need for guarantees. No end was envisaged to the alliance, for the oath of loyalty was not qualified and the sinking of lumps of metal implied that the alliance was for all time. In the same spirit the Phocaeans, to strengthen their determination to emigrate to the west rather than become subject to Persia, had sunk lumps of iron in the sea and sworn that they would not return until the iron swam.[1] Athens was formally justified later when she rejected, perhaps with the approval of the allies, Naxos' demand to leave the league. She was also formally correct when in 440 she interfered in the war between Samos and Miletus.

In his description of League meetings held at Delos Thucydides is perhaps ambiguous: ἡγούμενοι δὲ αὐτονόμων τὸ πρῶτον τῶν ξυμμάχων καὶ ἀπὸ κοινῶν ξυνόδων βουλευόντων.[2] Common meetings, κοιναὶ ξύνοδοι, might be of two kinds: they could be common to Athens and the allies or common only to the allies. The second Athenian League, of the fourth century, had a council of allies in which the Athenians were not represented, and policy decisions required the agreement of this council with the Boule and Assembly of Athens. Diodorus' description of the Delian League might be taken to imply a similar bicameral constitution: 'Aristides advised all the allies to form a common council and to make Delos their treasury;[3] but Thucydides' language points to a simpler organization. In the crucial sentence the Athenians are the subject in sense and grammar and it is logical that κοινῶν should refer to what is shared by them with their allies. Later when the allies are called ἰσόψηφοι the context implies that they each had an equal vote with Athens, not that their combined vote was equal with that of the Athenians.[4] The natural model for the constitution-makers consciously or unconsciously to follow was the Pelopon-

---

[1] Hdt. i. 165. 3.   [2] Thuc. i. 97. 1.

[3] Diod. xi. 47. 1: συνέβουλευε τοῖς συμμάχοις ἅπασι κοινὴν ἄγουσι σύνοδον ἀποδεῖξαι [τὴν] Δῆλον κοινὸν ταμιεῖον.

[4] Thuc. iii. 11. 4: ἅμα μὲν γὰρ μαρτυρίῳ ἐχρῶντο μὴ ἂν τούς γε ἰσοψήφους ἄκοντας, εἰ μή τι ἠδίκουν οἷς ἐπῆσαν, ξυστρατεύειν. The Mytilenaeans are explaining why they were left independent by Athens. It was partly to give an air of respectability to Athenian actions. Independent allies with an equal vote would not join in crushing a revolt (as Lesbos and Chios did against Samos) unless the victim was guilty.

nesian League, which was similarly described as 'the Lacedaemonians and their allies', and in which the allies met with
Sparta and not separately, and the Greek alliance under
Spartan leadership against Persia, in which there was again
no question of two separate bodies.[1]

A different kind of difficulty arises from Thucydides' statement that the declared programme of the League was to ravage
the king's territory in vengeance for the damage he had
inflicted.[2] This surely is not wide enough. A policy limited to
revenge and compensation is inadequate to explain the solemn
oaths that bound the allies in perpetuity. The primary need of
the allies was to maintain the independence they had won and
to liberate their fellows who were still under Persian control.[3]
Thucydides repeats his original statement later when he makes
Hermocrates at Camarina say in his attack on Athenian
imperialism: 'they became the freely accepted leaders of the
Ionians and of those allies who originated from Athens: their
professed aim was to take revenge on the Mede'.[4] We may
prefer the different motivation he attributes to the Mytilenaeans
when they explain to Sparta's allies at Olympia why they had
revolted from Athens: 'we joined the alliance not to enslave
the Greeks to Athens but to bring freedom to the Greeks from
the Mede'.[5]

Athens was from the outset the dominant power in the
League, but the allies each had an equal voice at first in the
meetings held at Delos. We are not told how often these meetings were held nor at what time of year, but it is reasonable to
believe that they were regular meetings, not specially convened,
and that they were held when the allies' representatives brought
their tribute to Delos. When later the tribute came to Athens
it was associated with the Athenian festival of the Dionysia, at
the close of winter and the coming of spring. Perhaps the earlier
association had been with the festival of Delian Apollo. This
was a little later in the year, but not far from the opening of
the sailing season, a good time for an annual meeting whose

---

[1] Hammond interprets the evidence differently, holding that both the Delian
and the Peloponnesian Leagues were bicameral. See App. 3, p. 459.

[2] Thuc. i. 96. 1: πρόσχημα γὰρ ἦν ἀμύνεσθαι ὧν ἔπαθον δῃοῦντας τὴν βασιλέως
χώραν.

[3] For a different view, see App. 3, pp. 463 f.

[4] Thuc. vi. 76. 3.   [5] Thuc. iii. 10. 3.

main topics were probably the summer's campaigning and a financial report from the *hellenotamiai*. What else the meetings discussed we can only guess. Two passages only in our sources give us any information and neither is completely reliable. Plutarch tells us that 'when the Samians proposed that the tribute reserve should be moved from Delos to Athens, Aristides commented that this would be expedient but not just'.[1] The story as it stands is not satisfactory because Aristides' epigram is part of a synthetic tradition; it is attached with minor variants to other episodes in his career and reflects the debasement of history by rhetoric. Invented stories, as the *Letters of Themistocles* in particular show, can be very circumstantial, but the inclusion of Samos may represent a genuine tradition. If Aristides was alive when the proposal was made it was not carried out, for Delos retained the treasury long after Aristides' death in the early sixties; but it may refer to the actual transference in 454, and the story could have assumed its present form from the rhetorical question: 'What would the noble Aristides have thought?' For our present purpose we accept no more than a probability that at some time in or before 454 the Samians at a meeting of the allies at Delos proposed that the tribute treasury should be moved to Athens; this implies what we should expect, that League meetings were concerned with general League policy. The other passage comes from Diodorus, probably drawing on Ephorus. In the period following the Thasian revolt, he tells us, there was widespread discontent in the Aegean: 'The Athenians' relations with their allies were no longer sympathetic, but they ruled with violence and arrogance. And so the majority of the allies, unable to stand the harshness of Athenian rule, discussed revolt together, and some of them ignored the common Council and acted independently'.[2] This passage will be considered later in its context. It implies that League policy was still in the late sixties based on League meetings, but it is very uncertain whether Ephorus had any independent evidence to justify the use of this language.

There are many other things which we should like to know. Did the Council exercise any powers of jurisdiction over individual members of allied states who could be regarded as traitors? Did it ever act as a court of arbitration in disputes

---

[1] Plut. *Ar.* 25. 3.   [2] Diod. xi. 70. 3–4.

between allies? When cities did not bring their tribute, did the Council consider themselves responsible for ensuring that arrears were collected? Was the tribute reassessed periodically before the treasury was transferred to Athens, and, if so, was the reassessment subject to the final approval of the Council? To such questions we shall probably never know the answers.

We know enough, however, of the original constitution of the Delian League to know that in several respects it was different from the Hellenic League formed in 481 when Xerxes' invasion was impending. Sparta had been elected leader of that League and could have been deposed from the leadership by the votes of the allies. Athens, on the other hand, was invited to be leader of the Delian League and the allies took oaths not just to the allies but to Athens (as leader) and the allies. The oath taken by the allies when the Delian League was formed was accompanied by the sinking of lumps of metal in the sea symbolizing its permanence. When the Hellenic League was formed it was almost certainly not expected to last indefinitely. But it was not formally dissolved when Sparta and the Peloponnesians withdrew from overseas fighting, and Sparta was still posing as the leader of a Greek alliance when she tried unsuccessfully to dislodge the Aleuadae in Thessaly and took a Greek, not merely a Peloponnesian, fleet with her.[1] This position Athens seems to recognize; for when her hoplites, sent on Sparta's urgent appeal to storm the helots' stronghold on Ithome, were dismissed she 'abandoned the alliance made with Sparta against the Mede'.[2] But the Hellenic League had no sound financial basis. According to Plutarch the states contributed to costs but there was no provision for regular payments based on an assessment of resources. The Delian League was in fact a new and independent creation having no formal relation with the Spartan-led Hellenic League.

There remain to be considered the two most difficult problems in the establishment of the Delian League. What was the original membership and what was the nature and total of the first assessment?

[1] Hdt. vi. 72; Plut. *Them.* 20. 1–2 refers to the force as ὁ τῶν Ἑλλήνων στόλος.
[2] Thuc. i. 102–4: ἀφέντες τὴν γενομένην ἐπὶ τῷ Μήδῳ ξυμμαχίαν.

4

THE FIRST ASSESSMENT

THUCYDIDES gives no secure hint of the original extent of the League: his purpose did not require it; elsewhere there is little firm evidence. Predominantly it was an Ionian League. The alliance was built up round the great offshore islands and the coastal cities of Ionia, and according to Thucydides kinship was the link between Athens and the allies.[1] They appealed to her κατὰ τὸ ξυγγενές, for traditionally she was the founder of the Ionian cities. It is not necessary to believe that all the Ionian cities were original members.[2] The two Magnesias are absent from all surviving tribute lists and Magnesia on the Maeander could be given by the Persian king to Themistocles when he fled from Greece.[3] We should not, however, exclude Ephesus on the ground that Themistocles is said to have landed there in his flight from Greece.[4] Athens' control was not yet being rigorously applied and it is doubtful whether in the sixties friends of Persia would feel very uncomfortable in such an orientalized city as Ephesus.

There is a strange absence of explicit evidence about the Aegean islands that had not in the sixth century shared Ionia's fortunes. By 443 at the latest these islands formed one of five (later four) districts into which the tribute-payers are divided in the lists of the *hellenotamiai*, and Melos and Thera, both Dorian, are the only important islands not included. The choice of Delos in the centre of the Cyclades as the League headquarters makes it highly probable that the surrounding islands joined at once; nor need we exclude Andros which had resisted pressure from Themistocles when he was raising funds for the

---

[1] Thuc. i. 95. 1.

[2] R. Sealey's view that very few cities of the mainland were original members is discussed in App. 3, p. 464.

[3] Thuc. i. 138. 5.

[4] Thuc. i. 137. 2. According to a tradition that may not be earlier than Ephorus, Themistocles landed at Cumae, Plut. *Them.* 26. 1.

war in the Aegean after Salamis;[1] the mood in the Aegean was now very different and Andros is likely to have followed her neighbours. It has been suggested that even Aegina should be added to the list and the suggestion cannot be summarily dismissed.[2] It is true that Athenian relations with Aegina had been continuously hostile down to the invasion of Xerxes and that Sparta had been persuaded to demand Aeginetan hostages before the Marathon campaign, but in 480 Aegina had joined the Greeks and had played her full part in the resistance. Though heavily outnumbered by the Athenians the Aeginetan ships won the greater glory at the battle of Salamis.[3] Her ships sailed with Pausanias in 478 and were probably at Byzantium when the leadership was accepted by Athens. While Sparta could regard the continuation of war against Persia as none of her business Aegina might have thought very differently. She was still one of the richest states in Greece and her wealth was derived from trade. She had been the only state from mainland Greece to be represented at Naucratis, where she had her own temple, and as late as 480 she was engaged in the corn trade from the Euxine.[4] Aegina could have had a very practical interest in carrying the war against Persia into the eastern Mediterranean. More positive evidence comes from Diodorus who writes of an Aeginetan revolt from Athens in 464–463 after the revolt of Thasos and before the outbreak of the First Peloponnesian War. The Athenians attack the island, but the account breaks off before it is completed. A little later, in the course of the war against the Peloponnesians, the Athenians again attack Aegina, though there is no reference back to the first passage, and the fighting ends in the reduction of Aegina and her incorporation in the empire.[5] Though the first passage speaks of a revolt and the second implies that Aegina was outside the League the language of the two passages is suspiciously alike and this would seem to be one of several occasions in this period when Diodorus creates two events from one.[6] While Diodorus is muddled Thucydides is quite clear. In his account the struggle of Aegina against Athens is a war and not a revolt,

---

[1] Hdt. viii. 111–12.   [2] D. MacDowell, *JHS* lxxx (1960), 118–21.
[3] Hdt. viii. 93. 1 : ἐν δὲ τῇ ναυμαχίῃ ταύτῃ ἤκουσαν Ἑλλήνων ἄριστα Αἰγινῆται.
[4] Hdt. ii. 178. 3; vii. 147. 2.   [5] Diod. xi. 70. 2–3; 78. 3–4.
[6] See App. 2, p. 456.

and each side has its own allies.[1] When he says that on Pausanias' first recall the allies, *except the Peloponnesians*, went over to Athens he implies that Aegina, with the other Peloponnesians, left the Greek fleet before the oaths of alliance were exchanged.[2]

The original membership cannot be confined to Ionians. Aeolian Lesbos had played a leading part in the preliminary negotiations and the leading Aeolian coastal cities normally shared the fortunes of the Ionians. We should also include some cities at least in Chalcidice, for one of the clauses of the Peace of Nicias that ended the first phase of the Second Peloponnesian War stipulated that Argilus, Stagirus, Acanthus, Stolus, Olynthus, and Spartolus should rejoin the Athenian alliance, but with certain safeguards. They were to have independence in jurisdiction and should pay tribute according to the original assessment of Aristides, as contrasted with the inflated assessments of the war years, particularly that of 425.[3] The inclusion of these cities need cause no surprise. They had been on the path of the invading Persian army, and they had drawn off by their restlessness part of the Persian force left in Greece at the end of 480.[4] But it is doubtful whether many if any of the Greek cities of the north Aegean coast were included in the original membership. Eion at the mouth of the Strymon certainly was held by a Persian garrison until 476 and Doriscus on the middle Hebros remained in Persian hands still longer.[5] Thasos, an island and therefore more secure, had already roused Persian suspicions before the war and probably joined at once, but the status of Abdera, Maronea, and the other coastal towns is considerably more doubtful. Herodotus tells us that before the war there were Persian military governors throughout Thrace and the Chersonese. 'All were expelled by the Greeks after the invasion with the exception of Eion and Doriscus.'[6] His words imply, though we should not demand precision in such matters

---

[1] Thuc. i. 105. 2: πολέμου δὲ καταστάντος πρὸς Αἰγινήτας . . . καὶ οἱ ξύμμαχοι ἑκατέροις παρῆσαν. Similar language is used for the forcible incorporation of Carystus in the League (Thuc. i. 98. 3), but not for the revolt of Thasos (i. 100. 2).

[2] Thuc. i. 95. 4; Diodorus (xi. 44. 6) says that the Peloponnesians sailed home before Pausanias was recalled, but he is unlikely to have had good evidence for this.

[3] Thuc. v. 18. 5: τὰς δὲ πόλεις φερούσας τὸν φόρον τὸν ἐπ' Ἀριστείδου αὐτονόμους εἶναι.

[4] Hdt. viii. 126–9.   [5] Hdt. vii. 106–7.   [6] Hdt. vii. 106. 2.

from Herodotus, that the garrisons were expelled not by the cities themselves but by the joint action of combined Greek forces, that is after the formation of the Delian League.

Though Hellespontine and Ionian contingents were probably with the Greeks at the capture of Byzantium in 478, it does not follow that all the coastal cities between the Aegean and Euxine were original members of the League. Some of the states in particular which were within easy reach of the satrap's capital at Dascylium may have hesitated. There is indeed some evidence that Lampsacus was not an original member, for when Themistocles took refuge in Persia the king assigned Lampsacus for his wine and Myus for his fish, while he ruled in Magnesia.[1] These assignments have usually been regarded as a gesture of empty vanity giving to Themistocles what Persia claimed but no longer controlled. The association of Themistocles, however, with Lampsacus seems too strong to allow this explanation. A Hellenistic inscription records the continuance in the third century of a festival instituted in his honour at which special privileges had been given to his son Cleophantus;[2] and the writer of one of the spurious *Letters of Themistocles* gives credit to him for lightening the burden of tribute that Lampsacus had to pay to the king.[3] On the other hand, better evidence proves that Lampsacus was a member of the League in the late fifties; the name appears unmistakably in the quota list for 452 and should almost certainly be restored in that of 450.[4] According to the earliest and best authorities Themistocles took refuge in Persia after the death of Xerxes in 465. It would be surprising if Lampsacus were outside the League in the years following the great victory of the Eurymedon and a regular tribute payer in the years following the Egyptian disaster of

---

[1] Diod. xi. 57. 7; Plut. *Them.* 29. 11.

[2] Lolling, *AM* vi (1881), 103–5, reproduced in Hill, *Sources*², p. 324 (B 122). See Highby, *Klio*, Beiheft xxxvi, p. 47, *ATL* iii. 111.

[3] Hercher, *Epistolographi Graeci*, p. 761 (Letter XX): καὶ Λάμψακον ἠλευθέρωσα καὶ πολλῷ φόρῳ βαρυνομένην ἄπαντος ἀφῆκα. Highby (loc. cit.) notes that the story may derive from Charon of Lampsacus. *ATL* hold that it is most unlikely that Lampsacus was politically under Persian control when 'given' to Themistocles. 'We suggest that Cleophantus, when restored to Athens, retained property in Magnesia and possibly in Myus, but waived his doubtful title in Lampsacus.' This compromise does not adequately explain the gratitude of Lampsacus to Themistocles.

[4] List 4. iv. 5; 2. v. 16.

454: surprising, but not impossible, for Lampsacus had been unreliable in the past. She had fought the Athenian establishment on the other side of the straits in the Chersonese;[1] Hippias of Athens when tyrant had married his daughter Archedice to Aiantides, son of the tyrant of Lampsacus, 'realizing that they had great influence with King Darius'.[2] Lampsacus joined the first Ionian revolt, but offered no more than token resistance when a Persian army approached.[3] The town was only a few miles from Dascylium, capital of the Phrygian satrapy. Similarly Myus was close enough to have been influenced by Magnesia. Her first preserved payment of tribute is in 451, and, like Miletus, she seems to have paid unnecessarily late in the early forties.[4]

While the Hellespont and Ionia had been bound up with the Greek successes of 479 and 478, the Carians had not been immediately involved. They had, however, fought strongly with the Greeks in the Ionian revolt and it is likely that most of the western Carians joined their Greek neighbours again. The attitude of Halicarnassus, however, is perhaps uncertain. In Xerxes' invasion Artemisia, ruler of Halicarnassus, came with him and Herodotus, himself from Halicarnassus, paints her portrait larger than life. Before the battle of Salamis she is Xerxes' wisest counsellor; in the battle she displays cunning and resource. She kept her position as ruler of Halicarnassus after the war and the rule remained in her family. Herodotus belonged to the faction that opposed her successor Lygdamis and was forced into exile, but Lygdamis must have held his position until near the middle of the century because an inscription survives suggesting that his position was more constitutional than might be supposed, and the lettering can hardly be earlier than 460.[5] An independent tyranny within a League led by a democracy will seem an anomaly to those who like their history to fall into regular patterns and it is often assumed that Halicarnassus' entry into the League was delayed until the tyranny was ended. This is possible, but not necessary. Athens was not doctrinaire in her relations with allies; there were oligarchies as well as democracies among them, more common probably in the early years than later; the names of individual

---

[1] Hdt. vi. 37–8.   [2] Thuc. vi. 59. 3.   [3] Hdt. v. 117.
[4] List 3. ii. 30; *ATL* iii. 35 f.; but see also p. 163.   [5] ML 32.

rulers in Caria appear on the tribute quota lists as late as the forties.[1] If the majority in Halicarnassus were content with the dynasty and the city fulfilled her obligations it is unlikely that Athens alone or the League as a whole would interfere. If Artemisia had much of the shrewd sense attributed to her by Herodotus she was fully capable of following an opportunist policy and linking herself with Delos rather than Sardis. Halicarnassus appears in the first quota list, of 453, the year after the Egyptian disaster; the tyranny seems to have lasted at least until 460. The years of the Egyptian expedition are not a convincing context for the admission of Halicarnassus to the League.

It is usually assumed that the Dorian pentapolis, Cos, Cnidus, and the three cities of Rhodes, revolted with Ionia after Mycale, but there is no clear evidence that they were original members. They are not mentioned in Herodotus' account of the Ionian revolt, and the initiative for the League had come from the Ionians. If they were primarily interested in trade in the eastern Mediterranean they might have decided to wait; but the evidence of the poet Timocreon provides a little foundation for including Rhodes. Plutarch in his *Themistocles* quotes some bitter lines in which Timocreon reviles Themistocles for failing to restore him to his native Ialysus;[2] he presumably refers either to the late summer of 480 when, after the battle of Salamis, Themistocles was exerting pressure in the Aegean to raise war funds: or, more probably, 478.[3] Timocreon implies that Themistocles had pocketed his fee and ignored his commitments, leaving his guest-friend in the lurch. Later, when Timocreon hears of the condemnation in absence of Themistocles at Athens on a charge of Medism, he celebrates the news: 'so Timocreon is not the only one who gives oaths to the Mede, there are other villains too. I am not the only one with a bushy tail, there are other vixens about.'[4] The natural implication is that Ialysus had renounced Medism before the end of 478 and that Timocreon was not able to return. It is a reasonable inference that the three cities of Rhodes, Lindus, Camirus, and Ialysus, accepted the invitation to join the Delian League. In the *Persae*

---

[1] *ATL* i. 297 f., e.g. Κᾶρες ὧν Τύμνες ἄρχει.　　[2] Plut. *Them.* 21. 4.
[3] Hdt. viii. 111–12. See also Endnote 2, p. 414, for a further discussion of the date.
[4] Plut. *Them.* 21. 7.

Aeschylus includes Cnidus and Rhodes in the Greek cities that threw off the Persian yoke after Salamis.[1]

There remains the more important but more elusive problem of Cyprus, which most historians have firmly excluded from the League.[2] The negative arguments are indeed strong, but not decisive, and the case for reopening the question at least deserves a serious hearing. Cyprus joined the Ionian revolt but was firmly under Persian control again before Lade was fought.[3] A Cyprian contingent was with the Persian fleet at Artemisium and Salamis, but the main cities at least of the island revolted when the decisiveness of the Greek victory was realized.[4] Such further incentive as was needed was provided when the Greeks made Cyprus their first objective in the year after Plataea and Mycale; the result of Pausanias' expedition should have been to strengthen considerably Greek feeling in the island. The Delian League was established within six months; instead of wondering how the Greeks could have accepted members from Cyprus so far to the east, we should ask: Is there any strong reason why Cyprus should not have joined or any good evidence that she did not join?

The main reasons why most historians have been unwilling even to consider seriously the inclusion of Cyprian cities are two. They think that the Greeks could not have contemplated extending their commitments so far east, and they think that the history of Cyprus from 478 to 450 shows that they did not. The first argument has already been considered; it is far from compelling. The second is stronger. In the best account of the battle of Eurymedon we are told that the main Persian fleet at the mouth of the river was expecting reinforcements from Cyprus;[5] this is held to show that Cyprus cannot have been brought under Greek control in 478. It is also reasonably argued that if the main cities of Cyprus had been original members, but part of the island had been lost to Persia between 478 and the date of the battle, Cimon would have at once sailed east after his victory to drive home his advantage in Cyprus: instead no attempt was made by League forces to help the Greeks in

---

[1] Aesch. *Persae* 891.   [2] Arguments for exclusion, *ATL* iii. 208.
[3] See p. 29.
[4] In the Persian fleet, Hdt. vii. 90. 1; viii. 68. 2. Revolt, Aesch. *Persae* 891–2.
[5] Plut. *Cim.* 12. 5.

Cyprus until at least six years later. The assessment of 425 has also been held to confirm this view. Beneath the decree providing for a sharply increased assessment was inscribed the list of cities from whom Athens demanded tribute and the amount they would now be required to pay. One of the striking features of this list is that it includes cities which have not been preserved in any of the earlier surviving quota lists which start in 453, and which are generally considered to have been previously recognized by Athens as coming within the Persian sphere. The inclusion of Celenderis on the coast of Cilicia is certain; another city was in Pamphylia, but its name is lost; probably it was Aspendus.[1] It is argued that this assessment included all states which had at any time been required to pay tribute. Had Cyprian cities been among the original members some at least of their names should have survived on the fragments of the list of 425. No Cyprian names can be read or reasonably restored.

This is a strong case, but not strong enough to silence doubt. The use of part of Cyprus by the Persians at the time of the battle of the Eurymedon can be explained by a Persian reaction at some time after 478 which recovered part of the island. The failure of Cimon to sail straight from his victory to Cyprus admits more than one possible explanation. The battle may have been fought towards the close of the summer; or Cimon may not have liked to risk a major action until he knew more of the situation in the island. But we must also explain why the League did not follow up the Eurymedon victory in the eastern Mediterranean. To anticipate the result of a discussion which must come later the reason could be that Athens was preoccupied with other urgent commitments and had to wait until her full resources were available.[2] In the years immediately following the victory she sent small forces only, under Ephialtes and Pericles;[3] as soon as her hands were free she led a major League force to Cyprus. As for the inferences to be drawn from the assessment of 425 there are too many uncertainties to regard an argument from silence as compelling. We cannot even be sure that no Cyprian names appear on missing fragments, for less than half the Ionian–Carian district survives. The force of

---

[1] See p. 329.   [2] See p. 79.
[3] Plut. *Cim.* 13. 4 from Callisthenes.

this particular argument is also weakened by a consideration of League strategy in the fifties. Athens during the early years of the decade seems to have been leading the League to a domination of the eastern Mediterranean.[1] From the evidence for Dorus in Palestine, Aspendus, and Celenderis it seems likely that all states on this coastline that claimed Greek origin were required to pay tribute. We should therefore expect Cyprian cities to be included in the fifties, though by the time the quota lists become available to us the great attempt to drive Persia out of Egypt had failed disastrously, and Cyprus had to be abandoned. But the recovery of Cyprus became a major objective of Athenian policy, and in 451 Cimon was attempting to restore the position that had been won in the early fifties.[2] If the absence of Cyprian names from the assessment list of 425 is a valid argument the conclusion should be not only that the Greek cities of Cyprus were not originally in the League, but also that they were not incorporated in the fifties. If, however, Dorus was incorporated then it is extremely unlikely that the Greek cities of Cyprus would be left to themselves. There is then still a case for believing that some cities of Cyprus joined the Ionians in the Delian League at the outset. This could have an important bearing on the vexed problem of the first assessment.

For this assessment Thucydides is again our basic source. 'The Athenians determined which states were to contribute money against the barbarian and which ships . . . *Hellenotamiai* were then first instituted as an Athenian office. They received the *phoros*, this being the name given to the money contributions. And the first assessment was 460 talents.'[3] Thucydides' account, following his general tendency, is impersonal; from other sources we know that Aristides, who commanded the Athenian contingent in 478, was responsible for establishing the first figures. The Aristotelian *Constitution of Athens* adds that the first tributes were assessed in the archonship of Timoxenus, that is roughly between July 478 and July 477.[4] How did Aristides proceed? If the authority of the *Constitution of Athens*

---

[1] *ATL* iii. 260 f.; below, p. 102. [2] Below, p. 111.

[3] Thuc. i. 96: οἱ Ἀθηναῖοι . . . ἔταξαν ἅς τε ἔδει παρέχειν τῶν πόλεων χρήματα πρὸς τὸν βάρβαρον καὶ ἃς ναῦς . . . καὶ ἑλληνοταμίαι τότε πρῶτον Ἀθηναίοις κατέστη ἀρχή, οἳ ἐδέχοντο τὸν φόρον. οὕτως γὰρ ὠνομάσθη τῶν χρημάτων ἡ φορά. ἦν δ' ὁ πρῶτος φόρος ταχθεὶς τετρακόσια τάλαντα καὶ ἑξήκοντα.

[4] Arist. Ἀθ. Πολ. 23. 5.

is accepted as final the work was completed in a very short time, less than nine months after discontent with Pausanias had led to negotiations for a new leadership and a new alliance. The Greek can admittedly be taken to mean that the first assessments of the first assessment were made in that year, i.e. that the work was begun but not completed then, but the natural implication is that the work was begun and ended within the year. The authors of *The Athenian Tribute Lists* infer that when the decision to form the League had been taken, but before the details had been finally agreed, invitations were sent to the Greek cities round the Aegean to send representatives to Delos at the beginning of the sailing season. With the help of these representatives Aristides, they think, completed his work on the island of Delos between March and July 477.[1]

There is, however, another tradition. Plutarch tells us that Aristides 'was asked to examine the land and revenues of the cities and to determine what each could and should pay'.[2] If this procedure was adopted the work cannot possibly have been completed in 477, and the result of the first assessment might not have been known for several years.[3] The total in that case would be considerably larger than if it were limited to states which joined the League at once in 478. Discarding the evidence of Plutarch is not always a serious risk, for, as we have already seen, his strength is the strength of his sources and many of his sources were late and unreliable. The statement that Aristides was asked to visit the cities might be no more than a guess of the fourth century or later. But even if only a guess it is a sensible guess; it may be doubted whether the representatives at Delos had enough knowledge or authority to commit their cities, and the Greeks must surely have hoped that there were other potential members of the League among those who were not represented at Delos. There is also an argument that has been generally overlooked. Aristides was the Athenian commander at Plataea and in the following year under Pausanias. By all accounts he was the main architect of the Delian League and

---

[1] *ATL* iii. 234 f.

[2] Plut. *Ar.* 24. 1: προσέταξαν αὐτῷ χώραν τε καὶ προσόδους ἐπισκεψάμενον ὁρίσαι τὸ κατ' ἀξίαν ἑκάστῳ καὶ δύναμιν. The use of ἐπισκεψάμενον does not necessarily imply visits to the cities, but Plutarch, in continuing πένης μὲν ἐξῆλθε, ἐπανῆλθε δὲ πενέστερος, assumes that Aristides had to travel.

[3] See Cavaignac, *Études sur l'histoire financière d'Athènes au ve siècle*, 37, 42 f.

his assessment is said to have been well received by all; yet in and after 477 he drops out of the record; it is Cimon who commands the allied forces in driving Pausanias from Byzantium, at Eion, and on Scyros. It is reasonable to believe that Aristides had not dropped out of favour, and that the reason why he did not lead the League forces is that he was otherwise engaged, assessing the original members and encouraging others to join. The best tradition that survives says that he died in the sixties on state business in the Euxine.[1] He was probably trying to attract the Greek colonies of the Euxine into the Delian League. To accept Plutarch is to reject the explicit statement of the *Constitution of Athens*, but behind that statement there may be only the record that Aristides was appointed in 478–477 to supervise the assessment.

In making an assessment it is possible either to calculate the total that is needed and then divide it among those who are to pay or to fix the amount that each can afford to pay, the grand total not being known until the assessment is completed. Diodorus, presumably drawing on Ephorus, tells us that Aristides was asked to follow the first method 'to assess the cities according to their ability to pay so that the grand total should be 560 talents'.[2] Many historians have followed Diodorus and have variously calculated how many ships could be maintained for how long at what rate of pay by an assessment of 460 talents.[3] In the period after 454 for which we have evidence this procedure does not seem to have been followed. In the decree ordering the assessment of 425 a general directive is given to the assessors to increase the scale of payments, but no specific total is laid down, and there is no reason to believe that earlier assessments had followed different principles. We should certainly reject Diodorus' total: it is not necessarily a textual corruption, but other sources confirm Thucydides and Ephorus' figures are notoriously unreliable.[4] We may also doubt whether Ephorus

---

[1] Plut. *Ar.* 26. 1. Plutarch also cites a tradition that he died of old age in Athens, and a third version by Craterus which rests on a confusion with Aristides, general in 425–424. Cornelius Nepos (*Ar.* 3. 3) says that he died some four years after the expulsion of Themistocles from Athens.

[2] Diod. xi. 47. 1: τάξαι φόρον ταῖς πόλεσι πάσαις κατὰ δύναμιν, ὥστε γίνεσθαι τὸ πᾶν ἄθροισμα ταλάντων πεντακοσίων καὶ ἑξήκοντα.

[3] e.g. 100 ships for 8 months at 3 obols a day, costing 400 talents (Busolt); 66 ships at 4 obols a day, costing 440 talents (Holm). See Busolt, *Gr. Gesch.* iii. 1. 82.

[4] For Diodorus' numbers see App. 2, p. 447.

had any reliable evidence for the methods adopted by Aristides. It is more probable that the total of the first assessment was not known until the work was completed.[1]

We have no contemporary judgement on the assessment of Aristides. Later it was regarded as a triumph of equity but it was then judged by comparison with the sharp increases that were imposed during the Peloponnesian War, and there is an air of unreality in the rhetoric of our sources. It was accepted, however, in the terms of the Peace of Nicias as providing fair figures for certain cities in Chalcidice, and no criticisms have survived.[2] Though Plutarch may have had no reliable evidence for saying that Aristides was asked to examine general revenues as well as the land of the cities the figures themselves suggest that the assessment was not based exclusively on land. The comparatively high tribute of Paros should be attributed to her marble quarries. Siphnos pays more than larger islands because of her silver mines, and the high tributes of the cities of the Thracian coast, Abdera, Maronea, Aenus are probably in part to be attributed to the wealth that they derived from trade with the interior.[3]

From 454 at least the tributes fall into a limited number of figures, making it clear that the assessment was not a precise percentage of public revenue; Aristides was content to aim at rough justice. His work will have been considerably simplified if, as many believe, he took over without change the figures established by the Persians in the areas which they had assessed. Herodotus tells us that after the collapse of the Ionian revolt Artaphernes made a careful survey of the territory of the Ionian cities and on this survey based a new assessment. His figures, Herodotus continues, 'remain in force right down to my day as they were fixed by Artaphernes'.[4] It might seem logical that the Ionians should be willing to pay to the League what they were already accustomed to pay to Persia, but the language of Herodotus should not be invoked as evidence. When he says that the tributes laid down by Artaphernes 'remain in force right down to my day' the natural inference is that he is

---

[1] *ATL* iii. 235.　　　　　　　　　　　[2] Thuc. v. 18. 5, quoted p. 52 n. 3.
[3] See the useful tables of tributes and areas, Beloch, *Gr. Gesch.*[2] ii. 2. 356–71.
[4] Hdt. vi. 42. 2 : τὰς χώρας σφέων μετρήσας κατὰ παρασάγγας . . . κατὰ δὴ τούτους μετρήσας φόρους ἔταξε ἑκάστοισι, οἳ κατὰ χώρην διατελέουσι ἔχοντες ἐκ τούτου τοῦ χρόνου αἰεὶ ἔτι καὶ ἐς ἐμὲ ὡς ἐτάχθησαν ἐξ Ἀρταφρένεος.

speaking of tribute still formally payable to Persia. And though by the middle of the century more than half the cities controlled from Sardis had been freed from Persia Herodotus' words imply that he is thinking of the assessment schedule at Sardis.[1] Nor would the statement if applied to the members of the League be correct; Herodotus should have known that there were many changes in the Athenian assessment of Ionian cities in the ten years following 454. Moreover if Aristides had adopted Persian figures for the larger part of the League we should have expected some echo of such a clear-cut principle in the sources. Various attempts have been made by comparing the tribute figures which Herodotus gives for the Persian satrapies with the Athenian figures derived from the quota lists to show that the Greeks paid less or more to the Persians than to the Greeks, but the evidence is not conclusive.[2] Tentatively we may believe that Aristides assessed the cities independently, perhaps paying more attention to revenue derived from trade than Persia had done. If Herodotus' account of Artaphernes' assessment is correct, the Persians considered only the land.[3]

Thucydides says that the first assessment totalled 460 talents; the figure has been widely questioned. Even before the first two stelae containing the record of the quotas of the period down to the Peloponnesian War were satisfactorily restored historians had felt that the evidence of the quota lists made an original total of 460 talents very difficult to accept. Walker, writing in the *Cambridge Ancient History*, was not alone in thinking that Thucydides had assumed for the seventies a figure that was only valid for the fifties and later.[4] The more accurate collocation of

---

[1] Cogently argued, Oswyn Murray, *Hist.* xv (1966), 142–6.

[2] According to Herodotus (iii. 90. 1) the annual tribute of the Ionians, Magnesians in Asia, Aeolians, Carians, Lycians, Milyans, and Pamphylians in the time of Darius was 400 Babylonian talents, the equivalent of 466 Attic talents. The Athenian assessment of the Ionian and Carian districts of the Delian League in 454 totalled *c.* 130 talents, to which should be added *c.* 100 talents for Samos, Lesbos, and Chios, still contributing ships. To be on the safe side we should estimate a grand total of not less than 200 talents and not more than 250. But without knowing the boundaries of the coastal cities we cannot compare with any accuracy the relation of the area occupied by members of the Delian League with that of those who were still under Persian control. It is safe to infer that there cannot have been a great difference between the Greek and Persian assessments. It is not safe to infer from the figures that Aristides took over the Persian assessments. The problem discussed, Cavaignac, *Population et Capitale*, 35; Beloch, *Gr. Gesch.*[2] ii. 1. 64.

[3] For the Persian indifference to trade, Hdt. i. 153. 1–3.   [4] *CAH* V. 45.

the fragments has increased the uneasiness. The assessment of 454 can be calculated with only a very small margin of error; it was about 490 talents.[1] But by 454 states were paying tribute who were not originally members of the League, and some of them were paying large sums. Aegina, for instance, independent until the early fifties, was assessed after conquest at 30 talents; Carystus, which had been forced to join the League in the late seventies, paid $7\frac{1}{2}$ talents. And in the late fifties many states which had originally contributed ships were regular tribute payers—Thasos certainly, Naxos probably, and others whom we cannot identify.[2] It is clearly difficult to reconcile an assessment of 490 talents in 454 with an original assessment of 460 talents.

The authors of *The Athenian Tribute Lists* found a novel solution to this dilemma, which has been widely accepted. They concluded that Aristides first assessed all states in terms of money and then, having decided which states should contribute ships, converted their money assessments into ships.[3] On this interpretation Thucydides' total would cover not only the assessments of the money payers but also the money equivalents of the ship contributions. That such a conversion could be reasonably made is shown by the reverse conversion later of ships to money. When ship contributors grew weary of the continuing obligation to provide ships they were allowed by Athens to pay instead τὸ ἱκνούμενον ἀνάλωμα, 'a corresponding payment'.[4]

To be satisfied, however, that Aristides could have worked in this way is not to be convinced that he did so, and there is a formidable objection to this view: it conflicts with what Thucydides tells us. This interpretation can indeed be wrung out of

[1] Gomme, *HCT* i. 275 gives 493 t.; *ATL* iii. 28 gives 498 t. 1,390 drs. Both estimates include all member states except Chios, Lesbos, and Samos, though some may still, as *ATL* believe, have been providing ships. Variations in estimates are caused by the irregularity in the payment of some cities and the uncertainty whether certain states were already in the League by 454.

[2] Thasos, Thuc. i. 101. 3. Ships are not mentioned in the brief account of the reduction of Naxos (i. 98. 4), but Naxos had naval traditions. Thucydides' language in i. 99 implies that the original ship contributors comprised a fairly large class. οἱ πλείους αὐτῶν . . . χρήματα ἐτάξαντο ἀντὶ τῶν νεῶν τὸ ἱκνούμενον ἀνάλωμα φέρειν in view of the article with νεῶν refers not to the original assessment (as Gomme, *HCT* i. 283) but to a later conversion from ships to money (more fully argued, *ATL* iii. 246–8).

[3] *ATL* iii. 236–43.   [4] Thuc. i. 99. 3.

his words, but the flow of his language makes it clear that he regarded the 460 talents as the total of the money contributions alone.[1] If this figure is impossible it is better to attribute a mistake to Thucydides than to force his words into a meaning that would never have been suggested unless the historical sense seemed to demand it. Such a mistake could easily be made. If the first assessment was made as suggested, the figure might have been recorded and remembered, but later it would naturally be assumed that the original assessment like the later assessments covered tribute alone. But before we reject Thucydides' figure we should inquire not whether it is likely but whether it is possible. Certain considerations entitle us to accept his figure until it is more decisively disproved.

It is often assumed that the assessment of Aristides cannot have been subsequently lowered, and that the allies in general cannot have been paying more tribute in the seventies than in the fifties, but the arguments that have maintained this thesis are not compelling. We cannot conclude that because in later tradition the Athenians claimed no credit for such a reduction no reduction was made; for we know that some thirty states had their tributes lowered in 446, but we hear nothing of this in the sources.[2] Tradition in fact preserved very little about the tribute after Aristides except the dramatic increases in the assessments of the war period, and a figure given by Thucydides for the amount of tribute being paid annually by the allies at the outbreak of the Peloponnesian War. It is at least possible that in the early and more dangerous years more tribute was paid than after the Eurymedon by which time a substantial reserve had probably been built up. The transference of the treasury from Delos to Athens, associated with the Egyptian disaster, could also have been an appropriate context for requiring less from the allies. No certain inference can be drawn from the stipulation in the Peace of Nicias that certain cities in Chal-

---

[1] Cf. M. Chambers, *CP* liii (1958), 26–32. S. K. Eddy, *CP* lxiii (1968), 189–95, explains φόρος as including things in kind as well as money. Similarly he thinks that in Thuc. ii. 13. 3 the 600 talents φόρος includes the value of ships from Chios and Methymna; he also suggests that a trireme was assessed at 1 talent. But his table, intended to show that this figure is confirmed by comparing tributes in the quota lists with the number of ships which the cities are reported to have had, includes sufficient anomalies to weaken the argument considerably.

[2] Below, p. 182.

cidice were to return to the assessment of Aristides.[1] The clause
need not mean that this was their lowest assessment in the whole
period of the League, but simply that it had been freely accepted
as fair and might tempt these rebel states to resume their allegiance to Athens. Thucydides' high figure will also be less
suspicious if we can believe that the Greek cities of Cyprus were
included (they might together have paid more than 50 talents)
and if we accept the view that the first assessment was not
completed in 477, but spread over several years; it will then for
instance have included the rich coastal towns of Thrace.

There is one further problem which is strictly relevant. The
authors of *The Athenian Tribute Lists* suggest that in the first
assessment less than 300 talents represented the assessment of
those who were to pay money. Yet by 454 a large reserve had
accumulated at Delos. Diodorus seems to give two variants for
the figure, 8,000 and 10,000 talents;[2] a reasonable inference
from a commentary on a speech of Demosthenes gives 5,000
talents.[3] Even if the figure is doubtful it is clear at least that
a very large sum had been accumulated, for only by such an
assumption can the extraordinary outburst of expensive public
building in Athens in the forties be explained, and Athens still
had a reserve of some 6,000 talents at the beginning of the
Peloponnesian War.[4] But if 5,000 talents or any such total had
been accumulated in the reserve and the annual yield of the
tribute had at first been less than 300 talents very little indeed
of the tribute revenue can have been spent. This conclusion the
authors of *The Athenian Tribute Lists* accept; they believe that
the year's tribute went almost entirely into reserve.[5] This is
difficult to believe. It does not seem true to the character of
Greek states to raise money for a remote contingency; the
tribute must surely have been designed to meet the expenditure
of the League. But what expenditure? Various alternatives
seem possible. League funds might have been designed to cover
the total cost of League campaigns; or, individual cities might

---

[1] Thuc. v. 18. 5, quoted p. 52 n. 3.

[2] Diod. xii. 38. 2 (8,000 t.); xii. 40. 1–2 (10,000 t.).

[3] *ATL* iii. 281. The document discussed, App. 10 (E), p. 515.

[4] Thuc. ii. 13. 3. The figure is reduced to 5,700 if we accept the text given by
a scholiast on Ar. *Plutus* 1193, advocated by *ATL* iii. 118–32. The small difference
does not affect the present argument.

[5] *ATL* iii. 238.

have provided the basic pay of their own crews while supplies needed in the course of campaigns were bought from League funds; or, League funds might have paid for the whole or part of the Athenian contingent on the ground that Athens was giving her services to protect the allies.

On this question there is, I think, only one piece of evidence which might be considered relevant. Ion of Chios, recording a dinner party in Athens which he attended as a very young man, tells us that Cimon, when asked on which of his exploits he most prided himself, chose his subtle dealing following the capture of Sestus and Byzantium. A large number of Persian prisoners had been taken, and Cimon dividing the spoil gave the allies the choice between the persons and property of the prisoners. The allies were tempted by the rich jewellery of the Persians; they had forgotten the high ransom that the prisoners would fetch. The money Cimon received provided maintenance for his crews for four months.[1] The story implies that Athens paid for her own contingent, but we need less anecdotal evidence and are left to assess probabilities. It seems probable that cities provided pay for their own crews but that campaign supplies were bought with League funds. It is also probable that League funds covered at least in part Athenian expenses. Later, when ship contributors converted to money payments we are told that the Athenians benefited because with the new tribute they increased the size of their fleet and became masters of those who provided the money.[2] In 478 the Athenians had contributed only 30 ships to the Greek fleet led by Sparta; when they took over the leadership and the Peloponnesian contingents were withdrawn a considerably larger number of Athenian ships will have been needed. Part at least of the expenditure should have fallen on the League treasury.

Even if we allow such expenditure from League funds the large accumulation is surprising. It may perhaps in part be accounted for by booty. The anecdote already quoted shows campaign booty being shared, as one might expect, between the contingents taking part in the operation. We are also told that Cimon built a new south wall for the Acropolis from the spoils

---

[1] Plut. *Cim.* 9. For the context of the episode, see pp. 465–8.
[2] Thuc. i. 99. 3: ηὔξετο τὸ ναυτικὸν ἀπὸ τῆς δαπάνης ἣν ἐκεῖνοι ξυμφέροιεν.

of the battle of the Eurymedon, which also paid for a handsome Athenian dedication at Delphi.[1] The windfall from this spectacular double victory must have been exceptional but cumulatively the booty won from some twenty-five years' intermittent fighting against the Persians should have been very considerable. It was normal to give tithes of booty to the gods; Delian Apollo may have benefited handsomely by 454.

[1] Plut. *Cim.* 13. 5; Paus. x. 15. 4.

5

THE EARLY YEARS

THUCYDIDES, having analysed the structure of the League, passes at once to a brief summary of its history. The first action, he tells us, was the capture of Eion from the Persians.[1] When Xerxes invaded he had organized his route well with supply bases and garrisons at key strategic points. Two of these commanded river crossings, Doriscus on the middle Hebrus and Eion at the Strymon's mouth, and these bases had to be defended if Persia was to retain any hold on her European conquests. The governor of Eion, Boges, did his duty bravely. Though the Persian position in Europe had disintegrated rapidly after the disaster at Plataea he defended Eion strongly and the siege lasted through the winter of 477–476.[2] It was probably not yet easy for the Greeks to finance such operations and we hear by chance of a rich Thessalian, Menon of Pharsalus, who received the Athenian citizenship for bringing to the allies a levy of 300 cavalry and 12 talents of silver.[3] When Boges saw that he could no longer hold out he built a pyre for himself and his family and threw his possessions into the river. Eion was occupied by Athenian settlers: it was too important strategically to be left to the local inhabitants and the allies may not have resented this Athenian military occupation.[4] A scholiast commenting on Aeschines in a confused note on the history of Athenian disasters at Amphipolis includes the failure of settlers sent to this up-river site in 476–475. The silence of Thucydides is not decisive against this evidence but the rest of the note does

---

[1] Thuc. i. 98. 1; Hdt. vii. 107; Plut. *Cim.* 7–8. 2.

[2] The capture of Eion is dated to the archonship of Phaidon (476–5) by the scholiast on Aeschines ii. 34, *ATL* iii. 158–60.

[3] Dem. xxiii. 199.

[4] Athenian occupation is not mentioned by Thucydides (contrast Scyros later); but we can accept Plut. *Cim.* 7. 3: τὴν δὲ χώραν εὐφυεστάτην οὖσαν καὶ καλλίστην οἰκῆσαι παρέδωκε τοῖς Ἀθηναίοις. Athenian occupation is the reason why Eion does not pay tribute.

not inspire confidence and we may doubt whether Athens was ready to push her interests on such a scale so early.[1]

After Eion had fallen the coastal cities to the east will have gone over to the Greeks without serious fighting; but Doriscus held out. The Persian governor Mascames, like Boges at Eion, did his duty and his descendants were still honoured by the Persian king with gifts. Herodotus tells us that Doriscus was never taken 'though many tried';[2] the first of the attempts probably followed the capture of Eion in 476. From Eion Thucydides passes to Scyros, Carystus, Naxos. The rocky island of Scyros was a notorious pirate base. The Athenians drove out the pirates and settled Athenians on the island, but what left a greater impression on the tradition was the recovery during the operation by Cimon of the bones of Theseus, which were solemnly brought back to Athens, a symbolic act which seems to have confirmed Athenian confidence in their growing naval power.[3] The allies are not mentioned in Thucydides' account of the Scyros operation, nor in any other source, but they are not likely to have protested, for the suppression of piracy would have been popular in the Aegean.

The Carystus episode was of a very different kind. Carystus, on the southern tip of Euboea, had no wish to join the League. Force was necessary and Thucydides implies strong resistance when he uses the word πόλεμος: 'The Athenians made war on Carystus without the rest of Euboea.'[4] We cannot properly assess the significance to contemporaries of the coercion of Carystus without more evidence. In the Marathon campaign the city had reluctantly served as a base for the Persians when they moved on Eretria. Carystus sent ships to the Persian fleet after Artemisium and it was only under severe pressure that she provided money when Themistocles was collecting funds in the Aegean for the Greek fleet after the battle of Salamis.[5] She had therefore a tarnished record in the Persian War but the action now taken can hardly have been justified by her attitude

---

[1] Schol. Aeschines ii. 34 (Dindorf): τὸ πρῶτον (ἀτύχημα) μὲν Λυσιστράτου καὶ Λυκούργου καὶ Κρατίνου στρατευόντων ἐπ' Ἠϊόνα τὴν ἐπὶ Στρύμονι διεφθάρησαν ὑπὸ Θρᾳκῶν, εἰληφότες Ἠϊόνα, ἐπὶ ἄρχοντος Ἀθήνῃσι Φαίδωνος.

[2] Hdt. vii. 106. 2. [3] Thuc. i. 98. 2; Plut. Cim. 8. 3–7.

[4] Thuc. i. 98. 3: πρὸς δὲ Καρυστίους αὐτοῖς ἄνευ τῶν ἄλλων Εὐβοέων πόλεμος ἐγένετο. Thucydides makes no mention of allies being with the Athenians.

[5] Hdt. vi. 99. 2; viii. 66. 2; viii. 112. 1–2.

then. It was too late merely for punishment and it seems most
unlikely that Athens should, after the capture of Eion, have
spoken of the danger from Carystus in the event of another
Persian invasion. More probably Athens maintained that Carystus was enjoying all the advantages of League membership
without any of the responsibilities. But it is difficult to find
arguments that would not have applied with equal or greater
force to Aegina.

The coercion of Carystus was followed by the revolt of Naxos.
Carystus did not wish to become a member; Naxos did not wish
to remain one. Thucydides again describes, but does not explain:
'The Naxians revolted; the Athenians besieged and reduced
them. Naxos was the first allied city to be enslaved contrary
to the original structure of the League', πρώτη . . . παρὰ τὸ
καθεστηκὸς ἐδουλώθη.[1] The words are strong but not precise;
Naxos was not literally enslaved, but she had to submit to
dictation and may have lost her vote at League meetings on
Delos. The actual terms of the settlement are not recorded; if
she had originally contributed ships she was now required
instead to pay money, and, like Thasos later, she may have had
to pull down her walls and surrender her fleet. Thucydides'
phrase παρὰ τὸ καθεστηκός does not necessarily imply the breaking of a formal agreement, but a change of status which was not
anticipated in 477.[2] Thucydides sees significance in the reduction of Naxos because it was the first example of what was to
become a recurring pattern.

In a short digression he gives us the main reason for revolts
and tells us why they failed:

There were other causes but the most important were the failure
to send tribute or ships and desertion during campaigns. The
Athenians insisted on discipline and were hard masters, using compulsion on men who were neither accustomed nor willing to face
hardships. In other ways too the Athenian command was no longer
so popular. On expeditions they no longer served as equals and they
found it easy to reduce rebels. For this the allies themselves were responsible, since most of them, resenting expeditions and wanting to
remain at home, converted ship contributions to a corresponding
money payment. And so the Athenian fleet grew in strength from the

---

[1] Thuc. i. 98. 4. An echo of the siege in Ar. *Wasps* 354 f.
[2] Gomme, *HCT* i. 282; *ATL* iii. 155-7.

money that they contributed, while the allies, when they revolted, were unprepared and had no experience of war.[1]

But Thucydides does not tell us why Naxos wished to secede. What we should like to know is what arguments were used on both sides, whether the issue was debated at a meeting of the allies and what were the reactions in the Aegean to the strong measures taken by Athens. We cannot exclude the possibility that party politics in Naxos had taken a dangerous turn and that one party, perhaps oligarchs, had once again as in 500 thought of looking towards Sardis.[2]

These are the only events recorded by Thucydides before his brief account of the battle of the Eurymedon, but he is not attempting a complete narrative. He is selecting what in perspective seems most important to an understanding of the development of Athenian power and we can expect him to omit what had little bearing on the future. We cannot therefore argue from his silence that after the capture of Eion the League gave up its early intentions to continue the war against Persia. Common sense demands that, in addition to the actions at Scyros, Carystus, and Naxos, operations were carried on against the Persians; and there are indeed hints that Athenian leadership was less one-sided than Thucydides seems to imply. Herodotus should be accepted when he tells us that there were several attempts to dislodge the Persian garrison from Doriscus;[3] more than one of these was probably made in the seventies. In more general terms Aristophanes makes the old jurors of the *Wasps* recall the days of their prime 'when they took many cities from the Medes'.[4] After the campaign that began with the capture of Eion we can imagine minor operations in the Hellespontine area and in Ionia freeing towns that retained Persian garrisons and perhaps others where the ruling party still looked to Persia.

Between the inauguration of the Delian League and the reduction of Naxos a context has to be found for the expulsion of Pausanias from Byzantium and Thucydides is here our only

---

[1] Thuc. i. 99.
[2] Hdt. v. 30. Naxian oligarchs, exiled by the demos, appealed first to the tyrant of Miletus, and through him to the Persian satrap at Sardis.
[3] Hdt. vii. 106. 2: οὐδαμοί κω ἐδυνάσθησαν ἐξελεῖν, πολλῶν πειρησαμένων.
[4] Ar. *Wasps* 1097–8: τοιγαροῦν πολ|λὰς πόλεις Μήδων ἑλόντες | αἰτιώτατοι φέρεσθαι | τὸν φόρον δεῦρ' ἐσμέν.

source. According to him when Pausanias was first recalled to Sparta, late in 478 or early in 477, he was tried on a charge of Medism and acquitted. He then went out privately in a ship from Hermione to Byzantium (and Thucydides emphasizes that he was not sent out by the state). He said he was going to join the Greeks in the war;[1] in fact, says Thucydides, he was intending to intrigue with the king, as he had begun to do before his recall when he had secretly sent back some high-ranking Persian prisoners to Xerxes. Pausanias was expelled forcibly from Byzantium by the Athenians and withdrew to Colonae in the Troad. At Sparta they heard that he was intriguing with the Persians and behaving suspiciously, so the ephors sent a herald to summon him home with the threat that if he did not come he would be declared a public enemy. Pausanias returned, was finally convicted, took refuge in the temple of Athena of the Brazen House, and was starved to death. The inadequacy of Thucydides' account is a separate issue; what concerns us now is the date and circumstances of Pausanias' expulsion from Byzantium.[2]

The earliest possible date would be 477, but this would allow too little time for Pausanias' conduct to develop to a point where force could be used without the risk of seriously straining relations with Sparta. A clue to a later date may be seen in the story told by Ion of Chios about Cimon distributing the spoils from Sestus and Byzantium. This requires a campaign in which prisoners are taken in Sestus as well as Byzantium. One of the *Letters of Themistocles* may here be invoked. Themistocles writes from Argos to Pausanias at Byzantium. He hears that Pausanias is in control of the whole Hellespontine area, that he has designs on Ionia, and that the king thinks highly of him. Themistocles is disturbed by this dangerous conduct.[3]

---

[1] Thuc. i. 128. 3: τῷ μὲν λόγῳ ἐπὶ τὸν Ἑλληνικὸν πόλεμον. In i. 112. 2 Thucydides uses Ἑλληνικὸς πόλεμος for a war between Greeks, and this is the more natural usage. Diodorus (xi. 50) does in fact speak of a serious threat of war between Athens and Sparta, but Thucydides follows a very different tradition in which the leadership against Persia passes from Sparta to Athens without serious friction. The Greek war in this passage must be the war between Greeks and Persians. It will have been easier for Thucydides to have used the same phrase with such different meanings in passages so close together if they were written at very different times (see App. 1, pp. 445 f.).

[2] Thuc. i. 128–35; discussed in detail, App. 4, p. 465.

[3] Hercher, *Epistolographi Graeci*, pp. 741–2 (Letter II).

The *Letters of Themistocles*, by different writers, are a strange mixture of empty rhetoric and plausible reconstruction. Some of their authors took the trouble to look for evidence which would make their letters convincing and from this letter we may infer that in one tradition Pausanias was not expelled from Byzantium until after the ostracism of Themistocles which cannot be dated earlier than 474. This would accord with a statement by Justin that Pausanias occupied Byzantium for seven years.[1] A date at the end of the seventies, 471 or 470, for Pausanias' expulsion conflicts with no specific evidence and allows an intelligible reconstruction. Pausanias returns to Byzantium in 477 or 476 and is accepted as governor of the town. The satrap at Dascylium may have aimed at recovering as much as possible of his lost territory and could count on support from Doriscus. With Pausanias' connivance Persians may have infiltrated into Sestus and Byzantium. Pausanias must have had considerable support since the city had to be besieged but it is very doubtful whether he was yet plainly guilty of active Medism. He was therefore able to withdraw to Colonae which was outside the Delian League. It was there probably that he began to negotiate seriously with the satrap at Dascylium, and it may be during this period that Arthmius of Zelea, whom the fourth-century orators recall to show how Athens treated traitors in the good old days, 'brought Persian gold to the Peloponnese' in the interests of Pausanias.[2] If such a reconstruction is even roughly right it helps to confirm that the early days of the Delian League were more eventful than Thucydides' brief summary suggests. It may help also to explain why in 465 there were still some Persians 'who were unwilling to leave the Chersonese', but this was after the main focus of action had shifted.

It is also possible that during these early years the League extended its frontier in the south. In his *Cimon* Plutarch says that 'no one humbled the great king more than Cimon. He gave him no respite when he had been driven from Greece, but followed hard on his heels before the barbarian could recover his breath and make a stand. Some cities he sacked and reduced; others he roused to revolt and won over to the Greek cause. As a result he stripped Asia, from Ionia as far

[1] Justin ix. 1. 3.   [2] See App. 4, p. 465; App. 10 (c), p. 508.

as Pamphylia, entirely of Persian arms.'[1] This passage, if taken
alone, implies that League forces operated in Caria and Lycia in
the seventies: an anecdote of the fighting survives. Frontinus in
his scrap book of cunning tactics used by Greek and Roman
generals quotes an attack by Cimon on a Carian town. He
burnt a sacred grove outside the walls and when the population
rushed out Cimon entered the city unopposed.[2] But the chronology of Plutarch's narrative becomes ambiguous when he proceeds immediately: 'then Cimon, hearing that the King's
generals had taken up a position in Pamphylia with a large
army and a large fleet, and wishing to strike fear into the Persians
and so close the sea within the Chelidonians to them, set sail
from Cnidus and Triopium', and there follows first the winning
over to the League of Phaselis and then a full account of the
victory of the Eurymedon. Plutarch is loose in his connections.
What interval if any he intended between the winning of the
coastline as far as Pamphylia and the campaign that ended at
the Eurymedon is not clear. He seems to imagine that he is
describing a single year's campaign, but the facts he gives
suggest that he has misunderstood his sources. A general campaigning as far east as Lycia and Pamphylia does not sail from
Cnidus and the Triopian promontory to fight the Persians at the
Eurymedon. Plutarch's text makes better sense if the fighting
in east Caria and Lycia is separated by an interval from the
battle of the Eurymedon.

It must be admitted that this reconstruction is inconsistent
with Diodorus who condenses all these operations in a single
campaign.[3] Cimon first sailed along the Carian and Lycian
coast, attacked the cities that were half Greek and half barbarian, drove out the Persian garrisons, and brought the cities
into the League. The Persians in defence built up an army and
a fleet. Cimon, learning that the Phoenician fleet was in Cyprus,
sailed against them. Diodorus' narrative of the Eurymedon
campaign is very close indeed to the text of a papyrus from
which several fragments have been found.[4] From Plutarch's
reference to Ephorus we know that this is the Ephoran version,
but the text seems too compressed to be that of Ephorus himself;

---

[1] Plut. *Cim.* 12. 1.   [2] Frontinus, *Strat.* iii. 2. 5.
[3] Diod. xi. 60. 3–62.
[4] *Pap. Ox.* xiii. 1610 = *FGH* 70 F 191 = Hill, *Sources*², 114 f.

more probably it comes from an epitome such as perhaps Diodorus normally used. In both Diodorus and the papyrus Cimon's operations from Caria to the Eurymedon come at the end of a catalogue of Cimon's main triumphs—Eion, Scyros, Caria, Lycia, and the Eurymedon. If Ephorus separated the annexations in Caria and Lycia from the Eurymedon by a not very conspicuous connection an epitome might well combine them. Diodorus' account is not a decisive objection to our interpretation of Plutarch.

Before we return to Plutarch's difficult version, the battle of the Eurymedon itself needs discussion, for our interpretation of Plutarch depends largely on our interpretation of the strategic conditions governing the battle. Thucydides once again is extremely brief: 'Next came the battle by land and sea at the river Eurymedon in Pamphylia fought by Athens and her allies against the Medes; led by Cimon son of Miltiades, they were victorious on the same day on both elements; and they captured and destroyed all the Phoenician ships, up to two hundred in number.'[1] Diodorus' account is detailed, picturesque, confused.[2] Cimon sails first to Cyprus where he wins a crushing victory and then on the same day sails back to the Eurymedon and wins further decisive victories by sea and land. One could not condemn this version on the ground that Thucydides makes no mention of Cyprus; but even without other evidence one would suspect the strategy and reject without question the possibility of action off Cyprus and at the Eurymedon falling on the same day. Any uneasiness of conscience that remains in dismissing Diodorus is dispelled by Plutarch's summary of another historian, Callisthenes, whose credentials admittedly are no better than those of Ephorus but who gives an intelligible account of the operations which is consistent with Thucydides. One important detail he adds and we can accept it. The Persians, he says, were not yet at full strength at the mouth of the Eurymedon; they were waiting for reinforcements from Cyprus. These reinforcements were also destroyed by Cimon sailing east immediately after the battle in the river's mouth.[3] Ephorus' strange confusion can be explained by the epigram preserved in Diodorus. A commemoration of Cimon's final

[1] Thuc. i. 100. 1.   [2] Diod. xi. 60. 5–62.
[3] Plut. Cim. 13. 3.

campaign in Cyprus was mistakenly referred to the Eury-medon.[1]

For the Eurymedon campaign, Plutarch tells us, a new type of trireme had been built, stronger and broader, designed particularly to carry more hoplites.[2] Even before they left Athens, therefore, Cimon was apparently expecting a different pattern of operations from those of the seventies. Fighting on land would be important; more hoplites would be needed. Plutarch's account of the campaign itself may be briefly summarized. Cimon assembled his fleet at the Triopian promontory and then sailed eastwards to meet the Persians who had made a camp for their land forces by the mouth of the river Eurymedon where their fleet was stationed. A demand to Phaselis that she should join the League was rejected and troops were deployed to besiege the walls; but the Chians in the fleet finally managed to get messages through and to persuade the city, with whom they had long-standing associations, to join them in the League: Phaselis submitted and paid an indemnity of 10 talents.[3] Her resistance, coming after the incorporation of eastern Caria and Lycia, is surprising. Probably her main concern was her trade with the eastern Mediterranean and Egypt, and she may have doubted whether the League would be strong enough to give her continuous protection.

Having won over Phaselis Cimon sailed at full speed eastwards. The Persian fleet, waiting for reinforcements, was afraid to offer battle in open waters and withdrew into the mouth of the river. Cimon attacked at once and won a complete victory, destroying all the Persian ships. He then landed and stormed the Persian camp, which offered no better resistance than at Mycale, and provided a rich harvest of booty for the Greeks. Having eliminated the main Persian forces Cimon sailed to meet the reinforcements expected from Cyprus and defeated them off Hydrus, some seventy miles east of the Eurymedon.

There is disagreement in our sources about numbers and names. Thucydides gives no figures for the Greeks, but his total

[1] Diod. xi. 62. 3; E. Meyer, *Forsch.* ii. 9–14. Wade-Gery argued that the epigram was composite, the first four lines commemorating the Eurymedon, the second four Cyprus, but see Peek, *Harv. Stud.* Suppl. i (1940), 97–108.

[2] Plut. *Cim.* 12. 2: ἐκεῖνος δὲ τότε καὶ πλατυτέρας ἐποίησεν αὐτὰς καὶ διάβασιν τοῖς καταστρώμασιν ἔδωκεν, ὡς ἂν ὑπὸ πολλῶν ὁπλιτῶν μαχιμώτεραι προσφέροιντο τοῖς πολεμίοις. [3] Plut. *Cim.* 12. 3–4.

in other major League operations, as in the Egyptian campaign
and in Cimon's campaign in Cyprus, is 200.[1] In Plutarch's
account Cimon sails from the Triopian promontory with 300
ships.[2] Diodorus has the best of both worlds: Cimon leaves
Athens with 200 ships but allied contingents bring the total to
300; the fleet sails along the south coast and as the cities are
brought into the League Cimon takes ships from them and so
increases the size of his fleet, but at the decisive engagement he
has only 250 ships.[3] A similar inconsistency recurs in Diodorus'
account of the Egyptian expedition; 'the Athenians resolved by
vote to help the Egyptians with 300 ships', but 200 is the number
given when they arrive in Egypt.[4] When there is discrepancy
and doubt about numbers the benefit of the doubt should go to
Thucydides: 200 ships may be accepted as the largest League
fleet commanded by Athenians. The variation in the number
of Persian ships is wider and even less subject to control.
Phanodemus' figure was 600, Ephorus' 350, but probably even
this lower figure should be reduced, for Thucydides implies not
many more than 200. According to Ephorus Tithraustes was
in command of the Persian fleet, Pherendates of the army;
Callisthenes said that Ariomandes, son of Gobryas, was in
supreme command and was himself with the fleet.[5] The two
accounts are not necessarily inconsistent: Tithraustes and
Phrendates may have been subordinate to Ariomandes.

The over-all strategy of the campaign must now be considered. Was the Eurymedon fought to break a Persian counter-
offensive before it could be effectively mounted, or because the
Persians, when they saw the Greeks advancing so successfully
along the coast, decided to make a stand at this point in order
to block any further advance? Were the Persians acting on the
defensive, or were they preparing an offensive? Diodorus'
answer is clear and it has been generally accepted. It was because the Greeks were advancing so successfully that the Persians decided to make a stand; the concentration of army and
fleet at the Eurymedon was defensive. And it is held that this
answer alone makes geographical sense. The mouth of the
Eurymedon is not a base from which an army can move westwards to attack Ionia; beyond the river there is no good coastal

[1] Thuc. i. 104–2, 112. 2.   [2] Plut. *Cim.* 12. 2.   [3] Diod. xi. 60. 3–6.
[4] Diod. xi. 71. 5, 74. 3.   [5] Plut. *Cim.* 12. 5–6.

road, and there is no easy route into the interior and so to Sardis. It is in Cilicia that Persian forces intended for the west muster and their route westwards lies through the Taurus mountains.[1]

This answer is not decisive if the Persians were placing their main emphasis on the fleet. In the Ionian revolt the final Persian move had come by sea and had resulted in the victory of Lade. When Datis and Artaphernes took a Persian expeditionary force across the Aegean in 490 they had brought their army to the Aleian plain in Cilicia and were joined there by the fleet, with horse transports.[2] Whereas Mardonius in 492 had separated his forces in Cilicia and sent his army overland to the Hellespont, Datis and Artaphernes embarked the infantry and cavalry on their ships. If a Persian offensive based primarily on the fleet was intended, the mouth of the Eurymedon would provide a suitable advanced base. It was here, at Aspendus, that a Persian fleet was held towards the end of the century when Tissaphernes, satrap of Sardis, was considering whether to commit himself to the fighting against Athens.[3] Plutarch uses the word ἐφεδρεύειν of the Persian fleet before the Eurymedon; it is perhaps more fitted to offensive than defensive tactics but both usages are found. It is more important to consider whether the idea of a Persian offensive is acceptable in the general context. To this question the answer generally given is an unhesitating no; the case should be reopened.

The disasters of 480 and 479 must have been a tremendous shock to Persian court circles and to the whole empire. Every satrapy had contributed to the invasion forces; every satrapy would know the decisiveness of the defeat. It is natural that Persia should be temporarily paralysed, but most unlikely that she should have accepted the humiliation indefinitely. The Ionian revolt had begun disastrously for Persia but had ended in the decisive victory of Lade. The Persian fleet, it could be argued, had not been fairly defeated in Greece; at Artemisium they had at least held their own in the fighting, at Salamis they had fought in an unfavourable position, misled by false intelligence; at Mycale, according to Herodotus, no naval battle was attempted, and the Phoenician ships had been sent away.[4] In fair open battle they might still hope to win. If the Persians

---

[1] See, e.g., *CAH* v. 55. [2] Hdt. vi. 95. 1–2.
[3] Thuc. viii. 81. 3, 87. [4] Hdt. ix. 96. 1.

were considering the use of their fleet for an offensive the first essential was to control the natural bases for the fleet, Phoenicia, Cilicia, Cyprus, and the Greek campaign of 478 had loosened Persian control. At the time of the battle of the Eurymedon the Persians were expecting reinforcements from Cyprus; the winning back of Cyprus or a considerable part of Cyprus may have been a preliminary stage in the Persian recovery. The next move will have been to build up a strong force which when it was ready would move into the Aegean and its mobilization point should be as far west as possible.

Such a conception can at least be read into Plutarch's account if we make a break between the campaigning in Caria and Lycia and the Eurymedon expedition, but if we hold that Greek cities in Cyprus had originally been members of the League and that Persia had regained even partial control the question naturally arises: Why did Cimon not follow up his decisive victory by liberating Cyprus? The reason why he did not sail east at once might be that he did not yet have adequate knowledge of the position and that little of the campaigning season remained. But there was no major expedition to the east in the following year. The only action following up the Eurymedon which is recorded is the sailing of two small task forces, 30 ships under Ephialtes, 50 under Pericles, at some time before 461.[1] They met no opposition, says Plutarch, emphasizing the decisiveness of the Eurymedon, but they achieved nothing memorable; their instructions presumably were to show the flag and not risk a major action. The most satisfactory explanation of the strange hesitation at this point would be the distraction of Athens by urgent commitments elsewhere. An understanding of the Eurymedon campaign therefore requires a reconstruction of the chronology.

In his *Cimon* Plutarch follows his account of the battle immediately by a minor operation in the Hellespont and then the revolt of Thasos. The operation in the Hellespont does not make convincing reading:

[1] Plut. *Cim.* 13. 4, from Callisthenes. Some historians have assumed that Pericles' expedition should be associated with the Samian revolt when he took a detachment of the Athenian fleet east to forestall any Persian attempt to help Samos (Thuc. i. 116. 3). But Thucydides gives sixty not fifty ships on that occasion and Pericles sailed no further than Caria. Both expeditions should be dated before the assassination of Ephialtes in 462 or 461.

Some of the Persians would not leave the Chersonese and were even encouraging Thracians from up-country to come to the Chersonese, for they thought nothing of Cimon who had sailed out from Athens with very few ships. So with four ships he attacked and captured the Persian squadron of thirteen ships. He drove out the Persians, defeated the Thracians and won for Athens the whole Chersonese.[1]

Sestus which, according to Herodotus, was the centre of resistance in the Chersonese, had been taken in the winter of 479–478. That any Persian forces could have remained in the area until the sixties is difficult to believe; Plutarch's story would in fact have been dismissed as one of his many confusions had not fragments of a casualty list been found which includes in the areas of fighting both places in or near the Hellespont and also Thasos.[2] The outbreak of the revolt of Thasos may be dated with some confidence to 465 ending in 463; the operations described by Plutarch fall in one of the years covered by the fighting in Thasos, probably the first. If the Eurymedon could be dated in 466 Athenian strategy in the eastern Mediterranean would be intelligible. Is there any strong reason why the battle should not be dated in this year?

The battle of the Eurymedon comes after the revolt of Naxos, and before the outbreak of the Thasian revolt. The revolt of Thasos can be dated in 465 but the revolt of Naxos can only be placed relatively in a series of events. It comes after operations at Eion, Scyros, and Carystus; the capture of Eion alone is firmly dated, in 476. One possible control exists in the career of Themistocles. According to our text of Thucydides Themistocles narrowly escaped the Athenian fleet at Naxos when he was fleeing from Greece to Persia. The insecurity of the chronology of the closing stages of Themistocles' life is notorious and few fifth-century subjects have attracted more attention with less result in the past generation.[3] Since our earliest authorities tell us that Artaxerxes, not Xerxes, was king when Themistocles reached Susa we can regard 465 as a secure *terminus post quem* for his arrival; the main problem is to determine the date when,

---

[1] Plut. *Cim.* 14. 1.

[2] *IG* i². 928, with *Hesp.* xxxvi (1967), 321–8 and *Hesp.* xxv (1956), 375. The headings include ἐπὶ Σιγείοι (ll. 32. 99); [ἐν Καρ]δίαι (l. 35); ἐν Θάσοι (ll. 43, 74); ἐ]ν Ἐίονι *Hesp.* xxxvi, 326 new fr. 1. 7,? also in 928. A. 37.

[3] A full review of the evidence, R. J. Lenardon, *Hist.* viii (1959), 23–48.

after his ostracism, he was condemned in absence at Athens. We have either to keep him longer in Greece than we should like or bring him to Ionia earlier than the date of his reception at Susa implies. Thucydides' account cannot be regarded as completely satisfactory, for he brings Themistocles past the Athenian fleet blockading Naxos and this cannot be later than 467. At least two years would be required to fill the gap between arrival in Ionia and reception by Artaxerxes; the narrative suggests a much shorter interval. Perhaps the least unattractive chronology can be based on one of the traditions regarding the flight. It is common to all the sources that Themistocles fled from Argos to Corcyra and this direction needs explanation if he intended from the outset to go to Persia. It might be that Athenian thalassocracy made the Aegean seem unsafe, but it should have been less dangerous to slip across by sea than to risk the long journey across Macedonia. Stesimbrotus provides us with the basis of an explanation when he tells us that Themistocles proceeded to Syracuse and asked Hiero for his daughter's hand in marriage, promising to bring Greece under his control; it was only when Hiero drove him out that he went to Asia.[1] This version as it stands contradicts Thucydides and is inherently improbable, but there is a plausible variant. The unknown writer of one of the *Letters of Themistocles* says that Themistocles had intended to proceed to Sicily but changed his plan when he heard of Gelo's death.[2] If there is substance behind this tradition the siege of Naxos will be dated by Hiero's death in 467 and the battle of the Eurymedon will follow in 466.[3]

The main objection to the dating of the Eurymedon in 466 is the strong positive argument advanced in favour of 469. This date is given by Diodorus, but in a very unconvincing context[4] More important is a passage in Plutarch's *Cimon* in which he illustrates the dominance in Athenian public life of Cimon by a story of the Dionysia. On one occasion the theatre audience was extremely restive and arrangements for the judging seemed likely to prove difficult. When Cimon with

---

[1] Plut. *Them.* 24. 7.

[2] Hercher, *Epistolographi Graeci*, p. 758 (Letter XX). Gelo is presumably a slip for Hiero.   [3] These dates are strengthened by M. E. White's chronology for Pausanias, *JHS* lxxxiv (1964), 140–52.

[4] Diod. xi. 60. 1. For the unreliability of the date see App. 2, p. 454.

his nine colleagues on the generals' board, one from each tribe, entered the theatre, they were acclaimed and asked to act as judges.[1] Plutarch gives the date: it was the memorable year of Sophocles' first victory, Apsephion was archon, 469–468. Plutarch loosely attaches the story to the recovery of the bones of Theseus which had brought special glory to Cimon, but these bones were recovered when Scyros was captured some years before 468. It has been held that the occasion must follow some spectacular success and no action brought such glory to Cimon as the battle of the Eurymedon. If the Eurymedon had been fought in the summer of 469 Cimon and his colleagues might naturally receive an ovation in the following spring.[2] This is an attractive deduction but it will not convince those who on other grounds have strong reasons for dating the Eurymedon later. Cimon was in very good repute so far as we know down to his return from Thasos. The occasion in the theatre was primarily a danger of the audience getting out of hand. If the generals entered together at a crucial point their appointment as judges needs no other explanation than the authority of their office. Unless and until new conflicting evidence is found we can believe that the Eurymedon battle was won in 466 and that the Athenians would have followed up the victory with a large-scale offensive in the eastern Mediterranean, had it not first been necessary to bring back security to the Chersonese and Hellespont, where the Persians from Doriscus and Dascylium may have been stirring up trouble. The revolt of Thasos in 465 interrupted Athens' more ambitious plans. Thasos was rich, had a substantial fleet, and was clearly prepared to offer much more than a token resistance.

The argument has been long and involved; a brief summary of the proposed reconstruction is needed. Thucydides in his brief summary of the early years of the League confines himself to events which seemed to be signposts to the future, anticipating the dominance of Athens which converted the League into an Empire. But we cannot believe that in the first ten years there was no fighting against Persians apart from the reduction

---

[1] Plut. *Cim.* 8. 7–8.

[2] *ATL* iii. 160. In Thucydides (i. 100. 2) the revolt of Thasos is linked to the battle of Eurymedon by χρόνῳ δὲ ὕστερον. This does not necessarily imply a long interval, cf. Thuc. v. 5. 3 (less than a year), and i. 64. 2.

of Eion. It is suggested that Cimon's successful operations in Caria and Lycia, not necessarily confined to a single year, should follow after the forcible incorporation of Carystus and before the revolt of Naxos, in the late seventies or early sixties. Meanwhile the Persians were preparing a counter-offensive, for which the revolt of Naxos could have given considerable encouragement. The striking force was intended to be sea-borne and was being built up by the mouth of the Eurymedon. But with the capitulation of Naxos in 467 Cimon was able to attack before Persian preparations were completed.

The revolt of Thasos needs more explanation than we are given by our sources. According to Thucydides the Athenians quarrelled with Thasos over the trading ports on the coast of Thrace opposite the island and 'the mine' which the Thasians worked on the mainland.[1] He does not explicitly identify the mine in question, but we can assume that it was the gold-mining area of Scaptesyle which Herodotus heard about when he visited the island.[2] Athens had developed a strong and profitable interest in the Strymon area when Pisistratus was tyrant. The expulsion of the Pisistratids from Athens and the occupation of coastal Thrace by the Persians presumably weakened the Athenian connection with the area, but the settlement of Eion after the expulsion of the Persian garrison in 475 provided a base for renewed infiltration; Thasos' decision to fight probably marks the end of a series of protests and arguments. Cimon defeated the Thasian fleet and settled down to besiege the city. At this same time, according to Thucydides, the Athenians sent out 10,000 settlers, Athenians and allies, to occupy Ennea Hodoi, the strategic site up-stream which commanded the easiest crossing of the river and the economic exploitation of the timber and metals of the area.[3] If the settlers were ready to sail when the Thasian fleet was defeated the colony was very probably planned before the fighting started; it may in fact have been the news of the colony which most alarmed Thasos. Thucydides implies that the quarrel over economic interests was between Thasos and Athens alone and

---

[1] Thuc. i. 100. 2: διενεχθέντας περὶ τῶν ἐν τῇ ἀντιπέρας Θρᾴκῃ ἐμπορίων καὶ τοῦ μετάλλου ἃ ἐνέμοντο.

[2] Hdt. vi. 46. 3: ἐκ μέν γε τῶν ἐκ Σκαπτησυλῆς τῶν χρυσέων μετάλλων.

[3] Thuc. i. 100. 3. For its economic importance, Thuc. iv. 108. 1.

it may be significant that he does not mention any share by the allies in the campaign; but the colony under Athenian leadership was open to the allies. It is doubtful whether in deciding to invite allied participation Athens was thinking primarily of the allies' interest; even Athens had not sufficient manpower available for military service to spare 10,000 men, but Athenian leadership and an Athenian nucleus among the settlers might be expected to safeguard the interests of Athens. The offer to the allies may have weakened opposition to the strong action taken by Athens against Thasos.

Thasos had become very prosperous in the sixth century. On her own island she had productive silver-mines, vines that yielded excellent wine, and abundant timber, a very marketable commodity in the Aegean. She was also well placed to exploit the gold- and silver-mines of the Strymon area and the trade with Macedon and Thrace. But the mines of the island were nearing exhaustion and Athenian encroachments on the mainland became increasingly threatening. Thasos must either resign herself to becoming a second-rate power or fight; she fought very hard. It was not until the third year that the city capitulated and the population meanwhile had endured crippling hardships. A story is preserved in a late source that when Thasos was being besieged by the Athenians a law was carried which stipulated the death penalty for anyone who proposed a settlement with Athens. The same author preserves a tradition that during an unspecified siege of Thasos, when there was a shortage of rope to assemble the defence works against the enemy, the women shaved their heads and their hair was used to bind the parts. Both stories probably refer to the siege of 465–463.[1]

The Thasians may have been encouraged to continue their resistance by the fate of the colony at Ennea Hodoi. The site was successfully occupied but the colonists, advancing into the interior, were attacked by a Thracian army at Drabescus and virtually annihilated.[2] The authors of *The Athenian Tribute Lists*

[1] Polyaenus ii. 35, viii. 67. The second passage is generally rejected on the ground that catapults were not used before the fifth century. I am grateful to E. W. Marsden for convincing me that catapults are not in question here. The reference is to improvisations such as Thucydides describes in ii. 75–6 (the siege of Plataea).

[2] Drabescus is probably the modern Drama, some ten miles north-west of Philippi. Herodotus (ix. 75) says Sophanes the Athenian, who with Leagros was in command of the forces, was killed by the Edonians ἐν Δάτῳ fighting for the gold-

reduce the losses considerably, arguing that only the military escort was destroyed, some 300 men.[1] This interpretation is not necessarily inconsistent with the first of two passages in which Thucydides refers to the disaster, but the meaning cannot be got from the second passage: ἐποίκους μυρίους σφῶν τε αὐτῶν καὶ τῶν ἄλλων τὸν βουλόμενον πέμψαντες, οἳ διεφθάρησαν ἐν Δραβήσκῳ ὑπὸ Θρᾳκῶν. In these words Thucydides surely implies what Isocrates repeats in the fourth century, that some 10,000 men were lost in Thrace.[2] The Athenians, however, did not relax their grip on Thasos and in the third year, 463, the island surrendered. Thucydides summarizes the terms imposed. The fleet was surrendered, the walls were dismantled, an immediate indemnity was imposed, and in future Thasos which had previously contributed ships to the League was required to pay annual tribute. She also had to surrender her mainland ports and mine.[3]

When our evidence begins, with the transference of the League treasury from Delos to Athens, the annual tribute of Thasos is 3 talents; in 443 and afterwards it becomes 30 talents. When the change was made is uncertain. It was after the list of 446 but there is no evidence for 445 and 444; it could have been at the regular assessment of 446, or after twenty years from the capitulation, 443 being the first year of the revised tribute. Two explanations have been given for the revision. The more widely accepted view is that the increase reflects the return to Thasos of their mainland mine or the Thasian coastal colonies; but the only Thasian colonies that pay tribute before 446, Neapolis and Galepsus, continue to pay tribute afterwards; about the mine there is no firm evidence.[4] J. Pouilloux in his detailed study of Thasian monuments and history has interpreted the increase as a mark of the revived prosperity of Thasos, but for this the increase seems to be too great and too sudden.[5] Perhaps the wrong question is usually asked. The

mines. Isocrates also (viii. 86) puts the disaster ἐν Δάτῳ. This was probably the name of the district.

[1] ATL iii. 106–10.

[2] Thuc. iv. 102. 2; Isocr. viii. 86. If the Drabescus casualties were included in the casualty list IG i². 928, some such number would be appropriate. I think they belong to a different year, Endnote 3, p. 416.

[3] Thuc. i. 101. 3.   [4] See also App. 14, p. 551.

[5] J. Pouilloux, Recherches sur l'histoire et les cultes de Thasos, 109–21. See the criticism by M. I. Finley, 2nd International Conference of Economic History, 1962 (Paris and The Hague, 1965), 28–32.

figure that needs explanation is not so much the 30 talents as the 3 talents. Even when Thasos lost her main revenues from the mainland she had rich resources on her own island. Her wine was in great demand,[1] and there should have been plenty of buyers for her timber; it would be very anomalous if her assessment was the same as that of Cythnos or Tenos. More probably 3 talents represents a special reduction in the light of the indemnity that had to be paid. Thasos, assessed at 30 talents, was paying no more than Aegina.

It is ironical that the victory of the Eurymedon should be followed so closely by the crushing of Thasos. The Eurymedon marked the culmination of Athens' leadership against Persia; it eliminated any serious threat to the Aegean and opened the way for a profitable offensive in the eastern Mediterranean. It was commemorated with impressive monuments at Athens and at Delphi. At Delphi the Athenians dedicated a bronze palm carrying a golden Athena. At Athens a new south wall was built for an extended Acropolis;[2] private dedications may have included a red-figure shield depicting Athena holding the decorative prow of a Phoenician ship, and a skyphos with a similar scene.[3] Thasos, on the other hand, was more significant for the future; it was the first unambiguous sign of tyranny.

The revolt of Thasos hastened changes in Sparta, in Athens, and in the League. When the allies refused to accept a Spartan successor to Pausanias in 478 the Spartans made no open protest. We have suggested above that Sparta was less united than Thucydides seems to have thought and that there were surely some who resented the surrender.[4] They were, however, unable to reverse the policy because Sparta had other pressing preoccupations. Her old rival Argos had begun to recover from the massacre of Sepeia in 494 and was again becoming politically active; there was restlessness in Arcadia; later there were rumours that Pausanias was tampering with the helots.[5] More important, Athens had fallen under the virtual control of a limited group of aristocratic families whose authority was

---

[1] Thasian wine, *Athen.* i. 28–31.   [2] Paus. x. 15. 4; Plut. *Cim.* 13. 5.

[3] U. Hausmann, *Charites* (ed. J. Schauenburg, 1957), 144–51.

[4] See pp. 40 f.

[5] Thuc. i. 132. 4: ἐπυνθάνοντο δὲ καὶ ἐς τοὺς Εἵλωτας πράσσειν τι αὐτὸν καὶ ἦν δὲ οὕτως. Thucydides' personal confirmation perhaps implies that in some quarters the story was discredited.

sustained by the political sagacity of Aristides and the continuing military successes of Cimon. The leading men of this group were on good terms with Sparta. Cimon, who had married the Alcmaeonid Isodike, called his eldest son Lacedaemonius; the wealthy Callias, uneasily married to the attractive Elpinice, Cimon's half-sister, was a *proxenos* of Sparta, as was the elder Alcibiades.[1] With such men commanding authority it was easier for Sparta to allow Athens to go her own way in the Delian League, but an undercurrent of frustration and opposition remained which was stimulated by Athens' aggression against Thasos. Thucydides reports that the Spartans promised to help the island by invading Attica, but were prevented by the great earthquake which roused the helots to revolt.[2] There is no good reason to reject this story. The promise will not have been made publicly in the Spartan Assembly but privately by 'the authorities', as the later promise in 433–432 to Potidaea;[3] and we may doubt whether the promise would have been fulfilled even if no earthquake had intervened. The Spartans did not invade Attica when Potidaea was attacked.

At Athens also there were potential divisions in politics. Themistocles had been cleverly driven from the leadership which he had exercised so effectively in 480 and, apart from a brief success when he outwitted the Spartans over the rebuilding of Athens' walls, he never recovered. Themistocles may have been more interested in policies than in political principles, but in order to regain his authority he needed the support of the common people; a further radical advance was his best hope of turning the Assembly against his rivals. But the leading families in the seventies, with the support of the Areopagus, were too successful to be effectively challenged, and Themistocles was ostracized. He now proceeded to develop a policy which he will have hoped to continue when he returned to Athens after his ten years of ostracism. Living at Argos he encouraged anti-Spartan movements among the states that

---

[1] Cimon's marriage, Plut. *Cim.* 4. 10; Callias *proxenos*, Xen. *Hell.* vi. 3. 4; Alcibiades, Thuc. v. 43. 2.   [2] Thuc. i. 101. 2.

[3] Thuc. i. 58. 1. The promise in 432 was given by τὰ τέλη, an ambiguous term (see A. Andrewes on Thuc. v. 77. 1 in *HCT IV*, 137 f.). Here more probably a promise by the ephors than a formal decision of the Spartan Assembly.

thought they had most to gain by the crushing of Sparta.[1] His political activity is probably reflected in the synoecisms that made Elis and Mantinea more democratic at about this time and it explains why Sparta was so desperately anxious to get rid of him.[2] When Pausanias was tried for Medism evidence was 'found' which implicated Themistocles, and Sparta worked on his enemies in Athens, where he was formally charged by an Alcmaeonid, Leobotes, and condemned in absence.[3] Themistocles made his way to Persia but his political associates at Athens continued to work for radical reforms. There are signs of the increasing strength of this opposition in the election as general of Ephialtes its leader and of Pericles his associate in the period following the victory of the Eurymedon; and the annihilation of the Ennea Hodoi colonists, though not the immediate fault of Cimon, probably affected his popularity. When Cimon returned from Thasos he was prosecuted by Pericles. According to Plutarch, our only source, he was accused of having failed to seize a large part of Macedonia because he had been bribed by King Alexander.[4] In his defence Cimon seems to have counterattacked: he was not, like so many, a *proxenos* of Ionians and Thessalians, an easy way to get rich. Presumably he was known to be friendly with Alexander and perhaps the Macedonian king was suspected of active sympathy with Thasos. But the main purpose of the trial was rather to provide a political demonstration, for Pericles is said not to have pressed the charges. Cimon was acquitted, but soon he had to face a more critical issue.

The great earthquake of 464 had been followed by the most serious helot revolt within living memory. After some initial successes the helots had been driven out of Laconia and had taken refuge on Mount Ithome, where they had an excellent defensive position. The circumference of the mountain was sufficiently large to make a complete blockade virtually impossible; the helots could produce some food on the mountain and could raid the rich plain of Messenia. A long siege was inevitable unless the position could be taken by assault. The

---

[1] Thuc. i. 135. 3: ἔτυχε γὰρ ὠστρακισμένος καὶ ἔχων δίαιταν μὲν ἐν Ἄργει, ἐπιφοιτῶν δὲ καὶ ἐς τὴν ἄλλην Πελοπόννησον.

[2] The synoecism of Elis is dated 471–470 by Diodorus (xi. 54. 1); Mantinea is said by Strabo (viii. 3. 2, = 337) to have been synoecized by Argos, but there is no evidence for the date.

[3] Thuc. i. 135; Plut. *Them.* 23. 1.   [4] Plut. *Cim.* 14. 3–5.

Spartans appealed for help to the members of the grand alliance formed in 481 against Persia and not yet formally dissolved. They particularly needed Athenian troops, for the early years of the Delian League had provided ample experience in storming fortified positions, and Caria should have been a good training-ground for Ithome.[1] But at Athens there was a tense debate in the Assembly. Ephialtes was realistic. Sparta was Athens' natural enemy and Athens should let her pride be trampled in the dust. Cimon appealed strongly to old loyalties: the Athenians must not allow Greece to be crippled; Athens must not lose her yoke-fellow. The Assembly was swayed by this emotional appeal and a strong force of hoplites was sent under Cimon.[2] In their absence Ephialtes was able to secure the passage of his reforms and when, in the same year, the Spartans dismissed the Athenians from Ithome, Cimon was discredited. In 461 he was ostracized.[3]

It is difficult to determine precisely the scope of Ephialtes' reforms but there is little doubt that they changed both the spirit and the forms of Athenian democracy considerably. The political power of the Areopagus, formidable though, or perhaps because, undefined, was broken and the popular organs of Boule, Assembly, and law-courts were considerably strengthened. The sharpness of political conflict which accompanied this democratic advance is vividly illustrated by the assassination of Ephialtes and the attempt of extremists soon afterwards to betray the city when a Spartan army was poised on the

---

[1] Thuc. i. 102. 1–2. Gomme (*HCT* i. 301) thinks that Thucydides has in mind assaults on palisaded camps as at Plataea and Mycale and perhaps Eurymedon. But the reduction of Naxos and Thasos and perhaps other rebels is more significant. For the relevance of Caria, cf. Ar. *Birds* 292–3: ὥσπερ οἱ Κᾶρες μὲν οὖν | ἐπὶ λόφων οἰκοῦσιν, ὠγάθ', ἀσφαλείας οὕνεκα, and Xen. *Cyropaed.* vii. 4. 1 : οἱ Κᾶρες ... ἅτε τὰς οἰκήσεις ἔχοντες ἐν ἐχυροῖς χωρίοις.

[2] Plut. *Cim.* 16. 8; Thuc. i. 102. 1; Diod. xi. 64. 2.

[3] There is no clear evidence for the relation in time of the reforms of Ephialtes and the Athenian expedition to Ithome. The reforms are dated 462–461 in Arist. *Ἀθ. Πολ.* 25. 2. The siege of Thasos lasted from 465 to 463. The expedition to Ithome should be in 462. Plutarch (*Cimon* 15) says that Cimon was campaigning when the reforms were carried; he tried to reverse them when he returned but was ostracized. In Plutarch the campaign was naval (ὡς δὲ πάλιν ἐπὶ στρατείαν ἐξέπλευσε). There is no good reason to believe that Cimon took his hoplites to Ithome by sea and there seems to be no time left for another expedition not otherwise recorded. Plutarch or his source may have changed a general word for campaigning into a more specific one, adopted because most Athenian expeditions were sea-borne.

borders of Attica.[1] This new radical Athens broke openly with
Sparta when the Athenian troops at Ithome were humiliated,
and her change of policy was made explicit by new alliances
with Argos and Thessaly.[2] Other Greeks will not have forgotten
that Thessaly Medized during the invasion of Xerxes and that
Argos sat on the wrong side of the fence.

In the League also the revolt of Thasos set up uneasy stirrings.
However high-handed Athenian leadership may have been
in dealing with Carystus and Naxos, the crushing of Thasos
must have seemed the most flagrant violation of the spirit
of the League that the allies had yet seen. Neither directly
nor indirectly were the Persians concerned. The issues were
economic, and the interests that were being protected were those
of Athens. Diodorus tells us that at this period, following the
revolt of Thasos, the majority of the allies were disaffected and
that some of them 'ignored the League council and remained
aloof'.[3] We would like to know whether Ephorus had evidence
for what he said or whether this is another product of his
rationalization. The picture, we think, is correct. The reduction
of Thasos was the most dangerous warning the allies had had,
and must have dulled the memories of the Eurymedon. It is
also likely that in the years following the Eurymedon most of
the states contributing ships converted their obligations into
money, but the evidence for this important development in the
League lacks precision. Thucydides summarizes the situation
in a short digression following his account of the reduction of
Naxos. He explains how it was that the revolts which followed
that of Naxos were so ineffective. One of the main reasons,
he says, was that the allies had grown weary of service away
from home and had preferred to pay tribute instead.[4] There is
no clear hint of date. The conversions could, so far as this
evidence goes, have come before Naxos, after Naxos, or both
before and after. Plutarch adds a little embroidery to the story.
Cimon, he says, was responsible, acting in contrast to other
generals who had inflicted penalties when states did not send
their ships or took their men away in the middle of campaigns.[5]

---

[1] Arist. *Ἀθ. Πολ.* 25. 4; Thuc. i. 107. 4: τὸ δέ τι καὶ ἄνδρες τῶν Ἀθηναίων ἐπῆγον
αὐτοὺς κρύφα, ἐλπίσαντες δῆμόν τε καταπαύσειν καὶ τὰ μακρὰ τείχη οἰκοδομούμενα.
[2] Thuc. i. 102. 4.   [3] Diod. xi. 70. 4.
[4] Thuc. i. 99.   [5] Plut. *Cim.* 11. 2.

This has been taken to indicate the period 452–450 when Cimon was back from ostracism and in command of League forces, following a period when his political opponents had been in control.[1] Plutarch cannot be so rigorously pressed, for his context may be no more than later rationalization. Even if it derives from good evidence it could suit a date in the late sixties, for the election as generals of Ephialtes and Pericles was, as we have seen, a sign that Cimon's authority was not unchallenged.

A more serious argument has been drawn from the quota lists of the first assessment period, 454–450. In the fragments of these lists most of the tribute-paying members are recorded one or more times. In the island district alone there is a substantial number of names that do not appear at all and this cannot be ascribed to coincidence. A special explanation is needed, and the inference that these states contributed ships down to the end of the fifties has been widely accepted.[2] This particular problem needs to be considered later in relation to its context. It will be maintained that most of these island states had never contributed ships and that the main process of conversion of ships to money had been completed by 460. The affair of Thasos seriously unsettled members of the League, but by the time that Athens became involved in war with the Peloponnesians all but the major islands of Chios, Lesbos, and Samos had probably lost such means of resistance as they had once had. Athens had already advanced a considerable distance on the way to Empire.

---

[1] A. B. West, *Am. Hist. Rev.* xxxv (1929–30), 267–75.
[2] West, loc. cit., accepted by *ATL* iii. 267 f.

6

WAR ON TWO FRONTS

WHEN Athens formally renounced the anti-Persian alliance of 480 and allied with Argos and Thessaly, war could be expected sooner or later. It could be expected sooner when Megara, attacked by Corinth, appealed to Athens and Athens accepted her into the alliance.[1] Thucydides, who records in such detail the incidents and arguments that led to the outbreak of war in 431, merely gives a list of the main events of the earlier war between Athens and the Peloponnesians, but since he insists so strongly on the importance of chronological accuracy we should accept his order of events unless he can be proved wrong. The Athenians, he tells us, were leading a League fleet of 200 ships to Cyprus when Inaros who had revolted in Egypt appealed to them for help; the League fleet left Cyprus and sailed to Egypt.[2] Questions arise thick and fast. Why did Athens commit herself and the League to a major offensive in the eastern Mediterranean when she had openly challenged Corinth and could expect war with the Peloponnese? What did she hope to achieve in Cyprus and how far was her decision to sail there influenced by the revolt of Inaros? And why, having committed herself to Egypt, did Athens involve herself in war on the Greek mainland?

It has sometimes been assumed that the radicals who came to power with the reforms of Ephialtes wished to reverse Cimon's foreign policy on both fronts, concentrating their forces against Sparta and her allies and coming to terms with Persia. This may have been their original intention, for a notorious passage in Herodotus can be naturally interpreted to imply this. He tells us that Argive envoys went up to Susa to inquire whether the friendly relations with Argos established by Xerxes were to be continued by his successor Artaxerxes; they happened to be at the Persian court at the same time as the Athenian Callias

---

[1] Thuc. i. 103. 4.   [2] Thuc. i. 104.

and his fellow envoys were there 'on other business'.[1] This has often been taken as a veiled reference to a Peace of Callias negotiated after Cimon's death in 450 or 449; but if this is the meaning Herodotus' language is unexpectedly cryptic and the context is inappropriate. There is no good reason why the Argives should want to renew relations with Persia in 450–449, for they had made a thirty years' peace with Sparta in 451–450 and were in no danger.[2] In 461 such a mission would have point and purpose, for by allying with Athens Argos had indirectly challenged Sparta and it would suit both Athens and Argos to be able to rely on the support or at least the neutrality of Persia. But if Callias was sent to explore the possibility of reaching an acceptable settlement he was not successful.

If Athens hesitated at this stage it was not for long. In 460 or 459 a full League force of 200 ships was sent to Cyprus. This vigorous offensive is intelligible as a reaction to the failure of Callias' mission, but it need be no more than a logical sequel, delayed by the revolt of Thasos, to the victory of the Eurymedon. Other factors combined to make the policy attractive. Successful fighting against Persia might settle the restlessness that had developed in the League at the time of the Thasian revolt, and there were good prospects of success. Xerxes had died in 465 and the succession had been disputed. More than a year of plots and assassinations passed before it was clear that Artaxerxes was to be king, and it was not at once clear how united the Persians would be behind him and how strong he would prove himself to be.[3] The news from Persia had encouraged revolt in Egypt, and Inaros the Libyan prince who led the movement from the western Delta had met with swift success. In a battle at Papremis he defeated the Persian garrison troops and killed Achaemenes, brother of Xerxes, who had been governor of Egypt for some twenty years.[4] It is probable that the battle had been fought before the Athenian fleet sailed for Cyprus and that when the Athenians decided to undertake that

---

[1] Hdt. vii. 151, quoted in App. 8, p. 487, T 1.

[2] Sparta's peace treaty with Argos was nearing its end when the Peace of Nicias was negotiated in spring 421, Thuc. v. 14. 4, 28. 2.

[3] Ctesias 61–2; Diod. xi. 69.

[4] Hdt. iii. 12. 4 with vii. 7. Herodotus implies that the battle of Papremis was fought before the Greeks arrived; Thucydides by his silence confirms this. For a different view, P. Salmon, *La Politique égyptienne d'Athènes*, 143–6.

expeditiǒn they knew the general pattern of events in Persia and Egypt. The situation was now ripe to win back Cyprus, but when Inaros appealed for help the rewards to be expected from the liberation of Egypt seemed greater. If Egypt could recover her independence Cyprus would offer little resistance and a Greek domination of the eastern Mediterranean could become more than a dream.

It may have been at this time and in this mood that the Athenians commissioned Phidias to make the great bronze statue of Athena Promachos. It was the first great public monument to be set up since the Persian wars and was to remain the most conspicuous landmark in Athens for those who approached the city by sea. The Promachos has usually been regarded as Cimonian in inspiration, but the credit for commissioning Athens' greatest sculptor, still a comparatively young man, to attempt the first colossal bronze statue in Athens should be given to the radical democrats. The crucial evidence lies in the public accounts which were inscribed on a marble stele when the work was completed and show that it had lasted nine years. Meritt considered that the letter forms pointed to the late fifties but this is consistent with the beginning of the work before Cimon's ostracism.[1] More important is an entry that recurs in each year's summary of expenditure; it shows that the work was controlled by a board of public commissioners with a secretary and assistant, and that they were paid by the state.[2] Plato in his *Gorgias* tells us that state pay was first introduced by Pericles.[3] In such matters one would prefer independent support for Plato's evidence, but at least there is no contradictory record. Other sources tell us that it was Pericles who introduced pay for the popular law-courts;[4] it is reasonable to believe that it was this step which established the precedent and that it was not till later that it was extended to the Boule, magistrates, and other officers of state. If this is right the Promachos cannot have been commissioned before the ostracism of Cimon in 461; it was

---

[1] The fragments in *Hesp.* v (1936), 362–80; vii (1938), 264–8; full text, *SEG* x. 243.
[2] e.g. col. 1, l. 67: μ[ίσθον ἐπιστ]άτεσι κα[ὶ γραμμα]|τ[ε̂ι καὶ hυπερ]έτει.
[3] Plato, *Gorgias* 515e:
[4] Arist. Ἀθ. Πολ. 27. 3. The general argument used here is invalid if jury pay, as many think, was not introduced until substantially later than the reforms of Ephialtes. I regard it as an essential corollary of the reforms. See Wade-Gery *Essays*, 235–8.

probably begun very soon afterwards and completed in the late fifties.[1] If these arguments are valid it is reasonable to look for reasons other than aesthetic for such a conspicuous monument.

If we accept Pausanias' statement that the statue commemorated Marathon, we may believe that Athens was reminding herself and other Greeks that she had defeated Persia, alone with the Plataeans, before the Spartan-led alliance, which she had now left, drove back Xerxes' invasion.[2] She would also be proclaiming that under Athena's protection she was still carrying on the struggle against Persia; and this may have needed stressing in view of her alliance with Argos and Thessaly, especially if she had negotiated unsuccessfully with Persia before resuming the offensive. Athena, it was hoped, would fight for Athens in Egypt.

Thucydides once again gives us a bare record of events and does not explain the reasons for the intervention in Egypt. No other reason may be needed than the hope of further crippling Persia, but it is probable that economic factors also appealed to Athens and her allies. By the time of the Peloponnesian War Athens seems to have depended on the Euxine for her corn supplies, but it is doubtful whether the Euxine alone could have provided adequate supplies for Athens before Pericles' expedition in the thirties. It is perhaps significant that when in 445–444 Psammetichus, an Egyptian 'King' sent a large gift of corn from Egypt to Athens it seems to have been badly needed.[3] The prospect of Egyptian corn may have influenced policy; more generally an independent Egypt from which Phoenician trade could be virtually excluded would be a richer market for the Aegean Greeks than a Persian province. The Ionians will have remembered the wealth that they drew from Egypt in the sixth century; the Egyptian enterprise was probably popular with the League so long as it seemed likely to succeed.

Operations had barely begun in Egypt, according to Thucydides, when hostilities broke out in Greece: 'The Athenians sent an expedition to Halieis. They were driven off by the Corinthians

[1] See Endnote 4, p. 416.

[2] Paus. i. 28. 2: ἄγαλμα χαλκοῦν ἀπὸ Μήδων τῶν ἐς Μαραθῶνα ἀποβάντων.

[3] Plut. *Per.* 37. 4; Schol. Ar. *Wasps* 718: σιτοδείας ποτὲ γενομένης ἐν τῇ Ἀττικῇ Ψαμμήτιχος ὁ τῆς Λιβύης βασιλεὺς ἀπέστειλε σῖτον τοῖς Ἀθηναίοις αἰτήσασιν αὐτόν. A small fragment from a decree, probably a little earlier (it has the three-bar sigma) also seems to refer to a corn shortage, *IG* i². 31. 6:]σεσσιτοενδε[ια. . . . .

and Epidaurians. Later the Athenians won a sea battle at
Cecryphalea. Open war followed with Aegina.'[1] Thucydides'
skeletal narrative suggests that the Athenians, already committed to a major offensive in the east, deliberately provoked
an unnecessary war with the Peloponnese. He may not have
given the full story, for it seems highly probable that an embarrassing piece of evidence, for which Pausanias is our only
authority, must be fitted within this period. In his account of
the Athenian Agora Pausanias describes in some detail the
famous paintings in the Stoa Poikile. Three of the subjects were
taken from the familiar repertoire of Athenian panegyric, the
battle against the Amazons, the sack of Troy, and the battle of
Marathon. The fourth subject belongs to a very different context. It portrayed fighting at Oenoe between Spartans and
Athenians who had come to the help of Argos, and the artist had
chosen the moment when battle was first joined.[2] This battle
of Oenoe in the Argolid was also commemorated by Argos at
Delphi, according to Pausanias, with a sculptured group of
the Seven against Thebes by the Theban artists, Hypatodorus
and Aristogiton.[3] The artists give a clue to the date, for one of
their names has been found at Delphi on a statue-base, and the
letters of the inscription require a date in the fifth century.
It would be more comfortable to ignore Pausanias but his
evidence is strong enough to override the silence of Thucydides;
a context has to be found during the period when Athens and
Argos were allies, between 461 and 451. It is not inconceivable
that Sparta attempted to intimidate Argos as soon as she heard
of the Argive–Athenian alliance by invading the Argolid and
that Athens quickly dispatched a force to help her ally.[4] The
result must have been the repulse of the Spartans and it seems
that the Athenians were so proud of the issue of the first clash that
they commissioned a painting of the battle to match Marathon.
And so by a strange irony the battle that emphasized the repudiation of Cimon's policy will have been commemorated in a
hall named after one of his partisans, the Stoa Poikile or, to give
it the original name, the Peisianakteion, named after Peisianax
the Alcmaeonid, probably brother of Cimon's wife Isodice.[5]

---

[1] Thuc. i. 105. 1.   [2] Paus. i. 15. 1.   [3] Paus. x. 10. 4.
[4] For further discussion see App. 5, p. 469.
[5] Plut. *Cim.* 4. 6: ἐν τῇ Πεισιανακτείῳ τότε καλουμένῃ Ποικίλῃ δὲ νῦν στοᾷ.

The battle of Oenoe could not have passed out of the historical tradition if it had been a major engagement, but even a minor engagement on the Argive border might have made Athens feel that Argos was in serious danger from Sparta. Concern for Argos could make the attack on Halieis more intelligible. The main importance of Halieis lies in its wide anchorage. It had the best harbour between Athens and Argos and besides offering easy access to Argos it could be a useful base for raids on the coastal towns of Hermione, Troezen, and Epidaurus which were normally in the Spartan camp.[1] There may also be some connection between the Athenian attack and an odd incident reported by Herodotus. The Spartan Aneristus, son of Sperthias, on whom the wrath of Talthybius was to fall in the second year of the Peloponnesian War, 'seized Halieis, founded from Tiryns, having sailed in with a merchant ship full of men'.[2] The incident is more intelligible at a time when Sparta is openly hostile. It may have preceded and even been the cause of the Athenian attempt to seize Halieis. That operation may have been designed to cement the alliance with Argos and to improve communications; the Athenians may not have expected opposition from Corinth and Epidaurus. If some such explanation of Oenoe is right Athens may have met with rather more sympathy in the Aegean than if the raid on Halieis was the first blow struck. Allies from the League fought with her at sea against Aegina and on land at Tanagra.[3] This new precedent has attracted less notice than it deserves.

The Delian League had been formed to fight Persians and we can be virtually certain that in 477 none of the allies envisaged that they would be called on to fight Peloponnesians. We should like to know how far they were now consulted and what arguments were used. Athens' formal justification may have been the original oath that the members had taken, either that they would not desert Athens and the allies, or that they

---

[1] These states were all raided by the Athenian fleet in 430, Thuc. ii. 56. 1–5. Athens had to give up Troezen under the terms of the Thirty Years' Peace in 446–445. The importance of Epidaurus as a link between Athens and Argos is emphasized in Thuc. v. 53.

[2] Hdt. vii. 137. 2.

[3] Thuc. i. 105. 2 (against Aegina); i. 107. 5 (Tanagra). Cf. the Spartan dedication at Olympia, Paus. v. 10. 4: δῶρον ἀπ' Ἀργείων καὶ Ἀθαναίων καὶ Ἰώνων, confirmed, by an inscription, ML 36.

would have the same friends and enemies;[1] but such formal argument could not have sufficed alone, and it is difficult to believe that Athens relied on compulsion. It seems more likely that she had at least some positive support. If she claimed that the Peloponnesians were treacherously trying to destroy her while she was fighting the allies' war in the east she might have been able to persuade a League meeting at Delos that this Athenian war was League business. But the allies' support of Athens depended on success; a serious setback in Greece or in Egypt might disrupt the League.

At first all went surprisingly well. Aegina, defeated at sea, was besieged and reduced.[2] In the seventh century she had been more prosperous than Athens; her trade remained more extensive through the sixth century and she could challenge Athens on equal terms. Themistocles' creation of the new Athenian navy upset this balance, but Aegina's coins were still circulating freely and widely after the Persian War. Now she was compelled to become a tribute-paying member of an Athenian League, assessed at 30 talents, the highest figure on the list. Corinth also soon exposed her limitations when the Athenian reserves under Myronides were able to deal with a Corinthian attack on Megara. From the landing at Halieis to this clash in the Megarid, Athens' war was with the states near the Isthmus, but Spartan leadership is implied by Thucydides when he says that 'the Peloponnesians, wishing to help the Aeginetans, transported 300 hoplites, who had previously helped the Corinthians and Epidaurians, to Aegina'.[3] Now, probably in 457, Sparta herself actively intervened. In response to an appeal from the traditional home of the Dorians against Phocis Sparta sent over the Corinthian Gulf a large force of 1,500 Lacedaemonians and 10,000 allies.[4]

Having restored the position in Doris they had to change their plans. Thucydides says that they were unable to return by sea because the Athenians had sent ships round into the Corinthian Gulf; he implies that the Spartans had gone by sea and intended to return the same way when they had fulfilled their mission in Doris. An immediate return by land was also ruled out as Athens held Megara and Pegae and was guarding the route through

---

[1] See p. 45.   [2] Thuc. i. 108. 4.   [3] Thuc. i. 105. 3.
[4] Thuc. i. 107. 2. For difficulties in Thucydides' account see Endnote 5, p. 417.

Geranea; the easier route by the shore of the Saronic Gulf had been sealed earlier when Athens built walls linking Megara with her port of Nisaea. The Spartans therefore decided to wait in Boeotia. Here they received encouragement from extreme oligarchs in Athens who hoped with the help of Sparta to undo the reforms of Ephialtes and stop the building of the long walls which would mean the abandonment of the farms of Attica in the event of war. There could be more than one reason why the Spartans chose to encamp at Tanagra. It was a good base for supplies, it commanded an easy route to Athens, and it may have been claiming to lead the Boeotian Confederacy.[1]

The Athenian leaders, however, had decided not to wait within the walls and allow the Spartans to ravage Attica; they had sent for contingents from their allies in the League and from Argos and Thessaly. With these allies the Athenians marched out, crossed the border and fought a pitched battle with the Spartan army at Tanagra. The Spartans won a hard-fought battle but the victory was not sufficiently decisive to encourage a march on Athens and they were content to with-draw across the isthmus through Geranea after a ravaging demonstration in Megara. According to Diodorus, and he may well be right, the Thebans had appealed to the Spartans after the battle; the Spartans strengthened their walls and supported their claim to the hegemony of Boeotia.[2]

The danger that threatened from Boeotia was quickly stifled by the dramatic Athenian victory at Oenophyta, two months after Tanagra, under Myronides. Thucydides gives no details; Diodorus, probably reflecting Ephorus, has only anecdotes, but he regards this as the greatest of all Athenian victories.[3] The victory of Oenophyta opened the way to the Athenian control of Boeotia, Phocis, and Locris, and in these areas Athens was able to dictate terms. The evidence is scattered and scanty but Athens seems to have acted with some moderation. When a little later she attempted to intervene in Thessaly, whose men had gone over to Sparta at the battle of Tanagra, contingents were taken from Boeotia and Phocis;[4] we may infer that Athens

[1] Coins with Tanagra's *TA* and Boeotian shield on the obverse, and the Boeotian *BOI* on the reverse, were probably minted when Thebes was humiliated after the invasion of Xerxes. For a possible reconstruction, B. Fowler, *Phoenix*, xi (1957), 164–70.   [2] Diod. xi. 81. 1–3.

[3] Thuc. i. 108. 2–3; Diod. xi. 82. 1–2.   [4] Thuc. i. 111. 1.

required the states that had submitted to her to accept Athens' foreign policy and send troops to fight for Athens when required. No mainland city, however, appears on the quota lists; unlike Aegina, they were presumably not required to pay tribute. The main controls were political; Athens attempted to promote elements that might be expected to favour Athens, and to keep in check hostile elements by requiring hostages and exiling the irreconcilable. She did not perhaps rigidly insist on democracies of the Athenian pattern; indeed she is said by the Old Oligarch at one time to have supported 'the best men' in Boeotia, and Athens may have hoped that by supporting anti-federal dynasts she could keep the Boeotian confederacy divided and weak; but the same writer admits that the experiment was unsuccessful and implies that it was short-lived.[1] The natural supporters of Athens were democrats.

The spectacular conquests of Myronides were followed, in 456 or 455, by a large-scale expedition round the Peloponnese under the command of Tolmides. Sparta had already renounced the offensive, but the war was now carried into her own territory. The dockyards at Gytheum were burnt and Laconia itself raided, and in the Corinthian Gulf Chalcis was captured.[2] For Athens the future had never looked so bright. The helplessness of Sparta had been exposed and Athens was emerging as the dominant power on the Greek mainland, while the Delian League under her leadership was keeping the Persians off the seas in the eastern Mediterranean and would soon crush the Persian remnants in Egypt—or so it was then hoped. The new radical democracy had abundantly justified itself.

It is possible that in this buoyant mood Athens had been prepared to consider commitments in Sicily. A large fragment survives of an Athenian alliance with Egesta in the west of the island, dated by the archon's name of which only the last two letters survive. The long-accepted date for this alliance was 454–453 because in that year Diodorus mentions a war in which Egesta was engaged and the archon's name for that year, Ariston, ends in the right letters. It has, however, been recently claimed that sufficient letter-traces can be read to demand the restoration of Habron, archon for 458–457. It is very doubtful

---

[1] [Xen.] Ἀθ. Πολ. 3. 11. See also pp. 209 f.
[2] Thuc. i. 108. 5.

indeed whether secure traces of the vital letters can be seen, but the new date may yet be right.[1] It would be surprising if Athens were to consider sending help to Egesta when she had lost the initiative in Egypt. In 458–457 she was riding high on the tide of success. The inscription suggests that the initiative came from Egesta, but without more evidence we can only guess at the motives of Athens in agreeing to an alliance. She may simply have been accepting an opportunity to feel her way politically in the west or the alliance with Egesta may have been linked with alliances with Ionian cities of east Sicily, anticipating later Athenian policy.

Meanwhile the brilliant Athenian successes in Greece were at first matched by the League force in the east. This force, according to Thucydides, consisted of 200 ships, and of these Athens may have supplied roughly a half. If Plutarch is right in ascribing a new model trireme to the Athenian fleet at the Eurymedon, the new type was probably also used now, for in Cyprus as at the Eurymedon hoplites might be as important as oarsmen and the standard trireme carried too few. The League fleet had probably begun operations in Cyprus before being diverted to Egypt, for the casualty list of the Erechtheid tribe, which seems to cover the first year of the Egyptian campaign, includes Cyprus among the areas of operations and Cyprus is listed before Egypt.[2] When the expeditionary force reached Egypt the situation was promising. Inaros had defeated the main army of occupation and killed its commander, but the garrison of Memphis still held out and there was a small Persian fleet in the river. This fleet was quickly eliminated. The Athenians and their allies 'got control of the river', Thucydides tells us; an inscription from the Samian Heraeum commemorates a battle near Memphis in which the Samians captured fifteen ships.[3] The two sources are not necessarily inconsistent, for the river battle was probably little more than a demonstration. The Greeks had moved at once on Memphis, the only surviving centre of serious Persian resistance, and, having swept aside the Persian fleet, they succeeded in capturing the main town; but a Persian

---

[1] ML 37. But see also Add., p. 599.   [2] ML 33.

[3] Thuc. i. 104. 2: ἀναπλεύσαντες ἀπὸ θαλάσσης ἐς τὸν Νεῖλον τοῦ τε ποταμοῦ κρατοῦντες. The epigram records a battle [Μέμ]φιος ἀμφ' ἐρατῆς, in which the Samians captured fifteen ships, ML 34.

garrison held out in an inner fort, the White Tower, as successfully as another small Persian force had held out at Doriscus.

After the initial successes we lose sight of operations in Egypt.
'The Greeks stayed on in Egypt, and there were actions of
many kinds.'[1] Thucydides' description is vague, but it suggests
that fighting was not confined to the siege of Memphis. There
may have been other pockets of Persian resistance and divisions
may have arisen between Greeks and Egyptians and between
the Egyptians themselves. Inaros was a Libyan prince from the
western desert who was not likely to carry the continuous support of more conservative Egyptians. As in the earlier revolt
under Darius and Xerxes Upper Egypt was probably much less
committed to the revolt than the Delta.[2] Nor did Greeks and
Egyptians always get on easily together; even the Saite kings
had found that Greek troops, though militarily effective, could
be politically dangerous. But the Greeks did not face serious
danger until the arrival of strong Persian reinforcements, and
in the first years the League did not confine itself to Egypt.
Frail wisps of evidence suggest that in the early fifties Athens
extended membership of the League into the eastern Mediterranean. A fragment of Craterus' collection of decrees preserves an entry from an Athenian assessment in which Dorus
and Phaselis were included among Carian cities. This Dorus
has been plausibly identified with the Dorus under Mount
Carmel and it is thought that Craterus selected for his collection an extract from the first assessment made at Athens, in
454.[3] Dorus traditionally had Greek roots. Another city of
Greek origin, Celenderis in Cilicia, is included in the extravagant assessment of 425, though it is not recorded in any
quota list as having paid tribute. The inference has been drawn
that Celenderis, and with it a city in Pamphylia, probably
Aspendus, were included in 425 because they had once been
assessed.[4] It is not too fanciful to believe that, while her fortunes
were rising in Greece and in Egypt, Athens attempted to
bring under her wing all cities in the eastern Mediterranean
that could, however tenuously, claim to be Greek foundations.

---

[1] Thuc. i. 109. 1: πολλαὶ ἰδέαι πολέμων.

[2] F. K. Kienitz, *Die politische Geschichte Ägyptens vom 7 bis 4 Jahrhundert* (Berlin,
1953), 69.

[3] See Endnote 7, p. 420.   [4] See pp. 329 f.

Artaxerxes' first reaction to the Greek success in Egypt had been to send Megabazus with money to bribe Sparta to invade Attica and so draw off the Athenians from Egypt.[1] Some of the money seems to have been spent, but with no result. If Artaxerxes was to save Egypt a new Persian army was needed. Megabyzus and Artabanus were put in charge of the mobilization, training, and leading of this force, which was probably not ready for action until 456. The numbers in our sources are very high, more than 300,000 infantry and cavalry, 300 triremes according to Diodorus, probably from Ephorus; Ctesias has 200,000 in the army, and a fleet of 300.[2] These numbers, as all Persian numbers at all times in all Greek sources, are almost certainly exaggerated but the sequel shows that the force was large and effective. On its passage down to Egypt it must have weakened the Greek hold on Cyprus and the coast; in Egypt Megabyzus in charge of the land forces defeated the Egyptians and their allies, drove the Greeks from Memphis, and finally blockaded them in Prosopitis, an island formed by a canal connecting the two western arms of the Delta. In the northern Delta was marshland difficult to penetrate and noted for its warriors, where Amyrtaeus remained king when the main revolt had collapsed. The Greek fleet still controlled the river and for eighteen months there was stalemate, but in the early summer of 454 the Persians diverted the water from the canal. The Greek ships now rested on mud, 'most of the island became mainland, and Megabyzus crossed and took the island with a land force'. Thucydides continues: 'So the Greek cause in Egypt was ruined after six years of war; and only a handful from a great force made their way through Libya and reached Cyrene safely; the majority were lost.'[3] Thucydides does not make it clear precisely how the end came, but we can accept from Diodorus and Ctesias that the Greeks, after fierce fighting, capitulated.[4] Under the terms of their surrender the survivors were allowed to escape to Libya, and they may already have burnt their ships. This was not quite the end. A relieving squadron of fifty ships, Athenian and allied, sailed into the Mendesian mouth of the Nile. According to Thucydides 'they knew nothing of what had happened', and this looks at first

---

[1] Thuc. i. 109. 2.   [2] Diod. xi. 75. 2, 77. 1; Ctesias 64.
[3] Thuc. i. 109. 4–110. 1.   [4] Diod. xi. 77. 4; Ctesias 65.

like a complete breakdown of communications between Egypt and Athens.[1] We cannot, however, believe that the news of the arrival of Persian reinforcements in Egypt and the relief of Memphis was unknown in Athens. More probably the final phase, completely unexpected, had been carried through at high speed. The relieving squadron knew that the Greeks were blockaded in Prosopitis, but they thought that the Greek fleet still controlled the river. Not expecting any opposition they were attacked both by troops from the banks and by ships on the river, and lost more than half their number. 'So ended the great expedition of Athenians and their allies to Egypt.'

How serious was this disaster in Egypt? Until this century it was generally assumed that the total force of 200 ships, originally sent to Cyprus, moved to Egypt, stayed there, and were destroyed; in the last twenty years this view has had very few supporters. According to current orthodoxy the greater part of the Greek fleet returned to home waters when they had won control of the Nile and blockaded the Persians in the White Tower. There were perhaps some fifty ships only left in Egypt to be lost in the final disaster, together with the majority of the relieving squadron of fifty.[2] There is some evidence that can be claimed for this view. Justin implies that the main Greek fleet had returned from Egypt by the time of the great sea battle of Aegina;[3] Ctesias introduces a more radical variant. He says that the Athenian force was of forty ships only, and the fact that he names the Athenian general Charitimides gives a circumstantial plausibility to his account. His description of the final scene is consistent with this figure; there were, according to him, more than 6,000 survivors.[4] The argument that is considered most decisive, however, is the interrelation of events in Egypt and Greece. At the battle of Aegina the Athenians, supported by allies, captured seventy Aeginetan ships;[5] their own fleet must have exceeded 100 ships and it is thought that Athens, even with League support, could not have had the resources to fight on this scale on two fronts. The main part of the Athenian

---

[1] Thuc. i. 110. 4.

[2] Detailed references in Salmon, *La Politique égyptienne d'Athènes*, 152 n. 6.

[3] Justin iii. 6. 6–7: 'parvae tunc temporis classe in Aegyptum missa vires Atheniensibus erant . . . interiecto deinde tempore post reditum suorum aucti et classis et militum robore proelium reparant'. See p. 475.

[4] Ctesias 63–4.   [5] Thuc. i. 105. 2.

contingent in Egypt will therefore have returned, probably between the battle of Cecryphalea and the battle of Aegina. This could also explain why the casualty list of the Erechtheid tribe lists men who died fighting in Cyprus, Egypt, Phoenicia, in that order. If, as is probable, these battle areas are recorded in chronological order the casualties in Cyprus will have been suffered before the fleet moved down to Egypt, and those in Phoenicia may reflect a raid on the Phoenician coast in the course of the main fleet's return to Greece.[1] On this interpretation the disaster in Egypt is considerably reduced in scale, a serious setback but not a crippling disaster. And it is claimed that this reappraisal is confirmed by the history of the next four years, which reveal no serious consequences of the disaster in the Aegean world. If more than 200 ships and their crews had been lost, the Athenians, it is thought, could not have maintained their position in Greece and in the League.

However attractive this modern view may seem, the evidence must be assessed before we turn to probabilities and we must turn to Thucydides before Ctesias. Some historians have satisfied their consciences by assuming that Thucydides' account is consistent with the modern view: he has merely, they suggest, omitted to mention the withdrawal of the greater part of the fleet; his mistake is one of omission and not of commission. This compromise is untenable. Thucydides' account is clear and consistent. 'The Greeks remained . . . a handful from a great force . . . so ended the great expedition.' The language recalls Thucydides' reflections on the Sicilian disaster; he may be wrong but he is deliberately saying that this was a major disaster.[2] It would be compatible with his highly condensed narrative to believe that small forces operated from Egypt in Cyprus and on the coastal route to Egypt and that some ships were absent on such operations in the final phase, but we cannot put Thucydides' view of the total losses, including the relieving squadron, at much less than 200 ships. If the modern view is right Thucydides is very wrong and his mistake is of an entirely

---

[1] *ATL* iii. 174 f.

[2] Thuc. vii. 87. 6: πανωλεθρίᾳ δὴ τὸ λεγόμενον καὶ πεζὸς καὶ νῆες καὶ οὐδὲν ὅτι οὐκ ἀπώλετο, καὶ ὀλίγοι ἀπὸ πολλῶν ἐπ' οἴκου ἀπενόστησαν. Cf. 1. 110. 1 (Egypt): καὶ ὀλίγοι ἀπὸ πολλῶν πορευόμενοι διὰ τῆς Λιβύης ἐς Κυρήνην ἐσώθησαν, οἱ δὲ πλεῖστοι ἀπώλοντο. A further parallel in iii. 112. 8 (Ambracia). See Westlake, *CP* xlv (1950), 209–16.

different order from a misunderstanding of the nature of the first assessment or of Spartan intentions in Boeotia before the battle of Tanagra. Thucydides was mature enough to see the significance of events in the mid thirties and to take detailed and accurate notes of what was happening. This was barely twenty years after the collapse in Egypt, when the main outline of the campaign would still be a live topic among relatives of the dead and in barbers' shops. Plutarch tells us that before the Peloponnesian War Pericles had to restrain extremists who had their eyes on Sicily already and wanted to make another attempt to secure Egypt.[1] Any talk about a return to Egypt would revive memories of the earlier campaign. Thucydides is supported in his main outline by Diodorus, reflecting Ephorus, and by Isocrates; it was the official version in the fourth century.

Some historians have appealed from Thucydides to Ctesias and at first sight Ctesias has good credentials. He was a doctor from Cnidus who worked at the Persian court in the early fourth century. He there had excellent opportunities to study Persian history and he himself claimed to have taken great trouble in consulting monuments and official records.[2] It might therefore be thought that in Ctesias' account of the Egyptian campaign we have the Persian version, and that if Ctesias puts the Athenian ships at only forty he must be near the truth because the Persians would not underestimate their enemies' strength. Such reasoning will be attractive only to those who have not read what remains of Photius' epitome of Ctesias. When he puts the total Persian land forces at more than 400,000 we cannot believe that he has consulted Persian records or thought realistically about the campaign. His account, perhaps not judiciously summarized in the epitome, does not make military sense and he makes no mention of any Greeks other than the Athenians. He ignores the final relief squadron and, by implication, dismisses the march of the survivors across the desert to Cyrene: but both these circumstantial details in Thucydides, repeated by Diodorus, must surely be right. It might seem surprising that Ctesias should minimize the size of the Athenian fleet, but his Greek numbers in the invasion of

---

[1] Plut. *Per.* 20. 3.
[2] For Ctesias, Diod. ii. 32. 4; Jacoby, *RE* xxii (1922), 2032–73.

Xerxes are similarly low. Herodotus tells us that there were 5,000 Spartiates at the Battle of Plataea; in Ctesias the number has shrunk to 300, presumably a confusion with Themopylae.[1] At Salamis he has 150 Athenian ships; Herodotus is probably nearer the truth in giving 180.[2] Just as in his account of the Egyptian expedition he has confused the order of events, so in the Persian war he makes Plataea precede Salamis. No serious attention need be paid to Ctesias except perhaps when he is retailing court scandal; he seems to have known a good deal about the royal ladies. There remains the evidence of Justin. If there were other passages in Justin's account of this period which seemed to derive from an independent and reliable source, his statement that the Athenian fleet had returned before the war with Aegina might carry some weight; since none can be found we need more than Justin, whose source could be merely rationalizing, to correct Thucydides.[3]

Before we can accept Thucydides' account, however, we must be satisfied that it is not impossible. Could Athens have fought on this scale on two fronts? Could she have sustained losses in manpower on this scale? On the first issue it can be pointed out that in attacking Halieis Athens was clearly risking a major clash with the Aeginetan fleet; she should therefore have felt confident that even with the large force in Egypt she had sufficient resources to face any fleet that she was likely to meet in Greek waters. As for manpower we lack the evidence we need. Any estimate of the total adult male population of Athens in 460 can be little more than a guess, nor do we know the complement of the ships if Cimon's new model was used. It is also often forgotten that the allies were strongly represented in Egypt. The epigram recording the capture of fifteen Phoenician ships by the Samian contingent at the battle of Memphis suggests that Samos had probably contributed a substantial contingent; the three big islands, Samos, Chios, and Lesbos, could have provided up to 100 ships without serious difficulty. The total number of Athenian ships need not have been more than 100 and these will not necessarily have been manned entirely by Athenian crews. In the later Peloponnesian War Athens drew

[1] Hdt. ix. 28. 2; Ctesias 25. [2] Ctesias 26; Hdt. viii. 44. 1.
[3] Justin iii. 3. 6. A further discussion of the sources for the Egyptian expedition, App. 6, p. 473.

heavily on the metics and allies to man her triremes;[1] the custom probably developed before the middle of the century. On such reasoning the Athenian losses could be reduced below 10,000. Thucydides' account cannot be lightly dismissed.

[1] See Endnote 24, p. 439.

7

THE AFTERMATH OF EGYPT

BEFORE judgement is passed on Thucydides' account of the Egyptian expedition it is necessary also to consider the sequel. The authors of *The Athenian Tribute Lists*, after a detailed examination of the evidence, conclude that the situation in the Aegean from 454 to 450 is incompatible with a major disaster in Egypt;[1] this evidence must be reviewed. From Thucydides we get very little help; the reconstruction rests primarily on the tribute quota lists of the first period, and substantial remains of at least three Athenian decrees. The record of the *aparchai* of the tributes paid to Athena was published annually on a high marble stele which was set up on the Acropolis for all to see. The natural inference is that from this date the tribute was brought to Athens and that the accumulated reserve had been transferred from Delos to Athens in 454. The first assessment period, covering the years from 454–453 to 451–450, is comparatively well represented in surviving fragments and in each list roughly half the names have been preserved. Moreover the precise relationship of the fragments has been established; the number of lines in each year's list is therefore known, and so the approximate number of states paying tribute.[2] Also in the first year, 454–453, though in that year only, the total of the year's quotas was recorded, but the most important figures are missing. This evidence flatters only to deceive. What we wish to know is what effect the Egyptian disaster had on the League's loyalty, and the evidence is ambiguous. The total of the first year's quotas can be restored to yield a total tribute of approximately either 350 or 400 talents.[3] Similarly,

---

[1] *ATL* iii. 262 f.

[2] The precise number will depend on the number of entries occupying two lines in the missing parts of the list.

[3] The total is expressed in Attic silver and a small balance of Cyzicene electrum staters. The silver total could be [⊢X]XXHHHΔΔ - - or [⊢T]XXHHHΔΔ - - -, giving a silver total of 333 or 383 talents. The number of Cyzicene staters was

though the first year's list is manifestly the shortest of the whole series, limited to some 140 states from a possible 170 or more, the significance of the figure depends on the identity of the absentees. Twenty small Carian states would together contribute less than Byzantium, Abdera, or even Miletus; the seriousness of the situation depends on the importance of the absentees. One other question has two possible answers. A large group of island states is absent from all our fragments. Absence from a single year's fragments can be coincidence, but outside the island district there are very few states indeed who do not appear in at least one of the four lists.[1] It has been suggested that their absence means only that they paid their tribute to generals in the field or to Athenian garrisons, but this solution we should reject. In later lists such payments were recorded with the others, and since the payment of the quota was a religious obligation we should expect it to be paid by all and recorded for all.[2] It is virtually certain that some at least of the islands were not paying tribute in the late fifties and there are two possible explanations: either they were contributing ships rather than money down to 450, or they were making their protest by withholding payment.

If it could be shown that the large number of absentees in the first list included several important states, that the year's tribute total was only 350 talents, and that the islands were not still contributing ships, Thucydides' account of the Egyptian campaign would be at least partially vindicated. It can only be shown that these answers are possible, perhaps probable. First, Thucydides. In his brief summary of events the Egyptian disaster is followed immediately by an unsuccessful attempt to restore a pro-Athenian dynast to power in Pharsalus and, a little later, an expedition round the Peloponnese led by Pericles.[3] It is possible that Athens was committed to these

56, 66, 86, or 96, but the value of the Cyzicene in Attic drachmae is uncertain; more than 24 drachmae and less than 28 drachmae. See W. E. Thompson, *Num. Chron.* 1963, 1–4, and Endnote 26, p. 442.

[1] The following island cities are missing from all four lists: Chalcis, Eretria, Hestiaea, and Styra (all in Euboea); Cythnos, Siphnos, Naxos, Paros, Tenos. Three other islands are found only in the last list (450), Ceos, Seriphos, Andros. For other absentees see App. 14, p. 558.

[2] Gomme, *HCT* i. 277 f. For later practice see lists 25 and 26: [μίσθον ἐτέλε]σαν ἡαίδε ἀπὸ τὸ φόρο | [τεῖ στρατιᾶι] (25. i. 59–60). [π]όλες αἵ[δ]ε ἀρχαῖς | [ἐδ]οσαν τὸμ φόρον (26. i. 11–12).   [3] Thuc. i. 111.

enterprises before the final news from Egypt was received, and they may even have come a little earlier than the capitulation on Prosopitis;[1] they are the last operations initiated by Athens in the First Peloponnesian War. After that, says Thucydides, 'there were three years of inactivity'.[2] Up to this point Athens had carried on a vigorous and successful offensive in Greece; the ending of operations is abrupt and the Egyptian disaster is the reason. From 454 Athens will have concentrated her resources on maintaining her hold on the League and building up her strength to meet Persia again and reverse the verdict of Egypt. Persia was now the main objective and even the radicals realized that it was no longer safe to fight on two fronts; if a large force was to sail east again there must first be a settlement with Sparta. For these delicate negotiations no one could match Cimon's authority. He was due to return to Athens after his ten years of ostracism in the late winter of 452–451, but we may accept the tradition that he was recalled by special decree and accept that part of the tradition which links his return closely with the making of peace.[3] Cimon was probably recalled in 452, and it was probably Pericles who proposed the decree.[4] The situation required the same kind of patriotism that Themistocles had invoked in 480 and for the moment there was no division on foreign policy.

When Athens decided to halt her offensive in Greece she was not in serious danger of attack. So long as Megara remained an ally and the Isthmus was held, the Peloponnesian army could not invade Attica. By sea the Aeginetan fleet had been eliminated, and Corinth had proved ineffective. Boeotia had not yet

---

[1] Thucydides seems not to have been rigorously chronological in his account of the Egyptian expedition. The opening year's campaign (104) is followed by a sequence of events in Greece (105–8). In returning to Egypt (109) he first sums up what has happened since he broke off, including the sending of Megabazus with money to Sparta. The point he chooses for resuming his account of the Egyptian expedition is the sending of Persian reinforcements which marked the decisive turning-point. From the dispatch of Megabyzus by Artaxerxes to the end the narrative is unbroken. For a different interpretation of Thucydides, *ATL* iii. 168–78.

[2] Thuc. i. 112. 1. ὕστερον δὲ διαλιπόντων ἐτῶν τριῶν.

[3] See Endnote 9, p. 422.

[4] Plut. *Cim.* 17. 8: καὶ κατῆλθε τὸ ψήφισμα γράψαντος αὐτοῦ Περικλέους. This could have been invented to explain why Pericles maintained his position, and to make a nicely moral story; but some at least of Pericles' decrees were preserved: ἔγγραφον μὲν οὖν οὐδὲν ἀπολέλοιπε πλὴν τῶν ψηφισμάτων, Plut. *Per.* 8. 7.

recovered from Oenophyta. Athens could therefore concentrate on maintaining the solidarity of the Delian League and preparing to renew the fighting against Persia. That the situation in the League was serious if not critical can be reasonably inferred from a combination of surviving decrees and of the quota lists. In the first year's list of 453 the Milesians in Leros pay 3 talents and the Milesians in Teichioussa are listed next to them. Leros and Teichioussa are not normally recorded separately, being dependencies of Miletus, but when they are listed their place, as we should expect, is immediately after Miletus; but in this list Miletus does not appear where we expect to find her. We infer that Miletus had not paid her tribute but that Milesian loyalists have taken refuge in Leros and Teichioussa. The small off-shore island of Leros was particularly well suited to a group in opposition; Hecataeus had advised the East Greeks in the last phase of the Ionian revolt to make it their base, and the name of Teichioussa, the walled town, suggests that it was a strong-point.[1] In 451 there is an entry for Miletus and we can infer that she has been brought under control by Athens.[2]

The nature of the trouble in Miletus is perhaps illumined by the evidence from near-by Erythrae. In the quota lists the states of the Erythraean peninsula sometimes make a single payment as Ἐρυθραῖοι καὶ συντελές, but in those pre-war assessment periods in which they are listed separately, their individual assessments apart from Erythrae herself are very small. But in 452 Boutheia is listed alone, paying as much as 3 talents, whereas later, when she is separately recorded, she pays only 1,000 drachmae. The natural inference has been drawn that Erythrae has seceded and that, just as Leros and Teichioussa remained loyal when Miletus revolted, so Boutheia, reinforced perhaps by refugees, continued to support the League.[3] There is explicit evidence for the political conflict at Erythrae in an Athenian decree which the French traveller Fauvel copied at the beginning of the nineteenth century. Unfortunately both the stone and the copy have since been lost; all that remains is the nearest approach to the copy that could be produced by the printer

---

[1] Hdt. v. 125. For Teichioussa, J. M. Cook and G. E. Bean, *BSA* lii (1957), 106–16.

[2] Meiggs, *JHS* lxiii (1943), 25–7; Barron, *JHS* lxxxii (1962), 1–6.

[3] *ATL* iii. 252.

whom Boeckh used for his pioneering *Corpus Inscriptionum Grae-carum* of 1842.[1] This decree which lays down new regulations for Erythrae begins with a clause specifying the obligations of Erythrae at the Athenian festival of the Great Panathenaea, held every four years, but Fauvel, who copied what he saw on the stone rather than what he thought he ought to see, must have found the opening lines extremely difficult to decipher; his copy makes nonsense and no coherent restoration can carry conviction. As the decree proceeds, however, Fauvel's text becomes increasingly closer to Greek and the sense at least of the central clauses can be restored with some confidence. Conditions are first laid down for the selection of a new democratic Boule at Erythrae; membership is to be confined to citizens of not less than thirty years of age, election is to be by lot, and a man may not serve more than once in four years. The establishment of the first Boule by lot is to be supervised by Athenian commissioners, *episkopoi*, and an Athenian garrison commander, *phrourarchos*; subsequently by the garrison commander cooperating with the outgoing Boule. This Boule is required to take a solemn oath:

> I will serve as a member of the Boule as well and as justly as lies in my power in the interest of the *plethos* of Erythrae and the *plethos* of Athens and her allies, and I will not desert the *plethos* of Athens nor the allies of Athens either of my own free will or at another's dictation; nor will I of my own free will or at another's dictation accept back anyonesoever of the exiles who have taken refuge with the Medes without the authority of the Boule and Demos of Athens; nor will I expel anyone that remains in Erythrae without the authority of the Boule and Demos of Athens.[2]

From this oath it is clear that there have been political troubles in Erythrae and since the party that has been driven out has taken refuge with the Medes it is reasonable to infer that the struggle in Erythrae has been between League loyalists and Medizers. Athens has presumably intervened to drive out the Medizers and retains firm control of the political purge. It might have been dangerous to give further play to political

---

[1] *CIG* i addenda 73b, p. 891. *IG* i². 10, revised in *ATL* ii D 10; ML 40. Detailed discussion, L. I. Highby, *Klio*, Beiheft xxxvi (1936). See also Meiggs, art. cit. 23–5; *ATL* iii. 254f. Plethos is a less neutral word than *demos*, emphasizing the power of numbers.

[2] Text, App. 16, p. 579.

rivalries in Erythrae, and the authority of the democratic
sovereign body of Athens is required before any modification
is made of the present settlement. An Athenian garrison is to
remain in Erythrae but it could be argued that the loyalists
needed protection against a possible reaction from the political
exiles or their Persian supporters. It is, however, clear that the
vital decisions have been taken by Athens and not by a League
meeting at Delos; Athens and not a League meeting decides
what elements are to be trusted in Erythrae. Lip-service, however, is still paid to the allies. The oath of renewed loyalty is
taken not to Athens alone, but also to her allies. Further recognition comes later:

> If an Erythraean kills another Erythraean he shall be put to death
> if he is found guilty, and if he is condemned to exile, he shall be
> exiled from the whole Athenian alliance and his property shall be
> the public property of the Erythraeans. And if anyone is convicted
> of betraying the city of Erythrae to the tyrants, he and his children
> shall be put to death and anyone who kills him shall be exempt from
> penalty.[1]

Erythrae retains the right to decide her own capital cases which
she was to lose later, and the League is still 'the alliance',
ξυμμαχίς and not yet 'the cities ruled by Athens', πόλεις ὅσων
οἱ Ἀθηναῖοι κρατοῦσι. The tyrants from whom trouble may be
expected are not tyrants in general, but specific tyrants who
could be named, leaders of the expelled Medizers. From this
point Fauvel's copy can once more provide only insecure hints
of the original, but if two fragments dealing with Erythrae,
which can still be studied in Athens and London, both belong
to the lost stone a little more can be added.[2] The London fragment mentions *phrouroi*, *phrourarchos*, and *episkopoi* and certain
judicial arrangements are laid down, but not enough survives
to define the nature of the cases and the responsibility for deciding them. The Athenian fragment comes from the last lines
of a decree and records an oath to be taken by the whole people
of Erythrae: 'I will not revolt from the *plethos* of Athens nor

---

[1] There are many uncertainties in the text but some important clauses seem
secure: in l. 31 φευγέτο [h]άπασ[αν] τὲ[ν] Ἀθεναίον χσυνμαχί[δα or αν, and in ll. 32–3
ἐὰν δέ τις [ha]λõ[ι προ|διδ]ὸς το[ῖ]ς τυράννοις τὲμ πόλ[ιντ]ὲν Ἐρυθραί[ο]ν.

[2] *IG* i². 11 (London); *IG* i². 13a (Athens); *ATL* ii. D 10. Texts of the oaths,
App. 15, p. 579.

from the allies of Athens either of my own free will or at another's dictation, but I will obey the judgement of Athens.' There are, however, difficulties in associating these two fragments with the lost decree; there may have been two separate interventions.[1]

Events in Miletus had probably followed a similar pattern. Perhaps a Medizing faction had gained control. Athens had intervened in the summer of 452 and by 451 Miletus was again outwardly at least loyal. But the settlement at Miletus appears to have been less decisive and less effective than at Erythrae. From the appearance of the Milesians in the quota list of 451 we may infer that Athens has driven out or underground the Medizing element in Miletus and imposed by decree a political settlement. There survive, however, substantial fragments of a decree passed by the Athenian Assembly in 450–449 which imposes a wide range of requirements on Miletus.[2] Provision is made for the sending of Milesian troops when required, and of the posting to Miletus of five political residents; a garrison is also mentioned. But there is no hint of the imposition of a democratic constitution and the new political residents are to cooperate with the magistrates of an oligarchic state. There may even be a barbed reference to this oligarchy in one of the very badly preserved clauses of the decree: ἐὰν σοφρονῶσι, if the Milesians pursue a 'sound' policy.[3] *Sophrosyne* was a virtue in which aristocracies tended to claim a monopoly. From this decree of 450–449 we conclude that the first settlement of 452 had proved inadequate and that Athens found it necessary to tighten control; but she still avoided the radical solution of giving power to the common people. A passage in the Old Oligarch's cynical analysis of Athenian democracy may add a little colour to the background. Having emphasized the political advantages gained by Athens from the support of democracies among her allies he drives his point home by showing that the exceptions proved the rule: 'Whenever the Athenians made it their policy to prefer the best men it did not serve their interest . . . when they preferred the best men in Miletus within a short time they revolted and cut down the Demos.'[4] This is good evidence for the support of oligarchy in Miletus and the most appropriate context is the troubles of the fifties. Perhaps Miletus, like Erythrae, had

---

[1] See Endnote 8, p. 421.
[2] *ATL* ii. D 11. Hereafter D 11.
[3] See also App. 15, p. 563.
[4] [Xen.] Ἀθ. Πολ. 3. 11.

in the mid fifties been controlled by tyrants; or at least Medizing oligarchs. In 452 Athens expelled the Medizers and decided
that a loyal oligarchy would provide the most reliable form of
government: it was necessary in 450–449 to maintain a closer
watch on Miletus, but the oligarchs were allowed to remain in
power. We shall see later the failure of this policy ending in the
establishment of democracy.

The situation that had developed in Erythrae and Miletus
is what we might have expected. Artaxerxes knew from the
assassinations that preceded his accession that his position was
precarious and that he needed to build up his reputation in the
empire. He reacted vigorously to the revolt in Egypt and is not
likely to have ignored Ionia. We can imagine him sending
instructions to the satraps at Dascylium and Sardis to intensify
their diplomacy and seize what opportunities they could make.
Themistocles, settled as governor of Magnesia, with a very
young daughter tactfully named Asia, must surely have been
sounded, but Themistocles knew how to play for time and he
may have died before the pressure became embarrassing. Even
in the early fifties there were factors that favoured Persia. The
revolt of Thasos had shaken the League, and the replacement
of Cimon's leadership by a radical and aggressive democracy
may have created political divisions in some of the allied cities.
Some oligarchs will have been less willing to follow a radical
democracy, and a Persian-sponsored tyranny or oligarchy may
have seemed to them the wisest insurance against their own
common people following the Athenian lead. When Megabyzus
won his first decisive success in Egypt Persian propaganda had
stronger backing, and the troubles in Miletus and Erythrae
probably reflect its success. What other states in Ionia and the
Hellespont were affected we do not know. Colophon, Clazomenae, and probably Ephesus survive from the first list; we
happen to have no evidence for Phocaea, Cumae, Teos. Similarly in the Hellespontine district we have no evidence for
Byzantium, Chalcedon, Selymbria, and other important cities.
The absence of states from the fragments of the first list can be
mere coincidence, since not more than half the list survives;
but it is also important to remember that states which are known
to have been paying tribute in 452 or 451 were not necessarily
loyal in 453.

The infiltration of Medism into Erythrae and Miletus was probably directed from Sardis. We may see the influence of the satrap at Dascylium in an Athenian decree of 451–450 which praises Sigeum for its continuing loyalty to Athens and promises protection 'against anyonesoever on the mainland'.[1] Such a decree implies a difficult situation in which Sigeum remained loyal under pressure, and the generalizing term used for Sigeum's potential enemies implies that the danger was not solely from Persia. We shall see later that there was trouble in the Hellespontine area in the early forties; this decree suggests that it may have begun earlier. Sigeum might be expected to remain loyal. It was an Athenian settlement and, though it had been closely linked with the Athenian tyrants, Salamis and Mycale should have put an end to the Medizing tendencies that Hippias encouraged. What we should like to know is how Lampsacus, Cyzicus, Byzantium, and other important towns in this area behaved. Any inferences from the first quota list to the security of Athenian control involve circular arguments. 'We cannot tolerate too great a discrepancy between the names assessed and the names from whom collection was made, for the good reason that defaulting by many cities would have had a deleterious effect upon discipline.'[2] But the effectiveness of discipline needs first to be independently established before we conclude that few important states were not paying in 453. We do not even know how long Miletus and Erythrae were in revolt before order was restored, nor what other measures of coercion were being used by Athens. The evidence does not justify a clear-cut decision in favour of the higher of the two figures for the tribute collection of 453.

Miletus was outside the League in 453 and was recovered by 451. Erythrae was outside the league when tribute was paid in 453 and 452; for the years 451 and 450 there is no evidence. The lost Erythrae decree can be restored to give the name of the archon for 453–452, Lysicrates.[3] It is a convenient economy to believe that Erythrae and Miletus were recovered by an Athenian

[1] *IG* i². 32, revised with new fragment, Meritt, *Hesp.* v (1936), 360, *SEG* x. 13; Meiggs, art cit. 28, *HSCP* lxvii (1963), 6. ll. 14–16: καὶ μὲ ἀδ|ικõνται μεδὲ ὑφ' ἑνὸς τõν ἐν τ|ε̑ι ἐπείροι.

[2] *ATL* iii. 267.

[3] *ATL* D 10.: Λ[υσι]κ[ράτες ε̑ρχε. The restoration is attractive but not certain, see Endnote 8, p. 421, and ML 40, p. 93.

force operating in Ionia in the summer of 452. Evidence of another Athenian expedition in the previous year has been seen in the second quota list, for 452. In this list a group of small Carian states head the preserved names from the first column. None of them appears in the fragments of the first list; their entry at the opening of the second list may represent their payment under pressure to an Athenian force in the late summer of 453, after the list for 454–453 was closed.[1] Our conclusion will be that after the Egyptian disaster Athens concentrated her resources on the League. Such control as she had exercised over Cyprus and the Greek coastal towns of the eastern Mediterranean was lost, but energetic steps were taken to retain Lycia and Caria. It is interesting that she seems to have chosen to make a display of force in Caria before tackling the more serious danger in Ionia; she may have thought that there was a danger of losing the whole of the southern coastline unless she showed at once that her spirit had not been broken by the capitulation of Prosopitis. What little evidence we possess suggests that Athens met with considerable success; but it would be wrong to assume that the Egyptian disaster was entirely to Athens' disadvantage in her relations with the League. The battle of the Eurymedon had temporarily paralysed the Persians; the loss of the League fleet in Egypt once again reminded the Ionians and their neighbours of their vulnerability. Faced with the very real danger of once again coming under Persian rule many of them may have been anxious to see Athenian strength and control restored.

It is more difficult to assess the repercussions in the islands. As we have seen, a significantly large group of islands do not appear in any fragments of the first assessment period, and some others are found only in the last list for 450.[2] West was the first to suggest that they were still contributing ships until the eve of Cimon's final expedition to Cyprus.[3] He also inferred that the criterion used by the Athenians in deciding what states were to contribute ships was the part that they had played in Xerxes' war; those who had fought with the Greeks should provide ships, the rest money. This latter inference has won little support. Such a clear-cut distinction should have been preserved

[1] ATL iii. 7–9.   [2] See p. 110 n. 1.
[3] West, Am. Hist. Rev. xxv (1929–30), 267–75.

in the tradition, nor does it seem likely that Athens in 478–477 would have excluded from the League fleet states such as Thasos which could have provided effective contingents. A more plausible explanation for the continuation of ship service by the islanders was found by Wade-Gery in their nearness to Athens. They were allowed, perhaps even encouraged, to provide ships for so long because they could be easily assembled at the Piraeus.[1]

It may be doubted whether Athens would originally have asked all these island states to provide ships. When Xerxes invaded Greece Chalcis had to borrow ships from Athens, Styra had produced two triremes only, Ceos two triremes and two pentekonters, Siphnos and Seriphos one pentekonter each and no triremes.[2] It is true that such small contingents were welcomed at Artemisium and Salamis, but in 478 Athens had the East Greeks also to draw on. It is more probable that she selected a limited number of the larger states. The argument from convenience of assembly, attractive at first, is not compelling. When Athens led a League force the natural assembly point for the fleets of Chios, Lesbos, Samos, and other allies was on the east side of the Aegean. When Cimon sailed for the Eurymedon 'he started from Cnidus and the Triopian promontory'; that is probably where the allies had joined the Athenian contingent. If the continuation of ship service by the islanders is rejected, an alternative explanation at least deserves consideration. Nesselhauf suggested that the absence of the islands from the quota lists reflected discontent. They do not appear on the fragments because they chose not to pay.[3] The authors of *The Athenian Tribute Lists* have no hesitation in ruling out this explanation on the grounds that if Athens succeeded in restoring control over Miletus and Erythrae she could not allow the islands, so much nearer home, to defy her.[4] This argument is not decisive. It might have been felt at Athens that the islands could be dealt with at leisure and that the greater urgency lay in Ionia and the Hellespont where the Persian danger was near and real. The islands' abstention may also have had different motives.

---

[1] *Hesp.* xiv (1945), 219, n. 16.   [2] Hdt. viii. 1. 2, 48.
[3] H. Nesselhauf, 'Untersuchungen der delisch-attischen Symmachie', *Klio* Beiheft xxx (1933), 11–13.
[4] *ATL* iii. 267 f.

To most of them Medism meant considerably less than in Ionia, but Delos meant considerably more. Archaeologically Delos is dominated by Naxos in the archaic period.[1] The Ionian festival which the Delian hymn to Apollo so vividly describes was primarily an island festival. Delos can be clearly seen from Naxos, Paros, Tenos, Syros, and Myconos. The refusal of the islands to pay tribute may in part have been their response to the removal of the treasury from Delos to Athens.[2]

There may even be evidence of Athenian police action in the islands before Cimon's expedition to Cyprus. Thucydides merely tells us that the Athenians broke off their war in Greece and sent an expedition to Cyprus; Plutarch, thinking naturally in terms of character, is more colourful and explicit in describing Cimon's motives:

When the peace was made [the five years' truce of 451] Cimon realized that the Athenians could not remain inactive, but wanted campaigns involving action and expansion. So [he led them to Cyprus] in order that they should not stir up trouble in Greece or by expeditions round the islands or the Peloponnese draw on the city responsibility for wars against fellow Greeks and lay the foundations for protests from their allies.[3]

This frail allusion to trouble in the islands in the late fifties may perhaps be strengthened a little by a passage from an unknown comedy in one of the less convincing chapters of Plutarch's *Pericles*. Pericles, he tells us, tended to hold himself in reserve like the *Salaminia*, for the great occasion:

at other times he worked through speakers who were his friends and close associates. They say that among them was Ephialtes who destroyed the power of the Areopagus, pouring, as Plato said, freedom out to the citizens in a heavy unmixed draft. The result, as a comic poet tells us, was that the demos became a wild horse 'and no longer dared to obey, but bit Euboea and leapt on the islands'.[4]

The writers of comedy are not normally conscientious in their chronology but this aggression against Euboea and the islands should not be too far removed from the reforms of Ephialtes.

[1] See p. 43 n. 4.
[2] Suggested by Meiggs, *JHS* lxiii (1943), 31, but not yet apparently taken seriously by anyone else.
[3] Plut. *Cim.* 18. 1.
[4] Plut. *Per.* 7. 8: πειθαρχεῖν οὐκέτι τολμᾶν, ἀλλὰ δάκνειν τὴν Εὔβοιαν καὶ ταῖς νήσοις ἐπιπηδᾶν.

THE AFTERMATH OF EGYPT

The conjunction of Euboea with the islands in this comic
fragment recalls the establishment of cleruchs in Euboea and
Naxos recorded by Diodorus, and the examination of these and
other cleruchies may further confirm the pattern that we propose. At some time near the middle of the century Athens developed a policy of settling Athenian citizens on land confiscated
from the allies. These cleruchs remained Athenians and were
liable to Athenian taxes and to service in the Athenian forces.
They were normally drawn from the two lowest property classes
and the grant of land would raise the *thetes* into the hoplite class.
Plutarch gives the fullest list of cleruchies that we possess and
he sets them within the framework of the political struggle
between Pericles and Thucydides son of Melesias after the death
of Cimon.[1] He or his source sees the policy as a vote-catching
bribe to the poor which also relieved the city of an idle and restless mob, and prevented revolts from the allies by intimidation.
For a closer dating we have to rely on the quota lists. Since the
confiscation of land weakened the resources of the state which
had to accept cleruchs, a natural consequence of a cleruchy was
the lowering of the state's assessment. Andros is among the
cleruchies listed by Plutarch. The island pays 12 talents in 450
and 6 in 449 and thereafter; the generally accepted explanation
of the decrease is that the cleruchy, 250 men according to
Plutarch, was established in the summer of 450.[2]

It is possible that on the same occasion cleruchs were also
settled in Naxos and Euboea. Naxos, to which Plutarch assigns
500 cleruchs, has no tribute preserved before 447 and in that
year and thereafter, though once the richest island in the
Cyclades, she paid only 6⅔ talents. We can infer that the cleruchy
was established before 447, and that on the same expedition
cleruchs were also settled on Euboea. Plutarch, who includes
the Naxian cleruchy in his list, makes no mention of this settlement in Euboea but both Diodorus and Pausanias include an
expedition settling cleruchs on Euboea and Naxos among the
achievements of Tolmides.[3] In both accounts the expedition
comes after the memorably aggressive cruise round the Peloponnese, probably in 456, and before the defeat and death of

---

[1] Plut. *Per.* 11. 5–6.   [2] Gomme, *HCT* i. 380; *ATL* iii. 298.
[3] Naxos *c.* 500 B.C. Hdt. v. 28: εὐδαιμονίῃ τῶν νήσων προέφερε. Cleruchy, Diod,
xi. 88. 3; Paus. i. 27. 5.

Tolmides at the battle of Coronea, in 446 or possibly 447. Diodorus gives a specific date, including the expedition in his record for 453–452; but there are strong grounds for rejecting this date. He opens the year's record with Pericles' expedition against Sicyon and to Acarnania, and this is followed by Pericles' settlement of 1,000 citizens in the Chersonese. 'At the same time Tolmides the other general crossed to Euboea with another 1,000 citizens and settled them [on land there] and on Naxos.' From Thucydides we can date Pericles' expedition against Sicyon in 454, or perhaps 455, and the quota lists make a date for the cleruchy in the Chersonese earlier than 448 virtually impossible. The reason for Diodorus' confusion we have seen elsewhere; his source was not annalistic but grouped Pericles' commands before 446 together, to be balanced by Tolmides' actions during the same period. No trust can be placed in the date 453–452 for the cleruchies in Euboea and Naxos; we are left only with the conclusion from the quota lists that Naxos, and with Naxos Euboea, was settled before 447.

The authors of *The Athenian Tribute Lists* suggest that these cleruchies were established in Euboea by Tolmides as part of the strategy that ended disastrously at the battle of Coronea, representing an attempt by Tolmides to seal off any help that might come to Boeotia from Euboea; their date would then be 446 or 447.[1] Neither date nor context is convincing. According to Plutarch Tolmides made the great mistake of underestimating the danger in Boeotia. Pericles tried publicly to restrain him 'with the well-known warning that if he did not listen to Pericles he would not go wrong if he awaited the wisest counsellor of all, time'.[2] The moral flavour and proverbial wisdom in this anecdote will not perhaps commend it to historians, but Tolmides' decisive defeat at Coronea does suggest that he misjudged the situation. Nor is the proposed date easily reconciled with the evidence of the quota lists. Already in 447 Naxos pays only $6\frac{2}{3}$ talents, and there is no subsequent decrease. If the cleruchy is established in 446 we should have to believe that no reduction was made in the island's assessment.[3] It is surely better to believe that the cleruchy was established before 447.

[1] *ATL*. iii. 294.   [2] Plut. *Per.* 18. 2.
[3] Both *ATL* (iii. 287) and Nesselhauf, op. cit. 128 f. accept a reduction of tribute in 450 *before* the cleruchy.

A better context for the Euboean and Naxian cleruchies is 450 when cleruchs were settled at Andros. There may be a hint in the quota lists of the state affected in Euboea, for Carystus' assessment was lowered from 7½ to 5 talents at the assessment of 450. This reduction might be explained on economic grounds, for several other states who, so far as we know, had no cleruchs also had their tribute reduced at this time, but Carystus is a likely centre of disaffection.[1] She had entered the League under compulsion and might be expected to take advantage of any Athenian weakness. Carystus is at the southern end of Euboea, cut off by high ground from the rest of Euboea, and more closely associated with the Cyclades than with Chalcis and Eretria. Like Naxos and Andros she was well known to Delos, for her 'treasury' is recorded in a Delian inscription and it was probably built, like the 'treasury' of Andros and the Stoa of the Naxians, in the archaic period.[2] The earlier date will also suit the Naxian evidence better. There is no question of Naxos, reduced to what Thucydides calls 'slavery' before the Eurymedon, contributing ships to the League in the fifties but Naxos is absent from all the quota fragments of the first period and was therefore very probably not paying tribute. If Athens was applying the cleruchy policy in Andros in 450 and neighbouring Naxos had been giving trouble she would surely have settled Naxos at the same time. It is an objection, but not a vital one, to this dating that Diodorus and Pausanias, probably drawing on a common source, do not include the settling of Andros in Tolmides' expedition to Euboea and Naxos; but Andros is a close neighbour to Carystus and, if Andros was settled from Carystus, it could have dropped out of the record.[3]

A coherent case can be made for widespread disaffection in the League following the disaster in Egypt, in Ionia and the Hellespont, in Caria, and in the islands. Athens, breaking off her offensive in Greece, concentrated on restoring her control over the League and succeeded in large measure. Carian dissenters who brought no tribute to the Dionysia in 453 were made

[1] *RE* Karystos, col. 2258.

[2] R. Vallois, *L'Architecture hellénique et hellénistique à Délos*, I (1944), 24–5.

[3] If we accept Plutarch's 500 for Naxos and 250 for Andros, the addition of 250 in Euboea (? Carystus) would give a total of 1,000 for Tolmides' expedition. This is the number of settlers sent to the Chersonese, and to Thrace (? Brea), Plut. *Per.* 11. 5, and perhaps to Hestiaea (Diod. xii. 22. 2).

to meet their obligations under pressure later in the summer. Miletus and perhaps Erythrae were recovered in 452, and in 450 trouble in the islands was met by establishing cleruchies to act as garrisons and maintain security. Such a reconstruction does not independently confirm Thucydides' version of the Egyptian campaign, but it makes his account more plausible than is commonly allowed. We have, however, attached considerable importance to the hypothesis of a large-scale cleruchy policy in 450 and two serious difficulties have to be met. Plutarch dates all the cleruchies after the death of Cimon, and Cimon's death is generally thought to come not earlier than the late summer of 450; a combination of Cimon's Cyprian campaign and widespread cleruchies might also be thought to overcrowd any single year, and the Cyprian campaign has seemed to most modern historians firmly rooted in 450.[1] The date of the resumption of fighting against Persia must therefore be re-examined.

Thucydides allows a three years' interval between the breaking off of Athens' offensive in Greece, in 454 or possibly 455, and the sailing of Cimon to Cyprus. Diodorus dates this campaign precisely. In his account the operations cover two archon years, 450–449 and 449–448; and these dates are not arbitrarily chosen to fill gaps or because he has used up the years down to 450, but because he accepts them from his source. But since other dates, presumably from the same source, are demonstrably wrong and no clear criterion can be established for determining which of his military and political dates are likely to be right we cannot regard his dating of the Cyprian campaign as final.[2] The reason why it has been commonly rejected is that better evidence suggests that measures were taken at Athens before the end of the archonship of Euthynos, 450–449, which presuppose the end of fighting against Persia.[3] If we reject Diodorus, we are not forced to accept 450 for the Cyprian campaign, though it is the only alternative date that has been strongly supported. We have two controls only that need attention. The first is Thucydides' statement that there was a three years' pause in the war in Greece before Cimon sailed; the second is the date of the five years' truce between Athens and Sparta negotiated by Cimon. If we are right in

[1] Gomme *HCT* i. 325; *ATL* iii. 178.
[2] For the Diodoran chronology see App. 2, pp. 456 f.   [3] Below, pp. 154 f.

believing that Cimon was specially recalled from ostracism shortly before his ten years had expired and that he began negotiations for peace as soon as he returned, we should date the truce with Sparta early in 451. This date we can roughly control from the events of 446. Sparta was sensitive about interstate agreements and it is most unlikely that a Spartan army would have invaded Attica before the truce had expired.[1] Pleistoanax led the Spartan army into Attica after the revolt of Euboea, in the summer of 446. The five years' truce was therefore made not later than the summer of 451. This is consistent with the evidence of Thucydides. If the last Athenian operation in Greece ended by June of 454 and the truce was made in April 451 διαλιπόντων ἐτῶν τριῶν would rightly express the interval. The Athenians, we think, had been building up their resources for an eastern campaign since 454; there is no reason why Cimon should not have sailed from the Piraeus in the summer following the truce with Sparta. It is suggested that Cimon died in Cyprus in 451.

The advantages of dating Cimon's death in 451 are considerable. The cleruchy policy no longer begins before the end of fighting with Persia, but after Cimon's death, as Plutarch's account requires; and the sequence of events between Cimon's death and the decision to use the tribute reserve on Athenian buildings no longer has to be too rigorously compressed. The time-table proposed in *The Athenian Tribute Lists* requires that after the return of the fleet from Cyprus Athenian envoys go up to Susa, negotiate the terms of a settlement, and return to Athens for the final ratification. Heralds are then sent out to invite the Greek states to a congress in Athens to discuss, with other topics, the rebuilding of the temples destroyed by the Persians. Sparta refuses to attend and the congress is abandoned. The Athenians then approve a decree proposed by Pericles that the tribute reserve shall be used on Athenian buildings and this decree is dated to the archonship of Euthynos which ends in midsummer 449.[2] Those who do not accept a Peace of Callias at this time need not be troubled by the dating of the Cyprian campaign in 450, but those who firmly believe in the peace must wonder whether so much can be crowded into less than

[1] For Spartan scruples in such matters see Thuc. vi. 105; vii. 18. 2.
[2] *ATL* iii. 277–81; table of dates, 178.

a full year. The strain is relieved if the campaign in Cyprus can be placed in 451.

The history of Cimon's last campaign cannot be recovered in detail and even its main outline is uncertain. Thucydides implies that sixty of his 200 ships were at the outset dispatched to Egypt in response to an appeal from Amyrtaeus who still held out in the marshes of the northern Delta; the remainder of his force besieged Citium. Cimon, however, died, food supplies ran out, and the siege was raised. The Athenians then sailed above Salamis and fought a double engagement by land and sea against Phoenicians, Cyprians, and Cilicians. They defeated their enemy on both elements and sailed home, taking with them the squadron that had been sent to look for opportunities in Egypt.[1] Thucydides' lean account can barely be recognized in Plutarch's much embroidered story. Even if we discard the omens and portents which dominate the narrative, the military record cannot be easily reconciled with Thucydides. The sending of the sixty ships to Egypt is followed by the defeat of the Persian fleet of Phoenician and Cilician ships. As a result 'Cimon won back the cities round about and watched events in Egypt; he had no mean ambition, aiming at the total destruction of the king's power'. The climax is hedged about with portents. Seers were sent by Cimon from Cyprus to Ammon to consult the god; they were dismissed 'for Cimon himself was already with him'. When the seers came to the Greek camp in Egypt they learnt that Cimon had died and understood the god's cryptic reply. Plutarch's account of the final stages of the campaign is distilled from many sources. Cimon's death at Citium Plutarch assumes to be non-controversial, but his sources did not agree whether death was due to sickness or a wound. As he was dying he advised those who were with him to conceal his death and sail away at once, 'and so it came about that they came safely home without the enemy or their allies knowing'; as Phanodemus says, 'they were led by Cimon though he was thirty days dead'.[2]

Diodorus' account is very different. Egypt is not mentioned, but the operations in and around Cyprus assume larger proportions. In the first year (450–449) Cimon secures control of the sea and reduces Citium and Marium. When ships come from

---

[1] Thuc. i. 112. 1–4.   [2] Plut. *Cim.* 18–19. 2= Phanodemus *FGH* 325 F 23.

Cilicia and Phoenicia Cimon sails out to meet them, sinks a large number, and captures 100 with their crews. The remnant he pursues to Phoenicia, where they take refuge with the Persian land forces. The Athenians disembark and force a battle. One of their generals, Anaxicrates, is killed fighting heroically but they defeat the enemy and sail back to Cyprus. In the next year (449–448) Cimon proceeds to reduce the rest of Cyprus and finally attacks Salamis which has a strong Persian garrison and a large supply of war equipment. Artaxerxes hearing of the Greek successes in Cyprus opens negotiations which lead to peace. The death of Cimon is added as a disconnected tailpiece: 'And it so happened that Cimon fell ill and died in Cyprus.'[1]

A more important piece of evidence must finally be added. As we have seen earlier, Diodorus' account of the Eurymedon campaign reflects the confusion that resulted from Ephorus' mistaken attribution to the Eurymedon of an epigram which commemorates the Cyprian campaign. Here is a contemporary document which any reconstruction must respect:

> Ever since the sea parted Europe from Asia and grim Ares stalks the cities of mortals, no deed such as this was ever done by men on this earth on land and sea together. For these men destroyed many Medes in Cyprus and a hundred ships they captured at sea with their crews, and Asia groaned mightily, stricken by them with both arms in the violent force of war.[2]

However broadminded we wish to be, there are irreconcilable contradictions within our evidence. In Plutarch and Diodorus the main sea battle comes early in the campaign; Thucydides mentions only one, at the end. The epigram records a sea battle in which 100 ships were captured, and which was accompanied by fighting on land. Diodorus' sea battle involves the capture of the hundred ships, but neither in his nor in Plutarch's account is the accompanying land fighting mentioned; Thucydides alone has a double engagement. We should accept his placing of the battle. Perhaps Phanodemus' neat comment that Cimon led the Greek fleet though he had been thirty days dead makes more point if he was referring to a battle than to an uneventful withdrawal. In Diodorus Citium is captured at the opening of the campaign; the majority of other sources, reflected

---

[1] Diod. xii. 3–4.   [2] Diod. xi. 62. 3.

in Plutarch, clearly agreed that Citium was still being besieged when Cimon died. But there are two episodes in Diodorus that seem to belong to history. Marium is not one of the most important towns in Cyprus and it is rarely mentioned in our literary sources; but graves of the late archaic period at Marium have yielded more imported pottery from Greece than any other site in the island and there were important copper mines in the area; its recovery would therefore have been a natural objective for a Greek force.[1] But if its capture is rightly linked by Diodorus with that of Citium perhaps it cannot belong to Cimon's campaign. Similarly the raid on Phoenicia does not look like invention, and it may be linked with the inclusion of Phoenicia in the battle grounds that head the casualty list of the Erechtheid tribe after Cyprus and Egypt. Perhaps these two episodes should be placed in the first year of the Egyptian campaign, the capture of Marium before the fleet was diverted from Cyprus, the raid on Phoenicia after the first engagements in Egypt.[2]

Cimon's posthumous fame has obscured the Athenian operations when they left Citium. We need not believe that Cimon on his death-bed advised the Athenians to return home at once; this is the kind of thing that the reading public expected great men to do, and that Epaminondas may actually have done. The question why the Athenians withdrew involves a wider and more difficult question. Diodorus says that the Persians opened negotiations for peace, but of this Thucydides says nothing. We have to consider whether Thucydides' silence is a decisive argument against a formal peace with Persia after the campaign in Cyprus.

---

[1] For the importance of Marium, App. 7, p. 480.

[2] For a different explanation of the confusion in Diodorus, J. Barnes, *Hist.* ii (1953–4), 163–76. I cannot follow him in introducing an expedition led by Cimon to Cyprus in 462.

8

THE PEACE OF CALLIAS

AFTER Cimon's campaign in Cyprus no further League operations against Persia are recorded. No Persian ships are known to have sailed west of Pamphylia and no Greek triremes sailed east. Fourth-century Athenian orators knew the reason; it was the famous peace, whose main terms were familiar to them and were repeated with minor variations to their audience when an emotional appeal to past glories suited their argument. The first clear surviving reference comes in Isocrates' *Panegyricus* of 380, when he contemptuously compares the humiliating Peace of Antalcidas dictated by Persia with the terms imposed on Persia by Athens when she was at the height of her power.[1] The next clear references come from Demosthenes in 351 and 343, and he is followed by Lycurgus in 328.[2] At some point in this complacent chorus Theopompus introduced a sour note. The peace, he insisted, was one of many fabrications invented for the greater glory of Athens.[3] Only one of his arguments survives: it must be a forgery because the letters on the stele were Ionic, and Ionic letters were not adopted by Athens until the archonship of Euclides in 403/2.[4]

The orators were not the only purveyors of the 'myth' against which Theopompus was protesting. He had probably already read the detailed account of the peace in Ephorus which survives in Diodorus.[5] Another historian may have reached the same conclusion as Theopompus, whether independently or following his lead. According to Plutarch Callisthenes denied that there was a formal peace after the victory of the Eurymedon, though the practical effect of the victory was to keep

---

[1] Isocr. iv. 120. The most important texts for the Peace of Callias are assembled in App. 8, p. 487.

[2] Dem. xv. 29; xix. 273–4; Lycurgus, *Leocr.* 73.

[3] Theopompus, *FGH* 115, F 153, 154.

[4] Harpocration, s.v. Ἀττικοῖς γράμμασιν, = F 154.

[5] Diod. xiii. 4–5.

the Persians east of the Chelidonian isles.[1] Without the full context we cannot be sure what points Callisthenes was making. Though he was probably denying the existence of any peace at any time in the fifth century his actual argument applies only to the sixties and he could possibly be refuting the confused versions of the later orators who associated the peace with this climax of Athenian success. With this confusion we need not be seriously concerned. If there was a peace the only convincing context is after the death of Cimon, where Diodorus records it.

It is typical of Plutarch that he remains puzzled by the dilemma, without making any attempt to resolve it. He seems to assume that the only issue in doubt is whether peace was made immediately after the Eurymedon. He reports Callisthenes' denial, but adds that Craterus included a copy of the peace terms in his collection of decrees.[2] He does not seem to know the comment that Craterus added to his text and he has not troubled to consult other sources. Had his interests been primarily historical he could at least have given us an outline of the controversy. Craterus' acceptance of the peace as genuine did not apparently end all doubt. Pausanias, coming to the statue of Callias in the Athenian Agora, describes him as 'Callias who, according to most Athenians, made peace with Artaxerxes son of Xerxes'.[3] There was still apparently in the second century A.D. a minority of sceptics. But the strongest voice, perhaps the only strong voice against the peace, was that of Theopompus, and it is very difficult to know how much weight should be attached to his judgement. He has sometimes been described as a careful scholar, but there is little in his fragments to support the claim. He was certainly widely read and had a strong influence on later writers, but a critical historical judgement was rare in the Hellenistic and Roman worlds, and malice and abuse were widely enjoyed. Theopompus was certainly not without bias and he seems to have had no love for Athens. His sympathies were with oligarchs and he went out of his way to denounce the leaders of Athenian democracy.[4] If the use of

---

[1] Plut. *Cim.* 13. 4.

[2] Plut. *Cim.* 13. 5: ἐν δὲ τοῖς ψηφίσμασιν ἃ συνήγαγε Κρατερὸς ἀντίγραφα συνθηκῶν ὡς γενομένων κατατέτακται.   [3] Paus. i. 8. 2.

[4] In his history of Greece during the reign of Philip of Macedon in twenty-five books he devoted a whole book (X) to an attack on the fifth- and fourth-century leaders of Athenian democracy, *FGH* 115, F 85–100.

Ionic letters in the public record of the peace was Theopompus' only argument we need not be disturbed, but it is well to remember that this argument is preserved only as a grammarian's note on Ionic letters; we do not know the full strength of Theopompus' case. The only firm inference that can be drawn from the one argument that survives is that at some time not long after the middle of the fourth century the terms of a peace with Persia were publicly displayed on a stele in Athens inscribed in Ionic letters. It is also a reasonable inference, and the point may be important, that this stele had not been set up recently. Theopompus' attack seems to be directed against the view that this was the contemporary fifth-century record. If it were generally known that the stele had been set up in or near the middle of the fourth century Theopompus' criticism would have had no sting.

Theopompus' acid attack would probably not by itself have weighed heavily against the concordance of Ephorus, the orators, and Craterus. What has influenced sceptics much more strongly is the silence of Thucydides and of all other fifth-century sources. If the Cyprian campaign was followed by a peace Thucydides should have recorded it, for, however much he compressed his review of the fifty years, a peace with Persia was too important to omit. His main theme was the development of Athenian power; a peace with Persia would have provided a much more stable background for the concentration of Athenian resources on the control of the Aegean than a mere cessation of hostilities. Hardly less surprising would be Thucydides' failure to mention the peace, if peace there was, in the speech of the Mytilenaeans at Olympia in 428. The Mytilenaeans were attempting to justify to Sparta's allies their revolt from Athens. They speak of Athens relaxing her hostilities against Persia and being more concerned with the suppression of the allies; they do not claim that Athens had made peace, though this would have been a stronger argument in their favour than any they use.[1] We might also have expected a reference when Pissuthnes, satrap at Sardis, intervened at the time of the revolt of Samos in 440, or when Thucydides reviewed in considerable detail the resources of both sides at the outbreak of the Peloponnesian

[1] Thuc. iii. 10. 4: ἐπειδὴ δὲ ἑωρῶμεν αὐτοὺς τὴν μὲν τοῦ Μήδου ἔχθραν ἀνιέντας, τὴν δὲ τῶν ξυμμάχων δούλωσιν ἐπαγομένους, οὐκ ἀδεεῖς ἔτι ἦμεν.

War. It is only in his last book that any evidence for an Athenian peace with Persia has been found; this evidence convinced Gomme, but it cannot be regarded as decisive against this silence in places where the context would seem to demand a reference.[1]

The silence of Herodotus would be less puzzling, for he deliberately ended his story of the Persian wars with the siege of Sestus; but digressions form a large part of his history and there are several contexts, as for instance in his description of Egypt, where he might have been expected to comment on the effects of a peace between Greeks and Persians. A reference has indeed often been seen in a passage which has already been discussed. Callias was with an Athenian embassy at Susa 'on other business' when some Argives went up to renew with the new King Artaxerxes the friendly relations that had been established with his father Xerxes. But there is no good reason why Herodotus should have referred so obliquely to a peace which, if made, was publicly accepted at Athens and well known throughout the Aegean world, and the natural context for the Argive embassy is soon after the new king was known to be firmly established.[2]

A further strong argument against a peace can be derived from a passage in Plutarch's *Pericles*, in which he is describing the opposition in the Assembly to Pericles' building policy by the followers of Thucydides son of Melesias.

But what brought greatest pleasure and glory to Athens, and most amazed the rest of the world; what alone bears witness to Greece that the tradition of Athens' power and wealth of old is no fable, her public monuments—this more than any other of Pericles' policies his enemies traduced and attacked in the Assembly. They shouted out that the Athenian people had lost its reputation and was disgraced for having brought the common treasury of Greece from Delos to herself; and the fairest excuse that could be made against this criticism, that it was in fear of the barbarians that they brought away the common funds and were guarding them in safety, Pericles had now made impossible. And Greece appears to be the victim of monstrous violence and manifest tyranny when she sees that with the money contributed under compulsion for the war we are gilding our city and decking her like a wanton woman, adorning her with extravagant stones, statues, and thousand-talent temples. So Pericles

---

[1] Thuc. viii. 56. 4. See pp. 142, 491.   [2] See pp. 92 f.

explained to the people that they owed no account to the allies for
the money, while they fought for them and protected them from the
barbarians. They contributed neither horse nor ship nor hoplite but
money only, and the money is the business not of those who give it
but of those to whom it is given, so long as they supply the services
for which the money is given.[1]

This vivid passage has generally been considered to be an
authentic echo of a real scene, and the date can be fixed within
narrow limits. The first year of the Parthenon accounts was
447–446 and the main annual grants to the commissioners both
of the temple and the chryselephantine cult statue were from
the outset paid by Athena's treasurers;[2] this implies that the
Delian League reserve had been amalgamated with Athena's
treasury before the Parthenon was begun. The critical debate
on the use of the allies' money should therefore have taken place
between Cimon's death in 451 and 447. In Plutarch's version
there is no hint of a peace with Persia; the natural inference
from the speeches of both sides is that the allies still think that
they are paying tribute for operations against Persia and that
a state of war still exists. If peace had been made, it should have
been at the centre of the argument on both sides and some clear
hint should have survived even in a short summary. The
strength of this argument was appreciated by Busolt, who
believed in a peace but concluded because of this passage in
Plutarch that it must have come later than the beginning of the
Parthenon.[3] This is an uneasy compromise because the most
natural context for the peace is where Diodorus sets it, immediately after the death of Cimon and the return of the Athenian
fleet from Cyprus. Moreover there is further evidence to be
considered later which suggests that the decree providing for
the use on Athenian buildings of the League reserve was proposed by Pericles in the archonship of Euthynus, 450–449.[4] It
remains for those who believe in the peace to explain Plutarch's
version.

The silence of the surviving sources of the fifth century combined with Theopompus' criticism makes a strong case against

[1] Plut. *Per.* 12.
[2] *IG* i². 339–53 (with *SEG* x. 246–56) and *IG* i². 354–62 (with *SEG* x. 257–63).
[3] D. Stockton, *Hist.* viii (1959), 69 f. strongly emphasizes this point in his attack
on the Peace of Callias. For Busolt's compromise, *Gr. Gesch.* iii. 349 with n. 1.
[4] See p. 155.

the Peace of Callias, but the reasons for accepting it, though not yet decisive, are stronger. If we could agree with Schwartz that this was a literary rather than a historical problem we could relegate the discussion to an appendix in small type; but one's view of the forties depends to a considerable extent on one's attitude to the peace. If no peace was made there can have been no public decision to abandon operations against Persia, and the allies cannot have known in the early forties that there would be no more League expeditions. If, on the other hand, peace was made it must surely have been publicly made, accepted by the Athenian Assembly, and known throughout the Greek world. It will have at once raised acute problems for Athens and for the allies. The pattern of events in the forties strongly supports the case for a peace but such argument, if unsupported, could reasonably be resented as circular. The firmer starting-point is the peace made by Athens with Darius, Artaxerxes' successor, in 423. The compelling evidence for this peace has been assembled by Wade-Gery; a brief summary will suffice.[1]

Andocides in his speech on the blessings of peace in 391 blames the Athenians for choosing the wrong friends, the weak instead of the strong:

> We made a treaty with the great king and pledged friendship for all time through the embassy on which served Epilycus son of Tisander, our mother's brother. Later we listened to Amorges, the king's slave and a fugitive; we discarded the king's power as if it were valueless and chose instead the friendship of Amorges, thinking it superior. This roused the king's anger, he became an ally of the Spartans, gave them five thousand talents for the war, until he destroyed our power.[2]

Andocides makes the wildest mistakes in this speech and he is always apt to trim facts to suit his needs, but even Andocides is not likely to invent from nothing an embassy to Persia, and his story is supported by an inscription. This inscription is a fourth-century copy of a fifth-century decree. It honours a certain Heraclides for his services to Athens and makes him a *proxenos*; an amendment is added mentioning the Persian king and a

---

[1] Wade-Gery, *Essays*, 207–11 (*Harv. Stud. Suppl.* i (1940), 127–32).
[2] Andoc. iii. 29.

treaty; it can be restored to mean that Heraclides has been praised by ambassadors returning from the king for his co-operation in negotiating a treaty with the king. A [N]eokleides was president at the Assembly which passed this decree and a Thucydides proposed the amendment. A Neokleides was secretary of the Boule for the tribe Aegeis in 424–423, and in the same year a Thucydides was one of the treasurers of Athena, and an Epilycus was first secretary of the Boule. We know from literary sources of a Heraclides who was given citizenship, in-creased pay for the Assembly, and served as general; he came from Clazomenae. If to Heraclides is added 'the Clazomenian' on the missing part of the stone the number of letters precisely fills the space available. Few things are more certain in fifth-century history than that the decree honours Heraclides of Clazomenae for helping an Athenian embassy on which Andocides' uncle Epilycus, a member of the Boule, served to negotiate a treaty with King Darius in 424–423.[1]

It is difficult to see why, if there had been no previous agree-ment, Darius should wish to make a treaty with Athens in the middle of the Peloponnesian War. There is considerably less difficulty if the treaty was a renewal. In the autumn of 425 an Athenian squadron sent out to collect money had captured a Persian envoy on his way to Sparta. The purport of his dispatch was that the Persian king needed a clear-cut statement of Sparta's proposals, since it was impossible through their changes of mind to know what they intended. The Persian was brought to Athens and sent back with an Athenian embassy, but at Ephesus they heard the news of Artaxerxes' death and returned.[2] When the Persian situation seemed settled, with Darius firmly on the throne, it was logical to send another embassy to forestall further Spartan approaches and restore stable relations with Persia. The treaty of 424–423 is a strong argument in favour of an earlier treaty, and, as Wade-Gery has pointed out, there may be a further link. Another decree of 424–423 is concerned with the payment of her annual dues to the priestess of Athena Nike. It is inscribed on the back of a stele which records the decision to appoint a priestess and build a temple of Athena Nike, and is also concerned with the payment

[1] *IG* ii². 8; ML 70. For the identifications, see Wade-Gery, op. cit. 208–10.
[2] Thuc. iv. 50.

to be made to the priestess.[1] The two decrees are closely associated and the second was proposed by a Callias. The proposer
of the first is not known, for the early part of the decree is
missing—but the three-bar sigma implies a date before 445,
and the frieze along the south wall of the temple of Nike
depicted scenes of fighting between Greeks and Persians. It
is tempting to believe that the decision to build the temple
followed the making of peace and was intended to represent it
as a victorious settlement.[2]

A further ground for accepting the peace is the evidence of
Theopompus that it was publicly recorded for all to see. If it
was a forgery it was a publicly accepted forgery set up officially.
As has been suggested above there would be no sting in Theopompus' criticism if the stele had been put up recently, for the
date of the copy would be adequate explanation of the Ionic
letters. This would seem to rule out the seductive suggestion
made by Habicht that the terms of the Peace of Callias were
among mid-fourth-century patriotic inventions used by Demosthenes and Aeschines to rally the Greek world against Philip.[3]
The stele referred to by Theopompus must have been considerably earlier than Philip's accession, and was probably known
to Isocrates in 380 when he wrote the *Panegyricus*. For his reference to the fifth-century peace is not merely general and vague:
'It will be seen that in that earlier peace we set limits to the
king's empire, and stipulated the assessments of some of his
tributes and prevented him from using the sea.' The first and
third of these clauses could be drawn from a vague literary or
oral tradition and would be obvious clauses to invent, but the
second clause is specific and unexpected. It presupposes a
specific peace with specific clauses, and these could be read.[4]

A more widely accepted view is that the Peace of Callias
was invented after and because of the King's Peace of 386 and
was designed to emphasize the humiliating contrast between
Athens' past pride and her present subservience, which Isocrates
himself stresses.[4] The fatal objection to this view is that the

---

[1] Wade-Gery, op. cit. 209. *IG* i². 24–5, ML 44 and 71.

[2] For the date of the decree, Meiggs, *JHS* lxxxvi (1966), 94–6. For the temple,
App. 9, p. 496 .

[3] Chr. Habicht, *Hermes* lxxxix (1961), 32.

[4] Isocr. iv. 120: εἰ παραναγνοίη τὰς συνθήκας τάς τ' ἐφ' ἡμῶν γενομένας καὶ τὰς
νῦν ἀναγεγραμμένας.

determining factor is the public policy of the Athenian state and not the personal views of Isocrates. In the eighties the Athenians, publicly at least, were supporting the King's Peace. When the Athenians made an alliance with Chios in 384 the decree, which sanctions the alliance and praises the Chian envoys who have come to Athens, recognizes the assurance of the Chians 'that they will uphold, like the Athenians, the peace and friendship and oaths and terms of agreement which the king swore and the Athenians and the Spartans and the rest of the Greeks', and the Chian envoys have brought with them from Chios 'assurances of goodwill to the people of Athens and all Greece and the king'.[1] Such language is quite inconsistent with the public sponsoring of a forged peace imposing very restrictive terms on Persia.

There may also be a reference to the peace earlier than 386. In his attack on the Peace of Callias Stockton urged as a strong argument the silence of Lysias in his *Epitaphius* delivered in 390.[2] Here was the dog in the night which did not bark. There may be a growl. 'They did not make the allies weak but they built up their strength. The power they displayed was such that the great king no longer coveted what belonged to others, but gave up some of what belonged to himself and lived in fear for the rest. No triremes sailed in those days from Asia; no tyrant arose among the Greeks; no Greek city was enslaved by the barbarians.' Most of this proud boasting is too general to be significant, but the statement that the king gave up some of what belonged to him—ἐδίδου τῶν ἑαυτοῦ—should imply a deliberate act on his part, a voluntary rather than compulsory surrender.

Against this background we may reconsider the arguments against the peace summarized at the outset of this discussion. The use of Ionic letters could be explained in various ways. Though Attic letters were normally used in public records that have survived from the middle of the fifth century a decree concerning Phaselis and another concerning Eretria used Ionic letters. The first of these, however, was set up at the expense of the Phaselites and the choice of lettering may have rested with them; the Eretrian inscription may have a similar explanation. It is, however, possible that Athens might as a gesture to the allies have used the alphabet with which they were more familiar,

<hr/>

[1] Tod, *GHI* ii. 118.   [2] Stockton, art. cit. 70; Lysias ii. 56–7.

in the same spirit perhaps as the surviving accounts of the Delian temples for 434–432, publicly displayed on the Acropolis at Athens, were in Ionic letters.[1] Another possibility is that the stele which could be seen in the fourth century recorded the treaty of 424–423 with Darius and not the original treaty with Artaxerxes; by this date Ionic letters, though not yet common, were being occasionally used in Athenian public inscriptions and the decree concerning the priestess of Athena Nike of this same year happens to begin in Attic and continue in Ionic.[2] A variant of this view has been suggested in *The Athenian Tribute Lists* that when the treaty was renewed in 424–423 the original text was retained but the prescript was erased. Darius was substituted for Artaxerxes, in Ionic letters, but the name of the proposer, Callias, and the terms of the treaty remained, in Attic.[3] This is perhaps possible, but not convincing: possible, because a parallel can be found for the erasure of the prescript to a treaty in the renewal in 433–432 of alliances made probably in the forties with Leontini and Rhegium. On these two stones it is clear that the prescript has been erased, and a new prescript added to an older text; it is a nice coincidence that the name of the proposer, retained from the original alliances, is a Callias, who might be the proposer of the treaty with Persia.[4] The more serious objection to this ingenious solution is that it makes Theopompus' criticism altogether too vulnerable. He may have been foolish, but not as foolish as that; we must believe that the stele was inscribed in Ionic letters throughout.

A third possibility is that the original, in Attic letters, was destroyed in the fifth century and set up again early in the fourth. We know of other decrees which were destroyed by the Thirty and replaced after the restoration of democracy in 403.[5] A better context for the destruction of a stele recording the Peace of Callias would be when Athens, shortly before 412, decided to support the revolt of Amorges; it might have been set up again when Athens began to dream again of empire towards the end of the nineties in the fourth century. All these three explanations will satisfy the known facts; the third is perhaps the most, the second the least likely.

---

[1] *IG* i². 377; ML 62.   [2] *IG* i². 25; ML 71.   [3] *ATL* iii. 276.
[4] *IG* i². 51, 52; *ATL* iii. 276–7, but see ML 63, 64.
[5] *IG* ii². 6, 8, 9.

The problem raised by Plutarch's account of the building debate is also not insuperable. We could believe that the account has passed through other hands before it is used by Plutarch and that some of the original arguments have been obscured or forgotten. The passage may also have suffered some rhetorical inflation in transmission. The statement, for instance, in Pericles' defence of his policy, that the allies contribute not a single horse, nor ship, nor hoplite, is not accurate. Allies, as we have seen, fought on sea at the battle of Aegina and on land at the battle of Tanagra; later, the regulations imposed in 450–449 on Miletus almost certainly provided for hoplite service.[1] It looks like a typical rhetorical elaboration of a simple argument. The long and detailed analysis of the social and economic advantages of a public-works policy, with its carefully balanced clauses, reads more like the fourth than the fifth century. The whole section may indeed have approached its present form in the late fourth century when Athens had again embarked on a public-building policy.[2] Cicero, for instance, tells us that Demetrius of Phalerum attacked the extravagance of the Propylaea.[3]

This does not deny that the debate in Plutarch may have an authentic nucleus, though it is difficult to identify the original source. So far as we know the passage is too colourful and detailed for Hellanicus and Thucydides asserts that, when he wrote, Hellanicus was the only writer who had written a history of the period between the Persian and Peloponnesian wars. Of the contemporary names known to us the least unlikely perhaps are Ion of Chios and Stesimbrotus of Thasos. Stesimbrotus certainly wrote of Thucydides son of Melesias, for the name was included in his title, but from the fragments that survive we should not expect him to allow such an effective reply to Pericles. Ion of Chios has perhaps a better claim. We know that he recorded the appeal made by Cimon in the Athenian Assembly when Sparta begged for Athenian help to reduce her helots on Ithome.[4] The language ascribed to Thucydides in the building debate would have appealed to him for he liked vivid words and colourful images. He too seems to have been no friend of Pericles, but he is more likely than Stesimbrotus to have been

---

[1] D 11, ll. 10 ff.
[2] See also F. J. Frost, *Hist.* xiii (1964), 389–94.
[3] Cic. *De Off.* ii. 60.
[4] Plut. *Cim.* 16. 10.

an honest reporter and such disparagement of Pericles as survives in his fragments concerns his personal qualities rather than
his political views. A brief account by Ion could have lost and
gained a good deal in its descent to Plutarch.

There is also, however, a possibility that the debate is fiction,
the product of a rhetorical exercise, showing the same ingenuity
as the best of the spurious *Letters of Themistocles*. When Cicero
wrote the *De Oratore* he believed that original speeches of
Pericles could still be read. 'The oldest orators whose writings
survive, Pericles and Alcibiades and in the same period Thucydides . . . they were followed by Critias, Theramenes, Lysias.'[1]
He refers to them again in the *Brutus* in similar terms: 'But
before Pericles, to whom some writings are attributed, and
Thucydides, who lived not when Athens was growing up, but
when she was already mature, there is no writing which has any
embellishment and which seems to be the work of an orator.'[2]
A century later Quintilian dismissed the supposed speeches of
Pericles: 'While Cicero says some of Pericles' alleged writing
had certain rhetorical embellishments I find in those I have
seen nothing worthy of his fame, and so believe they were
composed by others.'[3] The criticism sounds dangerously like
judgements which assume that all Rembrandts must be good
Rembrandts, but by Plutarch's day the issue was dead. Orthodox
opinion maintained that all that survived of Pericles was his
decrees and a few memorable phrases.[4] But once there had been
in the libraries speeches of Pericles and before they were generally condemned these speeches could have infected the tradition. Whether his ultimate source be genuine or spurious,
Plutarch's account of the building debate is not decisive evidence against a Peace of Callias.

Thucydides' silence is more embarrassing. No convincing
explanation has been given even by the strongest advocates of
the peace and the best that can be offered here is a palliative.
It has been held by some that Thucydides' omission of the treaty
with Darius is easily explained if this was a mere renewal of an
earlier treaty, and in fact the omission has been used more than
once as an argument in favour of the Peace of Callias. But this

---

[1] Cic. *De Oratore* ii. 93.   [2] Cic. *Brutus* 27.
[3] Quintilian iii. 1. 12 with xii. 2. 22, xii. 10. 49.
[4] Plut. *Per.* 8. 7, quoted p. 111 n. 4.

surely is special pleading. If Thucydides records an Athenian embassy that set out for Susa in 425–424 and returned when it reached Ephesus because it heard that the Persian king had died, there is no good reason why he should not have recorded the embassy on which Epilycus served in 424–423 that took over and completed the mission of the previous year.[1] It is true that he had probably been sent into exile before the embassy returned but he knew that relations with Persia were delicate and the news of the renewal of the treaty should not have escaped him. And even if it is tenable that the renewal of a treaty was not sufficiently important to demand a place in his narrative, his silence in the account of the fifty years before the war still needs to be explained.

A further anomaly in Thucydides' treatment of Athenian relations with Persia intensifies the general problem. Andocides mentions the Athenian decision to abandon their treaty with the Persian king and support the revolt of Amorges. Thucydides introduces Amorges for the first time in his narrative of 412, as 'Amorges, the bastard, who had revolted from the king'.[2] The Athenian decision to support this rebel is not mentioned in its proper context, probably some three years earlier, and it is never explained, but it is a very surprising step and had a significant bearing on the course of the war. There are then three silences and not only one in Thucydides to explain, and since two known events of some importance are unrecorded, the omission of the third is a rather less strong argument against its existence than it seemed at first. And since Thucydides introduces Amorges without having mentioned the decisive point in his relations with Athens, we may think it not impossible that Thucydides should have shown a knowledge of a treaty without having mentioned it at the two points where it was most relevant to his history.[3]

Such knowledge has been thought to be implied in Thucydides' account of the negotiations of 411. Alcibiades, hoping to secure his recall to Athens, held out the hope that he could secure Persian help. Athenian envoys were sent to negotiate with him

---

[1] Thuc. iv. 50.   [2] Thuc. viii. 5. 5.

[3] Andrewes in *Hist.* x (1961), 1–18, suggests that a primary reason for the comparative silence of Thucydides on Athenian–Persian relations is that he did not realize the importance of Persia until late in the war. He intended to make good the omissions in revision, but had only begun to fill the gaps.

but he soon realized that he had considerably less influence with the Persian satrap, Tissaphernes, than he had alleged. To avoid exposure he put forward in the name of the satrap terms which he assumed would be unacceptable in order to throw the responsibility for the breakdown on the Athenians. To his surprise the Athenians seem to have been prepared to sacrifice the whole of Ionia and the offshore islands; what they were not prepared even to consider was the demand that the King should be allowed to build ships and sail along his own coast wherever he wished and with as many ships as he wished.[1] No such clause is included in any of the quick succession of treaties made in 411 between the Spartans and Tissaphernes and it is considerably easier to understand if Persia had, under a previous treaty with Athens, accepted limits for her warships.[2]

The arguments against the Peace of Callias are not strong enough to destroy confidence. That confidence rests partly on the firm evidence for the treaty with Darius but no less on the pattern of events in the early forties which are most easily explained by the assumption that the tradition preserved by Diodorus is basically right. In succeeding chapters it will be assumed that peace was made by Athens with King Artaxerxes shortly after Cimon's death and that it was known by the allies that peace had been made.

The fighting against Persia could be ended because the climate of opinion in Athens and in the Aegean had changed sufficiently since 478 to make the new policy acceptable. In 479 when Mardonius sent peace proposals to Athens a councillor who proposed that they should be put before the people was lynched.[3] The victories of Salamis and Plataea exalted the national spirit but did nothing to lessen the hatred. When the Athenians returned to their homes after Plataea the city had been twice occupied and sacked. A few buildings which had

---

[1] Thuc. viii. 56. 4.

[2] Andrewes (op. cit. 15–16) draws attention to a clause in the third Spartan treaty with Persia, Thuc. viii. 58. 2: χώραν τὴν βασιλέως, ὅση τῆς Ἀσίας ἐστί, βασιλέως εἶναι· καὶ περὶ τῆς χώρας τῆς ἑαυτοῦ βουλευέτω βασιλεὺς ὅπως βούλεται. It is odd that it should be explicitly stated that the king may do what he wishes in his own territory. Andrewes suggests that the clause might relate to a clause in a Peace of Callias imposing restrictions on the King; but since this clause is not included in the first two Spartan–Persian treaties it may be a precaution against Sparta.

[3] Hdt. ix. 4–5.

served to house Persian officers had been spared, but all their temples had been burnt to the ground and very little else remained standing. Against this background it was difficult to think dispassionately of Persians. They were the national enemy, the barbarians, a subservient race ruled by an arrogant and cruel court. Something of this feeling remains in Aeschylus' *Persae*, produced in the spring of 472, but there emerges also in the tragedy something of the finer side of the Persian character.

Meanwhile through the years of intermittent fighting there were forces at work which brought the two peoples closer together. The Persians had developed a taste for Greek craftsmanship soon after the incorporation of the east Greeks in their empire. The great building inscription of Darius' palace records Greeks engaged in the transport of timber and in skilled labour on the building, and the sculpture at Persepolis shows clear traces of Greek influence.[1] Within Asia Minor there were several islands of Greek influence, where refugees or exiles held fiefs from the Persian king. Demaratus the Spartan king and a son of the Athenian Miltiades had been rewarded with estates and the sons of Gongylus the Eretrian, who had served Pausanias, were still living in Xenophon's day on land given to their father by Xerxes; Themistocles was allowed to live in state in Magnesia.[2] From such centres Persians in the western satrapies could become more familiar with the pattern of Greek living and thinking. Further east there were Eretrians and Milesians, forcibly removed from their homes, but stubbornly remaining Greek.[3] The partial Hellenization of Persians is reflected in the tradition that Datis, who with Artaphernes led the Persian forces at Marathon, claimed that the Medes and Athenians were brothers because the Athenians had founded the Median race.[4] This partiality for Greek myth is further illustrated in the opening chapters of Herodotus' history. Herodotus' starting-point for his account of the struggle between Greece and Persia is Croesus, for he was the first ruler in Asia to incorporate part of the Greek world in his empire; but as a prelude to the

[1] R. G. Kent, *Old Persian Grammar, Texts, Lexicon*, 142–4; G. M. A. Richter, *AJA* l (1946), 15–30.
[2] Xen. *Hell*. iii. 1. 6; Thuc. i. 138. 5.
[3] Hdt. vi. 20; vi. 119 1–2.
[4] Cf. Raubitschek, 'Das Datislied' in *Charites* (ed. J. Schauenburg, 1957), 234–42, discussing Diod. x. 26. 3.

historical account of causes and effects he gives us the version of
the Persian chroniclers who trace the feud between east and west
to the seizure of Io by the Phoenicians. It is not naïve to believe
that these λόγιοι τῶν Περσέων are real Persians who had learnt
to think in Greek terms. At the same time some Greeks were
coming to know more about the Persians. Herodotus' account
of Persian customs and character would have shocked his public
in the seventies. He emphasizes the respect for courage and
truth in the Persian nobility and their sense of loyalty and
honour.[1] The school of Isocrates who preferred to revive the old
feud between Greece and Persia did not approve such heresies;
Herodotus was condemned as φιλοβάρβαρος, but he is likely to
have met with more sympathy from some of his contemporaries.
Herodotus developed his respect for Persian qualities from his
own experience. He visited many parts of the Persian Empire
and seems to have met Persians of high standing; for some of
his material derives from Persian records, and not all of this
could be borrowed from Hecataeus, who had pioneered the
description of the east to Greeks. But Herodotus did not know
Persian. This is quite clear from his proud discovery that 'all
Persian names end in the letter sigma, which the Dorians call
san'.[2] This is true of Persian masculine names as pronounced
by Greeks, but some of these, including Xerxes, end in a
vowel in Old Persian. On both sides there were tendencies
that could lead to an understanding. This does not mean
that a policy of peace with Persia was non-controversial; it
was probably resented at Athens and elsewhere by many, but
it could be discussed in the Athenian Assembly without fear
of lynching.

The military situation provided a favourable context for
negotiations. The Athenian attempt to reverse the balance of
power in the eastern Mediterranean had not been an unquali-
fied success. The ships detached from his fleet by Cimon to
look for opportunities in Egypt had not provoked a general
rising against Persia. In Cyprus some successes had been
gained, but when Cimon died the fleet returned to Athens
without consolidating the ground they had won. As for the
Persians, their lack of success in Cyprus must have weakened
the confidence that came from the recovery of Egypt, and

[1] Hdt. i. 131–9.　　[2] Hdt. i. 139.

the final sea battle of the campaign had shown that Greek fleets were still superior to the Phoenicians. More important, Megabyzus, the hero of the Egyptian campaign, had fallen out with the King and was establishing a powerful independent base in Syria.[1]

The Athenian embassy which negotiated the treaty of peace was led by Callias son of Hipponicus, one of the richest Athenians of the day and a man who must have wielded considerable influence. His family, the Kerykes, shared with the Eumolpidae the supervision of the Eleusinian mysteries and he was himself a ceremonial torch-bearer. Religious prestige and wealth had kept the family prominent in politics through the sixth century. The first known Callias had been an associate of Solon; his son, Phaenippus, was a conspicuous opponent of the Pisistratids. Callias himself had the rare distinction of winning three Olympic victories with his chariot teams and must have been a powerful figure behind the scenes in the generation that followed the Persian invasion.[2] Plutarch accepted a tradition that he was related to Aristides, but the story is not above suspicion;[3] his marriage, however, to Cimon's half-sister Elpinice is certain.[4] It would have been difficult for a man with such associations not to have been a Cimonian in the seventies and sixties, and it is significant that, like the elder Alcibiades and Cimon, he was a *proxenos* of Sparta.[5] But at some time that cannot be determined Callias divorced Elpinice. The reason need not have been political, for Elpinice seems to have been an embarrassingly conspicuous figure, whose private life gave rise to abundant scandal; but the divorce may have had some effect on Callias' political sympathies. By the early forties, when most of his fellow aristocrats were rallying behind Cimon's political successor, Thucydides son of Melesias, Callias was playing a prominent part in policies that almost certainly derived from Pericles. He may have already led a mission to Persia in 461;[6]

---

[1] Ctesias 68–9.

[2] *PA* 7825. J. K. Davies warns me that schol. Ar. *Clouds* 64, the source of the three chariot victories, is confused and that there is little room for them in the victor list. They can, however, be fitted in 496, 492, 484; see C. Robert, *Hermes* xxxv (1900), 177. For the family, see D. D. Feaver, *Yale Class. Stud.* xv (1957), 127. A statue base on the Acropolis, possibly commemorating one or all of his victories, *DAA* 111.

[3] Plut. *Arist.* 25. 4.   [4] Plut. *Cim.* 4. 8.

[5] Xen. *Hell.* vi. 3. 4.   [6] See pp. 92 f.

he was later to serve on the embassy which negotiated the Thirty Years' Peace with Sparta in 446–445.[1] The choice of an aristocrat to head the embassy to Susa was wise, for the magnificence of the court at Susa could have been unsettling to men whose social horizon was limited to Attica.

We know perhaps another aristocrat in the party. Pyrilampes was sufficiently well connected and conspicuous to be remembered in Plato's circle. In the *Charmides* we are told that 'no one in Asia was more handsome or tall than Pyrilampes . . . when he went on embassies to the great king or elsewhere in Asia',[2] and on one of these journeys he brought back peacocks which caused something of a stir in Athens. An allusion in a fragment from a speech of Antiphon preserved in Athenaeus shows that they were brought back not later than the forties.[3] Pyrilampes' son Demos inherited them and at the time of the Archidamian War was well known in Athens for his beauty.[4] Aristophanes and Eupolis could rely on their audience knowing him, and Lysias mentions in passing a cup that the Great King had given him.[5] It is tempting to believe that Pyrilampes went to Susa in 450–449 and his son in 424–423. Like Callias, Pyrilampes had not joined Thucydides' party; Plutarch describes him as a close political associate of Pericles, and in naming his son Demos he demonstrated his political sympathies.[6]

The main sources for the terms of the peace treaty negotiated by Callias are Diodorus, reflecting Ephorus, and the orators from Isocrates to Lycurgus. We need not be surprised if there are minor variations in their versions for we can see from the parallel case of the decree condemning Arthmius of Zelea that orators were careless in quoting documents even when the original was on public display.[7] Directly or indirectly the terms that are quoted should derive from the stele which Theopompus criticized. The most generally quoted clauses of the peace

---

[1] Diod. xii. 7. [2] Plato, *Charmides* 158a.

[3] Athenaeus ix. 397c–d. There is a playful reference in Ar. *Acharn.* 61–3. Envoys returning from the Persian king are announced. Dicaeopolis is not enthusiastic: ποίου βασιλέως; ἄχθομαι 'γὼ πρέσβεσιν | καὶ τοῖς ταῶσι τοῖς τ' ἀλαζονεύμασιν.

[4] *PA* 3573. [5] Lysias xix. 25.

[6] The *Vita Anon. Thuc.* 6 records that Thucydides defended Pyrilampes, who had killed a boy in a love affair, when he was prosecuted by Pericles. This probably refers to the same man, but perhaps at an early age. Plut. (*Per.* 13. 15) describes him as a ἑταῖρος Περικλέους.

[7] See App. 10 (c), p. 508.

treaty are the restrictions imposed on the great king. By sea he was not to send his ships beyond points which are variously quoted: the Chelidonian islands, Phaselis, Cyaneae, the river Nessus. Wade-Gery suggested as the easiest explanation of the variants that they were all in fact mentioned in the treaty and that what was defined was a demilitarized zone.[1] The Greeks were not to sail east of Cyaneae on the south coast of Asia Minor and the Persians were not to sail west of Phaselis and the Chelidonians. This solution is not convincing. There is no early parallel for such a conception known to us and the only Cyaneae well known in the fifth century were the small islands at the mouth of the Euxine.[2] The more critical area was the southern coast, but Persian ships had operated in the Hellespont in 465 and if they were to be kept out of the Aegean the northern entry as well as the southern should be closed.[3] Phaselis and the Chelidonians seem to be interchangeable in the sources; we may follow Wade-Gery in believing that both were mentioned. Phaselis would be the limit for ships hugging the coast, the Chelidonians for ships sailing across the mouth of the bay. The river Nessus remains a mystery; it is mentioned in only one source, Aristodemus, and has not been identified;[4] it should be an alternative to Cyaneae in the north.

It is generally held that these limits were reciprocal and that while the Persians were to be kept out of the Aegean in this way the Greeks were not to sail east of Phaselis and the Chelidonians or into the Euxine. There is, however, no mention of such a clause in the sources and though orators would not hesitate to suppress it we should at least consider the text which Diodorus derived from Ephorus. He merely tells us that all the Greek cities in Asia were to be autonomous, but that the Greeks were not to attack the great king's territory.[5] With this we may couple a clause referred to by Isocrates in the *Panegyricus*: 'in that earlier peace we stipulated the assessments of some of his

---

[1] Wade-Gery, *Essays* 214.

[2] See J. H. Oliver, *Hist.* vi (1957), 254 f., quoting the limits given by Aristides, *Panath.* 153 (p. 249 Dindorf): πρὸς μεσημβρίαν μὲν Χελιδονέας, πρὸς δὲ ἄρκτον Κυανέας θέμενος. For Κυάνεαι as a boundary see Hdt. iv. 85. 1; Eur. *Andromache* 863.

[3] Plut. *Cim.* 14. 1.

[4] Aristodemos 13. 2: ἐντὸς Κυανέων καὶ Νέσσου ποταμοῦ καὶ Φασήλιδος . . . καὶ Χελιδονέων.

[5] Diod. xii. 4. 5.

tributes'.[1] The most likely interpretation of this clause is that the Greek cities east of the limits should not be penalized. There is good reason to believe that Greek cities of the eastern Mediterranean coast and Cyprus had been brought into the Delian League in the fifties and had been required to pay tribute to Athens.[2] They had been lost to the League by the failure in Egypt but Athens now did what she could for them. They were to pay tribute to Persia, but it may have been laid down that they should not be required to pay more than they had paid before they were won over by Athens; and they were to be autonomous, free to regulate their own affairs in their own way. A significant parallel, as Wade-Gery emphasized, can be seen in the terms which the Persian king offered in 395 to secure the withdrawal of Agesilaus from Asia Minor: 'The king thinks it right that you should return to Greece, and that the cities in Asia should be independent, but pay him the ancient tribute.'[3] If Diodorus is correct Athens did not renounce the right to send triremes into the Euxine, which she might want to do to protect her corn-supplies; the Greek towns in the Persian sphere had the right to associate with Athens, provided that they paid their tribute to the Persian king.

The restrictions laid on the Persians by land are more difficult to disentangle. The most-quoted clause has been described as the Sardis line. The Persian satraps were not to come nearer than a three days' journey from the coast, or, as others phrase it, a day's journey by horse.[4] Isocrates, however, in two passages says that the Persian army could not cross the Halys.[5] These

---

[1] Isocr. iv. 120: τότε μὲν γὰρ ἡμεῖς φανησόμεθα . . . τῶν φόρων ἐνίους τάττοντες. The fuller context is quoted in App. 8, T 5 (b), p. 487. Gomme (*AJP* lxv (1949), 33 f.), followed by O. Murray (*Hist.* xv (1966), 155), interpreted this clause to mean that in the fifth century Athens controlled some of the Greek cities which in the fourth century were subject to Persia. This, however, would be a very oblique way of saying something essentially simple and Isocrates would indirectly be admitting that the Ionian cities rightly belonged to the king. The context is concerned with the limitations imposed by the Athenians on the king. To balance the restrictions on what the king could do by land and by sea, the intermediate clause should mean the restriction on his right to assess some of the cities paying tribute to him. See also App. 8, p. 492.

[2] Above, p. 102.

[3] Xen. *Hell.* iii. 4. 25: βασιλεὺς δὲ ἀξιοῖ σὲ μὲν ἀποπλεῖν οἴκαδε, τὰς δ' ἐν τῇ Ἀσίᾳ πόλεις αὐτονόμους οὔσας τὸν ἀρχαῖον δασμὸν αὐτῷ ἀποφέρειν, Wade-Gery, *Essays*, 225.

[4] The terms are set out in App. 8, p. 487. See also H. Bengtson, *Die Staatsverträge der griechisch-römischen Welt von 700 bis 338 v. Chr.* ii. 152.

[5] Isocr. vii. 80 (357 B.C.); xii. 59 (339 B.C.).

variants Wade-Gery has combined by suggesting that the land
west of the Halys was to be a demilitarized zone which would
hold only token forces under the satraps.[1] This is difficult to
believe. The Persians had to maintain order in Phrygia and
Lydia as well as in Ionia; to renounce the right to move a large
army, if needed, beyond the Halys would be intolerable. It is
easier to believe that Isocrates' enthusiasm has led him astray
and that he has been careless. The Halys line was well remembered from Herodotus and Aeschylus,[2] and Isocrates may have
taken it as the three-day limit without thinking. What restrictions were placed on the Greeks is again uncertain. It is possible
that they merely covenanted in general terms not to attack the
great king's territory. Wade-Gery, however, has suggested that
the Athenians undertook to withdraw their garrisons from Ionia
and to dismantle all fortifications.[3] Certainly the absence later
of fortified city walls in Asia Minor needs explanation. More
than once in his last book Thucydides mentions, with apparent
emphasis, that Ionia was then without walls.[4] The question is
when and why were the walls pulled down. That this gesture
was made by Athens to satisfy Persia is possible, but, it seems
to me, unlikely. At best the peace would be difficult to justify
to the Ionians; if at the same time they were ordered to pull
down their walls in deference to the traditional enemy their
suspicions would be difficult to control. The status of garrisons
is rather different, for they had been installed nominally at
least to defend loyalists against Persians and Medizers; it would
be logical to withdraw them when peace brought security. But
we may wonder whether Athens was prepared to take this risk
and relinquish control. The fact that we have no clear-cut
evidence of garrison troops in Ionia between 450 and the outbreak of the Peloponnesian War is not significant, since even
in the period before the peace our knowledge is derived only
from the accidental survival of inscriptions. There is, however,
a passage in comedy which may imply garrison duty at Cyzicus

[1] Wade-Gery, op. cit. 213–21.
[2] Aeschylus, *Persae* 864–5: ὅσσας δ' εἷλε (sc. Δαρεῖος) πόλεις πόρον | οὐ διαβὰς
Ἅλυος ποταμοῖο; Hdt. v. 52. 2, 102. 1; vii. 26. 3.
[3] Wade-Gery, op. cit. 219 f.
[4] We have the good evidence of Thucydides (iii. 33. 2) that Ionia was unfortified
at the time of the revolt of Mytilene, ἀτειχίστου οὔσης τῆς Ἰωνίας. Wade-Gery (loc.
cit.) gives a list of towns said to have been without walls in the last phase of the war.

in the interval and if we are right in dating Cimon's death in 451 the Athenian regulations of 450–449 for Miletus will probably have been passed after the decision to make peace had been taken and when the terms may already have been known. A garrison is mentioned.[1]

The only logical alternative explanation of the defortification of the Ionian cities is an Athenian imperial decision. Faced with disaffection or potential disaffection Athens might have ordered the Ionians to pull down their walls. This had been one of the terms imposed on Thasos when her revolt was crushed, and it was repeated when Samos capitulated in 439. There are also signs of the use of this policy as a precaution rather than a penalty. When Potidaea in 433 grew restless the Athenians ordered her to pull down her southern wall facing Pallene;[2] in 425 Chios was suspected as soon as she showed signs of making her walls defensible.[3] There is a more interesting reflection of this policy in some lines of the comic poet Teleclides, a rather older contemporary of Aristophanes. Plutarch who quotes the lines does not name the play and we have no means of dating it, but what survives would be apposite in the forties. Teleclides who, like other writers of comedy, showed considerably less respect for Pericles than does Thucydides, is describing how the Athenians have allowed Pericles to exercise complete control of the state; the Athenians have put into his hands 'the cities' tributes, the cities themselves to bind and unloose, stone walls to build and others to destroy, treaty terms, power, control, peace, wealth, and happiness'.[4] It is dangerous to attempt to read too much into comedy, and we can resist the temptation to identify σπονδαί and εἰρήνη with the Thirty Years' Peace and the Peace of Callias, and the tributes with the use of the tribute on Athenian buildings, because they need be no more than the general areas of the state's policy, but the reference to the building up and the pulling down of stone walls is more specific and should refer to Athenian actions well known to the audience. Wall building might possibly refer to the building in the late

---

[1] Cyzicus, Eupolis, Πόλεις F 233, quoted p. 207 n. 2; Miletus, D 11.
[2] Thuc. i. 56. 2. [3] Thuc. iv. 51.
[4] Plut. *Per.* 16. 2:

πόλεών τε φόρους αὐτάς τε πόλεις, τὰς μὲν δεῖν, τὰς δ' ἀναλύειν,
λάινα τείχη, τὰ μὲν οἰκοδομεῖν, τὰ δὲ τἄμπαλιν αὖ καταβάλλειν,
σπονδὰς δύναμιν κράτος εἰρήνην πλοῦτόν τ' εὐδαιμονίαν τε.

forties of the middle wall at Athens which seems to have attracted the attention of comedy, but the destruction of walls makes very much better sense in relation to the allies. It is certain that Athens did at various times order cities to pull down their walls; it will be seen later that the early forties provided a context in which such a policy might have been pursued in Ionia.

The negotiations which resulted in the Peace of Callias probably began soon after Cimon's death in the late summer of 451 and should have been completed by the end of summer 450. Athens did not have to wait long for the reaction.[1]

[1] For the most recent articles on the Peace of Callias see Add., p. 598.

9

THE CRISIS OF THE FORTIES

THE Peace of Callias gave rise to crisis in the League and in Athens. With the end of hostilities against Persia the League had lost its original function; but Athens had no intention of relaxing her hold on the organization she had built up. There was widespread protest throughout the Aegean world but Athens made no attempt at compromise. The League would not be allowed to dissolve, the allies would continue to pay yearly tribute. These were the vital years of transition from League to Empire. Even the language changes; the 'alliance', ξυμμαχίς, becomes 'the cities which Athens controls', αἱ πόλεις ὅσων Ἀθηναῖοι κρατοῦσι. Athens was able to maintain a firm policy and weather the storm, thanks to the means of control she had already developed. In the fifties, if not earlier, she had learnt to send out constitutional advisers, to instal political residents and garrisons. The tools of empire had already been forged.

In the continuous narratives of Thucydides and Diodorus no emphasis is placed on the period that followed Cimon's last campaign and the end of war with Persia. The evidence, however, of inscriptions supplemented by secondary literary sources suggests that this was a period of considerable tension in Athens and in the Aegean. What may be the first document in the series we owe to Plutarch. He paraphrases in his *Pericles* an Athenian decree, which for convenience is known as the Congress Decree. The language seems to derive from an inscription and, since it is not closely linked with the preceding or following chapters, Plutarch may have found the document himself, either among the decrees collected by Craterus or in a collection of Pericles' decrees; there is no hint of it in any other source.[1] The decree, proposed by Pericles, provided for the sending out of heralds to invite the Greeks to send representatives to Athens

[1] Plut. *Per.* 17.

to discuss 'the problem of the Greek temples which the barbarians had burnt, the sacrifices which they still owed on behalf of Greece in fulfilment of the vows made to the gods when they fought the barbarians, and the sea, that all should sail in security and maintain the peace'. The areas to be covered by the heralds are specified, and the only Greeks not included are those of the Adriatic coast north of Ambracia, in Sicily, and Italy, and those east of Byzantium in the north, and of Rhodes in the south. If this is a genuine document and not an ingenious forgery, Pericles was nominally calling on the Greek world to set up another organization to do what the Spartan-led Greek alliance of 480 should have done but had failed to do, and to provide for the peacetime needs which the Delian League had hitherto satisfied, particularly the elimination of piracy by a fleet with adequate resources. But the meeting was to be held at Athens, the burnt temples were almost exclusively Athenian, and the fleet required to patrol the sea would have to be largely Athenian. It is not surprising that the Spartans led the way in refusing to attend, and it is probable that Pericles expected them to refuse. What the Athenians needed now that peace had been made with Persia was a new sanction for the Delian League; a panhellenic Congress sounded well and it may have been useful for propaganda. According to Plutarch, when the Spartans, followed by others, refused to attend, the Congress was abandoned. This is a little surprising because Athens would have had a good opportunity, even if only a minority attended, to justify her policy publicly at the expense of Sparta. The Congress proposal makes good historical sense, but Plutarch's account gives rise to doubts. It should not be used as the main foundation for the reconstruction of these years.[1]

With the Congress Decree is linked a problem presented by the tribute quota lists. In 450 a new assessment was made and remained in force until the Great Panathenaea of 446, but it is virtually certain that only three lists were recorded during the four years of this period.[2] Two of these lists resemble one another very closely, and seem to be interdependent; they should come

---

[1] The authenticity of the decree has been challenged by R. Seager, *Hist.* xviii (1969), 129–41. See App. 10, (D), p. 512.

[2] Some would say that 'virtually certain' is much too strong. The issue is discussed in ML, pp. 133–5.

from successive years. The list of 449 is dated; the remaining two lists are almost certainly from 447 and 446. Why is there no list for 448? The simplest explanation is that of *The Athenian Tribute Lists*; no list of quotas was recorded because no tribute was paid, and no tribute was paid because Athens had remitted the year's tribute pending the outcome of the Congress; when the Congress collapsed tribute was resumed. One may, however, wonder if Athens would have taken this risk. It would have sounded well for her to offer to forgo tribute if the Greek world generally would pay for the peacetime services that the Delian League performed, and the debt to the gods that had been incurred during the invasion of Xerxes; it would have been considerably more difficult to reimpose tribute once it had been remitted even for a single year. It is unsound to argue that the Athenians would have acted in the way we think more reasonable; there is, however, another possible interpretation. The reason why no quotas were recorded for 448 might be that the whole tribute of the year had been given to some other purpose.[1] A block grant, for example, to Athena Nike would be an intelligible commemoration of the Peace of Callias. Part of a decree survives which records the decision to build a temple of Athena Nike, and the early form of sigma with three bars suggests a date before 445.[2] The temple was not begun until considerably later, but the frieze on the south side represented scenes of fighting between Greeks and Persians, and Persian trophies were represented on the later balustrade surrounding the bastion on which the temple stands. It seems likely that those who supported the peace wished to represent it as a victorious conclusion to the fighting against Persia, in the same way as the last engagements in Cyprus were magnified; and a temple commemorating the fighting of the Delian League would be an appropriate use for the tribute of the first year of peace.[3]

We come to more secure ground with the main building programme of Pericles. From the accounts that survive we know that work on the Parthenon was begun in 447–446, and for the temple and the great cult statue the main payments to the

---

[1] As Meritt first suggested, *The Greek Political Experience* (Studies in Honour of W. K. Prentice), 53 (cf. Gomme, *CR* liv (1940), 67) though later he changed his mind.

[2] Meiggs, *JHS* lxxxvi (1966), 92–7.

[3] For the temple of Athena Nike, see App. 9, p. 496.

commissioners were made by Athena's treasurers. From this point Athena's treasury seems to finance extraordinary expenditures, both on buildings and on military operations such as the revolt of Samos. The explanation comes from a combination of the debate recorded by Plutarch with the evidence of a commentary on Demosthenes' speech against Androtion. From Plutarch's building debate we learn that Pericles was attacked for using the allies' tribute on Athenian buildings, and even if the speeches in Plutarch are derived from rhetorical sources, the central point around which the speeches are elaborated is likely to be historical.[1] It is confirmed by the commentator's note which is preserved in a papyrus of the second century A.D.[2] He seems to say that the Athenians decided to use the accumulated reserve of the Delian League, 5,000 talents, on the rebuilding of the Acropolis in the archonship of Euthydemos. Euthydemos was archon in 431–430 and Wilcken, who established the nature of the document, thought that the commentator was referring to the decree recorded by Thucydides, which set aside an iron reserve of 1,000 talents in the first year of the Peloponnesian War, and left 5,000 talents available for borrowing.[3] But this decree would seem to be completely irrelevant to a commentary on Demosthenes' speech against Androtion, and the note which includes a reference to the League reserve seems to arise from Demosthenes' reference to the buildings of the Acropolis. The most reasonable inference would seem to be that the commentator has made the same mistake as Diodorus, naming the archon of 450–449 Euthydemos instead of Euthynos. We should therefore place the Congress Decree and its sequel, the decision to use League funds on Athenian buildings, after the Peace of Callias which we have dated to 450, and before the change of archons in midsummer 449.

Fourth-century orators were proud to recall an oath taken by the Greeks before the battle of Plataea, which included an undertaking not to rebuild the temples which the Persians had destroyed.[4] A fourth-century copy was found in 1932 at Acharnae where it had been set up in the temple of Ares, together with a copy of the ephebic oath.[5] This Plataean oath was, like the Peace of Callias, contemptuously attacked by

---

[1] Plut. *Per.* 12. See p. 139. [2] Text and discussion, App. 10 (E), p. 515.
[3] Thuc. ii. 24. 1. [4] Lycurgus, *Leocr.* 80. [5] Tod, *GHI* ii. 204.

Theopompus and in modern times has been generally dismissed as a forgery.[1] The Acharnae text is almost certainly a fabrication, and it is very doubtful whether an original text survived into the fourth century, but it is difficult to see why an oath not to rebuild temples should be invented in the fourth century, when it was common knowledge that the most important temples had in fact been rebuilt. Pausanias in the second century A.D. could still quote the oath in relation to the temples of Demeter at Phalerum and of Hera on the road from Phalerum to Athens, but even the orators knew that the Parthenon and the Erechtheum dated from the second half of the fifth century.[2] The archaeological evidence accumulated over the last generation, particularly from the American excavations in the Agora, should make sceptics reconsider. It is surely significant that the shrines that were destroyed and for which we have evidence remained in ruins until the middle of the century. When the Athenians took the decision to rebuild the temples they may have argued that the Peace of Callias freed them from the oath that they had taken.

The strong policy now being pursued by Athens should be regarded as Periclean. Politically and militarily he was mature. He had served his political apprenticeship in the sixties and had identified himself with the reforms of Ephialtes. When the political revolution was consolidated by military successes in the early fifties Pericles was not yet a dominant figure; the more experienced generals, Myronides, Leocrates, and Tolmides, were probably the most powerful voices in the Assembly. But by 450 Pericles himself had made his reputation as a general, and Cimon, Leocrates, and probably Myronides were dead. Pericles was now in his forties, and politically he was determined to lead the radical democracy. His policies aroused strong opposition in Athens. The extreme oligarchs had been discredited by their exposure at the time of the battle of Tanagra, and the successes of the early fifties had closed divisions in the state, but on the death of Cimon his followers found a new leader, Thucydides son of Melesias, kinsman of Cimon and perhaps his brother-in-law.[3] Thucydides and his followers could see that Pericles' policies would give further strength to the

[1] App. 10 (A), p. 504.   [2] Paus. x. 35. 2.
[3] E. Cavaignac, *Rev. Phil.* lv (1929), 281–5.

radicals, and they also had doubts about the new imperialism. It is this aspect of policy that dominates Plutarch's account, the only source that preserves more than an echo of these critical years. Thucydides organized his followers to sit together in the Assembly, to give more noise and weight to their views. They attacked Pericles' use of allied funds on his new buildings, but what positive policies they advocated we are not told.[1]

It would probably be wrong to regard Thucydides as a sincere panhellenist who was supporting the allies on principle; he was more probably a shrewd politician whose primary aim was to discredit the radical leaders. He and his followers disliked Pericles' democracy more than his imperialism, but the two were bound up together. An ambitious public-building policy meant good wages for large numbers, and was later to mean public amenities at public expense rather than as the gifts of a benevolent aristocracy.[2] But an ambitious building policy could not be financed from domestic revenues alone; it needed League funds to make it practicable. The oligarchs had seen the significance of the long walls; they made the common people in the city militarily secure and the farms of Attica vulnerable. Pericles' policy of an ἔμμισθος πόλις would add economic security. But too many citizens had too much to gain from the building programme for the issue to be in doubt, and the emphasis on temples in the early stages of the programme could lull any consciences that were still tender. Thucydides continued his opposition, but must have changed his tactics; in the strong tones of the decrees passed at this time we may see the answer of the Pericleans.

While Athens' imperial policy provoked opposition at home it led to widespread protest in the empire, of which we catch glimpses in the quota lists and in other inscriptions. When the tribute of 450–449 came to Athens, in spring 449, peace, we think, had already been made with Persia and, even if the news was not at once made public in the Aegean, it would have been impossible for the Athenian embassy to have made its way to Susa unnoticed by any Greeks; there must at least have been rumours abroad in the Aegean. The quota list of 449 may reflect reactions. It is the longest list of the series to date, but the

---

[1] Plut. *Per.* 12 and 14.
[2] Public amenities, [Xen.] Ἀθ. Πολ. 2. 9–10.

arrangement of the list suggests that several states paid their tribute in two instalments, and that several others paid late in the year.[1] Among these latter were Miletus and a group of cities near her, and this may have been among the reasons that persuaded Athens to instal political residents in Miletus to watch the situation more closely. The decree providing for their appointment and dispatch was passed between midsummer 450 and midsummer 449.[2]

The discontent that can be inferred in 449 is much more emphatically illustrated in the list of 447, which, apart from the first list of 453, is the shortest of the series. Instead of some 175 names there is room for no more than 150, and the last nine, at the bottom of the last column, are listed under a special rubric, which has been restored to mean that they paid late, after the Dionysia.[3] Almost all the names are preserved or can be restored, and it is likely that the absentees included Miletus and the group of cities associated with her in 449, Colophon, and Athens' old enemy Aegina. Of the states listed, many again paid only part of their assessment. The next year's list, of 446, shows Athens' strong reaction. The order of states on the list is repeated, but some at least of the absentees of 447, including probably the Milesian group, are listed twice and other entries almost certainly represent the complements of partial payments for 447.[4] Athens seems to have brought pressure to bear on recalcitrants, and there is an indication of police action in two entries. One talent, probably the balance from an incomplete payment in 447 is paid by Abdera 'to Eion', Athens' settlement at the Strymon mouth which did not herself pay tribute; two other payments are made 'to Tenedos'. The most likely interpretation of these payments is that they were made to commanders operating in these areas.[5]

Further evidence of a force operating in the Thraceward area may perhaps be seen in the decree which provides for an Athenian colony at Brea. This decree lays down the formalities

---

[1] *ATL* iii. 30–6.

[2] D 11, passed in the archonship of Euthynos.

[3] Only the first letter survives: M[ετὰ Διονύσια], but no other plausible alternative has been found. It should be significant that the cities listed under this heading are inscribed in a different hand from the main list. See also Add., p. 599.

[4] Analysis of the list of 447–446, *ATL* iii. 39–52.

[5] List 8. i. 105; 8. ii. 108–9. *ATL* iii. 59–60.

followed in establishing the colony—the offering of sacrifices, the measuring of the land, the reservation of precincts for the gods, and the provision of settlers. It is also stipulated that if anyone attacks the colony the cities of the Thraceward area are to come to Brea's assistance according to the regulations already laid down.[1] This looks like an Athenian attempt to restore solidarity after a period of unrest, and the colony of Brea was also designed to strengthen Athenian control. It is probably to be identified with the 1,000 settlers sent out to live with the Bisaltae, whom Plutarch includes in his list of Athenians settled abroad at about this time.[2] When Xerxes invaded Greece the Bisaltae were independent, and in the archaic period they had issued coins, but in 453 Argilus, their neighbour, is listed as paying $10\frac{1}{2}$ talents, and in 445 only 1 talent.[3] It is at least a possible explanation that Argilus paid such a high tribute in 453 because she had absorbed the land of the Bisaltae and that this land was now confiscated from her. The date of the reduction in tribute would be consistent with what little evidence we have for the date of the Athenian colony.[4] Argilus was an Andrian colony, and Andros had been punished by the settlement of a cleruchy in 450.[5] There could have been reactions in Argilus.

The payments made 'to Tenedos' may indicate operations in that neighbourhood. It was at least about this time that an expedition was sent out under Pericles to re-establish Athenian

[1] *IG* i². 45, ML 49, ll. 13–17: ἐὰν δέ τις ἐπιστρα[τεύει ἐπ|ὶ τὲν γέ]ν τὲν τὸν ἀποίκον, βοεθέν τὰ[ς πόλες h|ος ὀχσύ]τατα κατὰ τὰς χσυγγραφὰς ha[ὶ ἐπὶ..|...6...]το γραμματεύοντος ἐγένον[το περὶ τ|ὸν πόλε]ον τὸν ἐπὶ Θράικες.

[2] Plut. *Per.* 11. 5; *ATL* iii. 60, 287 f. For the identification and date of Brea see also ML, pp. 132 f.

[3] No figure survives for Argilus between 453 and 445. In the assessment of 446 and 438 the figure was 1 talent. *ATL*, finding a payment of 10½ talents ($X\boxed{A}$) in 453 anomalous, transcribe ⟨H⟩$\boxed{A}$ representing a tribute of 1½ talents. This is not a natural mistake for the cutter to make, and the higher figure could be explained. 10½ talents, though not otherwise found as an assessment, is no odder than 7½ talents, the tribute of Ephesus from 454 to 446 and of Carystus before 450, and if Brea was carved out of the territory of Argilus the sharp reduction of tribute would be intelligible. The tribute of Argilus was further reduced from 1 talent to 1,000 drachmae after the foundation of Amphipolis; Brea was probably then abandoned, for it is not mentioned in Thucydides' detailed account of events in the Thraceward district from 424 to 421. See also Gomme, *HCT* iii. 576 n. 1. But see App., p. 602.

[4] The most significant letter is *rho* with tail (ℙ) which suggests a date before the Peloponnesian War, Meiggs, *JHS* lxxxvi (1966), 94; other arguments point to 446, ML, pp. 132 f.

[5] Thuc. iv. 103. 3: εἰσὶ δὲ οἱ Ἀργίλιοι Ἀνδρίων ἄποικοι. See above, p. 121.

control of the Chersonese with new settlers.[1] It is not surprising that the tradition inherited by Plutarch regarded this as one of Pericles' most memorable actions, because the Chersonese had a double usefulness; it provided a large area of fertile land which could support a substantial population, and it controlled a crucial section of the route of the corn transports sailing from the Euxine into the Aegean. A fringe of small colonies had been settled along the coast in the archaic period, but the interior was still held in the sixth century by the Dolonci. When in the time of Pisistratus this tribe came under heavy pressure from the Thracians, Miltiades occupied the peninsula and the principality remained in his family down to the end of the Ionian revolt, when the younger Miltiades was forced to evacuate. The expulsion of the Persians after the battle of Mycale restored Athenian control, but the land was not strongly held and the Thracians, always a threat, were again pressing down from the north; Athens once again intervened. The most reliable index of date comes from the quota lists. In the first list, of 453, the whole peninsula pays as a unit, Χερρονεσῖται, and the assessment is 18 talents. In 449 an incomplete payment of 13 talents is recorded and a second payment may have been included in the late payments of the final column. No entry survives from 447, but in 446, and thereafter, individual communities, Sestus, Madytus, and Elaeus pay separately, and the Χερρονεσῖται are later more closely localized as Χερρονεσῖται ἀπ' Ἀγορᾶς. The sum total of the new tribute is less than 3 talents and the large reduction is to be explained by the taking of land for Pericles' new settlers.[2] The quota lists show that the settlers were taken out between 449 and 446, probably in 447, but subsidiary operations in the area, explaining the payments 'to Tenedos' may have been needed in 446. A significant reduction in the Lemnian tribute also suggests that settlers were sent to Lemnos and Imbros between 450 and 446.[3]

A little further light may be thrown on Pericles' expedition by a well-preserved casualty list. This list, like its fellows, covers the fighting of a single campaigning year, and records the dead by tribe and by the scene of action. The largest number of casualties, including a general, were killed in the Chersonese and they are listed first; there were also casualties at Byzantium

[1] Plut. *Per.* 19. 1.   [2] *ATL* iii. 45 f.   [3] See Endnote 11, p. 424.

and 'in the other wars', a total altogether of 58. Across the bottom of the stone is an epigram commemorating those who fell by the Hellespont.[1] This casualty list was once commonly dated to the last phase of the Peloponnesian War when the Hellespontine district was the scene of almost continuous fighting. But the lettering seems inconsistent with such a late date, and one name certainly—and possibly another—suggest a date before the Peloponnesian War. Καρυστόνικος must owe his name to the forcible incorporation of Carystus in the Delian League in the late seventies; Ναχσιάδες has been thought to reflect the crushing of the Naxian revolt soon after, but the name could have been given by an Athenian friend of Naxos to his son at any time. These arguments have led to a general acceptance of 440 or 439 for the list on the ground that the only occasion on which we know that Byzantium was giving trouble was when she joined Samos in revolt. This solution, however, must be rejected. It does not explain why the main emphasis should be on the Chersonese, and it requires us to believe that Samos, which was the most critical field of action at this time and the scene of bitter fighting, should be included in 'the other wars' and should have fewer casualties than Byzantium. The document makes much better sense if it refers to Pericles' expulsion of the Thracians from the Chersonese. The casualties at Byzantium could be explained either by fighting against Thracians or by police action against the town; for the tribute payments of Byzantium are irregular in this period, and Byzantium was a colony of Megara, which was very soon to massacre its Athenian garrison; if there was trouble in Byzantium she would be anticipating her action in 440 when she joined Samos in revolt.[2] The 'other wars' of the casualty list could include the operations based on Eion, which have already been discussed, and other minor operations elsewhere.

One such minor operation was perhaps the recovery of Colophon in Ionia. Inland Colophon was likely to be an unreliable member of the Delian League. Her coinage was minted on the Persian standard, she no longer celebrated the Apaturia, and

---

[1] ML 48.

[2] Byzantium's tribute in 448–447 is incomplete; in 447–446 she makes at least two payments and probably a third. See Register, *ATL* i. 250. With Samos, Thuc. i. 115. 5.

she Medized openly soon after the beginning of the Peloponnesian War.[1] The name is preserved twice in the first assessment period, but does not appear in any surviving fragment of the second. This could be coincidence, but the reason is more likely to be the revolt of Colophon; for we have a substantial part of a decree passed by the Athenian Assembly at about this time which lays down regulations for Colophon and implies Athenian intervention to restore control.[2] The oath of loyalty now imposed on Colophon is not unlike the oath of the Erythraean Council, but it is more detailed and explicit. The text is lost at a crucial point and we cannot be sure whether loyalty was to be sworn to Athens alone, as later in the case of Chalcis, or to Athens and the allies, as at Erythrae; the former fits better the mood of these years. The formula of loyalty is also filled out: instead of the simple 'I will not abandon', the more explicit 'I will not abandon by word or deed'; and the Colophonians have to swear that they will not overthrow nor tolerate the overthrow of the democracy which has apparently been newly established by Athens.[3]

The decree also mentions settlers and officials to settle them, [οἰκέτ]ορες and οἰκισταί, in an uncertain context, and the authors of *The Athenian Tribute Lists* infer that Athens sent out an Athenian colony to watch Athenian interests in place of the garrison that she would have sent out in the fifties, but was now unable to send under the terms of the Peace of Callias.[4] Evidence for the colony, though not for its nature, they think, may be seen in the assessment of 446 in which the tribute of Colophon is reduced from 3 to $1\frac{1}{2}$ talents, and the tributes of her smaller neighbours, Lebedos and Dios Hieron, are also reduced.[5] They infer a second Athenian colony in Ionia from a fragmentary dedication by colonists proceeding from Athens to a colony. Only the first two letters survive; Erythrae is one of the few possible names.[6] Some support here too might be derived from the assessment of 446, for the tribute of Haerae, close neighbour to Erythrae, was reduced from 3 talents to 1, and there was a change at Erythrae. In the second period, from 450 to 446,

---

[1] Thuc. iii. 34. 1.
[2] *IG* i². 14/15; ML 47.
[3] For the text of the oath, App. 16, p. 580.
[4] *ATL* iii. 282–4.
[5] The tribute of Lebedos was reduced from 3 talents to 1 talent. For Dios Hieron, previously assessed at 1,000 drachmae, there is no evidence for the third period; after 445 she pays only 500 drachmae.
[6] *IG* i². 396; *DAA* 301.

Erythrae pays on behalf of her peninsula and the smaller cities are not separately listed. The figure for 450 is irregular but in 446 she makes two payments totalling 9 talents. In the assessment of 446 she is required to pay separately; her own tribute is 7 talents and the combined total of the smaller communities of the peninsula is roughly 1 talent. These changes do not seem to need an Athenian colony to explain them for there was a widespread reduction of tributes in the assessment of 446, and the increase of the peninsula's assessment in the thirties to 10 talents, 1,000 drachmae, the highest pre-war figure, more than offsets the reduction of 446. Athenian settlements in Asia Minor need firmer evidence, for they have left no traces in the literary sources. The colony of the dedication is more probably Eretria and the settlers at Colophon may have been drawn from other parts of Ionia, forming a precedent for the action taken in 430 at Notium.[1]

The evidence that we have examined suggests that Athens had to meet widespread trouble in the Aegean in 447, and that apart from the major operation in the Chersonese minor actions were fought at other points. In this reconstruction, however, we have made certain assumptions about the quota lists which have been questioned. There is no doubt that the list of 447 included many part-payments and probably some late payments, and that many cities are missing. The list of 446, in arrangement and content, is very closely related to its predecessor; it includes the complements of part-payments of 447, two payments for the two years by some states missing in 447, and payment in two instalments by some states for the current year. Are we right in assuming that part-payments and late payments indicate disaffection? For the late payments Miletus and the group of cities associated with her are a crucial case. The authors of *The Athenian Tribute Lists*, who were the first to identify these cities as a distinct group, have shown that their behaviour throughout this period is consistent; they always pay late. The only difference, in their view, between the list of 447 and those of 449 and 446 is one of book-keeping. 'The group appears to

---

[1] Thuc. iii. 34. 4: καὶ ὕστερον Ἀθηναῖοι οἰκιστὰς πέμψαντες κατὰ τοὺς ἑαυτῶν νόμους κατῴκισαν τὸ Νότιον, ξυναγαγόντες πάντας ἐκ τῶν πόλεων, εἴ πού τις ἦν Κολοφωνίων. Had there been two Athenian colonies in Ionia some trace could be expected in Thucydides, who in Books III and VIII covers events in Ionia. For Eretria as an alternative to Erythrae see p. 568.

be constant, except that in list 5 Mylasa paid (exceptionally) in good time, while in lists 7 and 8 Priene did the same. They may perhaps be distinguished from their appendix-fellows in that their late payment was very likely due to distance.'[1] This surely cannot be the explanation. If Phaselis and the cities of Rhodes could arrive in time distance cannot explain the lateness of Miletus, and in 447 at least the payments of this group cannot have been received by midsummer. It has indeed been suggested that for some reason that we cannot know, the books of the *hellenotamiai* were closed early in this particular year,[2] but since there seems to be a special rubric covering late payments it is much more probable that the list represents all tributes received by the end of the year of the *hellenotamiai* in midsummer. There is also good reason to suspect Miletus during this period. The Old Oligarch referred to Athens' support of oligarchy in Miletus and its failure; the oligarchs soon 'revolted and cut down the Demos'. The Athenian decree of 450–449 shows that Athens was then still tolerating oligarchy. At some time not long after this Miletus revolted; against this background the late payments of this period look like disaffection that has not yet led to a definite break with Athens.

The interpretation of part-payments is perhaps more controversial. The authors of *The Athenian Tribute Lists* set out three alternatives between which the choice must be made: that the part-payers are disaffected and unwilling to pay their full assessment, that they are temporarily weakened by enemy pressure or temporary economic difficulties, or that they are paying the balance of their tribute which is not recorded in the list of 447 to Athenian generals operating in their vicinity.[3] They themselves prefer the last of these interpretations, and believe that partial payments were made in advance to Athenian generals before the time of the Dionysia in early spring, when tribute was normally sent to Athens. These payments could not be recorded until the generals returned, and if this happened to be after the *hellenotamiai* of 447–446 had closed their books, the partial payments of 447 would appear in the record of 446. This solution cannot be disproved, but it is unlikely that when Athenian finances seem to have been buoyant the Athenian generals should be forced to collect the money they needed in so

---

[1] *ATL* iii. 35 f.   [2] Sealey, *Hist.* iii (1954–5), 327.   [3] *ATL* iii. 59 f.

many small instalments. Moreover, if they had acted in this way we should have expected some indication in the list as in the payments made 'to Eion' and 'to Tenedos'. In the early years of the Archidamian War when tribute was paid to Athenian officers in the Chersonese and to Athenian forces outside Athens, special headings were added.[1] We may therefore prefer to regard part payments as a mark of disaffection or special economic difficulties.

This interpretation would be considerably strengthened if an Athenian decree, which is not specifically dated, is rightly placed in 447 or 446. The main purpose of this decree is to ensure that the complete tribute is received from every state every year, and that payment is at once demanded from those who fail to pay. What has apparently been a serious loophole is now closed. Seals are to be agreed with the tribute-paying cities who in future are to seal their tribute with their own seal. The money is to be certified by the city authorities and entered on a tablet which is to be separately sealed.[2] This procedure is presumably designed to ensure that the cities cannot evade responsibility by maintaining that the full tribute was dispatched and that some of it must have been lost in transit. The decree also lays down stiff penalties for anyone found guilty of fraud in connection with the tribute, and invites anyone, Athenian or ally, to bring a prosecution against the offender. 'If any Athenian or ally commits an offence in respect of the tribute which the cities are required to record on a tablet for their couriers and send to Athens, he may be indicted before the *prytaneis* by any Athenian or ally who so wishes; and the *prytaneis* shall bring the case before the Boule or each be fined 1,000 drachmae for accepting bribes'.[3] The responsibility for tightening up the collection of tribute is to be shared between the Boule at Athens and Athenian officials operating in the empire: 'The Boule and the *archontes* in the cities and the *episkopoi* (travelling commissioners) are to ensure that the tribute be collected each year and brought to Athens.'[4] There is little evidence of gentle persuasion.

[1] See p. 110 n. 2.   [2] *IG* i². 66; ML 46.
[3] ll. 31–7. The general sense is clear but the translation is based partly on restorations.

[4] ll. 5–11: τὲ]μ β|ολὲν καὶ τὸς ἄρχ[οντας ἐν] τὲσ|ι πόλεσι καὶ τὸς [ἐπισκό]πος ἐ[πιμέλεσθαι hόπ[ος ἂν χσ]υλλέ|γεται ho φόρος κ[ατὰ] τὸ ἔ]τος h|έκαστον καὶ ἀπά[γεται] Ἀθένα|ζε.

This decree, which is primarily concerned with the tribute obligations of the allies refers in passing to their religious obligations: 'If any one commits an offence with regard to the sending of the cow or the panoply he shall be indicted and sentenced as in the case of a tribute offence.'[1] These offerings the allies were required to bring to the Great Panathenaea held in Athens every four years, and the very concise form in which the requirement is here specified suggests that the decree imposing these obligations on all the allies had been passed very recently. This clearly adds to the importance of dating the decree. When much less of the text was known than we now possess, it was dated during the Archidamian War, because in subject-matter it seemed closely associated with another decree, moved by Cleonymus, probably in 426, which also was concerned with tribute collection.[2] It was thought that these two decrees marked two stages in a continuing process, and at first epigraphists were satisfied with the dating. In 1940 a much earlier date, probably in the forties, was advocated by Raubitschek on the strength of some of the individual letters and the general style of the cutter, and this earlier dating won wider support when another large fragment of the decree was published, including the opening letters of the mover's name.[3] The restoration of $K\lambda\epsilon\nu i[\alpha s$ is almost inevitable, and, since the name is not common, it was thought that the proposer might be Clinias the father of Alcibiades, who was killed at the battle of Coronea in 446 or 447. It was a short step to suggest that this decree of Clinias was a reaction to the very unsatisfactory list of 447, and in turn the cause, in part at least, of the very successful collection of 446.[4]

The case for dating the decree in this context is still strong. The forms of some of the individual letters, and particularly the upsilon with curving strokes, favour a date earlier than the Peloponnesian War, and the stoichedon pattern is more crowded than we should expect in the twenties.[5] The suggestion that the decree was moved by the father of Alcibiades is less

[1] ll. 41–3: καὶ ἐ]άν τις περὶ τὲν ἀπα[γογὲ]|ν τὲς βοὸς ἒ [τὲς πανhοπλία]ς ἀδικε̂ι ...
[2] ML 68; see p. 323.
[3] Raubitschek, *AJP* lxi (1940), 477–9; new fragment, Meritt and Hill, *Hesp.* xiii (1944), 1–15.
[4] Meritt and Hill, op. cit. 9; Wade-Gery. *Hesp.* xiv (1945), 226–8. Meritt and Wade-Gery have changed their interpretation in *ATL* iii. 59 f.
[5] Meiggs, op. cit. 97.

bold than it might seem. One of the arguments brought against such an early date for this decree is the character of Athenian imperialism which it implies. Before the new fragment was found it was thought that the earliest reference to the obligation laid on all allies to bring offerings to the Great Panathenaea was in the Assessment Decree of 425, and there are those who think that such a policy would not have been adopted before the period of Cleon's ascendancy.[1] This argument will have serious force only if the rest of the evidence for the early forties is inconsistent with such high-handed action.

The closest parallel in tone and temper to the decree of Clinias is the so-called Coinage Decree. At various times and at various points in the Aegean, small fragments have been found which clearly derive from different copies of a single decree, and which, when put together, provide at least the general sense of most of the document. The decree imposes the use of Athenian silver coins, weights, and measures on the allies. Local mints are to be closed, the cities are to bring their money to Athens to be reminted, and individuals may do the same. The decree is to be rigorously applied, and a clause is to be added to the oath taken by members of the Athenian Boule when they enter office. 'If anyone mints silver coins in the cities and does not use Athenian coins, weights, or measures, I will punish and penalize him according to the former decree which Clearchus moved.'[2] Though most of the text is recoverable from a combination of the fragments, some of which overlap, there remain uncertainties. The ban on independent coinage refers only to silver coins and does not include electrum. In fact the electrum staters of Cyzicus are one of the commonest Greek currencies in the second half of the fifth century, and since many of their types are derived from Athens this minting cannot be regarded as defiance of the Athenian decree. Finds of Cyzicene staters are widespread in Thrace and the Euxine lands and we know that it was common practice in the fourth century for Athenian traders to change Attic drachmae into Cyzicene staters before entering the Euxine; for some reason the Euxine area preferred electrum.[3] In Athens Cyzicene staters were less popular.

---

[1] H. B. Mattingly, *Hist.* x (1961), 150–69, *CQ* xvi (1966), 188 f., *Ehrenberg Studies*, 202 f.
[2] ML 45; the Bouleutic oath in clause 12.   [3] Dem. xxxiv. 23.

Together with Lampsacene staters they were included in the first year's grant to the commissioners of the Parthenon, but it is significant that they were handed over from board to board each year without being spent;[1] presumably contractors insisted on Attic coin. It has also been thought that there may have been exceptions among the cities who still minted silver, and that the decree would not have applied to the large islands which still contributed fleets. But, however probable it might seem on general grounds that Chios, Samos, and Lesbos should have been treated differently from the rest, the evidence of the decree itself provides no support. The clause to be added to the Bouleutic oath should have been drafted with care, but it makes no allusion to exceptions. The decree in fact seems to apply to silver coinage throughout the empire, and the coins themselves do not disprove this. Lesbos is irrelevant to the issue because she normally minted electrum, and there may be traces of a break at Chios near the middle of the century.[2] For Samos there is more evidence, but its interpretation is better postponed until the date of the decree has been provisionally determined.

Before 1935 the commonly accepted context was between 425 and 414. The lower date was derived from the production in spring 414 of Aristophanes' *Birds*, which includes a parody of the decree;[3] the upper limit rested on the conviction that the decree showed the same high-handed imperialism as the assessment of 425, and is not likely to have been carried by the Assembly before Cleon's triumph at Sphacteria. These arguments still weigh considerably with some scholars, but we have more evidence now than was available when this dating became orthodox doctrine. In 1935 the Italians discovered on the island of Cos a new fragment of the decree which was inscribed in Attic, not the local Doric letters, and was reported to be on Pentelic marble from Attica.[4] The natural explanation of the anomaly seemed to be that the inscription was cut in Athens, and this could be accounted for by a clause in the decree which said that when an allied city refused to set up the decree publicly the Athenians would do it for them.[5] If the inscription was cut

---

[1] *IG* i². 339–53, with ML 59.
[2] J. Boardman, *BSA* liii–liv (1958–9), 308 n. 23.
[3] *Birds* 1040–2, see App. 17, p. 581.
[4] M. Segre, *Clara Rhodos* ix (1938), 151–78.   [5] Clause 10.

in Athens it could be compared with a long series of Athenian inscriptions, many of which are precisely dated, and since the Cos fragment uses the earlier form of sigma with three bars (𐅃) it could be dated before 445, by which time, so far as our present evidence goes, this form was obsolete.[1]

Segré, who first published the new fragment, did not hesitate to date the Coinage Decree to the early forties, and he was followed by Meritt and others. The coins themselves might be expected to provide the decisive control, but it may be doubted whether the dating of fifth-century coins is securely enough established to trace the closing of mints without a considerable margin of error. It may be a tribute to the security provided by Athenian sea power that so few hoards of fifth-century coins have been found, but it is a great handicap to the numismatist and historian; when coin hoards fail we are dependent on criteria of style and these can easily lead astray. Such descriptions as 'mature Parthenon style' have done more harm than good. The available evidence has been summarized by Robinson, who finds it consistent with a date for the decree in the early forties;[2] and it is interesting to note that already in 1912 Weil and Gardner were inclining towards the same approximate dating.[3] The main champions of a much later date have been historians and not numismatists.[4]

A new element was introduced into the argument when Professor Georgiades, who holds the Chair of Mineralogy in the University of Athens and has an unrivalled experience of Pentelic marble, demonstrated that the marble of the Cos fragment was not Pentelic but probably Parian. Professor Pritchett, at whose suggestion the stone had been examined, concluded that the stone must have been cut on Cos and not at Athens.[5] Island marbles are particularly difficult to identify and the Parian origin cannot yet be regarded as certain, but we should, provisionally at least, assume that the marble did not come from

[1] Meiggs, op. cit. 92 f.

[2] E. S. G. Robinson, Hesp. Suppl. viii (1949), 324–40.

[3] P. Gardner, JHS xxxiii (1913), 147–88; R. Weil, Zeitschrift für Num. xxv (1910), 52–62.

[4] Cavaignac, Rev. Num. xv (1953), 1–7; Tod, JHS lxix (1949), 105; H. B. Mattingly, Hist. x (1961), 148–69; CQ xvi (1966), 187–90; Ehrenberg Studies, 193–207.

[5] A. Georgiades and W. K. Pritchett, BCH lxxxix (1965), 400–40.

Attica. The inference that it must have been cut on Cos, though not certain, is highly probable, but the Attic script and the three-bar sigma still have to be explained. Pritchett suggests that they could be attributed to an Athenian mason who left Athens for Cos in the early forties, and came out of retirement to cut the decree, using the letters to which he had been accustomed when he left Athens.[1] This is surely stretching coincidence too far, especially when, apart from the early sigma, the letters cannot be regarded as old-fashioned. It is more probable that the mason was an Athenian sent from Athens to Cos, and probably other cities where the local authorities were proving stubborn. That Cos was giving trouble in the early forties is suggested by the tribute lists also. No figure is preserved for the first period, but in 449 she pays in two instalments; in 447 her payment is incomplete and in 446 she makes three separate payments. It looks from the figures as if she has been assessed by Athens to pay 5 talents and is trying to establish a lower assessment of 3 t. 3,360 dr. No payment is preserved from 445 to 443 but after 443 she seems to pay 5 talents regularly.[2] A somewhat similar pattern may be seen at Tenedos, whose assessment in the first period was $4\frac{1}{2}$ talents. In 445 and through the second period she seems to claim a reduction to 2 t. 5,280 dr. but, like Cos, she is made to pay the balance. Through the third period (445–443) the assessment is still $4\frac{1}{2}$ t. but in the assessment of 443 it is lowered to 2 t. 5,280 dr.

If the Coinage Decree is to be dated in the early forties the coinage of Samos assumes interesting significance. At some time in the fifth century the Samians issued a series of coins marked by letters, each of which probably represented a year's issue. These lettered coins have generally been dated a little after the crushing of the Samian revolt in 439, but Barron has shown, through a detailed examination of die-sequences, that a date near the middle of the century is much more probable for their

---

[1] Pritchett, *BCH* lxxxvii (1963), 20–3.

[2] See Register, *ATL* i. 326 and Meiggs, *Harv. Stud.* lxvii (1963) p. 35 n. 88. In that article (p. 21) I followed the orthodox view that Coan coins, with a Diskobolos on the obverse, were struck after 450 on the Attic standard. I suggested that they might be festival coins allowed by Athens as a special concession. Barron has now shown (*Essays in Greek Coinage presented to Stanley Robinson*, 75–88) that they are triple sigloi on the Persian standard. If they continue beyond 450, which is uncertain, they will represent the hostility to Athens that is reflected in the tribute lists.

introduction, and that if historical considerations are also taken into account the period from 454 to 440 seems to fit the evidence best.[1] Barron sees in the change of coin-type a change of government from democracy to oligarchy which persisted until the revolt. If Samian oligarchs continued to mint coins freely through the forties either they were defying the Coinage Decree or the decree must be dated later. We follow Barron in retaining the early date for the decree and believing that when the oligarchs took power, probably as a result of the Egyptian disaster, they proceeded to pursue an independent policy without openly breaking with Athens.

To many, however, the early date for the Coinage Decree is unacceptable. Their objections cannot be answered by pointing to the Clinias Decree or the Panathenaic Decree to which it refers for, as has been seen, the date of the Clinias Decree itself is uncertain. There is, however, further important evidence in the inscriptions of the period. A different language is used to describe the League. In the decree concerning Erythrae from the fifties the league is called a ξυμμαχίς; in two decrees which have the early sigma and are therefore to be placed before 445 the language is very different:[2] the allies are 'the cities which Athens rules', πόλες ὁπόσον Ἀθεναῖοι κρατῶσι. This is not a temporary change, it marks an open acknowledgement of empire, which is also reflected in Thucydides.

These two decrees are the earliest survivors of a long series offering special protection to friends of Athens in the cities of the empire.[3] Among the privileges given to a favoured *proxenos* is the safeguard that anyone who kills him shall be liable to the same penalty as one who kills an Athenian, and a collective fine of 5 talents is to be paid by the city.[4] Though the clause putting the killing of a *proxenos* on the same level as that of an Athenian frequently recurs, the collective fine, alluded to also much later in Aristophanes' *Peace* of 421, is explicitly recorded in only one surviving inscription.[5] This

---

[1] J. P. Barron, *The Silver Coins of Samos*, 59–67, 80–93.

[2] *IG* i². 27, 28a (Hill, *Sources*² B 34, 33) dated before 445 by the three-bar sigma, Meiggs, op. cit. 94; see also Endnote 12, p. 425.

[3] Meiggs, *CR* lxiii (1949), 9–12.

[4] *IG* i². 28a; *IG* ii². 38; Ar. *Peace* 164–72: P. Roussel, *REA* xxxv (1933), 383–5; Meiggs, loc. cit.

[5] *IG* i². 28a (Hill, *Sources*² B 33).

inscription should probably be dated after 450, because the language of empire is explicit, 'the cities which Athens controls', and almost certainly before 445 in view of its three-bar sigma. There may be found earlier inscriptions in the series, but until they are found the most reasonable historical interpretation is that in the early forties Athens became alarmed by the danger to Athenian citizens in the cities of the empire, and took drastic steps to protect them by adopting the principle of collective responsibility. A city that would have to pay 5 talents, as large a sum as the annual tribute of many cities, if an Athenian was killed in its territory, would attempt to tighten up its security measures. And since *proxenoi* were pro-Athenian and could be regarded by their fellow citizens as traitors, their killing was, in some cases, covered by the same penalties. These decrees are evidence both of the reaction against Athens in the Aegean after the Peace of Callias and of the uncompromising response by Athens. There is no need to hesitate in placing the Coinage Decree where the evidence of the Cos fragment seems to place it, soon after the Peace of Callias.

The language of the Coinage Decree is very similar to that of the Clinias Decree. It issues sharp instructions, and Athenian officers overseas are to take the lead in seeing that they are carried out. There is no suggestion that Athens is thinking primarily of the good of the allies and that Attic coinage is being imposed on them all for their own economic benefit. The language leaves little doubt that the main interest is that of Athens; there is not the slightest hint that the allies have been consulted and the free threat of penalties seems to anticipate resistance. Perhaps Athens had various objects in mind. Uniformity of coinage over most of the Aegean would facilitate trade, and as Athens was the dominant trader she stood to gain most from the change. She would also presumably attract more trade to the Piraeus, since Athens would in future exercise a monopoly in the issue of silver coinage, and cities and merchants who needed more coinage would find it convenient to bring goods to Athens to convert into Attic coins. Athens would also benefit when the tribute was paid only in Attic coin, apart perhaps from electrum staters; now that the principle had been decided to use League money for Athenian purposes most of the tribute would be spent in Athens, or at any rate paid to Athenians. We may also suspect that Athens was not thinking only in economic terms. The common Athenian coinage, together with the common obligations to the Great Panathenaea expressed the change from a Delian League to an Athenian Empire.

In this reconstruction the Peace of Callias occupies a crucial position. In the seventies and sixties, Athens had won an increasing dominance in the League, and was already using League resources for her own ends, notably in crushing Thasian economic competition and in fighting Sparta and her allies. But she was still intermittently fighting Persia and the language was still the language of a free alliance. The Peace of Callias faced Athens with the alternative of allowing the League to lapse or controlling it directly and explicitly. Athens decided that to remain great she must still command the resources of the League, but she no longer made any pretence about its nature. By a series of bold decisions she made it abundantly clear that henceforward she would rule an empire. It was her Assembly and not the meeting of allies that sanctioned the use of League funds for purely Athenian purposes, imposed Athenian coins, weights, and measures on the allies, and made of the Great Panathenaea an empire festival. We may doubt whether any League meetings were held after the peace.[1] The language of her imperial decrees is sharp and uncompromising, and there is little evidence of the velvet glove. The allies' reaction

[1] A. H. M. Jones (*Proc. Camb. Phil. Ass.* ii. (1954) 45) infers from Thuc. iii. 11. 3–4 with iii. 10 that there was a League meeting at the time of the Samian revolt. The Mytilenaeans at Olympia justify their revolt by the reduction of Athens' allies to subjects until only they and the Chians were left. They were left free only to make Athenian actions look more respectable. If Chios and Lesbos who had an equal voice with her served with Athens when she suppressed revolts there must, it would seem, be some justification. Having an equal vote implies a procedure for using the vote which in turn implies a meeting to take a vote before Chios and Lesbos were asked to support Athens in crushing Samos.

The difficulty of accepting Jones's inference is that we hear nothing in Thucydides or any other source of a League meeting so late. If a meeting had been called when Samos revolted there seems no good reason why a meeting should not have been called in 432 when the Peloponnesian War was clearly imminent. Thucydides was particularly careful to record in detail the steps that led to war; if a League meeting, however formal, had been part of the procedure he should have mentioned it; we should also have expected a stray reference or two in comedy. It is more probable that Thucydides has here lacked precision. He has in mind the long series of revolts which started with Naxos in the sixties and is using the specific term ἰσόψηφοι for the whole period, though it did not strictly apply when Samos revolted. The most likely context for the abandonment of League meetings is the reorientation that followed the Peace of Callias.

to the peace had less resolution because it had less unity. There was widespread disaffection illustrated in the quota lists, in a surviving list of Athenian casualties, and in the special measures taken to protect Athenian lives. But the allies did not act in unison and Athens had already evolved the means of restoring and maintaining order. If she had not built up a network of Athenian officers in the empire, as political residents, garrison commanders, and travelling commissioners, she would have found it much more difficult to weather the storm. Her success is reflected in the long quota list of 446, which seemed to indicate that after a temporary crisis she was once again secure. So it may have seemed in the early summer of 446.

10

THE THIRTY YEARS' PEACE

D URING the critical years that followed the Peace of
Callias Athens was able, with little interruption, to concentrate on the control of her allies in the Aegean; in
Greece she was protected by the Five Years' Truce which Cimon
had negotiated with Sparta early in 451. As Athens made her
imperial policy explicit there must have been at least a growth
of anti-Athenian feeling in the Peloponnese and in central
Greece, but the only action recorded is the so-called Sacred
War. Sparta intervened in 449 to restore Delphi, then under
Phocian control, to the Delphians.[1] Perhaps she intended to
show that although she would not attend a congress which might
enable Athens to make political capital out of religious issues,
she was still the champion of the most panhellenic religious
centre in Greece. Delphi's prestige had declined after the Persian wars, but the favour of Delphic Apollo was still politically
valuable. When Sparta had proposed to eject Medizers from
the Amphictyonic Council Themistocles had successfully led the
opposition;[2] he realized that this would give Sparta control of
a potentially useful instrument. When Athens after Oenophyta
secured control of central Greece she had made an alliance
with the Amphictyonic League.[3] So long as Athens dominated
Boeotia and Phocis, Delphi was more accessible to her than to
Sparta and she reacted strongly to Spartan interference. In the
same summer she placed Delphi again under the 'protection' of
Phocis.[4] But when Athens, by her defeat at Coronea, lost control
of central Greece her influence at Delphi weakened. At the

---

[1] Thuc. i. 112. 5.   [2] Plut. *Them.* 20. 3–4.
[3] *IG* i². 26; Meritt *AJP* lxix (1948), 312 f., with further revision lxxv (1954),
369–76. The decree recording the alliance is undated, but the three-bar sigma indicates a date before 445. It was only after Oenophyta that Athens was strong
enough to secure the alliance. See Endnote 6, p. 418, for M. Sordi's view that
the alliance preceded the battle of Tanagra.
[4] For the date, see Endnote 10, p. 423.

outbreak of the Peloponnesian War the Peloponnesians felt, with some justice, that they could rely on Delphi.

In the early spring of 446, Athens' position seemed to be stronger than ever; in the next six months she was in more critical danger than at any time since 479. The victory of Oenophyta had broken the Boeotian confederacy and, though Thebes herself was not taken, the rest of Boeotia came under Athenian control. Since the main danger to Athens was the formidable hoplite army of a united Boeotia, she made it her policy to encourage the appetite for independence in the cities. The federal coinage was replaced by individual issues of the various cities and political power was probably at first held by anti-federal leaders, among the aristocracies.[1] But this opportunist experiment seems to have failed and by 446 most of the Boeotian cities were probably democratic; there were certainly a large number of Boeotian oligarchs in exile. The Thebans, defending, after the capture of Plataea, their policy through the century, are made by Thucydides to declare that *stasis* was to blame for the weakness of Boeotia at this time.[2] Another reason why Athenian control could be maintained was that it was not too openly emphasized. The evidence suggests that no tribute was demanded; the cities were merely required to accept the commitments of Athenian foreign policy and send contingents when needed.[3] But the maintenance of Athenian control demanded the expulsion of leading men who would not co-operate. By 446 the number of Boeotian exiles had swollen considerably and they were not alone; anti-Athenian feeling had been mounting also in Euboea and throughout central Greece.

The first news of the growing danger to be received at Athens was that exiles were in possession of Chaeronea and Orchomenus. Quick action was needed and Tolmides was appointed to the command. He took a small force of only 1,000 Athenians and some allies, and later tradition said that he was warned by Pericles not to be rash.[4] This may be the invention of fourth-century rhetoric, but it seems clear that Tolmides did not expect serious trouble. He had little difficulty in restoring control at Chaeronea; the population was enslaved and an Athenian

[1] Head, *Coinage of Boeotia*, 25–9. For the political situation, see pp. 209 f.
[2] Thuc. iii. 62. 5.   [3] Thuc. i. 111. 1.
[4] Thuc. i. 113; Diod. xii. 6; Plut. *Per.* 18. 2–3.

garrison installed. But on his way home Tolmides was surprised at Coronea by a strong body of exiles from Orchomenus supported by Locrians, Euboeans, and others. The result was decisive defeat and the death of Tolmides. To save the remnants of their troops and recover prisoners the Athenians had to undertake not to interfere further in the affairs of Boeotia.[1]

The news of Coronea encouraged feelings that were already strong against Athens. Euboean exiles had fought against Athens at Coronea; they now succeeded in rousing most of their island to revolt. Pericles was appointed to command a large army, but soon after he had landed his troops in Euboea news came to Athens that most of her garrison at Megara had been massacred.[2] Megara had appealed to Athens in 461 for protection against Corinth, and Athens had gladly accepted the alliance; for Megara's port of Nisaea on the Saronic Gulf commanded the easiest route for a Peloponnesian army invading Attica and Pegae was a useful harbour on the Corinthian Gulf. When Myronides had defeated the Corinthian army with only the Athenian reserves of young and old, Corinth made no further major attack and the lessening of tension probably set up a reaction in Megara against the Athenian alliance. For it was soon clear that the Athenians were not disinterested in offering their protection. In building long walls from Megara to Nisaea their purpose was to block the route of a Peloponnesian army; before the battle of Tanagra they had sent a fleet round the Peloponnese to attack the Spartan army operating in Doris if it attempted to return across the gulf. The garrison that was massacred in 446 had probably been stationed in Megara soon after the alliance was made.

The news of the massacre led to the immediate recall of Pericles and his army from Euboea, and it seems that three of the ten tribal contingents were sent to Pegae; for an inscription from Athens records how Pythion, a Megarian, led 2,000 men from the tribes Pandionis, Cecropis, and Antiochis from Pegae through Boeotia to Athens. The inscription is not dated, but the circumstances fit the context of 446 and the Athenians were commanded by Andocides; he was probably the orator's grandfather, who served soon afterwards on the embassy which negotiated peace terms with Sparta, and was general again in 440.[3]

---

[1] Thuc. i. 113. 3–4.   [2] Thuc. i. 114. 1.   [3] *IG* i². 1085; ML 51.

It may have been the arrival at the isthmus of a large Peloponnesian army that caused the hasty withdrawal of Andocides from Pegae. It is at least possible that the revolt of Megara was encouraged by Sparta; it is certain that a large army under King Pleistoanax had soon crossed the border into Attica. The Peloponnesian army advanced as far as Eleusis and Thria; the Athenians took up a defensive position, prepared if necessary to give battle. But the battle was not fought; the Peloponnesian army returned to the Peloponnese, and though peace negotiations continued into the winter of 446–445, the general lines of the settlement had presumably been agreed before Pleistoanax withdrew. This withdrawal needs explanation, for never since 510 had the Spartans apparently been in a better position to dictate terms. The exile of Pleistoanax and of his chief adviser, Cleandridas, suggests serious division in Sparta on the policy to be pursued towards Athens.[1] The Athenians had more cause to be pleased. Plutarch preserves a tradition that Pericles had bribed the Spartans to withdraw and assigned the expenditure at his audit to 'state needs'.[2]

The withdrawal of the Peloponnesians released the Athenian army to return to the conquest of Euboea. Of the details of the fighting we know nothing, but one of the best-preserved inscriptions of the century reveals some of the terms of settlement with Chalcis, and various literary sources add a little. According to Thucydides Athens insisted on unconditional surrender at Hestiaea alone; with the other cities terms were negotiated.[3] Hestiaea was made an example because an Athenian crew had been killed there; the population was expelled and 1,000 Athenians were settled in their territory.[4] Chalcis and Eretria were also treated with severity and, though technically the terms were based on agreements, the agreements were in fact dictated by Athens. Plutarch says only that at Chalcis the Hippobotae

---

[1] Exile of Pleistoanax, Thuc. ii. 21. 1. Plutarch (*Per.* 22. 3) has the unlikely variant that the king was fined, but could not pay and so left Sparta. Cleandridas was the young king's adviser. According to Plutarch he was bribed by Pericles, and condemned to death in absence.

[2] Plut. *Per.* 23. 1.

[3] Thuc. i. 114. 3: τὴν μὲν ἄλλην ὁμολογίᾳ κατεστήσαντο.

[4] Thuc. i. 114. 3; Plut. *Per.* 23. 4. Diod. xii. 22. 2 gives 1,000 settlers, Theopompus, *FGH* 115 F 387 (Strabo x. 1. 3, 445), 2,000. The former is perhaps more probable, corresponding with the number sent to the Chersonese, the Bisaltae (= ? Brea), and possibly to Naxos with Andros and Carystus (see p. 122).

were expelled; the decree gives a much more detailed picture.[1]
It begins with an oath to be taken by the Athenian Boule and
dikasts. Military law is to be ended; no capital punishment will
be imposed without trial; the Chalcidians will not be expelled;
Chalcis will not be razed to the ground; the Chalcidians may
state their case before the Athenian people. More significant
is the oath which all Chalcidians of military age are required
to take. It follows the pattern of the Erythraean and Colophonian oaths but is more rigid and more detailed. The oath of
loyalty is taken to the Athenians alone and not even lip service
is paid to the allies. Loyalty must be observed in word and deed,
and the formula is fuller than before. And a new and more
sinister clause is added: 'if anyone stirs up revolt against
Athens I will denounce him'.[2] The revolt had shown that
Athens needed additional safeguards, but this clause is likely to
have encouraged denunciations and led to increasing bitterness
in local party politics. The Chalcidians are also required to send
help to the demos of Athens if it is attacked. No such clause was
included in the Erythraean and Colophonian oaths, but in the
regulations for Miletus of 450–49 a series of clauses, not forming part of an oath, seem to provide in some detail for military
service and to specify the rate of pay.[3] When the Peloponnesian
War breaks out Chalcis with other allies could be called upon
to implement this clause and Milesian contingents are often
recorded. Another clause, now found for the first time, concerns
the tribute. Irregularity in tribute payment had been a serious
problem in the forties. Chalcis has to undertake to pay tribute
regularly, but a qualification is added: 'I will pay such tribute
as I can persuade the Athenians (to impose).'[4] The clause may
look generally to the future or may be primarily concerned with
the reassessment that must follow the revolt. On this occasion
and at future assessments she will be able to state her case and
presumably appeal to an Athenian law-court. Such was the
procedure stipulated in the assessment decree of 425, when
Athenian assessors fixed the assessments provisionally, and the
allies were allowed to appeal to a specially empanelled jury

---

[1] Plut. *Per.* 23. 4; ML 52.
[2] ML 52. 25: ἐὰν ἀφιστῆι τις κατερῶ Ἀθηναίοισι. For full texts of the oaths, App.
16, pp. 578 f.
[3] D 11. ? 8 ff.
[4] ML 52. 25–7: κ|αὶ τὸν φόρον ὑποτελῶ Ἀθεναίοισιν, hὸν | ἂν πείθο Ἀθεναῖος.

court; the final word, however, lay with Athens. The oath ends with a promise of obedience to the Athenian demos.[1] There is no question of joint consultation; Athens will determine policy.

The oath is followed on the stone by a second decree which presupposes pleas made by a Chalcidian embassy in the Assembly for concessions in the terms imposed by Athens, and probably recorded on a separate stele which was originally affixed to the preserved stele.[2] The Chalcidians appealed on three points: for the right to change their hostages, for the right to tax all foreigners in their territory, and for the independence of their law-courts. The Athenian answers are polite but firm; no significant concessions are made. 'In the matter of the hostages the Athenians think it better that for the present the decisions taken by vote should stand, but when they think it right they will make arrangements for the exchange with the Chalcidians.'[3] 'The Chalcidians may tax any other foreigners in their territory but not those who pay dues to Athens or have been exempted from dues by Athens.' This clause has often been taken to refer to cleruchs settled on the Lelantine plain, but in an Athenian decree Athenian cleruchs would not be called ξένοι. It is probable that land belonging to oligarchs was confiscated by Athens, but not settled with Athenians.[4]

This clause marks the end of the original decree but an amendment is added which might represent an addition to or perhaps a correction of what was originally proposed: 'Chalcidians shall impose penalties on Chalcidians at Chalcis in the same way as the Athenians impose their penalties on Athenians at Athens, except in cases involving exile, death, loss of rights; in these cases there shall be *ephesis* to Athens to the Heliaea presided over by the *thesmothetai*.' This clause, whose meaning is disputed, will be discussed later in the general context of jurisdiction in the empire;[5] what is clear is that Athens intends to exercise a strong control over Chalcis through her law-courts and will not make any major change in the decision she has already taken. The amendment ends with an instruction that

[1] ML 52. 31–2: καὶ πείσομαι τôι δέμοι τôι Ἀθ|εναίον.
[2] For the physical factors see the introduction to ML 52.
[3] For the meaning of this clause (ll. 47–52) see ML, p. 142.
[4] For this clause (ll. 53–7) see ML, pp. 142 f. and App. 15, pp. 564–6.
[5] See pp. 224 f.

the generals 'take the best available measures for the security of Euboea in order to maintain Athens' interests'. The gods also are to be appeased. The original decree provided that 'three men with Hierocles shall carry out the sacrifices prescribed by the oracle as quickly as possible'. Thucydides' concentration on the historical core encourages us to forget that oracles were still state business.

The terms of the Chalcis decree have been described as fair and generous; this is to be misled by the politeness of the language. Chalcis has been punished severely and no important concessions are made. During the revolt the generals in the field have superseded the courts; martial law is now ended. Chalcidians who give trouble will still lose their lives or property, but only after a fair trial. Eretria seems to have received similar treatment; part of her oath survives and it closely follows that of Chalcis, as the Chalcis decree itself implies.[1] Reference is also preserved to a decree of 442–441 which required 'that a list should be made of Eretrian hostages, sons of the wealthiest citizens'.[2] The natural meaning is that the hostages were taken in this year and not that a list of hostages taken in 446–445 was to be inscribed in 442–441. The hostages may have been taken some three years after the end of the revolt as a result of continuing suspicion, and it is possible that at this time or in 445 a small colony was sent out.[3] What happened to the towns other than Hestiaea, Chalcis, and Eretria we do not know; we should particularly like to know the attitude of Carystus in and after the revolt.

The precise chronology of the year 446 cannot be determined. It is probable, as we have seen, that at the time of the Dionysia in early spring, when the tribute was brought, there had been no serious trouble. In the summer events moved very fast. The Spartans probably invaded in May when the corn was vulnerable, and by the end of July Euboea may have been reduced. The crisis will therefore have been over by the time of the Great Panathenaea in August when a new assessment was due, and though the details of the peace that was to be made with the Peloponnesians still had to be negotiated the main terms were

---

[1] ll. 41–3: ποέσθαι τὸν hόρκον Ἀθεναίος καὶ Χαλ|κιδέας, καθάπερ Ἐρετριεῦσι ἐφσεφίσατ|ο hο δêμος. For the Eretrian oath, D 16.

[2] Hesychius s.v. Ἐρετριακὸς κατάλογος.   [3] See App. 15, p. 568.

probably agreed before the Spartans withdrew from Eleusis. The assessment of 446 shows considerably more changes than that of 450 and the pattern is more uniform. In 450 five states had their tribute increased; twenty-one tributes were reduced; in 446 there were only three increases and as many as thirty reductions. Some of the reductions may be explained by special circumstances, such as the taking of land for Athenian settlers, but there was clearly a general tendency to lower tributes in 446.[1] This should be interpreted politically as an attempt to recover favour in the empire by concessions. It is significant that several of the tributes which were now reduced were raised again to the pre-446 figure in the thirties.[2]

Though the general principles governing the settlement must have been agreed before the Spartans left Attica the final formulation of the clauses had to be negotiated and peace terms had to be ratified by the Peloponnesian League and by the Assembly at Athens. The Athenian representatives included Callias and Andocides. Callias had been closely associated with Aristides and Cimon but by the early forties at the latest he was prepared to accept Periclean policies; his family remained loyal and prominent in the democracy. He could, however, be acceptable at Sparta, for his father had been a Spartan *proxenos*.[3] Andocides came from the same social class but he and his family also seem to have realized that the future lay with democracy.[4] The settlement that Callias and his colleagues drew up with the Spartans was remarkably favourable to Athens. Boeotia and Megara had already been lost, but Troezen and Achaea were still linked to Athens by treaty. These outposts in the Peloponnese Athens had to surrender, but this cannot seriously have disturbed her. Outposts in the Peloponnese were of value to Athens only if she intended an offensive against Sparta; now that Megara had returned to the Peloponnesian League and opened again the route into Attica, the policies of the fifties were out of date. Nor could Athens act effectively in the Peloponnese without an alliance with Argos, and already by the end of 451 Argos had made a thirty years' peace with Sparta. It was much more important that Athens did not have to surrender Aegina.

---

[1] For the details see App. 12, p. 526. [2] See p. 528.
[3] For Callias see p. 145. [4] *PA* 827.

This old rival of Athens had been a member of the Peloponnesian League, and a Peloponnesian force had tried to save her when she was besieged by Athens; but Aegina had eventually surrendered and had been forced to become a member of the Delian League. In the late fifties she was paying the high annual tribute of 30 talents, but the quota lists of the second period suggest that she had not finally accepted her humiliation. In 449 her recorded payment is incomplete; she is probably absent from the list of 447.[1] Perhaps she was adding her protest to the general discontent and hoping to regain her freedom in the disintegration of the empire. In 446 an Aeginetan, Aristomenes, won the prize for wrestling at Delphi and Pindar sang his praises.[2] It may be significant that he begins his ode with an invocation to the spirit of *Hesychia*, daughter of *Dike*, that makes cities great. Peace with calm was a quality that Athens conspicuously lacked, and when Pindar proceeds to the triumph of peace over violence it is difficult not to think of Athenian imperialism.[3] No clear allusion is made to Aegina's recent humiliation but she is 'the island where justice reigns'; if it would be tactless to mention her present troubles her proud early record can be remembered. The ode ends somewhat abruptly: 'Aegina, dear mother, in freedom guide this city with Zeus, and King Aeacus, and Peleus and good Telamon and Achilles.'[4] If Pindar was hoping that Aegina would secure her freedom in the peace that was being negotiated he was disappointed. For the sake of peace Sparta was prepared to sacrifice her former ally, but she hoped to salve her conscience by insisting on a guarantee that Athens would not interfere in Aegina's internal affairs. In 432, Thucydides tells us, the Aeginetans were among those who pressed most strongly for war against Athens, though they dare not come out into the open: 'they complained that they were not autonomous as the terms of the peace required'.[5] Autonomy is an ambiguous term, but it could be defined. When in 412 the Samian democrats rose successfully against the oligarchs who were appealing for Spartan intervention Thucydides tells us that the Athenians resolved by vote of

---

[1] For Aegina's tribute record see *ATL* i. 218.   [2] Pindar, *Pyth* viii.
[3] Wade-Gery, *Essays in Greek History*, 251 f. (*JHS* lii (1932), 214 f.).
[4] ll. 140–2. Αἴγινα φίλα μᾶτερ, ἐλευθέρῳ στόλῳ | πόλιν τάνδε κόμιζε Δὶ καὶ κρέοντι σὺν Αἰακῷ | Πηλεῖ τε κἀγαθῷ Τελαμῶνι σύν τ' Ἀχιλλεῖ.
[5] Thuc. i. 67. 2: Αἰγινῆται . . . λέγοντες οὐκ εἶναι αὐτόνομοι κατὰ τὰς σπονδάς.

the Assembly to give Samos autonomy; an inscription is preserved showing that the meaning of this autonomy was publicly expressed in a formal decree.[1] The precise formulation is lost but the main emphasis seems to be on the independence of the Samian courts. We may assume that so long as Aegina paid her tribute regularly she would not be required to send her most important trials to Athenian courts, nor be subjected to an Athenian garrison or political resident.

It is tempting also to believe that Aegina was now, as a special privilege reflecting her autonomy, allowed to mint her own coinage. In the early fifth century she was still using the turtle as her type and minting on a large scale as if she were consciously struggling against Athenian economic dominance. At some point the type was changed; the sea turtle was replaced by the land tortoise. Until recently it was generally inferred that the break occurred when Aegina surrendered to Athens in the early fifties and that her mint, closed then by Athens, was not reopened until Aegina was liberated and her expelled population restored at the end of the Peloponnesian War. But the discovery of an Aeginetan tortoise overstruck by a Phoenician dynast of Citium who is securely dated before the end of the fifth century demands the redating of the change in Aegina.[2] Historically the most attractive hypothesis is that the Aeginetan mint, closed when Aegina surrendered, was reopened when her autonomy was guaranteed. The numismatic evidence, however, slightly favours the continuation of minting after the surrender.[3]

While Sparta probably made a gesture on behalf of Aegina she did not impose any general conditions on Athens' control of her empire. Sparta's final demand before war broke out in 431 was that the Athenians should give back to the allies their autonomy, but Pericles could reply: 'We will give back their autonomy to the allies if they were autonomous when we made peace.'[4] Sparta in fact recognized the Athenian Empire and her

---

[1] Thuc. viii. 21; *IG* i². 101 with Lewis, *BSA* xlix (1954), 29–31.

[2] E. S. G. Robinson, *Num. Chron.* i (1961), 111. For the earlier view, Head, *Hist. Num.*² 377.

[3] P. Rajo, *Riv. Num.* lxv (1963), 7–15, argues from the large quantity of first-style tortoises, and the strong resemblance of the early tortoises to the latest turtles, that Athens allowed Aegina to reopen her mint soon after the conquest, but with a type demonstrating that she was no longer a sea power.

[4] Thuc. i. 144. 2: τὰς δὲ πόλεις ὅτι αὐτονόμους ἀφήσομεν, εἰ καὶ αὐτονόμους ἔχοντες ἐσπεισάμεθα.

later claim to be the great liberator rings hollow. But while the Athenian Empire was recognized there was to be no repetition of what happened in 460. Athens must not accept into alliance any member of the Peloponnesian League or their allies. The lesson of Megara had been learnt.

The evidence of the years immediately following the peace is pitifully lean, and there is no hope of recovering in detail the changes in mood of the Athenian Assembly. It might be thought that the peace which recognized the collapse of the land empire would have discredited Pericles, but when the crucial test came less than three years later it was his rival, Thucydides son of Melesias, who was ostracized. It may have been Myronides and Tolmides who were primarily associated with the expansion of Athenian conquest by land, and when in 446 the Peloponnesian army invaded Attica it was Pericles' leadership which saved Athens. The main policies with which he is credited in the sources are the consolidation of radical democracy and the maintenance of the Athenian Aegean Empire; in both these spheres he had been conspicuously successful. But the opposition persisted.

In 446–445 Athens seized an opportunity to feed her ambition in a different direction. The Sybarites, returning to the home from which they had been expelled by Croton in 510, ran into difficulties and appealed to the two major powers in Greece to stiffen their numbers. Sparta declined but the Athenians sent a small body of citizens to swell the Sybarite army. Relations between the two elements became strained, the Sybarites were once again driven out and by 443 Athens had decided to found a completely new settlement on a new site with a new name, Thurii.[1] This was to be a large foundation: it was to be open to all Greeks, under Athenian leadership, and its cosmopolitan nature was emphasized by the choice of non-Athenians to play a leading part in the venture. Protagoras of Abdera who had been first attracted to Athens in the fifties was to draw up the code of laws; Hippodamus who had remodelled the Piraeus was to design the town plan; the historian Herodotus of Halicarnassus also chose to go.[2] It has been suggested that

---

[1] The sources for the foundation of Thurii, Hill *Sources*[2], 345.

[2] Protagoras, Diog. Laert. ix. 8. 10; Hippodamus, Hesychius s.v. Ἱπποδάμου νέμησις; Herodotus, *Suda* s.v. Ἡρόδοτος.

in this sequence of decisions Athens spoke with two voices, that
Pericles was intending to press Athenian interests in the west
whenever opportunity offered, even at the cost of provoking
Corinth, but that his plans for Thurii were disturbed at the last
moment by Thucydides son of Melesias. Whereas Pericles had
originally intended an Athenian colony Thucydides was able
at the last stage to persuade the Assembly to make Thurii panhellenic.[1] The scraps of evidence on which this hypothesis
is hung are not convincing; in itself it seems unlikely. If
Thucydides had been strong enough to change the character of
the enterprise he surely could not have left the Periclean oecists,
Xenocritus and Lampon, in charge. The Pan-Hellenism was
deliberate, but probably not very high-minded. Athenian manpower could not have stood the strain of losing the 10,000 or
more men who were needed to give life to Thurii and, if the
majority had to come from outside Athens, there was little to
choose between allies, many of whom had recently been hostile,
and other Greeks. The gesture would look well in the after-glow
of the peace of 446–445, and Athens could be confident that
Spartans and Corinthians would not enrol in sufficient numbers
to be dangerous. The reasonable expectation was that the
majority of the colonists would be men living precariously on
marginal land in Arcadia and the other poorer parts of Greece.
Among these there would be no natural unity; Athenian leadership and a compact nucleus of Athenians, concentrated in an
all-Athenian tribe, should be sufficient to make Thurii in every
sense that mattered Athenian. It is doubtful whether Pericles
was thinking primarily in economic terms; his main concern
was more probably to raise the prestige and general influence
of Athens in the west.[2]

It is unlikely that the foundation of Thurii was the crucial
issue which resulted in the ostracism of Thucydides in 443, and
the attack on Pericles for using the allies' money on an Athenian
building programme must have lost such sting as it had when
first adopted. Plutarch alone suggests a new area of conflict, and
he is not necessarily wrong. In his *Pericles* he says that in the
final stages of the political struggle between the two leaders
Thucydides denounced the extravagance of Pericles. He was

---

[1] Wade-Gery, *Essays*, 256–8.
[2] Ehrenberg, *AJP* lxix (1948), 149–70.

'wasting the reserves and consuming the revenues'.[1] This makes sense. The Parthenon and the chryselephantine statue of Athena were not the only expensive works of the forties. In the same period there was much new construction in the Piraeus, and new temples were built on the hill of Colonus above the Agora, at Sunium, and perhaps at Rhamnus.[2] A fragment from a comedy of Cratinus, the *Thracian Women*, which was probably produced at the time, suggests that the Periclean Odeon was one of the points of attack: 'Here comes squill-headed Zeus with the Odeon on his head, now that the sherd season is securely past.'[3] Such an attack on the management of the state's finances might be reflected in a reorganization of procedure, and perhaps of responsibilities, that seems to have been introduced in the year of the ostracism. The facts that need explanation and might justify such an inference are an extraordinary assessment in 443 which was not normally due until 442, the recording for the first time in the quota list of 442 of the name of an assistant secretary who remains in office for a second year and the recording, again for the first time, of the name of one of the *hellenotamiai*, perhaps the chairman of the board. This looks like reorganization, and it is not accompanied by any change in policy; the assessment of 443 takes over with very few changes indeed the assessment of 446.[4]

The ostracism of Thucydides left Pericles for the first time in his career without a serious rival, and from this point for fifteen years he was elected general every year, with increasing authority. It is probable that he was primarily responsible for shaping Athens' imperial policy in the early forties; it is certain that he more than any other was responsible for the development of the empire in the next ten years. When incidents began to occur in 435 which could lead to war Pericles stiffened the Athenians against compromise or concession. By then he had made up his mind that war with the Peloponnese was inevitable and that Athens would merely weaken herself by attempting to appease Corinth and Sparta. It is likely that this

---

[1] Plut. *Per.* 14. 1 : τῶν δὲ περὶ τὸν Θουκυδίδην ῥητόρων καταβοώντων τοῦ Περικλέους ὡς σπαθῶντος τὰ χρήματα καὶ τὰς προσόδους ἀπολλύντος.

[2] See p. 289.

[3] Plut. *Per.* 13. 10: ὁ σχινοκέφαλος Ζεὺς ὅδε | προσέρχεται, τῷδεῖον ἐπὶ τοῦ κρανίου | ἔχων, ἐπειδὴ τοὔστρακον παροίχεται. For the date see p. 289 n. 3.

[4] See App. 12, p. 526.

was his view before 435 also, but we lack evidence. The strongest single hint is perhaps the building of the middle wall. It was almost certainly carried through in the years shortly following the peace, and it was purposeless if peace was likely to be permanent.[1] To convince the Assembly that the new wall was necessary someone must have argued that defence against the threat from the Peloponnese was still needed. Other evidence also suggests that Athenian imperialism soon recovered from the conciliatory mood of the assessment of 446.

Between 446 and 442 the Milesian oligarchs had carried through a purge of the demos. Athens, while imposing her garrison and political officials in 450–449 had tolerated the Milesian oligarchy, but, if we are right in attributing the late payments of Miletus and her neighbours during the second assessment period to disaffection, the settlement of 450–449 was unsatisfactory from the outset.[2] From 445 to 443 no Milesian payment is preserved on any of the quota list fragments; from 442 she pays regularly and her tribute has been reduced from 10 to 5 talents; it is a natural inference that during the three years following 446 Miletus had broken away from Athens. It is, however, difficult to believe that, after having reduced Euboea and made peace with Sparta, Athens would have allowed Miletus to defy her for as long as three years. Until more evidence comes to light it is better to date the recovery by Athens of Miletus 'between 446 and 442'.[3] With the recovery came almost certainly the establishment of the democracy which is attested in the last phase of the Peloponnesian War.

We may believe that Miletus emerged from these political troubles considerably weakened, and that her new democracy was less congenial to the Samian oligarchy. These factors will help to account for the Samian attempt to enlarge her territory on the mainland at the expense of Priene; but what began as a localized land-grab ended in a major clash with Athens. The

---

[1] Andoc. III. 7; Plato, *Gorgias* 455e with schol. says that Socrates heard the debate in the Assembly. In Plutarch's list of buildings (*Per.* 13. 7–8) the middle wall comes between the Parthenon and the Odeon. There is a possible reflection of the building of the wall in the Parthenon account for 443–442 (*IG* i². 343) in which the commissioners receive money $\pi]\alpha\rho\grave{\alpha}\ \tau\epsilon\iota\chi[\text{o}\pi\text{o}\iota\grave{\text{o}}\nu$ (l. 90).

[2] See p. 164, and App. 15, pp. 562 f.

[3] A more detailed discussion, App. 15, pp. 561 f.

incidents leading up to the revolt of Samos are only very briefly recorded by Thucydides. Hostilities broke out between Samos and Miletus, old rivals throughout the archaic period, on the mainland, where Samos like Chios and Lesbos controlled a stretch of the coastline. Samos appears to have been the aggressor and Miletus appealed to Athens.[1] Even if the allies had not sworn to have the same friends and enemies as Athens they had sworn loyalty to Athens and the allies; it could therefore be argued that fighting between members was against the letter as well as the spirit of the Delian League. Samos, however, regarded Athens' intervention as high-handed and continued to fight. At this point the potential seriousness of the situation was not fully realized at Athens. Pericles sailed with forty ships to Samos, imposed a democratic government, took hostages from the oligarchs, sent them for safe keeping to Lemnos, and installed a small Athenian garrison with officers combining military and political duties.[2]

The oligarchs were more determined than Pericles had thought. Many of them had not waited for the Athenians but had escaped to the mainland where they persuaded Pissuthnes, satrap at Sardis, to help them. Reinforced by 700 mercenaries from Pissuthnes they made a surprise descent on Lemnos and rescued their hostages. They then returned to Samos, captured the Athenian officers and troops and left them, embarrassing hostages, with Pissuthnes. For those who do not accept a Peace of Callias the Persian intervention raises no problem. There is, however, no serious difficulty in believing that the satrap was acting without the authority of the Persian king. In Samos the oligarchs resumed control of the government and made their defiance of Athens more explicit by reopening the war against Miletus. Byzantium joined Samos in revolt for reasons which have left no traces in the sources. Her payments had been irregular in the second assessment period and there had been fighting in her territory in or near 447, but she had paid her full tribute in 442 and 441, and in 440, on the eve of revolt, her payment was very nearly complete.[3] But Byzantium may have sympathized

---

[1] See Endnote 14, p. 428.

[2] Thuc. i. 115. 1–3; Plut. *Per.* 25. 1–3; Diod. xii. 27. 1–2.

[3] Byzantium's tribute record, *ATL* i. 250. In 442 and 441 she paid 15 t. 4,300 dr., in 440 15 t. 460 dr.

with the reaction of her mother city Megara against Athens and seen in the revolt of Samos an opportunity that might not recur. The Samian colony of Perinthus, however, apparently remained loyal to Athens.[1]

In describing the prelude to the Peloponnesian War Thucydides makes the Corinthians claim in the Athenian Assembly that they had resisted the proposal to send Peloponnesian help to Samos during the revolt: 'When the vote in the Peloponnesian league concerning help to Samos was divided we did not add our vote against you.'[2] The language is precise and should mean that Sparta formally called a meeting of her allies, and put the issue to a formal vote. Who provided the initiative? The Arcadian states and other smaller members of the League are not likely to have been concerned, and Corinth claims to have opposed action. Megara, whose colony Byzantium had joined Samos, and who may still have resented the recent Athenian occupation, might have agitated, but she alone had not enough authority to move Sparta. It is difficult to believe that a League meeting could have been called had not the majority of Spartans thought or been persuaded to think that if there was adequate support from their allies the Peloponnesians should take military action, whether by sending a fleet to Samos or by invading Attica.[3] That there was a serious risk of Peloponnesian intervention is also suggested by the terms of the settlement which followed the reduction of Samos. In a very fragmentary context near the opening of the decree the Peloponnesians may be mentioned, perhaps a reference to the Samian attempt to involve Sparta and her allies.[4]

The Peloponnesian League decided not to intervene but the Samian oligarchs persisted and the Athenians realized that nothing short of full-scale war was adequate. In the early summer of 440 they sent out a fleet of sixty ships and called on

[1] Tribute of Perinthus, *ATL* i. 374.

[2] Thuc. i. 40. 5: οὐδὲ γὰρ ἡμεῖς Σαμίων ἀποστάντων ψῆφον προσεθέμεθα ἐναντίαν ὑμῖν, τῶν ἄλλων Πελοποννησίων δίχα ἐψηφισμένων.

[3] A. H. M. Jones, *Proc. Camb. Phil. Ass.* ii (1953), 43, infers from the procedure of 432 when Sparta made her own decision before summoning her allies to meet that the Spartan Assembly had voted for war. There is no need to infer more than that Sparta thought that the subject deserved consideration. See App. 3, p. 461.

[4] *IG* i². 50. 12, ML 56: [Πελο]ποννεσ[—. cf. *IG* i². 101, ll. 3–4 (412 B.C.): Σ]|αμίον τὸς ἐπάγοντας Πελοπον|νεσίος ἐπὶ Σάμον.

the Chians and Lesbians to join them at Samos. Soon a further forty ships had come from Athens, and Chios and Lesbos had added twenty-five. The Athenians were now able to land and drive the Samians within their walls, and Pericles felt sufficiently secure to withdraw sixty ships from the blockade. This seemed a necessary precaution because the Samians had made a further appeal to Pissuthnes and a Phoenician fleet might sail into the Aegean. Pericles decided that if the Phoenician ships intended to intervene he would strike first. Stesimbrotus says that he sailed to Cyprus; Thucydides is more convincing in taking him only to Caria.[1] Of the Phoenician ships nothing more is heard. Their refusal to take any advantage of Athenian difficulties considerably weakens the argument against the Peace of Callias based on Pissuthnes' earlier sympathy; for had the Persians wished to reopen hostilities they could not have had a more favourable opportunity. The Samians had taken advantage of Pericles' absence; in a surprise sally they had attacked the Athenian camp, destroyed the ships on guard, and fought off the ships that put out to meet them. For fourteen days they controlled their home waters and built up their supplies, but when Pericles brought his squadron back the blockade was resumed. Further reinforcements now arrived, sixty ships from Athens and a further thirty from Chios and Lesbos, but it had been an ugly shock. Thucydides could even make the Athenians later admit that Samos came very close to taking from Athens the control of the seas.[2]

The Samians were now firmly blockaded but it was more than eight months before they were forced to submit. Various stories were told later illustrating the bitterness of the fighting. The Athenians, it was said, had branded their Samian prisoners with the Attic owl, the Samians had retaliated with the Samaina.[3] The Samian historian Douris went much further; he recorded that the Samian trierarchs and marines were taken to the market-place at Miletus, bound to posts, and left for ten days. By then they were in a distressing condition; Pericles gave orders that they should be taken down and their heads broken

[1] Thuc. i. 116. 3. Plutarch himself (*Per.* 26. 1), 'following the majority', rejects Stesimbrotus.
[2] Thuc. viii. 76. 4.
[3] Photius, s.v. Σαμίων ὁ δῆμος (Douris, *FGH* 76, F 66). Plutarch (*Per.* 26. 4) has reversed the roles and made the Samians brand with the owl.

with clubs; their bodies were to remain exposed, without attention.[1] This is not the kind of story that the kindly Plutarch likes,
and he could easily persuade himself to reject it. Douris had no
respect, he says, for the truth even when he had no personal
cause for bias; where Samos is concerned he cannot be trusted.
'Douris would appear to have made the sufferings of his country
more grim in order to slander Athens.' Plutarch finds confirmation of his suspicions in the silence of Thucydides, Ephorus, and
Aristotle. He is too easily satisfied. The story would have no
place in Thucydides' compressed account which studiously
avoids anecdote and subsidiary detail, nor should we expect to
find it in Aristotle's outline of the Samian constitution; had the
story been true and widely known it had a place in Ephorus'
history, but he was so notoriously partial to Athens that he
would probably have suppressed anything so discreditable.
Douris may have exaggerated, but the substance of the story
rings true. We can believe that Athenian feelings were strongly
aroused; there were probably excesses. It is significant that the
victims of this brutality were not ship's crews, but trierarchs
and marines. The Athenian purpose was to show that they were
fighting Samos to protect the new Milesian democracy from
Samian oligarchs.

Thucydides summarizes the settlement that followed the surrender. The Samians were required to pull down their walls,
give up their fleet, surrender hostages, and repay the expenses
of the war in instalments over a period.[2] The accounts had been
kept and are in large part preserved. They show a total expenditure by the treasurers of Athena of over 1,400 talents, which
is substantially higher than the 1,200 talents of the literary
sources.[3] The generally accepted explanation of the discrepancy
is that the published accounts included payments for operations
against Byzantium. The document may, however, refer to
Samos alone, for we hear of no fighting against Byzantium.
We do not expect understatements by orators and historians
where figures are concerned, but even Thucydides' figure for

---

[1] Plut. *Per.* 28. 2–3 (Douris F 67).

[2] Thuc. i. 117. 3; cf. Plut. *Per.* 28. 1; Diod. xii. 28. 3–4.

[3] *IG* i². 293; ML 55. Nepos, *Timotheus*, 1. 2, gives 1,200 talents. The same figure
can be read, by simple emendations, in Isocrates xv. 111 (ἀπὸ διακοσίων [νεῶν] καὶ
χιλίων ταλάντων) and in Diodorus xii. 28. 3–4 (τιμησάμενος αὐτὰς (sc. δαπάνας)
ταλάντων [χιλίων καὶ] διακοσίων).

the siege of Potidaea was probably too low.[1] The hard fighting and long siege must have heavily strained Samian resources, and it is not surprising that her payments of the debt stretched over a long period. There is a clear reference in a decree of the Archidamian war years, probably 426, and a less certain indication that she was still paying in 414–413. If this evidence is admitted the annual instalments may have been of 50 talents.[2]

The literary sources for the terms of settlement dictated by Athens are supplemented by substantial fragments from a decree passed by the Athenian Assembly in the archon year 439–438. Of the opening lines so little remains that detailed restoration would be irresponsible, but there is a tantalizing mention of the Peloponnesians which we have taken to give point to the Corinthian statement in Thucydides that Sparta and her allies seriously considered sending help to Samos. Restoration is easier in the oaths, for some of the formulae known from other inscriptions can be recognized in the letters that survive. The Athenian oath is of particular interest, especially when compared with the oath given to Chalcis. In their settlement with Chalcis the Athenians had merely covenanted to use the processes of law; the oath given to Samos is much more generous: 'I will act, speak and [counsel as well] as I am able in the interests of the Samian [demos]', and in the Samian oath there is further evidence of a change in tone. Chalcis had to swear allegiance to Athens alone; the Samians are to swear to remain loyal to Athens and her allies.[3] The language of the League is being revived. The impression given by the document is that Athens, having taken from Samos the source of her strength, decided to concentrate the blame on the oligarchs and show confidence in the new democracy. Thucydides does not mention the change of government but it could be inferred from the political character of the revolt and is confirmed by the emphasis on the demos in the Athenian oath and the explicit statement of Diodorus.[4] The fruits of this policy are

[1] See p. 310 n. 1. For the doubt about Byzantium see ML p. 150, note below text.

[2] The sources collected, Hill, *Sources*[2], B 63, pp. 306 f.; *ATL* iii. 334 f.

[3] For the texts of the oaths, App. 16, pp. 579–82.

[4] Diod. xii. 28. 4. The restoration in the Athenian oath (l. 22) τôι δέμοι τôι Σα]μίον is perhaps not quite certain. τêι πόλει is formally possible (Bradeen *Hist.* ix (1960), 265 n. 48).

seen in the unswerving loyalty of the Samian democrats even
after the Syracusan disaster and the bitter hostility of the
oligarchs to Athens. Our sources do not tell us the fate of
the oligarchs. We may imagine a purge of the leaders and confiscations; but some of them were able to establish a defensible
position on the opposite mainland at Anaea where they prepared
for bitter revenge: 'They kept the Samians of the city in a state
of alarm and welcomed refugees.'[1] In the Peloponnesian War
they gave what help to Sparta they could and by 412 they had
once again secured control of Samos.[2]

It would be tempting to infer from the oaths included in the
Samian settlement that Athens had decided to modify her imperial policy and rule the Aegean with a looser rein, but the
rest of the evidence does not encourage us to generalize from
the language used for Samos. The Samian revolt was crushed
in 439, and Chios and Lesbos had sent substantial contingents
to fight with Athens: before 431, and almost certainly before
433, Lesbos seriously contemplated following the example of
Samos, and appealed to Sparta for help. Our only evidence for
this surprising incident is a passing reference by Thucydides in
connection with the revolt of Mytilene in 428, but there is no
good reason to reject it.[3] Such action by Lesbos so soon after
the crushing of the Samian revolt is barely consistent with the
relaxation of Athenian pressure, and other wisps of evidence
suggest that Athenian control became tighter during the
thirties. When war broke out Pericles, according to Thucydides,
had no illusions about the nature of Athenian control: it was
a tyranny not a hegemony: ὡς τυραννίδα γὰρ ἤδη ἔχετε αὐτήν.[4]

There are hints in the tribute quota lists that the crushing of
the Samian revolt was followed by increasing Athenian pressure in the Aegean. In 439 for the first time the recorded payment of certain cities is followed by a second entry, described
as *epiphora*. The sums so paid are small in relation to the tributes
and the word means payment over and above what is due
or normal; it is, for instance, used of the extra pay given by
trierarchs to their crews in the Sicilian expedition. In the quota

---

[1] Thuc. iv. 75. 1.

[2] Thuc. viii. 21: ἐγένετο δὲ κατὰ τὸν χρόνον τοῦτον καὶ ἡ ἐν Σάμῳ ἐπανάστασις
ὑπὸ τοῦ δήμου τοῖς δυνατοῖς μετὰ Ἀθηναίων. The oligarchs had probably seized
power while Athens' main forces were engaged at Syracuse.

[3] Thuc. iii. 13. 1.   [4] Thuc. ii. 63. 2.

lists it should mean an extra payment imposed as a penalty.[1]
Something of the same mood is illustrated in the general
tendency to increase tributes in the assessments following the
Samian revolt. The evidence for the 438 assessment is very
scanty indeed but if the two assessments of the thirties are considered together there emerges a tendency to revoke the concessions made in 446 when in face of the crisis in the empire
widespread reductions of tribute had been made. Many of the
tributes are now restored to the pre-446 figures; so Ephesus
reduced in 446 from $7\frac{1}{2}$ to 6 talents was again required to pay
$7\frac{1}{2}$ talents, Miletus reduced from 10 to 5 was again assessed at
10, Aphytis reduced from 3 to 1 returns to 3 talents.[2] Increasing pressure is also reflected in the appearance of two new
headings in the quota list of 435–434. The precise meaning and
significance of these headings are not certain, but the cities are
small communities and most of them come from the periphery
of the empire. They are probably new to the empire and their
subsequent record suggests that they were not enthusiastic
volunteers. They were perhaps 'persuaded' that it was in their
interest to pay tribute for the benefits of membership.[3]

There is other evidence that Athens in the thirties was not
content merely to consolidate what she held. The record is
meagre and minor events have been completely lost, but two
events left their mark on tradition. In 437–436 the Athenians
established a large colony at Ennea Hodoi, now renamed
Amphipolis. The site commanded trade routes and an important crossing of the Strymon. The district was rich in timber,
which Athens lacked and needed for her fleet, and in silver, as
the Ionians had long ago realized. Histiaeus when invited by
Darius to choose his reward for loyalty on the Scythian expedition chose Myrcinus, a neighbouring site, and it was not long
before the Persian commander in Thrace advised his recall by
Darius on the ground that the district was rich in oars and
silver; Aristagoras similarly hoped to establish himself there
when the Ionian revolt began to collapse.[4] When Eion was
taken by Cimon in 476 there may have been an Athenian
attempt to settle, but if the attempt was made it was unsuccessful; the more ambitious colony of Athenians and allies which

---

[1] See Endnote 17, p. 432.   [2] For further details see App. 12, p. 528
[3] See pp. 250–2.   [4] Thuc. iv. 108. 1; Hdt. v. 23. 2; v. 126.

occupied the site during the Thasian revolt was virtually annihilated by the Thracians. Now at last Athens succeeded. Hagnon, who was to have a long and distinguished career as general and later as elder statesman, led the enterprise and left a well-settled city which provided a good living for the colonists and important revenues for Athens. But there was an inherent weakness in the colony which ultimately proved fatal. However attractive it might be to further Athens' political and economic fortunes by settlement overseas it was essential to retain at Athens sufficient manpower to maintain an adequate army and to provide at least a substantial nucleus of the crews for the fleet. Figures of Athenian manpower are notoriously speculative but it seems unlikely that the able-bodied male population of military age was more than 50,000, and it may have been less. The number of Athenians who could be released for Amphipolis was therefore small, as Thucydides later in his narrative notes in passing;[1] the great majority of the settlers were drawn from the allies and mainly, it seems, from the local allies of Chalcidice and Thrace. This was perhaps a deliberate gesture to retain the goodwill of the neighbouring states whose economies would be affected by the new colony; it may for instance be particularly significant that a strong Argilian element was included.[2] In 446, as has been seen, the assessment of Argilus was reduced to 1 talent and this may have been in compensation for the loss of Bisaltian land to the Athenian colony of Brea.[3] We now find a further reduction to 1,000 drachmae and no trace of Brea appears in Thucydides' detailed narrative of the Peloponnesian War. It is probable that Brea was abandoned and its population moved to Amphipolis; Argilus may have lost more land. When, however, in 424 the Spartan Brasidas appeared in Chalcidice, the Argilians in Amphipolis took the lead in encouraging him to move swiftly on their town.[4]

Athenian interest in the north-east is further reflected in her changing policies towards Perdiccas, king of Macedon. In 432 when Potidaea was on the point of revolt from Athens and an anti-Athenian mood was spreading in Chalcidice Perdiccas did his best to encourage the rebels. He was now, Thucydides tells

---

[1] Thuc. iv. 106. 1: οἱ δὲ πολλοὶ ἀκούσαντες ἀλλοιότεροι ἐγένοντο τὰς γνώμας, ἄλλως τε καὶ βραχὺ μὲν Ἀθηναίων ἐμπολιτεῦον, τὸ δὲ πλεῖον ξύμμεικτον.

[2] Thuc. iv. 103. 3.   [3] See p. 159 n. 3.   [4] Thuc. iv. 103. 4.

us, an open enemy of Athens, for the Athenians were supporting his brother Philip and Derdas; earlier he had been an ally.[1] Fragments of a decree setting out the terms of an alliance with Perdiccas survive, but there is no decisive evidence of date; a good case, however, has been made for placing it in the thirties.[2] Two of the clauses of the oath which Perdiccas is required to take can be confidently restored. He shall have the same friends and enemies as Athens, and he shall export oars to Athens only.[3] In the often-changing relations of Athens with Perdiccas the record of both sides is bad. It is doubtful whether Athens had any higher motive than opportunism for supporting the rivals of her ally.

The other expedition of the thirties that has not dropped out of the record is the expedition of Pericles into the Euxine. Plutarch tells us that the Athenian fleet was large and well equipped: 'Pericles attended to the needs of the Greek cities and established friendly relations with them; to their barbarian neighbours, their kings and chiefs, he displayed the greatness of Athenian power, their confidence and boldness in sailing where they wished, having made themselves complete masters of the sea.'[4] The only specific incident that Plutarch records is at Sinope. Thirteen ships and a small force under Lamachus were landed to stiffen a popular uprising against the tyrant Timesilaus. The tyrant and his followers were driven out and 600 Athenian volunteers were sent to take over their property and settle in the town. This is a very fragmentary skeleton, but some attempt must be made to determine the date and purpose of the expedition. If Plutarch's Lamachus is to be identified with the general known from Thucydides and Aristophanes his age should give a rough control. He was 'well on in years' but still energetic when he was elected in 415 to share the command in the Syracusan expedition; he was caricatured as a fiery young hothead by Aristophanes in his *Acharnians* produced in 425.[5] Lamachus is not likely to have been more than sixty when

---

[1] Thuc. i. 57. 2: Περδίκκας . . . ἐπεπολέμωτο, ξύμμαχος πρότερον καὶ φίλος ὤν.

[2] *ATL* iii. 313, n. 61. The date previously accepted was 423–422 for which date there are also strong arguments. See Endnote, 15, p. 428.

[3] *IG* i². 71. l. 20: καὶ τὸς] αὐτὸς φίλος νομιô καὶ ἐχθρ[ὸς hόσπερ Ἀθεν|αῖοι].
l. 23: οὐδὲ κο]πέας ἐχσάγεν ἐάσο ἐὰμ μὲ Ἀθε[ναίοις.

[4] Plut. *Per.* 20. 1–2.

[5] Plut. *Per.* 18. 1–2; Ar. *Acharn.*, e.g. 566 ff., 964 f.

he sailed to Syracuse, nor less than thirty when he took part in
the Euxine expedition. Some date after the Thirty Years' Peace
is indicated.

Two other lines of argument are more slender but not negligible. According to Diodorus a new dynasty secured control
of the Bosporan Kingdom in 438–437;[1] some time soon after its
accession would provide a suitable setting for the demonstration. The establishment of friendly relations with the new rulers
would help to explain how Athens by the beginning of the
Peloponnesian War felt no anxieties about her corn supply. In
the middle of the century there are signs that her supply may
have been precarious;[2] during the war she seems to have had
abundant supplies from the Euxine, which flowed freely until
the Sicilian disaster crippled Athenian naval power. There are
also indications that Athens established colonies in this area
during the thirties. Inference from the quota lists, encouraging
an attractive emendation in Diodorus, suggests that Astacus on
the Asiatic shore of the Sea of Marmara was colonized by Athens
in 435–434; it is interesting and perhaps significant that the
original foundation was Megarian.[3] Amisus on the south shore
of the Euxine may also have been colonized at this time. According to Theopompus it was a Milesian foundation which after
a phase of Cappadocian control was settled by Athenians under
the leadership of Athenocles.[4] This tradition is confirmed by
early fourth-century coins on which the city is named Peiraieus
and the reverse type is the Athenian owl, standing on a shield.[5]
Appian, in a brief summary of the town's history, says that it
was settled from Athens when she had command of the seas,
that it enjoyed democracy for a long time, but then came under
Persian control until democracy was restored by Alexander.[6]
These indications of time are vague, but a context between the
Persian and the Peloponnesian war is required, and at Amisus

---

[1] Diod. xii. 31. 1–2. I. B. Brashinsky, *Athens and the Northern Black Sea Area in
the sixth to second centuries B.C.* (in Russian, Moscow, 1963. pp. 60 ff.) emphasizes
that there is no evidence suggesting that Pericles visited the northern shore of the
Euxine and thinks that his expedition was confined to the southern shore.

[2] See p. 95 n. 3.

[3] Diod. xii. 34. 5, accepting Niese's emendation: ἔκτισαν οἱ Ἀθηναῖοι πόλιν ἐν
τῇ Προποντίδι τὴν ὀνομαζομένην Ἀστακόν (for MSS. Λέτανον); cf. Strabo xii. 4. 2,
563: Ἀστακὸς πόλις, Μεγαρέων κτίσμα καὶ Ἀθηναίων καὶ μετὰ ταῦτα Δοιδαλσοῦ.

[4] Theopompus F 389 in Strabo xii. 3. 14, 547.

[5] Head, *Hist. Num.*[2] 496.

[6] Appian, *Bell. Mithr.* 83.

and Astacus, as at Sinope, Athens was protecting Greek interests against the barbarian. All three incidents might well illustrate Plutarch's account of Pericles' expedition: 'he attended to the needs of the Greek cities . . .; to their barbarian neighbours . . . he displayed the greatness of Athenian power'.

A considerably earlier date has been suggested for this Euxine expedition on the ground that after 449 it would have been a violation of the Peace of Callias. That is why the authors of *The Athenian Tribute Lists* have advocated 450, which they think to be just consistent with the evidence for Lamachus' age.[1] The age of Lamachus, however, is not the only objection to such an early date. Between the Egyptian disaster and 446 Athens' energies were concentrated first on building up her resources against Persia and then in the maintenance of control over her allies. These years are not well suited to ambitious expeditions, magnificently mounted, beyond the limits of the empire. Pericles' expedition has a much more appropriate setting in the thirties, after the crushing of the Samian revolt, probably after the foundation of Amphipolis, but before the concentration of interest and tension on Epidamnus in 435.

Epidamnus, on the Adriatic coast north of Corcyra, had been founded by Corcyra, but the leader of the colony had come from Corinth, Corcyra's mother city. In 435 or a little earlier the democrats of Epidamnus, hard pressed by their oligarchs and by the barbarians of the interior, appealed for help to Corcyra. When Corcyra refused to intervene they appealed to Corinth, and when Corinth prepared to send help Corcyra resented what she regarded as Corinthian interference. There followed a large-scale battle off Corcyra in which 155 ships were committed and the result was a decisive defeat for Corinth. Throughout the next year Corinth made elaborate preparations to build up her forces with the help of Peloponnesian allies in order to reverse the verdict.[2] It was at this stage that Corcyra appealed to Athens for an alliance and the Corinthians stated their case before the same meeting of the Athenian Assembly. According to Thucydides the Athenians were at first inclined to accept the Corinthian arguments, but at a second meeting they decided to make a defensive alliance with Corcyra. They sent first ten and, later, twenty more ships to Corcyra and when

[1] *ATL* iii. 114–17.   [2] Thuc. i. 24–31.

the two fleets met off the Sybota Islands the Athenians saved
the Corcyraeans at a critical moment and the Corinthians returned home.[1]

This direct intervention by Athens in what Corinth could
with some reason regard as her own sphere revived the bitter
hatred that Corinth had felt for Athens in the fifties, and this
was the most important factor in bringing matters to a head in
432; in fact many historians have regarded the hostility of
Corinth to Athens as the main cause of the outbreak of war.
This was not the view of Thucydides whose judgement is unambiguous. 'The real cause . . . was the growth of Athenian power
which alarmed Sparta and forced her to go to war.'[2] Consistently with this view he says that the Athenians made their
alliance with Corcyra 'because they realized that war with the
Peloponnese was bound to come'.[3] We might perhaps question
this statement and regard it as a late insertion, to give more
body to revised views about the cause of the war; but there is
no need for such subtleties. Two contemporary decrees show
that this was the Athenian mood before the Corcyraeans
appealed to the Athenian Assembly.

At some point in the year 434–433 a Callias, probably the
son of Calliades, who was general in 433–432 and was killed in
Chalcidice in 432, moved two financial decrees at the same
meeting of the Assembly.[4] The first (A) provides for the repayment of the public debts to the gods and goddesses other than
Athena, and the appointment of ten treasurers of these other
gods. The second (B) is much less well preserved and its details
are more uncertain. It seems to be primarily concerned with
tidying up the Acropolis without completing the Propylaea and
imposing restrictions on public spending. These two decrees
came before the Assembly in a Great Panathenaic year, almost
certainly before the war and after the beginning of the Propylaea
(in 437–436). 434–433 may now be regarded as the generally
accepted date.[5] For our present purpose the most significant
decision is one that shortly preceded the first decree. Treasurers

---

[1] Thuc. i. 31–55.

[2] Thuc. i. 23. 6: τὴν μὲν γὰρ ἀληθεστάτην πρόφασιν, ἀφανεστάτην δὲ λόγῳ, τοὺς
Ἀθηναίους ἡγοῦμαι μεγάλους γιγνομένους καὶ φόβον παρέχοντας τοῖς Λακεδαιμονίοις
ἀναγκάσαι ἐς τὸ πολεμεῖν.

[3] Thuc. i. 44. 2: ἐδόκει γὰρ ὁ πρὸς Πελοποννησίους πόλεμος καὶ ὣς ἔσεσθαι αὐτοῖς.

[4] ML 58.   [5] The date further discussed, App. 11, p. 519.

of the other gods are to be appointed because the decision has already been taken to bring the treasures, in cash and in kind, from the temples of Attica and the lower city for security to the Acropolis where they are to be the responsibility of special treasurers and stored in the Opisthodomus.[1] Such a drastic decision could only be taken by the Assembly if it was convinced that there was serious danger of a Peloponnesian invasion, and this was either in the second half of 434 or the first half of 433. It is consistent with an anticipation of war that work on the Acropolis should be suspended and restrictions placed on the spending of public money from the reserve (as in B), and that in the first decree (A) any money remaining from the funds earmarked for the payment of debts to the gods should be spent on the walls and the docks.[2] From internal evidence the decrees are most likely to have been earlier than the summer of 433 because provision is made for the election of treasurers of the other gods 'when they elect the other officers', and it is generally held that Athenian elections were in late winter. Thucydides' evidence also would suggest a date before the hearing of the Corcyraeans, for the Assembly's decision seems to be closely followed by action. 'This is what the Athenians had in mind when they accepted the Corcyraeans as allies, and shortly after (οὐ πολὺ ὕστερον) the departure of the Corinthians they sent ten ships to support them.' We happen to know the approximate date of departure from the accounts of money paid out to the generals by the treasurers of Athena.[3] The first squadron of ten ships received 26 talents on the thirteenth day of the first prytany of the year 433–432. It is unlikely that the Assembly debate was earlier than June.

Though by 433 war may have seemed inevitable sooner or later, the intervention of Athens in the dispute between Corinth and Corcyra brought it very much nearer. From that point Thucydides gives the impression that Athens, while respecting the letter of the Thirty Years' Peace, was making it virtually impossible for the Peloponnesians to remain at peace. Immediately

---

[1] ML 58. 15–18.

[2] Ibid. 30–2: ἐπειδὰν δε ἀποδεδομένα ἐ τοῖς θεοῖς | [τὰ χρ]έματα, ἐς τὸ νεόριον καὶ τὰ τείχε τοῖς περιôσι χρεᾶσθαι χρέμασ||[ιν. The docks for the offensive, the walls against Spartan invasions. Cf. Ar. Banqueters, F 220: εἰς τὰς τριήρεις δεῖν ἀναλοῦν ταῦτα καὶ τὰ τείχη, | εἰς οἷ' ἀνάλουν οἱ πρὸ τοῦ τὰ χρήματα.

[3] ML 61.

after the fighting off Corcyra, according to Thucydides, Athens put extreme pressure on Potidaea, a Corinthian colony which still had visiting officials from Corinth. Thucydides writes as if Athens was taking tough precautions against trouble rather than reacting to pro-Corinthian intrigues.[1] There may, however, be more background to the Potidaea affair than Thucydides implies, for in the quota list of 432 we find Potidaea paying 15 talents tribute, whereas her normal tribute was 6 talents.[2] There is no evidence for 433, so we cannot know whether the increase was made at the assessment of 434. If it was made then or earlier it might have been a punitive assessment for suspicious attitudes; if only in 432 it might have been associated with the other demands.

While describing the Potidaea affair in some detail Thucydides has left historians very little guidance about an issue which to his contemporaries was considerably more important. When Sparta's allies brought their grievances against Athens before the Spartan Assembly in the summer of 432 three states only are mentioned. The Corinthians are naturally the most prominent; then the Aeginetans, who dared not come out into the open but complained that the guarantee of autonomy made to them in the Thirty Years' Peace was being ignored; finally the Megarians, who had many complaints, but the most important was 'their exclusion from the harbours of the Athenian empire and the Athenian Agora'.[3] The Megarian Decree, moved by Pericles, was parodied by Aristophanes in his *Acharnians* and is there made the main cause of the war.[4] No mention is made of it by the Corinthians at Athens in the summer of 433, though there is a reference to Athenian relations with Megara. The right context for the Megarian Decree still seems to be between the debate in the Athenian Assembly in the summer of 433 and the Spartan Assembly which hears the grievances of her allies in the summer of 432.[5] The Megarians complained that it was a breach of the Thirty Years' Peace. This Pericles, in Thucydides, denies: 'We will allow the Megarians to use our Agora and the harbours of the empire if on their part

---

[1] Thuc. i. 56. 2.   [2] See App. 12, p. 528.

[3] Thuc. i. 67. 4: δηλοῦντες μὲν καὶ ἕτερα οὐκ ὀλίγα διάφορα, μάλιστα δὲ λιμένων τε εἴργεσθαι τῶν ἐν τῇ Ἀθηναίων ἀρχῇ καὶ τῆς Ἀττικῆς ἀγορᾶς παρὰ τὰς σπονδάς.

[4] Ar. *Acharn.* 515–39.

[5] See Endnote 16, p. 430.

the Spartans will not expel us nor our allies from Sparta (for the peace terms forbid neither the one nor the other).'[1] The Megarian Decree violated the spirit rather than the letter of the peace. It was an extreme demonstration of Athenian imperialism for, while it was a harsh blow against Megara, it also ignored the economic interests of the allies.[2]

In the diplomatic manœuvring between the decision of the Peloponnesian League to go to war and the actual outbreak of hostilities Thucydides emphasizes the importance of the Megarian Decree in the demands made by Sparta. 'Above all and in the clearest terms they said that if Athens repealed the Megarian Decree, in which the Megarians had been forbidden to use the harbours in the Athenian Empire and the Agora of Athens, there would be no war.'[3] But it is not treated as a major issue in its own right, and recorded at the point in the narrative where it occurred. This is probably an illustration of one of the less attractive sides of Thucydides' character. He has no patience with the carelessness or stupidity of others and the very small space he gives to the Megarian Decree is his exaggerated reaction to what was the most popular view of the cause of the war.[4]

Thucydides has gone too far in the other direction but basically he was right. Throughout the century there had been men in Sparta who resented the confinement of Sparta within the Peloponnese and felt that what Athens was doing should have been Sparta's role. While Athens was led by Cimon and his associates friendly coexistence had been easy; but the radical reforms of Ephialtes, quickly followed by the ostracism of Cimon, ended that phase, and indecisive fighting lasted from 460 to 446. The Thirty Years' Peace patched matters up

---

[1] Thuc. i. 144. 2.

[2] Megara's customers in the islands may not have found it easy to buy elsewhere at the same price the goods they normally bought from Megara. Mattingly even suggests (*Hist.* xvi (1967), 1–5) that Aegina's complaint of her loss of the autonomy guaranteed in the Thirty Years' Peace may be explained by the Megarian Decree. This is an interesting suggestion, but it is not strengthened by dating and restoring *IG* i². 18 (which has $)$ to suit the context. Better restorations can be provided for the fifties or the forties.

[3] Thuc. i. 139. 1.

[4] Unnecessary criticism of other authors was a favourite weakness of Greek and Roman historians; it is not unknown in academic circles today. Thucydides is less good-tempered than most, as in i. 20 and vi. 54–9.

temporarily but there was too much restless energy in the air
for Athens to be content with stability. The Samian revolt was
a sharp warning and Sparta seriously considered intervention.
In the thirties the foundation of Amphipolis and Pericles'
Euxine expedition emphasized and increased Athens' resources. Phormio's operations in the north-west in aid of the
Acarnanians against Ambracia, which should probably be
dated in the early thirties, were a clear warning to Corinth.[1]
In the Athenian Assembly, according to Plutarch, there was
already talk of another bid for Egypt and of expansion in the
west.[2] It is not difficult to understand why the Spartans who
had seriously considered war when Samos revolted should in
432 feel forced to fight.

When war broke out in 431 the Delian League had become
an Athenian empire. This empire stood up to the strain of
large-scale war extremely well, but to appreciate the significance
of this we should first review the means which Athens had
elaborated to secure and maintain her control.

[1] Thuc. ii. 68. 7. The natives of Amphilochian Argos had been driven out of
their town by Ambraciots whom they had invited to settle there. They turned
for help to the Acarnanians and together they appealed to Athens. The Athenians
sent thirty ships and the joint forces recovered the town and enslaved the Ambraciots. Though the Ambraciots had been the aggressors Ambracia was a
Corinthian colony, and when the Athenians followed their action by a formal
alliance with the Acarnanians they were asserting their continuing interest in a
Corinthian sphere of influence. No mark of time is given by Thucydides, but if
the campaign had been earlier than 440 we should not have expected Corinth to
oppose action against Athens when Samos revolted. Gomme (*HCT* ii. 416) prefers a date in the fifties or early forties (but Thucydides' silence would be more
difficult to explain); Wade-Gery (*Essays*, 253 n. 5) suggests the spring of 432 (but
Thucydides would probably have recorded it at the end of his account of events
in the north-west, or made a reference to it when Phormio was sent to Potidaea).

[2] Plut. *Per.* 20. 3–4.

II

THE INSTRUMENTS OF EMPIRE

WHEN the danger from Persia seemed to have dissolved with the decisive victory of the Eurymedon, the Delian League would have disintegrated unless Athens had held it together. This she was clearly entitled to do so long as hostilities continued against Persia, and during the fifties in particular she took active steps to maintain control; but the Peace of Callias radically changed the situation and the transition to empire which had hitherto been a gradual process was now made explicit. Athens was able to show such decision because in the course of the fifties and perhaps earlier she had already developed the means of control. It was because her improvisations had proved so well suited to their purpose that she was able to hold her empire together even until the last stages of the Peloponnesian War. The means she employed must now be considered.

The foundation of Athens' power was her fleet. The Delian League was composed almost entirely of islands and coastal cities and could be controlled only by a powerful fleet. By the middle of the century when Chios, Lesbos, and Samos alone of the allies still contributed ships and Aegina had been crushed, Athens' fleet was strong enough to face the combined fleets of the Aegean; and when Samos had to surrender her ships the power of Athens was even more preponderant. The knowledge that Athenian triremes might appear at any moment in harbour was a deterrent to anti-Athenian elements. Strong walls could to a certain extent have neutralized the power of the fleet but it seems that in Ionia at least city fortifications were dismantled.[1] Moreover, nearly all Greek states required to import some essential materials and to find export markets for their own surplus. As the Old Oligarch points out: 'If a city is rich in ship timber, where will she market it if she does not persuade

[1] See pp. 149 f.

the power that rules the sea? If a city is rich in iron or copper or linen, where will she market it if she does not persuade the power that rules the sea?'[1] Athens was not the only state which needed to import corn from the Euxine, but her fleet could control the passage of the corn ships. Mytilene could build up supplies from the Euxine so long as her preparations for revolt were kept secret, but as soon as Athens had been warned the route was closed.[2] One of the privileges granted by Athens during the Archidamian war to Methone for her loyalty was the right to import corn from Byzantium.[3] The main function of the fleet in peacetime was to act as a police force. Each year, according to Plutarch, patrols were sent out.[4] They showed the Athenian flag, gave confidence to Athens' friends, and kept the seas clear of pirates.

But Greek moods changed quickly and Athenian dominance did not put an end to political rivalries; in some states Athens found it necessary to maintain garrisons. The first known example is at Erythrae, probably in the fifties,[5] but our evidence for the workings of Athenian imperialism comes almost exclusively from inscriptions: and from the first twenty years of the League no inscriptions recording Athenian relations with any of the allies survive; it would be dangerous to assume that no Athenian garrisons were installed in the sixties. The situation that gave rise to Athenian intervention in Erythrae has already been briefly described.[6] Tyrants had been in control and when expelled they had taken refuge with the Persians; presumably they had Medized earlier. An Athenian garrison could be justified as a necessary protection for the loyal democracy against the political group that had been expelled or any help that the satrap at Sardis might give them. In the same general context a garrison is recorded in the regulations laid down for Miletus in 450–449;[7] Miletus like Erythrae had shortly before deserted

---

[1] [Xen.] *Aθ. Πολ.* 2. 11. Exporting was of as much concern as importing to some states. The Corinthians tell their Peloponnesian allies in 432 that the inland towns depend on the coastal towns for both exports and imports (Thuc. i. 120. 2).

[2] Thuc. iii. 2. 2.

[3] ML 65. 34–6: $M[εθοναί|οις]$ $εῖν[αι$ $ἐχ]σα[γο]γὲν$ $ἐγ$ $Βυζαντίο$ $σῖτο$ $μέχ[ρι....$ $a|κισχιλίον$ $μεδίμνον$ $τὸ$ $ἐνιαυτὸ$ $ἑκάστο.$ A similar privilege was given later to Aphytis (D 21. 3–6).

[4] Plutarch (*Per.* 11. 4) says sixty ships for eight months every year, but this would have cost too much; see Endnote 13, p. 427.

[5] Erythrae, ML 40. 14–5.   [6] See pp. 112 f.   [7] D 11. 77.

the League.[1] When peace was made with Persia the need for protection against Medism was temporarily at least eliminated but garrisons were still maintained to protect Athenian interests. Chance references in Eupolis and Aristophanes speak of guard duty at Cyzicus and Byzantium and both passages seem to look back to the period of peace.[2] When Samos defied Athens in 440 and Pericles hoped for a quick settlement by striking at once against the oligarchs he installed a garrison to protect the democracy which he had set up, but the force was inadequate to deal with the serious rising that followed.[3] In Thucydides' narrative of the Peloponnesian War garrisons are found in many cities of Chalcidice, but they may not have been installed until war broke out or seemed imminent.[4]

More important than military control by small garrisons were the various forms of political control devised by Athens. The most consistent defence of their empire made with conviction by the Athenians was that they relied very little on force. The point is made with special emphasis in the speech of an Athenian envoy to the Spartan Assembly in 432, as reported by Thucydides: the stronger may be expected to use force to control the weaker, but Athens has relied on the processes of law.[5] This emphasis is reflected, as has been seen, in the terms of the oath sworn by the Athenians to Chalcis after the crushing of the revolt of 446.[6] Spartan behaviour in the Aegean when she attempted to take Athens' place provided a sharp contrast which Athenian orators appreciated: 'The Lacedaemonians put more men arbitrarily to death in three months than we brought to trial in the whole course of our empire.'[7] The people's law-courts played a very important part in safeguarding Athenian interests, but before we venture into the tangled field of jurisdiction some more direct forms of political control should be outlined.

---

[1] See p. 112.

[2] Eupolis, Πόλεις F 233: ἥδε Κύζικος πλέα στατήρων. | ἐν τῆδε τοίνυν τῇ πόλει φρουρῶν ποτ᾿ αὐτός . . .; Ar. Wasps 235–7: πάρεσθ᾿ ὃ δὴ λοιπόν γ᾿ ἔτ᾿ ἐστίν, ἀππαπαῖ παπαίαξ, | ἥβης ἐκείνης ἡνίκ᾿ ἐν Βυζαντίῳ ξυνῆμεν | φρουροῦντ᾿ ἐγώ τε καὶ σύ. For a list of garrisons, A. S. Nease, Phoenix, iii (1949), 102–11.

[3] Thuc. i. 115. 2–5.

[4] The force that attacked Eion, colony of Mende, in 425 was drawn mainly from local garrisons, Thuc. iv. 7: ξυλλέξας Ἀθηναίους τε ὀλίγους ἐκ τῶν φρουρίων καὶ τῶν ἐκείνῃ ξυμμάχων πλῆθος.

[5] Thuc. i. 77. 1–4. [6] ML 52. 5–10. [7] Isocr. iv. 113.

Writing during the Peloponnesian War the Old Oligarch, who had no love for democracy, admits that the Athenian demos was logical and shrewd in supporting the 'bad' men in the allied states rather than the 'good'. If they supported the 'good' their empire would quickly vanish; as it is, like supports like and they persecute the 'good': 'That is why they strip the "good" of their rights, confiscate their property, exile them and put them to death, while they uphold the "bad".'[1] He would not have used different language if he had written in the years between the Thirty Years' Peace and the outbreak of war. Aristophanes in a lighter but more cutting vein tells the same story. It is the few and the rich that his downtrodden jurors batten on.[2] There were still oligarchies in the empire in the thirties, but very few. The Samian oligarchy did not survive the Samian revolt, but oligarchs were in power at Mytilene when she revolted in 428 and Chios seems to have remained politically stable under a moderate oligarchy until she revolted in 412, and there may have been others of which we happen to have no evidence.[3] One has the impression from the combined evidence of the Old Oligarch and of Thucydides that the majority of the allied cities were democratic; it is less clear what part Athens had played in bringing this about. When the League was formed in 478–477 oligarchy was the common pattern in the Peloponnesian League, in Boeotia, and in Thessaly, but among the East Greeks democracy was the prevailing form. The tyrannies of the late sixth century were a symptom of Persian control; when Persia attempted reconciliation after crushing the Ionian revolt she dismissed the tyrants and established democracies.[4] In Thrace and Chalcidice oligarchs may have retained power longer but we lack evidence. In parts of Caria and Lycia tyrants could be expected and accepted long after they were an anachronism elsewhere.[5]

The governments of the allied cities were considerably more varied in form and spirit when the League was formed than when the Peace of Callias was made. At first all forms of government could work together because they had all agreed to common

---

[1] [Xen.] Ἀθ. Πολ. l. 14.   [2] Ar. *Peace* 639.
[3] There is no explicit evidence for the form of government in Chios at this time but Thuc. viii. 24. 4–5 suggests a moderate oligarchy.
[4] Hdt. vi. 43. 3.   [5] *ATL* i. 446.

objectives and the business of the League was primarily to carry on operations against Persia. But it was not long before politics obtruded. In most Greek states there was a division latent or patent between the few and the many, and when strains and stresses began to develop in the League it was to be expected that the few who thought that they had most to gain by independence should be most anti-Athenian. We know nothing of the political situation in Naxos at the time of the revolt or subsequently, but when Thucydides says that Naxos was enslaved we can believe that the terms dictated by Athens included political clauses. In 500 there had been sharp *stasis* in the island between oligarchs and democrats and when the olig- archs lost control they had appealed through Miletus to Persia.[1] It is at least possible that this pattern was repeated when Naxos attempted to secede and that Athens crushed the olig- archic party. One may doubt, however, whether in the seventies and sixties Athens crusaded for democracy. At home the spirit of government was conservative and the leaders of the people, Cimon and his associates, found no difficulty in main- taining friendly relations with Sparta. But when the under- current of unrest that had been growing through the sixties came to a head in the reforms of Ephialtes the mood may have been different. Oligarchs in the allied cities may well have felt more suspicious of the new Athenian leadership. The Old Olig- arch searching for cases where Athens has supported oligarchs can quote only two examples, and in both Boeotia and Miletus the experiment failed.[2] The Athenian commission sent out to Miletus in 450–449 was to co-operate with the magistrates of an oligarchy and not with a democratic council, but by 440 a democracy had almost certainly been installed.[3] So in the regulations dictated to Erythrae the main emphasis is on the appointment of a democratic council, and the Colophonians have to include in their oath an undertaking to be loyal to their new democracy.[4] At Samos it was the oligarchs who led the revolt and lost their position.

The pattern in Boeotia may have been different. There was probably, in some of the cities if not in all, friction between democrats and oligarchs, though Boeotian cities being primarily

---

[1] Hdt. v. 30.   [2] [Xen.] Ἀθ. Πολ. 3. 11.
[3] Above, p. 188.   [4] ML 40. 8–17; 47. 48.

based on agriculture were probably unlike Athens in their class structure; there were, however, probably also differences between federalists and anti-federalists. Athens' main concern being to break up a strong centralized Boeotian federation, she may have tried at first to rely on the support of oligarchs who preferred to exercise real power in their own cities rather than be submerged in a federation whose centre of power was Thebes. One can understand the experiment being tried by Athens, and one can understand it failing; anti-federal oligarchs are likely to have been too extreme for the common people. The experiment probably ended some years before Boeotia was completely lost to Athens at Coronea.

Athens was unsuccessful in preventing the consolidation of Theban power in a united federation; she was rather more successful elsewhere in preventing or breaking up powerful combinations. If in 428 Mytilene had succeeded in merging the smaller cities of Lesbos in an enlarged Mytilene she would have been considerably more dangerous. Athens crushed her revolt and Methymna remained independent; Mytilene also had to surrender to Athens the cities on the mainland which she had controlled. Samos and Chios had no other town on their islands to rival them but Rhodes was still divided between three rival cities, Lindus, Ialysus, and Camirus. Some of the small communities on the mainland opposite Rhodes had probably been controlled from Rhodes in the archaic period, as they were to be controlled later, but they pay tribute directly to Athens from the fifties onwards.[1] They probably owed their temporary independence to Athens. After the Syracusan disaster Rhodes revolted and became for a while the base of the Peloponnesian fleet; but the island was still raided by Athenian ships. It was primarily to concentrate their forces that the three cities in 409–408 together formed a new city and by now Athens had not the resources to interfere.[2]

In Thrace Athens was faced by hostile combinations throughout the Archidamian War. When trouble broke out in Potidaea in 432, many of the small cities on the coast were easily persuaded to move to Olynthus, and in very little time they became

---

[1] P. M. Fraser and G. E. Bean, *The Rhodian Peraea and Islands*, 95, suggest the Χερρονήσιοι.

[2] Diod. xiii. 75. 1.

a formidable force. At the western end of Chalcidice the Bottiaeans centralized power in Spartolus, and Athens had little
more success against them than against Olynthus. She seems to
have done better by diplomacy than by fighting. In the Peace
of Nicias she tried to ensure that Mecyberna, Gale, and Singus
were not absorbed by Olynthus and Acanthus.[1] She also seems
to have been able to detach at least some of the Bottiaean cities
from Spartolus, for in the record of an alliance made with some
of the Bottiaean cities at about this time Spartolus is not mentioned and the oaths have to be sworn in each city, by the
officers of each city.[2]

The Athenian democracy remained loyal to its friends. When
after the battle of Cyzicus Alcibiades took Byzantium he was
helped by men in the city: when Byzantium welcomed Lysander
after his final victory at Aegospotami, those who had helped
Alcibiades had to fly. 'For the time being', says Xenophon,
'they escaped to the Euxine, but later they went to Athens and
became Athenians.'[3] In 424 the Athenians hoped that Megara,
as a result of constant Athenian pressure since the beginning of
the war and political divisions, would be incapable of resisting
an Athenian attack, but the arrival of Brasidas at the crucial
point saved Megara. It is interesting to note that later there
were Megarian exiles fighting with Athens in Sicily.[4] The
Samians who remained loyal to Athens even after Aegospotami
were offered Athenian citizenship. In a sense this was a hollow
gesture because both the Athenian and the Samian democracies
were doomed; but when peace had been made and their democracy had been restored the Athenians stood firm by their offer
and passed a decree that what the people formerly voted for the
Samians should still be valid. Meanwhile the Samian democrats
had been unable to resist Lysander and had to leave Samos
without their possessions. The Athenians in their decree publicly thanked the men of Ephesus and Notium for the welcome
they had given to their Samian friends.[5]

In the Assembly debate which followed the surrender of
Mytilene in 427 Thucydides makes Diodotus claim: 'It is the

[1] Thuc. v. 18. 6: Μηκυβερναίους δὲ καὶ Σαναίους καὶ Σιγγαίους οἰκεῖν τὰς πόλεις
τὰς ἑαυτῶν, καθάπερ Ὀλύνθιοι καὶ Ἀκάνθιοι. See Gomme, HCT iii. 672 f.
[2] IG i². 90; Tod, GHI i. 68.   [3] Xen. Hell. i. 3. 18–19; ii. 2. 1.
[4] Thuc. vii. 57. 8.   [5] ML 94 with Tod, GHI ii. 97.

demos that is on your side in all the cities.'[1] As a broad general-ization this was true, but in most states there was also at least an undercurrent of opposition and even democrats sometimes needed watching. It was not therefore enough to know that in most of the allied cities the demos was in control; the political situation had to be more closely followed. The Erythraean decree refers to a *phrourarchos* and *episkopoi*. The first, as his name implies, is in charge of an Athenian garrison but his duties are not exclusively military. It is he who in future years is to co-operate with the outgoing Council in appointing the Council of the year;[2] he will also be expected to watch the play of local politics and nip any conspiracy in the bud. The function of the *episkopos* is less easy to define. The title did not survive the fifth century in Athens and late classical scholars could only make inferences from literary references similar to those we still possess. Antiphon in a speech concerning the tribute assessment of Rhodian Lindus had occasion to mention *episkopoi* and Harpo-cration commented that they seemed to be 'men sent by the Athenians to review the situation in the various cities'.[3] Theo-phrastus in the first book of his *Politics* compared the name un-favourably with the Spartans' *harmost* who fulfilled the same function and he gave φύλακες as an alternative name.[4] *Suda* gives a very similar definition: 'Those who were sent out by the Athenians to the subject cities to review the situation in the various cities were called *episkopoi* and *phylakes*; the Spartan title was *harmost*.'[5] The comparison with the Spartan *harmost* and the use of *phylakes* as an equivalent might imply that the *episkopos* was a resident official, but the surviving evidence barely allows this interpretation. At Erythrae the *episkopoi* are concerned with the establishment of the first democratic Council, but not its successors, which are to be the responsibility of the *phrourarchos*.[6] Moreover if the *episkopoi* were resident they would be indis-tinguishable from other Athenian officials, whereas in the Decree of Clinias they form a separate category: 'The Boule and the (Athenian) *archontes* in the cities and the *episkopoi* are to

---

[1] Thuc. iii. 47. 2: νῦν μὲν γὰρ ὑμῖν ὁ δῆμος ἐν πάσαις ταῖς πόλεσιν εὔνους ἐστί.
[2] ML 40. 12–15.
[3] Harpocration, s.v. ἐπίσκοπος: ἐοίκασιν ἐκπέμπεσθαί τινες ὑπὸ Ἀθηναίων εἰς τὰς ὑπηκόους πόλεις ἐπισκεπτόμενοι τὰ παρ' ἑκάστοις.
[4] Theophrastus, quoted by Harpocration, loc. cit.
[5] *Suda*, s.v. ἐπίσκοπος.
[6] ML 40. 13–14.

ensure that the tribute be collected each year and brought to Athens.'[1] We should regard the *episkopos*, as his name implies, as a visiting commissioner sent to investigate, report, and, when necessary, take action. In Aristophanes' *Birds*, when the inhabitants of Cloudcuckoobury are establishing their nice peaceful Utopia, it is the Athenian *episkopos* who first intrudes to find out what is happening and to spoil the innocent fun. His mission derives from an Athenian decree, he owes his appointment to the lot, and he brings two ballot boxes because he will be concerned with establishing democratic procedures.[2] Unlike the garrison commander the *episkopos'* work is temporary only, and when he has completed his mission of inquiry or action he leaves for Athens or another state. We do not know how many *episkopoi* there were, nor whether a regular number was regularly appointed for a regular time, but the decree of Clinias implies that their activities were widely spread, and the Erythraean Decree shows that they did not necessarily work singly.

The Milesian regulations of 450–449 open with provision for sending five Athenian officials to Miletus who are to take up residence and consult the local magistrates.[3] Such officials were widely distributed in the empire and they are often referred to in inscriptions. They are already well established by the date of the Coinage Decree, for the officials who are to be primarily responsible for the execution of the decree are described as 'the officials in the cities—οἱ ἄρχοντες ἐν ταῖς πόλεσι', and a later clause shows that these are Athenian and not local officials.[4] They are also referred to as a widespread class in the Clinias Decree, which requires them to improve the collection of tribute and in other decrees they are made responsible for the protection of friends of Athens who have been made *proxenoi*.[5] A much later decree, of which only a small fragment has been found,

---

[1] ML 46. 5–8: τὲ]μ β|ολὲν καὶ τὸς ἄρχ[οντας ἐν] τêσ|ι πόλεσι καὶ τὸς [ἐπισκό]πος ἐ|πιμέλεσθαι κ.τ.λ.

[2] Ar. *Birds*, 1022–52. See App. 17, p. 581.

[3] D 11. 4–7: hελέσθαι δ]ὲ πέντε ἄν[δρας τὸν δῆμον ἐχς hαπ]άντον a]ὐτίκα μάλα.... τούτος δὲ ἄρ]χεν καὶ συν[βολεύεν τôι τε αἰσυμνέ|τει καὶ τ]οῖς προσε[ταίροις. In ll. 41 and 47 they are hοι ἄρχοντες hοι Ἀθηναίον; in l. 64 hοι πέντε hοι ἄρχοντες, cf. l. 73.

[4] ML 45, cl. 3: ἐὰν δὲ [ἄλλος ἔξω τ]ῶν ἀρχόν[των ἐν τ]αῖς πόλεσι, cf. cl. 4: καὶ εἰ μ|ή εἰσι[ν] ἄρχοντες Ἀθηναίων.

[5] e.g. IG i². 56 (Hill, *Sources*², B 80), 2–7: ἐ[π]|ιμέλεσθαι δὲ αὐτὸ Ἀθένεσι μ|[ὲ]ν τὸς πρυτάνες καὶ τὲμ βολέ]ν, ἐν δὲ τêσι ἄλλεσι πόλεσι hο|ί τινες Ἀθεναίον ἄρχοσι ἐν τ|êι hυπεροπίαι.

seems to refer to 'the officials in the cities of Ionia'.[1] Further inscriptions record their presence on the island of Sciathos, and in Aphytis and Methone in the Thraceward area, but reveal little of their responsibilities.[2] Whether Miletus was exceptional in having a board of five we do not know, but Sciathos had only one.

The Milesian regulations also refer to a garrison in contexts which cannot be satisfactorily restored and the question naturally arises whether the officials at Miletus were different in kind from the *phrourarchos* at Erythrae. Formally a *phrourarchos* is misnamed unless he commands *phrouroi*, whereas *archontes* do not necessarily require troops though, as at Miletus and Samos, they could have *phrouroi* with them. It may be more than coincidence that after 450 we have ample evidence of the wide distribution of *archontes*, but no surviving reference in inscriptions or literature to a *phrourarchos*. The military title may have been deliberately dropped in favour of a title that was less explicit. The primary responsibility of these officials was to watch local developments and to ensure that local politics were not being steered into dangerous channels. A passage in Aristophanes' *Birds* reminds us that these political residents could be strongly resented. His decree-seller, hoping to find a brisk market for his wares in Cloudcuckoobury, offers among his samples 'If anyone drives out the (Athenian) *archontes* and does not accept them as the decree requires . . .' This specimen, like his parody of the Coinage Decree, probably derives from a genuine decree.[3]

There is also an embarrassing and unique reference in a late source to a more insidious form of interference: 'officials who were sent out to the subject cities to control secretly what was done outside Athens; that is why they were called the secret service'.[4] If such a service existed it is extraordinary that it has left no trace in comedy nor in any other surviving source. More

[1] *Hesp.* xxxii (1963), 39; *SEG* xxi. 57.

[2] Sciathos, ML 90, ll. 19–20: τὸν ἄρχοντα τὸν ἐν Σκι|άθωι ὃς ἂν ἦι ἑκάστοτε; Aphytis, D 21. 6–8; Methone, ibid. 8.

[3] Ar. *Birds*, 1050: ἐὰν δέ τις ἐξελαύνῃ τοὺς ἄρχοντας καὶ μὴ δέχηται κατὰ τὴν στήλην. See App. 17, p. 581.

[4] Bekker, *Anecdota Graeca* (Berlin, 1814) i. 273³³: κρυπτή· ἀρχή τις ὑπὸ τῶν Ἀθηναίων πεμπομένη εἰς τοὺς ὑπηκόους, ἵνα κρύφα ἐπιτελέσωσι τὰ ἔξω γινόμενα· διὰ ταῦτα γὰρ κρυπτοὶ ἐκλήθησαν. Ar. *Thesm.* 600 might refer, but the scholiast does not help.

probably the service is the creation of an imaginative scholar misinterpreting a passage in comedy.

The received text of the Aristotelian *Constitution of Athens* in its list of those paid by the state includes 700 officials overseas.[1] The number seems at first unduly large, for there were less than 200 cities paying tribute each year. But at Miletus, as we have seen, there was a board of five and in the first attempt to settle Samos Thucydides speaks of Athenian officials in the plural. The total will also include *episkopoi* as well as political residents, whether commanding garrisons or not, and perhaps other officials concerned with jurisdiction. We do not know enough to say that 700 is an impossible figure.

Athens also made it her policy to select and honour individual friends of Athens in the cities and to use their services. On them the Assembly conferred the formal title of *proxenos*, normally accompanied by that of benefactor, πρόξενος καὶ εὐεργέτης. They repaid the compliment with active loyalty. The series of decrees honouring individuals in this way during the period of the Athenian Empire is a long one and literary sources add to the number. The first surviving inscription comes from the middle of the century, but, according to Herodotus, Alexander of Macedon was already a *proxenos* of Athens before the invasion of Xerxes.[2] The institution, however, most common in Athens but found also in other cities, probably does not go back beyond the seventh century. In the period of monarchies and exclusive aristocracies as in Homer's description of the Mycenaean world, inter-state relations depended on the friendship of princes. When governments became less exclusive and emphasis in political organization and religion shifted from the feudal lords to the state itself, then the personal guest-friend was replaced by the state's friend and in public relations the *proxenos* succeeded to the function of the *xenos*. It is doubtful whether the new institution was widely used in the sixth century but it offered great advantages to an imperial power. In return for the honour of public recognition by Athens, commemorated on a marble

---

[1] Ἀθ. Πολ. 24. 3: ἀρχαὶ δ' ἔνδημοι μὲν εἰς ἑπτακοσίους ἄνδρας, ὑπερόριοι δ' εἰς ἑπτακοσίους. The repetition of the number makes it suspect.

[2] Hdt. viii. 136. 1. The first *proxenos* known from an inscription is Pythagoras of Selymbria, who was given a public burial in the Ceramicus to commemorate his services as *proxenos*, and the high quality of his forebears and himself (c. 455), *IG* i². 1034.

stele which all could see on the Acropolis or in some other
public setting, the *proxenos* was eager to defend her interests and
there could be no better source for political intelligence. When
Mytilene was making hurried preparations for revolt it was the
proxenoi of Athens who first gave the warning.[1] When in Aristophanes' *Birds* the *episkopos* arrives in Cloudcuckoobury to supervise the new constitution his first question is: 'Where are the
proxenoi?'[2] What he needed before intervening was an up-to-
date appraisal of the local situation. When Sophocles during the
Samian revolt was dispatched from the main fleet to bring reinforcements from Lesbos he dined with Hermesilaus, a *proxenos*
of Athens.[3] Ion of Chios, to whom we owe this minor footnote
to the Samian revolt, confines himself to some of the lighter talk
over the wine; it is unlikely that politics were completely
excluded.

Normally the men honoured as *proxenoi* would be reliable
democrats, but if the services to be gained were sufficiently important the Athenians were not politically pedantic. When the
Peloponnesian War broke out and Perdiccas of Macedon was
spreading unrest and disaffection among the Chalcidic cities it
was essential for Athens at least to neutralize Thrace and if
possible to secure her active help. The most promising agents
in diplomatic negotiations with the Thracian court would be
local Greeks and Nymphodorus of Abdera was particularly well
qualified for the task; the Thracian king Sitalces had married his
sister. But Nymphodorus had formerly been regarded as a public
enemy by the Athenians, πρότερον πολέμιον νομίζοντες; probably he was an Abderite dynast who disliked the undue power
that Athenian encouragement gave to the demos. Now that he
could be very useful his political record was forgotten and he
was publicly declared a *proxenos*. An Athenian alliance with
Sitalces was the city's considerable reward for this piece of
opportunism.[4]

A little later in his narrative Thucydides provides another
interesting glimpse of the importance of *proxenoi* in Athenian
politics. In 429 Phormio with only twenty ships had defeated a
fleet of Peloponnesians by masterly tactics in the Gulf of Corinth.

The Peloponnesians withdrew to build up their strength for another battle; Phormio sent an urgent appeal to Athens for reinforcements. But in spite of the urgency of the need the reinforcements, instead of making at full speed for the Corinthian Gulf, went first to Crete, 'for Nicias a Cretan of Gortyn, who was their *proxenos*, persuaded them to sail to Cydonia; this town was hostile to Athens and Nicias said he would bring it over'.[1] The attempt failed, but had perhaps been worth making. Cydonia was an Aeginetan settlement and the best harbour on the direct route to Egypt. The route from Egypt and Libya was important to the Peloponnesians; Athenian triremes based on Cydonia would have been a continuing threat to their merchantmen.[2]

The services commemorated on inscriptions are usually much more general. Oeniades from the island of Sciathos is typical: he is praised 'because he is loyal to the city of the Athenians and eager to do what service he can and helps Athenians who come to Sciathos'. He is honoured with the title of πρόξενος καὶ εὐεργέτης, which is to be hereditary.[3] Proxenides of Cnidus is similarly honoured 'because of his giving what help he can to the Athenians both now and in time past'.[4]

The importance of *proxenoi* is again well illustrated in the bitter political struggles that broke out in Corcyra in 427. Corcyra had made alliance with Athens in 433 and had been helped by Athens against Corinth at the battle of Sybota, but in 427 the Corcyraean prisoners taken in the engagements at Epidamnus and Corcyra had been released. It was said that they had been ransomed by *proxenoi*, but in fact they had been persuaded to bring over Corcyra to Corinth.[5] Opinion in Corcyra was evenly divided, and the main opposition to rejoining Corinth was led by Pithias, a would-be *proxenos* of Athens who was a leader of the people and at the time a member of the Boule.[6] He was brought to trial on a charge of attempting to enslave Corcyra to the Athenians. Acquitted, he in turn brought to court five of his wealthiest opponents on a religious charge. Their reaction

---

[1] Thuc. ii. 85. 5.

[2] Cf. Thuc. iv. 53. 3, on the importance of Cythera: ἦν γὰρ αὐτοῖς τῶν τε ἀπ᾽ Αἰγύπτου καὶ Λιβύης ὁλκάδων προσβολή.

[3] ML 90. 7–13. [4] D 23. 7–9. [5] Thuc. iii. 70. 1.

[6] Thuc. iii. 70. 3–6: ἦν γὰρ Πειθίας ἐθελοπρόξενός τε τῶν Ἀθηναίων καὶ τοῦ δήμου προειστήκει.

was to take daggers into the council chamber and murder Pithias with up to sixty of his associates.

Pithias was not the only member of an allied city who suffered for his political convictions. A fourth-century inscription concerning Athens' dealings with Iulis on the island of Ceos throws vivid light on what could happen to friends of Athens when oligarchs came into power. The secretary of the Boule who was responsible for publishing the decree had an unfortunate weakness for long sentences but there is no obscurity in his Greek:

> Since the men of Iulis who broke their oaths and the agreement and made war on the demos of Athens and the Ceans and the other allies and, though condemned to death, returned to Ceos, threw down the stelae on which were recorded the agreement and the names of those who broke their oath and the agreement, and of the friends of Athens whom the demos brought back to Iulis some they killed, others, Satyrides, Timoxenus, and Miltiades, they condemned to death and confiscated their property contrary to their oaths and the agreement because they prosecuted Antipater, when the Athenian Boule condemned him to death for killing the Athenian *proxenos* contrary to the decrees of the Athenian demos and in transgression of oaths and agreement, (for all these offences) they shall be exiled from Ceos and Athens and their property shall pass to the demos of Iulis; and the generals of Iulis now in Athens shall make a list of their names at once in the presence of the demos for the secretary of the Boule.[1]

This decree dates from 362 in the time of the fourth-century Athenian League, but it illustrates what must often have happened in the fifth century.

The Peloponnesian War, as Thucydides emphasizes, intensified political strains and stresses. Moderate elements tended to be submerged between extremes, and violence became the normal road to political power. During the revolution at Athens in 411 an Athenian general, acting for the oligarchs, suppressed the democracy in Thasos. It was thought that Thasian oligarchs would be loyal to those who had given them power. But the real leaders of Thasian oligarchy were men who could not compromise. They had been exiled from Thasos and were with the Peloponnesians. They now returned and with their partisans in Thasos collected ships and led Thasos into revolt from Athens.

[1] Tod, *GHI* ii. 142. 27.

A Thasian inscription probably of the period lists men whose property had been confiscated because of their Athenian sympathies.[1] Among them was Apemantus, whose five sons were made *proxenoi* of Athens before the end of the Peloponnesian War. The stele recording this honour was destroyed under the Thirty, but some years after the restoration of the democracy Eurypylus, one of the brothers, visiting Athens was able to have another stele set up: 'Menippides proposed that since the stele which recorded their proxenies was destroyed under the Thirty, the secretary of the Boule set up the record again on a stele at the expense of Eurypylus, and that they invite Eurypylus to public hospitality in the Prytaneum.'[2]

The work of *proxenoi* of Athens and of Athenian officials overseas was powerfully supplemented by the people's law-courts in Athens. The increasing use of Athenian courts to try allies' cases was one of the allies' main grievances; the dependence on courts rather than arbitrary purges was one of the Athenians' main defences of their rule. The complex problems of imperial iurisdiction require their own chapter.

[1] *IG* xii (8) 263.   [2] Tod, *GHI* ii. 98.

12

IMPERIAL JURISDICTION

THE Old Oligarch cynically admitted that the Athenian demos showed a shrewd understanding of its own interests in making the allies bring their cases to Athens. Apart from the material advantages to the state in Piraeus dues, and to those who had lodgings, horses, or slaves for hire, the central control of jurisdiction made the allies depend on the demos rather than on its generals and other officials; and the people's courts ensured that the right kind of justice was done.[1] He does not specify what classes of case came to Athens, but he implies that the volume was considerable and that this was one of the main features of Athenian imperialism. This also might be inferred from the speech given by Thucydides to Athenian envoys who happened to be at Sparta in 432 when the storm over Corcyra broke. One of the main criticisms that they tried to meet was that the Athenians were φιλόδικοι.[2] The meaning of this word and of the context in which it comes is still disputed but at least it can be inferred that the Athenian courts attracted strong criticism from the allies.

There is much evidence concerning judicial relations between Athens and her allies in literary sources good and bad and in inscriptions complete and fragmentary, but very few of the documents can be regarded as safe from controversy. Of some important passages the literal translation as well as the true meaning is uncertain, and the evidence for chronological development is particularly weak. No account yet published has reconciled all the evidence satisfactorily, but de Ste Croix's comprehensive review marks a considerable advance.[3] It might seem sound method to examine first the crucial passage in Thucydides, for he should be our most reliable authority; but

---

[1] [Xen.] Ἀθ. Πολ. 1. 16–18.   [2] Thuc. i. 77. 1. Below, pp. 228–33.
[3] G. E. M. de Ste Croix 'Notes on Jurisdiction in the Athenian Empire', CQ lv (1961), 94–112 and 268–80.

since translation and meaning are extremely controversial this passage cannot provide a firm foundation. It should be left to the later stages of the argument and we may be satisfied if the general view we adopt is not inconsistent with a defensible translation of Thucydides. We should also postpone discussion of συμβολαί which figure prominently in the evidence, for the conclusions to be drawn in this field are far from clear and they are less important to the subject than the space which they normally occupy in discussions suggests. It is better to take the risk of reconstructing in the light of the evidence that survives the situations that were likely to arise and the action that a democratic imperial state might be expected to take.

It is unlikely that much thought was given to questions of jurisdiction when the Delian League was formed. The autonomy of members was taken for granted and there was no question of their leader interfering in political cases. For disputes between individuals of different states there was already a customary procedure. Where frequent contacts were to be expected agreements were made between two states laying down the legal procedure to be followed; there was no reason why such agreements should be affected by the formation of the League. If it was anticipated that military action might involve judicial settlement it could have been assumed that the League Council meeting on Delos would be responsible. But when relations with the allies assumed more importance than fighting Persians politics were often involved and the Athenian custom was to use the Athenian courts, which were coming to maturity just when the League Council was fading in importance. While regular meetings were held on Delos the Council might be used as a judicial body in the same way as Councils in democratic and oligarchic cities had judicial powers; but when League meetings lapsed after the Peace of Callias it was natural that Athens should try in her own courts members of allied states whom she thought to be a threat to her control.

The earliest documents in our inquiry are the Athenian decrees which provide regulations for Erythrae and Miletus in the late fifties. It has often been emphasized that in the Erythrae Decree there is considerably more independence allowed to the local court than would have been the case a generation later: 'if any Erythraean kills another Erythraean he shall be put to death if he is found guilty'.¹ Later such a case would have been sent to Athens. This clause comes from a part of the decree which has long been lost, but if a fragment now in London once formed part of the same stone the impression that no Erythraean was to be tried by Athenian officials must be modified, for the fragment deals with problems of jurisdiction and covers some cases between Athenians and Erythraeans.² Similarly in the Miletus regulations it is clear that some cases involving Milesians are to go to Athens.³ One such category probably concerns military service. It seems that Miletus was required to send hoplites to fight with the Athenians when required: it is reasonable to assume, as the fragmentary text suggests, that offences connected with military service should be tried at Athens. Another clause seems to concern the judicial competence of the five Athenian officers who were being sent to Miletus; it has been plausibly restored to specify that they may decide minor cases but must send cases involving a penalty of more than a certain amount to Athens.⁴ This is an important clue.

When an Athenian garrison was installed in an allied city delicate questions could easily arise. The garrison commander would be responsible for the discipline of his men and could himself be expected to have the right of decision in minor cases, but it would not be consistent with the radical spirit of the new democracy of the fifties if magistrates at home or overseas could inflict serious penalties without appeal; such cases would have to be tried by the sovereign people through the people's law-courts. Offences confined to the garrison presented no serious problem. It was different when Athenian troops became involved with local inhabitants. What happened when a drunken soldier was hit on the head and robbed? What happened when an angry mother complained of her daughter's rape, or when a shopkeeper asserted that an Athenian soldier had taken one

---

¹ ML 40. 29–30.
² D 10. 57–62. For the relation of this fragment to the lost decree, see Endnote 8, p. 421.
³ D 11, 29–35.
⁴ D 11. 76–80, as restored by Schöll: [ἐὰν δέ τις ἀπειθεῖ αὐ|τοῖς τὸν Μιλ]εσίον ἒ [τὸ]ν φρουρὸν, κύριοι ὄ[ντον αὐτοὶ ζημιῶν μέχρι—δραχ|μῶν· ἐὰν δέ τις] μέζονο[ς ἄ]χσ[ι]ος ἐι ζημίας, Ἀθέ[ναζε προσκαλεσάμενοι αὐτὸν καὶ τὲν | ζημίαν ἐπιβ]αλόντε[ς h]οπόσες ἂν δοκεῖ ἀχσ[ιος ἔναι ἐσαγόντον ἐς τὸ δικαστέριο|ν].

of his best amphorae without paying for it? The evidence does not tell us but we may guess that all cases in which garrison troops became involved were tried in the first instance by the garrison commander and sent to Athens with a recommendation if the penalty exceeded his competence.[1]

Many more cases came to Athens directly without a preliminary hearing in the allied city. When, for example, Athenian decrees were passed which affected allied cities, provision had to be made for dealing with offences against the terms of the decree, and such cases we should expect to be tried at Athens. So in the Coinage Decree a clause has been persuasively restored to say that if there are no Athenian officers in the city the requirements of the decree shall be carried out by the magistrates of each city, and, if they do not act as the decree requires, these magistrates may be prosecuted at Athens and the penalty shall be loss of citizen rights.[2] The Clinias Decree which attempts to tighten up tribute collection includes a similar provision: 'If any Athenian or ally commits an offence in respect of the tribute which the cities are required to record on a tablet for their couriers and send to Athens, he may be indicted before the *prytaneis* by any ally or Athenian who so wishes.'[3] Such cases came before the Boule in the first place, but the Boule no longer had authority to decide them; their function was to prepare the case and send it with a recommendation to one of the people's courts.[4] There is no question of these trials taking place in local courts, nor is it likely that the Athenian claim to give judgement was ever formally discussed or formally defined. And when the Chalcidians are required to declare in their oath: 'if anyone stirs up revolt against Athens I will denounce him' we can assume that the denunciation would be made before an Athenian official who would, if he thought fit, initiate proceedings in an Athenian court.[5] Nor did the Athenians always wait for

---

[1] See previous note and *IG* i². 11, possibly a fragment of the lost Erythrae decree.

[2] ML 45, clause 4: καὶ εἰ μ]ή εἰσι[ν] ἄρχοντες Ἀθηναίων, ἔ[πιτελεσάντων ὅσα ἐν τῶι ψ]ηφίσματι οἱ ἄρχοντε[ς οἱ ἑκάστης τῆς πόλεως· καὶ] ἐὰμ μὴ ποιῶσι κατὰ τ[ὰ ἐψηφισμένα, ἔστω κατὰ τῶν ἀρχ]όντων τούτων περὶ [ἀτιμίας δίωξις Ἀθήνησι]. The penalty of ἀτιμία is restored from cl. 3.

[3] ML 46. 31–5: ἐὰν δέ τις Ἀθ[εναῖος ἒ χσύμμαχος ἀδικεῖ περὶ τὸ]|ν φόρον hὸν δεῖ [τὰς πόλες γραφσάσας ἐς γραμματεῖ]|ον τοῖς ἀπάγος[ιν ἀποπέμπεν Ἀθέναζε, ἔστο αὐτὸν γ]ράφεσθαι πρὸς [τὸς πρυτάνες τὸι β]ολομένο[ι Ἀθενα]|ίον καὶ τὸν χσ[υμμάχον.

[4] Ibid. 35–41.

[5] ML 52. 24–5: κ|αὶ ἐὰν ἀφιστεῖ τις κατερὸ Ἀθεναίοισι.

information from allies. One of the most unpopular features of Athenian imperialism was the informer who made it his trade to keep on the watch for anti-Athenian intrigues; and the complement of the informer was the summoner whose duty was to serve the writ and bring the suspected man to Athens.[1] Athens prided herself on the fairness of her courts but in such political cases political prejudice will have been a decisive factor. It is the oligarchs who were bruised and battered by the people's courts.[2]

In the fully developed imperial system there were more serious encroachments than these on the authority of the cities. One of the clauses at issue in the terms of settlement imposed by Athens on Chalcis after the revolt concerned the competence of the local courts. This competence had been severely restricted in the original decree and when the Chalcidians protested and appealed the Athenians were unwilling to reverse their decision: 'Chalcidians shall impose penalties on Chalcidians at Chalcis in the same way as Athenians impose penalties on Athenians at Athens, except in cases involving exile, death, and loss of rights; in these cases there shall be *ephesis* to Athens to the Heliaea presided over by the *thesmothetai*.'[3] Does *ephesis* in this clause mean compulsory reference in the first instance, compulsory reference after a preliminary hearing, or voluntary reference in the second instance by appeal? Common sense might seem to require one of the first two meanings, especially in the light of a passage in Antiphon's speech for the defence in the trial arising from the murder of Herodes. His opponents, he says, put a slave to death though 'even a city has no right to inflict the death penalty without the authority of Athens'.[4] But the two documents are not contemporary and the decisive criterion must be the normal use of the word. There is little doubt that *ephesis* and its cognates is the language of appeal.[5] It is used

---

[1] Ar. *Birds*, 1422–31 : Μὰ Δί' ἀλλὰ κλητήρ εἰμι νησιωτικὸς | καὶ συκοφάντης.

[2] Ar. *Peace*, 639 : τῶν δὲ συμμάχων ἔσειον τοὺς παχεῖς καὶ πλουσίους.

[3] ML 52. 71–6 : τὰς δὲ εὐθύνας Χαλκιδεῦσι κατ|ὰ σφὸν αὐτὸν ἔναι ἐν Χαλκίδι καθάπερ Ἀθ|ένεσιν Ἀθεναίοις πλὲν φυγῆς καὶ θανάτ|ο καὶ ἀτιμίας· περὶ δὲ τούτον ἔφεσιν ἔνα|ι Ἀθέναζε. Gomme, *HCT* i. 342 takes εὐθύνας as the examination of magistrates after their year of office. This would not give Athens the control she needed. Her main danger would come from oligarchs, probably not in office.

[4] Antiphon v. 47 : νῦν δὲ αὐτοὶ καταγνόντες τὸν θάνατον τοῦ ἀνδρὸς ἀπεκτείνατε ὃ οὐδὲ πόλει ἔξεστιν, ἄνευ Ἀθηναίων οὐδένα θανάτῳ ζημιῶσαι.

[5] Wade-Gery, *Essays in Greek History*, 192–5.

of a man whose claim to the citizenship has not been accepted
on his coming of age by his fellow demesmen and who takes his
case to the law-court; it is used also of a party who is not satisfied with the decision of an arbitrator.[1] No instance has been
cited where the word clearly means compulsory reference without even a preliminary hearing and the language of fifth-century
decrees suggests that when there is a preliminary hearing of a
case which has to go for final decision to another authority, such
compulsory reference is not described as *ephesis*.[2] This clause of
the Chalcis decree should mean that in cases involving the
major penalties there shall be the right of appeal to Athens and
since the decree does not specify who is to have this right we
should infer that both the prosecution and the defence could
appeal. This would be reasonable, for Athens was concerned to
ensure not only that the friend of Athens was not unfairly sentenced as a result of local prejudice, but also that the enemy of
Athens was not unfairly acquitted. A close parallel to this latter
use of *ephesis* is found in a later decree, probably from near the
middle of the fourth century, which provides for an Athenian
monopoly in the export of ruddle from the island of Ceos: 'if
anyone commits an offence whereby the export of ruddle to
Athens is hindered he shall be denounced before the local
magistrates, and the prosecutor may appeal if he is not satisfied
with the verdict to the *thesmothetai* at Athens, who shall bring
the case into court'.[3]

The *ephesis* that is specified in the Chalcis decree is said to be
'according to the decree'. This might possibly refer to a general
imperial decree applying this form of judicial control to all the
cities of the empire, but in the context it more probably refers
to the first decree concerning the settlement with Chalcis.[4] It
would be dangerous to generalize from the treatment of Chalcis; it would be even more dangerous to assume that the
Chalcis decree can be used to determine the meaning of the
passage from Antiphon about the death penalty. When Antiphon says that no city could put anyone to death without the

---

[1] Arist. Ἀθ. Πολ. 42. 1; 53. 2.
[2] ML 46. 37–9: [ἑὸ δ' ἂν] | καταγνôι ℎ[ε βολέ, μὲ τιμᾶν αὐτ]ôι κυρία ἔστο [ἀλλ'
ἐσ]‖φερέτο ἐς τ[ὲν ἐλιαίαν εὐθύ]ς.
[3] Tod, *GHI* ii. 162. 20–1: εἶν]|αι [δὲ] καὶ ἔφεσιν Ἀθήναζε καὶ τῶι φήναντι καὶ τῶι
ἐνδεί[ξαντι.
[4] ML 52. 76: κατὰ το φσέφισμα τὸ δέμο, cf. l. 49: κατὰ τὰ ἐφσεφισμένα.

authority of Athens he must mean either that cases involving the death penalty had to be referred to Athens for their first and only hearing, or that after a preliminary hearing the case had to be referred to Athens from the local court. He cannot only mean that in such cases an appeal could be made to Athens. The difference between the two passages need not disturb us. The Chalcis decree is dated in 446–445; Antiphon's speech was probably delivered between 416 and 413.[1] We should expect development in such a long interval, and a stiffening of control would not be surprising. Already when the Old Oligarch wrote, probably not later than 424, the principle of appeal seems to have been replaced by compulsory reference. The cases which concern the writer are those which carry the major penalties, and he writes as if such cases had without question to be brought before Athenian courts; and since no mention is made of a preliminary hearing at home it is probable that the process of law began and ended at Athens.[2]

It is interesting to note, as de Ste Croix emphasized, that the criterion adopted by Athens in withdrawing competence from the local authorities was not the nature of the offence but the nature of the penalty.[3] It might be thought that Athens should only have been concerned with political cases and that private murder, violent assault, serious offences in local administration, could and should have been left to local courts. The reason for not making such distinctions may be that it would have been extremely difficult to define unambiguously the categories of cases which did concern Athens' imperial interests, and still more difficult perhaps to ensure that political feuds were not fought out under irrelevant charges. The penalties included in this clause of the Chalcis decree are the major penalties. They all recur in the oath to be sworn by the Athenians to Chalcis and in the Old Oligarch's list of sentences passed by the popular courts on enemies of the Athenian people among the allies.[4] These two lists, however, also include among the penalties 'the confiscation of property', which is absent from the clause we have examined. This absence might perhaps be significant. In reply to an appeal for complete judicial independence Athens, while retaining control over cases involving the death sentence,

---

[1] K. J. Dover, *CQ* xliv (1950), 44–60. [2] [Xen.] *Ἀθ. Πολ.* 1. 16.
[3] De Ste Croix, art. cit. 270. [4] ML 52. 7–10; [Xen.] *Ἀθ. Πολ.* 1. 14.

exile, and loss of rights, might have allowed to the local courts full discretion to confiscate a man's property.

Athens also used her imperial position to give special protection in her courts to individual allies who had served her well as *proxenoi*. A long series of decrees in honour of *proxenoi* record these privileges and one of the earliest, which is probably to be dated near to the middle of the century, may serve as an illustration. A great deal of the text is missing but what survives is sufficient to give the sense of the main clauses and most of the restoration can be regarded as certain.

And if Acheloion is injured by anyone he may bring his case against the offender at Athens before the polemarch, and he shall not pay court fees apart from five drachmae . . . ; and if anyone kills Acheloion or any of his children in the cities which the Athenians rule, the city concerned must pay five talents, as when an Athenian is killed and the punishment of the killer shall be the same as if an Athenian were killed.[1]

The first form of protection offered here assumes that as a conspicuous friend of Athens Acheloion might not get a fair hearing in his local court; he is therefore allowed to bring his prosecution at Athens and Athens will see both that the defendant appears in court and that the decision of the court is carried out. The polemarch's court is specified because it is his responsibility to look after the interests of metics and favoured foreigners. This privilege of prosecuting at Athens recurs in other decrees, sometimes with minor variations. Acheloion's court fees are reduced; in other cases they are waived altogether.[2] Acheloion's life is also protected by the same deterrents that have been devised to protect Athenians, a heavy fine of 5 talents on the city concerned and the special punishment of the individual responsible.[3]

This privilege also recurs and in some inscriptions it is extended in a fuller formula: 'If anyone kills, arrests, or imprisons . . . the penalty shall be the same as has been voted for Athenians.'[4]

---

[1] *IG* i². 28a: *SEG* x 23 (= Hill, *Sources*², B 33), before 445 because it has Ϟ.

[2] D 23. 20–4. ἐὰν [δὲ ἀδικεῖ τις ἐ Ἀθεναίον]|ἐ τō[ν σ]υ[μμάχον τὸν Ἀθεναίον κατὰ| τ]ούτον λ[αγχανέτο Ἀθένεσιν πρὸς | τ]ὸμ πολέ[μαρχον τὰς δίκας ἄνευ πρ]|υτανείον.

[3] Ar. *Peace*, 170–2; Roussel, *REA* xxxv (1933), 383–5; Meiggs, *CR* lxiii (1949), 9–12. See also, p. 171.

[4] *IG* i². 154 (*SEG* x. 98), 10–13: [καὶ ἐάν τίς| τ]ιψας αὐτὸν ἀπ[οκτέν|ει βιαίοι θαν]άτοι ἐ δέσει ἐ [ἄγει, ε]ἶναι αὐτοῖς τὲ]ν τιμορίαν κ[αθάπε|ρ Ἀθεναίοις ἐφ]σέφισται. This fuller formula recurs in *IG* i². 141, ii². 32, 73, and, by restoration in *IG* i². 144

This is a very considerable extension and it almost certainly marks a later stage. None of the inscriptions with the fuller formula need be earlier than the Peloponnesian War, and none of those which offer protection only against killing need be later than the outbreak of war. The first stage reflects the sharp hostility that arose in the early forties when, with the end of fighting against Persia, it became clear to all that the League had become an Empire; the extension was probably a reaction to the increasing danger from anti-Athenian elements when Sparta's pose as the liberator of Greece heightened party feeling in the cities. The fact that these privileges are recorded in detail implies that they were not automatically enjoyed by all *proxenoi*, but were conferred only on the specially favoured or perhaps on those whose service to Athens might be expected to invite reprisals.

We should not expect Athenian citizens to be less favourably treated than their *proxenoi*, but while it is made explicit that favoured *proxenoi* are being treated in the same way as Athenians in the penalties established for their murder or arrest, no reference is made to citizens in the clauses which entitle *proxenoi* to prosecute at Athens. This suggests that Athenian citizens did not have the right to force members of allied cities to defend themselves in Athenian courts, and other evidence seems to point the same way;[1] but this brings us back to the Athenians' defence of their empire in Thucydides and the vexed problem of φιλόδικοι. Unfortunately Thucydides, who will have had no doubts himself about Athenian practice, has failed to make his meaning clear. The general sense of the Athenian argument in the context is that Athens relies on the law-courts rather than force although she has the power to coerce and might be expected as an imperial power to be impatient of the law. The passage that most concerns us runs as follows: "καὶ ἐλασσούμενοι γὰρ ἐν ταῖς ξυμβολαίαις πρὸς τοὺς ξυμμάχους δίκαις καὶ παρ' ἡμῖν αὐτοῖς ἐν τοῖς ὁμοίοις νόμοις ποιήσαντες τὰς κρίσεις φιλοδικεῖν δοκοῦμεν."[2] What is the charge and what is the defence?

The word φιλοδικεῖν and its cognates is not used elsewhere by Thucydides; in normal fifth- and fourth-century usage a

---

(*SEG* x. 108). The earlier formula, limited to killing, is more common; *IG* i². 27 (Hill, *Sources*² B 34) 28 (Hill 33), 56 (Hill 80), 72 (*SEG* x. 88), *IG* ii². 38 (*SEG* x. 99); also in *IG* i². 143 (*SEG* x. 52, a copy of *IG* i². 27, below, pp. 425 f.).

[1] De Ste Croix, art. cit. 276.   [2] Thuc. i. 77. 1.

φιλόδικος is a man who goes to court unnecessarily, who is litigious.[1] In view of the rest of our evidence this would be a strangely innocuous charge. What we expect to weigh most heavily with the allies is the withdrawal of their most important cases from the local courts and the political tyranny of Athenian jurors. To produce a possible translation that would approximate to this general sense φιλοδικεῖν would have to mean 'to be fond of dragging political suspects into (Athenian) courts'. Unfortunately the nature of the defence is even more obscure. We can be satisfied that ξυμβολαίαις δίκαις is equivalent to δίκαις ἀπὸ ξυμβολῶν, but the rest is uncertain. Are the two clauses co-ordinate or is the first subordinate to the second; is Thucydides referring to two sets of cases or one? If he is referring to only one set of cases the meaning would be: 'For finding ourselves at a disadvantage in cases with our allies deriving from judicial agreements, and having therefore provided for such trials to be held at Athens where the laws are equal for all . . . we are thought to φιλοδικεῖν.' If Thucydides had two sets of cases in mind he might mean 'For though allowing ourselves to remain at a disadvantage in cases with our allies deriving from agreements, and providing laws that are equal for all in the trials that we have transferred to Athens . . . we are thought to φιλοδικεῖν.' It is possible to feel that the Greek favours one meaning rather than the other, but neither can be decisively excluded. The nature of συμβολαί and the Athenians' use of συμβολαί in the fifth century must therefore first be considered.

The general nature of συμβολαί is not in serious doubt. They were inter-state agreements which laid down the procedure to be followed when disputes arose between members of two states.[2] Such disputes might most commonly arise from trading contracts, but fragments of agreements that survive show that the agreements covered very much more than trading matters. An agreement between Athens and Troezen included cases of assault and battery.[3] It was not necessary to have such agreements whenever one's citizens traded or travelled but it was a considerable convenience and Athens made abundant use of the

---

[1] E. G. Turner, CR lx (1946), 5–8.
[2] Harpocration, σύμβολα· τὰς συνθήκας, ἃς ἂν ἀλλήλαις αἱ πόλεις θέμεναι τάττωσι τοῖς πολίταις ὥστε διδόναι καὶ λαμβάνειν τὰ δίκαια.
[3] Woodhead, Hesp. xxvi (1957), 225–9.

practice. The main function of the agreement was to ensure that disputes could be fairly and quickly settled and judgements executed. This required agreement on the court before which cases should be heard, and what little evidence there is suggests that cases were normally at least tried in the defendant's court. This custom is attested in an agreement between Ephesus and Sardis of the first century B.C.[1] and it seems to be confirmed by a passage in the speech concerning Halonnesus wrongly attributed to Demosthenes.[2] The writer of that speech is trying to show that Philip of Macedon's sudden anxiety to have συμβολαί with Athens is insincere and based on ulterior motives. There was considerably more intercourse, he says, between Athens and Macedon in the days of the Athenian Empire but no formal agreement was made then, and the reason he seems to give is that συμβολαί would have involved considerably more travel. 'We were satisfied with their legal procedures and they with ours.' The passage is admittedly not without difficulty, but it seems to imply that under the terms of a normal inter-state agreement a Macedonian who intended to prosecute an Athenian would have had to come to Athens and an Athenian would have had to go to Macedon to prosecute a Macedonian.[3] That the defendant's court should be specified as the competent authority makes good sense, for this would protect the defendant from malicious prosecution and at the same time the prosecutor's interest would be served because the defendant's state would be in a better position to execute judgement than his own. The question that concerns us is whether Athens took advantage of her imperial position to modify such agreements in her own favour.

Our main evidence comes from inscriptions and they suggest, though they do not prove, that Athenian judicial agreements were not affected by political considerations. It is difficult otherwise to explain the terms of an Athenian decree concerning Mytilene which was passed at some time not long after the crushing of her revolt. Much of the restoration of this text is highly conjectural but there seems to be no doubt that the judicial relations between Athenians and Mytilenaeans are to

---

[1] *OGIS* ii. 437. 11 c. ll. 57–9: δι[κ]άζεσθαι τὸν ἀδι[κο]ύμενο[ν κατὰ τὰ προγεγραμ-μ]ένα ἐν [τ]ῆι [τ]οῦ ἀδικοῦντος πόλει.

[2] [Dem.] vii. 13.   [3] See Endnote 18, p. 433.

be governed by the same agreement as before the revolt.[1] Similarly in a decree from the end of the Peloponnesian War in which Athens offers full citizenship to the Samians it is laid down that any disputes which arise shall be settled according to the existing agreement.[2] The same continuity is implied in the inscription which records the Athenian settlement with Selymbria after Alcibiades' recapture of the town in 409.[3]

There is, however, one decree which has been thought to show that Athens used her power to change normal inter-state procedure to suit her own interest. This decree concerns Phaselis and may date from as early as the sixties. We can accept the current restoration of the critical clause: ὅ τι ἄμ με[ν] Ἀθ|[ήνησι ξ]υ[μβ]όλαιον γένηται|[πρὸς Φ]ασηλιτ[ῶ]ν τινα, Ἀθή[ν]η|[σι τὰς δ]ίκας γίγνεσθαι παρ|[ὰ τῶι πο]λεμάρχωι, καθάπερ Χ|[ίοις, καὶ] ἄλλοθι μηδὲ ἀμδ.[4] This clause was most commonly taken to mean that if a contract was made at Athens in future any case arising should be heard at Athens, whereas previously it might have been heard at Phaselis. This interpretation has now been challenged at two points in a detailed study of the decree by de Ste Croix.[5] Following Hopper he points out that though ξυμβόλαιον can mean a contract it can also, and more often does, mean any situation in which someone has, or believes himself to have, a legal right of action.[6] More important for our purpose, he holds that Athens is not in this decree bringing cases to an Athenian court which would previously have been tried elsewhere, but merely changing the court in Athens from the court normally used for cases arising from συμβολαί presided over by the *thesmothetai* to the polemarch's court. This change is a privilege because the polemarch's court deals with metics and specially favoured foreigners and probably was considerably less crowded than the courts of the *thesmothetai*. In this interpretation the emphasis is on παρὰ τῶι πολεμάρχωι and not on Ἀθήνησι. The clause does not mean that the case must be heard at Athens but that if it is heard at Athens it must be in the polemarch's court. Emphasizing practical considerations, de Ste Croix holds that the plaintiff must have the right to sue in

---

[1] D 22. 15–17: [καὶ ἀπὸ χσυμβολ]ῶν δί]κας διδόν[τα]ς πρὸς Ἀθεν[αίος καὶ δεχομένο|ς κα]τὰ τὰς χσυ[μβο]λὰς haὶ ἔσαν [πρὸ τõ].

[2] ML 94. 18.   [3] ML 87. 22–6.

[4] ML 31. 6–14.   [5] De Ste Croix, art. cit. 100–8.

[6] R. J. Hopper, *JHS* lxiii (1943), 38–45.

whichever city he prefers and that he will want to sue where he can get the most effective remedy.

De Ste Croix's interpretation of the Phaselis decree is very seductive, and it must be admitted that most earlier views are not consistent with the general tone of the decree which seems to be conferring a privilege and not a penalty on Phaselis. If we retain the restoration καθάπερ Χ[ίοις] in l. 11 the Phaselites are being treated like the Chians, who were one of Athens' firmest and strongest allies.[1] The decree is also being publicly displayed in the interests of the Phaselites and that is why they are paying for it. On the other hand, it is difficult to accept de Ste Croix's translation of Ἀθήνησι. In the structure of the Greek this word seems to carry emphasis, and is balanced by κατ[ὰ τὰς ὅσας] ξυμβολὰς πρὸς Φασ[ηλίτας]. The implication is that in the first half of the clause the procedure is a departure from what is provided by the existing συμβολαί.[2] We should, however, agree with de Ste Croix that this is not high-handed imperialism. To make sense of the general tone of the decree the Phaselites must have agreed to this change, and the reason is not difficult to envisage. The Phaselites' main concern presumably was to do business and get trade in the Piraeus, to hire ships, make loans, contract for the carriage of Athenian goods. If Athenians had to go as far as Phaselis to get satisfaction they would normally prefer to deal with nearer customers. The Phaselites could have willingly accepted what was plain common sense, especially when the change was coupled with the privilege of using the polemarch's court.

Returning to the passage in Thucydides it now seems more probable that he is referring to two sets of cases rather than one. The evidence of the inscriptions does not suggest that Athens insisted on all cases arising from ξυμβολαί being brought to Athens, and the Old Oligarch seems to have in mind allied cases against allies rather than against Athenians. It also seems unlikely that the Athenians at Sparta would have limited themselves to defending Athenian practice with regard to ξυμβολαί when so much imperial jurisdiction had no connection at all with ξυμβολαί. ἐλασσούμενοι γὰρ ἐν ταῖς ξυμβολαίαις πρὸς τοὺς

---

[1] The Chians had negotiated the entry of Phaselis to the Delian League when they resisted Cimon on his way to the Eurymedon (above, p. 76).

[2] R. Seager, *Hist.* xv (1966), 509.

ξυμμάχους δίκαις will not mean 'because we were at a disadvantage in cases arising from ξυμβολαί,' but 'though we *are* (and always have been) at a disadvantage'. The reason for the disadvantage was that Athens normally accepted the regular procedure of ξυμβολαί under which Athenians often had to prosecute in allied courts where local prejudice would be a serious handicap. In the second clause the Athenians are admitting that they have transferred some cases to Athens, but then (whereas in many allied courts there is no real justice) in Athens the laws are the same for all.

The difficulty of translating and interpreting this passage in Thucydides should not divert the emphasis from what most affected the allies. What they hated and feared most was a summons to appear at Athens on a political charge for suspicious talk or action. They also resented the undermining of their own authority by the need to refer their most serious cases to Athenian courts.

13

THE TRIBUTE

BETWEEN the assessment of Aristides and the disastrous end of the Egyptian expedition we lose all trace in the sources of the tribute. Thucydides in his concise summary of the original organization has told us that the Athenian *hellenotamiai* acted as receivers and deposited the tribute in the temple at Delos, presumably Apollo's temple;[1] the rest is guesswork and once again it is easier to ask the questions than to give the answers. How extensive were the duties of the *hellenotamiai* and to whom were they responsible? What records were kept by whom and where were they kept? What steps were taken on whose authority against defaulters? What provision was made for changes in assessments?

The *hellenotamiai* were Athenian officials and were probably elected by vote. For this there is no direct evidence, but the recurrence among the holders of the office of prominent names suggests that they were not chosen by lot, and they may, like the treasurers of Athena, have had to be members of the highest property class.[2] In the fully developed empire they entered office on the same day as the treasurers of Athena, on Hecatombaeon 28th, Athena's day, but there was no special reason for selecting this day in 478–477, and it may represent a change consequent on the removal of the League treasury from Delos to Athens.[3] Since the *hellenotamiai* held an Athenian office, and were elected by Athenians, they should have been formally responsible to the people who elected them, and even in the early days of the League they may have submitted to the same general examination as other Athenian magistrates at the end of their year of office. Their main work, however, was done at Delos and we

---

[1] Thuc. i. 96. 2.

[2] A list of known *hellenotamiai*, *ATL* i. 567–70. Among them are Sophocles the tragedian, general in 441–440 (Androtion F 38) and Pericles' son, general in 406–405.

[3] The period of office is inferred from ML 72. 25–8 and 84.

should expect them to have worked closely at first with the League Council. We may assume that the cities sent their tribute to Delos at the beginning of the sailing season or a little later at the time of Apollo's festival, and it is probable that the *hellenotamiai* reported the state of the treasury to the assembled representatives of the allies meeting in Council. Records need not have been elaborate but at the least the *hellenotamiai* must have maintained a copy of the assessment, lists of the amount of tribute brought by each city, and an account of annual expenditure. No fragment has ever been found on Delos of any such records; it is a safe inference that they were not inscribed on stone but on wooden tablets or some other perishable material.

It is unlikely even in the enthusiasm of the early years that all members paid each year their complete tribute; it probably rested from the outset with Athens, by consent of the allies, to issue reminders and, when necessary, enforce payment. The question of reassessment is more open. After 454 it was taken for granted that there would normally be a reassessment every fourth year when the Great Panathenaea were celebrated, but it is doubtful whether the discussions which preceded the formation of the League considered the need of revising Aristides' work. More probably it was assumed that the assessment of Aristides would be as permanent as the Persian assessment was intended to be. Situations, however, will have arisen which would demand adjustments. Natural disasters, a series of bad harvests, exhaustion of natural resources could make it impossible for cities to meet their full commitment; in such cases it may have rested with the League Council to sanction reductions. It is also at least possible that the general scale of payments was changed in the light of the accumulated reserve.

When the League treasury was moved to Athens, the Athenians had become used to the publication in permanent form of official records. The radical reforms of Ephialtes and his associates had emphasized the responsibility of magistrates to the people, and the sharp increase in the surviving number of inscribed marble stelae from the fifties is a reflection of this new emphasis.[1] For this reason we know considerably more about tribute procedure after 454 than before. Oddly enough, however, the record that provides most of our evidence for the

[1] See above, pp. 18 f.

period before the Peloponnesian War is the one that might seem to us the least important in the series. The basic records were the assessments and the annual lists of tribute-paying cities with the amount they paid. Fragments survive of three assessments from the war period, but not a single fragment has been found of the six assessments between 454 and 430; they may have been recorded on wood. Of the annual lists of tribute payments no fragment survives for any period, which suggests that they too cannot have been recorded on stone; but the Athenians did inscribe each year a list of the *aparchai* paid to Athena. The first of these lists records the payments of 454–453, inscribed in six columns at the head of a tall stele (height, at least 3·583 m.; width, 1·109 m.; thickness, 0·385 m.), clearly looking forward to a long series of such lists, which were subsequently inscribed on all four faces. The first stele when completed contained fourteen lists, covering the period from 454–453 to 440–439. The second (height at least 2·192 m.; width, 1·471 m.; thickness, 0·34 m.) began with the list of 439–438 and contained seven lists.[1] Subsequent lists seem to have been recorded singly on separate stelae.

The prescript at the head of the first list summarizes the procedure that had been followed. From the letters that still survive we know that the *aparche* was one-sixtieth of the tribute, that the list was prepared by the *hellenotamiai* and audited by the *logistai*. The full text has been restored to say: 'These *aparchai* were given to the goddess by the *hellenotamiai*, of whom —— was secretary, and were presented for audit to the thirty auditors from the tribute which the cities brought in the archonship of Ariston at Athens, a mina in the talent.'[2] The full formula is not repeated in subsequent lists, which record only the number of the list in the sequence, the name of the secretary of the *hellenotamiai*, and, in the second and third lists but not later, a shorthand indication that the list had been scrutinized by the

[1] The measurements are taken from *ATL* i. 3 and 67. The width is at the bottom of the stele. Pritchett has shown that there was a downward taper of the stele of up to 3 cm on the obverse and reverse faces (*CP* lix (1964), 272).

[2] *ATL* ii, List 1: [αἶδε ἀπαρχαὶ τêι θεôι παρεδέχθεσαν παρ]ὰ τôν hελλ[ενοτ]αμιôν hοῖ[ς...7....|... ἐγραμμάτευε καὶ τοῖς λογιστêσι τοῖς] τριάκο[ντα ἀπ]εφάνθεσαν [ἀπὸ τô φό|ρο hὸν ηαι πόλες ἀπέγαγον ἐπὶ Ἀρίστονος] ἄρχοντος Ἀ[θεν]αίοις μνᾶ ἀ[πὸ τô ταλ|άντο]. For the restoration of the last words cf. ML 60 (Propylaea Accounts), 12 f.: τὸ χσυμ[μαχ|ικô φόρο μ]νᾶ ἀπὸ τô ταλάντο, paid by the *hellenotamiai* to the Propylaea commissioners.

thirty auditors.[1] The implication of this *aparche* is not certain.
There is no suggestion in the wording that it was paid by the
allies or on the recommendation of the allies. It was paid, it
seems, by the Athenians and the decision was theirs. The simplest explanation is that Athens was translating into Athenian
terms the procedure that had been followed at Delos. If an
aparche had been paid to Apollo when the tribute was stored in
his temple, the transference of the *aparche* to Athena when the
tribute was placed under her protection would need no special
explanation. But the publication on permanent stone of these
lists suggests that payments to Athena were regarded as a serious
religious obligation.

The lists of the annual *aparchai* were presumably based by the
hellenotamiai directly on the lists of tribute payments. The
majority of these payments will have been made in the early
spring at the time of the Dionysia when the allies were expected
to bring their tribute to Athens,[2] but the books of the *hellenotamiai* remained open until the end of their year of office, late
in July or early in August, and the published list will presumably
have included late payers. But payments made or reported after
the change of boards could not be included, and if publicly recorded they would be recorded in the following year. In the
first lists there is no obvious explanation of the order of names.
It is not based on the assessment list because the order differs
from year to year. It is not geographical, though some neighbours are regularly listed together. It is not even alphabetical.
An inquisitive Athenian gazing at the year's list on the Acropolis
would have wasted much time in trying to find out whether an
Ionian town with which he had trading associations had paid
its tribute for the current year. The most natural inference is
that the order of names is the order in which payment was
received. This order for the most part will not be of great significance, it will tell us no more than the order in the queue when
the money was handed over in the Bouleuterion.

Most of the representatives will have arrived in Athens at
roughly the same time, and the counting of the tribute must
have been a slow business, for the highest payments of 30 talents
would have required 45,000 pieces in silver of the largest coin

---

[1] List 3: [ἐπ]ὶ τês: τρίτε[ς ἀρχês h[êι Διό[τ]ιμος ἐγραμ[μάτευε]: τοῖς τριάκοντα.
[2] Ar. *Acharn.* 502–6.

available. It would not have been surprising if some of these visitors chose to walk round the Acropolis before proceeding to the Bouleuterion. The only significant elements in the order inside the lists are probably the beginnings and the ends, for payments made after the Dionysia should be entered at the end of the list, and payments that were made after the *hellenotamiai* had closed their books should appear at the beginning of the next year's list. There is a little evidence that this was indeed what happened in the early lists. The second list, of 453–452, opens with an unbroken run of Carian names; none of the names survive in the fragments preserved from the first list, one of them is recorded a second time in the second list. This is the only clear instance of geographical grouping in the lists of the first period, and needs a special explanation, especially since most of these Carian communities are financially insignificant and are later very irregular in their payments. We may therefore accept the inference that these cities did not bring their tribute at the Dionysia, and that it was forcibly collected by an Athenian squadron which returned to Athens with the money after the *hellenotamiai* of 454–453 had already published their record.[1] No clear parallel to this anomalous recording is found in the surviving lists, but this is not surprising. Even when tribute had to be collected by Athenian squadrons the ships would normally be back in Athens before August. The evidence that late payers were listed last is a little stronger. Above the last nine names in the list of 448–447 is a heading of which only the first letter survives. The only plausible restoration that has been suggested would indicate that these nine cities paid their tribute after the Dionysia, *M[ετὰ Διονύσια]*.[2] This is the only list in which such a heading is found, but the composition of the last column in the list of 450–449 is best explained as a combination of late payers and complementary payments by cities which had previously paid only part of their normal tribute.[3] The Carian names at the end of the fourth list (451–450) also resemble in character those at the beginning of the second list and might reasonably be interpreted as late payers.[4]

The record of the first year includes for the first and only time a summation of the year's *aparchai* inscribed on the right face of

---

the stele. This comprises two totals, for silver and for Cyzicene electrum staters. The number of these latter is not fully preserved, but falls between 56 and 96, corresponding to between 13 and 26 talents of tribute.[1] This is the only direct indication that the tribute was not all paid in silver, for the *aparchai* are always recorded in drachmae and obols. Nor should we know from Cyzicus' normal tribute of 9 talents that she was paying in staters, but it is probably significant that this tribute is equivalent to 2,000 Cyzicene staters valued at 27 drachmae.[2] We may also be reasonably certain that Tenedos paid in Cyzicene staters. Her normal tribute seems to have been $4\frac{1}{2}$ talents, equivalent to 1,000 staters; but she makes several irregular payments in the second assessment period and all the other figures recorded for Tenedos are neatly divisible by 27.[3] Cyzicus and Tenedos alone will not account for the total of Cyzicene staters recorded in 453, but we cannot safely identify the others. Nor is it likely that the coins of Cyzicus were the only non-Athenian coins in the tribute. Though all figures are reduced to a common standard in the published record, states that still had independent mints are likely to have still paid their tribute in their own coin, and some of these at least could have been on the Aeginetan standard. When Athens enforced the use of her own silver coins in her empire she was simplifying her administration considerably.

Only six states with their payments survive in all four lists of the first period, but more than a hundred survive in at least two. With very few exceptions the payments are consistent through the period. In a few cases the recorded payment is a little higher than we believe the assessment to be, and this may represent a fine for late payment or refusal to pay;[4] when the payment is lower we can assume an incomplete payment. But basically the figures laid down in 454 were maintained until 450. In the list of 450–449, however, there are a significant

---

[1] List 1. Postscript 10–13 : [χ]ρυσίο σύμ[παντος Κυζικ]|ενô : κ[ε]φά[λαιον ἐν στατêρ]|ες Κυ[ζικενοί :.....έκοντ]|α héχ[ς. The maximum is based on the highest possible number of staters (96) at the highest rate of exchange (27 drachmae), the minimum on 56 staters at 24 drachmae, the lowest possible rate.

[2] The exchange rate of the Cyzicene stater is controversial. See Endnote 26, p. 442.

[3] The other recorded payments are 2·5280, 1·3720, 3240, 2160.

[4] *ATL* iii. 7. The few figures that seem to be higher than the assessment in the first period are from Carian communities whose later paying record is poor.

number of changes and the new figures supersede the old. It is clear that there was a new assessment in 450, and this was a year of the Great Panathenaea. There is similar evidence for a new assessment in 446 and a clause in the decree providing for a new assessment in 425 confirms that new assessments normally coincided with the Great Panathenaea.[1] It would be interesting to know when this policy was decided. It might not have been until after the Peace of Callias, when Athens was taking steps to make the Great Panathenaea an empire festival.

We are lucky in the survival of enough fragments of the decree governing the assessment of 425 to reconstruct the procedure adopted in that year.[2] Since this was an extraordinary assessment which did not coincide with the Great Panathenaea some of the clauses will not apply to earlier assessments but the basic outline probably follows a standard pattern. Ten assessors are elected to draw up a list of cities with the assessments that they propose; ratification rests with the Boule. The Assessment Decree of 425 provides for the establishment of a special court of 1,000 jurors to hear appeals from the allies against the assessments proposed by the assessors, and this was not an innovation; a court of 1,500 is recorded in the tribute list of 429 and it probably refers to a court set up in 434. The principle of appeal is also implicit in the oath administered to the Chalcidians when their revolt had been crushed: 'I will pay such tribute as I persuade the Athenians (to impose)', and it may even go back to the assessment of 450, the first which, in our reconstruction, could not be even nominally related to fighting against Persia.

Allies who wished to appeal could call on Athenian speech-writers to put their case in a form which would appeal to Athenian jurors, and fragments of two such speeches survive. They were both composed by Antiphon, who was later to be the master-mind of the oligarchic revolution of 411, and he wrote them for the peoples of Rhodian Lindus and Samothrace. Of the speech for Lindus only a few words survive.[3] There was a reference to an ἐπίσκοπος and to συνήγοροι, pleaders; the colourful word τριβωνευόμενοι probably refers to the use of delaying

---

[1] ML 69. 26–33: cf. [Xen.] Ἀθ. Πολ. 3. 5 (describing the duties of the Boule): τὸ δὲ μέγιστον εἴρηται πλὴν αἱ τάξεις τοῦ φόρου· τοῦτο δὲ γίγνεται ὡς τὰ πολλὰ δι᾿ ἔτους πέμπτου.   [2] ML 69.   [3] F 25–33 Thalheim.

tactics; and apparently there was a reference to Amphipolis, which is surprising and interesting. From such random pieces of cloth it would be irresponsible to try to make a coat. The fragments of the second speech, for the Samothracians, are more coherent and revealing.[1] In order to establish the point that the island could not afford to pay the proposed assessment the speech went back to origins, as Greeks so often did. 'It was Samians who settled on the island and we are descended from them. It was not any love of the island that sent them there, but sheer necessity; for they were driven out of Samos by tyrants and it was fortune that dictated their course. They had been taking plunder in Thrace and from Thrace they came to our island.' But it has also to be shown that the land is poor, with meagre resources. 'For the island which we occupy, as you can clearly see even from a distance, is high and rugged. Little of the land is useful and can be worked; most of it cannot be used, and it is a small island.' The mechanics of the collection were described: 'For those who seemed to be richest among us were chosen as collectors', and there is a rather puzzling statement presumably connected with the collection: 'They wouldn't have worried about the misery of other citizens and yet taken no thought of their own security', possibly a defence of rich collectors who looked after their own interests too well. The συντελεῖς who are mentioned are presumably those who pay tribute, perhaps in associations like the fourth-century symmories at Athens.

We can be more confident about the implications of ἀπόταξις. The word means the separate assessment of two or more communities which have hitherto paid together. The assessment of 422 includes two communities near the promontory of Serreium, Zone and Drys, which are not known to have paid tribute before. They lie opposite Samothrace and were probably controlled by Samothrace in the same way as Thasos, Lesbos, Chios, and Samos had all controlled stretches of the mainland opposite their islands. At the assessment of 422, or possibly 425, for which there is no surviving evidence, Athens required the mainland communities to pay separately; the reason perhaps was more economic than political. Athens may have thought it easier to increase the tribute in this way. When the decisions had been given by the tribute court it remained only for the

[1] F 49–56 Thalheim.

Boule to approve the revised list. The new assessments were then reported to the cities who were required to bring their tribute at the new level in time to be present at the tragedies and comedies of the Dionysia.

The assessment of 450 was conservative. Twenty-one reductions are known, five increases. In these changes there is no general pattern suggesting policy except in the island district. There we know six reductions—in Andros, Carystus, Ios, Rhenaea, Seriphos, Syros; and for Ceos, Cythnos, Siphnos, Naxos, Paros, Tenos and the Euboean states of Chalcis, Dion, Eretria, Hestiaea, Styra there are no first-assessment figures for comparison. To balance this loss in island tribute there is only one increase; the tribute of Athenai Diades is raised from 1,000 to 2,000 drachmae. Aegina, Grynchus in Euboea, and Myconos alone remain unchanged. On this evidence it is fair to speak of a deliberate policy of concession to the islands, and this fits well with the view outlined above that the islands resented the transfer of the League treasury from Delos to Athens more than the other districts.[1] Athens met their disaffection by planting cleruchies at Andros, Naxos, and probably Carystus and by treating the islands more leniently than the other districts in the 450 assessment.

But, while the assessment was conservative, the lists that follow are the most irregular of the series. The list of 449 differs from its predecessor in two respects. For the first time there is a clear tendency to group cities in districts. The list opens with at least thirteen Carian names, and Carian and Ionian names exclusively occupy the first two columns. They are followed in the third column by a long series of Thracian names, followed by a section which is predominantly Hellespontine. Last come the islands, in the second half of the fourth column. The second new characteristic is the occurrence of a significant number of partial payments, some of which at least are brought to their normal total by a complementary payment recorded in the final column, which probably also includes late payments. These partial payments we have interpreted as reflections of allied discontent with the strong imperialism of Athens following the Peace of Callias.[2] The list of 447 reflects a fuller growth of this discontent, but the list of 446 which records complementary

[1] See pp. 118–20.   [2] See pp. 164 f.

payments for 447, as well as current payments, seems to show the full recovery of Athenian control. After 446 there is no evidence in the lists of any state paying its assessment in two instalments, but it is possible, though perhaps unlikely, that this is due to a change in book-keeping methods rather than an increase of efficiency in collection.

The tendency towards a geographical grouping of cities, clearly marked in the list of 449, is not sustained through the second period, nor does the assessment of 446 bring any pronounced improvement. This assessment, unlike that of 450, has a clearly marked pattern. Only three cities had their tribute increased and of these the rise of Thasos from 3 to 30 talents is so sharp and abrupt, as we have seen, that it needs a special explanation.[1] Galepsus, on the mainland opposite Thasos, was now required to pay 1·3000 instead of the 450 figure of 1·2000, but the small increase merely marks a return to the assessment of 454. The third is Sermylia in the Thracian district. Her record in the first period is very irregular; in 453 she pays 7·4320, in 450 5·5500, and in 452 she almost certainly makes two payments, the first of more than 4 talents and less than 5. From these figures it is impossible to calculate her 454 assessment; it was probably more than 5 talents, and possibly 7½ talents. In 447 Sermylia is one of the nine cities recorded at the end of the list under a special rubric, probably as paying after the normal time at the Dionysia; her payment is 3 talents and the same amount is recorded for 446; but these two years are particularly marked by incomplete payments; 3 talents may not be the true assessment. In the 446 assessment and again in 438 Sermylia's tribute is 5 talents. Against these increases can be set thirty reductions to which should probably be added most at least of the twelve which are known only from the following period, for the 443 assessment seems to have made virtually no changes in the 446 figures.

These reductions are spread over all the districts except the islands, and the natural reason why the islands were excluded is that they had already enjoyed the benefit of a reduction in 450. Some of the decreases may have a special explanation, such as the establishment of a cleruchy, but the large number remaining will still require explanation. Economic factors are

[1] See pp. 85 f.

unlikely to give the answer, because it is barely possible that so many cities in different districts with different economic structures should be affected at the same time. We infer that the explanation is political rather than economic; it is significant that in the thirties there is a tendency to restore assessments to their pre-446 level. This policy of conciliation followed by the formal agreement of the Thirty Years' Peace must have considerably weakened opposition to Athens in the allied cities. While Athens was at war or liable to be involved in war on the mainland, it was easy for allied oligarchs to keep hope alive; when Athens and Sparta had made peace, resistance was foredoomed to failure. The new stability is reflected in the quota lists of the third period. The fluctuations in numbers of the first period, aggravated in the second, do not recur. Those who pay seem to pay regularly and seem to pay fully. It is strange that in this stability the Athenians should not have waited till the Great Panathenaea of 442 for their next assessment. The evidence, however, very clearly indicates that there was an extraordinary assessment in 443. This is not immediately evident from changes in the tribute; there are indeed very few, and of these few only two are clearly attested for 443–442. The main evidence for this extraordinary assessment lies in the form of publication.

In the list of 442 for the first time the cities are grouped in districts under district headings, Carian, Ionian, Hellespontine, Thracian, Island, and the order of the districts, though not of the names within the districts, is retained throughout the period. Two other new features also appear in this list. The practice is now instituted of recording on the stele, together with the name of the secretary, the name of one of the *hellenotamiai*, presumably the chairman of the board. This year Sophocles of Colonus was *hellenotamias*; within three years he was to win the first prize at the Dionysia with his *Antigone* and to be sent as general under Pericles to reduce Samos. The name is also added of an assistant secretary, Anticles, and he is recorded as still in office in the next year.[1] For this extraordinary assessment a special explanation

---

[1] He could be the Anticles who was at first assistant secretary and later secretary of the Parthenon commissioners (*IG* i². 343, 349, 350, 351). It is probably another Anticles who moves a decree concerning Chalcis in the Assembly in 446–445 (ML 52. 40), perhaps the Anticles who was general in 440–439 (Thuc. i. 117. 2).

is needed. It was not as in 425 an urgent need to raise more money, because the assessment of 446 was taken over virtually without change. The authors of *The Athenian Tribute Lists* have suggested that the assessment was moved forward a year because Pericles intended a specially magnificent celebration of the Great Panathenaea in 442, with the addition of a new musical event in the newly built Odeon.[1] Pericles, they think, was anxious that the Boule and the other officials concerned should not be preoccupied at the time with the detailed business of the assessment. We do not perhaps know enough of the procedure involved at this date in a new assessment to rule out this explanation, but if the procedure known from the assessment decree of 425 is to be our guide the main work of the assessment would come considerably later than the festival, when the allies were invited to come to Athens to appeal against the proposals of the assessors. We should rather seek a clue in the form of the record. The new principle of listing the cities under district headings is not a revolutionary step. The list of 449, as has been seen, had moved a long way towards the innovation. Nor does it follow that the division into districts is a reflection of a major change in administration. If a fragment of Craterus is rightly associated with the first assessment at Athens in 454, that assessment already used district headings, for Dorus and Phaselis are quoted as being Carian cities.[2] Moreover, some such divisions probably go back to the early days of the League. As soon as it was necessary to send out heralds to the allies to announce decisions of the Council at Delos, it would be logical to divide the allies up into districts. The headings that we find in 442 correspond to natural divisions.

The introduction of the name of one of the *hellenotamiai* need not necessarily imply a substantive change, but the mention of an assistant secretary who continues in office for a second year can only be reasonably explained if there was more administrative work than usual, and that something was initiated in 443–442 which needed a further year to complete or consolidate. It may, we have suggested, have been a financial reorganization following the ostracism of Thucydides, son of Melesias, who, according to Plutarch, had attacked the continuing extravagance of Pericles' building policy.[3] One other floating straw

---

[1] *ATL* iii. 206.   [2] See Endnote 7, p. 420.   [3] Plut. *Per.* 14. 1.

may be relevant. Antiphon, in his speech on the *Murder of Herodes*, referred to an incident which, he says, would be well known to the older members of the jury. The date of the speech is probably between 416 and 414, and certainly after 427; any date in the fifties or forties would therefore fit the story. Unfortunately no circumstantial detail is added to the bare facts, which are sensational. The whole board of *hellenotamiai* was condemned to death, but when all but one had been executed it was found that the charge was false.[1] It is strange that no allusion is made to this macabre incident in any of the surviving accounts of the condemnation of the Athenian generals after the battle of Arginusae, but the story cannot be an invention. Such an alarming miscarriage of justice might have led to a reorganization and redefinition of financial responsibilities. But at this point guesswork becomes irresponsible. It would be unwise to go further than suggest that the reason for the extraordinary assessment of 443 should be sought in the field of administration.

The years between the Thirty Years' Peace of 446–445 and the Samian revolt in 440 are years of consolidation. In contrast to the first and second assessment periods the number of cities in the annual lists varies little from year to year and there is no evidence in the figures of incomplete payments; the lists suggest that payment was regular and complete. There was, however, an exception to this uniformity. The record of many of the smaller Carian states, particularly those inland, had probably never been good. Nine of them are found only in the first period; a further nine have left no surviving record after 446 and for nine more there are no traces in the full lists of the fourth period (442–438).[2] It seems that Athens did not consider it worth the effort and expense to enforce payment until war sharpened the need for money and discipline. Apart from the Lycians, who paid 10 talents in 445, the combined assessments of the defectors was not more than 15 talents. From such poor communities there was little hope of extracting heavy fines or worthwhile confiscations; the small force sent to collect arrears would probably cost more than the money they collected, and Carian hill-towns were not easily intimidated.[3] Lycia, however, was more serious. The Lycians and Telmessians make a joint

---

[1] Antiphon, v. 69–71.   [2] See the table in App. 14, p. 553.
[3] Ar. *Birds* 292–3, quoted p. 89 n. 1.

payment in 451 and 450, but no figure is preserved; they do not appear in any of the fragments of the second period, but in 445 the Lycians pay 10 talents and the Telmessians independently pay 1 talent. This is the last appearance of either on the fragments preserved and, as the lists from 444 to 439 are well preserved, we can assume that payments lapsed before 440. Whether this was due to Lycian reaction against Athens or whether tribute was replaced by other services such as a responsibility for suppressing pirates along her coast line is uncertain. It is more probable that Lycia was asserting her independence, for a small force sent out by Athens late in 430 was intended to collect money in Caria and Lycia, and to stop pirates interfering with merchantmen from Phaselis and Phoenicia. Melesander, who was in command, was killed with the loss of part of his force when he penetrated into Lycia.[1]

Though during this period the Athenians relaxed their hold on the south-east periphery of their empire, their control over the remaining districts became more secure, and when the powerful island of Samos revolted in 440 there is no reflection in the tribute lists of serious trouble elsewhere; the number of states in all the district lists is normal. There is, however, one new feature which might be associated with the revolt. In the list of 439 for the first time some states are listed twice, credited first with their normal tribute and then with a second payment, *epiphora*.[2] The precise meaning of the word in this context is perhaps not quite certain, but it signifies an extra payment and should be a penalty of some kind. In 439 it appears in only two districts. There are no less than six cities affected in Ionia— Mysian Astyra, Dios Hieron, Notium, Cumae, Myrina by Cumae, Pitana; in the Hellespont there are only two cases— Dardanus and Lamponea. The institution persists through the thirties but unfortunately the lists from 437 to 430 are the most poorly preserved of the whole series. In 438 enough remains to show that four of the six Ionian cities who paid *epiphora* in 439 pay again, but no figures are preserved; of the other districts we can say nothing. Later, *epiphora* is applied to Thrace and Caria but the lists from 438 to 434 are too badly preserved to judge the scale. In 434 the Hellespontine and Thracian districts

[1] Thuc. ii. 69.
[2] For a detailed discussion of ἐπιφορά see Endnote 17, p. 432.

are almost complete and there is only one case in the Hellespont and one in Thrace. The preserved lists of 432 and 431 are more representative; in 432 there are two cases in Ionia and four in the Hellespont but none in Thrace, and in 431 there is only one case, in Caria. In 429 there is one reference to *epiphora* for the previous year, but none for the current year. This is the last we hear of *epiphora* in the tribute lists.

Sixteen states are affected in one or more of these years. The main incidence is in Ionia and the Hellespont, whereas Thrace has only one case, Stagirus, which was later to have the credit of defying Cleon, and no case is known yet from the islands. Most of the sixteen cities are of little account, paying not more than 2 talents; only Chalcedon (6 talents) and Cumae (9 talents) are among the higher payers. The amounts contributed in *epiphora* are small and the authors of *The Athenian Tribute Lists* note that the general rule seems to be that they are multiples of the one-sixtieth part of the assessed tribute. They suggest that *epiphora* represents the interest on late payments, a fine of 3 minae per talent per month (1 mina per talent per ten-day period).[1] If this is not the right explanation the natural alternative is a fine for some other reason; in either case it is a sign of new pressure. Whether the principle was abandoned when the entry seems to disappear from the lists is uncertain. We should not expect such pressure to be relaxed during the war; it may have been recorded elsewhere, and perhaps the quota was no longer given to Athena.

After the extraordinary assessment of 443 ,which was held a year before the normal date, the Athenians seem to have returned to the regular cycle, for the next assessment was in 438, a year of the Great Panathenaea. The evidence for the nature of this assessment is pitifully weak. Of the 437 list only a few names survive, from the 436 list nothing. Some two-thirds of the names from the Thracian district can be read or restored in the list of 435, but for half of these there are no figures; the list of 434 is rather better, for the Thracian district is almost complete and the Hellespontine district is also well represented. The Carian district now loses its identity and is amalgamated with the Ionian district. In the few cases where figures can be compared there are not many changes from the 443 assessment but

[1] *ATL* i. 452 f.

many of the changes first attested in the 434 assessment may have been made in 438; it is better to take the two assessments together and to speak less precisely of the changes in the thirties.

We can trace eight reductions and thirty increases in these assessments, and the changes are fairly evenly spread over the districts with the exception of the islands where there are no increases and only one reduction. The most striking changes are on the borders of the Odrysian kingdom in Thrace. Selymbria, on the European shore of the Propontis, which had paid 6 talents in the second period and 5 talents in the fourth (for the third there is no evidence), appears in 434 and 432 with a payment of only 900 dr.; Aenus, whose assessment had been 12 talents in the first two periods and 10 in the third and fourth, is absent from the lists of 434 and 431, and in 435 pays only 4 talents. By contrast Maronea, whose assessment had remained unchanged at 1½ talents for the first four periods, rises sharply to 10 talents in the fifth and sixth. We need to know more about the relations of the Odrysian kings with Athens and with the Greek coastal cities before we can understand the assessors' policy. Of the other increases at least twelve represent a return to the level preceding the widespread reductions of 446.[1] The remaining increases roughly balance the reductions. The assessments of the thirties in fact do no more than restore the tribute to its level before the Thirty Years' Peace; they do not suggest that Athens was seeing how much she could extort from the allies, and, as we have seen, she seems to have been content to accept the abstention of a large number of small Carian cities. In 442, a well-preserved list, there were 31 Ionian and 45 Carian cities, a total of 76; in 432 there are 51 names only which, however, for purposes of comparison should be regarded as 56 since the five small communities on the peninsula dominated by Erythrae are not independently recorded as they were in 442. A difference of twenty cities sounds serious but it probably represents less than 10 talents.

There are other features of the thirties that require explanation. In the list of 434 five states are listed as unassessed, ἄτακτοι. They are all in the Thracian district, but their tribute histories are very different. Pharbelus and Othorus had been regular payers; Chedrolus paid regularly in the second period but no

[1] For details see App. 12, pp. 527 f.

record survives from the third and fourth periods; Miltorus
appears now for the first time; the name of the fifth is missing.[1]
If they were all newcomers no problem would arise, but Pharbelus and Othorus had paid fairly regularly. The question is not
why they were included in 434, but why they were excluded
from the assessment of 438. The logical solution is that they
were removed from the official assessment list as a gesture by
Athens towards Perdiccas, king of Macedon, possibly part of
a formal agreement. The cities, however, preferred to have the
protection of Athens and were prepared to pay for it. Relations
between Athens and Macedon are so unstable during this
period that a change of mood between 438 and 435 is a reasonable hypothesis.[2] These Thracian towns first presumably paid
what they thought fit but in 434 they were put into two separate
categories which first appear in 433, the first year of the next
assessment period.

The assessment of 434 introduced two new rubrics—πόλες
αὐταὶ φόρον ταχσάμεναι and πόλες hὰς hοι ἰδιôται ἐνέγραφσαν
φόρον φέρεν. Three of the five Thracian ἄτακτοι pass into the
first group which also contains three other small settlements
in Thrace, two small islands, Casos and Amorgos, a community
on Carpathos, and Callipolis in the Hellespont. Together
these eleven cities pay 3 t. 2,500 dr. The remaining two Thracian
ἄτακτοι from 434 pass into the second group which has thirteen members, most of them in the Thraceward district,
with a small community near Chalcis in Euboea, a small island
in the Propontis, and possibly the small island of Syme near
Rhodes. Together they pay 2 t. 1,100 dr. The first group remains constant in 432, the second group is too poorly preserved
to compare, but in 431 the first group shrinks to five members
and of the seven from the Thraceward district only one remains;
the evidence for the second group is inadequate. In the assessment of 430 these two separate classes are preserved, but in 429
the αὐταὶ ταχσάμεναι have shrunk further to three members and
the second group which had eleven members in 433 now has
probably only four. Why were these special classes formed and
why was their special treatment maintained?

---

[1] See *ATL* iii. 86 f. with notes. For the ἄτακτοι and the two rubrics that follow,
ATL iii. 80–8; F. A. Lepper, *JHS* lxxxii (1962), 25–55.

[2] Perdiccas, previously an ally, had become an enemy by 432, Thuc. i. 57. 2.

Interpretation must start from the meaning of the Greek. It was once widely held, among others by the authors of *ATL*, that the πόλες αὐταὶ ταχσάμεναι were communities that now received an independent assessment by separation from a more important neighbour, a process of *apotaxis* that has several parallels in the tribute lists.[1] So, for instance, the small community near Chalcis might have been dependent on Chalcis; but in no case could *apotaxis* be proved and in some cases such as Callipolis there was no neighbour conveniently near. The small island of Amorgos might possibly have been dependent on Samos, but if she were lost to Samos on the crushing of her revolt Amorgos should have appeared on the tribute lists before 433. This view has not survived criticism and in *ATL III* the authors modified their position. Admitting that *apotaxis* would not satisfy all the cases they suggested a translation which would allow the inclusion of isolated or peripheral communities: 'Cities which accepted assessment by special arrangement', and the special arrangement was a guarantee for the future that their assessments would not be changed.[2] This, as Lepper has argued, is a strained interpretation of the Greek; he is surely right to follow Nesselhauf in accepting the normal meaning of the words, which would imply that the initiative for the assessment came from the cities themselves;[3] the πόλες hὰς hοι ἰδιόται ἐνέγραφσαν φόρον φέρεν should be cities in which the initiative was taken by individual members of the cities.[4]

Why did these small communities take or accept this special status? The answer must take account of the disappearance of almost all the Thracian members in 431 and the shrinking of the αὐταὶ ταχσάμεναι members from eleven to four by 429. This is difficult to reconcile with goodwill towards Athens: αὐταὶ ταχσάμεναι becomes a euphemism. Nesselhauf, whose interpretation has been elaborated by Lepper, seems to be on the right lines. These small communities may have thought that they gained more than they lost by paying tribute. In a crisis they might hope for Athenian protection; in their trading they might suffer if Athens was hostile. The Thracian communities may

---

[1] E. B. Couch, *AJA* xxxiii (1929), 502–12: *ATL* i. 456.
[2] *ATL* iii. 80–5.
[3] Nesselhauf, *Untersuchungen*, 60; Lepper, op. cit. 28.
[4] Nesselhauf, op. cit. 61; Lepper, op. cit. 29 ff. *ATL* i. 455 take the ἰδιόται to be Athenian citizens.

have preferred Athens to Macedon, but when a serious revolt
from Athens broke out among her 'allies' in Chalcidice and it
looked as if Spartolus and Olynthus meant business they preferred to take their chance with their Greek neighbours. Lepper
has carried the case considerably further than Nesselhauf
when he suggests that there was an Athenian decree (or decrees) defining trading rights.[1] This goes further than the evidence prompts, and is in itself unlikely. But the importance of
sea power in affecting the flow of trade was clearly appreciated
by the Old Oligarch: 'If a city is rich in ship timber, where will
she market it if she does not persuade the power that rules the
sea? If a city is rich in iron or copper or linen, where will she
market them if she does not persuade the power that rules the
sea?'[2] The Megarian Decree by which Athens closed the harbours of her empire to Megarian traders showed what Athens
could do when war was near. Earlier interference with the flow
of trade had probably been much more indirect.

Although by 435 it must have been clear to politically minded
men that there was a serious risk of imminent war, there is no
sign of restlessness in the tribute lists of 433 and 432. The list of
431 presents a very different picture. In 432 there were thirty-
eight in the Thraceward panel; in 431 the number has shrunk
to twenty-seven. The revolt of Potidaea early in 432, combined
with the propaganda of Perdiccas, had unsettled Chalcidice and
seriously affected the collection of tribute. Potidaea from 454
through the assessment of 438 had been required to pay 6
talents but by 432 she had to pay 15 talents.[3] The other two
main centres of revolt were Spartolus at the west end of Chalcidice and Olynthus at the east end. The tribute of Spartolus had
been raised from 2 talents to 3 t. 500 dr. in 434; Olynthus had
paid 2 talents. These two cities were the rallying points of those
who were encouraged by Perdiccas to revolt, mainly small communities paying not more than 1 talent, but Sermylia was more
important; her assessment was 4½ talents. Most of the absentees
came from Chalcidice, but Argilus was some distance to the
east; she probably still resented the foundation of Amphipolis,
neighbour and rival. East of the Strymon the tribute evidence
is much less easy to interpret. The absence of Maronea was

---

[1] Lepper, op. cit. 54.   [2] [Xen.] Ἀθ. Πολ. 2. 11.
[3] The date of the increase is not certain. See pp. 528 f.

financially serious; her assessment had jumped from $1\frac{1}{2}$ talents regularly paid from 454 to the end of the forties to 10 talents at the assessment of 438, retained in 434. There should be a special explanation of this sharp increase and there may be a special explanation for her absence in 431. Had she intended to break with Athens it would be a little surprising that she should bring her tribute in 429 and 428, though her assessment seems to have been reduced to 3 talents in 430. Aenus raises similar questions. Her assessment had been lowered from 12 talents to 10 in 446 but in 435 she pays only 4 talents and she is absent from a full panel in 434 and 431, nor is any payment preserved for the two intervening years. Unlike Maronea she is also absent in 429, but in 425 she sends auxiliary troops to Athens, and there is no literary evidence of revolt or strained relations.[1] The key probably lies in relations with the Odrysian Kingdom.

The Thraceward absentees of 431 meant a loss of some 40 talents tribute and the total collection can have been little if any more than 350 talents. This is in striking contrast to the natural interpretation of Pericles' summary of Athenian resources as reported by Thucydides: 'There come in every year some 600 talents tribute from the allies.' Thucydides' figure cannot possibly be inferred from the tribute lists. The list of 432 is particularly well preserved and there can only be a small margin of error in Tod's estimate of 388 talents.[2] Some such figure is consistent with the probable restoration of the *aparchai* for 444–443, which gives a total of 376 t. 4,550 dr. for the year's tribute.[3] It is indeed doubtful whether since 454 Athens had in any year received more than 400 talents. The assessment of 454 was considerably higher, about 490 talents, but in the late fifties payments were very irregular and a considerable number of islands withheld their tribute. In the second period some thirty talents were lost as compensation for cleruchies but there were no major changes in assessment thereafter. In the years from 454 to 431 Athenian assessment policy seems to have been moderate.[4]

Isocrates counts among the abuses of the fifth-century empire the display of tribute at the Dionysia, when porters, each carrying a talent, paraded in the orchestra when the theatre was full. This was probably a display of the tribute received for the year,

---

[1] Troops from Aenus, Thuc. iv. 28. 4; vii. 57. 5.   [2] Tod, *GHI* i, p. 56.
[3] *IG* i². 342. 36.   [4] See the table in App. 12 c, p. 529.

and there is no need to regard it, with Isocrates, as an act of wanton arrogance. We do not know when the decree which instituted the practice was voted, but there is no good reason to regard it as a war measure.[1]

The practice of sending out ships 'to collect money' is more likely to have been introduced after 431. In his record of the Archidamian War Thucydides three times mentions the dispatch by Athens of squadrons of 'money-collecting ships', νῆες ἀργυρολόγοι.[2] Two of these occasions at least, and probably the third also, coincide with assessment years, in 430, 425, and probably 428, which raises the question whether these ships have anything to do with tribute; were squadrons sent out, when a new assessment was declared, to collect arrears on the old assessment? The word used for these money-collecting missions, ἀργυρολογία, does not itself imply any connection with tribute. When Alcibiades wanted to raise money quickly in 407 to make his return to Athens more popular, he sailed to the Ceramic Gulf in Caria and collected 100 talents, which was considerably more than the pre-war assessment of the whole Carian district; Plutarch says he went 'to collect money', ἀργυρολογήσων.[3] The same term is used for the emergency levies raised by Theramenes and Thrasybulus in the winter of 411–410, when the Athenian fleet in the Hellespont had been forced to disperse to get money, as the generals could not otherwise pay their crews.[4] We may therefore accept the evidence of Aristides in his *Address to Rome*. In a summary of the grievances of the allies he separated the 'want of moderation in the tributes' from 'the money-collecting, over and above the tributes if any special need arose'.[5] Cleon is said in the *Knights* to be 'always demanding swift triremes to collect money'.[6] This suggests that the association with new assessments may be mere coincidence.

The forcible collection of extra money was probably a war measure, and with the war came also sharp increases in the tributes as Athenian reserves were drained. It was not until Athens saw that she was faced with a long war that she strained the resources of her allies.

---

[1] Isocr. viii. 82. See also Endnote 19, p. 433.   [2] Thuc. ii. 69; iii. 19; iv. 50. 1.
[3] Plut. *Alc*. 35. 4.   [4] Xen. *Hell*. i. 1. 8 and 12.
[5] Aristides, Εἰς Ῥώμην 45.   [6] Ar. *Knights* 1070–1.

14

THE BALANCE-SHEET OF EMPIRE

Of all the major aspects of Athenian imperialism the economic is the most elusive and that is not due only to the loss of so much Greek writing. Even if all that was written about Athens in the fifth century were available to us it would be impossible to answer the most elementary questions that our most modest economists naturally ask. It is indeed doubtful whether anything was written specifically about economic issues before the collapse of the Athenian Empire, and when such writing begins in the fourth century it has little interest for economists. Xenophon, composing a thesis on the public economy of Athens in the middle of the fourth century, realizes some elementary truths such as that prices rise when goods become scarce, but most of his proposals are very naïve. His main recipe for improving Athenian finances is to purchase some 30,000 slaves and with their labour exploit the Laurium mines intensively, on the assumption that they were inexhaustible.[1] Even Aristotle's *Oeconomica* is little more than an anthology of clever devices by which states and individuals have raised money and Xenophon's *Oeconomicus* is primarily concerned with the individual's management of his own property. Later writers were fascinated by the low prices recorded in Solon's day, but no one seems to have made a study of the rise and fall of prices; such conceptions as a price index or the total national product were alien to their thinking. It is strange that a people who reached such subtleties in mathematics did not develop an interest in economic theory or produce more specialized economic advisers. Even their accountancy remained crude and conservative.[2]

In Plato's *Gorgias* one of the main complaints against Periclean Athens is that the citizens were too fond of money;[3] to the

[1] Xen. Πόροι, iv.
[2] G. E. M. de Ste Croix, 'Greek and Roman Accounting' (in *Studies in the History of Accounting*, London, 1956), 14–74.   [3] Plato, *Gorgias* 515e.

aristocracy, and it was the aristocrats who still had the main influence on literary trends, money-making was not quite gentlemanly. Hipponicus and Nicias could both remain respectable though making big money through slave labour in the mines, but most of the old nobility lived on the modest yield of ancestral estates. It was partly because Cleon was so interested in money for the state as well as for himself that he became a natural target for Aristophanes. The wealth of Cleon's family had come partly at any rate from the making and selling of leather goods, and the affluence of Hyperbolus came from lamps. Such men could appreciate how money was made as well as spent.

No complete census, so far as we know, was taken in the fifth century, but there was plenty of evidence available for demographers. The deme registers included the names of all adult male citizens and for the purposes of the *eisphora* it was necessary to have a record of all property privately owned. Those who managed the tax that all metics had to pay could give the number of metics, and the number of slaves would also have to be recorded for tax purposes. If we had all these records we could answer some of the questions that most interest us. We would know how many men were available for military and naval service. We could calculate how many men had risen from the lowest class, the *thetes*, into the hoplite classes, how the birthrate had changed during the century, and what proportion of the population benefited from overseas settlement. Unfortunately we can never expect to recover such records; we do, however, have some useful figures in Thucydides who gives us a catalogue of Athenian resources at the beginning of the Peloponnesian War.[1] But, though recording the number of hoplites, divided between field army and home defence, he does not give any figure for the *thetes*, and this is a most serious gap in our understanding of political as well as military matters.[2]

On the material side we happen to have a figure for the import duty collected at the Piraeus. Andocides tells us that in one year the collection of the tax was sold for 30 talents and that 6 talents' profit was made.[3] Since the tax was levied at 2 per cent

---

[1] Thuc. ii. 13. 6–9.
[2] For the difficulty of estimating the number of *thetes*, Gomme, *The Population of Athens in the fifth and fourth centuries* B.C. (Oxford, 1933) 12–17.
[3] Andoc. i. 133–4.

one may deduce a value of some 1,800 talents for the goods that came into the harbour. This is an interesting figure, but it comes from 399, shortly after the total collapse of Athens; it provides a very uncertain basis for estimating the value of goods that came into the Piraeus in the generation before the Peloponnesian War. The first *eisphora* of the war yielded 200 talents; we should like to know what total of private capital this represented, and how private capital in 431 compared with the public reserve of 6,000 talents on the Acropolis. In 377 a census of property in Attica was taken and the total value quoted by Demosthenes and confirmed by Polybius was 6,000 talents.[1] The *eisphora* was voted in the form of a percentage levy; in the fourth century 1 per cent seems to have been normal and 2 per cent exceptional. If the *eisphora* of 428 was levied at 2 per cent the total of private capital will have been 10,000 talents; if at 1 per cent 20,000 talents. It seems to me more likely that the second figure is roughly right;[2] the war was to prove almost as destructive of private fortunes as of the public treasury.

It is difficult enough to reconstruct the economic history of Athens during the fifth century, but there is sufficient evidence to sketch a tentative outline; for 'the cities', as the members of the empire were often·called, we cannot do even that. We can roughly trace the political history of some of the more important members, especially Miletus, Thasos, and Samos, but even for these we have very little evidence indeed of economic conditions. We know from comedy and from stamped amphorae that Thasian wine had a good name and from inscriptions that the state took a practical interest in the trade, but we have no idea of the volume of wine exported nor whether in the second half of the century Thasos' share of the market was expanding or contracting. The tribute quota lists suggest the relative prosperity of the cities, but we do not know how far political factors modified assessments. When the evidence is so fragmentary there is a serious danger of making too much of too little and imposing a tidy pattern on developments for our own satisfaction.

[1] Dem. xiv. 9 (6,000 talents); Polybius ii. 62. 2 (5,750 talents).
[2] A. Böckh (*Die Staatshaltung der Athener*, i. 606 with n. 825) drew attention to Ar. *Eccl.* 823–9 where Euripides proposes a 2½ per cent tax which was to yield 500 talents. This could correspond nicely with a 1 per cent in 428, yielding 200 talents (Thuc. iii. 19. 1).

The most we can hope to do is to suggest in broad outline from such evidence as we have how Athenian imperialism affected the economies of Athens and her allies.

The Athenian's most tangible benefit was of course the tribute of which he was continuously reminded by the annual invasion of allies at the time of the Dionysia and by the splendour of the new buildings on the Acropolis. It was common knowledge that the Parthenon, the Parthenos, and the Propylaea had been paid for in large part from the tribute reserve brought from Delos in 454. The Bouleuterion, the Tholos, and the Stoa Poikile, all built before 450 from Athens' own resources, were in *poros*; the marble magnificence of the Parthenon and Propylaea was the permanent memorial of the empire's tribute. Without some such annual income from outside it would not have been possible to provide state pay for state services, from the jurors of the popular law-courts to the archons, and at the same time to maintain a large enough fleet to ensure command of the seas. In describing briefly how the allies were themselves responsible for their failure to preserve their independence Thucydides says that the majority of ship-contributors (in fact all except Chios, Lesbos, and Samos) preferred to commute to money payment 'and so the Athenian fleet expanded from the money that they contributed.'[1]

Thucydides' Pericles, summarizing Athens' resources at the outbreak of war with Sparta, says that some 600 talents of tribute came to Athens from the allies. This figure, as we have seen, is considerably higher than the tribute itself which in 431 was little if at all more than 350 talents.[2] But if the Samian and perhaps other indemnities and imperial revenues, such as the income received from Amphipolis, are included the total could be right, though Xenophon's term ὑπερόρια, overseas revenue, would be better than Thucydides' φόρος, tribute. Xenophon uses his term with reference to Athens' total income at the beginning of the war: from overseas and home sources combined it was 1,000 talents.[3] If both figures are right 400 talents would be the home income, from import and other harbour dues, court fees and fines, market and other taxes, leasing of mines and other public property: it is a reasonable figure, but we have no firm controls. We might calculate very roughly the cost of

---

[1] Thuc. i. 99. 3.   [2] Above, p. 253.   [3] Xen. *Anabasis* vii. 1. 27.

state pay for magistrates, members of the Boule, and jurors but we have miserably little evidence from which even to guess the annual expenditure on festivals, maintenance of public buildings, and administration. It is quite certain, however, that when these essential costs had been met there could not have been enough left to maintain a large fleet, let alone build up a reserve against war.

It was possible for the Spartans to fight a long war with very limited financial resources, because they were a land power and were trying to fight the war by land. Hoplites had to be fed on campaigns and Sparta's allies had to be paid, but an army could partly support itself on its ravaging and normally campaigns were short. Fleets were very much more expensive. The Egestans in 415 brought '60 talents of uncoined silver, being a month's pay for 60 ships';[1] the figures confirm those given in a misplaced chapter of Thucydides' text which may possibly not be by Thucydides himself.[2] We are there told that at the beginning of the war sailors received a drachma a day, which implies a talent a month for a crew of 200; and to the pay had to be added the incidental costs of maintenance. Seventy-six talents were drawn from the reserve by the generals who in 433 took the two squadrons, the first of ten, the second of twenty ships, to Corcyra though they left in August and could expect to return to Athens before the end of October at the latest.[3] But the greatest drain on the reserve came from sieges which tied down large forces and the crews of the triremes that transported them. More than 2,000 talents had been spent on Potidaea before it fell and the reduction of Samos cost at least 1,200 talents.[4] It is not surprising that new money had to be raised when Mytilene revolted in 428 and Athens was again faced with an expensive siege. Without the reserve on the Acropolis, which came mainly from tribute, Athens would have been unable to keep the initiative and maintain a naval offensive. The changed pattern of the fourth century shows what the tribute had meant to

[1] Thuc. vi. 8. 1.
[2] Thuc. iii. 17. 4, with Gomme, *HCT* ad loc.   [3] ML 61.
[4] Potidaea: Thuc. ii. 70. 2. Isocr. xv. 113 gives a total of 2,400. Samos: the published record of the grants made by the treasurers of Athena gives 1,400+ talents, but this may include money spent on the reduction of Byzantium, ML 55; Nepos, *Timotheus* 1. 2, gives 1,200 talents which probably corresponds with Isocr. xv. 111. and Diod. xii. 28. 3, both quoted p. 192 n. 3.

Athens. Whereas she may have had a total income of 1,000 talents in 430, in the fourth century it fell at one point as low as 130 talents.[1] As a result Athens lived from hand to mouth and could never sustain an aggressive policy for long in war.

The tribute from the empire directly or indirectly affected the living conditions of most Athenian citizens. The *thetes* and to a lesser extent the *zeugitai* found new opportunities overseas. The first Athenian settlement after the Persian invasion was at Eion by the Strymon's mouth; soon followed the expulsion of pirates from Scyros and the establishment of Athenians on the island. In both these cases Athens was occupying sites by the right of conquest. Soon after the middle of the century the policy of settling poorer Athenians overseas was more widely extended in a series of cleruchies. One thousand settlers were led by Pericles to strengthen the Athenian hold on the Chersonese, threatened by Thracian invaders, and at the same time or soon after new settlers were probably sent out to Lemnos and Imbros.[2] In 450 smaller settlements were established in the territory of restless allies, at Naxos and Andros and possibly Carystus.[3] A large fragment survives of the decree ordering the dispatch of a colony to Brea in the Thraceward district; it is probably to be identified with the 1,000 settlers sent out to live with the Bisaltae, and the date may be soon after the expedition to the Chersonese.[4] Many years later, in 443, Athenians led a colony to Thurii in south Italy but the colony was open to all Greeks and the Athenian nucleus was comparatively small, but at least 4,000 Athenian citizens received land abroad between 450 and 440. If earlier and later settlements were added the total would probably be doubled. The Brea inscription specified that the colonists were to be drawn from the *zeugitai* and *thetes*, but this was in an amendment;[5] the original proposal presumably made no explicit restrictions. Plutarch undoubtedly thinks of the settlers he lists as below hoplite status, for according to him one of Pericles' motives was to rid the city of an idle mob that gave trouble because it had nothing to do, and to relieve the poverty of the demos.[6] The cleruchs farming their lots could become potential hoplites and would at the same time

---

[1] [Dem.] x. 37, probably immediately after the Social War, 355 B.C.
[2] See Endnote 11, p. 424.   [3] See pp. 121–3.   [4] See pp. 158 f.
[5] ML 49. 39–42.   [6] Plut. *Per.* 11. 6.

act as garrisons of cities whose loyalty was unreliable. They remained Athenian citizens and presumably were eligible if required for military service.

It must be admitted, however, that the evidence for the status of cleruchies and the functions of cleruchs in the fifth century is thoroughly unsatisfactory. If the argument from silence were decisive we should have to accept the conclusion preferred by A. H. M. Jones that the cleruchs did not reside on their lots at all, for they are strangely absent from most of Thucydides' narrative;[1] but had that been the common practice there should have been some hint of it in the tradition, whereas the sources speak of *sending out* cleruchs.[2] In his account of the terms imposed on Mytilene when her revolt was crushed, Thucydides is quite explicit: 'They did not impose tribute on the Lesbians, but divided the island, with the exception of the territory of Methymna, into 3,000 lots; 300 lots they set aside to be the sacred property of the gods, to the remaining lots they sent Athenian cleruchs chosen by lot; the Lesbians negotiated a payment of two minae a year for each lot and worked the land themselves.'[3] There is no doubt that according to Thucydides the cleruchs left Athens and it is by no means clear that he regards the arrangement made with the Lesbians as unusual. Tantalizing fragments of an Athenian decree survive which is almost certainly associated with the Mytilenian settlement, but though cleruchs are mentioned there is insufficient of the text left to restore with confidence even the general sense of the clause or clauses concerning the cleruchs.[4] From Thucydides' account we should infer that 2,700 Athenians went to Mytilene and remained in the city receiving a rent of 2 minae a year for the land allotted to them. A garrison of this size would make military sense, for Mytilene had fought stubbornly and only the oligarchs mainly responsible had been put to death. When in the late summer of 425 a small Athenian squadron sent out to collect money found that Mytilenaean exiles had seized Antandrus and were preparing to make it a fortified base, they collected troops from their allies; but there is no word of the Athenian cleruchs[5] nor are they mentioned in the struggle for

---

[1] Jones, *Athenian Democracy*, 175.
[2] Isocr. iv. 107; Aristides, Εἰς ῾Ρώμην 45   [3] Thuc. iii. 50. 2.
[4] D 22; Gomme, *HCT* ii. 328–31.   [5] Thuc. iv. 75. 1.

Lesbos in the last phase of the war. It is possible that they were not called on in 425 through fear that the seizure of Antandrus by Mytilenaean exiles might encourage an anti-Athenian movement in the island. No such explanation can explain their absence from his narrative of 412 and 411. It is probable that by then they had been recalled to Athens, perhaps in 424 when Athens was attempting an ambitious offensive by land with a hoplite force severely depleted by the plague.

In publicizing attractive conditions for membership of her fourth-century alliance of 377 Athens renounced the policy of sending out cleruchs: 'From the archonship of Nausinicus no Athenian may privately or publicly acquire a house in the territories of the allies nor land by purchase or mortgage or in any other way.'[1] It is unexpected to find private acquisition linked in the same clause with the public acquisition of cleruchies. We must infer that this was a serious grievance in the fifth-century empire and that Athenians took advantage of Athenian dominance to buy up property overseas. In Athens no foreigner was allowed to own land or house property without a special vote conferring γῆς ἔγκτησις and the principle was widespread in the Greek world. The implication is that the principle was ignored. There may be examples in the stelae recording the confiscated property of Athenians found guilty at the time of the mutilation of the Hermae in 415. The possessions include holdings in Thasos and in Euboea.[2]

The dependence of tribute and cleruchies on the empire is self-evident. The relation of the growth of Athenian trade to the growth of imperialism is much less easy to determine. Athenian leaders had been interested in trade at least from the time of Solon, but it was Themistocles who first made the decisive developments possible by realizing the potential of the Piraeus and planning a large navy. If Themistocles, especially in his naval bill, was thinking primarily of the danger from Persia, he seems also to have thought in terms of an expanding trade to accompany an expanding fleet. This is a fair inference from his interest in the west and there may be a genuine tradition behind Diodorus' account of Themistocles' policy after the defeat of the

---

[1] Tod, *GHI* ii, n. 123. 35–46.
[2] ML 79 B. 55; *Hesp.* xxii (1953), 271 (vi. 545) and 273 (vi. 133), Thasos; Euboea, ibid., pp. 251 (ii. 90), 252 (ii. 178), 263 (iv. 18).

Persians: 'He persuaded the people to build twenty new triremes each year and exempt metics and craftsmen from all dues,
in order that large numbers should come to the city from all
quarters and increase the number of trades; for he judged that
both these policies were most useful for meeting the needs of a
sea power.'[1] Exemption from dues was a privilege that Athenians gave to individual metics, but it is extremely doubtful
whether they ever seriously considered giving it without dis-
crimination to all. We can, however, be certain that Athens
appreciated the value of metics and probably made better
provision for them than any other Greek state. They were
given a definite status in society and through *prostatai* were
able to go to law in the Athenian courts. They attended the
theatre with citizens and Aristophanes could call them the
city's bran.[2] Pericles encouraged Cephalus, father of Lysias,
to leave Sicily and settle in Athens;[3] he may have been
interested in the arms that his slaves made as well as in his
intelligence.

When, after the middle of the century, so much money was
circulating in Athens, men from other states and particularly the
islands, needed little encouragement to leave home and settle in
the Piraeus or Athens itself. The extent of the population increase caused by this influx we have no means of measuring
with any degree of accuracy. We can be reasonably confident
that the number of metics immediately after the expulsion of
Xerxes was very small indeed, nor probably was there any
dramatic increase before 450. The consolidation of empire, the
making of peace with Persia, and the decision to use the tribute
reserve on Athenian building must have been decisive in quick-
ening the flow. It was at this time that the Piraeus was virtually
replanned by Hippodamus. In 431 no less than 3,000 metics
could serve with the Athenian hoplite field force against
Megara.[4] These will have been men of substance, mainly large-
scale traders; the number of small shop-keepers, small-scale
tradesmen, and unskilled labourers must have been considerably larger. It is of such men that the Old Oligarch is thinking
when he says that slaves and metics enjoy considerable licence
at Athens and, a little later, 'Athens needs metics because of the

---

[1] Diod. xi. 43. 3. [2] Ar. *Acharn.* 508.
[3] Lysias xii. 4. [4] Thuc. ii. 31. 2.

number of trades and because of the fleet.'[1] A figure of 10,000 has become a common estimate for the number of metics; it was probably larger.

The considerable increase in the population of Athens and the Piraeus combined with a high level of employment meant a substantial increase in the volume of imports. The wide variety of markets that Athens could draw on is attributed to her control of the sea routes by the Old Oligarch, and this control depended on the large and effective fleet which the tribute made possible: 'Through control of the sea . . . the good things of Sicily, Italy, Egypt, Lydia, the Peloponnese, and everywhere else are all brought to Athens.'[2] A more impressive catalogue is given by Hermippus in a comedy produced in the twenties.

From Cyrene silphium and ox hides, from the Hellespont mackerel and all kinds of salted fish, from Italy salt and ribs of beef . . . from Egypt sails and rope, from Syria frankincense, from Crete cypress for the gods; Libya provides abundant ivory to buy, Rhodes raisins and sweet figs, but from Euboea pears and fat apples. Slaves from Phrygia, . . . Pagasae provides tattooed slaves, Paphlagonia dates and oily almonds, Phoenicia dates and fine wheat-flour, Carthage rugs and many-coloured cushions.[3]

Not all the cargoes that came to the Piraeus were intended for Attica. As the facilities of the Piraeus improved it probably became easier for many of the smaller states to buy what they needed from overseas in the Piraeus. This will apply particularly to luxuries but probably many states who could not subsist on their own crops will have come to Athens to purchase the corn they needed. The main sources of supply were the Euxine, Egypt, south Italy, and Sicily. Of these the Euxine was the most important and Athens, by her occupation of the Chersonese and her relations with the rulers of the Bosporus kingdom, could safeguard her own supply and interfere with the supplies of others. One of the Athenian decrees in favour of Methone on the Thermaic Gulf allows Methone to draw from Byzantium several thousand (the precise figure is missing) *medimnoi* of corn

---

[1] [Xen.] Ἀθ. Πολ. 1. 12: διότι δεῖται ἡ πόλις μετοίκων διά τε τὸ πλῆθος τῶν τεχνῶν καὶ διὰ τὸ ναυτικόν. διὰ τοῦτο οὖν καὶ τοῖς μετοίκοις εἰκότως τὴν ἰσηγορίαν ἐποιήσαμεν. The meaning here of τὸ ναυτικόν is service in the triremes.

[2] [Xen.] Ἀθ. Πολ. 2. 7.

[3] Athen. 1. 27e–28a (Hermippus, F 63).

a year.[1] This admittedly was during the early years of the Peloponnesian War, but even in peacetime Athens would have the power to control the shipping that passed from the Euxine into the Aegean. Many smaller states would probably find it more convenient to buy what they needed at the Piraeus, rather than make the long journey themselves to the sources of supply.

Among the material advantages of empire the Old Oligarch includes the centralization of jurisdiction in Athens.

Some think that the Athenian demos makes a mistake in this too, that they compel the allies to sail for their cases to Athens. The justification lies in the advantages that this brings to the demos of Athens. For, first of all, the court fees provide the jurors' fees for the whole year . . . In addition there are these gains for the demos of Athens when the allies' cases are heard at Athens: first of all the 1 per cent at the Piraeus which the state gets is increased; then anyone who has lodgings does better and anyone who has a carriage-pair or a slave to earn money for him; then the criers do better when the allies stay here.[2]

Nor in the general balance sheet should one forget the constant stream of embassies coming from the allies.

The material advantages that Athens drew from her empire were considerable. Did Athens grow prosperous at the allies' expense? Did the allies become poorer as Athens grew richer? These questions do not admit a clear-cut answer, and different areas probably fared very differently. How serious a burden the tribute was to the allies we cannot securely know without knowing more of their resources than the available evidence reveals, but we may doubt whether before the Peloponnesian War the allies were required to pay more than they could comfortably afford. Some of them almost certainly resented the tribute after 450 as a symbol of subjection, but that is another matter. When the Peloponnesians sacked Iasus in 412 Thucydides says that they found plenty of money, for the place was 'wealthy from of old'; the pre-war tribute was only 1 talent. Before returning to Athens in 407 Alcibiades sailed to the Ceramic Gulf and collected 100 talents; this much exceeded the pre-war tribute of the whole Carian district.[3] When the revolt of Thasos was

---

[1] ML 65. 34–6, quoted p. 206 n. 3. A similar privilege is accorded to Aphytis, D 21. 1–6.

[2] [Xen.] Ἀθ. Πολ. i. 16–18.

[3] Iasus, Thuc. viii. 28. 3; Ceramic Gulf, Xen. Hell. 1. 4. 8–9.

crushed in 462 she was required eventually to pay 30 talents a year, but during the Peloponnesian War 30 talents would only have kept a fleet of thirty triremes afloat for one month.[1] The war fleet which Thasos had to surrender to Athens must have been considerably larger than thirty ships for, according to Plutarch, she had challenged Athens in a sea battle and thirty-three of her ships were captured.[2] To surrender her fleet was a humiliation, but it was a considerable economy. However, Thasos had lost to Athens the virtual control of her mainland colonies and mining interests. In the sixth century Pisistratus had profited from the resources of the Strymon area, particularly silver and timber, but Athens lost her stake in the region when the Persians advanced along the north shore of the Aegean. The failure of Xerxes' invasion and the expulsion of the Persians from Europe with the exception of isolated pockets in Eion and Doriscus enabled Thasos to secure again the main economic control of the region. Thucydides is quite clear that the issue which led Thasos to revolt was a quarrel about economic interests. It is possible that Athens may have received some encouragement from Neapolis, the best sited of the Thasian colonies on the mainland, for the tribute of Neapolis, 1,000 drachmae before the war, was extremely low for a town that has nearly always been prosperous and even in 411, when Thasos revolted again and Athenian power was no longer formidable, Neapolis remained loyal to Athens. But we cannot cast Athens for the role of disinterested champion of the weak against the strong.

The Old Oligarch is fully alive to the economic aspects of thalassocracy: 'As for the cities on the mainland which are ruled by Athens the large are controlled by fear and the small by need. For there is no city which does not need to export or import; and these things it will not be able to do unless it accepts the bidding of the power that rules the sea.'[3] The extreme example of this power is the Megarian Decree by which Athens hoped to force Megara into submission. But by closing the harbours of the allies to Megarian ships she was also interfering with the trading interests of those who traded regularly with Megara.

---

[1] For the Thasian tribute see p. 85.   [2] Plut. *Cim.* 14. 2.
[3] [Xen.] *Ἀθ. Πολ.* 2. 3.

On the other hand, though Athens considerably increased her share of Greek trade during the fifth century it is also probable that the total volume of trade, at least after 450, became considerably larger. Aegean trade needed a strong fleet to suppress piracy and the sea lanes were probably more secure during the period of the Athenian Empire than at any other time in the Ancient World except perhaps during the first two centuries of the Roman Empire. The end of fighting against Persia, whether or not there was a formal peace, provided a further stimulus. Greek pottery, and particularly Attic pottery, came to Al Mina on the Levantine coast and to Naucratis in Egypt during the first half of the century but there is no clear indication of the volume in the published archaeological evidence and it is impossible to tell by what stages Attic red-figure pots came into the eastern Mediterranean. Before the battle of the Eurymedon Phaselis, not yet a member of the Delian League, may have carried on a brisk business, buying from Greeks and selling to easterners. It is true that throughout most of history the channels of trade have been much less affected by war than modern experience would suggest, but when up to 200 Phoenician ships had been captured or destroyed in the Eurymedon Greek merchantmen must surely have expected seizure if they sailed east. Even before the war there was armed rivalry between Phoenician and Greek. When the decisive battle of the Ionian Revolt off the island of Lade had been lost Dionysius, the Phocaean commander, 'sailed forthwith to Phoenicia, and having sunk merchantmen there and taken a great quantity of treasure he sailed to Sicily and using Sicily as a base plundered Carthaginians and Etruscans, but not Greeks'.[1] It is probable that the close of fighting against Persia brought a great change.

Herodotus, travelling in Egypt after the end of the Egyptian revolt, and almost certainly after the Peace of Callias, tells us that in his day wine came to Egypt from all parts of Greece and Phoenicia.[2] Two other passages suggest that in the second half of the century Greeks were widely tolerated in Egypt. In describing Egyptian sacrifice of bulls sacred to Epaphus, Herodotus says that those who have a market and Greek merchants living in their town bring the head of the bull to market and sell it.[3] It is doubtful whether Greeks could have circulated so freely in

[1] Hdt. vi. 17.   [2] Hdt. iii. 6. 1.   [3] Hdt. ii. 39. 2.

Egypt when Persians and Greeks were still at war, and under Amasis in the sixth century the Greeks seem to have been very restricted. Herodotus says that Amasis allowed the Greeks who came to Egypt to settle in Naucratis. If anyone entered any other mouth of the Nile he had to take an oath that he had not intended to come there and then he had to sail to the Canobic mouth. And if the winds were unfavourable and he could not sail he had to carry his cargo round the Delta in barges until he came to Naucratis.[1] Herodotus makes Amasis a philhellene in these dispensations, but Amasis won the throne as a nationalist reacting against the dependence of his predecessor Apries on foreign troops, mainly Greek. The concentration in Naucratis makes better sense as a policy of restriction.[2] Herodotus says that Naucratis was the only *emporion* in Egypt 'in former days', τὸ παλαιόν. The phrase is vague, but it implies that the situation was different in his own day.

The opening up of Egypt to the Greeks might have come when Persia first conquered Egypt in 525, or, perhaps more probably, as a result of the Peace of Callias. It is at least reasonable to believe that there was a considerable increase in the volume of Greek trade with Egypt in the second half of the century. In this connection a nice question arises concerning the gift of corn which Psammetichus 'king of the Egyptians' (also called 'king of Libya') sent to Athens in 445–444.[3] It has been held that this is an Egyptian rebel still resisting the Persians and hoping to enlist Athenian help. Certainly Amyrtaeus was still holding out in the marshes at the time of Cimon's final Cyprian campaign; but Herodotus emphasizes that the Persians behaved generously after the Egyptian revolt and allowed Thannyras and Pausiris, the sons of the two main rebel leaders, Inaros and Amyrtaeus, to take over the territories that their fathers had ruled.[4] Thucydides calls Inaros 'son of Psammetichus, a Libyan, king of the Libyans who are neighbours of Egypt'. Psammetichus who sent corn to Athens is probably brother and successor of Thannyras. He may have thought of reviving his father's cause and this very practical gift may have been designed to have a very practical response; Plutarch does indeed

[1] Hdt. ii. 178–9.   [2] R. M. Cook, *JHS* lvii (1937), 232 f.
[3] Plut. *Per.* 37. 4; Ar. *Wasps* 718, with schol. (Philochorus, *FGH* 328 F 119).
[4] Hdt. iii. 15. 3.

tell us that even before the Peloponnesian War there were some Athenians who wanted to make another attempt on Egypt.[1] But this is not a necessary inference. Psammetichus may have been thinking more of Greek trade than Greek triremes. Egypt was the main supplier of sails and rope.[2]

The history of fifth-century Greek trade in the Euxine is even less well attested than the trade with Egypt; but here too it is probable that the end of the fighting with Persia was followed by an expansion of Greek and particularly Athenian trade with the Euxine cities. The export of Athenian red-figure pottery to the area certainly increases, and the spectacular expedition led by Pericles into the Euxine in the thirties is likely to have encouraged an expansion of trade, but much more excavation is needed before important conclusions can be drawn.[3]

Along the north coast of the Aegean Abdera and Aenus pay high tributes (15 t. and 12 t., reduced to 10 t. in 446) and for some reason that we do not know Maronea rises from $1\frac{1}{2}$ talents in the first four periods to 10 talents in the thirties. The prosperity of these towns will have depended largely on the increasing wealth of the Odrysian Kingdom which reached its greatest extension in the last quarter of the fifth century. In exchange for their tribute they could expect the diplomatic and, if needed, the military support of Athens. West of the Strymon the Greek communities might have been engulfed by Macedon if they did not have Athenian protection. In 430 Athens, formally at peace with Perdiccas, sent envoys to tell him 'that justice requires him to allow the people of Methone free use of the sea and that he should not restrict them, but allow them to carry on their normal trade with the interior. He should neither harm them nor be harmed by them and he should not lead a military force through their territory against their will.'[4] It was much easier for Macedon to overrun Chalcidice in the fourth century when Athens had neither the means nor the will to defend her allies with adequate forces.

The least prosperous districts of the Athenian empire were the Ionian and Island districts. In the sixth century Ionian

---

[1] Plut. *Per.* 20. 3.
[2] Above, p. 264 (the catalogue of Hermippus).
[3] For the fullest account of Greek trade with the Euxine area in the fifth century see I. B. Brashinsky, op. cit. (p. 198 n. 1).
[4] D 3. 18–23 (= ML 65).

culture and trade could match the mainland, and Miletus was one of the strongest and most prosperous of Greek towns. She had been the main colonizer of the Euxine, she was strongly represented at Naucratis in Egypt, and her special relationship with Sybaris in south Italy presupposes a brisk trade with the west.[1] Silver-rich Tartessus, according to Herodotus, was first discovered by a Samian shipper, and it was the Phocaeans who exploited the market and established colonies from Sardinia through Massilia to Spain.[2] The greatest temples of the Greek world in the sixth century were at Ephesus, Samos, and Didyma near Miletus; and philosophy, geography, and science all had their roots in Ionia. Fifth-century Ionia seems but a pale shadow of this magnificence. In the catalogues of the sources of Athenian imports there is no mention of Ionia or of any of the cities of Ionia, though Milesian beds are included in the confiscated property of those who were condemned for mutilating the Hermae or making mock of the Eleusinian mysteries, and Critias singles them out together with beds made in Chios.[3] Milesian wool also retained a good name.[4]

Miletus was never required to pay more than 10 talents tribute before the war and no other Ionian mainland city paid as much. Phocaea's assessment was only 3 talents, and Erythrae paid no more than 7 talents in the third and fourth assessment periods when the smaller communities of her peninsula were paying independently; when she paid for the whole peninsula in the last pre-war period her tribute was still only 10 t. 1,100 dr. Aeolian Cumae alone in the Ionian district paid more than 10 talents, but her first-period assessment of 12 talents was reduced to 9 in the second period and thereafter. The Hellespont district represents a sharp contrast. The tribute of Byzantium rises from 15 talents in the second period to just over 18 talents in the last pre-war assessment. Lampsacus can pay 12 talents, Perinthus 10; Chalcedon and Cyzicus are both assessed at 9 talents. Such archaeological evidence as there is seems to confirm the decline of Ionia. No fifth-century buildings of any note have yet been traced but it is too early to look for firm conclusions from archaeology. Excavation has barely tapped the

[1] Hdt. v. 28; vi. 21. 1.   [2] Hdt. iv. 152; i. 163.
[3] *Hesp.* xxii (1953) 244 (i. 229, 233), 253 (ii. 244); Athenaeus i. 28b.
[4] Eupolis, F 227; Ar. *Lys.* 729.

surface of the Ionian cities; until the lower levels are reached over wide areas it is wiser to lean primarily on the literary and epigraphic evidence.

J. M. Cook, the excavator of old Smyrna, has associated the poverty of the Ionian cities at this time with the system of land tenure. He believes that most of the best land was still owned by landlords paying rent to the Persians, and that, for instance, very little of the rich Maeandrian plain was attached to the Greek cities.[1] It is true that in the Caicus valley where the Persian king had given fiefs to Demaratus, the Spartan king in exile, and the Eretrian Gongylus, Persian tenure came very near the coast, but it is difficult to believe that similar conditions obtained to the south. That Miletus, Clazomenae, and Ephesus should rest content while the profit from the best land near them went to the Persians seems quite incredible. It is more likely that the low tributes of the Ionian cities reflect the economic decline of Ionia. The decisive crushing of their revolt had sapped the strength and spirit of the Ionians. Miletus had seen most of her able-bodied men taken into captivity; Phocaea and Teos had been partly at least evacuated. Even if there had been no Athenian empire Ionia would have suffered increasingly from mainland competition.

The islands had not been significantly affected by the Ionian Revolt or the Persian wars, but there was little natural wealth in them. Siphnos had been rich in the sixth century when her silver mines were productive, but in the fifth century they seem to yield considerably less. Naxos was comparatively fertile, and Paros could export her marble; but most of the islands were rocky and had little good agricultural land. They could support themselves when populations were small and power dispersed but by the sixth century they had become a natural prize for a naval power. Athens first under Pisistratus, followed by Polycrates of Samos, became master of the Cyclades. Much later they were to look to the Ptolemies for patronage and protection and form a League of Islands to pool their resources. Their subjection to Athens in the fifth century dispensed them from the need to maintain their own fleets and under Athens' shield they could trade securely. More important, they probably

[1] J. M. Cook, 'The Problems of Classical Ionia', *Proc. Camb. Phil. Ass.* vii (1961), 9–18.

benefited more than other parts of the empire from well-paid service in the Athenian fleet and from the Athenian policy of unrestricted immigration which enabled them to settle as metics in the Piraeus or the city. Skilled islanders could probably make better money with their skills in Athens than at home and when the Athenians embarked on their great rebuilding policy there must have been a very large demand for sculptors, quarrymen, and masons.

From such evidence as we have it would be dangerous to conclude that the Athenians drained the wealth of the Aegean world and exploited the allies to improve their own standard of living. Athens profited considerably from the tribute but some of this wealth returned to the allies in payment for service on sea and land and from the opportunities opened to metics. Athens' secure control of the seas increased the total volume of trade, but though Athens was the main beneficiary others shared the benefits. The chief grievances of the allies in the period before the Peloponnesian War were not economic.

15

ATHENA'S CITY

I N his funeral speech of 431 Pericles is made by Thucydides
to claim that Athens was the school of Greece and that all
could share in her.[1] He was not thinking primarily of
philosophers, playwrights, and poets, but of her institutions,
character, and way of life. In this whole complex, however, the
development of Athens as the cultural centre of the Greek world
was of paramount importance and her development was closely
linked with the growth of Athenian power and wealth. Athens
could already be regarded as a culturally progressive state
towards the close of the sixth century but she was far from being
the leader of Greece. Pisistratus and his sons, especially
Hipparchus, had attracted men of talent to their court. Lasus
from Hermione had introduced the dithyrambic chorus to the
festival of the Panathenaea and Simonides of Ceos became the
most successful of the early competitors and something of
a court poet. When Polycrates, tyrant of Samos, was killed
and Samos submerged in the Persian empire, Anacreon moved
to Athens, but when the Pisistratids were driven out in 510 the
poets whom they had encouraged were dispersed. Simonides,
the greatest of them, went to Thessaly, but before the battle
of Marathon he was back in Athens and his epitaph for the
Athenian dead was chosen in competition against Aeschylus.
In 480 he commemorated the Spartan heroes of Thermopylae
and in his poems on the battles of Artemisium and Salamis he
paid full tribute to the part played by Athens in the resistance
to Persia, but Simonides left for Sicily in 476 and remained
there till his death in 468. There is a tradition that he was
a personal friend of Themistocles and the eclipse of Themistocles may have been a factor in his going but no special
explanation is needed.[2]

[1] Thuc. ii. 41. 1 : ξυνελών τε λέγω τήν τε πᾶσαν πόλιν τῆς Ἑλλάδος παίδευσιν εἶναι.
[2] C. M. Bowra, *Greek Lyric Poetry*², 308–72; A. J. Podlecki, *Simonides*, 480;
Hist. xvii (1968), 257–75.

T

In the years immediately following the repulse of the Persians there was little incentive for poets or philosophers to visit Athens. The city had been razed to the ground and private as well as public fortunes had suffered badly from the invasion; it was several years before living conditions could recover.

Pindar, who in this generation came to be the acknowledged poet laureate of the Greek world, had received part of his training at Athens in the period between the reforms of Clisthenes and the battle of Marathon. His devotion to Delphi made him a natural associate of the Alcmaeonids who had rebuilt the temple of Apollo more magnificently than their contract required, and he wrote an ode to celebrate the victory of Megacles in the four-horse chariot race at the Pythian festival in 486.[1] But by then Megacles had been ostracized and the Alcmaeonids were under a cloud. The temporary eclipse of this family may have affected Pindar's feeling for Athens, but after the repulse of Xerxes he commemorated in a dithyramb the part played by her in the great victories of 480 and 479—'Radiant, violet-crowned, famed in song, pillar of Greece, glorious Athens, city divine';[2] and no praise of Athens was to be more widely quoted. However, the striking contrast between the battle-pride of Athens and the humiliation of his native Thebes must have been an increasing embarrassment. In his later years he developed more sympathy for Athens' old enemy Aegina, and for patronage he relied above all on the Sicilian tyrants.

In these years Athens was no more attractive to sculptors than to poets. In the late sixth and early fifth centuries most of the foreign masters are represented by works in Athens, but foreign sculptors seem to have looked elsewhere in the seventies. Onatas, the Aeginetan master, is represented by three works in Athens before 480; later he is found at Olympia and elsewhere in the Peloponnese but not in Athens. Pythagoras, the Samian, who had migrated to Zancle and then, under the influence of the tyrant Anaxilas, became a citizen of Rhegium, had the greatest reputation of the day but his name has not been found on any base at Athens, nor do the literary sources record any of his work there. Calamis, possibly a Boeotian, made the famous Aphrodite for Callias, who negotiated peace with Persia, but this was probably soon after the middle of the

[1] Pindar, *Pyth.* vii. [2] Pindar, fr. 75 (Schroeder).

century, towards the end of his life; his earlier work seems to
have been distributed between Delphi, Olympia, and, significantly, Boeotia.[1]

Before 470 Athens had little to match the magnificence of
Syracuse, but the successes against Persia of the Delian League
under Athenian leadership, culminating in the great victory
of the Eurymedon, together with the growing maturity of
Athenian tragedy, considerably enhanced her prestige. Cimon
was the outstanding general of this generation and, supported
by strong family alliances, he seems to have extended his
patronage to distinguished foreigners. Ion of Chios[2] was later
happy to remember that when quite young he had been at a
dinner party attended by the great man at Athens. But though
he had associated with Cimon and his circle in his early years,
the radical reforms of Ephialtes did not apparently turn Ion
against Athens. He was proud to have his tragedies produced
at Athens in the period of Periclean leadership and he celebrated a victory at the Dionysia by a free distribution of Chian
wine to the citizens. Being rich and coming from Chios, whicn
was still probably ruled by oligarchs, he was almost certainly
attracted by Athenian culture rather than Athenian politics.
But his attachment to Athens was sufficiently strong to earn
him Athenian citizenship, and his son Tydeus remained a firm
friend of Athens, even when Chios had revolted in 412.[3] In 411
Pedaritus the Spartan harmost, who was prepared to be more
ruthless than the Chian magistrates, put him and his followers
to death for supporting Athens, ἐπ' ἀττικισμῷ.

Polygnotus, the greatest painter of his day, came from Thasos
and, like Ion of Chios, was an associate of Cimon and his circle,
one of the many victims of his half-sister Elpinice's charms
according to gossip.[4] He may have come to know Cimon during
the operations at Eion and Scyros and perhaps Cimon persuaded him to come to Athens when he returned from Scyros
with the bones of Theseus. If we accept a very reasonable
emendation, Polygnotus shared with Micon the paintings in
the shrine that was built to contain the hero's bones beyond

---

[1] Raubitschek, *DAA*, pp. 505–8. [2] See also above, p. 14.
[3] Thuc. viii. 38. 3 with Jacoby, *CQ* xli (1947), 1 n. 9.
[4] Plut. *Cim.* 4. 6. For an assessment of Polygnotus, C. M. Robertson, *Greek Painting*, 121–35; G. Lippold, *RE* xxi, cols. 1630–8.

the south end of the Agora.[1] Two of the paintings were to have a great influence on Athenian art through the century and beyond, the *Defence of Attica against the Amazons*, perhaps symbolizing the repulse of Persia, and the *Battle of Lapiths and Centaurs*, often interpreted as the struggle of civilization against barbarism, or constitutional government against tyranny.[2] These were the first of a great series of large painted panels that gave a special distinction to the buildings that can fairly be called Cimonian, and to later generations Polygnotus was the master, Micon, Panaenus, and others his associates. According to the Elder Pliny Polygnotus was the first to break down the stereotype formulae of the archaic period: 'He made the first great contribution to painting if indeed it was he who instituted the practice of opening the mouth, showing the teeth, and varying the expression from the stiffness of the archaic.'[3] Polygnotus repeated his partnership with Micon when they decorated the temple of the Dioscuri, not far from the Theseum. His subject was the *Marriage of the Dioscuri*; Micon painted the *Voyage of the Argonauts to the Land of the Colchians.*[4] The main home of the Dioscuri was at Sparta and one may suspect the influence of the philo-Laconian Cimon in the commissioning of the artists. Polygnotus' last commission in Athens was also probably Cimonian in inspiration. The building, famed for its paintings, was later called the Stoa Poikile, but its original name was the Peisianakteion, derived from Peisianax, the brother of Cimon's Alcmaeonid wife, Isodice. On the facing wall of the stoa there were three great paintings, the *Battle of Theseus and the Athenians against the Amazons*, the *Fall of Troy*, and, finally, the *Battle of Marathon*. Cimon had brought back Theseus to Athens; his father, Miltiades, the hero of Marathon, was duly emphasized in the painting of the battle and the *Fall of Troy* may have been intended to recall Cimon's victories over the Persians; Ladice in the painting was said to have the head of Elpinice, a pretty compliment.[5] Plutarch is very anxious to emphasize that Polygnotus was a gentleman, and did not have to paint for

[1] Harpocration (s.v. Πολύγνωτος): τὰς ἐν τῷ θησαυρῷ καὶ τῷ Ἀνακείῳ γραφάς. There was no monumental treasury in Athens; Θησείῳ is an almost certain emendation (not accepted by Lippold, op. cit. 1631 f.). For the site of the Theseum, *Hesp.* xxxv (1966), 40–8.

[2] Paus. i. 17. 2.

[3] Pliny, *NH* xxxv. 58–9.

[4] Paus. i. 18. 1.

[5] For the Stoa Poikile, see p. 96.

a living, and to prove his point he quotes two lines from a contemporary poet: 'At his own expense he adorned temples of
the gods and Cecrops' Agora with the brave deeds of heroes.'[1]
For his services he was granted Athenian citizenship, and it
was probably from his association with Athens that he painted
Odysseus after the Death of the Suitors for the forecourt of the temple
of Athena Areia at Plataea, and did another painting, whose
subject is not recorded, at Thespiae. Plataea had been under
the special protection of Athens since they first became allies
in 519, and Thespiae who refused to Medize in 480 was probably helped in her post-war recovery by Athens. As late as
the Peloponnesian War she was suspected by Thebes of
Atticizing.[2]

The painting in the Stoa Poikile was Polygnotus' last major
work in Athens. The building probably dates from the late
sixties, not far from the time when his native Thasos had to
surrender to Cimon and suffer the humiliation of pulling down
her walls, giving up her fleet, and paying a stiff indemnity.
Polygnotus' feelings must have been very mixed. He owed much
to his father's training, but if he had remained in Thasos and
not come to Athens his influence would not have been so great,
nor his fame so lasting. He may have felt differently when
Cimon was ostracized, for that meant the end of an age. We
hear no more of him at Athens and it may be at this stage that
he worked for the Cnidians on their pavilion at Delphi where
he repeated his subject for the Stoa Poikile and painted another
Fall of Troy on a larger scale with a more dramatic design.[3]
This was the grand climax of his painting career, and he may
have returned to Thasos in the fifties. Soon after the middle of
the century both he and his brother held office in Thasos.[4] He
may have helped to reconcile his countrymen to Athens.

[1] Plut. *Cim.* 4. 7.
[2] Plataean alliance with Athens, Thuc. iii. 68. 5; paintings, Paus. ix. 4. 2.
Relations of Thespiae with Athens, Hdt. viii. 75. 1; Thuc. iv. 133. 1; paintings,
Pliny, *NH* xxxv. 123.
[3] For the Cnidian *Lesche*, Paus. x. 25–31; J. Pouilloux, *Fouilles de Delphes* II, *La
Région nord du Sanctuaire*, 120–39. The archaeological evidence can only yield an
approximate date 'in the second quarter of the fifth century'. Cnidus claimed to
be a Spartan colony and Polygnotus seems to have adapted the story he painted
to suit Dorian tastes (Ch. Dugas, *REG* li (1938), 56; J. Défradas, *Les Thèmes de la
propagande delphique*, 151–6).
[4] See App. 15, p. 573.

Among other distinguished men who made Athens their second home was Hippodamus of Miletus, whose skills, interests, and eccentricities would have well fitted him for the society of Florence in the Renaissance. According to Aristotle he had long flowing hair and wore expensive ornaments on cheap garments. In the tradition of the Ionian physicists of the sixth century he made a wide study of the natural world, but he was also the first man known to us to construct in some detail an ideal state. At a time when Athens was encouraging all her citizens to take an active part in politics Hippodamus advocated a rigid functional division. His city, limited in size to 10,000, was to be divided into three classes, artisans, husbandmen, and armed defenders of the state. Land was similarly to be divided into three categories: sacred, public, and private; the same threefold division was to apply to laws, covering insult, injury, and homicide. Even the votes of jurors were to allow one of three verdicts; if they did not wish to acquit or condemn they could record their indecision.[1] It is doubtful whether this schematic approach to political problems would have appealed to radical democrats but it raised interesting questions and was not without influence on subsequent thinkers.

The common people of Athens will have appreciated Hippodamus more for his work in the Piraeus. How much deliberate planning had been attempted before the mid century we cannot yet discover, but it is certain that Hippodamus transformed the harbour town. The late lexicographers, Hesychius and Photius, both have an entry ʻΙπποδάμου νέμησις and explain it as the dividing up of the Piraeus by Hippodamus. The rectangular pattern of the streets that has been traced in parts of the area represents his work, and the Agora which took his name was presumably his creation. His commission was not merely to give a more dignified appearance to the town, but to improve the trading facilities of an increasingly busy harbour; the new buildings included a Corn Market attributed to Pericles.[2] His success in replanning the Piraeus led to a further commission to make a plan for Athens' great panhellenic

---

[1] Arist. *Pol.* 1267^{b}22–1268^{a}15.
[2] Ar. *Acharn.* 548 with schol.: τῆς λεγομένης ἀλφιτοπώλιδος, ἣν ᾠκοδόμησε Περικλῆς ὅπου καὶ σῖτος ἐπέκειτο τῆς πόλεως. For Hippodamus' work at Piraeus, Judeich, *Topographie*², 430 f., 448, 451 f. See Add. p. 598.

colony in the west at Thurii, but of his work there we know even less than of his work at the Piraeus. Athens must have won his loyalty, for his son was an Athenian citizen, well enough known in the city to be called simply son of Hippodamus by Aristophanes in the *Knights*. He is Archeptolemus of the deme Agryle, who supported peace with Sparta after the capture of Spartan prisoners on Sphacteria in 425. By 411 he had thrown in his lot with the extreme oligarchs and was condemned with Antiphon to death for attempting to betray Athens to Sparta. His house was razed to the ground and he was denied burial in Attica or within the Athenian empire.[1]

From Miletus at roughly the same time as Hippodamus came Aspasia, who was to live with Pericles for some fifteen years and give him a son who needed a special decree before he could become an Athenian citizen;[2] it was a sad irony, for his father had himself in 451–450 introduced the law that only those of Athenian descent on both sides were to be citizens. Though we know very little of her, Aspasia is perhaps the most interesting woman of the century. She was constantly attacked in comedy, accused of having a sinister influence over Pericles, and coarsely caricatured. In Aristophanes' *Acharnians* it was the seizure of two of her 'ladies in waiting' that provoked the Megarian decree which led to war between Athens and Sparta. But she must have been in part at least responsible for Pericles' Olympian calm. She could hold her own in the intellectual arguments of the day and was remembered by Socratics in the fourth century with affection and respect.[3]

Herodotus of Halicarnassus was roughly the contemporary of these two Milesians. The tradition that he gave public recitals in Athens is controversial, but he knew Athens and Athenian traditions well. Even in those parts of his work which many scholars believe to have preceded his decision to write a history of the Persian wars Athens is one of his common points of reference, implying either an Athenian public or a public familiar with Athens. So the outer ring-wall of the palace at Ecbatana is about the size of the Athenian circuit; the distance of Heliopolis from the sea is the same as the road from the altar

---

[1] Ar. *Knights* 794; *PA* 2384.   [2] Plut. *Per.* 37. 5.
[3] Ar. *Acharn.* 524–7; [Plato] *Menexenus* 235e with schol.; the Socratic Aeschines wrote a dialogue *Aspasia*.

of the Twelve Gods at Athens to the temple of Olympian Zeus
at Olympia; and the Tauric peninsula is very similar in shape to
the Attic peninsula that runs out to Sunium.[1] He has gathered
Athenian traditions of the great invasion, and has informed
himself in some detail of the history of sixth-century Athens.
He says strangely little of the city of his own day and appears
not even to have seen the great painting of the battle of Marathon in the Stoa Poikile, but there is little doubt that he
was fascinated by Athens.[2] The commonly held view that he
wrote his history of the Greek struggle against Persia primarily
as a defence of Athenian imperialism is considerably more
doubtful.[3] It was, however, surely as a friend of Athens that
Herodotus joined the colony of Thurii.

From a slightly later period, thanks to the selective tastes
of Athenaeus, we know something of another interesting visitor
to Athens. Hegemon of Thasos, nicknamed Lentil-soup, has
the credit, according to Athenaeus, of establishing parody as
a literary form. He had a great reputation in Athens for the
dramatic delivery of his verses, and his *Battle of the Giants* completely held his audience, though it was the day that brought
the grim news of the final Syracusan disaster. Athenaeus also
reports that once, when he was producing a comedy, he came
into the theatre with his cloak full of stones and proceeded to
throw them into the orchestra: 'Here you are: stones for
you. Throw 'em if you wish—Winter or summer, lentil soup
is good for you.' Such men could expect patronage, and
practical help in a crisis. When Hegemon had a case brought
against him at Athens he secured the support of the theatre
people and with them approached Alcibiades. Alcibiades
accompanied by Hegemon and his supporters proceeded to
the Record Office and wiped out the record of the charge.
The official on duty was too frightened of Alcibiades to do
anything and the prosecutor thought it wise to make himself
scarce.[4]

Doubtless there were mixed feelings at home when playwrights and poets made their mark and money in Athens;

---

[1] Hdt. i. 98. 5; ii. 7. 1; iv. 99. 5.
[2] I find no convincing trace of the painting in Herodotus' description of the
battle, but see L. H. Jeffery, *BSA* lx (1965), 44.
[3] See pp. 37 f.   [4] Athen. ix. 406f–407c.

Hegemon gives us a playful account of his reception in Thasos
when he returned:

> I came to Thasos, but when I came
> The air was filled with clouds of dung
> And all on target—the target, me.
> Someone came up and said: 'Who told you
> To walk on our nice clean stage with feet
> Like that? They stink!' So I replied
> With this simple tale:
> 'What made me come, although I'm old
> And hate the work, was my want of cash.
> Yes, want—that's the great spur that drives
> So many well-groomed stinkers away
> From Thasos on cargo ships, where it's kill
> Or be killed. This very minute they're croaking out
> Their croaky songs, and since I badly
> Wanted to eat, I've done the same.
> But another time I'll refuse to sell
> Myself. I'll stay in Thasos, harming
> No one, doling out the cash
> In handfuls. That way I won't be forced
> To hear those Greek women nagging my wife
> At home while she does her baking. . . .
> "Oh my dear", as the tiny cheese cake
> Catches their eye, "your husband won
> Fifty drachmae at Athens for writing verse
> And you go and cook him a midget like that!"
> All this was going through my head
> When Pallas Athene appeared at my side
> Holding a wand of gold. She tapped me,
> And then I heard her voice:
> "Stinking Peasoup, you've had the most
> Terrible treatment. But you must go
> And compete with the rest of them."
> So I plucked up courage, took a deep breath
> And sang right out at the top of my lungs.'[1]

Between the dinner party at which Ion of Chios enjoyed
Cimon's reminiscences and Hegemon's recital of his *Battle of
the Giants* there had been an intellectual revolution. In the sixth
century Ionia, and more particularly Miletus, had been the
main centre of speculation, and it is there that the foundations

[1] Athen. xv. 698d–699c, translated by Kenneth Cavander.

of philosophy, science, geography, and history were laid. The
Persian conquest of Lydia, quickly followed by the reduction
of the Greek cities, marked the beginning of a rapid decline
in creative energy. There were large-scale emigrations from
Phocaea and Teos and there were probably many men of
ability from other Ionian towns who, like Xenophanes of Colophon, left when the Persians came and looked for new homes
on the Greek mainland or in the west. In the generation following the loss of independence Heraclitus of Ephesus alone left
work that was still being read by philosophers a century later.
He was more widely remembered for his aristocratic arrogance
and his discovery that you can't stand in the same current
twice. When the attempt to recover independence in the Ionian
Revolt collapsed, the spirit of the East Greeks seems to have
been broken, and through the fifth century Ionia was something
of an intellectual backwater.

With the collapse of Ionia the pioneering in philosophy passed
to the western Greeks. Pythagoras of Samos had already laid
the foundations of a flourishing philosophical sect in south Italy.
They thought that an understanding of numbers was the key to
reality and evolved from their beliefs a very austere discipline.
A little later Parmenides and his pupil Zeno established an
influential school at Elea, which had been the final refuge of
the Phocaeans when they abandoned Phocaea and first tried
to settle in Corsica. Driven out by the combined pressure of
Carthaginians and Etruscans they had founded a new city on
the south-west coast of Italy. In passing to the west the main
emphasis of philosophy changed. Thales, Anaximander, and
Anaximenes had been primarily concerned with the physical
nature of the universe. The main question that they were asking
was: What are things made of? What are the basic constituent
elements? If a line can be drawn between physics and philosophy Parmenides and Zeno were more concerned with
philosophy than with physics.

Athens had played no part in the early growth of philosophy.
In the sixth century Solon and Clisthenes showed considerable
political wisdom but there is no evidence of intellectual
speculation for its own sake. Nor did the popular attitude to
religion encourage free thinking. Before the end of the sixth
century Xenophanes of Colophon, who wandered widely before

settling in the west, had accused the Greeks of accepting gods whose conduct was no better than that of humans and sometimes very much worse.[1] Nearly a hundred years later a decree was passed by the Athenian Assembly that all those who did not believe in things divine or who taught doctrines about the heavenly bodies should be impeached. This decree, Plutarch tells us, was aimed at Anaxagoras who was notorious for saying that the sun was a fiery ball larger than the Peloponnese.[2] It was Anaxagoras, a native of Ionian Clazomenae, who first brought philosophy to Athens. The chronology of his life is likely to remain in dispute since the sources are weak, late, and conflicting, but a probable reconstruction can be given which does not do too much violence to the evidence. A strong tradition says that Anaxagoras was the teacher of Pericles and exercised an important influence over him.[3] He should therefore have come to Athens before Pericles was fully grown up, probably in the early Cimonian period. At some point or points he had to leave Athens. One tradition says that he was expelled as a result of a prosecution for Medism brought by Thucydides, son of Melesias; which would point to a date before peace was made with Persia. A second tradition says that Cleon was his prosecutor, and this would suggest the time of the decree of Diopeithes shortly before the Peloponnesian War. It is very difficult not to accept the association of Anaxagoras with this decree because it seems, as Plutarch says, to be deliberately designed against him. The most satisfactory resolution of the dilemma is to accept both traditions, and two trials. The first trial will have been on a charge of Medism when Athens was committed to war with Persia. In many circles this could have seemed the worst of all possible crimes, but when peace had been made Anaxagoras' views about Persia might seem considerably less traitorous. When the Athenians had got used to the peace the Assembly could have accepted a proposal to cancel the earlier sentence. Anaxagoras would have been able to return to Athens and Plutarch preserves a good story that implies his presence. At a time when political feeling was running high between the followers of Pericles and of Thucydides son of Melesias someone brought a ram's head with

<hr>

[1] Xenophanes, F 10–13a.   [2] Plut. *Per.* 32. 2; Diod. xii. 39. 2.
[3] Plato, *Phaedrus* 270a.

a single horn to Pericles. Lampon the seer said that there were
two powers in the state, Thucydides and Pericles, and the victory would go to whichever of the two was given this portent.
Anaxagoras broke open the skull and explained the physical
cause of the 'portent'. Anaxagoras was admired by those who
saw his demonstration but a little later, when Thucydides had
been defeated and Pericles had complete control of all the
people's affairs their admiration turned to Lampon; 'and both',
adds Plutarch, 'were, I think, right, philosopher and seer. The
philosopher showed how, the seer why.' This is not the best
of evidence for dating Anaxagoras' activity in Athens but it
adds a little to the argument from the decree of Diopeithes.[1]
But while not believing that Anaxagoras left Athens finally
before the middle of the century, we are not committed to
assuming that he was continuously in Athens from the date of
his return. He must have spent long enough in Lampsacus to
have established a school of philosophy before he died and
to earn the considerable honour in which he was later held by
the town.[2]

Anaxagoras followed his Ionian predecessors in speculating
on the nature of matter, but in claiming that matter was not
self-moving but subject to an over-riding principle of intelligence he was breaking new ground. So far as we know he had
pupils but no rivals in the seventies and sixties; it was not till
near the middle of the century that Athens began to attract
philosophers from other centres. We then hear of a visit by
Parmenides and Zeno. Parmenides, who at the time was about
sixty-five, had long enjoyed a considerable reputation, but this
was apparently his first visit to Athens; Zeno, who was about
forty, was reading from his book which had not yet been
obtainable in Athens. They had come to a festival of the Great
Panathenaea and were attracting an interested following of
Athenian aristocrats.[3] In Plato's account the discussion was
wide-ranging, touching on the separation of philosophy from
physics, the possibility of cogent logical proof, and the object
and method of thought. This is not good evidence for the scope
of the discussion, for by the time of the *Parmenides* Plato was

[1] Plut. *Per.* 6. 2–3.
[2] For the chronology here adopted see Endnote 20, p. 435.
[3] Plato, *Parmenides* 127a.

more concerned with his own philosophy than with the historical accuracy of his Dialogues; but there is no need to question the reality of the visit. It is doubtful whether the two western philosophers had much influence in Athens beyond a small circle of aristocrats; though it was not difficult to appreciate superficially the puzzles of Zeno, the subtleties of Parmenides are not likely to have been widely understood. The Athenian public was considerably more influenced by the travelling teachers who began to come to Athens in the forties.

The development of democracy in the Aegean and in the west had brought an increasing emphasis on the popular Assembly and the law-courts, and to win a case or to carry a decree required special skills that had hitherto not been widely practised. The demand created the supply and by the time of the Thirty Years' Peace there was growing up a class of men who claimed to teach the art of citizenship. The study of rhetoric naturally formed an important part of the training which they imparted. Their pupils were taught how to present their arguments, how to make the best of a bad case, and how to construct the emotional rhythm of their speeches. Some were specialists in the precise use of words, others seriously considered the ends as well as the means of politics. Among them were philosophers; there were also grammarians and not a few frauds. Collectively they came to be known as σοφισταί, sophists.

Unlike the Ionian speculators these men were primarily teachers, and they taught for money. Though they were a product of the rise of democracy they found their pupils among men who could pay their fees and these were normally men of established families with inherited wealth. Most of them travelled from city to city, but the main focus of their activities was Athens; for in Athens they could depend on a quick appreciation of their cleverness, and more rich young men who had political ambitions than in any other Greek state. Athens also was an open city which welcomed strangers who had skills to display and, though the demand for the new training was greater in Athens than anywhere else, only Antiphon of the sophists who left their mark in the record was an Athenian.[1]

[1] For the present argument it is not of major importance whether the politician, the sophist, the interpreter of dreams, and the archon of 418–417 are four, three, two, or one.

What is almost equally surprising is the diversity of their origins. Protagoras, the first and the greatest of them, came from the rich trading centre of Abdera on the coast of Thrace, which became the home of refugees from Teos when they preferred evacuation to subjection under Persia. Prodicus, who was remembered mainly for his insistence on precision in language, came from the island of Ceos and is said to have made a great impression on the Athenian Boule when he came to represent his city's interests. Gorgias, who dazzled the Athenian Assembly in 427, came with an embassy from Leontini. Hippias who also served on embassies and was the most versatile of them all was from Elis. Euenus, to whom Socrates refers in the *Apology*, was residing in Athens at the time and was able to charge as much as 5 minae for one of his courses, but his home was Paros. Thrasymachus, who blusters his way through the first book of Plato's *Republic*, came from Chalcedon.

Plato's *Protagoras* provides a good reflection of the cosmopolitanism of the sophists and of the social status of the circles in which they moved in Athens. The dramatic date of the dialogue is during peace, before the outbreak of the Peloponnesian War. Socrates is roused early in the morning by a young Athenian, Hippocrates, son of Apollodorus, who has heard that Protagoras is in town. He begs Socrates to take him to see and hear the great man and together they set off. Protagoras was staying with Callias, the rich nobleman whose grandfather had negotiated peace with Persia and with Sparta and whose father was to be a general in 426. Callias was a weak man, consistently caricatured in comedy for his extravagance and for the flatterers who fed his vanity. He inherited a vast fortune and exhausted it on philosophers, sophists, and women.[1] Besides Protagoras he had staying with him Prodicus and Hippias, and with Protagoras was Antimoerus of Mende, the most famous of his disciples, and other followers from the various cities he had visited. Among the Athenians who came to listen were Paralus and Xanthippus, the two sons of Pericles by his first wife, Alcibiades, who had been his ward, Critias son of Callaeschrus of strong aristocratic descent, and his cousin Charmides, son of Glaucon, who was encouraged by Socrates

---

[1] *PA* 7826: Ar. *Birds* 281–6, especially 285–6: ἅτε γὰρ ὢν γενναῖος ὑπό ⟨τε⟩ συκοφαντῶν τίλλεται, | αἵ τε θήλειαι πρὸς ἐκτίλλουσιν αὐτοῦ τὰ πτερά; Lysias xix. 48.

to enter public life but discredited his master when with Critias
he became a member of the Thirty at the end of the war. The
house-party is a very aristocratic gathering and it is with
the best families that the sophists primarily associated. But the
subjects they discussed and the views they advocated soon
filtered through to a much wider public by way of the baths
and the barbers' shops.[1] When Aristophanes makes fun of their
new-fangled doctrines he knows that his audience knows what
he is talking about. He can mention Prodicus in passing without having to explain who he was.[2]

From Plato and Aristophanes we see the worst side of the
sophists. Training in rhetoric could easily lead to a concentration on form rather than substance. For Aristophanes the new
learning was excellent material for comedy; his contest between Right and Wrong, δίκαιος λόγος and ἄδικος λόγος is a good,
broad parody of the misuse of cleverness. And for once his
great enemy Cleon was with him: he warns the Assembly in his
speech in the Mytilene debate against the clever speakers 'who
wish to be thought wiser than the law. They always want to
have their own way in public discussion; they think that this
is their finest opportunity to display their intelligence, and their
folly generally ends in the ruin of their city.'[3] Plato's picture
is scarcely more favourable. He shows a certain respect for
Protagoras, but little for the rest. They suffer for being required
as a contrast and foil to Plato's Socrates. It would be wrong,
however, to think that the sophists were concerned solely with
debating success and political achievement. They were also
exploring areas which in the sixth and early fifth century had
been obscured by traditional religion. The rational inquiry
into the nature of the universe by the Ionian physicists was now
being extended to the nature of man and society.

The change is well illustrated by the difference between
Herodotus and Thucydides. Between them there is perhaps less
distance in time than a generation but the difference between
the presuppositions and preoccupations of the two men is
immense. Herodotus inherited from the Ionian geographers
the rational approach to physical phenomena, their interest

---

[1] Cf. Eupolis, F 180: καὶ πολλ᾽ ἔμαθον ἐν τοῖσι κουρείοις ἐγώ, | ἀτόπως καθίζων
κοὐδὲ γιγνώσκειν δοκῶν.
[2] Ar. *Clouds* 361; *Birds* 692.   [3] Thuc. iii. 38. 1–3.

in personal inquiry and in inference from visible evidence. He
can argue in a modern way about the formation of the Delta
and the causes of the Nile's flooding.[1] The river Peneus in
Thessaly flows to the sea through a gap in the mountains: 'the
Thessalians themselves say that Posidon made the channel
through which the Peneus flows; and that is likely enough, for
whoever thinks that Posidon is the earth-shaker would say
that it was the work of Posidon. The gap in the mountains
is certainly the result of an earthquake in my opinion.'[2] Anyone can see that the Delta is 'the gift of the river' (as, to his
annoyance, Hecataeus had already noted) 'from the shells on
the hills and the salt exuded from the ground'.[3] But when he
comes to the actions of men Herodotus is closer to the epic
poets and the early tragedians. Man's actions are still to a large
extent controlled by the powers above, whether it is ὁ θεός
or the more general τὸ θεῖον. The gods punish *hubris* but they
are also jealous of prosperity. Oracles are serious things, guiding
the actions of cities and men. Croesus was doomed because the
oracle had decreed that Candaules who had been killed by
Gyges, the first of the Mermnad kings, would be avenged in
the fifth generation.

In Thucydides there are only isolated survivals of this out-
look. The gods play no part in his analysis of the causes of the
Peloponnesian War; oracles are only for the superstitious.[4]
Behind Thucydides lies abundance of argument in Athens,
initiated by visiting philosophers or sophists and discussed
publicly and privately. Such questions as the relation of φύσις
and νόμος, the demands of nature and of man-made law, and
the rival claims of justice and expediency became talking-points
in the houses of the rich, and were reflected in the tragedies at
the Dionysia. The vital stages in the development of Athenian
imperialism took place while Athens was becoming intoxicated
with the new spirit of rational inquiry. It was a generation that
could look more realistically at the nature of power than could
the heroes of Marathon. The cold analysis of empire in the
speeches of Thucydides is not out of temper with the thinking
of the day. There is no difficulty in believing that Pericles as
well as Cleon could publicly call the empire a tyranny.

[1] Hdt. ii. 5; ii. 20–6.   [2] Hdt. vii. 129. 4.   [3] Hdt. ii. 12. 1.
[4] Thuc. ii. 21. 3; ii. 54. 2–3; v. 26. 3; but see ii. 17. 1–2, an interesting exception.

The intellectual growth of Athens in the second half of the fifth century was matched by the physical transformation of the city. After the Persian retreat living quarters were rapidly rebuilt for the population and public buildings, such as the Bouleuterion, which were required for the business of government, were restored, but the temples and public altars were left as heaps of rubble and ash, and such new public buildings as were erected were modest in scale and materials. The Stoa Poikile, built on the initiative and perhaps at the expense of the Alcmaeonid Pisianax, was to have a long history and remained famous for its paintings, but its walls were of *poros* not marble.[1] It was not until the state could command much ampler resources that the architects could be given an opportunity to make Athens an imperial city. The decisive impetus came with the Peace of Callias when on Pericles' proposal the Athenians resolved to divert the large reserve fund of the Delian League to the rebuilding of the temples of Athens and Attica. The temple of Hephaestus and Athena on Colonus hill above the Agora seems to have been the first of the new programme, closely followed by the Parthenon with its great gold and ivory cult statue of Athena. A little later followed three further temples by the architect of the Hephaesteum, the temple of Poseidon at Sunium, of Ares at Acharnae, and of Nemesis at Rhamnus.[2] A new concert hall was built on the south-east slope of the Acropolis, probably in the late forties; according to Plutarch it could hold a large audience and the roof was supported inside by a forest of columns.[3] In 437 work was begun on Mnesicles' Propylaea, the grand monumental entrance to the Acropolis, still unfinished when war became imminent and work was stopped. Never had so much scaffolding been seen in Athens before. The buildings that emerged, particularly

---

[1] *Hesp.* xix (1950), 323.

[2] W. B. Dinsmoor, *Hesp.* ix (1940), 44–7; *Hesp. Suppl.* v (1941), 153 f. Add. 289.

[3] Plut. *Per.* 13. 9–11; Judeich, *Topografie*², 306–8. A fragment (71) from Cratinus' *Thracian Women* seems to associate the Odeum with the ostracism of Thucydides, son of Melesias, in 443: ὁ σχινοκέφαλος Ζεὺς ὅδε | προσέρχεται τῳδεῖον ἐπὶ τοῦ κρανίου | ἔχων, ἐπειδὴ τοὔστρακον παροίχεται. Geissler, *Chronologie der altattischen Komödie*, 21 f., would date the *Thracian Women* later because it mentions Euathlus who is a young man in the *Acharnians* (l. 710), produced in 425; but this line only requires that Euathlus be considerably younger than the aged Thucydides (see J. M. Edmonds, *The Fragments of Attic Comedy*, i, p. 45, note f). There is also a probable reference to Psammetichus' gift of corn in F 73.

those on the Acropolis, became the wonder of the Greek world.
Elsewhere there were individual buildings that could match
them, as the temple of Hera at Samos, or of Artemis at Ephesus;
but none could match this concentration of great architecture.
The sight of the Acropolis from the lower city might not have
brought much comfort to an oligarch from Ionia awaiting trial
for suspected conspiracy, but traders and envoys will have been
impressed by what they saw. Some of them may even have
admitted to themselves that this was no bad use for the tribute
that had accumulated.

The allies were encouraged to feel pride in the imperial city.
When each year their representatives brought their tribute to
Athens they were invited to attend the Dionysia and hear the
latest Athenian tragedies and comedies. In comedy they could
see the rulers of the empire laughing at themselves, and could
appreciate the attacks, by no means all good-natured, on the
leading politicians of the day. In his *Babylonians*, produced in
426, Aristophanes may have gone too far, for he was brought
before the Boule by Cleon and the main charge was that he had
slandered Athenian officials before foreigners. In the *Acharnians*,
produced the next year, he tells his audience that he can speak
frankly 'for this is the Lenaea and the foreigners are not yet
here, for the tribute has not come, nor the allies from the cities'.[1]
In the three years following his trial he seems deliberately to
have avoided the Dionysia, for the *Acharnians*, *Knights*, and *Wasps*
were all winter plays; but the *Clouds*, the *Peace*, and the *Birds*
were produced at the Dionysia, and there is plenty of material
in them that a politically sensitive censor would have liked to
suppress. Few of the allies are likely to have known Athens well
enough to catch all the topical allusions, and the failure to
understand the reactions of the audience must have blunted
their own enjoyment. Tragedy they could enjoy on equal terms
and this was a spectacle that only Athens could provide.

The presence of the allies gave the Dionysia an imperial
flavour. Other Athenian festivals and cults of a more specifically
religious nature were used to strengthen the ties that bound the
allies to Athens.

[1] Ar. *Acharn.* 501–3, with schol.

16

RELIGIOUS SANCTIONS

THUCYDIDES tells us that when the Delian League was established 'Delos was their treasury, and the meetings were held in the sanctuary.'[1] This was Apollo's sanctuary; the tribute was stored in his temple and, like Athena later, he probably received an *aparche* from the annual tribute and perhaps a tithe of the booty won from the Medes. Since at the outset all members had an equal vote more than 150 representatives could be expected at meetings; the archaic temple was too small for such gatherings, which will have been held in the open air within the area reserved for Apollo. Delian Apollo was thus intimately associated with the League and it was fitting that at some time after its establishment, but substantially before the middle of the century, a larger and grander temple in marble should have been begun to supersede the modest tufa building of the archaic period.[2] The earlier temple had been either built or, more probably, restored substantially on Athenian initiative when Pisistratus ruled Athens and extended his power over Delos and the Cyclades; the initiative now probably came again from Athens.

At some time near the middle of the century work on this new temple was abandoned and it had to wait more than a hundred years for its completion.[3] No record survives in our sources of the building or abandonment of the temple but we can be reasonably certain that the occasion for stopping the work was the transfer of the treasury from Delos to Athens in 454. Athens did not, however, lose all interest in Delos. Fragments of the accounts of the administrators of the Delian gods' property covering the years 434–433 and 433–432 have been found on the Acropolis at Athens. They cover the financial

[1] Thuc. i. 96. 2.
[2] F. Courby, *Fouilles de Délos, Les Temples d'Apollon*, 97–106.
[3] Ibid. 104 f., 219 f.

affairs of the Delian temples, the lending of money at interest, and the leasing of property belonging to the Delian gods, including land, gardens, houses, and even fishing rights on Rhenea. The names with which the document now begins are Delian but we can assume that these Delians now as later in 411–410 are subordinate to Athenian Amphictyons.[1]

But after 454 Apollo no longer guarded the League funds and no longer presided over League congresses. Athena now received the *aparche* from the tribute and in various other ways she entered into Apollo's inheritance; Athens had to become the religious as well as the administrative and military centre of the empire. The allies had probably taken their tribute to Delos at the time of Apollo's festival; after the transfer of the treasury to Athens they brought it at the time of the Dionysia, and were encouraged to attend the new tragedies and comedies of the year in a ceremony that still had a religious framework.[2] A part was also assigned to them in the Great Panathenaea, the most splendid of Athenian festivals. The Panathenaea, re-organized shortly before Pisistratus became tyrant, consisted of special games and races and as a climax a great procession of priests, magistrates, and people passed along the processional way from the Dipylon gate through the Agora up to the Acropolis where a new robe was presented to Athena. Every fourth year the festival was celebrated with special splendour and it is no coincidence that it was normally in these years and at the time of the festival that the tributes of the allies were reassessed.[3]

We do not know what part, if any, the allies played in this festival in the first generation of the League, but already in the fifties Erythrae was required to participate. Though the lost decree which gives us our evidence is primarily concerned with the political settlement of Erythrae after a period of revolt, it opens with a long paragraph prescribing the obligations of Erythrae to the Great Panathenaea. These are set out in great detail, but the stone must have been very badly worn at this point when it was copied and the true text is beyond recovery.[4]

[1] ML 62; Courby, *BCH* lxi (1937), 364–79 (inscriptions from 410–409 and 408–407, which suggest that in the last years of the war Athens gave more authority to Delians in the management of the temples).
[2] Above, p. 290.   [3] Above, p. 240.   [4] ML 40.

One thing, however, can be safely inferred. When Athens made these provisions for Erythrae there was no standard obligation on all the allies. This was to come later.

On the stele which records the assessment of 425 the main decree was followed by a second which stipulated that all cities included in the assessment should bring a cow and a panoply to the Great Panathenaea.[1] It used to be thought that this sweeping measure reflected the extreme imperialism of Cleon and that it was introduced for the first time in 425; but the finding of a new fragment of the decree moved by Clinias to tighten up the collection of tribute requires a reconsideration of the date and purpose of the measure.[2] For the Clinias Decree, dealing primarily with the payment of tribute, refers briefly in passing to the cow and panoply: 'And if anyone commits an offence with regard to the sending of the cow and the panoply he shall be indicted and sentenced as in the case of a tribute offence'.[3] From this brief passing reference we can infer that a decree requiring all the allies to bring cow and panoply to the Great Panathenaea had been passed very recently. Reasons have been given above for dating the Decree of Clinias in or near 447, and the early forties, in our interpretation, provides an admirable context.[4] When the end to the fighting against Persia removed the common cause which had bound the allies together under Athenian leadership, positive steps had to be taken to prevent the disintegration of the League. The required participation of the allies in the Great Panathenaea and the enforcement of Athenian coins, weights, and measures were, we think, two of the measures taken by Athens in the early forties to express the new relationship of the allies to Athens.

In the Assessment Decree of 425 it is stated, if we accept a highly probable restoration, that the allies are to escort their offerings in the procession 'like colonists'.[5] Throughout the Greek world it was the recognized duty of colonies to maintain their links with their mother cities by participating in their main religious festivals, and Corcyra, according to Corinth, was acting outrageously in severing such connections. When the

---

[1] ML 69. 55–8. [2] ML 46; above p. 166.
[3] ll. 41–3. [4] Above, pp. 165–7.
[5] ML 69. 57–8: πεμπόντον | δ[ὲ ἐν] τῆι πομπῆι [καθάπερ ἄποι]κ[οι].

colony of Brea was sent out to Thrace in the forties the colonists were required to send a cow and a panoply to the Great Panathenaea and a phallus to the Dionysia,[1] and Athens claimed to be the founder of the Ionian cities. The earliest apparent reference to this claim is in a fragment of one of Solon's poems in which he refers to Athens as the oldest Ionian land, πρεσβυτάτην γαῖαν Ἰαονίας;[2] but this might mean no more than that Athens was the only Ionian state which was autochthonous and therefore the oldest. Many indeed have thought that the tradition of an Athenian foundation of Ionian cities is a late product of Athenian propaganda in the fifth century invented to justify Athens' claim to rule. Such light-hearted rationalism is less fashionable now than it was a generation ago, but this particular view has not been completely abandoned. We are not concerned so much with the question whether this tradition was based on real history as whether it was established before the fifth century and believed by others than Athenians. Of this there is no doubt.

Solon's line may be ambiguous, but the texts of Herodotus and Thucydides are sufficient to discredit scepticism. They could not both have been deceived by political propaganda built on no solid foundations in their own day. Herodotus reports what fifth-century Ionians believed about their origins and not what they were told by Athens to believe. He knows that the colonization of Ionia was a complex story; many races were mixed with the Ionians, but the real Ionians were those who derived their fire from the prytaneum at Athens and observed the Apaturia.[3] The claim of the aristocratic Neleids in Miletus to Athenian descent was not first made in the fifth century; Herodotus was right in making Aristagoras of Miletus appeal to Athens for help in the Ionian revolt because she was the mother city of Miletus.[4] And when Themistocles threatened that if the Peloponnesians left Salamis he would take the Athenians to Siris in south Italy 'which belonged to them' he implied that Athens could claim the site of Siris since it had been founded by Ionian Colophon, a colony of Athens.[5] The attendance of the Ionian cities of the League at the Great Panathenaea was an extension of a general tradition linking

---

[1] ML 49. 11–13. [2] Solon, F 4. [3] Hdt. i. 147. 2. [4] Hdt. v. 97. 2.
[5] Hdt. viii. 62. 2. Foundation by Colophon, Athen. 523 c.

colony and mother city. But no argument from common descent could apply to such Dorian allies as Byzantium, Cnidus, and the three cities of Rhodes, and participation was not voluntary.

As an extension of this emphasis on the role of Athens in colonizing the Aegean islands and the seaboard of Asia there is evidence in allied territories of a cult of Athena queen of Athens, Ἀθηνᾶ Ἀθηνῶν μεδέουσα, who is to be identified with Athena Polias. The most important evidence comes from Samos where a series of *horoi* (boundary stones) have been found in the plain which stretches from the old town of Samos to the great temple of Hera. The detailed description and analysis of these stones by Barron has rescued them from the status of puzzled footnotes, to which their difficulties had consigned them, and provided at least a firm basis for discussion.[1] Four of the *horoi*, in two pairs, mark reservations of Athena and one pair is inscribed in Attic script. Until recently these Samian stones were associated with the crushing of the Samian revolt in 439 and some scholars have inferred the imposition of a cleruchy, following the analogy of Mytilene where the city's territory was divided into 3,000 lots of which 300 were given to the gods. But though an Athenian settlement, whether cleruchy or colony, would have reservations for the gods, it does not follow that wherever such reservations are found there must be an Athenian settlement. There is no evidence, literary or epigraphic, for a cleruchy at this time on Samos and the silence of Thucydides is decisive. He records the main penalties imposed on Samos; had they included a cleruchy he must have mentioned it. The most plausible alternative explanation seemed to be the confiscation of some of the properties which had belonged to leading oligarchs, with the dedication of some or all of the confiscated lands to Athena and other cults. Similar *horoi* marking reservations for Athena, 'Queen of Athens', have been found at Cos and Chalcis and in both there is a mixture of Attic and local dialect and script.[2] There is also a probable reference to the cult in the decree recording an Athenian settlement with Colophon after a revolt.[3] With these three further examples should perhaps be associated four *horoi*

---

[1] J. P. Barron, 'Religious Propaganda of the Delian League', *JHS* lxxxiv (1964), 35–48.

[2] Hill, *Sources*[2], B 96, p. 319. [3] ML 47. 14.

from Aegina naming Athena, but with no title; they have a common Attic form and one of the stones is said to be of Pentelic marble.[1]

It would be convenient to accept the widely held view that all these *horoi* represent confiscations by Athens, but it is very difficult to date all the Samian stones as late as 439. The two *horoi* of Athena in Attic script and dialect have the three-barred sigma (ϟ) which in public documents from Attica seems to be obsolete after 446.[2] If these stones were found in Attica they would be dated roughly between 460 and 445, and reasons have been given for dating the Colophon decree, which also has the early sigma, in 447.[3] The stones from Cos and Chalcis are more difficult to date; the second pair of Athena's Samian *horoi* are in Ionic script and should be later, perhaps considerably later. Barron, following Preuner, argues from the title of Athena, Ἀθηνῶν μεδέουσα, that her cult originated outside Athens and that the Samian *horoi* in virtue of their date do not imply confiscation by Athens, but a cult established by Samian initiative.[4] For interpretation he leans on Plutarch's story of the ostentatiously moral reaction of Aristides to a Samian proposal that the League treasury should be moved from Delos to Athens.[5] Literally taken this proposal should be earlier than 460 by which time Aristides was dead, but the reaction of Aristides could be a later accretion. Barron, with *ATL*, refers the passage to the actual transfer of the treasury in 454, and suggests that it may have been accompanied by other proposals which would be consistent with the apparently strong support of Samos for Athens.[6] The dedication to Athena of *aparchai* from the annual tribute would be a natural corollary of the transfer. The proposal to consecrate reservations to her throughout the empire together with similar honours for heroes who were forebears of both Athenians and Ionians may have been a third clause in the same motion, which may also have included a direction to use the Attic dialect and script.[6]

Not all these arguments are convincing. Even Athena's title, Ἀθηνῶν μεδέουσα need not necessarily imply that the initiative

[1] Hill, *Sources*[2], p. 318.
[2] Meiggs, *JHS* lxxxvi (1966), 92–7.
[3] Above, pp. 161 f.
[4] Barron, art. cit. 41.
[5] Plut. *Ar.* 25. 3; above, p. 48.
[6] Barron, art. cit. 48; *ATL* iii. 262. Gomme (*HCT* i. 370, n. 2) differs.

came from outside Athens. It is used by Aristophanes in the *Knights* for Athena Polias and μεδέουσα is also applied to Aphrodite in his *Lysistrata*.[1] The use of the normal Athenian title, Ἀθηνᾶ Πολιάς, outside Athens could invite confusion with local Athenas; it was important to demonstrate that it was the cult of the Athenians' Athena that was being spread through the empire. Unfortunately the context of the very probable reference to the cult in the Athenian decree concerning Colophon has not survived, but since the decree records the terms imposed on Colophon after a revolt it seems more likely that the initiative comes from Athens rather than Colophon. The Chalcis stone might represent a confiscation after the revolt of 446 and, if we are right in inferring that Cos was hostile to Athens in the early forties, the Coan *horos* also may represent the will of Athens rather than Cos.[2] The Aeginetan *horoi* may refer to land taken by Athens from Aegina, and this could have happened at any time after the enforced incorporation of Aegina in the empire in the early fifties.

How do the Samian *horoi* fit such an interpretation? To Barron's suggestion that they represent the strong loyalty of the Samian democracy to Athens in 454, establishing cults in honour of Athens on their own initiative, there are two serious objections. It does not seem likely that a Samian proposal to honour Athens in this way would be accompanied by a requirement that Attic script and dialect should be used. We should expect that each city would use its own script, just as states which used the Ionic script inscribed their copies of the Athenian Coinage Decree in Ionic. The Attic script points to Athenian initiative. Nor is the year of the transfer of the treasury from Delos to Athens a favourable context for the launching of such cults either by the allies or by Athens. The Egyptian expedition had ended disastrously, and it has been argued above that there was strong resentment in the Cyclades that Delos was no longer to be the headquarters of the League.[3] During the three years following the final defeat in Egypt Athens was preoccupied with preparations to reverse the balance of power in the eastern Mediterranean. When peace had been made with Persia the prestige of the Athenian fleet

---

[1] Ar. *Knights* 581–5; *Lys.* 833–4.   [2] Above, p. 170.
[3] Above, p. 119 ff.

had been restored by the victory in Cyprus and there was greater need to find new links to bind the cities to Athens. As we have seen, it was probably in the early forties that Athens had required the allies to bring cow and panoply to the Great Panathenaea; she may at the same time have encouraged the spread of the cult of her patron goddess. If, however, this interpretation is on the right lines, we have to say either that the Samian stones, in spite of their script, should be associated with the Samian revolt of 440–439, or that there was earlier trouble with Samos which has left no traces in the literary record. This is not impossible. Barron has made a strong case for assigning a series of lettered Samian coins to the period 454–440 and he sees in them the reflection of a change from democracy to oligarchy in 454 continuing until the open revolt of 440.[1] At some time in these fifteen years Athens might have intervened and taken land from anti-Athenian oligarchs.

Two other cults associated with Athens are attested on Samian *horoi*. A pair of these *horoi* mark land dedicated to Ion of Athens and are in Attic dialect and script; two others show that land was also dedicated to the Eponymous Heroes of Athens, and have a mixture of Attic and Ionic vowels. Barron is surely right in identifying these Eponymous Heroes not with the heroes of the Clisthenic tribes, but with the four Ionic tribal heroes whose cult would be a natural complement to a cult of Ion.[2] Of these heroes of the Ionic tribes we hear very little in fifth-century Athens, but they are introduced with great emphasis by Euripides in his *Ion*, in association with Athens' Ionian origins and her colonization of the islands and the Asiatic coast.[3] One feels that Euripides had more than Athenians in mind; there would be allies as well in the audience. It is unlikely that these two cults were confined to Samos but there is not yet any evidence of their adoption by other members of the empire.

While encouraging the allies' involvement in Athenian cults and above all in the cult of Athena it was important for Athens to secure the goodwill of Delphic Apollo. Before and during the invasion of Xerxes Delphi had depended too much on cold calculation. Her advice to the Greek states had been at best

---

[1] Barron, *The Silver Coins of Samos*, 59–67, with 80–93.
[2] Barron, art. cit. 39 f.   [3] Euripides, *Ion* 1571–88.

ambiguous, at the worst defeatist. It was natural that she should expect Persia to overwhelm any Greeks who were rash enough to fight, but sufficient of her oracles could be re-interpreted to preserve her panhellenic importance. The Delphic Amphictyony was in fact used to deal with traitors after the war; they had declared that it was Epialtes who had shown the Persians the Callidromus path to cut off the Greeks at Thermopylae and had set a price upon his head. At this time the Spartans who had been the accepted leaders through the war were the dominant Greek power, but when they proposed that the Medizers should lose their place on the Council, Themistocles, who saw clearly the danger to Athens if Spartan influence extended outside the Peloponnese, managed to defeat the proposal.[1] We then lose sight of Delphi in our sources until the fifties when Sparta led a strong force from the Peloponnese to protect her mother country Doris against the Phocians, who may have been aiming at the control of Delphi. This move, as has been seen, led to a major battle at Tanagra which the Spartans narrowly won; but two months later Myronides won a decisive victory over the Boeotians at Oenophyta and for some ten years Athens was dominant in central Greece. It was probably soon after the victory of Oenophyta that Athens encouraged or at least allowed the Phocians to take control of Delphi and tried to consolidate her position by making an alliance with the Amphictyonic League. The evidence for this step is a fragmentary inscription which used to be interpreted as an Athenian alliance with Phocis, but some necessary corrections in the text by Meritt and new restorations make it more probable that an alliance is recorded with all the states of the Amphictyonic League.[2] It is likely that during the middle and late fifties Athens received favourable oracles from Delphi, and her Amphictyonic associations may be illustrated by the Congress Decree in which Pericles invited the Greeks of the mainland and east to meet in Athens to discuss problems still remaining from the Persian wars. Plutarch gives the routes that the heralds were to take and, as has often been observed, the pattern is closer to the Amphictyonic than to the Delian League.[3]

---

[1] Plut. *Them.* 20. 3.   [2] Meritt, *AJP* lxxv (1954), 369–76.
[3] For the Congress Decree see pp. 152 f., and App. 10 (D), p. 512. The authenticity of the decree is insecure.

It may have been as an immediate response to this initiative which had come to nothing owing to Spartan opposition that Sparta intervened at Delphi, took control from Phocis, and restored it to the Delphians. The Athenians, however, retaliated in the same summer and reinstated the Phocians; but their success was short-lived. In 447 or early 446 Boeotia revolted and the Athenian expeditionary force was routed at Coronea. To recover her prisoners Athens had to undertake to evacuate Boeotia completely, and, having lost control of Boeotia, she lost secure control of the natural route from Athens to Delphi.[1] When in 432 the Spartans had decided to go to war 'they sent to Delphi to inquire of the god whether they would fare better if they went to war, and the god, it is said, replied that if they fought with their full strength, victory would be theirs, and he would be on their side whether they called on him or not'.[2] Thucydides, in qualifying the record with 'as it is said', seems to imply that the Spartans rather than Delphi may have been responsible for the answer, but there is every reason to believe that Athens could expect no comfort from Delphic Apollo.

This may be one of the reasons that prompted the renewal of Athens' concern for Delos in the winter of 426–425, when they carried through a further purification and revived the Delian festival. This festival had once attracted Ionians from the mainland of Asia and the islands as well as Athenians to its singing, dancing, and athletic contests, but in the sixth century it declined. 'Later the islanders and the Athenians', says Thucydides, 'continued to send choruses and victims for sacrifice, but most of the competitive features lapsed as a result, it seems, of disasters until the Athenians then instituted the new competitive festival and for the first time introduced horse racing.'[3] Thucydides probably refers to the increasing pressures on Ionia, first from Lydia and then from Persia; the revival of the festival was in the summer of 425. It was preceded by a purification of the island. Pisistratus had provided the precedent when he cleared away the burials from the area around Apollo's temple and reinterred the graves' contents in a trench on Rhenea. The Athenians now took the more radical step of removing all

---

[1] Ar. *Birds* 188–9: εἶθ' ὥσπερ ἡμεῖς, ἦν ἱέναι βουλώμεθα | Πυθώδε, Βοιωτοὺς δίοδον αἰτούμεθα.

[2] Thuc. i. 118. 3.

[3] Thuc. iii. 104.

burials from the island; they also decreed that in future there should be no births nor deaths on Delos. The initiative, according to Thucydides, came from an oracle and we may accept Ephorus' addition that the purification of Delos was intended to commemorate the end of the plague.[1] Political motives, however, were probably also involved. The emphasis on the festival in particular looks like a bid for popularity in the islands and Ionia, which might in part offset the news from Chalcidice.

Some of the magnificence that the revival of the festival brought to Delos can be seen in Plutarch's description of Nicias' memorable display when he led the Athenian delegation:

> The choruses which the cities sent to sing in honour of Apollo used to approach Delos in an unorganized fashion. The crowd would go down to meet the boat and the choruses were made to sing without order or dignity as they got off their boat and put on their crowns and festival dresses. When Nicias led the Athenian delegation he landed on Rhenea with the chorus, the victims for sacrifice, and the festival equipment. He had brought with him a bridge built to measure in Athens and it had been magnificently decorated with gilt, dyed cloth, crowns, and curtains. At night he bridged the narrow channel between Rhenea and Delos, and when day came he led the procession to the god with his chorus splendidly attired, singing as it crossed the bridge. After the sacrifice, the contest, and the feasting, he set up a bronze palm tree to the god and bought an estate for 10,000 drachmae which he dedicated to the god. The revenue from the estate was to enable the Delians to offer sacrifices and to feast, calling on the gods to bring many blessings on Nicias. This he had inscribed on the stele which he left on Delos, and it was intended to protect his gift. But Nicias' palm was broken by the wind; it fell on the great Naxian statue of Apollo and overturned it.[2]

Plutarch would have had a better story if the great Naxian Apollo, which symbolized the dominance at Delos of Naxos in the archaic period, had been overturned when the Delian League was formed or when the revolt of Naxos was crushed.

The Delians were not allowed to enjoy the new dispensation for long; early in 422 they were expelled from their island. 'The Athenians thought that an offence of long ago made the Delians sacrilegious and unworthy of their religious function;

---

[1] Diod. xii. 58. 6.
[2] Plut. *Nic.* 3. 4–6. The date was probably 417 (Courby, op. cit. 220).

there was a shortcoming in the purification which I have recorded above, when they removed all burials and thought that they had made adequate provision.' Once again Diodorus, reflecting Ephorus, is more explicit; according to him the Athenians accused the Delians of trying secretly to make alliance with Sparta.[1] Ephorus is quite capable of adding such an explanation from his own imagination to make more satisfying sense of his narrative, but it is possible, when they heard of Athens' failure at Megara, her crushing defeat at Delium, and Brasidas' conquests in Thrace, that some Delians should have looked hopefully towards Sparta. The Delians were allowed by Pharnaces, serving under the satrap of Sardis, to settle at Atramyttium, but any danger that there may have been of their spreading Medism among Greek neighbours was ended when a Persian officer treacherously killed a large proportion of their men of military age for reasons which are not satisfactorily explained in our sources. In the summer of 421 'the Athenians brought the Delians back to Delos; they thought of their defeats in battle and the god at Delphi prompted them'.[2] It is doubtful whether the Athenians would have heard the call of Delphic Apollo if the war had not ended.

Later Delian inventories mention a temple of the Athenians, distinct from the small archaic temple and the large temple still unfinished at the end of the fifth century. Architecturally it has been dated to the last third of the fifth century and it may have been begun when Athens revived the Delian festival, an additional sign of her continuing concern for the birthplace of Apollo where Athenian hegemony had grown its roots.[3]

Not long after the revival of Delian ceremonies new emphasis was given to the cult of the two goddesses at Eleusis. Isocrates says that most Greek cities sent the first-fruits of their corn every year to Eleusis and that the Pythia ordered defaulters to comply with the practice.[4] The Eleusinian Mysteries make little appearance in literary sources during the archaic period but the archaeological evidence shows clearly that the site was of religious importance from the Mycenaean period onwards. In the fourth century the tradition was widely accepted that it was the duty of Greek states to offer annually first-fruits of

---

[1] Diod. xii. 73. 1.   [2] Thuc. v. 32. 1.
[3] Courby, op. cit. 107–205.   [4] Isocr. iv. 31.

their corn to the goddesses. How soon this tradition was established and how widely it was observed we do not know, but a new Telesterion was begun in the Periclean period and carried through by three successive architects. The first evidence, however, that we have of the bringing of first-fruits comes in a well-preserved decree approved by the Assembly.[1] The decree marks the acceptance of a report by a Commission. First the Athenians are ordered 'according to ancestral custom and the oracle from Delphi' to offer their first-fruits to the goddesses, 1/600th of their barley and 1/1,200th of their wheat, and 'the demarchs are to collect the first-fruits by demes and deliver it to the priests at Eleusis'. 'The allies also are to offer their first-fruits on the same basis; and the cities are to appoint collectors of the grain in such way as they think that the grain will be best collected; and when it is collected they are to send it to Athens and the carriers are to deliver it to the priests.' There follows a clause about cities outside the Athenian alliance: 'The hierophant and the torch-bearer at the Mysteries shall bid the Greeks offer the first-fruits of their corn according to ancestral custom and the oracle from Delphi.' 'The amount of the corn sent by each deme and by each (allied) city is to be recorded on a tablet at Eleusis and in the Bouleuterion, and the Boule is to announce to all the other Greek states, wherever it seems possible, how the Athenians and their allies are offering their first-fruits. They are not to give orders to them but to bid them offer their first-fruits, if they wish, according to ancestral custom and the oracle from Delphi; and the priests are to receive the first-fruits from these cities if any are brought.'

In this decree there is a very clear distinction between the allies and the other Greeks, though ancestral custom and the Delphic oracle are assumed to apply to all. The allies have no option in the matter, and to ensure that they do their duty they are required to appoint collectors of the corn following the pattern of the collectors of tribute whom they were required to appoint in 426. The other Greeks are to be approached very delicately and the wording suggests that no very widespread response is expected.

When and why was this decree passed? Of the persons named in the decree only Lampon is known. He moves an amendment

[1] ML 73.

which is in character with the seer who played a leading part in the colonization of Thurii and who was a familiar name to Aristophanes' audiences, but Lampon's active career covers a period of some thirty years. On general historical grounds any date after the Syracusan expedition would seem inconsistent with the imperial pretensions of the decree, and it would be completely out of place during years when annual invasions of Attica could be expected and Attica had to be abandoned. The years of the Peace of Nicias would suit the decree, but one of the last years of the Archidamian war provides a rather more convincing setting. The effect of the imprisonment of Spartans from Sphacteria was that Attica was free from invasion and crops could be sown each year with a confident expectation that they would be harvested; a grand gesture of this kind would raise morale. If the decree was passed in wartime it is easier to appreciate why the other Greeks were approached so delicately and why the Boule is to have the announcement made in the other cities, *wherever it seems possible*;[1] it would not be possible for Athenian envoys to call on cities that were at war with Athens. 'On those who do what is here prescribed many blessings shall come, and good crops and abundant crops, whosoever do no wrong to the Athenians nor to the city of the Athenians nor to the goddesses.' The politicians were thinking more of the Athenians than of the goddesses. The decree was devised for the greater glory of Athens.

The advanced rationalism of Thucydides tends to obscure the influence of traditional religion on the broad mass of Athenians, but the attacks made on Protagoras, Anaxagoras, and Diagoras should remind us that, however much the sophists might explain away, the majority of Athenian citizens still accepted the old gods;[2] and, though Thucydides dismissed oracles as idle superstition, a decree passed by the Assembly after the crushing of the Euboean revolt in 446–445 demanded 'that the sacrifices prescribed by the oracles should be carried out as soon as possible', and the generals were to see that there was no delay.[3] It was natural therefore that Athens should

---

[1] ML 73 l. 31 : *hόποι ἂν δοκεῖ αὐτεῖ δυνατὸν ἔναι.*

[2] G. Prestel, *Die antidemokratische Strömung im Athen des V. Jhdts. bis zum Tod des Perikles*; M. Derenne, *Les Procès d'impiété*.

[3] ML 52. 64–9.

invoke religion to support her claims to rule. The allies, sharing the cult of Athena and having the same rights and duties as colonies at the Great Panathenaea, were encouraged to regard the patron goddess of Athens as in part their own. They were also called on to give a lead to the Greek world in making the goddesses of Athenian Eleusis the patron goddesses of Greek agriculture to whom all Greeks should send the first-fruits of their corn crops.

After her defeat at Coronea Athens could do little to influence Delphi, but her generous patronage of the sacred island of Delos is likely to have impressed at least the islanders. How far participation in the cult of Athenian Athena sweetened the loss of autonomy we cannot say, but in the Great Panathenaea the allies were given a dignified role and those who actually took part in the procession 'like colonists' were probably proud to have done so. It is interesting, however, that almost all our evidence for Athens' religious policy towards the allies derives from inscriptions. This perhaps is an indication that religion played only a superficial part in determining the attitude of the allies.

17

THE ARCHIDAMIAN WAR

It was Thucydides' opinion that when war broke out between Athens and Sparta, the Greek world in general favoured Sparta, particularly as she had declared that the liberation of Greece was her aim. 'So roused were the majority against Athens, some wanting release from the empire, others fearing that they would be dragged into it'.[1] There may be some exaggeration here but Mytilene had apparently wanted to revolt before the war, and when Perdiccas began his intrigues from Macedonia he met at first with a widespread response from disaffected allies.[2] But in 431 there was no concerted rush to break away from Athens, and when she called on states for their contingents they sent them. The Spartans had declared in their final ultimatum that if the Athenians let the Greeks go free there could be peace; but the allies had no grounds for confidence in their liberators. They knew that Sparta had ignored them in the Thirty Years' Peace, that she had failed to support the Samian revolt, and discouraged Mytilene from coming out into the open. Nor could democratic parties relish liberation by Spartans who maintained their leadership of the Peloponnesian League by encouraging oligarchies. Even those who might have welcomed Spartan garrisons will have realized Sparta's military helplessness. The Old Oligarch was not the only one who understood the importance of sea power. Without a strong fleet Sparta would find most of the Athenian allies inaccessible.

There were only two areas where Athenian control was seriously threatened at the beginning of the war. In the assessment of 438 the Ionian and Carian districts, separate since 443, were merged and the total number of cities paying tribute in the Ionian–Carian district during the thirties sharply declined from the level of the forties. The lists of this period are very

[1] Thuc. ii. 8. 4–5.   [2] Thuc. iii. 2. 1; i. 57. 5.

fragmentary until 434–433, but it is a reasonably certain inference that the majority of the absentees are Carian. The further loss of tribute involved in Caria, however, was probably not more than 5 talents, for the individual assessments of inland cities in Caria were low; but the Lycians also had ceased to bring their tribute: their name does not survive in any of the lists after 445, when they paid 10 talents. During the peace Athens seems to have thought that it was better to sacrifice this tribute than to face the risk and expense of expeditions.[1] When war broke out, however, it was important to maintain a show of strength in the east, especially as the Carian and Lycian coasts were being used by pirates encouraged by the Peloponnesians to attack merchantment from the eastern Mediterranean.

This was the background of the Athenian decision to send, in the autumn of 430, six triremes to Caria and Lycia to collect money and to prevent Peloponnesian pirates making their base there and 'interfering with the merchantmen from Phaselis, Phoenicia, and those parts'. On the east side of the Aegean they were joined by levies from the allies, presumably loyal cities in Caria, but when the combined force moved up-country into Lycia, they were defeated by the natives and the Athenian general was killed.[2] In the autumn of 428 a further attempt was made to recover firm control over Caria, this time from the north-west. Lysicles had been sent out with twelve ships with a general commission to collect money. In the course of his operations he landed at Myus and advanced into Caria through the plain of the Maeander as far as the Sandian hill; there he was attacked by Carians and men of Anaea, presumably Samian refugees who were hostile to the democracy installed in Samos by Athens; Lysicles himself was killed, and with him a large part of his force.[3] It is doubtful whether inland Caria or Lycia was ever brought back into the empire, but they were not likely to have much influence on the coastal cities of the Aegean.

The factors affecting the other threatened area were very different, and the issues more important. Chalcidice was much

[1] But perhaps an attack on Carian Caunus should be fitted into this period. Ctesias 35–41; see Endnote 21, pp. 436 f.
[2] Thuc. ii. 69.
[3] Thuc. iii. 19 with L. Robert, *Anatolia*, iv (1959), 19–24.

less dispensable than inland Caria and Lycia. Strategically the loss of this area would cut Athens' land route to the Hellespont, and the important silver and timber supplies that were controlled from Amphipolis would be in continuous danger if Chalcidice became hostile. There had been trouble in this area in the early forties, which had led to the establishment of the colony of Brea, but the danger was more serious now because the Macedonian king Perdiccas was giving encouragement and aid. For this development Athens herself seems to have been primarily to blame. At some time before 433, perhaps at the time of the settlement of Amphipolis, she had made a formal alliance with Perdiccas, and part of the original Athenian decree, as we have seen, may survive.[1] A long list of Macedonian chieftains is included and there is no indication of political divisions in Macedonia; but in 433 Athens is supporting Perdiccas' brother Philip and his cousin Derdas.[2] As a result of the same policy Methone on the Thermaic Gulf which had been in the Macedonian sphere became a tributary ally of Athens, a further provocation.[3] Perdiccas, once an ally, was now a declared enemy. Thucydides, as is his custom, makes no comment, but Athens' change of policy would seem to be sheer opportunism. Perdiccas' natural means of retaliation was to stir up trouble for Athens by intrigues with the Chalcidic cities. He knew he could not protect small coastal cities from the Athenian fleet, but if they abandoned the coast and settled inland they would be considerably less vulnerable. Olynthus was well situated for the purpose, sufficiently far from the coast and sufficiently large to be defensible. It became a rallying-point to which many of the smaller cities migrated.[4] By the winter of 433–432 the situation was seen at Athens to be serious enough to need military action: preparations were made to send out an expeditionary force at the beginning of the summer of 432.

[1] See Endnote 15, p. 428.   [2] Thuc. i. 57. 2–3.

[3] The Thracian district is complete in the tribute quota list of 434 and Methone is not included. For 433 and 432 the lists are too incomplete to argue from absence. Methone should probably be restored in the list of 431 (23. ii. 67) where an *aparche* of 300 drachmae representing a tribute of 3 talents survives but the city's name is lost. Peparethos, Aphytis, Acanthus, Aenea, the only other Thracian cities known to have an assessment of 3 talents, are all preserved. Methone may have been incorporated in the empire at the time of the assessment of 434. See *ATL* iii. 136.

[4] Thuc. i. 58. 2.

Meanwhile a more important city of the area invited Athens' attention. Potidaea was a Corinthian colony which still received annually from Corinth visiting magistrates who exercised a special jurisdiction. When Athens' alliance with Corcyra in 433 made a break with Corinth inevitable and war with the Peloponnese probable, the situation in Potidaea was tense. Athens decided to make the first move, and ordered Potidaea to pull down her wall on the side that faced the isthmus of Pallene, hand over hostages, dismiss her Corinthian visiting magistrates, and not admit any successors.[1] Over the winter the Potidaeans were busy strengthening their defences and doing what they could to safeguard their position by diplomacy. Envoys were sent to Athens to plead for concessions, but Athens would not yield; at the same time Sparta was approached, and 'the authorities', perhaps the Ephors, assured them that if the Athenians attacked Potidaea the Spartans would invade Attica, a hollow promise. Potidaea came out into open revolt and made alliance, sealed by oaths, with Chalcidian rebels and Bottiaeans. Meanwhile many of the small coastal communities destroyed their cities and moved inland to swell the population of Olynthus.

The Athenian force of thirty ships and 1,000 hoplites had originally been intended for action against Perdiccas; the generals were now instructed to pull down the Potidaean wall, extract hostages, and to see that revolt did not spread among neighbouring cities. By the time they reached Macedon, however, they found that Potidaea was in revolt and that the revolt was spreading. Soon they knew that the Corinthian Aristeus, well known and liked in Potidaea, had reached the town with a mixed force of 1,600 hoplites and 400 light-armed. The Athenians, not strong enough to fight Macedon and the rebels at the same time, struck first at Macedon. They took Therma and were besieging Pydna when reinforcements arrived from Athens, forty ships and 2,000 hoplites under Callias, who took over the command. Potidaea now became the primary objective and Callias was able to bring pressure to bear on Perdiccas to accept an alliance. In the summer of 432 the siege of Potidaea began. The Spartans made no move, but Aristeus' troops gave heart to the defence, and the rebels in Olynthus were becoming

[1] Thuc. i. 56. 2.

a formidable force. The effect of these revolts in Chalcidice on the tribute was not inconsiderable; the cities of the area who paid no tribute in 431 had a combined assessment of some 40 talents. The siege of Potidaea was even more serious financially; it dragged on into the winter of 430–429 and cost at least 2,000 talents.[1] The Potidaeans were forced to negotiate surrender because their supplies were exhausted and it was clear that Sparta could do nothing to relieve the town; the Athenian generals were ready to offer acceptable terms because winter conditions were hard on their men. The inhabitants were allowed to evacuate with the minimum of clothing and money. The generals were attacked in Athens for making terms without the authority of the people; the Assembly's terms would probably have been harsher.

The Athenians occupied Potidaea with their own settlers, and in the following summer launched a major offensive against the remaining rebels of Chalcidice and their Bottiaean allies. They ravaged the territory of Spartolus, chief city of the Bottiaeans, when their corn was ripe and hoped that a pro-Athenian party would bring over the town to them, but it was saved by a strong force from Olynthus. In the actions fought outside the walls the Athenian hoplites at first more than held their own, but they were outmatched in cavalry and light-armed, and had to fall back on Potidaea with heavy casualties; they had lost 430 men and all three generals.[2] From this point the Athenians abandoned their attempts to break the power of Olynthus and concentrated on the protection of the cities that still remained loyal. Thucydides records the capture of Eion, a Mendaean colony which was hostile to Athens, in the summer of 425, but it is significant that the Athenian force was limited to a handful of men from Athenian garrisons and local allies, and that a party within the town had offered to betray it. This minor offensive was not directed from Athens, and the success was ephemeral. A force of Chalcidians and Bottiaeans drove out the Athenians with heavy losses.[3]

It was some time before the empire as a whole felt the pressures of war seriously. Chios and Lesbos were required to

---

[1] Thuc. (ii. 70. 2) says that when Potidaea was on the point of surrender the Athenians had already spent 2,000 talents on the siege. Isocrates (xv. 113) gives 2,400 for the total cost.   [2] Thuc. ii. 79.   [3] Thuc. iv. 7.

contribute contingents to the Athenian fleet's offensives, but
hoplites were not yet needed.[1] Nor did the Athenians yet feel
any anxiety about finance. In 431 Athens still had a reserve of
6,000 talents which seemed enough to sustain a long war;[2] it is
not therefore surprising that the assessment of 430 was conservative in spirit. Two lists partially survive from this assessment, for 429 and 428; the tributes of some sixty states are
preserved in one or both. Six are lowered and only five are
raised. These are mainly larger cities such as Byzantium and
Torone, and this may indicate policy; perhaps the assessors of
430 aimed at a small total increase at the expense of a few of
the richer cities.[3] But it is doubtful whether Athens received as
much tribute in 429 as in 433. The 40 talents from Chalcidice
which were lost in 432 had not been recovered; no improvement is noticeable in the Ionian–Carian district, and the expulsion of Aeginetans in the summer of 431, though it gave land to
Athenians, took from the tribute a further 30 talents. The total
amount of tribute received in the first years of the war probably
did not amount to more than 400 talents.

By 428 much of the Athenian optimism of 431 had evaporated.
Potidaea had at last been reduced, but the siege had been long
and expensive; the more general revolt in Chalcidice had been
contained but not broken. The Spartan invasions of Attica had
proved no more effective than Pericles had led the people to
believe, and in the only naval action of the first three years
Phormio had confirmed the decisive superiority of Athenian
seamanship. But the plague had more than balanced any such
successes. The losses among Athens' fighting forces had been
catastrophic and the effect on the people's morale had been
almost as serious. At the end of 430 they had even deposed
Pericles and made peace overtures to Sparta. They were
recovering well from this mood when they heard that Mytilene
was preparing to revolt. The news came from Tenedos and
Methymna and from *proxenoi* of Athens in Mytilene. The ruling
oligarchs were strengthening the fortifications, rushing in

---

[1] Allies are not recorded by Thucydides in the campaigns of 431; in 430 Lesbos
and Chios together contributed fifty ships to Pericles' expedition against Epidaurus, ii. 56. 2.

[2] Thuc. ii. 13. 3. If the text given by a scholiast on Ar. *Plutus* 1193 (preferred by
ATL iii. 118) is accepted, the reserve would be 5,700 talents.

[3] A discussion of these lists in App. 13. p. 531.

supplies from the Euxine, and attempting to synoecize the smaller cities of the island in Mytilene.[1] Aristotle in his *Politics* preserves a tradition that traced the causes of the revolt to a dispute about heiresses. A rich Mytilenaean left two daughters. A *proxenos* of Athens, Dexander, wished to secure the heiresses for his two sons. When he failed 'he stirred up *stasis* and roused the Athenians to intervene'.[2] We are reminded of the personalization of the causes of the Peloponnesian War by Ephorus. There was indeed *stasis* at Mytilene but heiresses are not needed to explain it. Relations with Athens were the crucial issue and it had been an issue for several years. Mytilene had seriously considered revolt before the war; it was natural that friends of Athens, whose standing in Mytilene depended largely on good relations with Athens, should become increasingly suspicious of their government.

When she heard the news, Athens detained the crews of ten Mytilenaean ships which 'happened to be at the Piraeus as their alliance required', and sent out a fleet.[3] Mytilene had gone too far to draw back. She could not hold her own at sea but determined, in spite of the lessons of Samos and Potidaea, to withstand a siege. Lesbos, according to tradition, had been settled from Boeotia, and Boeotians helped to stiffen feeling against Athens; it was assumed that Sparta would actively help. A friendly reception was indeed given to the Mytilenaean envoys who went to Sparta and they were taken to Olympia to address the allies, but those who hoped for decisive action were soon disillusioned. Sparta had neither the heart nor the money to put an effective fleet on the sea, and her leadership was inadequate to stir her allies into unorthodox efforts. When she summoned them to mobilize at the isthmus for an invasion of Attica much later than usual and therefore perhaps more unexpected and damaging, the allies were very slow in assembling; they were too busy with their harvests.[4] Meanwhile the Mytilenaeans were offering stiff resistance. Athens had sent out only forty ships at first, hoping to surprise them at a festival outside their walls, but news of their coming preceded them and the city was prepared.

---

[1] Thuc. iii. 2. 3.   [2] Arist. *Pol.* 1304^{a}9.

[3] Thuc. iii. 3. 4. The Athenians were told that the Mytilenaeans were speeding preparations μετὰ Λακεδαιμονίων καὶ Βοιωτῶν ξυγγενῶν ὄντων.

[4] Thuc. iii. 15.

The Athenian generals, according to their instructions, delivered an ultimatum requiring Mytilene to pull down her walls and surrender her fleet. The terms were too humiliating to be accepted, but a truce was allowed while envoys went to Athens to plead their case. They could not secure what they regarded as reasonable concessions and there was no alternative to open war. Though the second city of the island, Methymna, refused to join her, Mytilene had won over the smaller towns and in their first attack on the Athenian lines they at least held their own. Later they attacked Methymna without being able to take it and strengthened the defences of Antissa, Pyrrha, and Eresus. This offensive was sufficient to convince the Athenians that their numbers, particularly of hoplites, were inadequate to force a decision; in the autumn they were reinforced by 1,000 hoplites from Athens and a new commander.[1] By the summer of 427 supplies in Mytilene were near exhaustion. The Spartan commander, Salaethus, who had slipped through the blockade towards the end of the winter, armed the common people for a desperate attack on the Athenian lines; but the people now demanded that their rulers should share out the remaining corn supplies; otherwise they would hand over the city to the Athenians. The oligarchs realized their helplessness and, afraid that if they were deserted by the people they might fail to secure any agreement from the Athenian generals, they surrendered to Paches. The terms of the surrender were that Mytilene's fate should be decided at Athens; meanwhile they would let the Athenian army come into the city and themselves send envoys to Athens to plead their case. Until they returned Paches was not to imprison, enslave, or kill anyone. Those who had been primarily responsible for negotiating with Sparta had little confidence in this agreement, and took refuge at altars; Paches promised them safe conduct and sent them to Tenedos until a decision should be reached at Athens. Paches had perhaps seen the reaction at Athens against the Athenian generals when they made their settlement with Potidaea, without reference to the Assembly; it is doubtful whether he or the Mytilenaeans anticipated the people's ruthlessness now.

When at last a Spartan fleet of forty triremes sailed across the Aegean it was too late; at Myconos they heard that Mytilene

[1] Thuc. iii. 18. 3.

had already fallen. The Spartan commander Alcidas showed neither spirit nor sense. Following unimaginatively the policy laid down at Sparta when the war began, that all crews caught on the high seas should be put to death, he killed Athenian allies who came into his hands. This, as Samian exiles from Anaea sharply reminded him, was a poor way to liberate Greece.[1] He was advised to make a surprise attack on Mytilene or establish a base in Ionia or at Aeolian Cumae and build up an Ionian war against Athens; but Alcidas felt too uncomfortable in alien surroundings with an untested fleet, and made all speed back to the Peloponnese. He should have shown more resolution, for an enterprising Spartan could have made considerable headway. The Persians had interfered at just this time at Notium after taking Colophon,[2] and a Spartan document shows that there was support to be had in money as well as words. Walled up in a church near Sparta is a list of gifts from cities, groups, and individuals to the Peloponnesians for the war. The gifts include money, raisins, corn, and other supplies for ships' crews; among the donors are the 'neutral' island of Melos, with two separate contributions, the Ephesians, and friends of the Spartans in Chios. The list is not dated but it must precede the enslavement of Melos in 416, and therefore should fall in the Archidamian War.[3] Chios was to become the most substantial supporter of Sparta in the last phase of the war; there were Chians with Alcidas, and two years after the surrender of Mytilene, in 425, Athens was sufficiently suspicious to intervene sharply; the Chians were ordered to pull down the new wall which they were building and to give pledges.[4] Had Alcidas shown energy and determination Chios, which had the largest fleet after Athens in the Aegean, might have anticipated the course she was to follow in 412.

The helplessness of Sparta discredited her in Ionia. It was now clear that the East Greeks could expect no aid from the Greek mainland. When Paches heard the surprising news that Spartan ships were putting in at Ionian harbours, he set off at full speed in pursuit, but Alcidas had too long a start and

---

[1] Thuc. iii. 32. 1–2. For the policy adopted by Sparta at the beginning of the war, Thuc. ii. 67. 4.
[2] See below, p. 315.
[3] ML 67. F. E. Adcock makes a strong case for 427, *Mélanges Glotz*, 1–6.
[4] Thuc. iv. 51.

Paches returned to settle affairs on Lesbos. On his way he was able to check Persian encroachment at Colophon's harbour town of Notium. In 430 *stasis* had broken out in Colophon, probably along lines that had divided the city in the forties, and one party called in Persia.[1] The opposite faction took refuge in Notium, but there too the same conflict of interests developed and mercenaries supplied by the satrap at Sardis were virtually in control when Paches arrived. The conduct of Paches at Notium was strangely different from the moderation he had shown when Mytilene surrendered. While the commander of the mercenaries was engaged in a conference, his men were attacked off their guard and only the Greeks among them were spared; he himself was cynically led back to his fort to fulfil the pledge that had been given and shot down. Notium was now given to the Colophonian refugees and all other Colophonian loyalists who could be found in Ionia were encouraged to join them. An Athenian commission was sent out to establish the new community on a basis of Athenian laws.[2]

The Mytilenaean revolt which exposed Spartan helplessness was also accompanied and followed by increasing pressure on the allies from Athens. Thucydides says that by the end of the summer of 428 the Athenians needed more money for the siege and imposed for the first time (in the war) a capital levy, ἐσφορά, on their own citizens.[3] It is probable that at the same time the allies were required to increase their contributions. The evidence for an extraordinary assessment, not normally due until 426, is strong though not decisive. Thucydides records the dispatch of a squadron to collect money, ἀργυρολόγους ναῦς, in the autumn of 428, and the only other two occasions on which such squadrons are mentioned are in the autumns of assessment years, 430 and 425. There survive also small fragments of a quota list which on internal evidence does not belong to the assessments of 430 or 425, and should be probably dated in 427. Only sixteen payments are preserved; four of them show increases on the last known figures, and there is only one 'normal' reduction. The sample is much too small for firm inferences, but it is likely that the total tribute claimed by

---

[1] Cf. above, pp. 161 f.   [2] Thuc. iii. 34.

[3] Thuc. iii. 19. 1: καὶ αὐτοὶ ἐσενεγκόντες τότε πρῶτον. The implication in πρῶτον is that later in the war the ἐσφορά became a recurring feature; but see also App. 11, p. 520.

Athens was substantially higher than in 430 and moving towards the inflated figures of 425.[1]

Politically also Athens was adopting a harder attitude. When Samos surrendered there was no question of enslavement; hostages were required, but the newly established demos was treated with generosity and respect. When Potidaea surrendered, the inhabitants' lives were spared though they had to abandon their town, and Thucydides implies that the Assembly would have insisted on stiffer terms. But when Mytilene surrendered in the summer of 427 the first decision of the Athenian Assembly was that all adult males should be put to death and the women and children enslaved. This was the policy advocated by Cleon, who by now was the most persuasive voice in the assembly, a violent man, but a shrewd judge of the interests and moods of the demos. The next day, however, there was, according to Thucydides, a general revulsion of feeling and the Mytilenaean envoys at Athens, who will have probably included *proxenoi*, and their Athenian friends, were able to persuade the *prytaneis* to summon a second meeting. Thucydides, who passes rapidly over the first decision, summarizes the critical second meeting of the Assembly in two considerable speeches; clearly he thought that in the history of the Athenian Empire this was a moment to stress.[2] Cleon made an aggressive defence of his policy but the vote went narrowly against him; he had to be content with carrying a proposal that those most responsible for the revolt should be put to death. The manuscripts give the number as 'rather more than 1,000', but that is a considerably larger number than we should expect from the previous narrative; it is not, however, easy to emend the text convincingly.[3] In addition the Mytilenaeans, like the Samians, had to pull down their walls and surrender their fleet; they also had to hand over to Athens the cities which they controlled on the mainland opposite, of which Antandrus, commanding good timber supplies, was the most important. No indemnity was

[1] Meritt, *Athenian Financial Documents*, 3–25. Further discussed in App. 13, p. 531.
[2] Thuc. iii. 37–48. For these speeches see p. 380.
[3] Thuc. iii. 50. 1. Palaeographically the easiest emendation is $\overline{\Lambda}$ for $\overline{A}$, τριάκοντα, but this number is surely too small. In 412 the Samian demos killed up to 200 and exiled as many as 400 oligarchs (Thuc. viii. 21). This makes the Mytilenaean figure more credible. I would keep the text but do not feel sufficiently confident to base general arguments upon it. See Gomme, *HCT* ii. 325 f.

imposed, but the island, with the exception of Methymna's territory, was divided into 3,000 lots. Of these a tithe, 300, were given to the gods; to the rest the Athenians sent cleruchs selected by lot. But before long the land was restored to the natives who paid an annual rent of 2 minae for each lot.[1] Presumably the Athenian cleruchs stayed on Mytilene as a garrison, but they pass out of recorded history and may have been recalled to the mainland when in 425 and 424 Athens needed more manpower.[2] There were, however, Athenian officers on the island when Antiphon composed his speech on the *Murder of Herodes*, probably between 416 and 414.[3] We should know more of the situation in Mytilene after the revolt if more survived of a decree passed by Athens, probably in response to representations made by a Mytilenaean embassy. Most of the details are uncertain, but the tone is friendly and two concessions are beyond reasonable doubt. The Judicial Agreement (συμβολαί) between Athens and Mytilene is to remain unchanged, and the Mytilenaeans are to be αὐτόνομοι, which should mean either that they may try their own cases, or that they may have whatever constitution they choose.[4]

The emergence of Cleon as a dominant force in the Assembly marks a new phase in Athenian politics at home and abroad. He was the first of what we may call for convenience the new radicals to leave a strong mark on the tradition that has come down to us. He was supported by Cleonymus, Hyperbolus, and probably Thudippus; he was followed after his death by Androcles, Archedemus, and Cleophon. Contemporary reaction against any use of the language of modern politics to describe the democratic processes of the city state is so strong that even such innocuous language as is used here perhaps needs a little definition. It is not implied that there was a party organization in the modern sense with party headquarters and party whips. Athenians did not enrol in any such party and every vote in the Assembly was a free vote. Nevertheless the Assembly

---

[1] Thuc. iii. 50. 2–3, the equivalent of a tribute assessment of 100 talents.

[2] Above, p. 261.

[3] Antiphon v. 47. For the date of the speech, K. J. Dover, *CQ* xliv (1950), 44–60 (416–413).

[4] *IG* i². 60 ; *ATL* ii D 22. 12–13, καὶ αὐτο[νό]μος δοκ[εῖ ἐ]ν|[αι αὐτός] ; ll. 15–17, καὶ ἀπὸ χσυμβολ|ôν δί[κας διδόν[τα]ς πρὸς Ἀθεν[αίος καὶ δεχομένο|ς κα]τὰ τὰς χσυ[μβο]λὰς ἁὶ ἔσαν [πρὸ τô.

recognized leading personalities and soon came to know their views. It would be naïve to believe that Cleon had no associates, and that the views he expressed in the Assembly were not shared by associates. Despite the strong animosity of Thucydides and Aristophanes one can reconstruct something of Cleon's politics, and can see how they influenced those who took or tried to take his position after his death.

Cleon's main power rested on the Assembly; his manner was violent and he had the great advantage for meetings in the open air of a penetrating voice;[1] Thucydides admits his power of persuasion.[2] In home politics he sharpened the division between the rich and the poor which Pericles' moral and political ascendancy had concealed; his main weapon was the law-court, taking advantage of the compulsory examination of magistrates at the end of their year of office, or bringing charges of conspiracy against dangerous oligarchs. It may also have been Cleon who was mainly responsible for introducing in 428 the *eisphora*, which by imposing increasing obligations on the rich encouraged a polarization of rich and poor round peace and war. The measure should not, however, be regarded simply as a political tactic against the rich. By 428 the reserve, though by no means exhausted, was running out dangerously fast, and unless strong measures were taken soon the Athenians would no longer be able to maintain the initiative.[3] Cleon is made by Aristophanes in the *Knights* to claim credit for the money he brought in when he was a member of the Boule, and this may have been in 428–427.[4] Even if he was not directly responsible for the financial measures taken in that year he seems to have had an effective influence on public finance.

In foreign policy Cleon stood for a strong line against the allies. There is no evidence that he tried to build up more positive and idealistic support for Athens among the democrats of the cities; his chief aim seems to have been to ensure that Athenian control was firmly maintained and that the cities

---

[1] Ar. *Knights*, 137: ἅρπαξ, κεκράκτης, Κυκλοβόρου φωνὴν ἔχων.

[2] Thuc. iii. 36. 6: τῷ, δήμῳ, ἐν τῷ τότε πιθανώτατος.

[3] Thuc. iii. 19. 1. In 431–430 alone the Athenians had taken more than 1,300 talents from the reserve, *SEG* x. 226.

[4] Ar. *Knights* 773–5. Cleon claims credit ὃς πρῶτα μὲν ἡνίκ' ἐβούλευον, σοὶ χρήματα πλεῖστ' ἀπέδειξα | ἐν τῷ κοινῷ, τοὺς μὲν στρεβλῶν τοὺς δ' ἄγχων τοὺς δὲ μεταιτῶν. This would be a very appropriate description of the εἰσφορά.

contributed as much as they could to the war. It is true that almost all our evidence comes from Thucydides and Aristophanes, who had no sympathy for Cleon, but there can be no doubt that he was the first to propose the death penalty for all males in an allied city after revolt. Mytilēne was saved, but Cleon had his way later with Scione.[1] Thucydides implicitly condemns Cleon for refusing Sparta's offer of peace when Pylos had been occupied, but though Pericles would have used different language it is by no means certain that he would have acted differently. Both thought that a lasting peace could only be won if Sparta was broken or completely humiliated. This had been Themistocles' view and it is interesting that in this year Cleon boasted his rivalry with Themistocles. He may partly have been thinking of his attempts to win over neutral Argos.[2] There is only one reference to this interesting development, in Aristophanes' *Knights*, but there can be no doubt that Cleon visited Argos while at the height of his power.[3] Like Themistocles before him and Alcibiades after him Cleon perhaps realized that the most effective way to fight Sparta was in the Peloponnese with her discontented allies. This policy depended on an alliance with Argos.

Cleon, however, cannot be directly associated with an attempt to revive the Athenian land empire of the fifties, and indeed he probably had no part in the plans of 424 which ended so disastrously at Megara and Delium. The evidence of Aristophanes' *Clouds* is decisive that Cleon was elected general for 424–423; he is not, however, even mentioned by Thucydides in connection with the operations of the summer of 424, which seem to have been directed by Demosthenes and Hippocrates.[4] We can believe that Cleon, extremely effective at a mass meeting,

---

[1] Thuc. iv. 122. 6; v. 32. 1.

[2] Ar. *Knights* 811–13, 817–19: ὁ Θεμιστοκλεῖ ἀντιφερίζων. It is interesting and perhaps significant that the Sausage Seller's reaction to Cleon's claim to have done Athens more good than Themistocles begins (l. 813) ὦ πόλις Ἄργους, κλύεθ᾽ οἷα λέγει. σὺ Θεμιστοκλεῖ ἀντιφερίζεις;

[3] Ar. *Knights* 465–6: οὔκουν μ᾽ ἐν Ἄργει γ᾽ οἷα πράττεις λανθάνει. | πρόφασιν μὲν Ἀργείους φίλους ἡμῖν ποιεῖ.

[4] Cleon's generalship in 424–423 is doubted by Gomme, *HCT* iii. 505–6, 526–7, but the evidence of Aristophanes is decisive (*Clouds* 581–94: εἶτα τὸν θεοῖσιν ἐχθρὸν βυρσοδέψην Παφλαγόνα, | ἡνίχ᾽ ᾑρεῖσθε στρατηγόν, τὰς ὀφρῦς συνήγομεν | ... οὐ φανεῖν ἔφασκεν (sc. ὁ ἥλιος) ὑμῖν, εἰ στρατηγήσει Κλέων. | ἀλλ᾽ ὅμως εἵλεσθε τοῦτον. But Cleon's generalship will be a blessing in disguise because when he is examined at the end of his year of office we shall have him at our mercy).

carried considerably less weight and felt considerably less confident when the generals discussed strategy in the *strategion*. But Cleon and his followers do seem to have aimed at the expansion of the empire in the west and possibly also in the east.

Plutarch records that during Pericles' ascendancy there were those who wished to go further and faster than he was prepared to lead:

> Pericles did not yield to the ambitions of the people when their strength and good fortune encouraged them to try once again to win Egypt and to raid the King's coastline. And many were seized with the ill-starred and fatal passion for Sicily which Alcibiades and the speakers who supported him later fanned into flame. And some even dreamt of Etruria and Carthage.[1]

Athens had been interested in the west throughout the fifth century but apart from her intervention at Sybaris and settlement of Thurii she had limited herself to diplomacy and alliances; so far as we know she had never seriously contemplated sending a fleet or army to Sicily. In 427 twenty ships were sent under Laches and Charoeades, and Thucydides assigns two objectives to the expedition. The excuse was the appeal of Ionian allies, Leontini and Rhegium, for protection against Syracuse; the real motives were to prevent the sending of supplies to the Peloponnese and to assess the chances of conquest in Sicily.[2] By the end of the summer of 426 it was clear that the chances were less good than optimists had expected. Messana had been won and lost, indecisive engagements had been fought, Syracuse showed no signs of being intimidated, and one of the Athenian generals had been killed and the other discredited. In the winter of 426–425 the Sicilian allies appealed to Athens for a stronger force, and the Athenians decided to send a new commander at once and forty more ships in the spring. They took this decision, according to Thucydides, because they thought that it would bring the war to an end in Sicily more quickly, and at the same time they wanted to keep their fleet in training.[3] The new Athenian fleet was delayed on

---

[1] Plut. *Per.* 20. 3–4.

[2] Thuc. iii. 86. 4: πρόπειράν τε ποιούμενοι εἰ σφίσι δυνατὰ εἴη τὰ ἐν τῇ Σικελίᾳ πράγματα ὑποχείρια γενέσθαι.

[3] Thuc. iii. 115. 4: ἅμα μὲν ἡγούμενοι θᾶσσον τὸν ἐκεῖ πόλεμον καταλυθήσεσθαι, ἅμα δὲ βουλόμενοι μελέτην τοῦ ναυτικοῦ ποιεῖσθαι.

its way to Sicily, and when finally it arrived in the early summer of 424 there was no war to fight. The Syracusan Hermocrates had persuaded the Sicilian cities at Gela to agree to a general peace, and the Athenian generals could only accept the terms and return to Athens. There they received a rough welcome; two of them were exiled, the third fined, 'on the ground that they could have reduced Sicily but had been bribed to leave the island'.[1]

Athenian policy in Sicily between 427 and 424 seems to reflect an uncertainty of aim, a compromise between a scheme of conquest, and a defensive interference to prevent the domination of Syracuse and to deny Sicilian supplies to the Peloponnese. Ambitious designs on Carthage are associated by Aristophanes in a playful passage of the *Knights* with Hyperbolus;[2] Laches was probably prosecuted by Cleon on his return to Athens,[3] and the savage treatment of the generals who had had to accept the agreement of Gela came at a time when Cleon's influence was still at its height after his spectacular success on Sphacteria. It is probably the new radicals who nursed the ideas of conquest rather than the more limited aim of maintaining the balance of power against Syracuse. And by conquest they meant the incorporation in the empire as tributaries of some at least of the Sicilian cities. Their interest in the east is more controversial and will be discussed later.[4]

They were probably also responsible for increasing pressure in the Aegean. In the summer of 426 Nicias was sent with a strong force of sixty ships and 2,000 hoplites against the island of Melos.[5] With Thera Melos, which according to tradition had been settled by Dorians from Sparta, was independent of both Athenian and Spartan alliances at the beginning of the war. Thera appears on the tribute quota list of 428 and may be restored in 429.[6] She probably was 'persuaded' to enter the Athenian empire at the time of the assessment of 430, and

---

[1] Thuc. iv. 65. 3: ὡς ἐξὸν αὐτοῖς τὰ ἐν Σικελίᾳ καταστρέψασθαι δώροις πεισθέντες ἀποχωρήσειαν. The formal charge may have been that they accepted the peace without reference to the Assembly.

[2] Ar. *Knights* 1303–4: φασὶν αἰτεῖσθαί τιν' ἡμῶν ἑκατὸν ἐς Καρχηδόνα | ἄνδρα μοχθηρὸν πολίτην ὀξίνην Ὑπέρβολον.

[3] Ar. *Wasps* 894–7. It is probable that the mock trial in which Λάβης is prosecuted by Κύων derives from a real trial. It might, however, be mere fantasy.

[4] Below, p. 330.   [5] Thuc. iii. 91. 1–3.

[6] Thuc. ii. 9. 4. List 26. iii. 23; 25. ii. 54.

Melos is likely to have been 'invited' at the same time. Melos, however, refused to comply and she is recorded as having made two contributions to Spartan war funds during the Archidamian War;[1] there can have been little doubt where her sympathy lay. The Athenians seem to have expected that the Melians would be intimidated by the size of the Athenian force and surrender without fighting, but when they ravaged the land the Melians neither surrendered nor offered battle. At this stage the Athenians had no intention of risking another long siege and withdrew.

In his plays produced during the Archidamian War Aristophanes consistently associates Cleon with the allies. He accepts bribes from them, he bullies them, he watches like a tunnyfisher from the rocks their tribute shoaling in; he is always asking for swift triremes to collect money.[2] Cleon's passion for the courts is concerned with allies as well as Athenian oligarchs, and it is always the rich who are being shaken;[3] successful prosecutions of suspected oligarchs might be regarded as essential to Athenian security. At the same time the allies were made to contribute more money to the war. There was probably, as has been seen, an extraordinary assessment in 428 when the revolt of Mytilene emphasized the dangerous fall in Athenian reserves. Since normally new assessments were made at the time of the great Panathenaea, the question of a new assessment may have become a political issue in the next Great Panathenaic year, 426. The assessment decree of 425 includes a clause which insists in the strongest terms that there shall in future be an assessment at the time of the Great Panathenaea, and stringent penalties are laid down for members of the executive who fail to carry out their responsibilities.[4] The natural inference from the polemical tone is that there was no new assessment in 426, and it is at least a possible inference that there had been some support for one. It is tempting to believe that the associates of Cleon had wished to raise the tribute again but had been successfully opposed by Nicias and his group who consistently followed a more moderate policy towards

---

[1] Above, p. 314; ML 67 side 1–7, 13–17.

[2] Ar. *Knights* 312 : κἀπὸ τῶν πετρῶν ἄνωθεν τοὺς φόρους θυννοσκοπῶν. Ibid. 1070–1 :
οὐ τοῦτό φησιν, ἀλλὰ ναῦς ἑκάστοτε | αἰτεῖ ταχείας ἀργυρολόγους οὑτοσί.

[3] Ar. *Peace* 639.   [4] *ATL* ii A 9; ML 69. 26–33.

the empire. A decree standing in the name of Cleonymus may represent something of a compromise. This decree was probably passed in the second prytany of 426–425, not long, that is, after the Great Panathenaea of 426; it makes provision for the appointment of collectors in the allied cities who are to be personally responsible for the collection of tribute.[1] The new radicals, having perhaps failed to secure a new assessment, were at least determined to see that the current assessment was actually realized, and the pinning of responsibility on collectors, who would naturally be selected from the rich, is typical of their methods.

The financial aspect of the war was becoming increasingly serious. It had been thought necessary to increase revenue in 428 because of the heavy drain of the early war years on the reserve; but expenditure continued to exceed income. The assessment may have been increased in 428, but the decree moved by Cleonymus shows that collection was far from satisfactory. The *hellenotamiai* were required within ten days of the Dionysia to report to the Assembly which cities had paid their tribute, which had not paid, and which had paid only in part. It was some advance to improve the machinery of collection in the cities, but, if we are right, Cleon and Cleonymus would have preferred a new assessment. This they were not able to secure in the Assembly in 426, for the opposition of the moderates was too strong. Twelve months later they had their opportunity and seized it.

[1] D 8; ML 68.

18

THE ASSESSMENT OF 425

THE story of the occupation of Pylos and the capture of Spartiates on Sphacteria does not need retelling in detail. Demosthenes, the most imaginative of the Athenian generals in the Archidamian War, had occupied the promontory of Pylos in Messenia. The Spartan army, hastily recalled from an invasion of Attica, had attacked the position unsuccessfully, and had occupied the off-shore island of Sphacteria. The Athenians, taking advantage of an alleged breach of a truce agreement, had secured possession of the Spartan fleet, but the blockade of Sphacteria proved unexpectedly difficult. Cleon, in the course of a full-blooded attack on the generals in the Assembly, boasted that if he were in command he would bring the Spartans home alive to Athens within twenty days or kill them on the island. The command was thrust on him and he fulfilled his boast.[1] Two hundred and ninety-two prisoners were brought back, including one hundred and twenty Spartiates. It was against this background that the Assembly accepted the proposal to make a new and higher assessment of the empire.

Some twenty fragments of the decree survive, their relative position has been established, and, though several individual restorations remain very uncertain, the general import of most of the clauses is clear.[2] Ten assessors are first to be appointed by the people; they are to draw up a list of cities to be assessed and to fix a provisional assessment for each. In no case are they to assess a lower figure than before, unless the city is incapable of paying more. Heralds are to take news of the assessment to the allies and to invite them to come to Athens in the month Maimakterion (November/December) to state their case if they think that the new assessment is too high. Their cases are to be brought before a specially constituted court of 1,000 jurors

[1] Thuc. iv. 1–40.
[2] ML 69. For the basic reconstruction, Meritt and West, *The Athenian Assessment of 425 B.C.*; translation, *ATL* iii. 71–3.

and hearings are to be completed before the end of Posideion (January/February). The final decision is to rest with this special law-court and the Boule. Below the decree are inscribed under district headings the cities and their assessments, some half of which are preserved. The grand total of the new assessment was recorded below the list but the vital first figure is missing. Formally it could be either 500 or 1,000 talents, yielding a total of between 960 and 1,000, or between 1,460 and 1,500.[1] Surviving district totals make it clear that the higher figure must be restored: the new assessment was higher than 1,460 talents.[2] How spectacular an increase this represents depends on the figures for 430 and 428, and for the latter especially we have very little evidence indeed. The assessment of 454 had been approximately 500 talents.[3] It is doubtful whether the assessment of 430 had been as high, but the figure could have risen considerably in 428, perhaps to some 800 talents. That there was a stepped increase and not a sudden meteoric rise is the tradition recorded by Plutarch: 'After Pericles' death the demagogues raised it (the assessment) little by little until it came to a total of 1,300 talents.'[4]

Plutarch's source maintained that the tribute increases during the war were the work of the 'demagogues'. Many modern scholars have been more sceptical and have regarded as irresponsible all attempts to associate the assessment of 425 with any particular political group.[5] Our only direct evidence indeed comes from Plutarch and his authority is weak, but other arguments point the same way. The decree was proposed by a Thudippus; it may be coincidence that in the early fourth century there is a Cleon son of Thudippus in Athens, but the

---

[1] $[\kappa\epsilon\phi\acute{a}\lambda a]\iota o\nu\,[\tau]\hat{o}\,\chi o\acute{\upsilon}\mu\pi a\nu\tau o\varsigma : [\chi]\,$ ⊢⊢⊢⊢⊢ ₧⟨ - -.

[2] ₧ instead of χ would give a total of 960–1,000 talents, which the preserved figures show to be too low. The Thracian total was between 310 and 350 talents, the Hellespontine between 250 and 300; the island total is not preserved, but most of the individual figures survive, totalling 150 + talents. These figures alone yield a minimum total of 710 talents which would leave less than 300 talents for the Ionian district, the Actaean cities (on the mainland opposite Lesbos, taken from Mytilene in 427), and the cities in the Euxine. The lower total could only be possible if the Ionic–Carian district was treated very much more lightly than the other districts. Surviving figures rule out this possibility.

[3] *ATL* iii. 9–28 calculate 498 t. 1390 dr.; Gomme, *HCT* i. 275 gives 493 talents.

[4] Plut. *Ar.* 24. 3: $\epsilon\pi\iota\tau\epsilon\acute{\iota}\nu o\nu\tau\epsilon\varsigma\,o\acute{\iota}\,\delta\eta\mu a\gamma\omega\gamma o\grave{\iota}\,\kappa a\tau\grave{a}\,\mu\iota\kappa\rho\grave{o}\nu\,\epsilon\grave{\iota}\varsigma\,\chi\iota\lambda\acute{\iota}\omega\nu\,\kappa a\grave{\iota}\,\tau\rho\iota a\kappa o\sigma\acute{\iota}\omega\nu$ $\tau a\lambda\acute{a}\nu\tau\omega\nu\,\kappa\epsilon\phi\acute{a}\lambda a\iota o\nu\,\acute{a}\nu\acute{\eta}\gamma a\gamma o\nu.$

[5] Gomme, *HCT* iii. 501 f.

suggestion by Wade-Gery and Meritt that this may be the son of the Thudippus who proposed the assessment decree, married to a daughter of Cleon and naming a son after his famous father-in-law, is at least a reasonable hypothesis.[1] More important is the language of the decree, which displays the violence associated with Cleon and his associates. Penalties are threatened at every turn, and in the clause insisting on regular assessments in the years of the Great Panathenaea there is a strong suggestion of polemic.[2] The general tone is reminiscent of the decrees of the early forties, which also threatened the executive with penalties on a liberal scale, and the two periods have something in common. In both there were sharp divisions of opinion and strong feelings. It is doubtful whether the decrees of the thirties when Pericles' ascendancy was not seriously questioned were of this temper.[3] Moreover Thudippus' decree was passed, if not immediately, at least very soon after Cleon's triumph, when his reputation and influence were at their height.[4] The view that Thudippus was the mouthpiece of Cleon's group has, however, to admit one objection. Aristophanes' *Knights*, produced at the Lenaea of 424, is primarily concerned with attacking Cleon, but the play has no clear reference to the assessment decreed only a few months earlier. Cleon is associated by Aristophanes with the tribute: he watches like a tunny-fisher from the rocks the tribute shoaling in; he is always asking for swift triremes to collect money; but neither passage requires a new assessment to give it point.[5] It is difficult, in view of its temper, to believe that the decree was non-controversial, and Aristophanes' attitude to the allies elsewhere makes it unlikely that he would have approved the sharp increase now made. Did he perhaps remember the *Babylonians* and feel that anything which could be construed as an attack on the new policy, especially when the final list had not yet been approved, might lead to another prosecution?[6] Thucydides

---

[1] Isaeus ix. 17; Meritt and Wade-Gery, *AJP* lvii (1936), 392 n. 36.

[2] ML 69. 26–33.

[3] The evidence for comparison is inadequate, but the decrees of Callias, carried in 434–433 (ML 58) are very different in tone though they cannot have been non-controversial.

[4] Meritt and Wade-Gery (op. cit. 377–94) associate the decree directly with Cleon's return, but see ML, pp. 194–6.   [5] References quoted, p. 322 n. 2.

[6] Aristophanes had been brought before the Boule by Cleon for his *Babylonians* produced at the Dionysia of 426, schol. Acharn. 503. See above p. 290.

also ignores this assessment, but that is perhaps less surprising. He does not choose to give details of Athens' financial history, though he fully appreciates the importance of money in war. He reviews Athens' financial resources at the beginning of the war, draws attention to her recovery before the Syracusan expedition, and emphasizes her bankruptcy after the Syracusan disaster. He also records the introduction of the *eisphora* in 428 and the replacement of tribute by a tax on imports and exports in 413; but if the high assessment of 425 proved unrealistic and seemed to have no effect on the course of the war, his decision to ignore it is a little easier to understand.

The assessors were instructed to aim at a higher assessment to meet the costs of the war, and it is clear that this part of their instructions was carried out. The island figures, which are almost completely preserved, show an increase in total from a pre-war 63 to *c.* 150 talents, and it seems that the islands were treated more leniently than the other districts. The Thraceward area which had an assessment of some 120 talents before the war was now required to pay between 310 and 350 talents; the Hellespontine district, formerly assessed at roughly 85 talents, now had an assessment of between 250 and 300 talents. But the sharpest increase was in the Ionian–Carian district, where a pre-war assessment of a little over 110 talents was raised to some 500 talents. The list of figures shows no signs of a standard percentage increase throughout the empire; the wide variation in the scale of increase rather suggests that the resources of each city were individually considered. The special court is likely to have been kept busy with appeals, and it may have been on this occasion that Antiphon wrote his speeches on the Samothracian and the Lindian tribute, of which small fragments survive.[1]

The assessment of 425 aimed not only at getting higher payments from those who were already paying tribute, but also at extending significantly the number of payers. The highest number of cities paying in any one year before the war was not more than 180; the assessment of 425 included not less than 380 cities and possibly more than 400. The list includes several cities who are not known to have paid before, and not all of these will have consented freely to inclusion. The island of

[1] Antiphon F 25–33, 49–56 Thalheim. See pp. 240 f.

Melos, assessed at 15 talents, had certainly shown no signs of submitting to Athens. Thucydides in reviewing the allies of both sides at the beginning of the war expressly states that Melos and Thera were neutral, but Thera appears on the quota list of 428 and may perhaps be restored in 429.[1] It is likely that this island was included for the first time in 430 and incorporated by the gentleness of pressure. In the decree concerning the tribute moved by Cleonymus, probably in the summer of 426, Thera is mentioned in company with Samos as owing money to Athens which she pays in instalments.[2] This might represent the cost of incorporation; perhaps a small detachment of the Athenian fleet called at Thera in 430. It is a reasonable inference that some pressure was put on Melos at the same time, but with no success. From the Spartan inscription already referred to we know that at some time in the Archidamian War, possibly 427, Melos made two donations to Spartan war funds, and Thucydides records an expedition led by Nicias against the island in 426.[3] The considerable force of sixty ships and 2,000 hoplites met with resistance and did not stay to force an issue, but the resistance meant war. The inclusion of Melos in the assessment of 425 implies that the island is to have a further chance to submit to Athens without fighting. The three small neighbours of Melos were also now assessed for the first time. Two of them at least submitted;[4] Melos preferred to cling stubbornly to her independence.

The assessment list also includes for the first known time cities from the Euxine. This district is not represented in the quota lists before the war, nor in those of the 430 assessment, but we have too little evidence to exclude the possibility that the innovation dates from the assessment of 428. Under the heading [ἐκ τô] Εὐ[χσείνο] are listed cities on both north and south coasts.[5] There is room for not less than forty and not more than fifty cities, but none of the twenty-one tributes preserved in whole or in part is more than 5 talents. The total assigned to the district is not likely to have exceeded 100 talents, and may have been as little as 50. It is perhaps more surprising that these

---

[1] See above, p. 321 n. 6.   [2] *ATL* D 8; ML 66, 21–2.   [3] Above, p. 314.

[4] Payments are preserved for Sicinos in 421 and 418, for Pholegandros in 418.

[5] *SEG* xviii. 5. The restoration is questioned by I. B. Brashinsky (*Vestnik drevnej hist.* (1955), 148–161), who prefers [φόρος] ἐκ τô ἐσ[χάτο (*sc.* τês ἀρχês vel τês Θράικης); but see J. and L. Robert, *REG* lxxi (1958), 226–7 n. 173.

cities did not appear in the lists before the war than that they should appear now. If, as one tradition holds, Aristides died in the Euxine, it seems probable that he was there on League business, and Pericles' expedition into the Euxine in the thirties would have provided a good opportunity for encouraging some of the cities to pay tribute.[1] What negotiations preceded the inclusion of these cities in the assessment of 425 we do not know, but the squadron of money-raising ships that sailed into the Euxine under Lamachus soon after the assessment had been drawn up did nothing to convince unwilling states; a severe storm swept away the ships and Lamachus had to lead back his small force overland to Chalcedon.[2] However, the quota list of 420 almost certainly includes a Euxine district;[3] we can infer that some at least of the cities were willing to join the empire. It has sometimes been held that the assessment of Euxine cities must have been a breach of the Peace of Callias. The cities of the north coast, intimately bound up with Athens' corn supply, were in no sense subject to Persia, but the south coast was the Great King's territory; a compromise has therefore been suggested that the claim to tribute from the cities of the south coast was dropped in 423, and that only the northern cities remained on subsequent assessment lists.[4] Positive evidence is unfortunately limited to one city; we are told that Nymphaeum on the north coast remained in the empire after the Syracusan disaster until it was treacherously abandoned by Demosthenes' grandfather.[5] If, however, the suggestion made earlier that under the peace terms the Greek cities within the Persian sphere were guaranteed autonomy, they could have paid tribute to Athens as well as to Persia.

A similar problem arises from the inclusion in the Ionian–Carian list of cities east of the Chelidonian Islands and Phaselis, which marked the boundary in the Peace of Callias between Athenian and Persian spheres. Celenderis on the coast of Cilicia is fully preserved; another state whose name is lost is

---

[1] Plut. *Ar.* 26. 1 ; *Per.* 20. 1–2.   [2] Thuc. iv. 75. 2.

[3] List 34. iii. 78. On this line there seems to be no numeral and a district heading has to be restored. This would make the Euxine district the last on the list as in the assessment of 425.

[4] *ATL* iii. 114–17.

[5] Aeschines iii. 171 ; cf. Craterus, *FGH* 342 F 8: ὅτι Ἀθηναίοις τὸ Νύμφαιον ἐτέλει τάλαντον, probably from the 410 assessment (see Endnote 23, p. 438).

described as 'in Pamphylia'; this was probably Aspendus.[1] Ilyra, Perge, Sillyon, also lie within the Persian sphere. These cities and perhaps others in the eastern Mediterranean may have been induced to pay tribute at the time of Athens' maximum expansion in the early fifties. They do not appear in any of the fragments of the first assessment period (454–450) nor subsequently; presumably they had been abandoned after the collapse of the League expedition in Egypt.

Though the assessment of these southern cities and of the Euxine district may not have been contrary to the letter of the Peace of Callias, it was contrary to the spirit, and the context needs closer attention. When the assessors drew up their list Artaxerxes was still alive, or so the Athenians thought. Soon afterwards came the arrest by an Athenian squadron of a Persian envoy proceeding to Sparta, whose message was that the Spartans had sent so many conflicting statements that the great king was completely confused and required clear-cut propositions.[2] The incident is a reminder that the Peloponnesians realized from the outset of the war the potential value and the potential danger of help from Persia. In 430 their first envoys had been seized while preparing to cross over to Asia, thanks to the action of the Thracian king's son Sadocus, recently made an Athenian citizen;[3] negotiations must, however, have been proceeding for some time before 425. The Persian envoy now arrested was taken to Athens where it was decided to send him back to Susa with an Athenian commission. They crossed the Aegean but at Ephesus the Athenians learnt that Artaxerxes had died and they returned home; they will have remembered the period of uncertainty and assassinations which followed Xerxes' death. By the end of 424 it must have been known that Darius was securely established, and before the end of 424–423 Athenian envoys, including Andocides' uncle Epilycus, had gone to Susa and reached agreement with the king.[4] Presumably the Peace of Callias was renewed, perhaps with minor modifications, and the aggression implicit in the assessment of 425 was renounced; on his side the king will have undertaken to break off negotiations with Sparta. By this time Athens was probably

---

[1] ML 69 (A9) ii. 146; ii. 156–7. See also Endnote 7, p. 420.
[2] Thuc. iv. 50. 1–2.
[3] Thuc. ii. 67.   [4] Above, pp. 134f.

in a less aggressive mood. The assessment reflected the high optimism that followed Cleon's triumph at Sphacteria. By the end of 424 the Athenians had failed in a promising attempt to seize Megara, they had been heavily defeated by the Boeotians at Delium, and Brasidas was making serious inroads into their empire in Chalcidice.

To see the assessment of 425 in proper perspective we need much more information than has come down to us. It will have been less sensational than most modern accounts suggest if, as seems probable, the assessment of 428 had already aimed at a substantial increase. More important, we need to know much more than we do about the changes in the value of money during the fifth century. How in terms of purchasing power did an assessment of 10 talents in 425 compare with an assessment of 3 talents in the late fifties? We have nothing but frail hints. The daily pay of jurors was probably 2 obols when it was first introduced; it was raised to 3 obols in 425 or 424.[1] The pay of hoplites seems to have been 4 obols a day in 450–449; it was a drachma in 431.[2] Such indications as this suggest that prices may have risen since the mid century; it is what we should expect from the increased scale of public expenditure at Athens, particularly on public buildings. There was almost certainly more coinage circulating in the second half of the century than in the first, and money should have been worth less. But it is doubtful whether prices had doubled; on any reasonable estimate the burden on the allies was considerably heavier in 425 than before the war.

The total aimed at was over 1,460 talents, but Melos will not have been the only state which refused payment. The ships sent out to collect money in the winter of 425–424 were the largest such squadron recorded by Thucydides, but it did not provide the decisive display of force that was needed. It is true that in Ionia they nipped in the bud a serious threat from Mytilenaean oligarchs in exile. As at Samos in 439 some of the leaders of the revolt against Athens had escaped to the mainland, and they were now attempting to regain a strong base in

---

[1] Schol. Ar. *Wasps* 88: ἐδίδοτο δ' αὐτοῖς χρόνον μέν τινα δύο ὀβολοί, ὕστερον δὲ Κλέων στρατηγήσας τριώβολον ἐποίησε.

[2] Four obols mentioned in a poorly preserved section of the Miletus decree of 450–449 D 11. 13. For the drachma rate, Thuc. iii. 17. 4.

the cities which had been taken from Mytilene by Athens under the settlement of 427. They had seized Rhoeteum and were on the point of taking Antandrus, which commanded ample timber resources for the building of a fleet, when the Athenian collectors forestalled them; Ionia may have been impressed.[1] But Lamachus' ships which he took into the Euxine were lost.[2] The only figure for the actual collections of this period comes from Plutarch, who tells us that the maximum reached was 1,300 talents. If this applied exclusively to tribute in the strict sense it would mean a short-fall of nearly 200 talents, but if, as is more likely, it included such imperial revenues as the annual payments of the Samian indemnity the short-fall might be as much as 400 talents.[3] Even so the Athenians will have received considerably more in this assessment period than in any other.

This increased financial pressure on the allied cities was accompanied by an increased demand for allied manpower. Chios and Lesbos had regularly sent their contingents to serve with the Athenian fleet in the early years of the war, but for her hoplite forces Athens was at first content to rely on her own citizens and metics. In 425, however, soon after the capture of Spartiates on Sphacteria, the expedition led by Nicias into Corinthian territory included allied contingents; there were Milesians, Andrians, and Carystians as well as 2,000 Athenian hoplites.[4] For the attack on Cythera in the next year the allies outnumbered the Athenians; there were 2,000 Athenians, 2,000 Milesians, and smaller contingents unspecified.[5] It was fortunate for Athens that there were no contingents from the allies when the main Athenian field army was decisively defeated by the Boeotians at Delium later in the year;[6] the actual sight of a large Athenian army in rout might have had a very unsettling influence.

---

[1] Thuc. iv. 52.   [2] Thuc. iv. 75. 2.

[3] Plut. *Ar.* 24. 5. It may be doubted whether literary sources drew a sharp distinction between tribute and indemnities. Thucydides' figure of 600 talents φόρος in 431 is either much too large or includes other moneys coming from the allies, Thuc. ii. 13. 3. Above, p. 253.

[4] Thuc. iv. 42. 1.

[5] Thuc. iv. 53–4: τῶν ξυμμάχων Μιλησίους καὶ ἄλλους τινάς, possibly again from Andros and Carystus.

[6] Thuc. iv. 94; cf. iv. 90. 1: the Athenians had marched out πανστρατιᾶς ξένων τῶν παρόντων καὶ ἀστῶν γενομένης. These were not contingents of allies, but little more than an unarmed rabble.

Failure in Boeotia was not the only bad news that Athens had to face in 424. Before Delium, Demosthenes and Hippocrates had carefully planned a surprise attack on Megara and were on the point of taking possession when a Peloponnesian force led by Brasidas saved the city. The Athenians managed to hold Nisaea, but without possession of Megara itself and Pegae the Athenians could not hope to guarantee Athens against invasion from the Peloponnese. And Brasidas was to do more serious harm to Athens, for his force had been collected to attack the Athenian empire in the north. Such a strategy had been contemplated at the outset of the war, but orthodox Spartan commanders did not relish the risks involved, and the humiliating ineffectiveness of the attempt to relieve Mytilene did not encourage enterprise. Brasidas, however, as Thucydides emphasizes, was not a typical Spartan. He had imagination as well as courage, and could talk as well as fight. It suited the Spartan government to let him go, because it enabled them to send with him potentially dangerous helots. His force was small in number and lacked distinction in quality, 700 helots and 1,000 men hired from the Peloponnese, but his leadership made them more dangerous to Athens than the full Spartan army under an orthodox leader.[1] Having saved Megara he moved quickly north and by skilful diplomacy brought his small force safely through Thessaly, which was still nominally allied to Athens, but contained strong anti-Athenian elements. Brasidas had powerful friends in Pharsalus which had resisted Athenian interference in 454.[2]

The situation in Chalcidice had changed little since the fall of Potidaea in 429. The Greek and Bottiaean rebels who had come into open revolt in 432 had rallied round Olynthus and Spartolus and were still independent. In the late summer of 429 a major attempt to take Spartolus had failed with heavy losses.[3] In 425 minor operations with a small force drawn from local Athenian garrisons had met with only limited success.[4] In the early summer of 424 when Sparta took her decision to give Brasidas official support the circumstances were favourable to the enterprise. The rebels were alarmed at the Athenian successes of 425 and feared that Athens might now feel free to

---

[1] Thuc. iv. 80. 5–81.   [2] Thuc. iv. 78; i. 111. 1.
[3] Thuc. ii. 79.   [4] Thuc. iv. 7.

send a major force against them. They appealed urgently for help to Sparta, and cities which still nominally accepted Athenian control secretly added their pleas. The recent announcement from Athens of the sharp increase in tributes heightened resentment and fear. Behind the Greeks and Bottiaeans, as in 432, was Perdiccas, anxious to undermine Athenian influence in his country, but even more concerned to force the Lyncestians under Arrhabaeus on his border to recognize his authority. It is not surprising that Brasidas made considerable headway in Chalcidice; what is at first surprising is that he did not make more, even after the Athenian defeat at Delium. But the situation was complex and there were elements which were not fully within his control.

Perdiccas' interests did not coincide with those of Brasidas. The Spartan needed above all Macedonian money and supplies to maintain his force in Chalcidice; but the price he had to pay was service under Macedonian command against the Lyncestians. When the second expedition ended in open quarrel Perdiccas abandoned Sparta and once more made his terms with Athens.[1] Nor could Brasidas rely on the Spartan government. He needed them to sustain him with reinforcements and a steady determination to crush Athens; they used him to win a bargaining position for negotiating peace. They were more concerned with recovering the prisoners they had lost on Sphacteria than in taking Athenian possessions in the north. Brasidas assured the people of Acanthus that the Spartan authorities had bound themselves by oaths not to interfere with the independence of any allies who joined him; it was not long before young Spartans were being sent out to act as governors of Amphipolis and other cities.[2] Nor was the support in Chalcidice for Brasidas as resolute and as unambiguous as he had hoped. The progress of his campaign soon made it clear that in most of the Greek cities, if not in all, there were sharp divisions and that there was a surprising degree of support for Athens among the common people. Brasidas' personal example, according to Thucydides, was long remembered and, after the Athenian disaster in Sicily, was an important factor in encouraging the spread of revolt.[3] But in 424 Brasidas had a great

---

[1] Thuc. iv. 132. 1.   [2] Thuc. iv. 86. 1; iv. 132. 3.
[3] Thuc. iv. 81. 1-2, 108. 2-3.

deal of Spartan history to disown; in 424 many of the Greeks in Chalcidice will have thought more of Sparta's failings in 446 and 427, at the times of the Thirty Years' Peace and the revolt of Mytilene.

Brasidas, having disentangled himself from the Macedonian campaign against the Lyncestians, moved first on Acanthus, and Thucydides records his speech. Brasidas' main appeal is that he comes as a liberator. His concern is not to give power to one party rather than to another, but to give autonomy: that was Sparta's proclamation at the beginning of the war, and that was the Spartan tradition.[1] The most interesting aspect of Brasidas' speech is its defensiveness. The Acanthians did not rush out to welcome him; they shut their gates at first and needed persuasion. What they clearly feared was that freedom from Athens could mean subservience to an oligarchy relying on Spartan support. After due deliberation they opened their gates, but, Thucydides implies, their motives were mixed. They were affected not only by the noble arguments of Brasidas; they feared for their crops still unharvested.[2] If they refused entry they would lose the product of a year's work and their main means of support through the winter.

The surrender of Acanthus was followed by that of Stagirus. But Brasidas' main objective was Amphipolis, strategically and economically the most important base of Athenian influence. The city which had suffered most from the Athenian occupation of Amphipolis was her neighbour Argilus. This city came over to Brasidas without hesitation, and it was through Amphipolitans who had originally come from Argilus that Brasidas was able to occupy Amphipolis. Acanthus, Stagirus, Argilus, Brasidas' first three gains, were all colonies of Andros. This may be mere coincidence, for all were on the direct route to Amphipolis, but it is possible that Andrian ill feeling against Athens had influenced her colonies; Andros had been subjected to a cleruchy as early as 450.[3] Incorporation in the Delian League did not mean the severance of a colony's relations with her mother city and even when cities had become virtually subjects of an Athenian empire

---

[1] Thuc. iv. 85–7.
[2] Thuc. iv. 88. 1: διά τε τὸ ἐπαγωγὰ εἰπεῖν τὸν Βρασίδαν καὶ περὶ τοῦ καρποῦ φόβῳ ἔγνωσαν οἱ πλείους ἀφίστασθαι Ἀθηναίων.
[3] Above, p. 121.

they were open to unsettling influences from outside. It is notable that Boeotians supported revolt in Lesbos, and that a Megarian was among the most active in persuading Byzantium, a Megarian colony, to come over to Sparta in the last phase of the war.[1] Corinth's violent hostility to Athens when she accepted a defensive alliance with Corcyra in 433 was mainly responsible for unsettling her colony Potidaea. The capture of Amphipolis was primarily the work of the Argilian element in the population; it was made easier because the number of Athenians in the colony was small.[2] But the loss of Amphipolis proved less serious than was at first feared. It robbed Athens of an important source of silver and timber, but the Spartans failed to take advantage of its command of the land route to the Hellespont. From Amphipolis Brasidas made a quick move on Eion at the mouth of the Strymon, once a key point on Persia's line of communications and occupied by Athenians since 475; but Thucydides, stationed with a small squadron at Thasos, arrived in time to save the place. Brasidas rested for the winter.

Early in 423 Brasidas, having secured his main objective, turned back to Chalcidice to exploit the feeling against Athens on a wider front. Of the three promontories Athos was the least Greek, the least populous, and the least wealthy. There were no large settlements and little co-ordination among the small communities. Most of these came over without fighting but Sane, an Andrian colony breaking the pattern of 424, and Dion held firm. They were not sufficiently important to justify the expense and delay of sieges; Brasidas wisely decided to move quickly on to richer prizes while his prestige was at its height. He moved on to Torone, the largest and wealthiest city of Sithonia, and events in Torone during the next eighteen months are an illuminating reflection of a conflict of feeling that was widespread in the empire. The city had been stiffened by an Athenian garrison of fifty men with two triremes in attendance and at least a token defence was made, but Brasidas had active partisans within the walls and found no difficulty in getting his men in. The Athenian garrison fell back on Lekython, a fort overlooking the sea, and there they were joined by Toronaeans 'who were well disposed to them', a small minority but sufficiently

---

[1] Thuc. iii. 2. 3; viii. 80. 3.
[2] Thuc. iv. 106. 1: βραχὺ μὲν Ἀθηναίων ἐμπολιτεῦον, τὸ δὲ πλέον ξύμμεικτον.

hostile to those who had intrigued with the Spartans to risk an unpleasant death as traitors. When the fort was captured, more by Athenian misunderstanding than Spartan judgement, few of the friends of Athens escaped. But it is notable that when Cleon came north in the late summer of 422 he was able to reoccupy Torone without much difficulty.[1]

Brasidas, having made provisional arrangements for the government of Torone, now heard that the authorities at Sparta had agreed to a year's truce with Athens. But the movement that his successes had encouraged could not suddenly be halted. Two days after the truce had been declared Scione revolted and Mende shortly afterwards followed her lead. There was some dispute whether the truce had preceded or followed the revolt of Scione, but Thucydides, who admired Brasidas' character, felt quite confident that technically the acceptance by Brasidas of these rebels was a breach of the truce.[2] Scione and Mende, however, were in no mood to argue refinements of this kind; they had made up their mind. These new acquisitions were spectacular gains for Brasidas, but dangerous. For the neck of the peninsula of Pallene was held by Athenian settlers who had been sent to Potidaea in 429, when the population had been expelled following the crushing of their revolt; and Mende and Scione were very accessible to the Athenian fleet. When the news of the revolts reached Athens Cleon who had been in eclipse in the latter part of 424 and had not been re-elected general for 423–422, seized his opportunity. His great strength was criticism and the main reason for his effectiveness was his forcefulness as a critic in the Assembly. In 427 his proposal that all adult males in Mytilene should be put to death had been carried, but almost immediately reversed; he now perhaps reminded the Assembly that mercy had not paid. A decree was carried in his name that the penalties he had proposed for Mytilene should be applied to Scione.[3]

It was some considerable time before the terms of this decree could be carried out. An army was sent north under Nicias and Nicostratus, but Scione showed no weakness. Mende provided some compensation, for there the demos had not been wholly behind the revolt and refused to cooperate with the Spartan

---

[1] Thuc. iv. 110–14; v. 2. 2–3. 5.   [2] Thuc. iv. 122. 6.
[3] Thuc. iv. 122. 6.

'liberators'. It was not long before the more resolute among them were leading Athenians in a surprise occupation of the commanding position in the town. Mende was occupied with little loss of life and was treated generously. She was allowed to try in her own courts those who were primarily responsible for the revolt, though normally such cases, involving the extreme capital penalties, would have been referred to Athens.[1] Scione resisted to the end, the decree gave her little option; and when at last she had to surrender in 421 the sentence was carried out. In Thucydides' narrative the butchery of the Scionaeans carries very much less emphasis than the narrow escape of the Mytilenaeans, but it was remembered as a war crime in the Greek world through the fourth century.[2]

The resistance of Scione produced at Athens the mood that Cleon had capitalized in 425. Once again Nicias and his colleagues were exaggerating the military difficulties and causing unnecessary expense and delay. The truce had expired in the spring of 422; in the late summer Cleon was appointed to a special command in the north.[3] But Cleon's problem in Chalcidice was considerably more difficult than at Sphacteria in 425. He had no Demosthenes to advise and support him; his force was composed mainly of hoplites, and he had against him the best general of the Archidamian War. The campaign, however, began well. He caught Brasidas unprepared and succeeded in winning back Torone before Spartan reinforcements could arrive. His failure to take Stagirus was balanced by his recovery of Athos and he seems to have met with rather more success than Thucydides implies.[4] But he showed poor judgement in his reconnaissance before Amphipolis; caught off his guard, he was killed with a large number of his men. In the engagement Brasidas also lost his life, and the removal of the two men who had done most to keep the war alive opened the way for the renewal of negotiations. In the spring of 421 peace was made.

It was soon found that the Peace of Nicias had settled nothing. Sparta had ignored the interests of her strongest allies, and Corinth, Megara, Elis, and Boeotia had voted against the terms

[1] Thuc. iv. 130. 7. For the significance of this privilege see pp. 224 f.
[2] Isocr. xii. 63.   [3] Thuc. v. 2. 1.
[4] Meritt and West, *AJA* xxix (1925), 159–69, but it would be dangerous to infer from their inclusion on the assessment list A10 (?422, see pp. 340–3) that Trailus and Bromiscus had been captured or recovered by Cleon.

which Sparta had agreed with Athens;[1] but the smaller Peloponnesian states, who stood to gain nothing from the war, supported Sparta, and by the constitution of the Peloponnesian League the vote of the majority was binding on all. Athens also had misgivings and a politician to exploit them. It was soon found that Sparta could not fulfil her undertaking; though she was formally willing to restore Amphipolis, the population was not willing to be restored. But in spite of the loss of Amphipolis, which proved to be permanent, Athens' position in her empire was strengthened by the peace. Sparta's pose as the great liberator was shown to be mere opportunism; once again as in 446–445 she was prepared to sacrifice those she had undertaken to free if she could not otherwise satisfy her own immediate interests. She stood by while the men of Scione were butchered and all she could do to satisfy her conscience was to persuade Athens to agree that the cities which had not yet returned to the Athenian fold should not be penalized if they repented; they were to be autonomous and to pay not the inflated assessment of 425 but the original tributes fixed by Aristides.[2] In the same spirit in 446–445 Sparta had secured similar guarantees for Aegina.

[1] Thuc. v. 17. 2.   [2] Thuc. v. 18. 5.

19

THE PEACE OF NICIAS

I T has for long been an accepted view that the Peace of
Nicias marked a temporary change in Athens' attitude to
her allies, and that this change is reflected in an assessment which has been dated in 421. The evidence for this
assessment is derived entirely from inscriptions. A few fragments of the assessment itself survive, and we have also the
very worn stone on which some of the tribute quotas of 420 can
be read. The accepted view of the date and nature of this assessment, reflected most fully and authoritatively in *The Athenian
Tribute Lists*, derives from an impressive study by West, published in 1925.[1] Comparing the figures available with the pre-
war figures and the assessment of 425, he maintained that the
new assessment showed in general very considerable reductions.
This he thought was implied also in the clause of the Peace of
Nicias which guaranteed to certain rebel cities in Chalcidice
a return to the Aristidean assessment if they resumed loyalty to
Athens.[2] Could Athens have treated her loyal allies worse?
West regarded this return to the spirit of Aristides as a gesture
of generosity to the allies which accompanied the making of
peace; the assessment on this view had to be dated when peace
had been made, or at least assured. One further conclusion
reached by West has since been modified. He inferred from the
literary evidence that in the assessment of 418, following the
peace-assessment, the tributes were once again sharply increased. Since he wrote, however, fragments of the island district from two lists of this assessment have been found, and they
show no significant changes from the preceding assessment.[3]
There are also serious objections to West's main thesis.

As has been emphasized above, the assessment decree of 425
insisted sharply, to the accompaniment of strong threats, that

---

[1] West, *AJA* xxix (1925), 135–51; *ATL* iii. 347–53.
[2] Thuc. v. 18. 5, quoted p. 52 n. 3.   [3] Lists 38 and 39 in *ATL* ii.

in future new assessments should be made at the time of the Great Panathenaea.[1] In July/August, therefore, of 422, a new assessment was due and a marble stele on the Acropolis that all could see made it quite explicit that the members of the prytany on duty at the time of the festival would all be held personally responsible if they failed to set the assessment procedure in motion. In August 422 peace was not inevitable, far from it. The year's truce, begun in spring 423, which had been intended by its sponsors to lead to a peace settlement, had lapsed and fighting was still going on in Chalcidice. Cleon had stirred up the Assembly to take stronger action and had gone north to put an end once and for all to the rebellion.[2] Before Cleon's death the majority of the Assembly was in no mood for peace. Unless, therefore, there is clear-cut evidence that the assessment following that of 425 was made in or after the spring of 421 we should expect it to have been completed in 422 and to reflect the influence of Cleon rather than Nicias.

There are in fact two pieces of evidence which suggest that the assessment was closer to the 425 figures than to those of the thirties. The first is a very small part of a quota list which records the quotas of Sigeum, Cyzicus, and Artacus, and they are considerably higher than the pre-war figures.[3] The pre-script of this list originally included the archon's name and the only two names which satisfy the space available on the stone are those of the archons of 422–421 and 418–417, Alcaeus and Antiphon. After some hesitation the authors of The Athenian Tribute Lists chose Alcaeus, the archon of 422–421, and included the list within the 425 assessment period; but, as Meritt himself recognized, there are strong arguments in favour of the later date, and more recently Meritt and McGregor have revised their view.[4] The chairman of the hellenotamiai in 418–417 was Ergocles of the deme Bessae;[5] in the list under discussion all the hellenotamiai are named in official tribal order and the restoration ['Εργοκλês Βεσσ]αιεύς precisely fills the number of

---

[1] ML 69. 26–33.
[3] ATL List 33; ML 75. Sigeum pays 1 t., pre-war 1,000 dr.; Cyzicus 20 t., pre-war 9 t.; Artacus probably 4,000 dr., pre-war 2,000 dr.
[4] Meritt, Hesp. viii (1939), 54–9 (422–1); AJP lxii (1941), 1–15 (418–7); Hesp. xvii (1948), 31 f. (418–417); ATL ii. List 33 (422–1); Meritt and McGregor, Phoenix, xxi (1967), 85 f. (418–417).
[5] IG i². 302. 11 = ML 77.

[2] Thuc. v. 2.

letters required for the representative of the tenth tribe, Aiantis. It is also at least possible to restore the prescript to give the same secretary of the *hellenotamiae* as in 418–417.[1] Logically then the list should belong to 418–417 and since other evidence suggests that few changes were made in 418 we should infer that there was little if any of the spirit of Aristides in the assessment of the Hellespontine district in 422.

A further piece of evidence seems to confirm more directly the inference about the Hellespontine tribute derived from this very fragmentary list. Part of the total for the Hellespontine district is preserved in the surviving fragments of the assessment, but the vital first figure is lost. The total was either 96 or 196 talents as compared with a total in 425 of between 250 and 300 talents.[2] In 425 the numerals of the total were indented one space; if, as might be expected, the same practice was followed by the cutter of the next assessment, the Hellespontine total should be restored to give 196 talents. And this figure is the more likely on other grounds. If the lower figure, 96 talents, were restored we should have to imagine an almost complete return to pre-war level in the Hellespont. For the tribute actually paid by the district in 443–442 was 77 t. 880 dr. and to this must be added the assessment of those cities which did not pay in that year, and of cities such as Callipolis, Bysbicus, and Sombia that were added after 442. Even in the evidence to which West was limited, the increase above pre-war level in the tributes that are preserved is larger than this.

What then of the evidence collected by West, which seemed to show a return to the assessment of Aristides? Even in the figures available to him there were striking exceptions to his general rule. Clazomenae, for instance, had maintained an assessment of only 1½ talents from 454 to 431; in 425 her new assessment was 6 talents; her quota in 420 represents a tribute of 15 talents! It must be admitted, however, that in the majority of cases the new figures were considerably lower than in 425; but the evidence is almost exclusively from the islands and it is possible that the islands were more generously treated than the other districts of the empire. It is a reasonable conclusion from the limited evidence that the assessment was carried through in 422, and that, apart from the island district, the

[1] See ML 75, p. 226.   [2] Phot. *ATL* i. 115, fig. 164; 119, fig. 173.

figures were slightly but not dramatically reduced. Such reductions are more likely to have been made on practical than
sentimental grounds. There had perhaps been too many protests, active and passive, against the 425 figures; if Athens
demanded a little less she might get a little more. The islands
seem to have been more favourably treated than the other
districts, and this may have been because they were more vital
to Athens and particularly to her fleet. If this interpretation of
the evidence is right the Peace of Nicias will not seriously have
affected the tribute, and we may not be forced to reject the
evidence of Andocides. In extolling the blessings of peace he
claimed that after the Peace of Nicias more than 1,200 talents
of tribute came in to Athens each year.[1] If this figure is strictly
limited to tribute in the technical sense, it should be dismissed,
but a tribute of 1,000 talents together with other imperial
revenue of 200 talents might well be near the mark. It would
be dangerous to infer from the tribute evidence a change of
heart at Athens towards the allies, and the treatment of Scione
is barely consistent with a spirit of reconciliation. When the
town fell Cleon's decree was carried into effect though Cleon
himself was dead. The men were killed, the women and children
sold into slavery.[2]

Peace had been made in the spring of 421; in the late summer
of 418 an Athenian contingent fought with allies from Argos
and Mantinea against Sparta; war between Athens and Sparta
had not formally been reopened, but the peace was dead.
Fundamentally Periclean imperialism had generated too much
energy and appetite to allow the Athenian demos to settle down
to a stable peace. Had there been the will the way could have
been found, but underlying suspicions were too deep-rooted.
Incidents were bound to arise and it needed only an ambitious
and unscrupulous politician to exploit them. Alcibiades was
more than any other single individual responsible for the breakdown of the peace, but had he not led Athens into aggressive
policies his place would probably have been taken by the
followers of Cleon led now by Hyperbolus.[3] Alcibiades first

---

[1] Andoc. iii. 9.   [2] Thuc. v. 32. 1.
[3] Hyperbolus was a more powerful figure than Thucydides' contemptuous dismissal implies (viii. 73. 3). He was a member of the Boule in 421–420 and one of
the main speakers in the Assembly, Ar. *Peace* 680–1.

revived the policy pioneered by Themistocles of building up an alliance against Sparta in the Peloponnese in order to crush her in the field. This policy was not doomed to failure; in fact Alcibiades was fully justified when he later claimed that he had 'united the strongest powers in the Peloponnese without involving you (the Athenians) in any danger or expense, and made the Lacedaemonians stake everything on the issue of a single day'.[1] The battle of Mantinea was lost because Athens was not fully united and therefore did not wholeheartedly support Alcibiades' plans, and because Elis objected to the allied strategy and withdrew her considerable contingent. When Alcibiades' grand design on the mainland failed Athenian restlessness found a new outlet in the expansion of the empire by sea.

Within the Aegean one important island only had resisted persuasion and pressure. The fragments of evidence that throw light on Athenian relations with Melos during the Archidamian War have already been reviewed.[2] It seems clear that Melos, though technically neutral, showed her sympathy for Sparta by making two contributions to Spartan war funds; and that when Melos resisted an Athenian expedition to the island in 426 a state of war was accepted by both sides. After her inclusion in the assessment of 425 we hear nothing of Melos until 416, when a strong force was sent to compel the island to submit. There were thirty triremes, 1,200 Athenian hoplites, and no less than 1,500 allies, mainly if not exclusively from the islands.[3] Even this display of strength did not intimidate Melos. Though she could have surrendered on terms that might have been regarded as tolerable she determined to resist until finally she had to surrender unconditionally. The men were killed, the women and children were enslaved.[4]

Thucydides gives great emphasis to the Melian episode. It is related in great detail; it reaches a climax in a dialogue which is technically unparalleled in the rest of the history. Athens' ruthless policy is carried out in cold blood, and no justification is given other than the natural law that the stronger rule the weaker. As Thucydides tells the story Athens is guilty of unprovoked aggression against a harmless neutral. Most modern scholars have reacted strongly against this

---

[1] Thuc. vi. 16. 6. [2] Above, p. 328.
[3] See Endnote 22, p. 437. [4] Thuc. v. 84–116.

account. They believe that the dialogue between Athenian and Melian representatives which precedes the last grim phase bears little relation to what was actually said. Athens, they think, must have had some substantial reason, or at least excuse, for aggression, and this must have figured prominently in any talks that were held between the two parties. It has also been suggested that the inclusion of so many islanders in the Athenian force is ample evidence that there was much more to be said for Athens than Thucydides allows. On this view Thucydides is using the Melian episode to analyse in the form of imaginary speeches his own conception of Athenian imperialism and to show what the conquest of Melos really implied. It must be admitted that there is a more continuous and intelligible background to the expedition than Thucydides provides, but though no proper motive is explicitly given the attack is linked up with the expedition of 426.[1] Thucydides' treatment of the Melian episode cannot be satisfactorily judged in isolation and we shall return to it when we consider his many speeches on Athenian imperialism.[2] For the present it is enough to emphasize that the defiance of Melos in 426 is an adequate explanation for the attack, when combined with the restlessness of the Athenian demos and the ambition of Alcibiades, who may have been primarily responsible for the policy.[3] Islanders were included in the force because after her crippling losses in the plague Athens called increasingly on the allies for hoplites and the islands were the main area of recruitment.[4]

Melos was a minor episode to Alcibiades; he needed a larger stage and a bigger prize. When Egesta and Leontini appealed to Athens early in 415 he saw his chance and turned all his considerable energy into schemes for a western empire. Once again Thucydides fails to bring out the continuity in Athenian policy. His long introduction on the history of Sicily gives the impression that Sicily is now entering the orbit of Athenian

---

[1] Thuc. v. 84. 2: τὸ μὲν πρῶτον οὐδετέρων ὄντες ἡσύχαζον, ἔπειτα ὡς αὐτοὺς ἠνάγκαζον οἱ Ἀθηναῖοι δῃοῦντες τὴν γῆν, ἐς πόλεμον φανερὸν κατέστησαν.

[2] Below, pp. 376 ff.

[3] Thucydides (v. 84. 1) merely says Ἀθηναῖοι ἐστράτευσαν. Plutarch (Alc. 16. 5) makes Alcibiades mainly responsible for the treatment of the Melians after their surrender; so also [Andoc.] iv. 22.

[4] See Endnote 22, p. 437.

imperialism for the first time, but his own narrative shows that the great expedition of 415 was in a sense the logical outcome of earlier policy. Ideas of conquest as opposed to alliances in the war are referred by Plutarch to the years preceding the war; they appear first in Thucydides when he tells the story of the Athenian campaign in Sicily between 427 and 424. The reason for the harsh treatment of the three generals on their return in 424 was, according to Thucydides, that they had accepted bribes to leave when they could have reduced the island. This, however, was not the directive that Thucydides attributes to their mission, and it seems that they were the victims of the people's new optimism lighted by Cleon's out-standing success at Sphacteria; the formal charge may have been that they had accepted terms without reference to the Council and Assembly.[1]

The conference of Gela did not permanently resolve the differences between Syracuse and the Ionian states. Leontini, one of Athens' earliest western allies, soon had cause to com-plain of Syracusan interference: the demos had been expelled and a bargain struck with the oligarchs.[2] Athens could now have justified further intervention and she did seriously con-template action. Phaeax, a noted orator, was sent with two colleagues to approach the old allies of Athens and other cities in south Italy and Sicily, to see what support Athens could expect in a major expedition against Syracuse.[3] At first he met with some success, but he failed to persuade Gela and made little headway in the west of Sicily. No action followed his report, but this was not only due to the inadequacy of the western response; during his absence the Athenian mood had changed. He had been sent out when Cleon was reviving Athenian aggressiveness in the summer of 422; when he returned Cleon was dead and a considerable majority of the Assembly was firmly resolved on peace. When Leontini appealed more urgently in 415 the mood had once more changed, and Alci-biades was eager to exploit the new situation.

The formal Athenian justification when the Assembly was persuaded by Alcibiades to send a large force to Sicily was that it was their duty to save their Ionian allies from Dorian

<hr/>

[1] Above, p. 321 n. 1.   [2] Thuc. v. 4. 2–3.
[3] Thuc. v. 4–5.

Syracuse and Selinus. Alcibiades, however, was thinking in no such limited terms. His ambition was to conquer Sicily, build up an Athenian empire in the west, possibly including Carthage, and then, with the overwhelming resources of the west, to crush the Peloponnese.[1] According to Thucydides, the people supported him because the conquest of Sicily would substantially increase the wealth at the state's disposal which, in one way or another, would be distributed to Athenian citizens.[2] We are not told what the allies thought but they were to play a very large part in the expedition. Of the 5,100 hoplites more than 2,000 were drawn from the cities of the empire, and Thucydides catalogues their contingents; they came from Euboea, Andros, Naxos, Samos, and Miletus. In the fleet were thirty Chian triremes, ten from the loyalists of Lesbian Methymna, and two pente-konters from Rhodes.[3] The bulk of the triremes, as always, were Athenian, but the crews seem mainly to have been drawn from non-Athenians. A decree concerned with preparations for the expedition has been restored to provide for the recruiting of volunteers from the cities of the empire,[4] and when Nicias addresses the sailors before the decisive engagement in the Great Harbour, he implies, in Thucydides' account, that the majority were not Athenians;[5] we can be confident that the metics and allies considerably outnumbered the citizens. It is very doubtful whether they were seriously disturbed by the moral issues involved. The rowers were volunteers who were glad to have the high pay. The hoplites may have been con-scripted but they too probably thought more of the booty to be won than of Athens' justification. It might be thought that the preponderance of allies in the expedition would be a serious source of weakness, especially when the arrival of the Spartan Gylippus and the prospect of reinforcements from the Peloponnese began to force the Athenians on the defensive. But, though we hear of individual desertions under stress, the

[1] Thuc. vi. 90. 2–3. There may be some exaggeration in Alcibiades' boasting at Sparta, but the objectives are credible.

[2] Thuc. vi. 24. 3: ὁ δὲ πολὺς ὅμιλος καὶ στρατιώτης ἔν τε τῷ παρόντι ἀργύριον οἴσειν καὶ προσκτήσεσθαι δύναμιν ὅθεν ἀίδιον μισθοφορὰν ὑπάρξειν . . . διὰ τὴν ἄγαν τῶν πλειόνων ἐπιθυμίαν.

[3] Thuc. vi. 43.

[4] ML 78, with IG i². 98b. 5–6: μισθ]όσθον δὲ καὶ τὸν χσυμμάχον hοπόσ[ος ἂν ναύτας ἐπαγ|γέλλονται hαι π]όλες ἐς τὲμ βολὲν τὲν Ἀθεναίο[ν.

[5] See Endnote 24, p. 439.

contingents remained loyal, and even in the final retreat the majority of them refused to accept the preferential terms offered to them by the Syracusans.[1] Nicias reminded the sailors that the empire was no less theirs than Athens'. They had helped to win it and they shared in the advantages that it brought. There was some truth in this. They felt closer to Athens than to the Syracusans. The allies at Syracuse remained loyal to the Athenian commanders to the bitter end and there is no evidence of widespread trouble in the Aegean while the main Athenian forces were preoccupied in the west. There was, however, probably at least one serious setback. When the revolt of Samos, which had been led by oligarchs, was crushed in 439, the terms of settlement suggest that Athens relied largely on the goodwill of the new democracy to maintain her control.[2] By 412 Samos was ruled again by an oligarchy which was soon to attempt to break away from Athens with Spartan support.[3] At the time of the revolt of Mytilene, in 427, exiled Samian oligarchs were still at Anaea offering a welcome to political refugees and keeping Samos in a state of constant tension.[4] We are not told when the oligarchs succeeded in gaining power; the most likely context is when the news from Syracuse became increasingly encouraging to Athens' enemies. But it is significant that even a hostile oligarchy at Samos did not risk an open break with Athens until the news of the final catastrophe in Sicily reached the Aegean. We learn, by the chance survival of an inscription, of Athenian forces in the Thermaic Gulf and in Ionia;[5] the Athenian fleet still ruled the Aegean. Stasis may have developed in the cities but revolt was not yet a critical issue.

Further evidence confirms that the mood at Athens was not so black and tense as one might think when the crisis developed in Sicily. In the spring of 414 Aristophanes could still afford to poke fun at Athenian imperialism. Indeed there is no better caricature of Athenian methods than the scene in the *Birds* where a series of Athenians appears without warning to protect, guide, and suppress the innocent constitution-makers of

---

[1] Thuc. vii. 82. 1. [2] Above, pp. 193 f.
[3] Thuc. viii. 21; Diod. xiii. 34. 2; *IG* i². 101.
[4] Thuc. iii. 32. 2; iv. 75. 1.
[5] ML 77. 78–9: ἐν τôι Θερμαίοι κόλπο[ι - - - καὶ στρατεγôι ἐν Ἐφ[έσοι.

Cloudcuckoobury.[1] But at the time of the Dionysia most Athenians could still feel confident. By the following winter there was at least cause for anxiety about the outcome, and the financial situation was becoming alarming. It was now that the Athenians decided to change the system of tribute and replace fixed assessments by a 5 per cent levy on imports and exports in the harbours of the allies. It is possible that the Athenians thought that this change would be popular among the allies, since it would relate tribute more directly to the benefits of Athenian sea-power, but the main motive, according to Thucydides, was to raise more money.[2] The new system required a much more detailed control to counter evasions, but the Athenians do not seem to have doubted their capacity to make the system work. More important and more significant is Athenian policy towards Persia.

Near the beginning of Thucydides' narrative of 412 in his last book, we unexpectedly read that Amorges, bastard son of Pissuthnes, former satrap at Sardis, is co-operating with Athenians.[3] For an explanation we have to descend to Andocides. In his speech on the necessity of peace in 391 he warns his Athenian audience not to repeat the mistake that they have so often made in the past of choosing the wrong friends, as when they allowed themselves to be persuaded by the King's fugitive slave and threw away the peace which his uncle Epilycus had helped to negotiate with the great king.[4] Ctesias fills out the background. Pissuthnes had revolted from Darius, and the King sent Tissaphernes, Spithradates, and Parmises to suppress him. Pissuthnes came out with some Greek troops under the command of an Athenian, Lycon. Lycon and his Greeks were bribed by the king's generals to desert Pissuthnes, who was taken to the Persian king and, in spite of the pledge given to him, put to death.[5] We should welcome a more reliable source than Ctesias, but the outline in his epitome is credible. We need, however, to know much more. When did Pissuthnes revolt? Why was an Athenian in his service? Had Lycus been hired to sustain Pissuthnes' bid for independence, and was the Athenian state a party to the business? It is better to leave such

[1] Ar. *Birds* 1021–55, App. 17, p. 581.   [2] Thuc. vii. 28. 4.
[3] Thuc. viii. 5. 5.   [4] Andoc. iii. 29.
[5] Ctesias, 52.

questions, which Thucydides strangely ignored, unanswered, but even if Pissuthnes made his bid while Athenian prospects in the west looked bright in 415 or 414, and this seems the more probable chronology, the Athenians made no attempt to reverse their policy and disown Amorges when the tide began to turn against them in Sicily.

20

THE IONIAN WAR

WHEN the news of the final humiliation in Sicily reached Athens the position seemed desperate. Thucydides' description is typically economic and vivid:

When they saw that there were no longer enough ships in the docks, no money in the treasury, and no trained men for special duties on their ships, . . . they determined to do what they could. They would take whatever steps were possible to secure timber for ship-building and they would break into the iron reserve of 1,000 talents which they had set aside at the beginning of the war.[1]

The empire meanwhile, according to Thucydides, threatened collapse as the allies competed fiercely to be the first to revolt, now that Athens' power was broken.[2] His detailed narrative does not fully bear out this gloomy analysis. Athens could fight on for eight more years and there was even a period when disinterested observers might have expected her to win the war. Athens had weaker enemies and more friends than was realized when the scene of war shifted to Ionia.

In 412 Sparta seemed poised for victory. The army at Decelea under King Agis had penned the Athenians in the city and denied to Athens the mines and agricultural resources of Attica. In quick succession Euboea, Lesbos, Chios, and Erythrae offered their active help in return for Spartan support. Sparta's allies of the Peloponnesian League might be expected to throw their full weight into the fighting now that the prospects seemed so much brighter, and especially Corinth, whose colony Syracuse had been saved by the leadership of the Spartan Gylippus. But it was not long before the inherent weaknesses beneath the surface were exposed. The focus of war naturally shifted to the east side of the Aegean and the Spartan system was poorly adapted to sustain overseas operations. She lacked ships, experienced naval commanders, and finance, and

[1] Thuc. viii. 1. 2–3.   [2] Thuc. viii. 2. 2–4.

of these finance was perhaps the most serious stumbling-block. The Peloponnesian League had no reserves and no regular income; the overseas contingents were financed by their own states, but Sparta herself did not even use a normal currency. To maintain a large fleet ready for action the crews had to be regularly paid, and regular pay required regular subsidies from the only source with an available surplus and common interests. Sparta had attempted to secure Persian aid during the Archidamian War but her approaches were half-hearted and the Peloponnesian prospects must have seemed unconvincing to Persia while the Athenian fleet dominated the Aegean.[1] The elimination of the Athenian fleet at Syracuse completely changed the picture. Sparta now seemed to have the spirit and means to break Athens and Persia might consider financial aid to her a profitable investment.

Sparta did not find it difficult to open negotiations with the satrap at Sardis; the difficulty lay in finding a basis of agreement which would be acceptable to the east Greeks in whose interests, nominally at least, Sparta had crossed the Aegean. She could not afford to sacrifice Greeks to Persia; on the other hand, Persia could not be expected to provide aid unless Sparta helped her to recover some of her lost dominion. The result was hesitation, opportunism, and suspicion. The first treaty, made in the summer of 412 after the revolt of Miletus, stipulated that 'all the territory and all the cities which are in the possession of the King or were in the possession of his forefathers shall be the King's and whatever revenue or other advantages the Athenians derived from these cities the King and the Lacedaemonians and their allies shall combine to prevent them from receiving such revenue or advantage'.[2] There was an obvious danger in the vagueness of the definition of the King's rights and nothing was clearly laid down about the payment of Spartan forces. This particular weakness was remedied in the following winter but it required a third treaty before it was made clear that the King's claim to the territory in Europe that the Persians had occupied before and during Xerxes' invasion could not be recognized.[3]

This third treaty, which defined more closely what Persia was to get and what she was to give, was the work of a com-

---

[1] Thuc. iv. 50. [2] Thuc. viii. 18. 1. [3] Thuc. viii. 37. 2; 58. 2.

mission sent out from Sparta owing to the ineffectiveness of
her forces in Ionia.[1] It reflected an uneasiness that persisted
in Sparta through the war. While most Spartan commanders
in Ionia realized that they were dependent on Persian finance
and had to pay a price for it, at Sparta, away from realities,
it was less easy to be reconciled to sacrificing the tradition of
Thermopylae and Plataea. This ambivalence was brought into
sharp relief when Callicratidas succeeded Lysander in 406.
Lysander had established cordial relations with his Persian
paymaster; Callicratidas found Persian pretensions intolerable
and came out boldly for a Hellenic policy.[2] But Callicratidas'
cause was lost when he was defeated and killed at the battle of
Arginusae. Nor was policy towards Persia the only source of
indecision in Sparta. Power was divided between King Agis at
Decelea and the authorities at Sparta, and the ephors needed
little encouragement to be jealous of Agis. Early in 412 Euboea
and Lesbos appealed to Agis; Chios and Erythrae sent to
Sparta. It was some months before the policies of Agis and his
home government could be reconciled. Athens, as Thucydides
emphasizes, could not have had a more convenient enemy.[3]

In a naval war which depended so largely on money, Persia's
should have been the decisive voice, but Persia had her own
problems. While the central direction of policy rested with the
King far in the east, distance was bound to give considerable
independence to the satraps. In the west power was divided
between Tissaphernes at Sardis and Pharnabazus at Dascylium.
Each was anxious to secure the main credit for recovering
Persian control over the Greek cities; as a result they pursued
rival policies and never co-ordinated their actions. While Tissaphernes was determined to concentrate the war in Ionia
Pharnabazus independently sent Greek agents to Sparta, hoping
with the aid of a Spartan fleet to win back the Athenian subjects
in his satrapy. It was not until Cyrus the King's son was sent
down from Susa to take supreme command in the west in 407
that Persian intervention became decisive. The main responsibility for the earlier ineffectiveness of Persia rested with
Tissaphernes. He had been appointed to Sardis when Pissuthnes' revolt had been crushed and his instructions were to
drive out the Athenians and send Amorges, who was trying to

[1] Thuc. viii. 39. 2.   [2] Xen. Hell. i. 6. 7–11.   [3] Thuc. viii. 96. 5.

carry on what Pissuthnes had started, to the King dead or alive. Now that the Athenians had broken the peace of 424–423 by supporting Amorges Darius had no hesitation in insisting on the tribute of the Greek cities which had for so long been paid to Athens.[1]

Tissaphernes had small forces at his disposal under subordinate commanders whom he used when good opportunities offered, but major objectives could only be won by the Peloponnesian troops. Had he from the outset paid them regularly and generously the impetus achieved early in 412 might have been maintained and the war ended within two years, but Tissaphernes was dilatory and evasive and a spirit of frustration spread through the Spartan command. Much of the credit for this Persian paralysis should go to Alcibiades. Recalled from the Syracusan expedition he had gone to Sparta and played a large part in shaping their policies. In particular he had persuaded them to make the island of Chios their first and main objective. From Chios he hoped to exploit his personal magnetism in spreading revolt rapidly and widely in Ionia. At first he met with considerable success and it was his personal contacts with leading Milesians that won Miletus for the Spartans early in the summer of 412.[2] But by midsummer Alcibiades was no longer tolerated by the Spartans. He was too clever altogether for them; they resented his vanity, and fundamentally distrusted him. If he had seduced the wife of Agis in his duller days at Sparta the king's influence may have contributed to his eclipse; whatever the reasons, Alcibiades by the late summer of 412 was no longer safe among Spartans. Since there could be no question yet of his return to favour at Athens he went to Sardis and imposed his considerable charm on Tissaphernes, who even called his finest park *The Alcibiades*.[3] Tissaphernes was susceptible to the attraction of Hellenism, and displayed

---

[1] Thuc. viii. 5. 5: ὑπὸ βασιλέως γὰρ νεωστὶ ἐτύγχανε πεπραγμένος τοὺς ἐκ τῆς ἑαυτοῦ ἀρχῆς φόρους, οὓς δι' Ἀθηναίους ἀπὸ τῶν Ἑλληνίδων πόλεων οὐ δυνάμενος πράσσεσθαι ἐπωφείλησεν. Even though the Persian king may not have formally renounced his right to tribute from the Asian cities in the Athenian Empire he cannot now have demanded the arrears from 478. He probably demanded tribute from the time when Athens supported Amorges (and possibly Pissuthnes before him) and Tissaphernes was sent to Sardis with instructions to recover the lost cities.

[2] Thuc. viii. 17.

[3] Plut. *Alc*. 24. 7: παραδείσων τὸν κάλλιστον . . . Ἀλκιβιάδην καλεῖν ἔθετο.

his taste when he issued coins with a very Hellenic portrait of himself.[1] There can be no doubt that a clever and handsome Athenian would appeal more to a Persian nobleman with Hellenic tastes than rather dull-witted and stubborn Spartan commanders. Alcibiades had little difficulty in convincing Tissaphernes that the right policy for Persia was to wear down both sides so that neither would be capable of interfering in Asia. In his general direction of policy the Persian king had commissioned a fleet from the forest lands of the eastern Mediterranean to assemble at Aspendus and be available for use in the Aegean when opportunity offered. One hundred and forty-seven ships came to Aspendus, but no further, because Tissaphernes had no intention that they should. When the delay became embarrassing he went personally to Aspendus, giving the impression to the Spartans that the Phoenician fleet would now join them, but there was no movement. Alcibiades, who was by now attempting to win his way back to Athens, claimed the credit and he may be right. The mystery fascinated Thucydides but he was not certain of the solution.[2] He mentions various motives attributed to the satrap, but he was personally convinced that Tissaphernes' intention was to play for time and weaken both Spartans and Athenians. Trouble in Egypt and Arabia was probably the decisive factor ultimately in his not using the ships in the Aegean, but in the early summer of 411 it was more probably Tissaphernes' responsibility.[3]

Tissaphernes' relations with Sparta and Athens required delicate calculation; the Ionians also proved more troublesome than might have been expected. Sparta had explicitly recognized Persia's claim to the Greek cities of Asia, but the cities themselves had not been consulted. Tissaphernes instituted a small garrison in a newly built fort in Miletus; the Milesians attacked the fort without warning and drove out the garrison.

---

[1] E. S. G. Robinson, *Num. Chron.* viii (1948), 48–55 with pl. v. 8. *Obv.* Bearded head wearing Persian tiara. *Rev.* Owl r., above owl, olive spray with berry and waning moon exactly as on an Athenian coin; on rev. downward, *ΒΑΣ* replacing *ΑΘΕ*. The weight, 16·96 gr. is equivalent to an Attic tetradrachm. 'Style and alphabet show that they were made by and for Greeks.' Robinson gives reasons for the identification and for dating the issue not later than 410.

[2] Thuc. viii. 87.

[3] Diodorus' source (in xiii. 38. 5) knows of the return of the King's ships to Phoenicia before the end of the summer of 411. For the important evidence from Egypt see D. M. Lewis, *Hist.* vii (1958), 392–7.

Sparta's allies approved their action, and not least the Syracusans, but Lichas, the Spartan governor, felt uncomfortable; he
knew that under the third treaty Persia was entitled to control
Miletus. 'The Milesians', he said, 'and the others in the great
King's territory must be subjects of Persia and show their proper
respect until the war ends in victory.'[1] This cannot have sounded
very comforting or convincing to his Milesian audience; when
Lichas died they refused to let the Spartans choose his burial
ground. Later in the year there was another clash, at Antandrus.
The city had sent its men with the Peloponnesians into the
Hellèspont, but they had to hurry back over Mount Ida to save
their city, which was being roughly treated by the Persian
Arsaces, serving under Tissaphernes. They remembered how
this same Arsaces had called out the Delian refugees in Atramyttium and had treacherously surrounded and shot them down.[2]
In the same summer Cnidus, which had voluntarily gone over
to Tissaphernes, drove out its Persian garrison.[3] Ephesus seems
to have been an exception in accepting Persian control willingly.
Tissaphernes sacrificed conspicuously to Ephesian Artemis:[4]
the other Ionians might have told him that she was not a very
Greek goddess.

The ambivalence of Tissaphernes, and the lack of resolution
and imagination in the early Spartan leadership are in part
responsible for the continued survival of Athens, but no less
important was the support she retained or recovered in the
cities of the empire. The welcome that so many of them offered
to Sparta in 412 soon grew cold when they learnt at first hand
more of Spartan manners and methods. Mixed crews were
considerably more difficult for Spartan commanders to control
than Spartan hoplites, and the tough independence of their
western allies from Syracuse and Thurii was unfamiliar to
Sparta. The harmosts whom they sent out to hold cities that
they had won over lacked the political sensitiveness of their
Athenian counterparts. Agreements with Persia made talk of
liberation a mockery and revolt stirred up sharp divisions
between democrats and oligarchs, though the pattern was not
uniform. In 412 Chios, Samos, and Lesbos, who had taken the
lead with Athens in the formation of the Delian League, and

---

[1] Thuc. viii. 84. 5.   [2] Thuc. viii. 108. 4–5.
[3] Thuc. viii. 109. 1.   [4] Thuc. viii. 109. 2.

who had retained their autonomy longest, all revolted; the
different histories of these three islands in the next seven years
illustrate the danger of generalization.

At Samos in 412 the democrats rose up against the oligarchs,
who had recently seized power, and the crews of three Athenian
triremes which happened to be at Samos joined them.¹ Diodorus adds what Thucydides omits, that the Samians invited the
Peloponnesians to help them to revolt, and a partly preserved
inscription confirms him. But the democrats were successful and
Athens wisely gave them full support and a formal guarantee of
autonomy; it was probably now that Samos whose mint had
been closed in 439 began to issue her own coins again, but on
the Attic standard.² Samos remained Athens' main naval base in
the eastern Aegean until the fleet was lost at Aegospotami. There
was temporary indecision among some leaders of the Samian
demos when Athens herself carried through an oligarchic
revolution, but the bulk of the demos stood firm and a
unique Athenian tetradrachm which has Athena's head with
ethnic on the obverse and the Samian oxhead on the reverse
reflects her close union with Athens.³ Even when Athens'
position was desperate Samos refused to surrender to Lysander.
This striking loyalty Athens recognized generously, and when
the end was near she conferred on all Samians Athenian citizenship. This may have seemed an empty gesture when Athens
herself was on the point of surrender to Sparta, but when the
Samian democrats had been expelled by Lysander and the
Athenian democracy had been restored in 403 by Thrasybulus
the old decree was set up again and a new one added confirming the grant of citizenship and thanking the cities that had
given refuge to the Samian friends of Athens.⁴ The stability of
Samos in these last years was due largely to the ruthless action
taken against the oligarchs in 412. Two hundred of their
leaders were killed, 400 were exiled and lost their property,
land, and houses; their class, the *geomoroi*, were forbidden to
intermarry with commoners. Among the exiles whose property

¹ Thuc. viii. 21.
² Diod. xii. 34. 2, *IG* i². 101 with Lewis, *BSA* xlix (1954), 29–31, l. 4; Barron,
The Silver Coins of Samos, 97–101.
³ Thuc. viii. 73; Barron, op. cit. 101; Seltman, *Greek Coins*² (1955), 137 f.,
pl. xxvii. 8–9.
⁴ ML 94 with Tod, *GHI* ii. 97.

was confiscated was Cleomedes. His name is preserved on the inscription recording Athens' grant of autonomy; he was later honoured with a statue at Delphi as one of Lysander's ship commanders at Aegospotami.[1]

The events of 412 in Samos were the culmination of party feeling that had been festering for a long time. The oligarchs had gained, or possibly retained, power in the middle of the century and had led Samos into revolt against Athens in 440. When Samos surrendered the democrats assumed control under Athenian protection, but there were sufficient oligarch refugees at Anaea on the mainland to keep party feeling alive in the island, and by 412 they were back in power. The grim revenge of the democrats in 412 is not surprising but it is ironical that the pro-Athenian party should win its most decisive victory when to most of the Aegean world Athens seemed not far from collapse.

The history of Chios had been very different and Thucydides was fascinated by her fortunes in these years. Chios alone, he thought, apart from Sparta, was able to combine moderation with prosperity: 'the greater the wealth and power she developed the more stable and secure she became'.[2] The fortunes of once powerful states such as Corinth and Aegina had declined under the shadow of Athens' growing dominance. The Ionian cities of the mainland had never fully recovered from the Ionian revolt, and Mytilene, Erythrae, and Colophon were probably not the only cities where political instability had led to unsuccessful revolt. Athens herself, with minor setbacks, had grown in power and wealth but Thucydides thought that she had lost moderation. An empire needs financial resources and judgement; Pericles had provided both but after his death, according to Thucydides, the Assembly became the victim of irresponsible leaders selfishly pursuing their own ambitions. Not so Chios: she avoided the mistakes of Samos and Lesbos and, as Thucydides emphasizes, her land had been unravaged since the Persian wars. Her revolt was consistent with her record of political sense; she delayed until Athens' survival after the Sicilian expedition seemed precarious even to Athenians, and many other cities were joining her in revolt.

---

[1] Thuc. viii. 21; *IG* i². 101. 5: τὸν ἀγρὸν τὸν Κλεομέδεος in an uncertain context; probably the property had been confiscated; memorial at Delphi, Paus. x. 9. 10.

[2] Thuc. viii. 24. 4.

The revolt of 412 had indeed older roots. The record of contributions to Spartan war funds in the Archidamian War, mentioned earlier, includes a payment of Aeginetan staters by 'the friends of the Lacedaemonians in Chios'.[1] This could have been a small group acting independently without any hope of influencing state policy, but in the winter of 425–424 Athens felt sufficiently suspicious to intervene. 'The Chians pulled down their new wall on the instructions of the Athenians who suspected that they were going to adopt an anti-Athenian policy. The Chians, however, gave firm pledges, and their leading men gave security that they would not change their policy towards Athens.'[2] This was but a ripple on the surface. Chios still sent her contingents to serve with the Athenian fleet, she was the only independent ally left. 'A noble city', Eupolis could say, 'she sends you warships and men when needed and in all she does she nobly follows our lead.'[3] Athens even paid her the supreme compliment of coupling Chios with Athens in the Assembly's prayers.[4] But in 412 Chios thought that Athens was doomed. Her leading citizens appealed to Sparta and took the initiative in spreading revolt as widely as possible in Ionia.

There were conflicting claims in 412 on Sparta's resources. Appeals came from cities of both western satrapies and to both Spartan sources of authority, to Agis at Decelea, and to Sparta where the main power rested with the ephors. The two most attractive appeals were from Lesbos and Chios, the first made to Agis with strong support from Boeotia, linked traditionally with the settlement of Aeolian Lesbos, the second to Sparta, where Alcibiades threw his restless energies into the scale. A compromise was finally reached. The Peloponnesian force should proceed first to Chios, then to Lesbos, and then to the Hellespont.[5] The Hellespont was the most critical area, for the cutting of the corn route from the Euxine could have starved Athens to surrender, as it did later; but control of the Hellespont required decisive naval superiority and Chios had the largest Greek fleet in the east and the widest influence in Ionia.

The men who had steered Chios into revolt had every reason to be pleased by the operations of the early summer. Though the main Peloponnesian fleet was surprisingly blockaded by

---

[1] ML 67. 9–10. See p. 314.   [2] Thuc. iv. 51.   [3] Eupolis, Πόλεις F 232.
[4] Schol. *Birds* 880; Theopompus, *FGH* 115 F 104.   [5] Thuc. viii. 8. 2.

an Athenian squadron, Alcibiades, partnered by the Spartan Chalcideus, succeeded in slipping into Chios and maintaining the impetus of the revolt. Erythrae had come over without hesitation and a token force of three triremes persuaded Clazomenae to join the rebels. Teos was the next objective. The Athenians, now based at Samos, had shown the flag at Teos but withdrew when they found themselves heavily out-numbered. The Chian fleet of twenty-three ships sailed in and land forces from Clazomenae and Erythrae approached by land and were admitted; the wall that the Athenians had built for the defence of Teos was destroyed.[1] Alcibiades' new objective was Miletus. This had once been the wealthiest and most powerful city of Ionia and it still derived prestige from its history and the natural wealth of its land; moreover Alcibiades could exploit his connections with the political leaders and was anxious to secure for himself and Endius, his most influential Spartan supporter, the main credit for spreading revolt before larger forces under a new commander arrived from the Pelo-ponnese. Miletus was won and at Miletus was made at once the first agreement with the Persians. A little later Lebedos and Haerae joined the swelling number of rebels.[2]

Still anxious to strengthen their own position as much as possible as soon as possible, the Chians moved on Lesbos which, according to Spartan strategy, was to be won over before the united forces from the Peloponnese and Ionia moved to the Hellespont. Methymna, which along with Chios had continued to contribute ships after the reduction of Mytilene, came over at once and it was thought that four ships were sufficient to hold it; the rest of the Chian fleet meanwhile persuaded Mytilene to revolt again. So far all had gone well; but it was soon seen that appearances were deceptive. Astyochus the Spartan nauarch for the year now arrived in Chios to take over the high command, but, before he had settled down, an Athenian force of twenty-five ships under two capable democratic generals, Leon and Diomedon, sailed to Lesbos. Astyochus at once led out his fleet to give what help he could. He came first to Pyrrha, next day to Eresus, and there he learnt with a shock that Mytilene had been taken by the Athenians 'with no more than a shout'. The Athenians had sailed into the

---

[1] Thuc. viii. 12–16.   [2] Thuc. viii. 17–19.

harbour completely unexpected and had had no difficulty in
seizing the Chian ships at anchor; they had later landed and
overcome the half-hearted resistance of the Mytilenaeans.
Astyochus had no hope with his existing resources of reversing
this decision; he had to be content with securing the revolt of
Eresus which he put into a state of defence. His infantry he
then sent to Antissa and Methymna, hoping to win support.
But the expedition to Lesbos had failed and soon Athenian
troops were landing on Chios itself; three times the Chian
forces were defeated with heavy losses. 'After this the Chians
no longer went out to fight and the Athenians ravaged the land
which was well equipped and cultivated, and which had not
suffered from the time of the Persian wars to that day.'[1]

The explanation of this dramatic reversal of fortune at
Chios is in part military. The Spartans showed less resolution
than the occasion demanded; the Athenians recovered more
quickly than could reasonably have been anticipated. But
political factors contributed seriously to the failure of Chios.
In spite of Thucydides' emphasis on their stability and political
sense the Chians were not firmly united when they declared
against Athens. At first they had carried out their negotiations
with Sparta secretly but before any ships sailed from the Peloponnese the Athenians had wind of the plot. They sent one of
their generals, Aristocrates, to Chios to protest and when the
Chians pleaded innocence they were required to send ships
to Athens according to the terms of their alliance. The Chians
sent seven ships, but Thucydides adds the significant comment
that they were dispatched because the oligarchs who were
planning the revolt did not wish to have the common people,
who knew nothing about their negotiations with Sparta, against
them until they had secured their ground.[2] When Alcibiades
and Chalcideus approached Chios early in 412 they took the
precaution of landing first on the mainland where they made
their plans 'with some of the Chians who were collaborating with
them'. When they landed on Chios 'the common people were
amazed' but the leaders of the revolt had made arrangements

[1] Thuc. viii. 24. 3.
[2] Thuc. viii. 9. 3. There is no firm evidence of the precise form of government
in Chios before the revolt. For a discussion see T. J. Quinn, *Hist.* xviii (1969),
22–30.

for a Council meeting to be in progress at which Alcibiades and Chalcideus were able to paint a more rosy picture of the prospects of help from the Peloponnese than the blockade of the fleet at Spiraeum warranted.[1] It seems clear from Thucydides' account that the oligarchs had no real confidence in the people and were not themselves unanimous; it is not therefore surprising that when the first serious reverses came there should be some Chians who wanted to steer the city back to Athens. What follows is almost more revealing. 'The magistrates', Thucydides says, 'were aware of this movement. But they did nothing themselves and called Astyochus the Spartan nauarch back from Erythrae with his four ships, and discussed with him the most moderate means of suppressing the conspiracy, whether by taking hostages or some other means.'[2]

The outcome of these discussions is not related and we are surprised to find a little later that the situation has sharply deteriorated: 'The Chians had suffered seriously already in several engagements and their internal affairs were not in a healthy state.' Tydeus son of Ion and his followers, who remained loyal to Athens, had already been put to death by Pedaritus, the Spartan harmost, and the rest of the population had been compelled to accept a narrow oligarchy.[3] As a result they suspected one another and made no move. The opposition to the government came no doubt partly from the poor, but if Tydeus is son of the Ion whose plays were produced at Athens he is likely to have been wealthy; his loyalty to Athens will not have been due to a class hatred of oligarchs, but to an attachment to Athens inherited from his father. By the end of 411 Chios was apparently controlled securely by Sparta through a narrow oligarchy of pro-Spartans. We hear nothing more until 409–408 when we are surprised to find the Spartan admiral Cratesippidas restoring Chian exiles who proceed at once to attack their political opponents and exile up to 600. The new exiles occupied Atarneus, a strong point on the mainland opposite Chios, and maintained a state of war against their home government.[4] This does not seem to be a clash between

---

[1] Thuc. viii. 14. 1–2.   [2] Thuc. viii. 24. 6.
[3] Thuc. viii. 38. 3: τῆς ἄλλης πόλεως κατ' ἀνάγκην ἐς ὀλίγους κατεχομένης. I take this to mean a narrow as opposed to a moderate oligarchy.
[4] Diod. xiii. 65. 3–4.

oligarchs and demos but between two groups of oligarchs. The friends of Sparta in Chios who gave financial support to Sparta during the Archidamian War were probably a small minority. In 412 they were able to win over the broad support of the propertied classes, but when the realities of Spartan help were seen the moderates went into opposition. Between 411 and 408 they succeeded in overthrowing the pro-Spartan regime and exiled the Laconizers, probably as an indirect result of the Athenian victory at Cyzicus in 410. But when Sparta had built up a new fleet the Laconizers were reinstated and the moderates went into exile at Atarneus. They were still there after the war, defying the puppets of Sparta in Chios and out of sympathy with the other Ionian cities who were not prepared to fight for their liberties.[1]

In Lesbos the conflict of interests between rich and poor was not the only issue. While we hear only of one city in Samos and Chios, in Lesbos Methymna, Pyrrha, Antissa, and Eresus recur in the narrative as well as Mytilene. In all accounts of the early days of the Delian League Lesbos is grouped with Samos and Chios and it seems likely that the island had one vote only and sent one contingent to the League fleet. Presumably Mytilene had for long exercised a general hegemony over the island and there was no reason to make a change in 478-477. But in 428 we are told that 'all Lesbos except Methymna revolted from Athens'. One of the charges was that Mytilene was forcibly synoecizing the island, presumably bringing pressure on the smaller towns to transfer their populations to Mytilene.[2] This charge could frighten Athens, for her imperial policy was normally opposed to the absorption of smaller cities by their more powerful neighbours. In 432 Olynthus became dangerous when she attracted refugees from small coastal cities of Chalcidice in revolt, and it was the union of her three cities in the last phase of the war that gave Rhodes the strength to sustain her revolt. The other small cities of Lesbos fought with Mytilene in 428-427 and suffered with her, for the whole land of Lesbos, excluding only Methymna, was confiscated. From that point Methymna was a favoured ally of Athens, and there may have been some bitterness against her in Mytilene. Against this background it is easier to see why when Methymna declared

---

[1] Xen. *Hell.* iii. 2. 11. [2] Thuc. iii. 2. 3.

for Sparta in 412 Mytilene could be so easily recovered by Athens.

In Thasos also we can trace the rough pattern of events and there too political divisions led to instability; as on Lesbos, the differing interests of the dominant city and her dependencies complicated developments. Thasos had been under democratic control since her revolt had been crushed in 463, and she did not at once come out in revolt when she heard of the Syracusan disaster. The impetus in fact came indirectly from Athens, for when in the spring of 411 the Athenian oligarchic leaders in Samos were preparing to bring the revolution in Athens to a head, they decided to accompany and support their own revolution by setting up oligarchies in the allied cities. Diitrephes, the Athenian general who had been appointed to the command in the Thraceward area, overthrew the popular government, but this did not reconcile all Thasian oligarchs to Athenian rule. Soon after Diitrephes had gone they began to rebuild the city walls which they had been forced to dismantle in 463: 'They no longer wanted aristocratic government dependent on Athenian support; they daily expected the Spartans to win them freedom. For there were with the Peloponnesians Thasians who had been exiled by the Athenians and they with their associates in the city were doing everything in their power to bring ships and effect the revolt of Thasos.'[1] Less than two months after the overthrow of the democracy a Peloponnesian fleet had arrived and Thasos could openly disown Athens.[2] There was, however, a price to pay for Peloponnesian support. To the natural conflict between democrat and oligarch was added the developing friction between Laconizers and independents. The resilience of the Athenians who continued to maintain a fleet in Thracian waters kept these divisions alive.

Growing tension in Thasos is reflected in decrees both in Thasos and in Athens. It was probably in the autumn of 411, after naval successes in the Hellespont had revived Athenian hopes, that the Thasians issued a decree offering rewards to informers who exposed plots in Thasos against the government, and this was followed later by a further decree extending the scope of the first to plots formed against Thasos, not only in

[1] Thuc. viii. 64. 2–4.   [2] *Hell. Ox.* (Teubner, 1959), vii. 4.

the island but also in her dependencies on the mainland.[1] A
Thasian decree of the time also survives recording the banishment of two Neapolitans and four Thasians for supporting
Athens, and the confiscation of their property.[2] An Athenian
decree of 410–409 throws more light on the background. In it
the city of Neapolis, a colony of Thasos on the mainland, is
praised for her loyalty to Athens and her help to Athenian
forces in the area, though she was attacked by the joint forces
of Thasos and the Peloponnesians.[3] Neapolis had been taken
from Thasos when the revolt of Thasos was crushed and appears
regularly in the pre-war quota lists. She made no attempt to
return to her old allegiance when her mother city revolted and
she continued to support Thrasybulus who was in command of
Athenian operations in the area. The pressure mounted as
Athens' general fortunes improved, until in 407 Thrasybulus
defeated the Thasian troops in battle, penned them behind
their walls, and instituted a tight blockade. Thasos capitulated
before the end of the year. She was forced to recall the friends
of Athens who had been sent into exile, and an Athenian
garrison was installed.[4] Neapolis had played her small but
important part in the long struggle, and when Thasos was
recovered a further decree was passed at Athens in gratitude
for her services.[5]

The story of Thasos between 411 and 407 is a striking illustration of the decisive importance of naval power in the Aegean
world. The fortunes of Euboea during these years point the
same way. Envoys from Euboea were the first to appeal to
Agis at Decelea and they were confident that if help was guaranteed they could bring the island out in revolt. Agis knew the
importance of Euboea. Now that Attica was permanently
threatened by the Spartan occupation of Decelea, food supplies
from Euboea were vital to Athens.[6] Agis gave the Euboean
envoys a friendly reception and sent to Sparta for two governors
to assume control when the island had openly declared itself.

---

[1] J. Pouilloux, *Recherches sur l'histoire et les cultes de Thasos*, 139–53. New light
on the Thasian calendar has shown that the interval between the two decrees was
considerably longer than Pouilloux conjectured. See ML 83. For a fuller discussion of Thasian history from 411 to 407, see App. 15, pp. 570–8.

[2] *IG* xii. 263.   [3] ML 89.

[4] Xen. *Hell*. i. 4. 9; Diod. xiii. 72. 1.   [5] ML 89. 48–64.

[6] Thuc. viii. 95. 2: Εὔβοια γὰρ αὐτοῖς ἀποκεκλῃμένης τῆς Ἀττικῆς πάντα ἦν.

They came with a force of some 300 newly enfranchised helots, but Agis was persuaded by urgent pleas from Lesbos, strongly supported by the Boeotians, to transfer these forces to the Lesbian operation. Early in the next year the Boeotians occupied Oropus, which commanded the easiest crossing to Euboea and was held by an Athenian garrison. Even now, however, the Euboeans, who no doubt remembered the failure of their revolt in 446, did not dare to come out into the open, and we find the strange anomaly of Eretrians going to Rhodes, where the main Peloponnesian fleet was temporarily stationed, to beg for help.[1] It was not until the late summer of 411 when the revolutionary government of the 400 at Athens was losing control that Euboea at last received help. Forty-two ships under a Spartan commander sailed from Laconia, ravaged Aegina, threatened the Piraeus, and passed on to Oropus. The Athenians, who had a small squadron on guard in the Euripus, hurriedly sent reinforcements but they could only muster thirty-six ships. Athenian morale was low, they had a hostile population in Eretria behind them, and after a short engagement they turned back to the land. Those who took refuge in Eretria were massacred; others escaped to an Athenian fort outside the city and some ships which made for Chalcis were also saved. Revolt now spread through the whole of Euboea, with the exception of Oreus in the north which had been occupied by the Athenians when the Hestiaeans were expelled for their part in the revolt of 446.[2] We hear too little of Euboea to know what opposition existed or developed against the revolt and whether there remained Atticizing democratic parties in the cities, but the help given by Eretria to the Peloponnesians before and after the battle of Oropus suggests a widely based hostility to Athens. When, however, with the fall of the 400 and the return of Alcibiades to the navy, Athens began to recover confidence, Euboea felt sufficiently nervous to persuade the Boeotians to help them build a mole linking the island with the mainland.[3]

Diodorus says that the mole was built by the Euboeans, without specifying any of the cities separately. In implying that

[1] Thuc. viii. 60. 2.

[2] Thuc. viii. 95. It would be interesting to have specific evidence concerning Carystus which was geographically cut off from the rest of Euboea and had been well treated in the assessment of 425.

[3] Diod. xiii. 47. 3–6.

they joined forces he may be right, for at some time near the
end of the fifth century two issues of a new coin were struck
with the legend *EYB* suggesting a League of Euboean cities.
The lying heifer of the obverse is so like the heifer of early
Eretrian coins that we can be confident that Eretria supplied
the initiative and became the minting centre; it is what we
should expect from her appeal a little earlier to the Spartan
fleet at Rhodes. The coins are not on the Attic standard, but
the Aeginetan, emphasizing their new alignment with the
Peloponnesians. The first issue was probably struck soon after
the liberation of Chalcis and Eretria.[1]

In most of the cities of the empire that broke away from
Athens after the Syracusan disaster revolt was led by oligarchs
and resulted in oligarchy: among the common people there
often remained a continued loyalty to Athens. In Miletus the
pattern was different. In the middle of the century the Athenians
had tolerated a Milesian oligarchy even after a revolt, but the
experiment had failed and when the Milesian oligarchs forcibly
suppressed their opponents Athens intervened and established
a democracy.[2] This democracy was still in control when Alcibiades persuaded Miletus to revolt in 412; it was not until the
winter of 406–405 that oligarchs with Lysander's unscrupulous
support seized power and, as earlier in the century, carried out
a drastic purge of their democratic opponents.[3] It is a strange
irony that, in contrast to the mid century when Milesian oligarchs Medized, democrats should now take refuge with the
Persians. This almost certainly represented a sharp change of
attitude. Earlier the Milesian democrats had shown increasing
resentment at Sparta's subservience to Persia, and when Tissaphernes established a garrison in Miletus, as he had every right
to do under the terms of his agreement with Sparta, the
Milesians had dismantled his fort.[4]

Spartan lack of imagination, political divisions in the cities,
and strains arising from relations with Persia, helped Athens
to survive, but the new tones of Athenian imperialism made it
easier for her to capitalize her military successes. In these years
Athens was not vindictive when she recovered rebels. The

---

[1] For the identification and dating of this coinage see W. P. Wallace, *The Euboean
League and its Coinage* (*Numismatic Notes and Monographs*, no. 134 (1956). 1–7.
[2] Above, p. 188.   [3] Diod. xiii. 104. 4–5.   [4] Thuc. viii. 84. 4.

brutality of the Scione decree was not repeated and we hear of no sweeping political purges instituted by Athens. Alcibiades was able to control his men and put an end to plundering when he recovered towns in the Hellespont, and the terms of the Selymbrian settlement which in part survives illustrate the new mood. They were dictated by the generals when Selymbria surrendered in 408 but formally ratified by the Assembly at Athens when Alcibiades returned to the city in 407. The Athenians released all the hostages they held and encouraged political tolerance in Selymbria. Exiles were to be allowed to return provided that they accepted the city's foreign policy; disputes should be duly settled by process of law. Athenians and allies could go to law to recover land or house property, but no other claims for losses during the war could be accepted.[1]

An even more surprising illustration of Athenian generosity is the treatment of the Rhodian Olympic victor Dorieus when they captured him. Dorieus had done as much active harm to Athens as he could. A leading figure of the oligarchic opposition in Ialysus, he had been condemned to death by an Athenian court and had, like many other political exiles, found refuge and a new citizenship in Thurii. This colony, founded by Athens in 443 with colonists from many parts of Greece, had become more panhellenic than Athens intended; Dorieus, like the Spartan Cleandridas before him, will have played his part in undermining Athenian influence. After the Athenian defeat at Syracuse he returned in command of a small Thurian squadron, which he maintained at his own expense, to the Aegean. In 412 he played a leading part in consolidating the revolt of Rhodes and in the following year he continued to serve with the Spartan fleet. In 407, however, he was caught by an Athenian squadron and must have expected a quick death; the Athenians released him without even imposing a fine. This was a tribute to his athletic record. He had won the pancratium at three consecutive Olympics, in 432, 428, 426, and had a long record of victories at the other main Hellenic centres. The Athenians perhaps were more influenced by his four victories at their own festival of the Panathenaea.[2] The Spartans were considerably less generous

[1] ML 87.
[2] Xen. *Hell.* i. 5. 19; Diod. xiii. 38. 5; Paus. vi. 7. 5. For his athletic record, *SIG* 82; Paus. vi. 7. 4.

later. In 394 Rhodes changed sides and made approaches to the Athenian commander, Conon. Dorieus at the time was in the Peloponnese and can hardly have been in sympathy with the new policy; the Spartans condemned him to death.[1]

Further light on Athens' relations with her allies might be reflected in the tribute lists of this period, but our evidence is confined to a few small fragments of an assessment list, and the date of this list is not quite secure. In 413 the Athenians had substituted for fixed tribute assessments a 5 per cent duty on imports and exports by sea, hoping to increase by this means their revenue.[2] They were probably soon disillusioned, for while the amount of an assessment was beyond dispute the amount accruing from harbour dues depended on honest and conscientious book-keeping. Athenian resident officials were presumably expected to exercise what control they could, but their task would have been difficult even if Athens' Syracusan expedition had prospered; when it failed they will have had considerably less authority. It used to be thought that the change instituted in 413 was maintained until the end of the war, since Aristophanes speaks of an *eikostologos* in his *Frogs* produced in the spring of 405;[3] but Xenophon includes among the terms of settlement when Chalcedon was recovered in 409, that the city should regularly pay her normal tribute, implying a fixed sum rather than an annually varying figure.[4] The implication of Xenophon's text seemed to be confirmed when in 1933 five fragments were found in the Athenian Agora of an assessment list later than any yet known. This assessment was probably introduced at the time of the Great Panathenaea of 410 when the Athenian victory at Cyzicus and the restoration of radical democracy had revived Athenian confidence.[5] Among the six names that survive is a Milesian settlement, probably Miletoteichos which is not found earlier and may have been incorporated when Cyzicus was recovered. The survival of an *eikostologos* at Aegina in 405 may imply that the 5 per cent duty had to be paid by Athenian settlements as well as allies, and that their obligation was retained when the tribute system was reimposed.

[1] Paus. vi. 7. 6.   [2] Thuc. vii. 28. 4.   [3] Ar. *Frogs* 363.
[4] Xen. *Hell.* i. 3. 9: ὑποτελεῖν τὸν φόρον Καλχηδονίους Ἀθηναίοις ὅσονπερ εἰώθεσαν.
[5] Meritt, *Hesp.* vi (1936), 386–9; *ATL* ii A 13. For a different view, see Endnote 23, p. 438.

It was easier to draw up a list of assessments in Athens than to collect the money, nor could Athens afford the delay between collecting the tribute at the time of the Dionysia and distributing it to the generals with the fleet. When the iron reserve of 1,000 talents had been exhausted, by the end of 411 at the latest, the city had no money to send out. The home revenues had been drastically reduced by the Spartan occupation of Decelea and what was collected in Piraeus dues, court fines, and *eisphora* was needed for state pay for state officials and the 2-obol dole which was now desperately needed by those who were cut off from their normal source of livelihood.[1] When money was urgently needed to prevent the desertion of crews the generals in the eastern Aegean had to collect such tribute as they could themselves, and often no doubt when they could extract more they would do so. In presenting their account of the year's expenditure from Athena's revenues in 410–409 the treasurers of Athena included payments to four generals and two trierarchs stationed at Samos. The money is described as coming from Samos and supplied by the allies; it may have been collected by the officers themselves.[2]

By the end of 411 the weaknesses in Sparta's position had been clearly exposed. Her allies on the mainland gave her considerably less help than might have been expected. Corinth, who had clamoured so loudly for war in 432, delayed the sailing of the first Peloponnesian fleet across the Aegean and contributed very little to the war.[3] Megara was actively interested in helping her own colonies, Byzantium and Selymbria, to free themselves from Athens, but provided very few ships or men. The Boeotians agitated for their kinsmen of Lesbos, but considering that their ample resources had been less strained by the Archidamian War than those of any other of Sparta's allies, and that they were the main beneficiaries from the occupation of Decelea, their contribution to the fighting forces was negligible. Nor did the support that Sparta received from Athens' allies fulfil expectations. A majority of states in Ionia, the Hellespont,

---

[1] ML 84. 10, 12, 14, 22, 23.

[2] Ibid. 34–7: τὰ ἐχσάμο ἀνομολογέσα[ντο ℎοι σύ]μμαχ[οι|: το]ῖς στρατεγοῖς ἐς Σάμοι.

[3] Very little indeed is said of Corinth in the narratives of Xenophon and Diodorus, but the *Hellenica Oxyrhynchia* (vii) records the exploits of the Corinthian Timolaus, μάλιστα λακωνίζων, in charge of a small squadron.

and in the Thraceward area could be persuaded to revolt if they were assured of protection, but in most cities there were Atticizers waiting to reverse policy if the Athenians gained even temporary successes. The natural divisions in the cities were aggravated by the political insensitivity of Spartan officers. In the Archidamian War a system of harmosts had been evolved to maintain control in cities such as Torone and Amphipolis that came over to Sparta.[1] More diplomatic skill was needed by harmosts than Spartan training normally produced and their unpopularity had been an embarrassment to Brasidas in Chalcidice. It is not surprising that Lichas in Miletus, Pedaritus in Chios, and Eteonicus in Iasus failed to gain the full confidence of the cities they were sent to help; in many cases the result was further political division, between Laconizers and independents, extreme and moderate oligarchs.[2] It was much easier, as Lysander demonstrated later, to govern through a small determined minority who knew what they wanted and were prepared to be ruthless to get it, than through a broadly based government of reasonable men. Military and political difficulties were accentuated by financial weakness. Hoplite armies, on which Sparta's hegemony within Greece had rested, could largely live off the land; crews had to be regularly paid to remain afloat. Before she faced realities Sparta had expected Persia to finance her war. Before the end of 411 she had found that Persian support was irregular and embarrassing.

By this time Athens was much stronger than she had been when fighting began in 412. So far from collapsing she had more than held her own in Ionia and was strong enough to follow the Peloponnesians when Mindarus moved his forces at the end of the summer from Ionia to the Hellespont. In two engagements before the end of the year she outfought the Spartans and before midsummer of 410 she had won a decisive victory at Cyzicus.[3] This victory which eliminated the main Spartan fleet and its commander Mindarus was primarily due to Alcibiades. After a year's diplomatic juggling, he had been recalled in the summer of 411 by the Athenian fleet at Samos, which had refused to accept the oligarchic revolution at

---

[1] Thuc. iv. 132. 3; H. W. Parke, *JHS* l (1930), 37–50.
[2] Thuc. viii. 38. 3–4; Xen. *Hell.* i. 1. 32, emending Θάσῳ to Ἰάσῳ (see p. 577).
[3] Xen. *Hell.* i. 1–20.

Athens. In spite of his dubious record his personality was strong enough to control a dangerous situation and he did a signal service, as Thucydides emphasizes, when he prevented the democratic fleet from sailing back to Athens to overthrow the 400.[1] The firm stand of the fleet was fatal to the extreme oligarchs, and it is to Alcibiades and the generals at Samos that the main credit should go for the bloodless counter-revolution which transferred power to the 5,000. The winter of 411–410 was spent by the Athenian commanders in raising money by forced levies wherever they could; when the dispersed squadrons reassembled in the Hellespont it was Alcibiades who persuaded them that they must fight.[2] The victory of Cyzicus not only tilted the balance of naval power sharply in Athens' favour; it seemed likely also to restore the financial resources which were essential to naval power. Soon after the battle a special customs station was established at Chrysopolis near Byzantium, where a charge of 10 per cent was levied on all ships' cargoes coming out of and entering the Euxine;[3] Athenian control, and with it tribute, was gradually restored through most of the Hellespontine district. Sparta even made proposals for a peace which would stabilize the position now reached; but Cleophon, perhaps remembering Sparta's similar offer in 425 and the dramatic successes that followed its failure, led the Assembly to reject the Spartan proposals.[4] He was not mad. There was now good reason to believe that Athens could recover her empire completely and force Sparta to admit her helplessness.

In the bitterness of defeat most Athenians may have forgotten the mood of the years that followed the victory of Cyzicus, but Thucydides, who was particularly fascinated by the unexpected in history, saw the period clearly in perspective. Between 410 and 406 Athens seemed likely to win the war. Thucydides had no illusions about Alcibiades' character. He knew his ambition, vanity, and irresponsibility, but Alcibiades had also magnetism and ability. For four years Athens went from success to success and this was largely the work of Alcibiades.

---

[1] Thuc. viii. 82. 2–3.

[2] Xen. *Hell.* i. 1. 14. The account of the battle of Cyzicus in Diod. xi. 49. 2–51 suggests that Xenophon may have exaggerated the dominance of Alcibiades.

[3] Xen. *Hell.* i. 1. 22 mentions only ships coming out of the Euxine; Polybius iv. 44. 4 adds ships entering.

[4] Cleophon led the Assembly to reject peace in 410, Diod. xiii. 53. 1–2.

As Thucydides says: 'his war leadership was unrivalled.'[1]
By the summer of 407 the Hellespont had been recovered,
ending the threat to the corn route, at long last Thasos had
surrendered, and the Athenian fleet could sail and raid at will
along the coast of Ionia. Alcibiades was welcomed home in
triumph and given full command by land and sea. Within six
months he had been rejected by the Athenians and was concentrating on his own personal interests in Thrace. The occasion was the failure of his helmsman Antiochus who at Notium
had accepted battle against instructions.[2] The real reason was
that the new radicals, led by Cleophon, had a debt to pay. They
remembered how Alcibiades had stolen their following during
the Peace of Nicias and had been indirectly responsible for the
murders of Androcles and Hyperbolus. They could work up
feeling when Alcibiades was out of Athens and they seized their
first opportunity to discredit him. Alcibiades was not condemned in court, he was not even formally accused; but he was
not elected general for 406–405. He knew what this meant and
left the fleet.

Sparta's minor victory at Notium had been won by Lysander
who changed the whole course of the war. It was not merely
that he was an able general. He succeeded also in two spheres
where previous Spartan commanders had failed. He made
firm political friendships in the Ionian cities which bound
small but strong groups to Sparta, and more particularly to
himself; he was also able to secure and maintain good relations
with the Persians. In this fortune favoured him, for in 407
Cyrus, the King's younger son, had been sent down by Darius
to the coast to take supreme control of the two western satrapies.
Cyrus had abundant resources to finance Sparta and he found
Lysander personally congenial. The overriding importance of
Lysander is best judged by what happened when he handed
over his command, after the normal year's tenure, to Callicratidas. The new commander had little sympathy with a policy
that depended on Persian support and he was not prepared to
accommodate himself to Persian etiquette. He preferred to
fight a Greek war in a Greek way but his decent instincts
needed success to nourish them. At the battle of Arginusae in

[1] Thuc. vi. 15. 4: δημοσίᾳ κράτιστα διαθέντι τὰ τοῦ πολέμου.
[2] Xen. *Hell.* i. 5. 11–14; *Hell. Ox.* iv.

the summer of 406 the Spartan fleet was heavily defeated and Callicratidas lost his life.[1] It was now clear in Ionia and even in Sparta that the restoration of Lysander was an essential condition of Spartan victory, even of recovery. Lysander was sent out, nominally as second-in-command since a renewed tenure of the nauarchy was illegal; he at once began to revive his relations with Greek oligarchs and with Cyrus. Meanwhile the Athenians had squandered the fruits of victory. The crews of twelve sinking ships had not been rescued after the battle of Arginusae. The probable reason was that a storm made rescue impossible, but the thought of so many dead men floating unburied roused extremely bitter feelings. There had to be scapegoats and by an emotional vote in the Assembly it was decided to try all the generals together. In the heat of the moment they were condemned.[2] The Athenians had sacrificed some of their best commanders; more important they had completely undermined the morale of the fighting forces at Samos. Lysander was able to take the initiative and sail to the Hellespont. The Athenians had to follow because the Hellespont was their vital life-line. At the battle of Aegospotami they were trapped into total defeat; only twelve ships out of 180 survived the battle.

The utter destruction of the Athenian fleet meant that Athens faced starvation. She depended on the corn from the Euxine and the corn transports were now at the mercy of the Spartan fleet. Athens settled down to siege conditions and Lysander reaped his reward. The cities of the Aegean realized that at last Athens was broken, and opened their gates. Samos alone stubbornly held out, but the democrats surrendered before they were destroyed and were allowed to leave the island. Delos was purged of Athenian influence and for a brief interlude the Aegean world thought that it was free. When Athens finally surrendered the terms of peace were dictated. She had to pull down her long walls which alone gave her security against the Peloponnese and Boeotia, and she had to surrender what was left of her fleet except twelve ships which she was allowed to retain for police duty. All her overseas possessions she had to resign, including her cleruchies. There was no longer an Athenian empire.

[1] Xen. *Hell.* i. 6. 26–33.   [2] Xen. *Hell.* i. 7. 34.

21

FIFTH-CENTURY JUDGEMENTS

IN modern times widely varying judgements have been passed on the Athenian empire. It is more difficult but more interesting to try to discover what contemporaries thought. From Herodotus and Thucydides we might expect to get a clear picture of the empire as seen by ruler and ruled, but Herodotus tells us nothing. He knew the Aegean world well when the Delian League was changing into the Athenian Empire in the middle of the century. In Samos and Sparta at least he must have heard the sharpening of Athenian imperialism discussed with feeling and he himself must often have pondered the rise and anticipated the fall of Athens; but he ignores even what would seem the most attractive opportunities to make his comment. He emphasizes the troubles that fell on Greeks and Persians in the reigns of Darius, Xerxes, and Artaxerxes;[1] why does he not mention the close of the chapter, when hostilities against Persia were abandoned even if no Peace of Callias was made?

Some have thought that Herodotus was dazzled by the greatness of Athens and that in his history of the Persian War he was deliberately defending her against contemporary attacks on her imperialism. This cannot be disproved and there is little doubt that Herodotus admired Athenian leadership in literature and the arts; it does not, however, follow that he misunderstood or approved Athenian methods of controlling her allies. A panegyrist would surely have dwelt proudly on Athens' decision to send ships to help the Ionians in their revolt in 499; Herodotus is positively cynical. 'It is easier, so it seems, to persuade a multitude than to persuade one man.'[2] And the Athenian ships were not, in Herodotus' narrative, blazing a trail of glory; they were like the ship that took Paris to Sparta, 'the beginning of troubles'.[3] He implies that the Ionians did not deserve to be

[1] Hdt. vi. 98. 2.
[2] Hdt. v. 97. 2.
[3] Hdt. v. 97. 3: αὗται δὲ αἱ νέες ἀρχὴ κακῶν ἐγένοντο Ἕλλησί τε καὶ βαρβάροισι.

free, but he never says so. He knows that Athenian hegemony derived originally from the discrediting of Pausanias; he is less confident than Thucydides that the official verdict on Pausanias was honest. Nominally the transfer of hegemony was correctly managed; Herodotus, however, automatically thinks of Athens *taking* the hegemony from Sparta.[1] When he considered the Athenian empire we may guess that the question uppermost in his mind was: 'How will it end?'

Herodotus remains elusive through his silence; Thucydides supplies abundant material, but delicate problems of interpretation arise. The development of Athenian imperialism clearly preoccupied him. He sees the period between the establishment of the League and the outbreak of the Peloponnesian War as a gradual change from ξυμμαχίς to ἀρχή, alliance to rule. At first the allies join in common council with the Athenians;[2] later they take their instructions from Athens. From independent allies they become subjects, ὑπήκοοι. When Naxos revolted it was reduced to slavery; obedience, πείσομαι, becomes the key word in oaths of allegiance. On the eve of war Sparta poses as the great liberator: 'Men's sympathies leaned strongly toward the Spartans, especially as they claimed that they would free Greece.'[3] When Brasidas seized Amphipolis in 424 'the subject cities of Athens, learning of his moderation, were more than ever encouraged to revolt and they sent secretly to him urging him to come; each wanted to be the first to revolt'.[4] After the Syracusan disaster the Athenians 'expected that their enemies in Sicily would at once sail with their fleet to the Piraeus . . . and that their enemies in Greece would redouble all their preparations and attack Athens in force by land and sea; their allies, they thought, would revolt and join their enemies'.[5]

Apart from recording the main events of the history in his narrative Thucydides devotes no less than eight long speeches to an analysis of its nature, and these speeches between them cover the period from the outbreak of war to the Sicilian expedition. We miss such an analysis in the period before the war, but Thucydides deliberately intended only a summary

[1] Hdt. viii. 3. 2; above, p. 40.
[2] Thuc. i. 97. 1: ἡγούμενοι δὲ αὐτονόμων τὸ πρῶτον τῶν ξυμμάχων καὶ ἀπὸ κοινῶν ξυνόδων βουλευόντων.
[3] Thuc. ii. 8. 4.   [4] Thuc. iv. 108. 3.   [5] Thuc. viii. 1. 2.

narrative of events. We also find no speeches in his last unfinished book, but had he completed his history he might have
introduced further speeches illustrating the relations between
Athens and her allies. The speeches in Thucydides present a
broadly consistent picture; the basic problem is to determine
whether they reflect what the speakers actually said or whether
they express Thucydides' own views on the real nature of
Athens' empire.

There may be considerable doubt about Thucydides' practice, but there should be none about his profession: 'The
speeches have been composed as I thought the speakers would
express what they had to express (τὰ δέοντα) on the several
occasions, but keeping as closely as possible to the general sense
of what was actually said'.[1] The phrase τὰ δέοντα is ambiguous
and has tempted some scholars into lengthy speculation, but
such extravagances should have been excluded by the qualifying clause: ἐχομένῳ ὅτι ἐγγύτατα τῆς ξυμπάσης γνώμης clearly de-
notes an intention to reproduce the main substance of an actual
speech delivered by an actual person and not what, in Thucydides' opinion, the realities of the situation ideally demanded.
Some have thought that Thucydides' clear and explicit statement settles the matter; a much larger number of scholars have
found his statement in varying degrees unacceptable.[2]

The views on the Athenian empire expressed in these
speeches, some of which are said to have been delivered in the
Athenian Assembly, are candid, almost cynical. There is no
question of the moral rights or moral duties of empire and comparatively little about the benefits that Athens brought to her
subjects; the dominating element throughout is the interest of

---

[1] Thuc. i. 22. 1: ὡς δ' ἂν ἐδόκουν ἐμοὶ ἕκαστοι περὶ τῶν αἰεὶ παρόντων τὰ δέοντα
μάλιστ' εἰπεῖν, ἐχομένῳ ὅτι ἐγγύτατα τῆς ξυμπάσης γνώμης τῶν ἀληθῶς λεχθέντων,
οὕτως εἴρηται.

[2] A full bibliography would be impractical. The following selection is intended
to reflect the wide range of interpretation: E. Meyer, Forschungen, ii. 379–400;
A. Grosskinsky, Das Programm des Thukydides, Abt. Klass.-phil., Berlin, 1938; A. W.
Gomme, Essays in Greek History and Literature (1937), 156–89; J. H. Finley 'Euripides
and Thucydides', Harv. Stud. xlix (1938), 23–68 (= Three Essays on Thucydides)
(1967); J. de Romilly, Thucydide et l'impérialisme Athénien (1947), (trs. P. Thody,
1963); H. Strasburger, 'Thukydides und die politische Selbstdarstellung der
Athener', Hermes, lxxxvi (1958), 17–40; F. E. Adcock, Thucydides and his History
(1963), 27–42; A. Andrewes, 'The Melian Dialogue and Pericles' last Speech',
Proc. Camb. Phil. Soc. vi (1960), 1–10, 'The Mytilene Debate', Phoenix, xvi (1962),
64–85.

Athens. The first review comes in 432 when Athenian envoys, present at Sparta on other business, are allowed to address the Spartan Assembly, which has been urged to war by a Corinthian speaker. It opens with what must have been a stock fifth-century theme, Athens' contribution, particularly at Marathon and Salamis, to the defeat of Persia.

If our services then are remembered our empire should not be so unpopular. We took the hegemony not by force but because you did not wish to continue fighting Persia and the allies asked us to lead them. Circumstances compelled us to convert the alliance into its present form. Fear was the main motive, then pride, and finally profit too. It no longer seemed safe to give up our position when we had become generally unpopular and some of our allies had revolted and been reduced, and you were no longer friendly, but suspicious and hostile. . . . We have done nothing unusual or unnatural if we accepted empire when it was offered and if pride, fear, and profit do not allow us to let it go. We are not the first to have followed this course; it is a law of nature that the weaker should be controlled by the stronger. . . . Praise should be given to those who accept empire naturally and rule with greater respect for justice than power requires.

This point is then developed in greater detail. Athens controls her empire largely through her law-courts and not by arbitrary rule. If Sparta took her place she would soon lose her present popularity.[1]

Two years later Pericles expresses himself in very similar terms.[2] By the end of 430 the lack of spectacular success and the unforeseen calamity of the great plague had undermined the morale of the Athenians and had turned them against Pericles. His purpose was to convince them that his policy was right: it was necessary to fight and Athens was worth fighting for. He concentrates on the pride of empire. 'It is right that you should help to maintain the honour that comes from empire, in which you all rejoice, and that you should not shirk the labours unless you abandon the honours.' They will leave behind them the record that no Greeks ever ruled more Greeks. But fear also again enters as a motive force. 'Remember that you are not just fighting for slavery or freedom; the loss of empire is also at stake, and the risks that unpopularity in the

---

[1] Thuc. i. 73–8.   [2] Thuc. ii. 60–4.

empire brings. This empire you can no longer relinquish . . . it is already a tyranny.[1] It may be thought unjust to have taken it, but to let it go would be dangerous.' In these two speeches there is no attempt to cloak imperialism in fair words. Athens is a tyrant in the sense that her rule rests neither on the free consent of those she rules nor on a formal constitutional settlement. She has no moral right to empire, but the weak will always be subject to the stronger and Athens exploits her imperial power much more moderately than others have done in the past or would do in the future.

In neither of these two speeches did the occasion demand a full development of the benefits that the empire brought to the allies. We could expect less uncompromising realism when the Athenian Euphemus in 415 addresses the Assembly at Camarina in Sicily. Syracuse and Athens were competing for the support of Camarina when the issue of the expedition was still in the balance. The Syracusan leader Hermocrates, who in 424 had succeeded in uniting Sicily in a general peace which forced the Athenians to withdraw, now made a frontal attack on Athenian imperialism. The Athenians claimed to have come to help their Ionian allies, Leontini and Egesta; their real motive was to destroy Syracuse and add Sicily to their empire. 'Is it credible that while destroying cities in Greece they should build up cities in Sicily, that they should show a real concern for Leontini which is Chalcidian on grounds of kinship and hold in servile submission the Chalcidians of Euboea from whom the colonists of Leontini came?' 'They became the freely accepted leaders of the Ionians and of those allies who originated from Athens: their professed aim was to take revenge on the Mede, but on charges of desertion, or of making war on one another, or on whatever other grounds seemed plausible, they reduced their allies to subjection.' The issue was not freedom. 'They were not fighting for the Greeks to be free, nor were the Greeks simply fighting for their freedom from the Mede. The Athenians were fighting that the Greeks should be their subjects rather than the Mede's; the Greeks were fighting for a change of master, for one who would not be less intelligent, but who would use his intelligence to more evil purposes.' Athenian imperialism, according to Hermocrates, meant the enslavement of allies; the

[1] Thuc. ii. 63. 2: ὡς τυραννίδα γὰρ ἤδη ἔχετε αὐτήν.

Sicilians must show that they were not spineless like the Greeks of Ionia, the Hellespont, and the islands.[1]

In meeting this savage attack Euphemus does not attempt to challenge Hermocrates' general picture of the Athenian empire. He does not deny that the allies are subjects rather than partners, nor does he attempt to claim that the empire rests on their goodwill. He even goes so far as to say that they deserved what they got. 'For they came against Athens their mother city, and they had not the courage to revolt and destroy their property and to abandon their cities as we did. They wanted to bring to us the same slavery that they endured. And so we deserve our empire, because we provided the largest fleet and gave the most whole-hearted support to the Greek cause.' 'We will not use fine words and say that our empire is the natural result of our destroying the barbarian alone; and we will not say that we faced danger then simply in order to free those who became our allies.' In defending Athenian policy in Sicily Euphemus echoes again the motive of fear, which is stressed in both the earlier Athenian speeches on empire. 'As we have said, it is fear that makes us retain our empire in the Aegean, and it is fear that brings us to Sicily to build up our security with the help of our friends; not to reduce them to subjection, but to save them from subjection.' This argument is logically developed to show that Athens' interests require a balance of power in Sicily and that without Athenian intervention Syracuse would dominate the island. Athenian policy is consistently based on a realistic appreciation of expediency:

Our leadership in Greece varies with an ally's usefulness to us. Chios and Methymna provide ships and are autonomous; the majority of our allies are under more compulsion and bring money; others, though they are islands and easy to take, are completely free allies, because they are strategically sited round the Peloponnese. It is natural therefore that we should deal with Sicily according to our interests and, as we have said, fear of Syracuse is the decisive factor.[2]

Athenian imperialism is reviewed in a different context when Mytilene surrenders in 427. Cleon had carried a decree that all adult males should be put to death and the women and children sold into slavery. The next day there was a change of

---

[1] Thuc. vi. 76–80.   [2] Thuc. vi. 82–7.

feeling in Athens; they realized that the destruction of a whole
city should not have been so lightly decided. Mytilenaean
envoys with the support of Athenian sympathizers took advantage of the new mood and persuaded the *prytaneis* to call a second
Assembly and reopen the question.[1] Thucydides says that there
were many speeches on both sides; he selects two only. Cleon
made a forceful and logical attack. Irresolution is a weakness
of democracy; there was no reason to change their decision.
Mytilene had not the same excuse as other cities; she was
independent and Athens had honoured her. Her action was
conspiracy rather than revolt and deserved the supreme penalty:
Athens must make an example of Mytilene to prevent other
allies following her example. Recalling perhaps his main argument in the original debate he insists that the demos should
not be spared. 'For they all alike joined the revolt when they
could have turned to us and been back again in their city by
now. But they thought they would be safer if they took the risk
with the oligarchs and joined the revolt.' 'I still maintain, as
I did at the beginning, with all my strength that you should
not reverse the decisions you have already taken, nor allow
the three greatest dangers to empire to lead you astray: these
are pity, persuasive talk, and human sympathy.'[2]

The reply of Diodotus, who also spoke in the original debate,
is the more surprising of the two speeches. Cleon has declared
that it was irresponsible to reconsider a decision; Diodotus
appeals to reason. What is dangerous is an emotional decision
reached without due consideration of every aspect of the case.
Calm reflection is never to be regretted. He is not concerned
with the guilt of Mytilene; the only relevant consideration is
what judgement will best suit Athens' interests. The capital
penalty has never proved a deterrent:

> We must not be hard judges if harsh judgement will do us harm.
> Our security should not be based on the full rigour of the law but
> on a careful consideration of what we should do. Our aim should not
> be the severe punishment of men of free spirit when they revolt;
> rather should we take every possible precaution before they revolt
> and try to ensure that they do not even think of revolt. If they do
> revolt and we crush them we should pin the guilt on as few as
> possible.

[1] Thuc. iii. 36. 5.   [2] Thuc. iii. 37–40.

Diodotus then comes to a more specific point:

As matters now stand the demos in every city is your friend; either they do not join the oligarchs in revolt or, if they are compelled to join, they soon oppose the leaders of revolt and so when you go to war you have the common people on your side. If you destroy the Mytilenaean demos, which did not take part in the revolt and which, when once it got possession of arms, voluntarily surrendered the city, you will in the first place be killing your benefactors and that is wrong; you will also be presenting to the men who wield power what they most desire. When they lead their cities into revolt they will at once have the demos on their side, for you will have shown that the same penalty applies to the just as well as to the unjust.

Cleon's proposal is to be rejected not because it is not fair but because it is not expedient. Diodotus admits Cleon's point that pity and liberal human feelings are bad counsellors. On grounds that have nothing to do with such human weakness he urges the Athenians to try the oligarchs whom Paches has detained and to ignore everyone else.[1] After a close vote Diodotus' proposal was carried and the fate of the men whom Paches had selected as being primarily responsible for the revolt was separately debated. This time Cleon had his way. On his proposal they were all put to death.[2]

In the Melian dialogue there is an even more ruthless exposition of Athenian imperialism. The preface is casual and calm: 'In the following summer (416) Alcibiades sailed to Argos with twenty ships and seized those Argives who were still thought to be suspect and to favour Sparta, three hundred in number, and the Athenians deposited them on the near-by islands which they controlled. And the Athenians sailed against the island of Melos.'[3] Thucydides describes in detail the size and composition of the force and tells us that before opening hostilities the generals sent envoys to the Melians to present the Athenian case. The Melians would not introduce them to a popular Assembly, but asked them to state their case before the magistrates and oligarchs. There then follows the presentation of the Athenian case and the Melian reaction to it in dialogue form, used here by Thucydides for the first and only time. After brief preliminaries the Athenians state their case bluntly:

---

[1] Thuc. iii. 42–8.   [2] Thuc. iii. 50. 1.   [3] Thuc. v. 84. 1.

We are not going to use high-sounding phrases saying that we
deserve our empire because we overthrew the Mede or that we are
coming against you because we are the victims of injustice . . . We
ask you not to think that you will convince us by saying that it is
because you are colonists of the Spartans that you did not join us . . .
but to do what is practicable in the light of what we both genuinely
know . . . The strong do what they can and the weak follow. . . . We
will show you that we are here for the benefit of our empire and
what we are going to say now will be aimed at preserving your city.
We wish to rule over you without trouble and we want you to be
spared to our joint advantage.

When the Melians ask how their enslavement could be to their
advantage the Athenians reply that they will be spared destruction. The Melians offer to be neutral, to become friends
rather than allies; this the Athenians reject outright. 'Your
hostility does not harm us. Your friendship would be a sign to
our subjects of weakness; your hatred is a sign of our strength.'
The Melians then appeal to Athens' own interests. The destruction of Melos will antagonize all neutrals. The Athenians
counter by saying that the cities they now fear are the islands
which they do not control and those who are restive under
Athenian rule. The Melians then fall back on the gods. The
gods will not allow the righteous to perish, and the Spartans
cannot afford not to help them. The Athenians reply:

We do not think that we shall suffer by comparison in respect of
the gods' goodwill. For what we claim and what we do is not inconsistent with what men think about the gods or wish for themselves.
We think that the gods apparently and men demonstrably carry
their rule as far as their power extends by a necessary law of nature.
We did not make this law, nor are we the first to use it . . . ; we know
that you too and others if they had the same power as we have would
act as we do.

Spartan aid is an idle hope: 'Most conspicuously of any people
we know the Spartans think that honour is what pleases them
and justice what suits them.' Finally the Athenians appeal for
a sense of realities: 'You will not think it humiliating to submit
to the greatest city in Greece when it makes only moderate
demands, that you should be our allies, paying tribute but keeping your land. When you are given the choice between war and
survival do not let vanity lead you to the wrong decision.'[1] The

[1] Thuc. v. 87–111.

Athenians withdrew and gave the Melians time to reflect. The
Melians maintained their position. The Athenian generals led
their troops into action. During the winter (416–415) the
Melians met with temporary success, but the arrival of reinforcements from Athens soon led to unconditional surrender.
'The Athenians killed all the adult Melian men that they captured; the children and women they enslaved. The land they
occupied themselves, subsequently sending 500 settlers.'[1]

Thucydides makes many other comments on the Athenian
empire both in his own person and through his speeches, but
these are his main set pieces. Through minor variations a consistent picture emerges. The empire is a tyranny. If the allies
were free they would claim their independence but they are not
free. At no point is it suggested that the Athenian empire is
maintained for any other purpose than the interest of Athens.
The main forces that sustain it are the material benefits it
brings, the pride that an imperial power feels, and the fear
that to give it up would be regarded as weakness and would
invite attack. In the days of public relations officers, politicians'
speeches to world audiences and leading articles in the best
papers which must not give offence, such frankness is very
refreshing, but what inferences are we to draw from it? Is
this what speakers said in the Assembly? Is this what the
majority, or a substantial minority, of Athenians thought? Or is
Thucydides merely analysing his own judgement without
relation to the arguments actually used?

Thucydides was a creative artist and the architecture of most
of his history was designed with considerable deliberation. He
has carefully selected the context of his main speeches and in
the context he has sometimes had to select from a number of
speeches. The Mytilenaean debate in which the proposal to put
to death all the males was rejected is recorded at length; the
proposal that all the men of Scione should be put to death is
passed over without emphasis, though in fact it was carried
out. The speech of the Athenian envoys at Sparta in 432 and
of Pericles at Athens in 430 were the only relevant speeches
made on those occasions, but in the Mytilenaean debate there
were many speeches from which he selects only two, presumably
those in which the main issues were most clearly crystallized.

[1] Thuc. v. 116. 4.

But such selection is quite consistent with the profession he has made about his speeches. He has promised to keep to the general sense of what was said. It would not be a relevant criticism that several speeches in the Assembly in 427 dwelt on the innocence of women and children, nor that some speakers must have argued primarily about what was the just rather than the expedient punishment for the offence. Nor should we be surprised if both Cleon and Diodotus speak in Thucydidean Greek and argue more coherently than we expect in crowded open-air meetings. This was a recognized convention, illustrated in Tacitus' version of the Emperor Claudius' speech recommending to the senate the admission of Gallic nobles. What we need to know is: 'Was Diodotus the decisive speaker against Cleon and did he use the arguments that Thucydides attributes to him?'

The natural reaction, especially of those who are familiar with modern political speeches and debate, is to insist that, whatever intelligent or cynical Athenians may have thought to themselves, they cannot possibly have used such cold-blooded language before a large popular audience. They must, it is thought, have claimed more positive merits in their empire and more positive support from their allies. Appeals are made to the language of panegyric, to the speeches of Lysias and Isocrates, and the fine praises of Athens in the tragedians as evidence for the language that was really used.[1] The Melian dialogue in particular has come under continuous criticism, in respect of both substance and form. From other sources we know that Melos had contributed to Sparta's war fund, and had been included in the Athenian assessment of 425. This evidence suggests a more complex pattern in the relations of Athens with Melos.[2] Athens, it is thought, must have had, if not a good reason, at least some specific excuse for attacking Melos in 416, and the fact that she could call on a large number of islanders suggests that the Athenian action may not have seemed like unprovoked aggression to the Aegean world.[3] Specific Athenian charges against Melos should have figured prominently in the talks; Thucydides ignores them. Instead his debate is focused on general principles. Some of the rare lapses from the abstract

---

[1] See especially H. Strasburger, 'Thukydides und die politische Selbstdarstellung der Athener', *Hermes*, lxxxvi (1958), 17–40 (= *Thukydides* (1968), 498–530).
[2] See p. 328.
[3] See Endnote 22, p. 437.

have come under heavy fire. Many scholars for instance would rule out the possibility that Athenian representatives in 416 could have suggested, even as an unlikely hypothesis, the defeat of Athens. The use of the dialogue, unparalleled elsewhere in Thucydides, has been held to confirm the suspicions aroused by the substance of the debate; the reason for its use would be the desire to emphasize the incident and its significance in the development of Athenian imperialism. It has even been held that the juxtaposition of Melian dialogue and Sicilian expedition is deliberate artifice. This, it is thought, is tragedy not history.

Some of the critics' points are blunt. In the narrative Thucydides is nearly always very economic in editorial comment. Events are recorded but not explained. They are concisely described in chronological order, the relation between them is rarely elaborated. Thucydides' treatment of the Melian episode is not isolated and there is nothing unusual in the apparent concealment of relevant factors; we also know more than he tells us about the history of Methone during this period. But the attack on Melos is not entirely unexplained. Thucydides has already recorded how in the summer of 426 Nicias sailed with a substantial force of sixty ships and 2,000 hoplites to Melos: 'for the Melians were islanders and did not wish to submit to Athens nor to join her alliance; and so the Athenians wished to bring the island over'. They ravaged the land but the Melians did not offer battle, and the Athenians withdrew. From that point there was a state of war between Athens and Melos, as Thucydides reminds us in a passage that is sometimes misunderstood and more often overlooked. Having described the composition of the Athenian force in 416 Thucydides adds: 'the Melians are colonists of the Spartans and were unwilling to submit like the rest of the islands to Athens. At first they supported neither side and remained neutral, but when the Athenians ravaged their land they accepted open war.'[1] Thucydides is not here referring to operations in 416 because open hostilities are then preceded by a debate behind closed doors; he is referring to Nicias' expedition of 426. It is not therefore necessary to assume that there was any special charge against Melos in 416. Her continuing independence after the direct challenge in 426 could be regarded as ample provocation and

[1] Thuc. v. 84. 2.

the expedition of 416 could be explained in terms of the situation in Greece and the ambition of Alcibiades. His first grand design had been to revive the policy of Themistocles and crush Sparta with an alliance of Sparta's potential enemies in the Peloponnese. This design had collapsed on the battlefield of Mantinea. It was natural that the Athenian restlessness which Alcibiades had exploited should find an alternative outlet, by sea. The incorporation of Melos in the empire was the most attractive opportunity open to the Athenian fleet.

If it could be firmly proved that the Melian dialogue was written after the end of the war we should have more reason to dismiss it from the history of the war, but the strong division of opinion on this point is sufficient to show that the arguments are not compelling.[1] To us it may seem very strange that the Athenians should even hypothetically contemplate total defeat before the Syracusan expedition, but Athenian audiences knew from the tragedies which they watched each year that prosperity was unstable, and that reversals of fortune could be swift and sudden.[2] The pattern of tragedy is reflected throughout Herodotus' history; it must have strongly influenced Athenian thinking in the fifth century. The juxtaposition of Melos and Syracuse is indeed dramatic, but unless it can be shown that significant events occurred between the surrender of Melos and the arrival of envoys from Leontini and Egesta we cannot fairly accuse Thucydides of sacrificing history to art. Even the use of dialogue which inevitably recalls the technique of tragedy is adequately explained, by Thucydides himself. The Melians for good reasons refused to introduce the Athenian representatives to their popular Assembly, for they knew very well that among the common people there might be some support for Athens and there would certainly be considerable reluctance

---

[1] The Athenian statement (v. 99. 1) that they have no cause to fear what Sparta would do if Athens were to fall, since ruling powers are not vindictive to those they defeat, seems to point to a date after the war when Spartan moderation had saved Athens from the destruction advocated by Thebes and Corinth. The following statement, however, that the real danger lies in the successful revolt of her allies, points to a date before the end of the war. Both passages, however, could have been written either early or late.

[2] The instability of fortune is emphasized by Herodotus at the outset of his history (1. 5. 3–4). It is a recurring theme in Euripides, e.g. *Supplices* 269–70: τῶν γὰρ ἐν βρότοις | οὐκ ἔστιν οὐδὲν διὰ τέλους εὐδαιμονεῖν. Cf. *Andromache* 105 f., *Heraclidae* 865 f., *Troades* 509 f.

to fight. They therefore asked the Athenians to appear before a
selected audience and the Athenians are made by Thucydides
to insist that if they are to abandon the emotional medium of
an uninterrupted speech before a popular audience they should
carry the implication to its logical end and avoid long speeches
altogether. The Melians should answer the Athenian case point
by point.

In view of the nature of the negotiations Thucydides' difficulties in getting a reliable report of what was said on both sides
must have been considerably greater than for the speeches from
the early years of the war. He probably himself heard Pericles'
Funeral Speech and his last great speech in 430. He was in
Athens during the Mytilene debate and he could have cross-
examined at the time the Athenian envoy who addressed the
Spartan Assembly in 432. But in 416 he was an exile and it may
have been some time before he could find an Athenian or
Melian who took part in the negotiations. It is unlikely that
participants would have remembered for long the exact sequence
of the various points raised, and there is probably more free
composition in the Melian Dialogue than in the other speeches
we have considered; Thucydides, however, will have been true
to his undertaking if he was told little more than that Athens
brought no specific charges against Melos, but offered to spare
her if she became a member of the Athenian empire; and that
Melian appeals to justice and religion had no effect.

Thucydides no doubt had his own reasons for elaborating the
dialogue with such care. Some have thought that he gave it this
emphasis to show the full extent of Athens' moral degeneration
after Pericles' death. But there is strangely little emphasis on the
final penalty, the killing of the men and the enslavement of the
women and children. Thucydides' interest seems to be concentrated on the analysis of power and the logical implications
of the natural law that the strong rule the weak. It is embarrassing that less than two years later Aristophanes could speak of
the Melian famine in a very light-hearted way.[1] Had Thucydides been in the audience when the *Birds* was performed would
he have been repelled?

The difference in tone between the Melian Dialogue and
the other expositions in Thucydides of Athenian imperialism

[1] Ar. *Birds* 186.

has perhaps been exaggerated. Common threads link them all together: policy is determined by self-interest; it is natural that those who have power should exercise it over those who have not. But did the Athenians really think and talk about their empire in this cold-blooded way? It might be thought for instance that Thucydides' narrative adequately explains the Melian expedition, but that the Athenians' case must have been developed along very different lines. They might have used the argument that the Melian oligarchs were suppressing the common people and that the champions of democracy had come to liberate Melos. They might have claimed that Melos was enjoying all the benefits derived from Athenian thalassocracy without contributing to the cost. If we compare the language of modern imperialism in the nineteenth and early twentieth century it is very difficult to regard these Thucydidean speeches as genuine reports of public utterances.

We can be certain that we shall never be able to compare a speech in Thucydides with an official record of the speech as in the case of Claudius' speech to the Roman Senate on behalf of Gallic nobles. The nearest we can get to a control of the authenticity of Thucydides' speeches is by reviewing the writings of his contemporaries and trying to understand the intellectual climate of his generation. This is the generation of Euripides rather than Sophocles or Aeschylus and there is much in common between the two writers. Finley has shown in detail how the leading ideas in Thucydides' early speeches are reflected in the early or middle plays of Euripides.[1] The dialogue between Theseus and the Theban herald in the *Supplices* bears striking resemblance to the idealistic analysis of Athenian democracy in Pericles' Funeral Speech.[2] The need for the spirit of action and the danger of 'doing nothing to disturb the peace', on which Pericles dwells in his final speech, is also reflected in the *Supplices*.[3] These were common topics of the day. The repudiation of fine words, καλὰ ὀνόματα, emphasized in the Melian Dialogue and in the speech of Euphemus at Camarina, is echoed in Euripides' *Hippolytus*.[4] More important, a fascination

---

[1] J. H. Finley, *Three Essays on Thucydides*, 1–54.
[2] Euripides, *Supplices* 403–55; Thuc. ii. 37–44.
[3] Ibid. 576–7; Thuc. ii. 63. 3.
[4] Eur. *Hipp.* 487; Thuc. v. 89; vi. 83. 2.

for the rival claims of self-interest and right, τὸ συμφέρον and τὸ δίκαιον, and the contrast between νόμος and φύσις, law, convention, or custom and what is natural, pervades both authors.

Thucydides and Euripides reproduced the same ideas because they were both profoundly influenced by Protagoras and the sophists who followed him. The papyrus fragments of Antiphon the sophist's *Truth* are typical of their time in emphasizing the artificiality of man-made law in contrast to the overriding demands of nature; the view that it was a law of nature that the strong should rule the weak was not invented by Thucydides. Even the Melian Dialogue becomes less remarkable against the background of the sophists. Protagoras had expounded political philosophy in *Antilogies* and Socrates was by no means the only philosopher to proceed by question and answer; Thucydides' first readers would probably have been less surprised than we are by the form and substance of the dialogue. The sophists challenged all conventions and stretched rationalism to the limit. The attitude to the empire of Thucydides' speakers is credible in such a climate and Euripides is not the only author who can persuade us that leading men could have thought and spoken in this way.

Among other writers the most unambiguous witness is the anonymous oligarch who wrote a short pamphlet on Athenian democracy while Thucydides was collecting the material for his history. He does not like democrats and he does not attempt to disguise his prejudices. Democracy is bad because it gives power to the worthless and not to the best elements. The constitution is designed to suppress the best elements, but since all the machinery of government is directed to that end power will remain in the hands of the worthless. Everywhere the best elements are opposed to democracy; Athens knows this and applies the knowledge to her control of the empire.

The Athenians who are sent out bring charges against the good men among the allies and hate them. They know that the ruler must be hated by the ruled and that if the rich and the good grow strong in the cities the rule of the Athenian demos will last a very short time. That is why they strip the good of their rights, confiscate their property, exile them and put them to death, while they uphold the bad.[1]

[1] [Xen.] Ἀθ. Πολ. 1. 14.

They are right also in compelling the allies to bring their cases to Athens because it brings in money to individuals and to the state and allows the Athenian demos through the popular law-courts rather than its representatives abroad to control the empire. 'As matters stand individual allies are compelled to flatter the Athenian demos when they realize that they must come to Athens to try and to be tried before the demos and nowhere else; for that is the law at Athens.'[1] The analysis is throughout cynical. Self-interest is the decisive criterion and the Athenian demos knows how best to serve its own interests at home and abroad. The author cannot withhold a grudging admiration for the system he hates; it is thoroughly bad but it knows its business. The writing of this pamphlet is considerably less studied and successful than Thucydides' style, even at its most tortuous. The author shows, however, something of the same spirit as Thucydides' speeches on imperialism. But the author is not talking in an Assembly; he is writing primarily for fellow oligarchs, and we should expect him to be prejudiced against the men who controlled the popular Assembly.

Aristophanes is a more important witness, for the audience which he addresses is the Assembly on holiday; but to infer his political views from his comedies is hazardous. The nineteenth and early twentieth centuries, with few exceptions, felt confident that his personality and politics were self-evident. Modern scholars have tended to be much more sceptical, and for this change a powerful article by Gomme has been largely responsible.[2] To ask what were Aristophanes' political views or to what party he belonged were, Gomme maintained, wrong questions. Aristophanes' aim was to extract the comedy in a situation and he could adapt his attitude as plot and context required. The men who fought at Marathon are both the heroes of the good old days, who should be a model to the decadent rising generation and, at other times, tedious bores. Old men hate war, but the angry old Acharnians of the chorus are the most bellicose of men in the play that takes their name. Aristophanes attacks the new learning, but his contest between Right and Wrong shows that he has learnt all the tricks of the trade.[3] His

[1] Ibid. 1. 18.
[2] A. W. Gomme, 'Aristophanes and Politics', *CR* lii (1938), 97–109.
[3] Ar. *Clouds* 889–1111.

main purpose is to win the prize. He does not think it his primary duty to give advice to the state, and even in the *parabasis* he is normally more concerned with his art than with politics.

In spite of Gomme's warning, more recently reinforced by W. G. Forrest, the historian should not meekly surrender.[1] One thing at least is clear. Aristophanes takes the empire for granted and never questions its justification. He does, however, attack the means by which Athens and particularly Cleon and the demagogues who follow him controlled the cities. For them the empire is merely a source of easy money. Cleon takes 10 talents from Potidaea, more than 40 minae from Mytilene and is going to get a talent for a decree in the Assembly about Miletus.[2] In the contest between Paphlagon (Cleon) and his rival, the Sausage-seller, in the *Knights* to prove which of the two best serves the people, the Sausage-seller asks how Cleon, who was responsible for the rejection of Sparta's offer of negotiations in the previous year, could possibly call himself a friend of demos. Cleon claims that his motive was 'to make the people rulers of all the Greeks; for the oracles foretell that the demos shall have jury service at 5 obols a day in Arcadia, if they persevere'. 'Yes', says the Sausage-seller, 'but you were not thinking of ruling over Arcadia, but of your plunder and bribes from the cities.'[3] Aristophanes has no qualms about Athens' right to exact tribute, it is the misuse of it that he attacks. It is the demagogues, the men who say 'I'll always fight for the common people' who get their 50-talent bribes from the cities and who terrify and bully with their 'Give me the tribute or I'll call up the thunder and destroy your city.'[4] Everything goes into their pockets, the common people get nothing. In the *Wasps* he harks back to the good old days when what mattered most was how a man shaped as an oarsman: 'For then they captured many cities from the Medes and it was they above all who were responsible for our getting the tribute which the younger generation now squander.'[5] He is also well aware of the important part played by the law-courts in controlling the empire. Sycophants and summoners are among his commonest targets and he knows that it is the rich who suffer most.

[1] W. G. Forrest, 'Aristophanes' *Acharnians*', *Phoenix*, xvii (1963), 1–12.
[2] Ar. *Knights* 438, 834, 932.   [3] Ibid. 801–2.
[4] Ar. *Wasps* 666–71.   [5] Ibid. 1098–1101.

In the *Knights* the chorus echoes Thucydides' language: 'O demos, a fine empire is yours when all men fear you as a tyrant.'[1] It is reasonable to infer that Pericles and Cleon also could have called Athens a tyrant city without profoundly shocking their audience. In this speech of the chorus in the *Knights* and in many later passages of the play we feel that the popular audience in the theatre was listening to language not dissimilar to that of Thucydides' speeches. But what may have been the most important evidence offered by Aristophanes is lost. In his *Acharnians*, produced in 425, Dicaeopolis exclaims: 'Cleon will not now attack me for abusing the city in the presence of foreigners: we are alone, this is the Lenaea and the foreigners are not yet here, for the tribute has not come, nor the allies from the cities.' A scholiast explains that Cleon had prosecuted Aristophanes in the Boule for defaming the city in the *Babylonians*, produced at the Dionysia of 426.[2] Unfortunately very few fragments of this intriguing play survive and no reconstruction of the plot can claim to be much better than guesswork. It was once commonly held that the chorus was composed of allies, working as slaves for a hard task-master in a mill, but the foundation for this hypothesis is much too frail to carry weight.[3] It is, however, reasonable to infer that the play did seem to criticize Athenian methods of imperial rule. Aristophanes' replies through the chorus of the *Acharnians* that he has put an end to insincere flattery: 'and in so doing I have brought you much advantage, as I have done also by exposing what democratic government means in the cities; and so those who bring your tribute from the cities will want to come and see your best of poets who had the courage to say at Athens what was true and right.'[4]

During the Archidamian War Aristophanes continually harks on peace and this is surely not because the idea is comic. In his *Peace*, produced at the Dionysia of 421 very shortly before the terms of the Peace of Nicias were agreed and formally ratified, he made his views more explicit. Trygaeus asks: 'What then should we do? Should we not put an end to war, or should we rather determine by lot which of us should suffer more, when we

---

[1] Ar. *Knights* 1111–14.   [2] Ar. *Acharn.* 502–6.
[3] G. Norwood, 'The Babylonians of Aristophanes', *CP* xxv (1930), 1–10.
[4] Ar. *Acharn.* 641–5.

could make peace and rule Greece together?'[1] In the *Lysistrata*, produced ten years later, Laconia celebrates the agreement with which the play ends by recalling the time when Athens and Sparta fought side by side against the Mede. In this play his hatred of war is more strongly emotional than in the plays of the twenties. Amid the broad farce of the strike of women Aristophanes through Lysistrata makes a moving plea for peace. She upbraids both Spartans and Athenians: 'You sprinkle water on the altars from the same source, like members of the same family, at Olympia, Thermopylae, and Delphi (and how many other places could I name, had I the time?), and while the barbarians are there in arms you kill Greeks and destroy Greek cities.'[2] He knows and feels what war means for women: 'When a man comes home from the war, even if his hairs are grey, he soon finds a girl to marry; but a woman's time of opportunity is brief, and, if she does not seize it, none will marry her. She sits alone with her grief.'[3]

Aristophanes looks back to the time when Athens and Sparta could live together and they had a common enemy in Persia. And Persia is still the natural enemy. If Athens and Sparta continue to fight, Greece will be helpless against the barbarian. Trygaeus in the *Peace* says that he is going to Zeus to ask him what he is going to do about the Greeks: 'If Zeus doesn't reconcile the Greeks, I will charge him with betraying Greece to the Medes.'[4] In the *Knights*, produced at the Lenaea of 424, Paphlagon (Cleon) threatens to go to the Boule and expose the Sausage-seller: 'I will tell them about your meetings at night in the town and your negotiations with the Medes and the King.'[5] This may have been topical, for Artaxerxes had died in 425 and an embassy was to proceed to Susa early in 423. In the *Thesmophoriazusae* again Aristophanes links the Medes with Euripides as the natural enemies: 'If any one plots against the demos of women or makes overtures towards Euripides or the Medes to harm the women, or plans a tyranny. . . .'[6] The play was produced at the Dionysia of 411, when relations with Persia were again topical.

Aristophanes disliked πολυπραγμοσύνη, 'dynamic' policies, and he probably disapproved of the aspect of Periclean leader-

---

[1] Ar. *Peace* 1080–2.   [2] Ar. *Lys.* 1128–34.   [3] Ibid. 588–93.
[4] Ar. *Peace* 107–8.   [5] Ar. *Knights* 477–8.   [6] Ar. *Thesm.* 335–8.

ship which virtually drove Athens to war. His place is among those whom Pericles in 430 attacks for accepting the empire but declining the risks that are the inevitable price: 'Inactivity is safe only if it is accompanied by the readiness for action.'[1] These men increasingly regretted the failure to accept Sparta's terms when the Pylos operation swung the balance of war in Athens' favour, and when peace was made in 421 Nicias was able for a brief moment to revive the hope that Sparta and Athens could work together. The alliance between Athens and Sparta, which was intended to intimidate those who were discontented with the terms of Nicias' peace, includes a very Cimonian clause: 'If the slaves revolt the Athenians will send help to the Spartans with all their strength and to the full extent of their ability.'[2]

While hoping for a Greece in which Athens and Sparta could live without fighting one another Aristophanes and the many who shared his views had no wish to abandon the empire. Sparta had after all in the Thirty Years' Peace accepted the right of Athens to rule her allies; it was only the provocative policy of Pericles that had led to war. There were, however, elements in Athens whose overriding ambition was a comprehensive reform of government which would put the city under the control of 'the best men'. They had seen the importance of the long walls to the democracy and at the time of the battle of Tanagra they had been prepared to open the gates to Sparta in order to stop the consolidation of Ephialtes' reforms.[3] This small minority of reactionaries had little hope in the Periclean period, but when Athenian power was crippled at Syracuse they had their chance. It was they who were the driving force behind the establishment of the Four Hundred in 411 and the suppression of the policies of the moderates.

While the moderates were minded to carry on the war to maintain the empire the extreme oligarchs preferred to negotiate with Sparta, and when their power collapsed in Athens they fled for refuge to the Spartan force at Decelea. Intellectually distinguished and strong-minded, they would probably have accepted the diagnosis that Plato later attributed to Socrates. In the *Gorgias* Socrates replies to Callicles' claim that

---

[1] Thuc. ii. 63. 3: τὸ γὰρ ἄπραγμον οὐ σῴζεται μὴ μετὰ τοῦ δραστηρίου τεταγμένον.
[2] Thuc. v. 23. 3.   [3] Thuc. i. 107. 4.

Athens' political leaders made her great: 'They say that these leaders made Athens great. They do not realize that it is these leaders of an earlier generation who are responsible for the festering sickness of our state.'[1] 'Abandoning *sophrosyne* and justice they have filled the city with harbours, docks, walls, tribute, and suchlike futilities. When therefore the collapse comes they will blame the advisers of the day, and praise Themistocles, Cimon, and Pericles. But it is these men who will be responsible for the fate of Athens.'

While we hear a little of what some Athenians thought about the empire, we hear very little indeed of the allies' feelings. We should know a little more if Stesimbrotus' pamphlet *On Themistocles, Thucydides, and Pericles* had survived. Stesimbrotus from Thasos had enjoyed Athenian hospitality as a Homeric scholar and rhapsode, but he wrote with bitterness, probably from the oligarchic point of view; and in Thasos during the last quarter of the century the tension between demos and oligarchs became increasingly acute. Hellanicus of Lesbos was very different. He wrote his chronicle of Athens after the end of the war. Jacoby is surely right in regarding it as a significant gesture and a tribute that was badly needed when a ruined Athens was struggling to revive her self-respect.[2]

[1] Plato, *Gorgias* 518e–519c.   [2] *FGH* 323a Comm. text 20 f.

22

FOURTH-CENTURY JUDGEMENTS

ACCORDING to Thucydides the three greatest motive forces of the Athenian empire were fear, pride, and profit. Of these we hear least of pride and when it is introduced it is an arrogant form of pride rather than the complacent panegyric that we should expect. For this we have to wait until the fourth century; it begins with Lysias. In a funeral speech we do not expect undue modesty, and had Pericles in 431 chosen to speak primarily about the empire rather than about Athens herself his language might have been very different from the cold analysis in the speeches that concern us. There is no ambiguity in Lysias:

What speech, what orator, however long his speech, could do justice to the high qualities of those who lie here? They faced the hardest toils, the most conspicuous struggles, and the most glorious dangers to make Greece free and to display the greatness of their own city. For seventy years they ruled the sea; they kept their allies free from civil strife; they did not believe that the many should be slaves to the few but they insisted on equal standards for all. They did not make their allies weak but built up their strength. The power that they displayed was such that the Great King no longer coveted what belonged to others, but gave up some of what belonged to himself and lived in fear for the rest. No triremes sailed in those days from Asia; no tyrant rose among the Greeks; no Greek city was enslaved by the barbarians. So great was the sense of restraint and the fear that the high qualities of these men spread abroad. For these reasons they and they alone can become the champions of Greece and lead the cities.[1]

It was easier to say this in 390 when the Aegean world had had time to experience the nature of Spartan liberation; but some of the speakers in Thucydides would have smiled a wry smile.

Lysias sets the general tone for the orators who follow him. The most prominent note is the military achievement of

[1] Lysias ii. 56–8.

Athenian hegemony which provided such a striking contrast with the humiliations of the fourth century. Lycurgus recalls the fighting against Persia:

> For seventy years they led the Greeks. They sacked Phoenicia and Cilicia. At the Eurymedon they won victories on land and sea and captured one hundred triremes from the barbarian. They coasted along the whole of Asia, raiding as they went, and to crown their victories they were not content with the trophy set up at Salamis, but they made a settlement in which, to secure the freedom of Greece, they fixed boundaries for the barbarian and would not allow him to pass beyond them.[1]

Isocrates points the contrast more explicitly:

> One can see the greatness of the change most clearly by comparing the settlement made in our day with the settlement that has now been recorded. It will be seen that in that earlier peace we set limits to the King's empire, and stipulated the assessments of some of his tributes and prevented him from using the sea. But now it is he who manages the affairs of Greece and tells every city what it must do.[2]

The achievement against Persia was non-controversial and is frequently recalled, but the Athenians also liked to be reminded that they had been in their great days the champions of democracy. In the recollections of the fourth-century orators there is none of the cynicism of the Old Oligarch, and very little relation to reality. Isocrates can claim: 'Our fathers persuaded the allies to adopt the constitution which they themselves continued to enjoy; and this is a sign of goodwill and friendship when men advise others to adopt what they themselves consider to be in their own interest.'[3] Not all fourth-century writers, however, expressed such naïve views; Aristotle knew what this kind of persuasion involved: 'Constitutions can be overthrown from inside and from outside when faced with a hostile constitution that has power behind it, whether it be near or distant. This is what happened with the Athenians and Spartans. The Athenians overthrew oligarchies everywhere; the Spartans overthrew democracies.'[4]

Even Isocrates knew that some charges still clung to the fifth-century empire:

[1] Lycurgus, *Leocr.* 72–3.   [2] Isocr. iv. 120.
[3] Isocr. xii. 54.   [4] Ar. *Pol.* 1307^{b}22–4.

I believe that those who do not care to hear what I have now said will not dispute its truth. They will not, I think, produce other matters in which the Spartans served the Greeks particularly well. Rather I think they will try, as they constantly do, to bring charges against our city. They detail the most unsavoury acts of our maritime empire. They will attack the bringing of suits and cases to Athens and they will distort our exaction of tribute. In particular they will dwell on the sufferings of Melos, Scione, and Torone, thinking that by these charges they will tarnish the benefits our city brought, which I have a little while ago described.[1]

For most criticisms Isocrates had a defence and nowhere is the defence of Athenian imperialism more fully developed than in his first major speech, the *Panegyricus*:

I think that all will agree that those are the best leaders of Greece who have brought greatest prosperity to those who followed them. We shall find that when we led Greece private households were more prosperous and the cities greater than they have ever been. For we were not jealous of the cities that expanded, nor did we stir up internal trouble, by establishing new and conflicting forms of government which would make the two parties fight against one another while both cultivating us. Instead we regarded the peaceful harmony of our allies as a benefit to all and we used the same laws to look after all the cities. We considered our policy towards them as allies and not as masters; we were in general control of policy, but in private affairs we allowed each state to be independent. We helped the common people and were declared enemies of narrow oligarchies, for we thought it monstrous that the many should be subject to the few, and that those who had less property but in all other respects were in no sense inferior should be driven out of office, and that, while some arbitrarily ruled the country they all shared, others should have to leave it . . . Such objections and more they felt to oligarchy, and so they set up in the other cities the same form of government as we enjoyed ourselves. This form of government I do not, I think, need to praise at length, especially as a brief word makes the position clear. Under this form of government they continued for seventy years without experiencing tyrannies. They were at peace with all men.[2]

Carried away by his own eloquence Isocrates can even expect his audience to believe that the cleruchies should have been popular:

[1] Isocr. xii. 62–3.   [2] Isocr. iv. 103–6.

Men of judgement should feel very grateful for these benefits rather than attack us for the cleruchies which we sent to cities that were becoming depopulated, not because we wanted the land, but to protect it. This can be proved. We had the smallest territory in relation to our numbers and the largest empire. We had twice as many triremes as all other states put together, and we were prepared to face twice the number. Euboea lay close to Attica; it was well situated for the control of the sea and in all other respects it was the best of the islands. We controlled Euboea more securely than our own territory and we realized that among Greeks and barbarians the greatest reputation goes to those who destroy their neighbours and so win ease and plenty for themselves. Yet none of these considerations led us to do what would have been wrong to the people of the island. We alone of those who have held great power allowed ourselves to live more poorly than those who are alleged to have been our slaves. Yet had we wished to take advantage of our position we would not, I imagine, have coveted the land of Scione which, as all can see, we handed over to the Plataeans who came to Athens for refuge, and kept our hands off such a large territory as Euboea's which would have made us all more prosperous.[1]

Isocrates here defends Athens against charges of greed and aggression. His real view of the empire was probably very different. When during the Social War he is pleading for peace he emphasizes the futility of the continuous fighting of the fifth century:

Their folly was so much greater than other men's that whereas other men learn restraint and judgement from disasters they failed to learn anything. And yet they experienced more disasters and more serious disasters in this period of empire than Athens has known throughout her history. Two hundred ships sailed to Egypt and were destroyed with their crews, and 150 in Cyprian waters. They lost 10,000 Athenian and allied hoplites at Datum, in Sicily 40,000 men and 240 ships, and finally 200 ships in the Hellespont. And the losses of fifteen or more ships, and casualty lists of 1,000 and 2,000 men who could count?[2]

In the same speech he criticizes the public parade of tribute in the theatre orchestra at the Dionysia, but even here there is no basic criticism of the way in which Athens controlled her allies.[3] It would be more interesting to know what Isocrates

[1] Isocr. iv. 107–9.   [2] Isocr. viii. 85–8.
[3] Isocr. viii. 82; Endnote 19, p. 433.

really thought about Athenian political interference. The experience of the Thirty following the Four Hundred had made oligarchy an ugly word at Athens, which was not likely to attract even lip service in public, but Isocrates was very far from being a radical. The common people should have their say, but not much more; the responsibility of government should lie with the best men. He spread a sentimental haze over the days when the Areopagus exercised a wise and benevolent control of the state. His real thoughts were probably closer to the Old Oligarch than to his own public utterances.

Thucydides never suggests that the Athenian empire rested on the allies' free consent; the fourth-century orators never suggest that it did not. Fortunately we have a reliable corrective in the decree which followed the foundation of the second Athenian Alliance in 377. We can learn more of what the fourth century thought about the empire from what their politicians did than from what their orators said. Xenophon, our main contemporary source, strangely ignores the foundation of this second Alliance, but Diodorus preserves a summary account which is probably derived from Ephorus.[1] The opportunity to revive the fifth-century alliance came when the Aegean world had become increasingly disillusioned by Spartan leadership. The overthrow of Athens had not led to a general liberation but to the replacement of one tyrant power by a worse. Sparta's attempts to champion the East Greeks against Persia had been desultory and ineffective. In order to control the Greek cities she had imposed unintelligent Spartan governors and unpopular local boards of ten. To finance her expeditions she had exacted tribute as harshly as Athens. Meanwhile Sparta had lost the support of some of her strongest allies in Greece. By the end of 395 Boeotia and Corinth were prepared to carry on war in alliance with Athens and Argos against her. The first phase ended in 387 when peace terms were negotiated with Persia and imposed on Greece, but Sparta broke both the spirit and the letter of this peace by treacherous attacks on Thebes and Athens. It was to defend the independence of Greek states against Sparta that Athens in 378–377 built up a new alliance.

Diodorus briefly describes the preliminaries. The main heads of agreement were first worked out at Athens in consultation

---

[1] Tod, *GHI* ii. 123; Diod. xv. 28. 2–5.

with a small group of allies, Chios, Rhodes, Byzantium, later joined by Thebes and Mytilene. The alliance was then thrown open to all cities who would agree to the proposed terms, and the basic constitution of the alliance was supplemented by a declaration of policy. In Diodorus this declaration takes the form of a renunciation of cleruchies and any other form of overseas possession, public or private, by Athenians. This, however, was only one clause, though perhaps the most important. It can be seen in context in the decree moved in the Assembly by Aristoteles in the spring of 377. In this decree the purpose of the new alliance is defined. It is to ensure 'that the Spartans allow the Greeks to be free, independent and unmolested in full possession of their own territory, and that the common peace to which the Greeks and the King pledged themselves by oath should have full authority and remain in force for all time according to the agreements then made.'[1] Prospective allies are given unequivocal guarantees: 'If any Greek or barbarian on the mainland or in the islands who is not subject to the King so wishes he may be an ally of Athens and her allies. He shall be free and independent and may have whatever form of government he chooses. He shall not be required to accept a garrison, nor an Athenian official, nor to pay tribute.'[2] But the clause which carries the greatest emphasis in the decree as in Diodorus is the renunciation of property rights:

From the archonship of Nausinicus no Athenian privately or publicly may acquire in the territory of any city either house or land, by purchase, mortgage or any other means. And if any one buys or acquires or accepts in security any such property by any means soever, any ally who so wishes may denounce him before the representatives of the allies, and the representatives of the allies shall sell the property and they shall give the half to the informant; the other half shall be the common property of the allies.[3]

In these guarantees can be seen the features of fifth-century imperialism which it was politic to disown, political and judicial interference and concentration of authority in Athens. In the second alliance Athens was again the leader, and her generals led the combined forces of the alliance without question, but the allies had their separate Council—instead of a single

---

[1] Tod, loc. cit. ll. 9–11.   [2] Ibid. ll. 15–23.
[3] Ibid. ll. 35–46; cf. Diod. xv. 29. 8.

Council presided over by Athens, a bicameral organization in which policy was decided by agreement between Athens and her allies. There were decrees of the allies as well as Athenian decrees; the agreement of both was needed. Even the *phoros* is transformed. The second alliance no less than the first needed money, but the word *phoros* had been too long associated with subjection. A new word was found, *syntaxis*, implying an agreed contribution rather than a tribute imposed from above.[1]

The second Athenian alliance was formed in very different circumstances from the first. Athens was still suffering from the effects of her total defeat in the Peloponnesian War. Politically and economically she had made an impressive recovery, but she had no financial reserves and her navy was neither as large nor as efficient as it had been in the fifth century. She could not hope to dictate and diplomacy had to take the place of force. Even so the declaration of policy in the decree of Aristoteles is an admission that the forms in which she exercised her control in the fifth century had been unpopular, and not only among oligarchs. The history of the second alliance in some respects repeated the pattern of the first. Early enthusiasm was followed by apathy. Contributions, at first freely given, had later to be collected under pressure. When trouble broke out Athens again had recourse to garrisons and governors, but only, it seems, at vulnerable points. The allies' council, however, continued to meet and when peace was made with Philip in 346 an allied delegate accompanied the Athenian negotiators.[2]

[1] For the structure of the alliance, S. Accame, *La Lega Ateniese del sec. IV. a.c.* (Rome, 1941), 27–68.
[2] Aeschin. ii. 20.

23

EPILOGUE

THE surviving literature of the fifth century provides no
clear corrective to Thucydides' powerful picture of the
Athenian empire as an unpopular tyranny, and the
panegyric of the fourth century has all the hallmarks of unconvincing rhetoric. It is not surprising that posterity has largely
accepted Thucydides' verdict and even heightened his colours.
But the fifth century comes to us through men whom the Old
Oligarch would have recognized as 'good men', and just as
the history of Rome in the late Republic is coloured by the
political allegiance of contemporary historians, who had little
sympathy with the needs and interests of the *plebs Romana*, so we
are apt to see the Athenian empire largely through the eyes
of well-educated men who did not have to worry about their
material needs.

In attempting to form our own judgement two questions,
which are often confused, need to be distinguished: How did
the Athenians regard their empire? and: How did the 'allies'
regard Athens? The evidence that has so far been examined
suggests that the Athenians, both rich and poor, thought
primarily of the benefits that empire brought to them and
were not ashamed to say so. If the speeches and judgement of
Thucydides are to be discounted, as evidence only for the views
of Thucydides, and if Aristophanes is not to be cross-examined
on his views, we can appeal to the content and style of the
imperial decrees that survive; for here we have policies that
were discussed and approved, not merely by the political
leaders, but by the whole people in the Assembly; and the words
that are on the stones are the words that were drafted by the
author of the decree and read out by the herald. The strong
language of the Coinage Decree, the Decrees of Clinias and
Cleonymus providing for the tightening up of tribute collection, and the Assessment Decree of 425 is the language of ruler

to subjects. There is no suggestion in any of these decrees that the Athenians are concerned with the interests of anyone save Athens. Orders are given and penalties are laid down for resistance to the orders. The Coinage Decree prescribes that 'if there are no Athenian resident officers, the officers of the city shall carry out the terms of this decree and if they do not do what has been decreed (about the enforcement of Athenian coins, weights, and measures) they shall be tried at Athens and the penalty shall be loss of citizen rights'. 'If the allies themselves refuse to publish the decree the Athenians shall do it for them.' 'The herald [who is to be sent out] shall require them to carry out the commands of the Athenians.'[1] When Clinias introduces a measure to ensure that no tribute is 'lost' on the way to Athens he tries to safeguard the new procedure against interference: 'If any Athenian or ally commits an offence in respect of the tribute which the cities are required to record on a tablet for their couriers and send to Athens, he may be indicted before the *prytaneis* by any Athenian or ally who so wishes' and the procedure is to be the same 'if anyone commits an offence with regard to the sending of the cow or the panoply (to the Great Panathenaea)'.[2] The decree of Cleonymus, probably passed in 426, and the Assessment Decree of 425 are stronger, but less important for the general argument, because the pressure of war and the growing concern for the depletion of the financial reserve could be expected to harden the tone of decrees. Most of the surviving oaths imposed on allies who had revolted and been reduced emphasize the subjection of the ally even when oligarchs have been replaced by democrats. Samos is here a striking exception. When their revolt was crushed in 439 the Athenians bound themselves by oath to watch over the interests of the new democracy.[3] It is significant that the Samian democracy alone of the allies remained loyal even after the loss of the Athenian fleet at Aegospotami which meant the final defeat of Athens.

The firm tone used towards the allies in the imperial decrees to which we have referred is used also towards the Athenian executive. It would seem that obstruction or evasion is anticipated not only from the allies but also from Athenian magistrates.

---

[1] ML 45, cls. 4, 10, 11. [2] ML 46, ll. 31–5, 41–3.
[3] Above, pp. 193 f.

The Coinage Decree contains a clause safeguarding the decree against amendment or repeal: 'If anyone makes a proposal or puts to the vote a proposal that foreign coinage may be used or lent he shall be indicted at once to the Eleven.' To make doubly sure that the policy will not lapse or be reversed a clause is to be included in the oath taken by all members of the Boule at the beginning of their year of office: 'If anyone mints silver coins in the cities (of the empire) and does not use Athenian coins, weights, and measures, I will punish and penalize him according to the former decree which Clearchus moved.'[1] Clinias in his decree to improve the collection of tribute attempts to ensure that offenders will be punished: if a case is brought before the *prytaneis*, 'the *prytaneis* shall bring the case before the Boule or each be fined 1,000 drachmae for accepting bribes'.[2] But the most forceful of all decrees in the suspicions that it suggests against the executive is the Assessment Decree of 425. Heavy penalties are laid down for the assessors, the oath-administrators, the *eisagogeis* (who are to introduce tribute cases to court), the *prytaneis* responsible for bringing the decree before the people, and for the future *prytaneis* on duty at the time of each celebration of the Great Panathenaea, if they do not carry out their instructions. Such precautions, which are very reminiscent of the *sanctio* introduced by Roman democratic politicians in controversial laws in the late Republic, make little sense unless it was thought that there was at least potential opposition to be controlled. This opposition is probably to be found among those who supported Thucydides son of Melesias against Periclean policies in the forties, and during the Archidamian War among men of property who for personal and political reasons disliked the style and policies of Cleon and his associates. Athenian oligarchs will also have tended to sympathize with the oligarchs in the allied cities who suffered most from Athenian financial demands. The recognition of some such opposition at Athens, however, does not invalidate the impression given by the decrees as well as by the writers that her imperial policies were governed by self-interest.

The conviction that Athens thought almost exclusively in terms of her own interest does not necessarily imply the belief that her rule was universally unpopular. In the Mytilenaean

---

[1] ML 45, cls. 8, 12.   [2] ML 46. 35-7.

debate Diodotus claims that 'in all the cities the demos is your friend',[1] and in Thucydides' narrative there is ample evidence of support given by the popular parties to Athens. Mende followed Scione into revolt very shortly after the year's armistiee in 423, but when a substantial Athenian force arrived from Athens there was *stasis* in the city and the demos refused the order of the Spartan commander to go out and fight. Instead they attacked the Peloponnesians, who had been sent to stiffen their resistance, and their political opponents, presumably the oligarchs.[2] A somewhat similar sequence of political fluctuations had taken place in Mytilene at the time of her revolt. When it seemed that the Spartan fleet which had been expected would not arrive in time, the Spartan Salaethus, who seems to have taken command of the defence, issued arms to the demos intending to make a sally in full force from the town against the Athenian lines. The people, however, hitherto unarmed, now asserted themselves and refused to fight unless those who were in control brought what was left of the corn into the open and distributed it to all. If this demand was not met they would make terms with Athens and hand over the city. The authorities decided that it was the lesser evil to surrender themselves.[3] It is true that we do not know how the demos felt towards Athens before the revolt, nor in the opening stages of the siege. As Cleon emphasizes, they did not take positive action until there was danger of starvation and no hope of Mytilene winning her independence: it would be unsafe to infer either that they were discontented with the oligarchy before the war or that they were not.

It was the demos who paved the way for Cleon to recapture Torone, and at Acanthus, the first city which Brasidas approached, the demos was opposed to admitting him to address the Assembly; it was only the fear of losing their crops that made them give way. Even though Brasidas made a very persuasive speech and insisted that he did not intend to interfere with the political independence of Acanthus there were speeches on both sides after his address and a secret ballot was demanded. The majority, according to Thucydides, voted for revolt from Athens partly because Brasidas spoke convincingly, but partly also because they were still afraid for their crops. Even when

[1] Thuc. iii. 47. 2.   [2] Thuc. iv. 130. 3–4.
[3] Thuc. iii. 27. 2–28. 1.

Athens was crippled by the tragic failure of the Syracusan expedition she was not without support in the cities. When the Athenian oligarchs staged their revolution in 411 there was little resistance to the overthrow of the democracy in Thasos, but there were still Atticizers in Thasos who had to be exiled, and Thrasybulus could restore democracy in 407. But the demos was not everywhere the friend of Athens. Miletus remained stubbornly hostile to Athens after her revolt in 412 though the democrats were in power. The small communities in Chalcidice that had emigrated to Olynthus maintained their secession from the empire, and when the Athenians tried to recover Carian cities which had lapsed in or before the thirties, they were roughly handled and returned empty-handed. In Euboea, in spite of the stringent controls imposed by Athens after the crushing of the revolt of 446, there was sufficient threat to Athens in 424–423 to require Athenian interference and when the greater part of the island revolted again in 411 there is nothing in Thucydides' account to suggest that the demos in Chalcis or Eretria made any protest or gave Athens any help. But in most cities during the war it is true not only that, as the Old Oligarch emphasizes, Athens supported the demos, but also that the demos supported Athens.

There is then an apparent conflict between the unfavourable picture of the empire given by Thucydides in his own person and through his speeches and the widespread evidence in his narrative of support for Athens in the cities. This conflict has been brought into sharp relief by de Ste Croix, who in a very influential article used Thucydides to attack Thucydides.[1] The political sympathies of Thucydides are with the moderates, as is shown particularly by his somewhat extravagant praise for the government of the five thousand in 411–410; he therefore thinks primarily of the men in the allied cities who share his political views. Democracy is dangerous when it is no longer controlled by men of standing; his sympathies are closer to the oligarchs in the cities than to the demos. But Thucydides is too honest a historian to falsify his narrative and change the pattern of events to suit his own prejudices.

[1] G. E. M. de Ste Croix, 'The Character of the Athenian Empire', *Hist.* iii, (1954), 1–41. Reactions: D. W. Bradeen, *Hist.* ix (1960), 257–69; T. J. Quinn, *Hist.* xiii. (1964), 257–66; J. de Romilly, *Inst. Class. Stud. Bull.* xiii (1966), 1–12.

This is a strong case, and one naturally asks whether Thucydides himself was aware of the apparent inconsistency and how he would have answered the criticism. I suspect that he would have drawn attention first to his detailed analysis of the *stasis* in Corcyra during the Archidamian War. Through the fifth century the policy of Corcyra seems to have been to maintain neutrality and concentrate on increasing her own prosperity. When, however, Corinth began to interfere in what Corcyra regarded as her own sphere of interest old enmities were revived, and, faced with the prospect of a formidable attack by Corinth and her allies, Corcyra was forced to appeal to Athens. By making an alliance with Athens in 433, although it was only defensive, Corcyra became indirectly involved in the Peloponnesian War. Corinth could not tolerate an actively hostile Corcyra and attempted through Corcyraean prisoners whom she released to bring Corcyra over to the Peloponnesian side. Envoys from Athens and Corinth addressed the Corcyraean Assembly and a compromise decision was reached. Corcyra would maintain her defensive alliance but would also renew her former friendship with the Peloponnesians. The men working for Corinth in Corcyra wanted more than this. They realized that the democratic leader Pithias, the most influential man in the Boule, was their main obstacle, and, having tried unsuccessfully to secure his downfall by accusing him in court of trying to enslave Corcyra to Athens, they entered the Boule with daggers, and killed Pithias with up to sixty others. They then assembled the people and explained that their action had been necessary to save Corcyra from enslavement to Athens; and a motion was forced through that neither side should be allowed to enter a Corcyraean harbour with more than one ship.

But the murder of Pithias had made neutrality impossible. The demos now looked to Athens and the oligarchs to Sparta, and as the Athenian fleet could keep the Peloponnesians off the seas the advantage swung strongly towards the demos. There were two massacres of oligarchs in cold blood and heavy losses on both sides during the fighting. It was the war which sharpened the latent hostility between rich and poor, oligarchs and demos. Before the war both parties seem to have worked together under democratic forms, but the choice between Athens and Sparta meant a choice between democracy and oligarchy.

'The people's leaders in the cities brought in the Athenians, the oligarchs the Spartans. In time of peace they would have had no excuse for appealing to them nor would they have been prepared to do so, but it was those who wanted a change of government who were easily encouraged to appeal for an alliance which would harm their enemies and win support for themselves.'[1]

A further interesting illustration of political patterns is provided by the fortunes of Megara during the Archidamian War. Megara had the misfortune to be between two more powerful states. In the archaic period Corinth had been her main enemy and border disputes between them continued into the fifth century. But after the Persian War Megara had much more to fear from Athens. In 461 Corinthian aggression had persuaded her to ally with Athens, but by 446 she was disillusioned and put to death the majority of the Athenian garrison which had been settled in her territory to 'protect' her. We know nothing further of Megara until the decree which excluded her from the harbours of the Athenian empire and the Agora of Athens. The causes seem to have been trivial, the working of sacred land and the. harbouring of Athenian runaway slaves; but Pericles' purpose was to put pressure on Megara which held the key to the invasion of Attica from the Peloponnese. This pressure was intensified when war broke out: Athenian hoplites invaded Megarian territory twice each year and a blockade of the port of Nisaea was maintained at first from Budorum on Salamis and later, more closely, from the small island of Minoa. The increasing pressure caused political strains and in or before 427 a considerable body of intriguers had been exiled. When Plataea surrendered, Sparta allowed them to settle there for a year; by 424 they had occupied Pegae, the Megarian port on the Corinthian Gulf. Meanwhile a Peloponnesian garrison had been installed in Nisaea under a Spartan commander to make certain that the Peloponnesian invasion route was kept open. In this desperate situation there was a general feeling in Megara that the exiles should be recalled and political differences sunk. This did not suit the leaders of the people, who thought that the demos would not be strong enough to hold their own; they therefore approached two of the Athenian generals, Demos-

[1] Thuc. iii. 82. 1. For Pithias, see also above, p. 217.

thenes and Hippocrates, and planned to hand over the city to them. Plans, however, miscarried. The Athenians captured the long walls linking the city with Nisaea, and Nisaea itself, but the tactics for opening the city gates to the Athenians were betrayed.

At this point the Spartan Brasidas arrived with a hastily levied Peloponnesian force, but it is significant that he was not at once admitted to Megara. It was only when the Athenians had refused battle and withdrawn that the friends of the exiles could welcome the Peloponnesians. The leaders who had hoped to bring Megara over to Athens escaped while they could and the friends of the exiles from Pegae had little difficulty in persuading the people to recall the exiles. The majority of Megarians probably hoped that political feuds could now be buried but the exiles were bitter men. They took oaths not to revive the past and to give the best counsel that they could, but when they obtained office they held a review under arms, selected some hundred of their enemies who were thought to have played a leading part in the negotiations with the Athenians, and made the people vote on them openly. The men were found guilty and executed, and a narrow oligarchy was established to control the city.[1]

As Thucydides says in his analysis of developments at Corcyra the effect of *stasis* in the Peloponnesian War was that moderate men of the centre were destroyed by both sides either for not joining the struggle or because others resented their survival. States like Corcyra and Megara could live in reasonable harmony in peace, but the war affected the whole Greek world. Oligarchs saw in Sparta a hope of regaining power, the demos naturally looked to Athens. The alternative to the protection of Athens could be subjection under local oligarchs. The internal struggle in the cities became one of the dominant factors in the war, and numbers were on the side of democracy. Though control by Athens was the price to be paid for Athenian protection it does not follow that the cities preferred to be subjects, rather than independent. They would almost certainly have preferred a free democracy to a subject democracy, but for most of them a subject democracy was better than an uncontrolled oligarchy.

---

[1] Thuc. iii. 68. 3, iv. 66–74. A more detailed discussion of Megarian politics at this time, P. Legon, *Phoenix*, xxii (1968), 211–23.

The allies would have liked to be rid of Athenian officials, garrisons, and tribute if without them the many were not suppressed by the few. Had this not been so there would have been no need for the Athenians to renounce these features in their fourth-century Alliance when they were appealing to cities most of whom were democracies.

Phrynichus in Thucydides realized this clearly when in 412 he addressed those who were preparing for an oligarchic revolution at Athens. They had been persuaded by Alcibiades that there was a good prospect of the Persians supporting Athens with money, if the democracy was overthrown and he was restored. Phrynichus distrusted Alcibiades and thought that their calculations were unrealistic.

The King was not likely to join the Athenians whom he distrusted when he could have the friendship of the Peloponnesians who had never done him any harm, whose naval power was now a match for Athens, and who held cities of some importance in his dominion. As for the allied cities to whom they had promised oligarchy . . . he knew full well that this would not make those who had revolted return to Athens nor those who had not revolted remain loyal. They would prefer independence under any form of government to subjection, whether by an oligarchy or a democracy.[1]

The Aegean world gained considerably from the use made by Athens of the wealth that she drew from the cities and, as the Athenians claimed at Sparta in 432, they made considerably less use of force than imperial powers are expected to use; but they could have made more concessions to the general Greek passion for autonomy without undermining their position.

[1] Thuc. viii. 48. 4–5.

ENDNOTES

1. The Council of Samos

THE course of the debate after the battle of Mycale in 479 is uncertain. Thucydides (i. 89. 2), normally our most reliable source, does not mention this Council of Samos, but in a short summary he has no need to do so. He merely says that 'after the battle of Mycale the Spartan king went home with the Peloponnesian allies; the Athenians with the allies from Ionia and the Hellespont, who had already revolted from the king, remained with the Athenians and besieged Sestus which was held by the Medes'. He seems to have thought that the Ionians and Hellespontines had already joined the Greek alliance.

Herodotus (ix. 106) is naturally more detailed. 'The Greeks came to Samos and there discussed the removal of the Ionians and where in those parts of Greece which the allies controlled they should settle the Ionians, leaving Ionia to the barbarians; for it seemed impossible to them that they should act as a shield protecting the Ionians for ever, and they had no hope that the Ionians would get good terms from the Persians. In the circumstances the Peloponnesian authorities thought that the best solution was to expel the Greek peoples who had Medized from their towns and give their land to the Ionians. The Athenians, however, did not even agree that Ionia should be abandoned or that the Peloponnesians should make proposals about Athenian colonies. The Ionians supported them enthusiastically and the Peloponnesians gave way. And so they took into their alliance Samos, Chios, and Lesbos and the other islanders who happened to be with them.' They then sailed north to destroy the Persian bridges over the Hellespont, but, when they reached Abydos, they found them completely destroyed. Leotychidas decided to sail home, but the Athenians settled down to the siege of Sestus.

The account of Diodorus (xi. 37) is rather different. 'The Greeks under Leotychidas and Xanthippus sailed to Samos. There they admitted the Ionians and Aeolians to their alliance and then advised them to leave Asia and settle in Europe. They undertook to expel the peoples who had Medized and give their land to the Ionians and Aeolians; for if they stayed in Asia they would be living next to an enemy very considerably stronger than themselves, while their allies would be on the other side of the Aegean, and would be unable to bring them help in time. When the Ionians and Aeolians heard what was offered they decided to do as the Greeks suggested and were preparing to sail with them to Europe. But the Athenians had second thoughts and advised them to stay where they were; even if no other Greeks sent help, the Athenians would help them alone for they were their kinsmen. They calculated that if the Ionians were settled jointly by the Greeks they would no longer regard Athens as their mother city; and that is how the Ionians came to change their mind and to decide to stay in Asia. And this is how power in Greece came to be divided; while the Spartans sailed back to Laconia the Athenians with the Ionians and islanders proceeded against Sestus.'

There are several differences between the accounts of Herodotus and Diodorus:

1. In D. the Greeks admit mainlanders into the alliance before the council of Samos. In H. it is only the islanders that are admitted and that is after the council.

2. D. speaks of Ionians and Aeolians, H. of Ionians only.

3. The proposal to evacuate Ionia is at first regarded as non-controversial in D, and Athens only opposes it when the Ionians had already decided to accept the offer of a new home in Greece.

4. In D. the main Athenian motive in changing their mind is the fear of losing the allegiance of the Ionians. In H. they merely say that it is not for the Spartans to give advice about Athenian colonies.

5. In D. the council was the immediate cause of the splitting of the Greek forces (which lasted through the fifth century and culminated in the Peloponnesian War). In H. the Greeks remain together after the council and proceed to the Hellespont to break down the bridges.

There is no reason to believe that Diodorus, or rather his source, had anything more to go on than Thucydides and Herodotus. In (2) he adds the Aeolians because Herodotus often uses Ionians to include Aeolians; but Ephorus, the main source of Diodorus, came from Aeolian Cumae and had a tendency to bring in his native town or the Aeolians whenever he had the opportunity. In (1) D. may have been influenced by Thucydides who could be thought to imply that the Ionians were incorporated in the alliance as soon as they revolted. If, however, Leotychidas had decided on the evacuation of Ionia, it is unlikely that he would have stopped to make alliances before the principle of evacuation had been decided: H.'s version is much more convincing. It is very doubtful whether in (3) and (4) D. is doing more than reading between the lines of Herodotus and making the story more dramatic. In (5) again we should accept Herodotus rather than Diodorus, perhaps here interpreting Thucydides, who omits the sailing of the whole Greek fleet to the Hellespont to break down the bridges. In retrospect the council of Samos could seem considerably more important than it did at the time. In 478 the Greeks were still united. There is also a suggestion of later colouring when Herodotus makes the Athenians tell the Spartans that the Ionians were none of their business.

2. Timocreon on Themistocles

'You may praise Pausanias, you may praise Xanthippus, you may praise Leotychidas. I praise Aristides, the very finest man that ever came from the holy city of Athens; for Lato showed her contempt for Themistocles, liar, villain, traitor, who, persuaded by ill-gotten silver pieces, would not bring his guest-friend Timocreon back to his native Ialysus. He accepted

3 talents of silver and sailed away to the devil; some he unjustly restored, others he expelled, others he killed. Loaded with money he entertained all comers at the Isthmus and they laughed at him; his meats were cold. They ate them and prayed that no good would come of it to Themistocles.'

This outburst by Timocreon (quoted in Plut. *Them.* 21. 4) is surprisingly difficult to explain satisfactorily. Since Pausanias and Leotychidas can still be regarded as heroes, neither can have yet been disgraced. We cannot be certain when Pausanias' reputation collapsed, but Leotychidas cannot have been invoked after his conviction and exile following his unsuccessful expedition to Thessaly in 477–476. The only passage in our literary sources which seems to offer a possible context is Themistocles' activities in the Aegean after the battle of Salamis when he extorted money from the islands (Hdt. viii. 111–12). Herodotus, however, makes no mention of political activity and limits the range of Themistocles' operations; he confines himself to the Cyclades and goes no further than Andros. Kirchoff, *Hermes*, xi. (1876), 44 ff., suggested that Themistocles, while going no further than Andros, sent instructions further afield. This explanation has been widely accepted but it is an unsatisfactory compromise (see Beloch, *Gr. Gesch.*[2] ii. 2, 144 n. 1). The poem implies that Themistocles actually went to Rhodes, and *ATL* (iii. 185 with n. 10 and 191 n. 26) have accepted the apparent logic of the evidence. Themistocles, they think, went to Rhodes in 480, possibly only with a small detachment. On his return he went to the Isthmus and there his unpopularity was conspicuous (a situation also reflected in Hdt. viii. 123). Aristides is praised for his command of the Athenian contingent under Pausanias in 478.

Herodotus' evidence is not perhaps decisive for the range of Themistocles' operations in 480, but even without his evidence we should strongly doubt whether any Greek fleet would have gone so far so early. Herodotus is no doubt exaggerating when he pictures the Greek fleet in 479 waiting at Delos, terrified of what lay beyond (Hdt. viii. 132. 3), but in the immediate aftermath of Salamis the Greeks did not know what naval resources were left to the Persians nor how they were distributed. In 478 the situation was transformed. The Persian fleet had been destroyed at Mycale, Pausanias had sailed in the early summer unopposed to Cyprus. Themistocles' star had not yet set. He had been temporarily eclipsed in 479, but after the rout of the Persians he came into his own again when he outmanœuvred the Spartans and was mainly responsible for the refortification of Athens (Thuc. i. 90–1). During this crisis Aristides and Themistocles seem to have co-operated (Thuc. i. 91. 3). In the early summer of 478 Aristides led the Athenian contingent to join Pausanias, but he had only thirty ships. Pausanias' expedition to Cyprus showed conclusively that the Persians were temporarily paralysed, and it is possible that, while Pausanias sailed to Byzantium, Themistocles was sent to consolidate the Greek cause in Rhodes and other islands. The Isthmian festival to which he returned will then be that of 478, and the emphasis on Aristides will more probably be to his role in establishing the Delian League, a role that Themistocles would have dearly liked; and, as Bowra first suggested (*Greek Lyric Poetry*[2], 353 f.), Lato may refer to Delos, the centre of the League.

3. *IG* i². 928

The recent study by Bradeen (*Hesp*. xxxvi (1967), 326) of *IG* i². 928, arising from the discovery of a new fragment, has brought the problems of this casualty list into clearer focus. We can at least accept his conclusion about the form of the monument. It was not, as has often been thought, a large square stone inscribed on all four sides but a series of ten stelae, one for each tribe, a form of casualty list which Bradeen illustrates from other examples and from a vase painting. It was already known that this monument commemorated men who died at various points in or near the Hellespont and others who died at Thasos; it was also widely believed that the Drabescus casualties were included. The new fragment adds the unexpected name of Eion to the places where men died. Bradeen's explanation is that the Thracians following up their victory at Drabescus attacked Eion and the year, he suggests, is 464.

This chronology raises difficulties. In Plutarch's narrative (*Cim.* 14. 1) the operations in the Hellespont precede the fighting at Thasos. If this is right it is difficult to include the casualities of Drabescus in the same year's list. The precise relation in time between the attempt to colonize Ennea Hodoi and the naval battle against the Thasian fleet is not clear in Thucydides. He merely says that 'the Athenians sailed against Thasos, defeated her fleet in battle, and landed on the island; at about the same time (Thuc. i. 100. 3: ὑπὸ τοὺς αὐτοὺς χρόνους) they sent 10,000 settlers, Athenians and allies, to the site then called Ennea Hodoi'. Even on the assumption that the colony was planned before the fighting against Thasos, the Athenians could not have proceeded with the colony until the Thasian fleet had been eliminated. How long after settling at Ennea Hodoi the colonists waited before advancing into the interior we cannot deduce from Thucydides. It is, however, very unlikely that the operations in the Hellespont, the battle of Thasos, and the Drabescus disaster could all be contained in a single year.

It is a reasonable inference that the losses at Drabescus were not included in the casualty list we are considering, and indeed Pausanias suggests that the Drabescus casualties had a monument to themselves (Paus. 1. 29. 4: πρῶτον δὲ ἐτάφησαν οὓς ἐν Θρᾴκῃ ποτὲ ἐπικρατοῦντας μέχρι Δραβησκοῦ τῆς χώρας Ἠδωνοὶ φονεύουσιν ἀνέλπιστοι ἐπιθέμενοι). The casualties at Eion will not be connected with the disaster at Drabescus; the most likely explanation is that Thasos tried to get what help she could from her colonists and from the Thracians in order to relieve the pressure on Thasos. The most natural form of aid would be an attack on Eion which Athens had occupied some ten years earlier.

4. Blocks Attributed to the Promachos

An earlier date would be needed if we accepted the identification by Stevens and Raubitschek of two large blocks found on the Acropolis as coming from the pedestal of the base of the Promachos (*Hesp*. xv (1946), 107–14;

Raubitschek, *Dedications from the Athenian Acropolis*, 172). These two blocks have three large letters each from a dedicatory inscription which was restored to read: [Ἀθεναῖοι ⋮ ἀν]έθε[σαν] ⋮ ἐκ τ[ôν ⋮ Μεδικôν]. The most significant letter is the early form of theta, ⊕, on the basis of which Raubitschek suggested that the statue probably commemorated the Eurymedon, being begun *c.* 465 and completed by *c.* 445. This, however, is considerably later than the theta suggests, for this form seems to be obsolete before 470 (I know of no certain example after 479).

Dinsmoor (Χαριστήριον εἰς Ἀναστάσιον Κ. Ὀρλανδον (1967), 151–5) has given more important reasons for dissociating these blocks from the Promachos. They are both stippled on all four sides with smooth margins, and therefore should have stood free. The tops are smoothly dressed, and were entirely exposed. They must have been separate blocks placed at some distance apart. Dinsmoor attractively suggests that they were designed to carry some of the cables from the Persian bridges over the Hellespont (Hdt. ix. 121).

5. The Tanagra Campaign

Thucydides' account of the Tanagra campaign is not immediately convincing (i. 107. 2–108. 2). Nicomedes takes 1,500 Spartans and 10,000 allies from the Peloponnese to protect the Dorian mother country from the Phocians. Having fulfilled their mission they find that they cannot return across the Gulf of Corinth (the implication being that they had crossed by sea) because the Athenians had sent a squadron into the gulf; and the land route was difficult because the Athenians held Nisaea, Megara, and Pegae and had troops on Geranea. They therefore decide to wait in Boeotia and consider what would be the safest way to return. They receive encouragement from elements in Athens who wanted to overthrow the democracy. The Athenians, however, come out to fight, with contingents from Argos, Cleonae, and allies of the Delian League. The Spartans win a hard-fought battle and so are able to return to the Peloponnese, raiding Megara on the way. Two months later the Athenians invade Boeotia and win a decisive victory at Oenophyta.

Why was such a large army taken from the Peloponnese? What were the Boeotians doing while the Athenians were being fought on their territory? The answer of most historians is that Sparta's real purpose was to make a strong display of force and thereby restore Theban leadership over the Boeotian League, which had been broken by Thebes' humiliation in Xerxes' invasion. Diodorus is often invoked to support this interpretation, and he does indeed mention help given by Sparta to Thebes (Diod. xi. 81. 1–3); but the help in Diodorus is given after and not before the battle, and the approach comes from Thebes. D. W. Reece (*JHS* LXX (1950), 75 f.) resolves the dilemma by assuming that of the 10,000 allies under Nicomedes the majority are Boeotians. Sparta's original intention (as Thucydides implies) was limited to teaching Phocis a sharp lesson. It was only when their return was cut off that the Spartans called in the Boeotians.

There is indeed some evidence that Boeotians fought at Tanagra. Pausanias (i. 29. 9) refers to the Athenian battle at Tanagra 'against Boeotians and Lacedaemonians', and a Platonic dialogue (*Alc. Mai.* 112c) refers to 'the casualties of Athenians, Spartans, and Boeotians at Tanagra'. On the other hand, the Thebans in Thucydides (iii. 67), answering the Plataean attack, lay great emphasis on the help they gave Sparta indirectly at the battle of Coronea but say nothing of Tanagra. The positive evidence of Pausanias outweighs the silence of a speech in Thucydides and the battle of Oenophyta is much easier to understand if some Boeotians had helped the Spartans at Tanagra.

Thucydides has made a serious mistake of commission or omission. The nearest we can reasonably get to his account is to accept his figures and his clear implication that the 10,000 allies came from the Peloponnese, and to believe that the Spartans entered Boeotia only when an unopposed return seemed impossible. They were joined at Tanagra by some Boeotians, but not a large force, and they did after the battle do what they could to restore the credit of Thebes.

6. Athens and the Amphictyonic League

There is little doubt that Meritt is right in making changes in the text of *IG* i². 26 and interpreting the document as an alliance between Athens and the members of the Amphictyonic League. The questions that need to be answered are—when? and why? Meritt thought that the alliance reflected Athenian policy when, after Tanagra, the Spartans had withdrawn into the Peloponnese and the victory over the Boeotians at Oenophyta had given Athens control of central Greece. Athens' main concern would be to gain the support of Apollo at Delphi and become the acknowledged leader of Greece.

M. Sordi gives the inscription a different date and a different purpose (*RF* xxxvi (1958), 48–65 with *BCH* LXXXI (1957), 61–5). Emphasizing that Thessaly controlled half the votes in the Amphictyonic Council she thinks that Athens could not hope to dominate the Council unless Thessaly was friendly to her or completely crushed. The Thessalians made an alliance with Athens soon after the dismissal of the Athenian hoplites from Ithome in 462, and they sent a cavalry contingent to fight with Athens at Tanagra; but in the battle they went over to the Spartans. An Athenian alliance with the Amphictyonic League could have no practical value after Thessaly had deserted Athens in battle and the Athenian attempt to repair the damage by restoring Orestes son of the Boeotian 'king' to Pharsalus achieved nothing. Professor Sordi sees the alliance as a call by the Thessalian-controlled Amphictyonic League to Athens to lead in a sacred war against Sparta and the Boeotians. When the Peloponnesian army led by Nicomedes intervened to save Doris from the Phocians the real issue was the control of Delphi which Phocis had usurped during the period of Thebes' humiliation after the Persian War. When Sparta took Delphi from Phocis in the interests of the Boeotians the main body of the Amphictyons called for a sacred war under the leadership of Athens against the Spartans and Boeotians. The battle of Tanagra was the result, the beginning but also the end, because there had been a decisive shift of power in Thessaly.

For this bold reconstruction support can be claimed from two sources. Plutarch in his *Cimon* (17. 4) does say that the Spartans came to Tanagra after freeing Delphi from the Phocians. More specifically Philochorus (*FGH* 328 F 34, quoted by a schol. on Ar. *Birds* 556) is reported to have referred to a sacred war fought by the Athenians against the Boeotians who wanted to take the oracle from the Phocians. In spite of these floating straws the silence of Thucydides and the improbability of the reconstruction weigh heavily against the thesis. Thucydides' account of the Tanagra campaign is not completely satisfactory (see Endnote 5 above), but if Athens was fighting a sacred war he should have known, and we should have heard more about it in the fourth century when Delphi again became a political prize and the notion of the sacred war was revived. The reconstruction also seems unrealistic. Was there time for a sacred war to be launched in the interval between Sparta's completing her task in Doris and camping at Tanagra? And where are the other Amphictyons beside Thessaly? And why is Argos fighting in a sacred war? And would Thessaly have appealed to Athens to support Phocis, her traditional enemy?

Raubitschek sees in the alliance part of a grand Athenian design, initiated by Pericles, to convert the Delian League from an instrument of war to an instrument of peace, carrying out the principles of the Amphictyonic League. It follows the making of peace with Persia and will in turn be followed by the Congress Decree, inviting the states of Greece to discuss the problems left over from the Persian War and the consolidation of peace. This attractive thesis depends on a radical revolution of orthodox chronology. Raubitschek puts the beginning of the Egyptian expedition in 462 when Plutarch says that at the time of the reforms of Ephialtes Cimon was away on a naval expedition (Plut. *Cim.* 15. 2: ὡς δὲ πάλιν ἐπὶ στρατείαν ἐξέπλευσε). This was the Cyprian expedition which was diverted to Egypt to support the revolt of Inaros (Thuc. i. 104. 2). The fighting in Egypt lasted six years and will have ended in 457–456. Cimon died in 456 and peace was negotiated with Persia in 456–455. Raubitschek finds support for his dates in an anecdote recorded by Plutarch (*Cim.* 18. 7–8). Cimon, while commanding the fleet in Cyprus, sent messengers to the oracle of Ammon. The god ignored the purpose of their visit, but said that Cimon was already with him. The messengers realized his meaning when they came to the Greek camp in Egypt and heard that Cimon had died. Raubitschek assumes that the Greek camp 'must have been the one in Cyrene where the last remnants of the Egyptian expedition assembled'. This reconstruction means the rejection of Thucydides, Diodorus, and Plutarch and these do not represent a single tradition. The camp to which the messengers came was περὶ Αἴγυπτον, and this surely cannot mean Cyrene. It is presumably the base used by the sixty ships which Cimon detached from his main fleet at Cyprus, and which rejoined the main fleet after Cimon's death. But this was not part of the great expedition that was destroyed after six years' fighting; both Thucydides and Diodorus distinguish clearly the Egyptian expedition which is not associated with Cimon and the Cyprian expedition which Cimon led. The proposed chronology does too much violence to good evidence. We can agree with Meritt in seeing Athens' Amphictyonic policy as the sequel to Oenophyta. It probably lapsed with the defeat in Egypt but could be revived again when peace had been made with Persia.

7. The Assessment of Dorus

Stephanus of Byzantium quotes Craterus' *Collection of Decrees* for a note on Dorus: ἔστι καὶ Καρίας Δῶρος πόλις, ἣν συγκαταλέγει ταῖς πόλεσιν ταῖς Καρικαῖς Κρατερὸς ἐν τῷ περὶ Ψηφισμάτων τρίτῳ. "Καρικὸς φορός· Δῶρος, Φασηλῖται." Though Phaselis is regularly included in the Carian district no Carian Dorus is known, and it is assumed that Dorus under Mount Carmel, a Greek foundation, was at one time included in the Delian League, though the name does not appear on any surviving fragment. If Dorus was included it is reasonable to assume that other Greek foundations also in the eastern Mediterranean were brought in and listed with the Carian cities and not under a separate district heading. So in the Assessment Decree of 425 Celenderis in Cilicia and, probably, Aspendus are included in the Ionian–Carian district. The Dorus fragment comes from Craterus' third book and in the fourth book he quoted a clause from a decree: ἐὰν δέ τις ἐξ ἀμφοῖν ξένοιν γεγονὼς φρατρίζῃ διώκειν εἶναι τῶι βουλομένωι, 'if anyone whose parents are both foreigners becomes a member of a phratry, anyone who wishes may prosecute him'. This clause has been associated with Pericles' law of 451–450 restricting Athenian citizenship to those whose parents were both Athenians and this points to the first assessment at Athens in 454 after the transfer of the League treasury. During the early fifties Athens had been highly successful in Egypt and probably also in Cyprus and it is credible that she should have added Greek cities in the eastern Mediterranean to her League. The ultimate result of the Egyptian disaster was the Athenian withdrawal from the area, but this decision was not taken until Cimon had died in Cyprus and Athens was ready for peace with Persia. Another assessment fragment from Craterus comes from the ninth book which also included a record of the condemnation of Antiphon in 411. The hypothesis of *ATL* that Craterus included samples from the first and last assessment decrees, of 454 and 410, is economic and convincing; other assessment fragments whose place in Craterus is not recorded can be conveniently fitted into one or other of these two assessments.

There is, however, the difficulty that in the tribute lists district headings are not given until the fourth assessment, in 443. That is the only assessment period when a separate Carian district was recorded, for in 438 and thereafter the Ionian and Carian districts were amalgamated under the heading Ἰονικὸς φόρος. This worried Jacoby who dated the Dorus fragment in 443, but without conviction and with a question mark (*FGH* 342 F 1 with Comm. p. 68). He also questioned the association of the phratry fragment with Pericles' citizen law. Pritchett was bolder (*BCH* lxxxix (1965), 434–6, *Hist.* xviii (1969), 17–21). He argued that the quota lists were not valid evidence for the date of the transfer of the treasury from Delos; they merely told us when the Athenians first decided to give an *aparche* of the tribute to Athena. Leaning on the story in Plutarch (*Arist*. 25. 3) of Aristides' noble reaction when the Samians proposed that the League funds should be transferred to Athens, Pritchett would date the transfer before the death of Aristides, and, following Krech (De Crateri *ΨΗΦΙΣΜΑΤΩΝ ΣΥΝΑΓΩΓΗ*, 10–11), he would date Craterus' first fragment soon after the Eurymedon victory. 'It would strain credulity to argue that a city having been incorporated into the Alliance withdrew before making even one payment.'

These arguments are not strong. The only conclusion that should be drawn from Plutarch's anecdote is that at some unknown time the Samians probably proposed the transfer of the League treasury to Athens. Aristides is not necessarily part of the original version of the story; in transmission 'What would the noble Aristides have said?' could soon become what the noble Aristides did say. Nor does the story necessarily imply that the proposal was accepted. In the building debate recorded by Plutarch in his *Pericles* (12) it is said that fear of the Persians was given as the reason for the transfer and it is implied that it was not long before the building of the Parthenon. Even without the tribute quota lists 454 provides the most likely context. The quota lists, however, provide strong confirmation. It is much more probable that the giving of the *aparche* to Athena should be an immediate consequence of the transfer than that it should have been introduced more than ten years later. The absence of Dorus from all surviving fragments of the lists creates no difficulty. When the Persians had destroyed the League fleet in Egypt Greek states in the eastern Mediterranean would not have risked reprisals by sending tribute to Athens, but so long as Athens was actively preparing to resume the fighting with Persia these states would remain on the assessment list. By the Peace of Callias Athens renounced her eastern ambitions and all states east of Phaselis were excluded by the assessors until the extraordinary assessment of 425 (see pp. 329 f.). Had records been preserved in Delos Dorus would probably have been found among the tribute payers in 458 and 457. She would almost certainly not have been included in an assessment or quota list in the sixties. The Athenians did not follow up the Eurymedon victory in the eastern Mediterranean until after the fall of Thasos in 463 (see p. 79).

It need not surprise us that there were district headings in the assessment list of 454, though the lists of tribute quotas show no signs in the first period of geographical ordering, and headings do not appear until the list of 442. Assessment lists and quota lists were drawn up by different boards and it is not unnatural that the *hellenotamiai* should at first have followed the order in which they received the tributes.

8. The Erythrae Decree

Reasons, based on letter forms, for disassociating the two fragments that survive in London and Athens (*IG* i². 11, 12–13A) from the lost decree copied by Fauvel are given in ML, p. 93. In the fragments the rho is consistently angular with no tail (Ρ); on the lost decree the regular form in *CIG* is angular with tail (Ρ̄), and the fact that in l. 18. ΙΕΚΟΝ almost certainly represents ΗΙΕΡΟΝ confirms that this was the form on the stone. Of the various hypotheses offered in ML the most probable seems to me that the lost decree was dated by the archon's name of 453–452, and represents the recovery of Erythrae by Athens, and that the surviving fragments are from a second decree. This would mean a parallel sequence in Miletus and Erythrae. Revolt probably followed soon after the news of Megabyzus' success in relieving the White Fort at Memphis. Athens intervened in the summer of 452 and brought both cities back into the League. She made lenient settlements in both cities, but soon had to intervene again. In 450–449, probably after the death of Cimon and the making of peace with Persia, she tightened her hold on Miletus by appointing five resident Athenian officials (D 11); at roughly the same time she made the whole demos of Erythrae take an oath whose terms were considerably stronger than those in the oath to be taken by the Boule in the decree of 452.

9. The Recall of Cimon

According to Theopompus Cimon was specially recalled from ostracism (*FGH* 115 F 88): 'Before five years of the war [against Sparta] had passed the demos sent for Cimon, for they thought that as he was a *proxenos* of Sparta he was best suited to make peace quickly. Cimon returned to the city and ended the war' (*FGH* 115 F 88). The same tradition probably lies behind Plutarch who says more specifically that after the battle of Tanagra the Athenians, anticipating further trouble from Sparta, recalled Cimon. 'He returned to Athens and at once ended the war and reconciled the two cities.' A special decree was needed; it was proposed by Pericles (Plut. *Cim.* 17. 8–18. 1). Nepos (*Cim.* 3. 3) also drew on this tradition. 'After the fifth year of his ostracism he was recalled to his city. Because of his friendship with the Spartans he decided to go to Sparta; he set off on his own initiative and made peace between these two most powerful states.'

Many historians have accepted the evidence of Theopompus as decisive (e.g. Busolt, iii. 216 n. 1.), but the history of the immediately following period is very difficult to reconcile with this date. Had he been sufficiently indispensable to be recalled there should remain some trace of his presence in Athens before 451. The policies pursued in these years are the negation of what he had stood for; the offensive against Sparta and the Peloponnese is pressed more vigorously than before. If he was the wrong man to attack the Peloponnesians, he could surely have been sent to Egypt. We would at least expect some anecdote associated with these years. A more important objection is that both Theopompus and Plutarch imply that the motive for recalling Cimon was the desire for peace with Sparta and that peace was made by Cimon when he returned. This is a natural inference also from Andocides (iii. 3) who in an admittedly confused passage says that 'when we held Megara, Pegae, and Troezen and had war on our hands in Euboea, we were anxious for peace and welcomed back Miltiades, son of Cimon, who had been ostracized and was living in the Chersonese, for this very reason that we should be able to send him, a *proxenos* of the Spartans, to Sparta to negotiate a settlement. And then we had a fifty-year peace with Sparta and kept the peace for thirteen years.' There is a rich confusion here between the five years' truce of 451 and the Thirty Years' Peace of 446–445, and between Miltiades and his son, but there is nothing in the passage remotely suggesting the year of the battle of Tanagra, and Andocides is considerably earlier than Theopompus.

There was no peace after Tanagra. Diodorus records a four-month truce (xi. 80. 6) but large-scale operations followed in the next years. Busolt suggested as a compromise that Cimon made the truce after Tanagra, but realized that he could not accept Athenian policies and withdrew again to the Chersonese. This has the worst of both worlds (Busolt, iii. 318). Since the first recorded act of Cimon after his return is the five years' truce in 451, many historians have preferred to believe that there was no special recall, and that the tradition has no more value than the sentimental romancing about Cimon's appearance on the battlefield of Tanagra (Plut. *Cim.* 17. 4–6). The evidence for a special recall going back at least to Andocides is too strong to be dismissed. There is no good reason why the decree should not have been preserved with others moved by Pericles, and Pericles had reason to take the initiative. The crisis created by the Egyptian disaster demanded unity among Athens' leaders; all knew that the Egyptian disaster had to be avenged and that it was too big a risk to send a large expedition into the eastern Mediterranean if there was any danger of attack from the Peloponnese.

Jacoby, *CQ* xli (1947), 16 f., also rejects the earlier date for Cimon's recall, but suggests that Pericles' decree of 451–450 limiting Athenian citizenship to those who were Athenian-born on both sides was intended as an insurance in case Cimon or his friends did not keep the bargain (of dividing power). This is a much too clumsy gesture for Pericles. There was, I think, a genuine closing of the ranks after the Egyptian disaster.

10. The Second Sacred War

In a confused note a scholiast, commenting on Aristophanes' *Birds* 556, says that in the third year from the first war (when Delphi was restored by Sparta to the Delphians) the Athenians fought against the Lacedaemonians on behalf of the Phocians and restored the temple to the Phocians, as Philochorus says in his fourth book. It is not quite certain whether the mark of time should be attributed to Philochorus and one may well doubt whether he thought that the Athenians fought the Spartans in the second war. *ATL* accept the attribution of the date to Philochorus and date the two 'wars' in 449 and 447. Jacoby thinks that the Athenians must have reacted at once and this surely is the implication of Thucydides (i. 112. 5): καὶ αὖθις ὕστερον Ἀθηναῖοι ἀποχωρησάντων αὐτῶν στρατεύσαντες καὶ κρατήσαντες παρέδοσαν Φωκεῦσιν. Would Thucydides have written ἀποχωρησάντων αὐτῶν if he thought that this interval was more than two years?

11. The Status of Lemnos and Imbros

The status of Lemnos and Imbros has been recently discussed by *ATL* (iii. 290–3); A. J. Graham, *Colony and Mother City in Ancient Greece*, 174–88; and P. A. Brunt, *Athenian Oversea Settlement in the Fifth Century* (Ehrenberg Studies, 77–80). On the major issues they are agreed. Herodotus' story (vi. 137–40) of the capture of Lemnos by Miltiades, probably at the time of the Ionian revolt, is confirmed by inscriptions. A late Corinthian helmet inscribed Ἀθεναῖοι [τ]ὸν ἐγ Λέμν[ο] was found at Olympia (E. Kunze, *Festschrift für Carl Weickert*, 7–21), and an inscription (*c.* 500) from Lemnos listing names under Athenian tribal headings (*IG* i². 948, note) also shows that Athenians were settled on the island before the invasion of Xerxes. Herodotus (v. 26–7) implies that the native population of Pelasgians had been earlier driven out or killed by the Persians, but he probably exaggerates, as in his accounts of the sacking of Miletus and Eretria (Hdt. vi. 18; 101. 3).

In 480 the Lemnians sailed in Xerxes' fleet and one of them, Antidorus, was said by Herodotus (viii. 11. 3) to have been the only Greek who deserted the King. When the Delian League was established Lemnos, like Sigeum, which had also been an Athenian possession in the sixth century, was required to pay tribute. The settlers, whether colonists or cleruchs, can surely not have been accepted as full Athenian citizens after their unresisting Medism in the crisis of 480. The island's assessment in the first period of the tribute lists (454–450) seems to have been 9 talents; later it was reduced to 4½. The reduced tribute is divided between the two main towns of the island, Hephaestia paying 3 and Myrina 1½ talents. In 451 the 9 talents is paid by the 'Lemnians' (3. i. 3), but in 452 ['Εφαισσ]τιές is restored and no other restoration seems possible (2. v. 14). Presumably Μυριναῖοι would also have appeared in this list, but we cannot tell what significance to attach to the difference. The first evidence of the reduced payment comes in the list of 446, but both towns are restored in *ATL* for the year 449 (5. iv. 39–41).

A reduction in tribute is not always a sign that land has been taken for Athenian settlers, but there is other evidence which suggests that there was a fresh infusion of Athenian stock near the mid century. In a casualty list set up in Athens, probably during the Peloponnesian War, there is a heading Λημνίων ἐγ Μυρίν[ης] and beneath it two columns of names under Athenian tribal headings (*IG* i². 947); on another stone (*IG* i². 948) Λήμνιοι are listed under a tribal heading. It was probably the new settlers, cleruchs rather than colonists, who made a well-known dedication on the Acropolis; Pausanias (i. 28. 2) says that the most remarkable of the works of Phidias was an image of Athena, called the Lemnian Athena after the dedicators (G. M. A. Richter, *The Sculpture and Sculptors of the Greeks*³ (1956), 227 f.). For Imbros there is no separate evidence, but the island is not preserved in any of the fragments of the first tribute period and *ATL* suggest (iii. 57 n. 50) that the tribute of Imbros was included in the large single payment of the Chersonese. When she pays separately she eventually pays 1½ talents.

The tribute evidence suggests that the cleruchs were sent out between the spring of 451 and the spring of 446, and the date will depend on the validity of the restorations at the bottom of the fourth column in the list of 449. *ATL* (i. 175) suggest the restoration of the two Lemnian towns here, because of the 16 names surviving in the last 23 lines all are in the Island district except one (Sigeum). In l. 35 [Νάχσιο]ι is restored on the assumption that an island name is needed. Then there follow three blank lines. For the last three lines *ATL* restore ΧΧΓᴿΔΔ [Αἰγινῆται], ΗΗΗ ['Εφαισστιῆς], Η [Μυρι- ναῖο]ι. The restoration of Aegina (with an incomplete payment) is certain, because no other assessment in the first two periods is higher than 15. There is therefore a strong case for inferring that the last two names are island names and, if so, by elimination they are almost certainly the two Lemnian cities. There is, however, the objection that Myrina's payment would be 1 talent, whereas in the third period and afterwards it is 1½ talents. There is therefore almost an even chance that the run of island names ends with Aegina.

If the restorations in the list of 449 are right the cleruchs will have been sent out between 451, when the payment of 9 talents by the 'Lemnians' is preserved, and 449. 450 would provide a possible context for, as we have seen (above, p. 121), cleruchies were established in that year on Andros and probably also on Naxos and in Carystus. If the restorations are found to be wrong the Lemnian cleruchy should probably be associated with Pericles' expedition to the Chersonese in 447 (p. 160). Historically I prefer the later date.

Men from Lemnos and Imbros, presumably cleruchs, fought for Athens in the Peloponnesian War against Lesbos (Thuc. iii. 5. 1), at Pylos (iv. 28. 4), at Amphipolis (v. 8. 2), and in Sicily (vii. 57. 2) where they are described as 'still using the same language and customs as the Athenians'.

12. *IG* i². 27 and 28A

The evidence that the language of alliance was changed to the language of empire in or by the early forties depends on the dating of *IG* i². 27 and 28A. In both inscriptions the cities are called πόλεις ὅσων Ἀθηναῖοι κρατοῦσι (with minor variations). 28A also mentions the collective fine of 5 talents imposed on cities where an Athenian was killed, to which only two other references are known, in Aristophanes *Peace* (169–72) and *IG* ii². 38 as revised by Wilhelm, *Attische Unkunden*, iv. 23–4, pp. 25–31 (*Sitzungsber. Ak. Wien*, 1939). These two inscriptions have been dated before 445 because they both use the three-bar sigma. This criterion has been repeatedly attacked by Mattingly and against 27 in particular he has marshalled an impressive array of arguments (*BCH* lxxix (1968), 479–81).

The foundation of his case against the orthodox dating of 27 is its relation to *IG* i². 143. The prescripts of these two decrees are strikingly similar:

IG i². 27	*IG* i². 143
Λεον[τὶς ἐπρυτάνευε, ...]	Λ-
οστρατος [ἐπεστάτε...7....]	[εοντὶς ἐπρυτάνευ]ε Ἀρισ[το]κράτε-
ράτες ἐγρ[αμμάτευε ...7....]	[ς ἐγραμμάτευε...6...]ρ[....] ἐπ[ε]-
χος εἶπε Ἀ[—	[στάτε—

They have the same tribe in prytany, and the same names can be restored for the president and secretary. Wilhelm (op. cit. 29–31) drew attention to the association of the two decrees, and Meritt at first (*Hesp.* x (1941), 315–17) held that 143, which is dated *c.* 433–404 in the Corpus, was a reaffirmation of the much earlier 27. He later, however, changed his mind (*Hesp.* xxi (1952), 346 f.) on the ground that the two inscriptions honoured different men. The 'later' decree was headed by two columns each of four names. Those on the right, which alone survive, are all sons of an Iphiades, and this name recurs in *SIG* 187, honouring Iphiades of Abydos. The men honoured in *IG* i². 27, Meritt thought, were Delphians: ll. 5–6: χος εἶπε. Ἀ[. . . . . 10 . . . . . καὶ τὸ-]|ς ἀδέλφος [ἐκείνο τὸς Δέλ-]|φος. The coincidences should not be pressed: there was a Leontis in prytany every year, different restorations were possible for the president and secretary. 'Our judgement is that *IG* i². 143 honours men from Abydos and that *IG* i². 27, which is an earlier inscription honouring Delphians, has no connection with it.'

Mattingly is right in reopening the case. It is a very striking coincidence that the space available allows precisely the same names for president and secretary in the two decrees. Pritchett (*Hesp.* xi (1942), 231 n. 5) also pointed to the fact that in 27. 5 where the last surviving letter is Ἀ the number of letter spaces available fits the name Ἀλεχσόμενος, the last of the four brothers listed in 143. Mattingly added another coincidence: in both the name of the president precedes that of the secretary, whereas in standard practice this order is reversed. Mattingly's conclusion is that 27 must have the same date as 143, *c.* 420. He should at least have considered the possibility of changing the date of 143 to match 27. There are good photographs of 27 and 143 in Wilhelm's study (op. cit., pls. i and ii). The sigma in 143 (pl. ii) has four bars but there are other letter-forms which would be out of place in the twenties. The vertical of the phi is contained within the circle (Φ), a form which seems to be out of date by 445 (see the table in *JHS* lxxxvi (1966), 92). The form of upsilon which is very close to V would, I think, be impossible to parallel after 430. Minor features in mu (the central strokes would be expected to come lower in the twenties) and lambda (the sloping vertical and acute angle) also favour the earlier date. Mattingly restores Νικόστρατος as president in both inscriptions, identifies him with the general of the twenties, and argues that there is no Nicostratos of the previous generation in the family, since the general's grandfather was Euthoinos. But Nicostratus is a not uncommon name, and Δημόστρατος is a possible alternative. In 27 the three-bar sigma is not the only sign of an early date. Both photo and squeeze suggest that the rho in l. 3 has a tail (Ρ). There is no epigraphic difficulty in dating both 27 and 143 in the early forties.

Mattingly brings forward two further arguments in favour of dating *IG* i². 27 and 28A in the late twenties. Taking them to be two copies of the same decree he infers that the decree provided for two copies to be made and set up in different places, probably on the Acropolis and in the Bouleuterion. This requirement is found in only four other fifth-century decrees— the Assessment Decree of 425 (ML 69), a decree honouring Leonidas of Halicarnassus, dated *c.* 430 in the Corpus (*IG* i². 56 = Hill, *Sources*² B 80), where one copy is to be set up in Halicarnassus; and two decrees honouring *proxenoi*, which provide for a stele on the Acropolis and a record on a wooden board in the Bouleuterion (*SEG* x. 54a; xii. 41). Since none of these examples have been dated earlier than 430 Mattingly infers that 27 and perhaps 28A (for which there is no evidence) should join them in the twenties. This argument would only have force if at least three examples of decrees earlier than 430 in favour of *proxenoi* could be shown to have provided for only one copy. The final clause providing for publication does not survive in any *proxenos*-decree earlier than the decree in favour of Leonidas of Halicarnassus.

Mattingly also argues that the imperialistic phrase αἱ πόλεις ὅσων Ἀθηναῖοι κρατοῦσι is not otherwise found before the beginning of the Peloponnesian War. Apart from 27 and 28A all the other examples (*IG* i². 56; ii². 32, 38) are later. This statistic also only becomes significant if Athenian inscriptions of the forties and thirties can be found where a different phrase is used for the cities of the empire. At present there is no such evidence.

13. Peace-time Patrols

Plutarch in his *Pericles* (11. 4) says that Pericles sent out each year sixty triremes which provided pay for many of the citizens for eight months. We do not know Plutarch's source but we cannot accept the statement as it stands. S. K. Eddy (*Gk. Rom. Byz. Stud.* ix (1968), 141–56), allowing seventy-six days without pay for festivals (but would sailors on patrol not be paid on holidays?), calculates that the annual cost to the state would have been prohibitive, more than 300 talents. This calculation, however, is based on a daily rate of 1 drachma which was paid to sailors during the Peloponnesian War. In the forties it might have been substantially less, possibly not more than 3 obols, the rate to which Athens was reduced in the last phase of the war (Thuc. viii. 45. 2); but even at this rate the cost would have been dangerously high. Eddy suggests as a solution that the number of ships should be sixteen rather than sixty, and he appeals to Thuc. i. 116. 1, where sixteen ships in two squadrons are detached from the fleet of sixty ships that sailed against Samos in 440. This is not a convincing number for routine duty, where we should expect a round number as in the expeditions of the Peloponnesian War or in the force recorded in *IG* i². 97 which was sent out to collect tribute (see p. 432). The source may have said that sixty ships were sent out annually to train the crews, and in transmission the circumstantial detail of eight months, representing the full sailing season, might have been added.

However dubious the details in Plutarch, his source, probably an *Atthis* (cf. Arist. Ἀθ. Πολ. 24. 3), is not likely to have invented the basic fact that routine patrols annually cruised in the Aegean.

14. Priene and the Samian Revolt

Thucydides merely says that war broke out between Samos and Miletus over Priene. This state bordered on the Samian possessions on the mainland, and there survives a record of a Rhodian arbitration between them concerning disputed land from the second century B.C. (*SIG* 599). In the archaic period Priene had fought wars against both Miletus and Samos and she had remained independent of both. In the Ionic revolt she had sent her own contingent to the battle of Lade (Hdt. vi. 8. 1.) and down to 441 she paid her own annual tribute of 1 talent to Athens. The scholiast notes: 'It was near Miletus and the Milesians were trying to get control of it', but it is doubtful whether this is more than a guess. It seems more likely that Samos, taking advantage of Milesian weakness, following the suppression of the demos by the oligarchs and of the oligarchs by Athens, was hoping to coerce Priene. Miletus will have attempted to defend Priene and have appealed to Athens when she found that she was no match for Samos. It has been suggested by Nesselhauf (*Untersuchungen*, 48 n. 4) that the Samians may have been reacting to the loss of Marathesium. This town was, later at least, included in the Samian Peraea (Strabo xiv. 1. 20, 639); it appears for the first time in the tribute list of 441 and may be restored in 442. If Athens had encouraged Marathesium to claim her independence Samos might have been tempted to try to compensate by the incorporation of Priene.

Both Marathesium and Priene are absent from the full Ionian list of 439 and we do not know the reason. *ATL* (iii. 307) suggest that the Samians were in possession, but it seems more likely that by the time of the Dionysia of 439 the Samians were being blockaded. Gomme (*HCT* i. 350) thought that they might have paid their tribute to Athenian generals, or been released from payment because they had suffered in the fighting. The objection to the first of these explanations has already been noted (p. 110); the second is the more probable.

15. The Athenian Alliance with Perdiccas

Fragments of an Athenian treaty with Perdiccas have been recovered from the Acropolis (*IG* i². 71; *SEG* x. 86; Bengtson, *Staatsverträge*, 186). They include part of an oath to be taken by Perdiccas: he is to have the same friends and enemies as Athens and must undertake not to allow anyone except Athenians to take oars from Macedon. A second decree on the same stone concerns the Lyncestian king, Arrhabaeus; the intention seems to be to offer him friendship (? and the use of ports controlled by Athens) with a view to reconciling him with Perdiccas. At the bottom of the stone there was a long list of Macedonian nobles who presumably took the oath.

While there was continuing discussion about the relation of fragments, the length of line, and about restorations, the date was generally agreed, 423–422. In that year Perdiccas, who had broken with Brasidas, turned once again to Athens. 'He made overtures to the Athenian generals (who were besieging Scione) and reached an agreement with the Athenians' (Thuc. iv. 132. 1). In 424 and 423, though formally allied to Athens, he had tried to subdue Arrhabaeus, who was a threat to his frontier, with the help of Brasidas. In the first year the armies withdrew without fighting, because Brasidas wished to negotiate before invading Lyncestian territory and Arrhabaeus was apparently willing to accept Brasidas as a mediator. In 423 the joint armies of Brasidas and Perdiccas defeated the Lyncestians, but Brasidas, who was anxious for his allies in Chalcidice, would not support Perdiccas who wanted to follow up his victory. Both armies withdrew and there was an open breach. An Athenian stele combining an alliance with Perdiccas with a decree about Arrhabaeus suits this context well.

The general consensus about date was broken when *ATL* (iii. 313 n. 61) suggested that the decree should rather be identified with the original alliance with Perdiccas which by 432 had broken down (Thuc. i. 57. 2: Περδίκκας . . . ἐπεπολέμωτο ξύμμαχος πρότερον καὶ φίλος ὤν). Epigraphically they showed that the length of line adopted by previous editors was too short, and a line of 100 letters allowed them to restore, among the Macedonians who took the oath, Philip brother of Perdiccas, whom Athens later supported, and his son Amyntas. They also considered that the inscription was much more suited to the original alliance than to the 'patching up of differences which Athens had with Perdiccas near the close of the Archidamian War'.

This attractive case has been widely accepted, but not by all. Gomme, while appreciating the neatness of the restorations, was inclined by the combination of Perdiccas and Arrhabaeus to return to the date 423–422 (*HCT* iii. 621 f.). Bengtson (*Staatsverträge*, 186) also felt the strength of the argument from Arrhabaeus, and thought that an Athenian monopoly of Macedonian oars was intelligible in a state of war but not in peacetime. Mattingly (*BCH* xcli (1968), 472–4) accepted these arguments and added more. He showed that other appropriate Macedonian names could be restored that would provide the same number of letters as Philip and his son. He also argued in favour of the later date that this stele was inscribed by the same hand as two other decrees (*SEG* x. 87, coinage regulations, and *SEG* x. 215, concerning two golden Victories), which in turn are better suited by the later date.

None of these arguments is decisive. Gomme reminds us that the most elaborate of treaties were often the shortest-lived, and Thucydides implies that, though Perdiccas first negotiated with the generals in the field, the agreement was made by the Athenian people in Athens. In 422 Cleon, before attempting to recover Amphipolis, could send to Perdiccas, asking him to bring a force to join him, as the alliance required (Thuc. v. 6. 2: πέμψας ὡς Περδίκκαν πρέσβεις, ὅπως παραγένοιτο στρατιᾷ κατὰ τὸ ξυμμαχικόν). On the other hand, Athens would not wait for war to break out to secure a monopoly of Macedonian oars, if an opportunity arose in peace. The argument from the letter-forms is circular because the other two decrees are also not dated. The argument from Arrhabaeus is perhaps stronger, for he is at war with Philip's successor Archelaus who became king of Macedon not earlier than 414. But there was always a potential feud between Macedon and her neighbours; Arrhabaeus could have ruled from 440 to 410.

I remain sadly undecided. Purely epigraphic arguments, the letter-forms and the unusually long line, favour the later date, but not decisively. I find the content more appropriate to the original alliance. Among the Macedonians who took the oath is Arrhabaeus who would be included at either date. Derdas also is almost certainly listed (l. 61—Δέ]ρδας). He had joined Philip against Perdiccas by 432; would he have been trusted by Perdiccas in 423–422?

16. The Date of the Megarian Decree

In Ephorus' account of the cause of the Peloponnesian War, as reflected in Diodorus (xii. 38–9, esp. 39. 4) and Plutarch (*Per.* 29. 4), the decree by which the Megarians were banned from the Athenian market and from the harbours of her empire, assumes considerable importance; similarly Andocides could say (iii. 8) that the war broke out because of the Megarians. In Thucydides the decree is not a major factor in the causes of the war. The real cause was Sparta's fear of the growing power of Athens; the most important incidents that led to the fighting concerned Corinth. Thucydides seems to regard the Megarian Decree as less important than the Athenian alliance with Corcyra or her ultimatum to Potidaea; he does not even tell us when it was passed.

The first mention of the decree is when the allies of Sparta were putting their grievances before the Spartan Assembly in the summer of 432. 'The Megarians had many other complaints to make, but their main grievance was their exclusion, contrary to the terms of the peace, from the harbours of the Athenian empire and the Agora of Athens' (Thuc. i. 67. 4). The decree is not mentioned by the Corinthians in their speech to the Athenian Assembly in the summer of 433, though had it then been operative it should have been emphasized. A reference is indeed made to Megarian relations with Athens (Thuc. i. 42. 2): 'It would be wiser to remove the suspicion that you once aroused because of Megara.' The Greek is difficult because the Corinthians speak of suspicions that formerly existed (τῆς δὲ ὑπαρχούσης πρότερον διὰ Μεγαρέας ὑποψίας) whereas removing (ὑφελεῖν) implies current suspicion. The meaning, however, is not obscure. By accepting the Megarians into alliance in 461 Athens had provoked Corinth; Athens by refusing to make alliance now with Corcyra could show that she had learnt her lesson (but see Gomme, *HCT* i. 175 f.).

In Aristophanes' playful account (*Acharn.* 515–39) the decree is the climax to a series of incidents. The first phase was unofficial: nasty little men went round the Agora denouncing Megarian cloaks and other goods, which were at once confiscated and sold. Then some gay drunkards went to Megara and stole a prostitute, whereupon the Megarians retaliated by seizing two of Aspasia's girls; and so Pericles pronounced the formidable decree. Aristophanes implies that in the first phase it was not strictly legal for Megarian goods to be sold in the market, but no public action was being taken. Possibly a decree had been passed when the Megarians massacred their Athenian garrison in 446; it may have lapsed with the Thirty Years'

Peace without being formally repealed. The date that suits our evidence best for the decree of Pericles is between the late summer of 433 when Athens decided to make an alliance with Corcyra and the summer of 432 when the Megarians complained before the Spartan Assembly. At such a time it would have been a deliberate act of provocation and this is not inconsistent with Pericles' unconciliatory attitude in these critical years: τῆς μὲν γνώμης, ὦ Ἀθηναῖοι, αἰεὶ τῆς αὐτῆς ἔχομαι, μὴ εἴκειν Πελοποννησίοις (Thuc. i. 140. 1).

It is, however, strange that, if this is the right date, Thucydides does not mention the passing of the decree in his narrative of the course of events after the battle of Sybota in the late summer of 433. This is one of the reasons that have convinced some historians that the decree was passed before the train of events started by the troubles at Epidamnus: the arguments are persuasively presented by P. A. Brunt (*AJP* lxxii (1951), 269–79). His main argument is that Thucydides, having said that he will set out the reasons why they broke the peace and the points at issue (i. 23. 5), does not mention the passing of the decree in his narrative of events. Aristophanes' witness is discredited on the ground that 'it is doubtful how far sober history can ever be reconstructed from the jests of comedy'. But appeal is made to Aristophanes' statement that when the Megarians appealed to Sparta they were *slowly* famishing and 'we were unwilling to repeal it in spite of their *repeated demands*' (535–8: ἐντεῦθεν οἱ Μεγαρῆς, ὅτε δὴ 'πείνων βάδην, | Λακεδαιμονίων ἐδέοντο τὸ ψήφισμ' ὅπως | μεταστραφείη τὸ διὰ τὰς λαικαστρίας· | οὐκ ἠθέλομεν δ' ἡμεῖς δεομένων πολλάκις). This language, Brunt maintains, implies a longer interval than a year between the passing of the decree and the appeal to Sparta. But it is quite possible that the first year of the decree caused considerable discomfort at Megara. If the Megarians' regular means of selling exports to buy food was cut off it would take some time to adjust. Later, when Corinth was committed to war she will have seen that Megara's supplies did not fall dangerously low. Nor can πολλάκις be regarded as very significant; the frequent appeals to Athens against the decree come in Aristophanes after the complaint has been made to Sparta and that was in the summer of 432. It is usually dangerous to argue from silence, but the silence of Thucydides in the Corinthians' speech of 433 still seems a very strong argument against an earlier date. The belittling of the Megarian Decree by Thucydides should not be exaggerated. The Megarians are next in importance to the Corinthians at Sparta in 432, and when in the winter of 432–431 the Spartans presented their demands to Athens in order to comfort their consciences when they went to war, 'they told the Athenians to abandon the siege of Potidaea and to allow Aegina their independence. Above all they declared in the plainest terms that if the Athenians repealed the Megarian Decree there would be no war.' The reason, we have suggested, why Thucydides did not mention the decree when it was passed, and did not make more of it, was probably because others had made too much.

17. Epiphora

Tod judiciously described ἐπιφορά as 'a small additional charge, the nature of which is not yet clear'. We need to know whether it is a voluntary offering or a charge imposed by Athens. For the first meaning there is a parallel in Thucydides vi. 31. 3, where ἐπιφορά is used of money paid by trierarchs to their crews on the Syracusan expedition in addition to their pay from the state; for the second there is a Delphic inscription (*CIG* 2266 p. 17) in which the word seems to mean a penalty for late payment. Boeckh thought that this was the right parallel and Nesselhauf (*Untersuchungen*, 51 f.) supported him with detailed argument. *ATL* (i. 452 f.) carried this interpretation further. *Epiphora*, they suggest, represented the interest on late payment, calculated at 3 minae per talent per month, the unit of division being the tripartite ten-day division of the Athenian month. This thesis explains the figures that survive.

S. K. Eddy (*AJP* lxxxix (1968), 129–43) prefers to follow the Thucydidean usage. The payments, he thinks, are voluntary contributions, and in 439 the contributions from Ionia and the Hellespont reflect a fear that the activities of Pissuthnes, satrap at Sardis, during the Samian revolt may foreshadow renewed Persian interference on a larger scale. The two payments from Thrace, in 434 and 433, reflect fear of Macedon. Eddy's main arguments against *ATL* are that in list 7, where there is a special heading for late payers (M[ετὰ Διονύσια), there is no extra payment; nor are the payers of *epiphora* listed last in their districts as they would be if the general assumption is correct, that the order on the stele is the order in which cities paid. The distribution also is odd if it refers to late payers, for only one city in the Carian district is known to have been affected, though the Ionic–Carian lists of 432 and 431 are well preserved. The distribution is indeed unexpected but there remain strong reasons for regarding *epiphora* as a penalty. The entry in the list of 429 referring to a payment due in the previous year (25. i. 46): [Πυγε]λῆς ἥνες ἐπιφορᾶς is difficult to reconcile with a free contribution, but easy to understand as a penalty incurred in 431–430 but not paid until the following year. The use of the word in *IG* i². 97 also points to a penalty. This inscription used to be attributed to the expedition against Melos in 416, but Meritt has shown conclusively that, though some of the figures of the forces serving on the expedition are the same, there are more significant differences (*Robinson Studies*, ii. 298–303). He assigns the inscription to a force of thirty ships sent to collect tribute, probably soon after the beginning of the Peloponnesian War. The phrase ἐντελὲ τὸμ φορόν (l. 7) and, possibly, of [κατὰ μ]έρος in l. 5 point to the collection of tribute, and in close association there is mention of [τ]ὸν ἐπιφορὸν (l. 9). This is not a likely context for free-will offerings, but well suited to payments demanded by Athens. It is true that there is no clear sign in the tribute lists before 439 of a cash penalty for late payments, but by the time of the Samian revolt Athenian imperialism had grown harder. The cities paying *epiphora* are not listed last in their districts, but though in the lists of the first period (454–450) the order of the cities does seem to represent the order of payment (see p. 237), it is very uncertain whether the same principle was applied after 443 when the cities were listed by district.

We may still regard *epiphora* in the tribute lists as a penalty, probably but not necessarily for late payment.

18. [Dem.] vii. 13

[Dem.] vii. 13: ἀλλ' ὅμως οὐδενὸς τοιούτου ὄντος τότε, οὐκ ἐλυσιτέλει σύμβολα ποιησαμένους οὔτ' ἐκ Μακεδονίας πλεῖν Ἀθήναζε δίκας ληψομένους, οὔθ' ἡμῖν εἰς Μακεδονίαν, ἀλλ' ἡμεῖς τε τοῖς ἐκεῖ νομίμοις ἐκεῖνοι τε τοῖς παρ' ἡμῖν τὰς δίκας ἐλάμβανον.

De Ste Croix follows the interpretation of A. R. W. Harrison in *CQ* (1960), 248–52. Harrison considers two alternatives. By the first the effect of a formal agreement would be that Macedonians wanting to bring a charge against Athenians would have to come to Athens and Athenians would have to go to Macedon to prosecute Macedonians. The objection to this interpretation is that δίκας λαμβάνειν has to be taken in two different senses, meaning in the first clause 'to get satisfaction' and in the second 'to give satisfaction' (for the second meaning see Liddell and Scott, s.v. λαμβάνω, ii. 1. e). Harrison therefore prefers a second possible translation: 'There was nothing to be gained by making a treaty to regulate the procedure of Macedonians who came to sue in Athens and Athenians who went to sue in Macedon, but we sued under the existing laws of Macedon and they under the existing laws of Athens.' The change would be not in the place but in the law. This seems to me a very oblique way of expressing something very simple; the coming from Macedon to Athens and from Athens to Macedon is quite redundant. It is a much lesser evil to accept the use of δίκας λαμβάνειν in two different senses. In the first clause it will mean 'sue', in the second 'sue or be sued'.

That the speaker is thinking primarily of the extra travelling that a treaty would involve is supported by what immediately precedes the passage under discussion: καὶ ἐμπορικαὶ δίκαι οὐκ ἦσαν, ὥσπερ νῦν, ἀκριβεῖς, αἱ κατὰ μῆνα, ποιοῦσαι μηδὲν δεῖσθαι συμβόλων τοὺς τοσοῦτον ἀλλήλων ἀπέχοντας. The argument understood is that the introduction in the fourth century of ἐμπορικαὶ δίκαι, which guaranteed traders a quick hearing of their case, made σύμβολα much less necessary, and particularly for those states a long distance from one another. The point of introducing τοὺς τοσοῦτον ἀλλήλων ἀπέχοντας here is that such states would be particularly relieved not to have to travel the long distances required by σύμβολα because the special ἐμπορικαὶ δίκαι at Athens gave them all the security they wanted.

19. Tribute Display at the Dionysia

Isocrates viii. 82: οὕτω γὰρ ἀκριβῶς εὕρισκον, ἐξ ὧν ἄνθρωποι μάλιστ' ἂν μισηθεῖεν, ὥστ' ἐψηφίσαντο τὸ περιγιγνόμενον ἐκ τῶν φόρων ἀργύριον διελόντες κατὰ τάλαντον εἰς τὴν ὀρχήστραν τοῖς Διονυσίοις εἰσφέρειν, ἐπειδὰν πλῆρες ᾖ τὸ θέατρον·

καὶ τοῦτ' ἐποίουν καὶ παρεισῆγον τοὺς παῖδας τῶν ἐν τῷ πολέμῳ τετελευτηκότων·
ἀμφοτέροις ἐπιδεικνύοντες, τοῖς μὲν συμμάχοις τὰς τιμὰς τῆς οὐσίας αὐτῶν ὑπὸ
μισθωτῶν εἰσφερομένας, τοῖς δ' ἄλλοις Ἕλλησι τὸ πλῆθος τῶν ὀρφανῶν καὶ τὰς
συμφορὰς τὰς διὰ τὴν πλεονεξίαν ταύτην γιγνομένας. In reconstructing the scene
difficulties arise over both text and translation. In the passage underlined
some manuscripts have τῶν πόρων for ἐκ τῶν φόρων and that was the reading
preferred by most nineteenth-century editors. The reference, however, to the
allies makes φόρων much more appropriate to the occasion. The more serious
difficulty concerns τὸ· περιγιγνόμενον. This verb, when applied to things,
normally means to remain over and above, and this is what it means in a very
similar phrase in Xenophon (*Hell.* ii. 3. 8): ἀργυρίου τετρακόσια καὶ ἑβδομήκοντα
τάλαντα, ἃ περιεγένοντο τῶν φόρων, οὓς αὐτῷ Κῦρος παρέδειξεν εἰς τὸν πόλεμον. This
can only mean 470 talents which still remained from the tributes which
Cyrus gave to Lysander. *ATL* (iii. 16 f.), accepting this meaning, translate
the phrase as 'the surplus of the funds derived from the tributes of the allies'
and, since the reserve had been built up, mainly at least, from the tribute
brought to Athens from Delos in 454 and subsequent tribute not spent, it
would be the changing amount of the reserve that was displayed. There are
two main objections to this interpretation. Even when the reserve was being
drained in the Archidamian War the display would require not less than
2,000 porters. It is also very doubtful whether the spectacle would in fact,
as *ATL* believe, have reassured the allies and convinced them that Athens
was not short of money, even though there was less to display each year.
Some of the allies would remember that the reserve had stood at some 6,000
talents in 431; for them there could be little reassurance in a parade of
2,000 talents.

These difficulties disappear if we follow Raubitschek (*TAPA* lxxii (1941),
356–62) in translating 'the annually incoming tribute money'. There is
a good parallel to this use in Arrian, *Anabasis* vii. 17. 4 and ample justification in Liddell and Scott, s.v. περιγίγνομαι ii. 3. We should therefore imagine
the dramatic festival opening with a parade of men, hired for the occasion,
each carrying a bag or jar filled with 1,500 tetradrachms or their equivalent.

Isocrates associates the tribute display with a procession of war orphans,
and he condemns both. The tribute display was an unnecessary insult to
the allies, 'showing them the value we attached to their property, given to
hired men to carry'; the orphans brought home to the rest of Greece 'the
number of war orphans and the disasters to which our restless ambition
led us'. The intention in bringing the orphans into the orchestra of the
theatre was to demonstrate the state's care for them and to encourage them
to play their part in serving the state in war (see Aeschines iii. 154). The
tribute display may have been intended as a collective receipt.

ATL assume that the decree dates from the early years of the Archidamian War. This is possible but the text does not require it: τῶν ἐν τῷ
πολέμῳ τετελευτηκότων does not mean those who died in any particular war
but those who died in war (cf. Aeschin., loc. cit.).

20. The Chronology of Anaxagoras

The main sources for the life of Anaxagoras are collected by G. S. Kirk and J. E. Raven in *The Presocratic Philosophers*, 362–5. Most of our information comes from Diogenes Laertius, an honest compiler who collected what he could find in accredited authors and made no attempt to analyse his sources critically:

1. The main tradition, canonized by Apollodorus, seems to have been that he was born *c.* 500 and died in 428–427 (accepting a necessary emendation by Scaliger).

2. He is said to have been twenty years old when Xerxes invaded.

3. According to Demetrius of Phalerum in his *Register of Archons* he embarked on philosophy when he was twenty years old, in the archonship of Callias (456–455). The repetition of twenty years is odd, and there is no authority for beginning his life in 476. The most favoured resolution is to emend Callias to Calliades, archon of 480–479 (but see below).

4. They say that he spent thirty years in Athens.

5. There are two traditions of his trial: (*a*) Sotion in his *Succession of the Philosophers* made Cleon the prosecutor, and the charge was impiety, in that he called the sun a burning mass of metal. Pericles defended him, he was fined 5 talents and banished. (*b*) Satyrus in his *Lives* made Thucydides, Pericles' political opponent, the prosecutor and the charge was Medism as well as impiety. He was condemned to death in absence.

6. Finally he withdrew to Lampsacus and there died.

7. When the magistrates of Lampsacus asked him what he would like them to do for him he asked that the children should be given an annual holiday in the month that he died. 'The custom is still observed.'

8. When he died the people of Lampsacus buried him with full honours.

A. E. Taylor (*CQ* xi. (1917), 81–7) made a strong case for dating his career at Athens from 480 to *c.* 450, when he was driven out of Athens by Thucydides son of Melesias. Taylor's main arguments were; (*a*) Since Pericles was taught by him, presumably when he was growing up, Anaxagoras must have been active in Athens before *c.* 470. (*b*) Anaxagoras cannot have been in Athens when Socrates began to study philosophy, for Socrates was taught by Archelaus, pupil of Anaxagoras, and seems from Plato first to have known Anaxagoras' philosophy from his book. (*c*) The charge of Medism would have been obsolete after the ending of hostilities with Persia, *c.* 450. (*d*) Sufficient time must be allowed for Anaxagoras after leaving Athens to establish a school of philosophy at Lampsacus and receive such honours from the town. Taylor's case, coming from such a distinguished Platonist, has been very widely accepted (see, e.g., *Cambridge Ancient History*, v. 478). The main difficulty that it raises is the rejection of a trial arising from the decree of Diopeithes, which seems to be aimed primarily at Anaxagoras, as Plutarch (*Per.* 32. 2) says and Diodorus implies (xii. 39. 2); in both cases the source was probably Ephorus. There is therefore much to be said for Davison's suggestion that both trials are authentic and that the first sentence was repealed in the forties when peace had been made with

Persia (J. A. Davison, *CQ* xlvii (1953), 33–45). Davison, accepting the archonship of Callias (456–455) in the text, inferred that this must have been the date of some important event in his life and assigns the attack by Thucydides to that year. This seems to me less attractive, though possible. A date in the late fifties would seem to suit the climate in Athens better for a charge of Medism, perhaps just after Cimon's death when Pericles was thinking of peace and Thucydides was trying to step into Cimon's political leadership. From *c.* 445 Anaxagoras may have divided his time between Athens and Lampsacus; there need be no difficulty in giving him sufficient time in Lampsacus to become an adopted Lampsacene. The association indeed probably goes back to the time when he 'foretold' the fall of the famous meteorite on the Chersonese across the water in 467–466. Finally we may doubt whether he began to practise philosophy at Athens in the year of Xerxes' invasion. He would have had a poor audience and poorer accommodation.

It is more probable that he took up the serious study of philosophy at the age of twenty (in Clazomenae) and came to Athens in the middle or late seventies. If his thirty years in Athens rests on a good tradition, it could represent the sum total of his stays in Athens.

21. The End of Zopyrus

Herodotus, after describing the siege of Babylon, adds that Zopyrus the son of Megabyzus, the hero of the siege, deserted the Persians and went over to Athens (Hdt. iii. 160. 2): Μεγαβύζου δὲ τούτου γίνεται Ζώπυρος, ὃς ἐς Ἀθήνας ηὐτομόλησε ἐκ Περσέων. Ctesias (66–72) provides the background and the sequel. When Megabyzus recovered Egypt he took the rebel leader Inaros and Greek prisoners back to Persia with a promise that their lives would be spared. Five years later the king under pressure from his mother allowed them to be crucified. Megabyzus withdrew to Syria in revolt, sent back the remaining Greeks to Greece, gathered together a large army, and defeated two generals sent against him. He was then persuaded by the royal family to make his peace and returned to court. On a hunting expedition he killed a lion that was about to attack the king, but the king, furious that he had been deprived of the honour, exiled Megabyzus to Cyrta on the Red Sea. After five years he escaped, disguised as a leper. Once again the royal ladies arranged a reconciliation with the king. Megabyzus died at the age of seventy-six and the king was deeply grieved. Then, after a chapter of scandal about the royal ladies, Ctesias records the death of Megabyzus' wife. 'When both his parents had died Zopyrus deserted the king and went to Athens, for his mother had done a good service to the Athenians (κατὰ τὴν τῆς μητρὸς εἰς αὐτοὺς εὐεργεσίαν). With his following he sailed to Caunus and demanded the surrender of the city. The Caunians said that they would hand over their city to him, but not to the Athenians who were with him. When Zopyrus entered the walls a Caunian threw a stone which hit him on the head and killed him. Amestris his grandmother crucified the

Caunian.' Then follows a brief note of the death of Amestris and of King Artaxerxes (in 425).

It would be irresponsible to accept all the embroidery of this story, especially where the royal ladies are concerned, and we may doubt the prominent part that Inaros plays in the plot, in view of the apparent contradiction in Thucydides (i. 110. 3). But, in view of Herodotus' statement, the basic outline that Megabyzus, after recovering Egypt, revolted from the king and that after his death his son went over to Athens, should be true. The end of the story is circumstantial and plausible. Caunus on the southern coast of Caria has revolted from Athens and is apparently under Persian control. Zopyrus, himself a Persian, would seem a useful man to negotiate with Persians or Medizers, but the plan miscarries and Zopyrus has been too short a time in Athens even to invite a joke from Aristophanes. When is the revolt of Caunus to be dated? The indications in Ctesias suggest at least fifteen years after the end of the Egyptian campaign, 439 or later. Our only control is in the tribute quota lists. Caunus is a very regular payer down to 439. From 436 to 433 we have no evidence. A payment is preserved for 432, and is possible in 431. From 430 to 425 too little is preserved of the Ionian–Carian district to argue from silence. The assessment of Caunus down to the 438 assessment had been $\frac{1}{2}$ talent. For the following four assessments there is no evidence, but in 425 the figure is 10 talents (for details, see *ATL* i. 304 f.).

On this evidence the revolt should come either between 437 and 433 or between 431 and 425. Perhaps the most likely context is after the failure of Melesander's expedition to Caria and Lycia in 430 (Thuc. ii. 69. 1). The revolt may help to explain why an assessment which had remained unchanged from 454 to 438 should be twenty times as high in 425.

22. The Allies in the Melian Expedition

The force that reduced Melos included τῶν δὲ ξυμμάχων καὶ νησιωτῶν ὁπλίταις μάλιστα πεντακοσίοις καὶ χιλίοις (Thuc. v. 84. 1). This is a strange formulation because the islanders were allies. Thucydides could possibly be referring to allies such as Argos who were not in her empire but there is no campaign before this in which such allies had served in significant numbers. Most scholars therefore, including Stahl and Steup, followed more recently by Andrewes (*Cambridge Class. Phil. Papers*, vi. (1960), 3) have inferred that the allied force was confined to islanders, and Andrewes sees in this an indication that the Athenian case must have had substantial support in the Aegean—'1,500 allies, and islanders at that!' But if Thucydides had wished to emphasize the point, we should expect him to have done it less cryptically; the point is nowhere developed. It is perhaps defensible to take the phrase to mean other allies (e.g. Miletus) and islanders, for the islanders seem to have been regarded as having a special relationship with Athens: Ar. *Peace* 296 ff.: ἀλλ' ὦ γεωργοὶ κἄμποροι καὶ τέκτονες | καὶ δημιουργοὶ καὶ μέτοικοι καὶ ξένοι | καὶ νησιῶται; ibid. 759 f.: ἀλλ' ὑπὲρ ὑμῶν πολεμίζων | ἀντεῖχον ἀεὶ καὶ τῶν ἄλλων νήσων; Thuc. vi. 68. 2. In 425 against Corinth Nicias had with him contingents from Miletus, Andros, and Carystus; in 424 in his capture of Cythera he had allies with him but Thucydides mentions only Milesians. In the Syracusan expedition the allied troops are predominantly islanders, though Milesians are again included. Closer to the description of the force against Melos is Thucydides' account of the reinforcements taken by Demosthenes to Syracuse (vii. 20. 2: ὁπλίταις δὲ ἐκ καταλόγου Ἀθηναίων δια-κοσίοις καὶ χιλίοις, καὶ νησιωτῶν ὅσον ἑκασταχόθεν οἶον τ' ἦν πλείστοις χρήσασθαι, καὶ ἐκ τῶν ἄλλων ξυμμάχων τῶν ὑπηκόων, εἴ ποθέν τι εἶχον ἐπιτήδειον ἐς τὸν πόλεμον, ξυμπορίσαντες.

23. The Last Assessment

In 413 (Thuc. vii. 28. 4) the Athenians replaced the annual tribute by an import and export duty of 5 per cent in all the harbours of the empire; their reason, according to Thucydides, was that they would raise more money. Since no further change is recorded in any of the surviving sources it was naturally assumed that the new system was continued until the empire collapsed. The assumption seemed to be confirmed by the mention of an εἰκοστολόγος in Aristophanes' *Frogs* (363), produced in 405.

In 1936 Merritt published five small fragments found in the Agora excavations which came from an assessment list of which nothing was previously known. The inclusion of Ionic eta and lambda suggested a date towards the end of the century and Meritt recalled that Craterus had quoted from an assessment in his ninth book which included a record of the trial of Antiphon in 411–410. Assuming that Craterus chose the first and last assessment from which to take samples it was tempting to associate the new fragments with a last assessment in 410. This date seemed particularly appropriate to the new fragments which included Miletoteichos (later Miletopolis), a city that has not been preserved in any other quota or assessment list. It is a considerable distance inland behind Cyzicus, and the year of the great Athenian victory at Cyzicus provides the best context we know (Meritt, *Hesp.* v. (1936), 386–9; *ATL* i. 120 and 208; iii. 91 f.).

Mattingly has reopened discussion, suggesting that this assessment should be dated in 418 (*BSA* lxii (1967), 13). The presence of Miletoteichos shows that the assessment was being rigorously pressed in that part of the empire. This could correspond with the impression given by the high Hellespontine figures of tribute quota list 33 which Mattingly dates in 418–417 (in agree-ment with ML 75). He further suggests that the statement of [Andocides] iv. 11 that Alcibiades as an assessor doubled the assessments of the allies should be referred not to 425 but to 418. Craterus in quoting from the last assessment, or in commenting on a later event, could have referred back to the 418 assessment. Certainly the Ionic letters and script can be paralleled as early as 418 but the arguments from Miletoteichos and Craterus are con-siderably stronger in 410; nor was the summer of the Mantinea defeat an appropriate context for doubling the assessment (see ML 75 for a different pattern). Both Merritt and Mattingly assume that 414 can be eliminated, owing to the introduction of the *eikoste*, but according to Thucydides the change was made in 413 when the occupation of Decelea sharpened the Athenian financial crisis. There should have been a regular assessment in 414. But 410 still has considerably the strongest claim (followed in order by 414, 418, 406).

Meritt justified his dating of this assessment after the introduction of the *eikoste* by Xenophon's statement that Chalcedon, on its surrender to Athens in 410, agreed to pay her normal tribute (Xen. *Hell.* 1. 3. 9: ὑποτελεῖν τὸν φόρον Καλχηδονίους Ἀθηναίοις ὅσονπερ εἰώθεσαν). Some may think that this text alone is not enough to destroy the inference from Aristophanes' *eikosto-logos* in 405. It is, however, a change that we should have expected even without evidence. Harbour taxes might be an effective substitute for a fixed tribute so long as Athenian power was strong enough to provide an effective control, but after the disaster at Syracuse it would have been extremely difficult to check evasion. It is significant that the *eikostologos* in the *Frogs* comes from Aegina which was occupied by Athenians and so paid no tribute. Such communities might have been required to pay the *eikoste*, since the state was virtually bankrupt, and might have continued to pay it rather than φόρος.

24. The Composition of the Athenian Crews

Most of the evidence for the composition of Athenian crews in the fifth century has been assembled by Amit and his study has (or should have) usefully narrowed the field of discussion (M. Amit, *Athens and the Sea*, 30–49). Amit has removed any doubts that there may have been on two points: (1) Slaves were used only in an emergency, as for the battle of Arginusae. (2) Citizens formed a considerable proportion of the crews. What remains uncertain is the degree to which metics and mercenaries (ξένοι) were used.

That mercenaries were an important element in the navy is suggested by one of the Corinthian attempts to reassure the members of the Pelopon-nesian League who had no wish for war in 432. They had to be persuaded that the issues concerned them as well as the leaders and, more important, that the Peloponnesians would win the war. They would borrow money from Delphi and Olympia and draw away Athens' mercenaries by higher pay (Thuc. i. 121. 3). In answering the point Pericles does not deny the use of mercenaries: 'There might be serious danger if we and our metics alone were not still a match for them.' But the mercenaries would not in fact be tempted: 'No one would choose to fight with the Peloponnesians for the sake of a few days' high pay, when by so doing he would make himself an exile, and face greater danger' (Thuc. i. 143. 1–2). The natural inference is that it was abnormal not to use at least some mercenaries when large fleets were needed. Thucydides' description of naval dispositions in 428 points the same way. When Mytilene came out in revolt, forty ships were sent, and a further thirty were sent round the Peloponnese. The Spartans then appeared in force at the Isthmus and the Athenians decided on an immediate show of strength to make it clear that the revolt of Mytilene would not exhaust their resources. They manned 100 ships to raid the coast of the Peloponnese and Thucydides says that the crews were composed of citizens of the zeugite class as well as the *thetes*, and metics (Thuc. iii. 16. 1). This passage suggests that when there were seventy ships at sea it was impossible to find the crews for 100 more ships from *thetes* and metics alone. The reason why foreigners were not recruited for the 100 ships is that the essential purpose of the demonstration was to make a show of force at once.

But though the evidence for the normal use of foreigners is adequate, we must allow for considerable exaggeration in Isocrates' sweeping indictment in the *Peace* (viii. 79): 'Who could have stood the callousness of our ancestors who assembled the idlest and most criminal men from the whole of Greece and filled the triremes with them, and so were hated by the Greeks.' In the same speech (viii. 48) he draws a rhetorical contrast between the fifth and fourth centuries: 'Then, slaves and foreigners were sailors—the citizens, hoplites; now foreigners are hoplites—the citizens, sailors.' The contemporary evidence makes it perfectly clear that the crews were not mainly composed of mercenaries, and that there was a ναυτικὸς ὄχλος of citizens, but even Isocrates could not make such sweeping statements if the recruitment of foreigners was not normal.

This point needs to be made, because there is a passage in Thucydides, which seems to point the other way. Before the final sea battle in the Great Harbour at Syracuse Nicias tried to raise the morale of his men (vii. 63. 3–4). He first addresses the soldiers who are going to fight a land-battle on sea, and then turns to the sailors. They must not be discouraged by their disasters; they now have more ships, better equipped: 'Think of the privilege you enjoy and how worth preserving it is. You have long been regarded as Athenians, though you are not. Because you know our language and adopt our ways you have been admired throughout Greece. You gain as much as we from the benefits of empire. . . .' These words seem to be addressed to metics, and so the scholiast understood them: ναῦται: τοὺς μετοίκους λέγει. Does this mean that there were no foreigners and no citizens, or very few, in the crews? We should not expect this, and there are slight indications that the impression given by Thucydides is misleading. In one of the decrees concerned with preparations for the expedition there is a tempting restoration which could imply the recruitment of allies: μισθ]όσθον δὲ καὶ τὸν χσυμμάχον ηοπόσ|[ος ἂν ναύτας ἐπαγγέλλονται ηαι π]όλες ἐς τὲμ βολὲν τὲν Ἀθεναίο[ν (ML 78 b, with IG i². 98). The presence of ηεχσέκοντα νεõν in the following line makes some such restoration probable. Diodorus also implies that there were foreigners in the crews. In his description of the forces that took part in the expedition he includes τῶν συμμάχων πλείους τῶν ἑπτακισχιλίων ἐκτὸς τῶν ἐν τοῖς πληρώμασι (Diod. xiii. 2. 7). Diodorus does not normally carry great weight, but this passage probably means that his source either knew that there were mercenaries in the crews or assumed that there would be.

There is no explicit evidence that the crews included citizens, but unless Thucydides has completely misrepresented the mood in which the expedition set out many of the *thetes* must have been anxious to serve for the pay was good and the prospect of booty was bright. Thucydides says that the trierarchs gave a bonus to the *thranitai* in addition to their pay, for these were the most skilled oarsmen (Thuc. vi. 31. 3). Aristophanes called them the saviours of the city (Ar. *Acharn.* 162–3: ὁ θρανίτης λεώς, | ὁ σωσίπολις); it is reasonable to assume that they were normally citizens.

We are left with no firm conclusions, and certainly no statistical analysis that could be taken seriously. Isocrates' implication that Athens relied entirely on non-citizens to man her triremes can be dismissed without qualms. The Old Oligarch's grudging admission about the people's 'right' to power would be meaningless unless citizens formed the nucleus of the crews ([Xen.] *Ἀθ. Πολ.* 1. 2, emphasized by Amit, op. cit. 40–2.): 'Since it is the demos which rows in the ships and is the source of the city's power, much more than the hoplites, the nobles, and the better elements, it is fair (δίκαιον) that in the lot all should be eligible for office and that anyone who wishes should be able to speak.' Though the evidence is not satisfactory it seems on balance that metics played a bigger part than mercenaries (who would probably be mostly allies). Sometimes there was ample notice of expeditions; but many were required to sail soon after the decree that authorized them. For practical purposes it was better to be in Piraeus when the crews were wanted, and islanders for instance who were good oarsmen would naturally tend to become metics.

25. Electrum Staters of the Ionian Cities

Towards the end of the nineteenth century numismatists became interested in a number of east Greek electrum staters which had a common weight and a common reverse, an incuse square divided into four. Of the obverses some were clearly city heraldic types such as the sphinx of Chios and the winged boar of Clazomenae, others might have been derived from such types, but there remained some which had no recognized associations. The early investigators assumed that the differences in the obverses reflected different minting centres, but Six, emphasizing the common features, suggested that all the coins came from a single mint, and he suggested the rich and powerful island of Chios as the centre (M. J. P. Six, *Num. Chron.* x (1890), 215–19). P. Gardner, in a paper read to the British Academy in 1908, was the first to attribute these coins to the Ionian revolt, and his case was strengthened when several more coins of the series were found in a hoard at Vourla, the site of Clazomenae (P. Gardner, *PBA* 1908, 119–24, more fully developed in *A History of Ancient Coinage* (1918), 91–103; Vourla hoard, R. Jameson, *Rev. Num.* xi (1911), 60–8). Gardner thought it more likely that each city minted its own coins; Seltman reverted to Six's position; he thought that to issue the same type of coins from a number of minting centres required a degree of organization that was most unlikely. 'It is much more probable that the rebel states pooled their financial revenues and placed them under the control of a board of monetary officials who caused their numerous badges to be stamped on the coins' (C. Seltman, *Greek Coins²* (1955), 87 f.).

Seltman exaggerated the difficulties. A central mint controlled by representatives of the cities would in fact be more complicated than agreeing material, weight, and reverse and leaving the cities to mint their own coins. Mr. Martin Price, of the Department of Coins and Medals at the British Museum, has very kindly drawn my attention to two coins of Clazomenae in the museum's collection which puts the matter beyond reasonable doubt. An electrum stater of the 'revolt series', BMC Clazomenae 2, and a silver half-stater (BM. Ford 1918. 143) use the same obverse die and the same reverse die, and must both have been minted at Clazomenae. If therefore there was a single federal mint it was at Clazomenae and few Ionian cities would be less likely candidates. This, together with the lack of die-links among the reverses, makes it virtually certain that the rebel cities minted their own coins; but the common weight and common reverse indicate a remarkable degree of co-ordination, which is also reflected in the central direction of the revolt in the early stages by τὸ κοινὸν τῶν Ἰώνων.

26. The Cyzicene Stater

The evidence for the value of the Cyzicene stater at Athens in the middle of the fifth century and later is inadequate.

1. Payments of Cyzicene staters by the treasurers of Athena are preserved in the accounts of the financial period 418–414 (IG i². 302. 13, 57, 65) and of 409–8 (IG i². 301. 93 ff., and 120 ff.). In every case the equivalent in Athenian currency is added, but in no such text are the figures complete.

2. Demosthenes, in a court case soon after the middle of the fourth century, says the Cyzicene stater was then valued at 28 drachmae in the Bosporan kingdom (Dem. xxxiv. 23). Cyzicenes were the commonest currency in the Euxine area (Xen. Anab. v. 6. 23); we should expect them to be worth less in Athens.

3. The mercenaries who marched east to win the Persian throne for Cyrus were paid a daric a month (Xen. Anab. i. 3. 21), and the daric was worth 25 drachmae in Athenian money. When, in their retreat, they reached the Euxine, they were offered a Cyzicene stater a month and the same rate was later offered by the Thracian king Seuthes. From this it has been inferred that the Cyzicene stater was also worth 25 drachmae; but all that necessarily follows is that the two rates were not far apart.

Schwahn (RE, s.v. φόρος, 635 f.) assumed without argument that the Cyzicene was valued in Athens at 27 drachmae. ATL (iii. 266 n. 6) accepted 24 drachmae on the strength of an article by Woodward (JHS xxxiv (1914), 276–81). Thompson, however, has shown that Woodward's conclusion was based partly on restoration where other restorations are possible, and partly on what is very probably a wrong reading; and the Attic equivalent of the Cyzicene staters recorded in IG i². 302. 57, which ends in 3½ obols, cannot be reconciled with an exchange rate of exactly 24 drachmae (W. E. Thompson, Num. Chron. 1963, 1–4). There is the further objection that the Cyzicene stater is heavier than the Lampsacene, which is firmly fixed at 24 drachmae. Thompson inclines to a fractional figure near 25 drachmae.

Since the maximum number of Cyzicene staters in the summation of the *aparchae* of 453 is only 96, the difference between an exchange rate of 24 and 27 is not, financially, of great importance. It would, however, be interesting to know whether the Athenians, in assessing Cyzicus and other cities which also paid in her staters, chose figures which could easily be translated into Cyzicenes. The normal pre-war tribute of Cyzicus was 9 talents, which reveals nothing, but in 446 she makes a part payment of 4,320 drachmae which is a very un-round figure. Tenedos also makes odd payments which seem to require a special explanation, especially her assessment in 443 and later of 2 t. 5,280 dr., which has no parallel in the lists. In the accompanying table the various recorded pre-war payments of Cyzicus and Tenedos are translated into Cyzicene staters at exchange rates from 24 to 27 drachmae.

CYZICUS			TENEDOS			
Rate	9 t.	4,320 dr. 4·3000	2·5280	1·3720	3240	2160
24 dr.	2,250 st.	180 st.	1,125 st.	720 st.	405 st.	135 st.	90 st.
25 dr.	2,160	170	1,080	$691\frac{1}{5}$	$388\frac{4}{5}$	$129\frac{3}{5}$	$86\frac{2}{5}$
26 dr.	$2,076\frac{12}{13}$	$166\frac{2}{13}$	$1,038\frac{6}{13}$	$664\frac{8}{13}$	$373\frac{11}{13}$	$124\frac{8}{13}$	$83\frac{1}{13}$
27 dr.	2,000	160	1,000	640	360	120	80

At the two rates of 24 and 27 drachmae all the preserved pre-war payments of Cyzicus and Tenedos can be converted into an exact number of Cyzicene staters, but a rate of 27 drachmae gives the more convincing totals. We should also expect the Cyzicene to be at a higher rate than the Lampsacene (at 24 drachmae) partly because it is heavier and partly because it was a much more widely distributed currency. An exchange rate of 27 drachmae is the easiest way of explaining the odd payments of Cyzicus and Tenedos. Athens deserves the credit of adapting her assessments to the convenience of those few cities who paid in Cyzicenes.

APPENDIX 1

Thucydides' Account of the Pentekontaetia

I HAVE shown considerably less respect for Thucydides' account of the period from 478 to 433 than for the rest of his history, and this attitude needs defence. Though there are no decisive arguments, there are respectable reasons for believing that these chapters are later than the main period of composition and less fully considered than most of his text.

The shortcomings have been often enough rehearsed (see Gomme, *HCT* i. 361–413); a brief catalogue of some of the more serious must suffice. The purpose of the digression is to explain the growth of Athenian power which had made her so formidable that Sparta felt forced to go to war. The narrative starts well enough by selecting from the early years of the Delian League those incidents which added to Athenian power. So we have the capture of Eion which enabled Athens to occupy a key harbour town through which she could have access to valuable forests and mines, the settlement of Scyros which gave Athens increased control over the sea route to the north and north-east, the reduction of Carystus which was the first state to be forced to join the League, and the reduction of Naxos which established a precedent for the strong handling of secessions. We should not complain that he tells us nothing of the fighting against Persia in the seventies; it was of less significance in the growth of Athenian dominance. But towards the middle of the century Thucydides seems to lose sight of his objective. In his account of the First Peloponnesian War there is little explanation of strategy or tactics, and, while the hostilities on the mainland are briefly recorded, the transference of the League reserve from Delos to Athens is ignored; nor is anything said of the ending of the fighting against Persia. Even if no formal peace was made there were no further League expeditions into the eastern Mediterranean and no Phoenician fleet came into the Aegean; this meant that the Athenian fleet was free to maintain control of the empire.

There is nothing in Thucydides to suggest that the forties were a period of high tension in the Aegean and of a sharpened Athenian imperialism; nothing to suggest that the early Pericles was less Augustan than the elder statesman who in his period of unchallenged power after the ostracism of Thucydides, son of Melesias, so fascinated the historian. Had Thucydides given as much thought to this period as to the war years and his brief summary of early Greek history his silence would be seriously damaging to some of the main contentions of this book (and especially ch. ix). The objection loses much of its force if the account of the Pentekontaetia is late and hurried and much less well digested than most of the history. It begins well, but ends badly. After the detailed account of the Samian revolt he passes at once to the incidents in the north-west which were to lead inevitably to war. To substantiate his ἀληθεστάτη πρόφασις much more is needed on the period after the Thirty Years' Peace, and particularly the early thirties; much less would have sufficed for the period before the peace.

If Hammond were right in dating the composition of book i, with the exception of minor additions not essential to the main structure, before 415 (*CQ* xxxv (1946), 146–52) the thesis that the digression on the Pentekontaetia was a hurried piece of work would be barely tenable. I believe it to be late, but the evidence is not decisive. Thucydides says that he wrote his account because other writers had not covered the period, with the exception of Hellanicus whose account was unsatisfactory: τούτων δὲ ὅσπερ καὶ ἥψατο ἐν τῇ Ἀττικῇ ξυγγραφῇ Ἑλλάνικος, βραχέως τε καὶ τοῖς χρόνοις οὐκ ἀκριβῶς ἐπεμνήσθη (Thuc. i. 97. 2). Hellanicus included in his *Atthis* a reference to the Athenian emergency gold coinage of 407–406; his history probably went to the end of the war, and there are no good grounds for inferring an earlier edition that ended before this (as Gomme, *HCT* i, p. 6 n. 3). Jacoby was satisfied that the reference to Hellanicus was added to a completed draft, but the Greek allows either interpretation and cannot be regarded as firm evidence. A little less ambiguous is the reference to Pissuthnes who was satrap in Sardis at the time of the Samian revolt. Thucydides adds that he was satrap at Sardis *at that time*: ὃς εἶχε Σάρδεις τότε (Thuc. i. 115. 4). This clause was surely written when Pissuthnes no longer ruled at Sardis, and we know that his rule ended when he revolted and was killed (Ctesias, *Persica* 52); but we cannot give a precise date to his revolt. After his death the revolt was carried on by Amorges who had joined forces with the Athenians by 412 (Thuc. viii. 5. 5, 19. 2, 28, 54. 3 and above, p. 349). Beloch dated the original revolt *c.* 420 (*Gr. Ges.* ii². 1. 377) but this seems too early, for Tissaphernes who succeeded Pissuthnes does not seem to have been long in office when the king demanded from him the arrears of tribute from the Greek cities (Thuc. viii. 5. 5). It is not impossible that the note on Pissuthnes is a later addition but it is more probably part of the original text. 'Not earlier than 415' is perhaps a safer inference than Hammond's 'not later than 415'.

There is one other passage which suggests that the digression on the Pentekontaetia was not originally intended. In describing the events that led to the change in the leadership of the Greeks against Persia Thucydides records the recall and acquittal of Pausanias but says nothing at this point about his subsequent actions (i. 95). Similarly Themistocles passes out of the story when the rebuilding of Athens' walls in 479–478 has been described (i. 91). Later, however, Thucydides devotes a long digression to the closing stages of Pausanias' career, balanced by the story of Themistocles' ostracism, flight, and end (i. 128–38). The digression arises from the diplomatic manœuvring before the opening of the Peloponnesian War. The Spartans, on their first demand, required the Athenians to drive out the curse of the goddess; the Athenians countered with the Tainaros curse and the curse of the Brazen House. This was the temple at Sparta in which Pausanias had taken refuge and in which he was walled up until he was on the point of death. The story of Pausanias' end is therefore relevant, but the account of his sailing out privately when he had been acquitted on his first recall, his occupation of Byzantium, and his forcible expulsion by the Athenians should more properly have come after his first recall. The light measure given to Pausanias and Themistocles in the narratives of the Pentekontaetia would be easier to understand if Thucydides had already written a long digression on the two men.

If Thucydides did not originally intend to record the period between the Persian and Peloponnesian Wars, why did he change his mind? When he began his history he probably did not contemplate the possibility of Athenian defeat. When Athens surrendered and the empire was dissolved there was more need to tell the story of her rise to greatness.

The Use and Misuse of Diodorus

THOUGH Diodorus lived some 400 years after the events which concern us there still survived in his day important sources which are lost to us, and, however unimpressive his narrative may seem, we cannot afford to ignore him unless we are satisfied that his source is worthless. The main difficulty in using Diodorus is to decide the principles that should be applied. This brief survey will be divided into three sections, on numbers, on dates, and on narrative.

Numbers. It is noticeable that in Diodorus' account of the fifth century his numbers often differ from those of Thucydides. Have they any independent value? A series of parallel passages will focus the problem:

I. THE ATHENIAN FORCE AT TANAGRA

T. i. 107. 5. 'The Athenians came out with their full force and 1,000 Argives and contingents from the other allies. The grand total was 14,000.'

D. xi. 80. 1. 'They went out with the Argives and Thessalians intending to attack the Spartans with 50 ships and 14,000 troops.'

2. THE CORINTHIAN FLEET, 433

T. i. 46. 1. 'The Corinthians sailed against Corcyra with 150 ships. There were 10 from Elis, 12 from Megara, 10 from Leucas, 27 from Ambracia, one from Anactorium; the Corinthians themselves provided 90 ships.'

D. xii. 33. 3. 'The Corinthians manned 90 triremes themselves and received 60 from their allies.'

3. ATHENIAN HELP TO CORCYRA, 433

T. i. 45. 1, 50. 5. 'They sent 10 ships to help Corcyra . . . [later there are] 20 ships which the Athenians sent after the 10, because they were afraid that Corcyra might be defeated.'

D. xii. 33. 2. 'They sent 10 well-equipped triremes at once, and promised to send more later if they were needed.'

4. CORCYRAEAN FLEET, 433

T. i. 47. 1. 'The Corcyraeans . . . manned 110 ships . . . and the 10 Athenian ships were with them.'

D. xii. 33. 4. 'The Corcyraeans put out against them with 120 triremes including the Athenians.'

5. THE ESCAPE FROM PLATAEA

T. iii. 20. 2. (At first all had intended to make the attempt) 'but half shrank back because they thought the danger too great; up to roughly 220 maintained their resolve.'

D. xii. 56. 2. 'When they were at a loss and wondering how they could escape, the majority thought that no action should be taken, but the rest, some 200, resolved to force their way by night past the guards.'

6. PAUSANIAS' EXPEDITION, 478

T. i. 94. 1. 'Pausanias was sent out with 20 ships from the Peloponnese; with them sailed the Athenians with 30 ships and a number from the other allies.'

D. xi. 44. 2. 'Pausanias took 50 ships from the Peloponnese and sent for 30 from Athens. . . .'

7. THE ODRYSIAN KINGDOM

T. ii. 97. 3. 'The tribute from all the barbarians and from the Greek cities which they controlled, under Seuthes the successor of Sitalces, who brought it to its highest point, was worth some 400 talents, including only the gold and silver. And gifts in gold and silver worth no less were also brought.'

D. xii. 50. 2. 'Ruling such an extensive territory he collected an annual revenue of more than a thousand talents.'

8. THE THRACIAN EXPEDITION OF 429

T. ii. 98. 3. 'The total number is said to have been not less than 150,000; and of these the majority were infantry, and about one-third were cavalry.'

D. xii. 50. 3. 'When he was at war during this period he mustered for Thrace more than 120,000 infantry and 50,000 cavalry.'

9. PLAGUE LOSSES

T. iii. 87. 'Not less than 4,400 hoplites from the ranks ($\dot{\epsilon}\kappa$ $\tau\hat{\omega}\nu$ $\tau\acute{\alpha}\xi\epsilon\omega\nu$, the field army) and 300 cavalry died. Of the rest of the people the number was impossible to discover.'

D. xii. 58. 2. 'They lost more than 4,000 infantry and 400 cavalry, and of the rest of the people, free and slave, more than 10,000.'

10. PERICLES' REVIEW OF ATHENIAN RESOURCES

T. ii. 13. 3–9.	D. xii. 40.
'Some 600 talents' tribute came in yearly from the allies.'	'Each year there was an income of 460 talents of allies' tribute.'
'There were still 6,000 talents of coined silver on the Acropolis (the highest point reached was 10,000 talents less 300, from which they had drawn for the Propylaea of the Acropolis and the other buildings, and for the siege of Potidaea)'.	'From the 10,000 talents in the common fund they had spent 4,000 talents on the building of the Propylaea and on the siege of Potidaea.'
'There was also uncoined gold and silver in public and private dedications and sacred vessels used in processions and games, Persian spoils and the like worth not less than 500 talents.'	'In addition vessels used in processions and Persian spoils worth 500 talents.'
He added also treasures from the other temples.'	'And he reminded them of the dedications in the temples.
'If the position were desperate they could use the gold plate on the goddess herself. He told them that the refined gold of the statue weighed 40 talents which could all be taken off.'	'And the statue of Athena which had 50 talents of gold, with the fine dressing of the statue all removable.'
'13,000 hoplites apart from the 16,000 on garrison-duty and manning the battlements, drawn from the oldest and youngest and metic hoplites.'	'Apart from allies and men on garrison duty 12,000, and more than 17,000 men on garrison duty and metics.'
'1,200 cavalry, including mounted archers, and 1,600 archers.'	
'300 triremes fit for service.'	'300 triremes available.'

There can be little doubt that in all these examples the ultimate source for the numbers is Thucydides. In the first four the Thucydidean numbers are followed but an appearance of independence is given by a change in the phrasing. In (1) Thucydides mentions only the Argives by name among Athenian allies at Tanagra but he refers generally to other contingents. Diodorus adds the Thessalians (mentioned a little earlier in Thucydides) but he omits the other allies. In (2) Thucydides gives the numbers of ships supplied by each of

Corinth's allies; Diodorus simply gives the total of all the allied contingents. In (3) Diodorus, like Thucydides, says that the Athenians sent two squadrons of ten and, later, twenty ships to help Corcyra but in his version the Athenians promise in sending ten to send more if they are needed. Thucydides implies that the decision to send a second squadron was not in mind when the first was sent. In (4) Diodorus in his total has merely added the Athenian to the Corcyraean ships instead of recording them separately.

In the next six examples there are minor differences between Thucydides and Diodorus. In describing the siege of Plataea (5) Thucydides gives the number of those who attempted to break out, some 220. Diodorus instead gives the number who remained, some 200. This number which at first looks independent is probably based on Thucydides' statement that half were deterred by the danger. For Pausanias' expedition to Cyprus and Byzantium in 478 (6) Thucydides gives the number of ships only from the Peloponnese and from Athens. He does not specify who the other allies were or how many. Diodorus gives the same number for Athens, but gives fifty ships from the Peloponnese and ignores the other allies. But there were certainly ships from some of the islands on the campaign. If other figures suggested real independence one might believe in a second source, but the rest of our examples are against it. In (7) Thucydides has detailed the resources of the Odrysian kingdom in tribute and in gifts. Diodorus has given a global figure based on Thucydides' 400 talents' tribute, which was equalled by gold and silver gifts; then the 800 talents implied by Thucydides are brought up to 1,000 to allow for the miscellaneous gifts of cloth, etc. In (8) Diodorus has slightly altered the context for the Thracian army. For him it is the potential strength of the army at a given period; Thucydides is giving the figures for a specific campaign. Thucydides says that the cavalry was roughly a third of the infantry which was not less than 150,000. In Diodorus the division is done and he gives 5,000 cavalry. Thucydides' 'not less than 100,000 infantry' becomes in Diodorus 'more than 120,000'. So also in the record of Athenian losses from the plague (9). Thucydides' 'not less than 4,400 hoplites and 300 cavalry' becomes 'more than 4,000 hoplites and 400 cavalry'. Similar differences can be seen in the two accounts of Pericles' review of Athenian resources at the beginning of the war. The structure in Diodorus clearly derives from Thucydides; but in Diodorus capital is put before income, whereas Thucydides gives income first. Diodorus' statement of the capital is, on the surface, different from Thucydides, but it is clearly derived from Thucydides, in roughly the same way as Thucydides' figures for the Thracian army are expressed differently by Diodorus. Thucydides' emphasis is on the present level of the capital, 6,000 talents; subordinate is the explanation that it had once been 9,700 talents, but the expenses of the Propylaea and other buildings and the siege of Potidaea had reduced it. Diodorus subtracts 6,000 from 9,700, rounds it off and reaches his main statement, the expenditure of 4,000 talents. For Athens' income from the allies, however, the figures are quite different; why Diodorus gives 460 talents where Thucydides gives 600 is most uncertain. For the gold on the statue of Athena Thucydides gives 40 talents, Diodorus 50; Philochorus, probably from the official record, gives 44 talents.

These examples are sufficient to warn us that when Diodorus' numbers differ from those of Thucydides we cannot necessarily infer that his source is correcting Thucydides on good evidence. Even in major differences, such as the number of ships from the Peloponnese in Pausanias' expedition of 478, or the 460 talents for Athens' tribute income where Thucydides has 600, we cannot believe that Diodorus' figures have serious value. Fifty talents for the gold on Athena's statue is probably given arbitrarily in order to be different from Thucydides. And Diodorus' 560 talents for the first assessment (xi. 47. 1) should not be regarded as a serious rival to Thucydides' 460.

The manipulation of Thucydides' figures that we see in Diodorus is almost certainly to be attributed to his source rather than to Diodorus himself, and there is little doubt that his main source for most of the fifth century is Ephorus. He specifically attributes to Ephorus his account of the causes of the Peloponnesian War (xii. 41. 1); his account of Cimon's exploits from the capture of Eion to his victory of the Eurymedon (xi. 60–2) is extremely close to a series of papyrus fragments covering the same events in the same order (*Pap. Oxy.* xiii. 1610 = Hill, *Sources²*, pp. 114 f.), and two important details in this account, the names of the Persian commanders and the number of the Persian ships, are attributed by Plutarch (*Cim.* 12. 5, 6) to Ephorus (the papyrus and Diodorus have 240 ships, Plutarch 250), but the alternative number attributed by Plutarch to Phanodemus is very different. There are also typically Ephoran features in Diodorus' narrative. Though annalistic in form, he often arranges his material by subject, and will not, for example, begin his account of the First Peloponnesian War until he has completed his account of the Egyptian expedition. Like Ephorus (T11) he prefers to write κατὰ γένος.

While there is good reason to ignore Diodorus' numbers when they conflict with Thucydides, it is more difficult to decide his value when there is no comparison with Thucydides. In his narrative of the First Peloponnesian War Thucydides gives few details and no numbers for the expeditions of Tolmides and Pericles. Diodorus assigns fifty ships to each expedition and as many as 4,000 hoplites to Tolmides (xi. 84. 6). The number of ships is credible but it need be no more than Ephorus' guesswork. The number of hoplites assigned to Tolmides seems too large and is built up by a suspicious anecdote which carries little conviction; but it is quite possible that both figures come ultimately from Hellanicus.

There is one particularly puzzling variant in numbers. None of the fleets of Athenians and allies engaged in fighting the Persians has more than 200 ships in Thucydides. This is his figure for the fleet that was sent to Cyprus and thence to Egypt (i. 104. 2), and also for Cimon's fleet in his final expedition to Cyprus (i. 112. 2). Thucydides gives no figure for the Eurymedon, but it is reasonable to believe that he regarded 200 as the full strength for practical purposes of the League. In the secondary sources the figure of 300 appears fitfully. According to Diodorus, on the Eurymedon campaign Cimon took 200 ships from the Piraeus, and increased his force to 300 by calling on the Ionians and their allies. This fleet he further increased by taking more ships from the cities which he liberated (Diod. xi. 60. 3–5), but in the decisive engagement off Cyprus he has only 250 ships (xi. 60. 6). There is the same ambivalence in Diodorus' account of the Egyptian expedition. On hearing the appeal of Inaros the Athenians resolved (ἐψηφίσαντο) to send 300 triremes to the aid of the Egyptians (xi. 71. 5), but they arrived in Egypt with only 200 ships (xi. 74. 3). To account for this inconsistency it has been suggested that the difference represents a change in policy, or that the first figure is a textual slip. The figure 300 is, however, confirmed later in Diodorus in a speech at Syracuse attributed to Nicolaus. He is warning the Syracusans of the resilience of the Athenians: 'Once before in Egypt Athens lost 300 ships with their crews and forced the King who seemed to be the victor to accept humiliating terms' (Diod. xiii. 25. 2). Plutarch gives Cimon 300 ships on his final campaign (*Cim.* 18. 1); Diodorus, like Thucydides, gives 200. Plutarch also gives 300 as the number of ships with which Cimon started from the Triopian promontory for the Eurymedon (*Cim.* 12. 2). The figure 300 appears sufficiently often to require a special explanation. Behind it may lie a confusion between a total including the allies and a total excluding them. If 200 was a correct figure and was composed of 100 Athenian ships and 100 from the allies, it might have been mistaken for a purely Athenian total to which 100 allies were added. But the most likely source for the figure is Ephorus, and he is capable of introducing it merely to seem independent of Thucydides. Whatever the origin of the number 300 the combination of figures in Diodorus' accounts of the Eurymedon and the Egyptian expedition is a clumsy conflation for which surely Ephorus cannot be blamed. It undermines the very prevalent view that Diodorus used only one source at a time.

Dates. The problem of Diodorus' chronology is even more complex. What system of chronology was used by Ephorus we do not know, but

he was certainly not annalistic and he arranged his material by subject, κατὰ γένος. This treatment has made a considerable impression
on Diodorus' narrative but he has combined it with an annalistic
form, giving the Athenian archon and the Roman consuls for each
year. These dates certainly do not come from Ephorus and it is
generally assumed that he will have got them from a chronological
handbook. From the same source he can have got his dates for the
accession and deaths of kings and tyrants (e.g. xi. 48. 2; xi. 69. 1;
xii. 31. 1). Certain other events also seem to stand outside the flow of
the narrative. In the year 471–470 the names of archon and consuls
are followed by the brief note that Elis was synoecized, though this
synoecism is completely unconnected with what precedes or follows
(xi. 54. 1). Similarly the founding of the colony of Amphipolis is
placed at the end of the account of 437 (xii. 32. 3). It is loosely connected with what precedes by a formula much overused by Diodorus:
ἅμα δὲ τούτοις πραττομένοις, but the events with which it is thus linked
are the preparations for further fighting by Corcyra and Corinth.
Diodorus has got the right date for Amphipolis (see Thuc. iv. 102. 3),
but the wrong date for the clash between Corinth and Corcyra.
Entries such as the synoecism of Elis and the foundation of Amphipolis come from a source that is particularly concerned with chronology and is likely to be reliable. The right date is given for the Thirty
Years' Peace (Diod. xii. 7) and it stands independently at the end of
a chapter, though it is not irrelevant to the rest of the chapter and
could have come from a historical source. There is a stronger case for
attributing Diodorus' date for the dispatch of Athenian settlers to
Hestiaea, 445–444, to the chronological source (xii. 22. 2). Diodorus
has described the expulsion of the Hestiaeans under the year 446–445.
He would naturally have linked the resettlement with the expulsion
if he had not had a firm date from a source that was independent of
Ephorus.

Such dates as these are more likely to be right than wrong, but one
of them we should reject. Under the year 454–453 Diodorus notes
that the Athenians and Peloponnesians agreed to a truce of five years,
negotiated by Cimon. This comes at the beginning of a chapter otherwise devoted exclusively to western history (xi. 86. 1). Gomme finds
the date attractive and tentatively suggests that διαλιπόντων ἐτῶν τριῶν
may have got displaced in Thucydides' manuscripts. 'Three empty
years are so much more likely to have followed a truce than to have
preceded it' (Gomme, HCT i, 325). Thucydides' dating in 451, however, makes better sense of the Spartan invasion of Attica in 446, and
Sparta would be more prepared to come to terms when Athens had
recovered from the Egyptian disaster than when she was at her
weakest immediately after it (in 454–453). On such an issue as this

we should choose Thucydides before the later chronographers. Reigns and foundation dates are not the only insertions in Diodorus' historical narrative. His notes on literary figures, the acme of Pindar, the beginning of Thucydides' history, and such entries as the Metonic cycle (xii. 36. 2) are not taken from the main historical source or sources that he is following. They could all come from the main chronological source or from a separate handbook.

The serious difficulties begin with the dating of historical events. The artificiality of many of his year divisions has long been generally recognized. Under 477–476 he describes the policy of Themistocles immediately after the defeat of the Persians, Pausanias' expedition to Cyprus and Byzantium, his high-handed behaviour, his unpopularity with the allies at the establishment of the Delian League, his recall and eventual death. The next year 476–475 is devoted exclusively to western history. Then for 475–474 Diodorus describes the resentment of Sparta at the loss of the command against Persia, the eagerness for war with Athens, and the intervention of Hetoimaridas who persuades the Spartans to maintain peace (xi. 41–50). This seems to be the immediate result of what Diodorus described under 477–476; it has only been postponed because Diodorus has devoted the intervening year to the west. Similarly for the three years 474–471 no events are recorded for the mainland; all three years are devoted to western affairs, and again later for 467–466 and 466–465 there is nothing but the west.

The Ephoran pattern is clearly seen in Diodorus' treatment of the closing phases of Themistocles' career and in the series of Cimon's victories. The story of Themistocles from a trial at Athens before his ostracism, through his ostracism, flight, settlement at Magnesia, and death is crowded into a single year, 471–470 (xi. 54–59). From Themistocles Diodorus passes to Cimon, and the capture of Eion, the discovery of the bones of Theseus with the resettlement of Scyros, and the Eurymedon campaign, which must have covered a span of more than five years, are also compressed within the year 470–469 (xi. 60–2). It has often been suggested that these two years have been chosen by Diodorus, because one of the events recorded in each career is known to belong to that date. The Themistoclean date would be either the date of his ostracism, or of his condemnation and flight; for Cimon the Eurymedon would be the natural choice. It is indeed possible to build a plausible chronology round 470 for the dates of Themistocles' flight and 469 for the battle of the Eurymedon. But if this were Diodorus' practice we should be able to apply it more generally. If it works for Themistocles and Cimon why does it not work for the Egyptian expedition? Diodorus is elsewhere so arbitrary in his dating that it is easier to believe that 471–470 has been assigned to Themistocles and

470-469 to Cimon because these were the years available when he had reserved three years for western events. Cimon's campaigns are followed immediately by the Spartan earthquake and Helot Revolt (xi. 63-4). But again it would be dangerous to regard this as reflecting a strong tradition correcting Thucydides, who seems to date the revolt in 464; the year 469-468 may have been given by Diodorus simply because that is the point he has reached. The murder of Xerxes and the accession of Artaxerxes are correctly dated (xi. 69), they come from the chronological source; but instead of continuing with the events that were direct sequels of Xerxes' death he interposes a year for events in Greece.

Under the year 464-463 Diodorus records the revolt of Thasos, the 'revolt' of Aegina, the growing resentment of the allies at Athens' growing imperialism, and finally the attempt to colonize Amphipolis and the destruction of the colonists (xi. 70). This would seem to be a very abbreviated version of a digression on the growing power of Athens and the attitude of the allies to her at the time of the Thasian revolt, derived probably from Thucydides' digression after the revolt of Naxos (Thuc. i. 99). But the revolt of Aegina is not so easy to explain away. From Thucydides' narrative it has generally been assumed that Aegina was not an original member of the Delian League and only became one when she had been crushed by Athens and was forced to pay tribute. We should indeed expect Aegina to have withdrawn with the other Peloponnesians when Sparta lost the leadership. Diodorus does in fact follow Thucydides when he comes to the narrative of the First Peloponnesian War. The great sea-battle between Athens and Aegina is recorded in its right place after the battles of Halieis and Cecryphalea. After their crushing defeat the Aeginetans were forced to join the League and pay tribute to Athens (Diod. xi. 78. 4: ἠναγκάσθησαν εἰς τὴν Ἀθηναίων συντέλειαν κατα-ταχθῆναι). There is no question of a revolt here and it would be dangerous to lean on Diodorus for support of the view that Aegina was a member of the League from the outset. Perhaps Ephorus used the two examples of Thasos and Aegina to illustrate the growth of Athenian power, and since the digression was mainly about the relation of Athens to her allies, Diodorus carelessly assumed that Aegina, like Thasos, was an ally (see also above, p. 51).

It would be convenient if we could accept Diodorus' chronology as it stands from 459-458 to 455-454, but it would create as many difficulties as it would solve. Whatever system we adopt, the evidence of the Erechtheid casualty list must be respected. Men from this tribe died in the same year at Halieis, Aegina, and Megara (above, p. 101). These events are distributed by Diodorus between two archon years, 459-458 and 458-457. To reconcile the inscription with Diodorus we should have to date Halieis and Aegina in the first half of 458 and Megara in the second half. But the Erechtheid casualty list includes for the same year losses in Cyprus, Egypt, and Phoenicia. The fighting in these areas also would have to be included in 458, which would mean (if we accept 454 for the final disaster and Thucydides' six years for the duration of the expedition) that it could not be the first year. This is formally possible, but it is considerably more probable that the list of battle areas does reflect the fighting in Cyprus preceding the diversion to Egypt, the first fighting in Egypt, and a raid on Phoenicia. Thucydides also suggests that events moved very rapidly after the dismissal of the Athenians from Ithome (i. 102. 4–105). A reasonable compromise is to believe that the dates given by Diodorus for the early fifties are neither random nor arbitrary, and may go back to an *Atthis*, but that they are not necessarily right. It must have been very difficult in the fourth century or later to date battles in the Pentekontaetia. If Hellanicus was inaccurate (Thuc. i. 97. 2) how were later writers to correct him?

After 454 Diodorus relapses into his more careless habits. For 453–452 he records an expedition led by Pericles against Sicyon. After winning a battle outside the town he failed to take it by storm and withdrew to Acarnania where he plundered the territory of Oeniadae (Diod. xi. 88). The narrative remains very close to Thucydides (i. 111. 2–3), but in Diodorus the expedition takes place after a five years' truce has been made with Sparta (in 454–453) and Diodorus does not seem to realize that he has already described the expedition, though more vaguely, under 455–454 (Diod. xi. 85). Sicyon in this earlier account is not mentioned but from the Peloponnese Pericles 'crossed to Acarnania and won over all the cities escept Oeniadae'. The easiest explanation of this particular doublet is that Diodorus here passed from one source to another. In the same year Diodorus dates the expedition of Pericles to the Chersonese and the settling of cleruchs by Tolmides in Euboea and Naxos. This dating we can ignore without any qualms. The evidence of the tribute lists shows convincingly that the Chersonese was resettled in 447 (above, pp. 159 f.). All that we can infer from Diodorus about Tolmides' expedition is that it was not earlier than 453–452 and probably not later than 447. Diodorus' dating in 453–452 is worthless.

At the end of Book XI Diodorus makes it clear that it was his intention to begin Book XII with Cimon's expedition to Cyprus. 'We have now come to the year preceding the Athenian expedition led by Cimon to Cyprus and bring this book to an end according to the plan announced at its beginning.' His date for the Cyprian expedition, 450–449 and 449–448 is not arbitrary and allocated by Diodorus himself, but taken from a presumably reputable source. This, however, does not mean that the date is necessarily right; it cannot command the same confidence as Thucydides' dates within the Peloponnesian War. For those who believe both in a Peace of Callias and in the interpretation of the Strasburg Papyrus by *ATL* it would require a heavily overcrowded programme. We think it more probable historically that Cimon set out for Cyprus very soon after Sparta's agreement to a five years' armistice early in 451 (above, pp. 124 f.).

Narrative. It is only very rarely that we can rely on Diodorus for numbers or dates. His main value is that he occasionally helps us to fill out the narrative with material that is not in Thucydides. He remains our fullest source for the western Greeks in the fifth century and provides our only evidence for the organization of the colony of Thurii. His account of the revolt of Samos is ultimately based on Thucydides but he adds the detail that Pericles in his first interference exacted a fine of 80 talents as well as taking hostages, and, in our text, he records that the indemnity to be paid by Samos was 200 talents (probably a textual error for 1,200, the figure given by Isocrates xv. 111 : reading ἀπὸ διακοσίων [νεῶν] καὶ χιλίων ταλάντων κατεπολέμησε). When Diodorus differs from Thucydides we can usually ignore him. From his main source Ephorus he derives a partisanship for Athens, and a taste for filling in gaps by plausible rationalization. In Thucydides the First Peloponnesian War starts with a setback for the Athenians: they land at Halieis but are defeated by the Corinthians and Epidaurians (Thuc. i. 105. 1); later they win a sea battle off Cecryphalea. In Diodorus operations open with an Athenian victory (with no clues to location). The Athenians then sail with a large fleet to Halieis, land, and cause heavy casualties among the enemy. The Peloponnesians rally, collect a formidable force, and fight a battle against the Athenians by Cecryphalea which the Athenians again win. This has added nothing but confusion to Thucydides and converted an Athenian defeat into a victory (Diod. xi. 78. 1–2). But not all Diodorus' additions to the Thucydidean narrative are valueless. Diodorus records (xiii. 34. 2) that in 412 Samos was among the Athenian allies that revolted to the Spartans. Thucydides in this year merely records a rising of the demos in Samos against their nobles. A fragment from an Athenian decree, however, which rewards the Samian demos for its loyalty does refer to 'the Samians who brought in the Spartans' (*IG* i². 101 with Lewis *BSA*. xlix (1954), 29–31). More interesting is the comparison of the two accounts of the expulsion of the Delians from Delos in 422. Thucydides says the Athenians considered that an old offence made them impure and that the purification carried out in 426 needed the expulsion of the Delians to complete it (Thuc. v. 1). Diodorus says that the Athenians accused the Delians of secretly making an alliance with the Spartans (Diod. xii. 73. 1.). This is a more attractive explanation, but it is the kind of explanation which Ephorus was quite capable of inventing.

The chapters of Diodorus that add most to our other sources are those which record Cimon's final campaign in Cyprus and the peace with Persia that followed it. We have no means of controlling the details of Cimon's campaign but at the least we can believe that Marium was important to the Greeks at this period, and the reason for that should be the copper mines of the area (App. 7, p. 480; Diod. xii. 3–4). The terms of the peace are almost certainly the terms recorded on a stele at Athens that could be read in Ephorus' day. Theopompus declared that it was a forgery; we believe that he was wrong (above, pp. 129 ff.).

Diodorus was not a critical historian. He was not capable of asking the kind of questions that interest us most about the Athenian empire, nor would he have known where to find the kind of things we want to know. He does, however, fill a few gaps, and it is fair to remember that he is writing a universal history of which the fifth century is a very small part.

The following articles have been of most value to me:

E. Schwarz, *RE s.v.* Diodoros, v, 633–704; F. Jacoby, *FGH* ii A 70 (Ephorus); W. Kolbe, 'Diodors Wert für die Geschichte der Pentekontaetia', *Hermes*, lxxii (1937), 241–69; A. von Mess, 'Untersuchungen über die Arbeitsweise Diodors', *Rh. Mus.* lxi (1906), 244–66, 'Untersuchungen über Ephoros', loc. cit. 360–407; R. Drews, 'Diodorus and his Sources', *AJP* lxxxiii (1962), 383–92; L. Holzapfel, *Untersuchungen über die Darstellung den griech. Geschichte* (1879).

APPENDIX 3

The Origins of the Delian League

HAMMOND has now developed more fully the views which he outlined in his *History of Greece* (*JHS* lxxxvii (1967), 41–61). The various steps in his argument need discussion.

1. Thuc. i. 89. 2: οἱ δὲ Ἀθηναῖοι καὶ οἱ ἀπὸ Ἰωνίας καὶ Ἑλλησπόντου ξύμμαχοι, ἤδη ἀφεστηκότες ἀπὸ βασιλέως, ὑπομείναντες Σηστὸν ἐπολιόρκουν. Hammond (p. 46), accepting from Herodotus that after Mycale the Greeks admitted to their alliance only Samos, Chios, Lesbos, and other islanders, takes οἱ ἀπὸ Ἰωνίας in Thucydides to mean only the Ionian islanders. But Ἰωνία in Thucydides always means primarily the mainland and sometimes excludes the islands (Thuc. viii. 56. 4; i. 12. 4). His natural meaning here is that there were Ionians from the mainland with Athens at the siege of Sestus; nor is it easy to separate Aeolian Lesbos from Ionian Samos and Chios. Herodotus mentions only the Athenians as staying to besiege Sestus; on the other hand, it is only the Peloponnesians who decide to sail home (Hdt. ix. 114. 2). It is doubtful whether Herodotus weighed his words carefully; we can understand him to imply that the islanders stayed with the Athenians.

2. Ἀθ. Πολ. 23. 5: καὶ τοὺς ὅρκους ὤμοσε (sc. Ἀριστείδης) τοῖς Ἴωσιν ὥστε τὸν αὐτὸν ἐχθρὸν εἶναι καὶ φίλον ἐφ' οἷς καὶ τοὺς μύδρους ἐν τῷ πελάγει καθεῖσαν. Hammond (p. 50) presses the literal meaning of this passage. 'As the wording runs, the treaty is between Athens on the one hand and the Ionian League on the other; consultation must have been between two chambers, the Athenian state and the Ionian League.' Hammond thinks that Athens made a separate alliance with Aeolian Mytilene (alluded to in Thuc. iii. 10. 2: ἡμῖν δὲ καὶ Ἀθηναίοις ξυμμαχία ἐγένετο πρῶτον ἀπολιπόντων μὲν ὑμῶν ἐκ τοῦ Μηδικοῦ πολέμου) and 'during the winter, we may suppose, Athens made a number of such alliances'. But the Ἀθ. Πολ. links the oaths sworn by Aristides to the Ionians with the assessment of tribute. In both he is surely referring to the formation of the general alliance, as is also suggested by the following passage in Plutarch's *Aristides*.

3. Plut. *Arist.* 25. 1: ὁ δ' Ἀριστείδης ὥρκισε μὲν τοὺς Ἕλληνας καὶ ὤμοσεν ὑπὲρ τῶν Ἀθηναίων, μύδρους ἐμβαλὼν ἐπὶ ταῖς ἀραῖς εἰς τὴν θάλατταν. Hammond (p. 52) refers this scene to a separate and later

alliance between Athens and all the allies, Ionian, Aeolian, and
Dorian. It is much easier to believe that both sources are referring to
the same famous occasion, without weighing their words carefully.
There is no trace in either source of the two stages inferred by
Hammond.

4. There remains Hammond's most important conclusion that the
Delian League was bicameral, the Boule and Assembly of Athens
being balanced by a Council of Allies (pp. 51 f.). Briefly the following
arguments converge:

(a) This is the natural implication of the most significant passages in
    Thucydides.
(b) This is what Diodorus expressly says.
(c) This is what the parallel of the Peloponnesian League, οἱ
    Λακεδαιμόνιοι καὶ οἱ ξύμμαχοι, reflected in οἱ Ἀθηναῖοι καὶ οἱ
    ξύμμαχοι, suggests.

The passages in Thucydides are ambiguous and cannot decide the
issue.

i. 97. 1 : ἡγούμενοι δὲ αὐτονόμων τὸ πρῶτον τῶν ξυμμάχων καὶ ἀπὸ
κοινῶν ξυνόδων βουλευόντων. Hammond takes this to mean that the
allies conferred in common Congresses, 'which comprised their dele-
gates and no others' (p. 52). Clearly the Greek could mean this, but
it could also mean Congresses which Athens and the allies shared.

iii. 10. 5 : ἀδύνατοι δὲ ὄντες καθ' ἓν γενόμενοι διὰ πολυψηφίαν ἀμύνεσθαι
οἱ ξύμμαχοι ἐδουλώθησαν. Hammond takes this to mean that the allies'
Council, unlike Athens, was unable to unite because of its many and
diverse votes. The statement makes equal sense if the Athenians presided at their meetings.

iii. 11. 4 : ἅμα μὲν γὰρ μαρτυρίῳ ἐχρῶντο μὴ ἂν τούς γε ἰσοψήφους
ἄκοντας, εἰ μή τι ἠδίκουν οἷς ἐπῇεσαν, ξυστρατεύειν. Hammond trans-
lates the reasoning attributed to Athens by the Mytilenaean representatives at Olympia in 428: 'if those we are attacking were not in the
wrong, the group of states whose vote is equal to ours would not be
joining us in the campaign; for they would be unwilling.' But the
passage could equally well mean that the Mytilenaeans and Chians
each had an equal vote with Athens.

While these passages from Thucydides are ambiguous there is little
doubt about the more natural meaning of Diodorus xi. 47. 1 : ὁ μὲν
Ἀριστείδης συνεβούλευε τοῖς συμμάχοις ἅπασι κοινὴν ἄγουσι σύνοδον
ἀποδεῖξαι [τὴν] Δῆλον κοινὸν ταμιεῖον. Diodorus envisages a Congress
confined to allies. Hammond infers that behind Diodorus is Ephorus
and behind Ephorus an earlier source which is neither Thucydides nor
Herodotus, but probably Hellanicus or a writer of τὰ Μηδικά. This is
possible but by no means necessary. All that Diodorus says could be

derived from Thucydides, interpreted by Ephorus in the light of the second Athenian Alliance in the fourth century, when the allies had a separate council presided over by a chairman from the allies.

If the evidence of Diodorus is considered inadequate to resolve the doubts raised by the ambiguities in Thucydides it becomes more important to determine the structure of the Peloponnesian League, for this was at least a possible model for the Delian League. Hammond believes that in this League there were two chambers, the Spartan state and the Allies' Congress: the two partners had an equal vote and each had the power of veto. In this he follows the conclusions of U. Kahrstedt (*Griechische Staatsrecht I: Sparta und seine Symmachie*, 1922) who argued mainly from the procedure followed by Sparta and her allies, according to Thucydides, in 432. This procedure is described in some detail. The Corinthians called the allies to Sparta and Sparta invited them to bring their grievances before the Assembly. The allies were then dismissed and the Assembly was addressed by King Archidamus and Sthenelaidas an ephor. The Assembly decided that the peace had been broken and that they must go to war (i. 88). The Spartans then summoned their allies again in order to put to the vote the question whether there should be war: the majority voted for war (i. 125. 1). In this case there are two separate votes, but the allies' Congress is not presided over by one of the allies as was the fourth-century Athenian Alliance, but by Sparta. Nor does it necessarily follow that Sparta herself always reached a definite decision before summoning her allies. If that were the rule we should have to believe that in 440 when Samos revolted from Athens the Spartans voted for war, because the allies were certainly convened (i. 40. 5): οὐδὲ γὰρ ἡμεῖς Σαμίων ἀποστάντων ψῆφον προσεθέμεθα ἐναντίαν ὑμῖν, τῶν ἄλλων Πελοποννησίων δίχα ἐψηφισμένων εἰ χρὴ αὐτοῖς ἀμύνειν. This in itself is by no means impossible, but we should first review other passages that may throw some light on the problem.

Pericles emphasizes one of the main weaknesses of the Peloponnesian League (i. 141. 6): ὅταν μήτε βουλευτηρίῳ ἑνὶ χρώμενοι παραχρῆμά τι ὀξέως ἐπιτελῶσι, πάντες τε ἰσόψηφοι ὄντες καὶ οὐχ ὁμόφυλοι τὸ ἐφ᾽ ἑαυτὸν ἕκαστος σπεύδῃ. The more natural meaning here surely is that all the allies, including Sparta, had an equal vote. If there were two separate bodies whose agreement was necessary why is not the point made that Sparta can do nothing without her allies' agreement? Kahrstedt (loc. cit.) refers to a fourth-century decree of the allies quoted by Xenophon (*Hell.* v. 4. 37): εἰ δέ τις πόλις στρατιᾶς οὔσης ἔξω ἐπὶ πόλιν στρατεύσοι, ἐπὶ ταύτην ἔφη πρῶτον ἰέναι κατὰ τὸ δόγμα τῶν συμμάχων. Formally this could be a decree passed by a meeting confined to Sparta's allies, but it is more probable that Sparta was a party to the agreement, and that the 'decree of the allies' is a decree of the whole alliance, including Sparta. A similar conclusion would seem to follow even more clearly from a passage in Thucydides. In 421 Sparta tries to dissuade a disillusioned Corinth from adopting an independent policy; she argues that Corinth is breaking the rules of the League in not accepting the peace with Athens which had been accepted by the majority: παραβήσεσθαί τε ἔφασαν αὐτοὺς τοὺς ὅρκους, καὶ ἤδη ἀδικεῖν ὅτι οὐ δέχονται τὰς Ἀθηναίων σπονδάς, εἰρημένον κύριον εἶναι ὅτι ἂν τὸ πλῆθος τῶν ξυμμάχων ψηφίσηται (Thuc. v. 30. 1). If τῶν ξυμμάχων does not include Sparta, it would mean that Sparta was bound by what the majority of her allies decided; this surely is a condition that Sparta would never have tolerated while she remained strong.

We may then believe that in both the Peloponnesian and the Delian Leagues the meetings of the allies were presided over by the leaders who, as in modern international bodies, could rely on the weaker allies voting as their leaders wished.

Sealey has advocated an even more radical departure from traditional views (*Ehrenberg Studies*, pp. 233–55). His strongest point is his insistence that in Thucydides' view 'the purpose of the League was to exact vengeance for their sufferings by ravaging the King's land' (i. 96. 1: πρόσχημα γὰρ ἦν ἀμύνεσθαι ὧν ἔπαθον δῃοῦντας τὴν βασιλέως χώραν) and that the further motive of freeing the Greeks is put forward not by Thucydides himself but in the speeches of the Mytilenaeans (iii. 10. 3), who have a case to plead, and by Hermocrates (vi. 76. 3–4), whose interest it was to show how far Athens had departed from the original purpose of the League. 'The original purpose of the Delian League was to plunder the King's land.'

Others have assumed that the admission of Asiatic Greeks of the mainland to the League can reasonably be called liberation. Herodotus, according to Sealey, implies that the mainland cities paid tribute to Athens at the same rate as they had previously paid to Persia (Hdt. vi. 42. 2). 'The adding of such cities to the Delian League was as much akin to conquest as to liberation.' The mainland cities would be the first victims of any Persian reprisals, if they joined in anti-Persian enterprises, and this was clearly realized at the Council of Samos after the battle of Mycale when the allies admitted only islanders to the Hellenic League. The operations of 478 did not alter the strategic situation in Asia Minor. 'It follows that, when the Delian League was founded, among its members Asiatic mainlanders must have been very few.' 'It may well be incorrect to suppose that the mainland cities of Asia Minor were the scene of a large popular movement, such as could be carried away by the first enthusiasm of victory.'

Sealey rounds off his study by offering an almost Herodotean explanation of the immediate context of the establishment of the

ℓ

Delian League. We discuss later the difficulty of explaining the story recorded by Ion of Chios and preserved in Plutarch (*Cim.* 9) concerning the disposal of Persian prisoners from Sestus and Byzantium. Sealey suggests that the prisoners taken at Sestus at the end of winter 479–478 were not disposed of at once, but left in Sestus. When in the following summer Pausanias brought the Greek fleet from Cyprus and captured Byzantium the prisoners from Sestus were brought to Byzantium. Pausanias' arrogance led to his recall and the command was offered to the Athenians, who now had to undertake the task of distributing the booty of Sestus and Byzantium. 'Two Athenian generals were present, Aristides and Cimon, but it was the junior of them who later told his friends at a drinking party how he had distributed the spoils. Perhaps Aristides passed on a task that might have hurt his reputation.' 'The student must beware of the dogmas of sentimental liberalism. The League of Delos was founded because of a dispute about booty and its purpose was to get more booty.'

This interpretation of Ion's story of the distribution of the spoils from Sestus and Byzantium is not essential to Sealey's main thesis and can be lightly dismissed. It is most improbable that Persian prisoners would have been left in Sestus when the Athenian fleet sailed home. Had the Persian prisoners from both towns been available when Byzantium was captured, would Pausanias have waited so long before dividing the spoils? We should also need a better reason for Cimon rather than Aristides becoming responsible for the distribution. A context is needed where Cimon is in command (see App. 4, p. 465).

The more important points in Sealey's case need more serious discussion. In emphasizing plunder as a main objective Sealey is straining the use of δηοῦντας. As A. W. Jackson has pointed out (*Hist.* xviii (1969), 12–15) the word means 'ravage' and does not necessarily imply booty; when booty is included it is secondary. Nor was plunder a main objective in the campaigns of 478. The reduction of a large part of Cyprus (Thuc. i. 94. 2) was not a piratical raid, and Byzantium was chosen because of its strategic importance. In Thucydides' summary account of the early years of the League there is no mention of plunder. It remains true, however, that Thucydides' statement of the purpose of the League does not include the liberation of Greek cities. This, however, is a legitimate inference from what the League forces did in fact do and also from the sinking of metal in the sea to emphasize that the allies were binding themselves to remain permanently in the alliance. That they should solemnly pledge themselves to ravage the king's territory indefinitely is difficult to believe. That they should realise that only by a permanent alliance could they be independent of Persia is only what experience had taught them. Why at this point

Thucydides should seem to narrow his vision we cannot understand, but even Thucydides should not be blindly followed.

Thucydides' statement about the purpose of the League would be more credible if Sealey were right in his judgement about the Ionian mainlanders. If the League was virtually limited to islanders and mainlanders were deliberately excluded, a policy of raids would be intelligible. But neither Herodotus nor Thucydides justifies the somewhat cynical conclusions of Sealey about the mainlanders' mood after the Greek victory at Mycale. 'So for the second time Ionia revolted', says Herodotus (ix. 105) and by this he surely means that the majority at least of the cities of the seaboard were anxious to become independent. Sealey emphasizes the opposition of Phaselis to the Greeks on their Eurymedon campaign and implies that it could be typical; but it would be misleading to argue from Phaselis' attitude to the feelings of Miletus, Teos, Phocaea, or their Ionian neighbours. Phaselis was in a very vulnerable position at the limits of Greek settlement and may have relied largely on trade with the east.

APPENDIX 4

The Latter Days of Pausanias

The story recalled by Ion of Chios, which Plutarch preserves (*Cim.* 9), concerning Persian prisoners from Sestus and Byzantium (above, p. 66) has provoked continuing controversy and there are excellent arguments against all the solutions that have been proposed. There was a capture of Sestus by the Athenians under Xanthippus early in 478, and Byzantium was captured in the late summer of 478 by the Greek fleet under Pausanias. At some later date Pausanias had to be forcibly expelled from Byzantium to which he had returned after his first recall to Sparta. At no time do our other sources speak of a capture of Sestus and Byzantium in the single campaign which Ion implies. Sestus is a positive embarrassment.

Ion of Chios had come to Athens as a very young man (μειράκιον) almost certainly before 462, for he recorded Cimon's famous appeal in the Ithome debate of that year. Jacoby thinks that he is probably also the source for Plutarch's story of Cimon's judgement in the theatre at the Dionysia of 468, but this is far from certain (Plut. *Cim.* 8. 7–8). Cimon's story was told when the wine was flowing freely (τοὐντεῦθεν οἷον εἰκὸς ἐν πότῳ τοῦ λόγου ῥυέντος ἐπὶ τὰς πράξεις τοῦ Κίμωνος) and Ion was young. It would be convenient to assume with Jacoby and Meyer that his memory was at fault, but that is a counsel of despair (Jacoby, *CQ* xli (1947), 2, n. 4; Meyer, *Forschung.* ii. 64 f.). If we are to avoid the unattractive hypothesis of three captures of Byzantium between 479 and 462 we are virtually forced to associate Ion's capture of Sestus with the expulsion of Pausanias from Byzantium by the Athenians. Our context for Ion's story will therefore depend on our reconstruction of Pausanias' career after his recall to Sparta late in 478, or, improbably, early in 477. When did he sail out to Byzantium, how long did he stay there, and what was he doing?

Our main source for this period is here surprisingly unsatisfactory. Had Thucydides' account been written by any other Greek historian it would not have been taken seriously. Beloch long ago pointed out the most serious of the difficulties (*Gr. Gesch.*[2] ii. 2, 154–9), and Miss Lang has recently given a fuller, perhaps a little too full, catalogue (M. L. Lang, 'Scapegoat Pausanias', *Class. Journ.* lxiii (1967), 79–85). The most glaring is the use of Pausanias' correspondence with Xerxes. It is just conceivable that Pausanias kept a letter from Xerxes, but it is very unlikely that, knowing he was suspected, he would have allowed it to get into the wrong hands. We cannot believe that he would have kept a copy of his reply. In that letter he asked for the king's daughter; in Herodotus it is the hand of the satrap's daughter, a much more plausible ambition, and Herodotus regards even this as doubtful (v. 32: εἰ δὴ ἀληθής γέ ἐστιν ὁ λόγος). The chronology also is unconvincing. During his first occupation of Byzantium Pausanias sends a letter to Susa and receives a reply. This reply goes so much to his head that in his tours through Thrace he has a bodyguard of Medes and Egyptians; all this before his recall which comes while the Greek fleet is still together at Byzantium, presumably before the end of the sailing season, or, at the latest, early in 477. If we accept 478–477, the date given by the Aristotelian Ἀθ. Πολ. (23. 5) for the assessment of Aristides, the change in leadership from Sparta to Athens cannot be later than the spring of 477 and should more probably fall in 478. In his account Thucydides seems to realize that he is dealing with controversial issues. He says that on his first recall the main charge against Pausanias was Medism, 'and it seemed to be perfectly clear' (i. 95. 5: κατηγορεῖτο δὲ αὐτοῦ οὐχ ἥκιστα μηδισμὸς καὶ ἐδόκει σαφέστατον εἶναι); similarly of the last phase Thucydides, having recorded that the Spartans found out that Pausanias was also intriguing with the helots, adds 'and so it was' (i. 132. 4: ἐπυνθάνοντο δὲ καὶ ἐς τοὺς Εἵλωτας πράσσειν τι αὐτόν, καὶ ἦν δὲ οὕτως). We cannot be so easily satisfied. If the evidence of Medism in his first occupation of Byzantium was as evident as Thucydides thought it was, Pausanias would surely not have been given so much rope. Even Thucydides says that at the time of his second recall he was still held in high regard at Sparta as regent for Pleistoanax, son of Leonidas, and he held the σκυτάλη, a sign of official standing, when he was summoned from Colonae (i. 131. 1).

The reason for the first recall of Pausanias need be no more than the hostility of the East Greeks, who had very much more to gain from Athenian than from Spartan leadership. One may also seriously wonder whether Pausanias' conduct could have become sufficiently flagrant to give the Athenians acceptable grounds for besieging and finally expelling him from Byzantium before the end of 477. Tentatively we suggest that Pausanias, though not acceptable to Lesbos, Chios, Samos, and the other East Greeks, had a solid following in Byzantium which, as a Megarian colony, may have felt less affinity than the Ionians with Athens.

It is therefore reasonable to join the revival of interest in Justin's statement that Pausanias occupied Byzantium for seven years (Justin ix. 1. 3: 'condita primo a Pausania, rege Spartanorum, et per septem annos possessa fuit, dein variante victoria nunc Lacedaemoniorum nunc Atheniensium iuris habitus est'); the actual date of his expulsion will depend on the date of his arrival (477 or 476) and so be 471 or 470. By this time Pausanias' conduct must have been very suspicious, but if there had been clear-cut evidence of Medism he would have surely been disowned by Sparta. It is more likely that it was from Colonae that he began negotiations with Persia through the satrap at Dascylium. Such an interpretation seems to me more probable than the more exciting and more radical view proposed by Miss Lang. She suggests that Pausanias from 478 onwards had no wish to continue the war with Persia, but wanted peace, and it was because the east Greeks saw that he wanted peace that he was first recalled. He was sent out a second time to continue peace negotiations, but when, as a result of Cimon's victories, any talk of peace became discreditable, he was sacrificed by the authorities at Sparta and made a scapegoat. This strays much too far from the evidence.

There are many advantages to be gained from dating the expulsion of Pausanias from Byzantium in the late seventies. Miss White has shown that it is extremely difficult to date the death of Pausanias earlier than the early sixties (M. E. White, *JHS* lxxxiv (1964), 151). On our reckoning this could mean a comparatively short stay at Colonae of not more than two or three years. It is also rather easier to accept a second capture of Sestus about 470 than in 477 or 476. During Pausanias' seven years in Byzantium Sestus could have become infected from Dascylium, Byzantium, or Doriscus. This context will accord with the general situation assumed by the writer of the second *Themistocles Letter* (above, p. 72); and will give a more realistic background to Cimon's operations in the Hellespont in 465.

It remains to re-examine the case for the most commonly accepted date for the expulsion of Pausanias from Byzantium. The expulsion is placed by *ATL* early in 477 because Ephorus says that Cimon took the fleet from Byzantium to Eion, and the attack on Eion was, according to Thucydides, the first operation (against Persia) of the Delian League. There must have been a campaign in the first year of the League, but before proceeding against Eion the vitally important Byzantium had to be made secure. The capture of Sestus, associated by Ion with the capture of Byzantium, will probably reflect an attempt by the Persians who held Doriscus to make contact with the satrap at Dascylium. This involves a too crowded time-table. In not more than six months Pausanias has to return to Sparta, appear before a Spartan court, sail out to Byzantium, and become sufficiently suspect to be expelled without creating a serious situation with Athens. The expulsion, moreover, has to be a minor operation. Thucydides' ἐκ τοῦ Βυζαντίου βίᾳ ὑπ' Ἀθηναίων ἐκπολιορκηθείς (i. 131. 1) is too lightly dismissed; his language implies that the Athenians were denied entry, and that the resistance was sufficiently serious to make a quick assault impracticable. Thucydides' description of Pausanias' end (i. 134. 2 : προσκαθεζόμενοι ἐξεπολιόρκησαν λιμῷ) is quoted as a parallel showing that the siege could have been short, but in both cases it is the length of the siege that is emphasized. Pausanias had to be starved out and it was not till he was on the point of death from starvation that the 'siege' was ended. So Byzantium could not be taken quickly nor did the city surrender early in the siege.

ATL's main reason for choosing 477 is the evidence of Ephorus that the capture of Byzantium immediately precedes the attack on Eion, for Ephorus implies that the Athenians came from Byzantium to Eion, and they can only have been at Byzantium to expel Pausanias. The passage in question comes from a papyrus which is clearly Ephoran, but may be an epitome rather than Ephorus himself (*Pap. Oxy.* xiii. 1610; *FGH* 70 F 191 ; Hill, *Sources*[2], pp. 114 f.) : Ἀ[θη]ναῖοι [δ]ὲ Κ[ί]μωνος τοῦ Μιλτιάδου στρατηγοῦντος ἐκπλεύσαντες ἐκ Βυζαντίου μετὰ τῶν συμμάχων ['Ηι]όνα τὴν ἐπὶ Στρ[υμό]νι Περσῶν ἐχόν[τω]ν εἷλον. Before this passage Ephorus, as Diodorus (xi. 54–9), seems to have given the post-war career of Themistocles down to his death, and before that will have come the story of Pausanias which probably Ephorus like Diodorus continued from his first capture of Byzantium to his death at Sparta. The record of Cimon's victories in the papyrus seems to follow a digression (op. cit. 36 f.) : ὅθεν] παρεξ[έβ]ημεν. In Diodorus and presumably in Ephorus also the digression is a moralizing discourse on the virtues and vices of Themistocles, and it is very doubtful whether the Eion campaign was linked in any way with the expulsion of Pausanias from Byzantium. Byzantium may have been chosen by Ephorus because Eion was the next campaign to 478. He may have assumed that the fleet remained at Byzantium over the winter of 478–477 while the Delian League was established.

One other hypothesis should perhaps be briefly examined. Since Ion's story hinges on the taking of Persian prisoners at Byzantium it is tempting to identify the occasion with the first capture of Byzantium in 478 when Persian prisoners figure prominently in the record. The prisoners from Sestus will then be those that were captured in or at the end of the winter of 479–478. This solution was suggested by Woodhead (*Proc. Camb. Phil. Soc.* v (1952), 9–12) and developed further by Sealey (*Ehrenberg Studies*, 248–52). It seems unlikely that the prisoners would have been held so long rather than being sold at Sestus or Athens; it is much more unlikely that Cimon would have been responsible for distributing the booty in 478. Pausanias was in command when the Persian prisoners were captured ; it would have been his responsibility to dispose of the spoils. If the distribution was delayed beyond Pausanias' recall the responsibility should have passed to Aristides who commanded the Athenian contingent.

APPENDIX 5

The Battle of Oenoe

The battle of Oenoe is mentioned in our surviving sources only by Pausanias. He tells us (i. 15. 1) that there was a painting of the battle in the Stoa Poikile at the north end of the Agora. The painting showed the Athenians drawn up in battle-line against the Spartans at Oenoe in the Argolid; the action was just beginning. The battle was also commemorated by the Argives at Delphi (x. 10. 3). Near the sculptured horse was a group of the seven Argive heroes against Thebes, and the Argives themselves attributed the dedication to the victory which they and the Athenians who came to help them won against Sparta. Pausanias adds that he personally thinks that the group of the Epigoni was also set up by the Argives to commemorate the battle. On two counts this evidence is very surprising. In the Stoa Poikile such a painting is a very odd companion to the other three great paintings, and we should not expect such an apparently important event to have left no trace in our literary sources. But the evidence is impressive: it needs to be either explained or explained away.

Until near the end of the nineteenth century it was generally held that the most appropriate context for the battle of Oenoe was in the early fourth century, when Athens with Argos and Corinth was ranged against Sparta. This solution was encouraged by the identification of Hypatodorus, one of the two sculptors of the Delphi dedication according to Pausanias, with a Hypatodorus mentioned by the Elder Pliny (*NH* xxxiv. 50), who flourished in the 102nd Olympiad (372–369 B.C.). A dedication base at Delphi with the name Hypatodorus in archaic letters had been recorded by Dodwell, but the stone was temporarily lost and it was assumed that the letters were archaistic rather than archaic. This attempt to reconcile the evidence had to be abandoned when the stone was found; the letters were clearly early and not archaistic (*FD* iii. 1. 388 f., pl. 12; *Klio* viii (1908), 188; *LSAG* 45, no. 17). C. Robert (in *Hermes*, xxv (1890), 412–22) demonstrated that the battle of Oenoe must be placed in the period of the mid-fifth-century alliance of Athens and Argos, between 462–461 and 451–450.

An alternative solution was offered by Löwy and revived by H. F. Stier (*Eine Grosstat der attischen Geschichte*). They suggested that the name Oenoe was on the painting but that it represented the nymph Oenoe and that the battle was the Athenian victory over the Boeotians at Oenophyta in 458 (or 457). This desperate attempt to explain Thucydides' silence has, rightly, won very little support. Oenophyta was indeed a memorable victory, but the meaning of a picture on constant public view near the centre of the city would not have been so singularly distorted, and the evidence from Delphi would still need to be explained. Pausanias says that shields captured from the Spartans on Pylos or Sphacteria were hung in the Stoa Poikile (Paus. i. 15. 4. One of the shields was discovered near the temple of Hephaestus, *Hesp.* vi (1937), 347 f.). It would have been highly appropriate to hang shields captured from Spartans near the painting of an earlier triumph against Sparta.

The context should be sought in the ten years following 462–461. Robert thought the battle fitted best in the very early days of the alliance before Thucydides' record of the so-called First Peloponnesian War began. Busolt, *Gr. Gesch.* (iii. 323 n. 3) preferred the year following Tolmides' expedition round the Peloponnese in which no operations are reported by Thucydides. He is similarly silent about the capture of Troezen, which we know only from the fact that the town had to be surrendered under the terms of the Thirty Years' Peace (Thuc. i. 115. 1). The capture of Troezen and the battle of Oenoe, Busolt thought, might have been two episodes in a single expedition. The controversy showed every sign of becoming dormant, ignored, or relegated to a modest footnote, when Miss Jeffery reopened the issue with a battery of fresh arguments and a very original hypothesis (L. H. Jeffery, *BSA* lx (1965), 41–57). She raised two objections to the early date. Herodotus (ix. 35) refers to an oracle promising Sparta a series of five consecutive victories and the last of the five is Tanagra; the series should not be interrupted by a defeat at Oenoe. She also thinks that Athens would not have been able to command the sea-route while Aegina was still free, and was not strong enough to risk the land-route. Miss Jeffery also thinks that an Argive dedication by two Boeotian sculptors when there was a flourishing school of Argive sculptors needs a special explanation. Her own hypothesis is bold and persuasively presented. The Argives sent a contingent of 1,000 men to fight with the Athenians at the battle of Tanagra. After the battle they waited in Athens, needing Athenian transport to return home, and fought again with the Athenians at the battle of Oenophyta, the spoils of which included the sculptured group which the Argives dedicated at Delphi. They were escorted back to Argos by Tolmides in his famous *periplous* and the battle of Oenoe was fought by Tolmides' hoplites with the Argives. This reconstruction Miss Jeffery supports by a scholiast's note on a passage in Aeschines (ii. 75): 'He told him to emulate the command of Tolmides who with 1,000 picked Athenians proceeded through the middle of a hostile Peloponnese without fear.'

These arguments are of uneven weight. Even the scholiast whose record elsewhere is very unimpressive does not mention a battle in this context, and Tolmides' exploits were so frequently invoked that if they included a victory over a Spartan force we should have heard about it. Nor should the earlier years be ruled out on the ground that the sea route was not safe while Aegina had a strong fleet. If Athens could attempt to seize Halieis before her great battle with the Aeginetan navy (Thuc. i. 105. 1) she could send a force to assist Argos. A victory, however small the scale, would seem more significant in the early days of the alliance than after the major battles of Tanagra and Oenophyta.

We should, however, discard one of the main arguments that have been used in support of the early date. It has normally been assumed that the painting of Oenoe is contemporary with the other paintings of the Stoa Poikile. This would be embarrassing because there are good reasons for associating the building with the circle of Cimon, and an open clash between Athens and Sparta marked the abandonment of Cimon's policy. The archaeological evidence is not yet decisive but the evidence so far collected is thought to point to a date c. 460 (Hesp. xix (1950), 328; AJA lxviii (1964), 200). The building was originally named the Peisianakteion (Plut. Cim. 4. 6), and Peisianax was probably the brother of Cimon's Alcmaeonid wife, Isodice (Beloch, Gr. Gesch.² ii. 2. 32); Polygnotus who painted the Fall of Troy recognized Cimon as his patron. Cimon had planted plane trees in the Agora; it was appropriate that a Cimonian should be associated with a new public building in the Agora with magnificent paintings. From Pausanias' account of the paintings it is reasonable to infer that the battle of Oenoe was not part of the original design. He says (i. 15. 1) that the Stoa first shows the battle of Oenoe, then 'On the middle wall are the Battle of the Athenians against the Amazons, the Fall of Troy, and finally the Battle of Marathon.' The three subjects recur in most of the panegyrics of Athens and they were particularly appropriate for Cimonians. Miltiades, father of Cimon, had been mainly responsible for the victory of Marathon and Cimon had brought to Athens the bones of Theseus who was primarily responsible for driving out the Amazons. The natural inference from Pausanias is that the Battle of Oenoe was on one of the shorter walls and that the other three were on the long wall facing you as you entered. Robert, assuming that there would be symmetry in the distribution of the paintings suggested that the Fall of Troy and the Battle with the Amazons, both mythical subjects, were on the facing wall and that the two historical battles were on the short walls. This, however, is contrary to Pausanias' natural meaning; he implies that all three paintings were on the facing wall, ἐν τῷ μέσῳ τῶν τειχῶν. Miss Jeffery has tentatively suggested that there was perhaps a fifth painting, the Suppliant Heraclids (op. cit. 43) opposite Oenoe, but this is attested by only one indifferent source.

From the arrangement of the paintings I infer that Oenoe was added after the other paintings. For this there may also be some archaeological evidence, for which I am deeply indebted to Professor Homer Thompson, who writes: 'The paintings were done not directly on the walls but on wooden tablets; so much is clear from Synesios' use of the term *sanides* and also from his statement that the paintings had been removed by a proconsul. If the paintings had been intended from the beginning proper provision should have been made for fastening the wooden plaques to the walls; we should have expected a framework of wooden scantlings set with slots in the face of the wall as in the early Propylon on the Acropolis at Athens (M. H. Swindler, *Ancient Painting*, p. 424 n. 14a; W. B. Dinsmoor, *Architecture of Ancient Greece*[3], p. 198) and in the Stoa of Attalos I at Delphi (G. Roux, *BCH* lxxvi (1952), 153, fig. 25). Yet, if the Agora excavators are right in their attribution of fragmentary wall blocks to the Stoa, the wooden panels were fastened to those blocks by means of iron spikes: a much less effective arrangement and one that has the appearance of an after-thought. Can it be that the part of the wall represented by the surviving fragments was prepared to receive a painting after the completion of the Stoa, conceivably the Battle of Oenoe?'

Miss Jeffery has argued that no fifth-century battle between Greeks would be commemorated by a painting of the actual battle. The painting, she thinks, must have been of a mythical subject; it probably reflected the championship of the Argive cause by Athens when the seven Argive champions marched against Thebes and Athens procured their burial. Oenoe figured in the painting because the Seven left Argos by the road leading to Mantinea which passed Oenoe (Paus. ii. 25. 2). The Athenians in that case would have been fighting Thebans, but the names, probably originally on the picture, were gradually obliterated. This explanation of the name Oenoe on the painting is very strained; it is easier to believe that the battle of Oenoe was celebrated in paint by a picture of the battle, because at the time a victory on land over Sparta was an amazing achievement. After the major engagements that followed, Oenoe was seen in perspective as a minor relief and when Thucydides came to write his summary of the period it was almost forgotten; at the time it must have been a splendid encouragement to the new democratic leadership. The immediate context eludes us but the Spartans may have attempted with a small force to take the Argives by surprise when they heard of the Argive–Athenian alliance. The site of the battle, over the border in Argive territory, shows that the Spartans were the aggressors.

APPENDIX 6

The Sources for the Egyptian Expedition

There are three main sources for the Egyptian Expedition, Thucydides (i. 104, 109–10), Ctesias (63–7), and Diodorus (xi. 71. 3–6, 74–5, 77). The account of Thucydides is brief and reduced to essentials; that of Ctesias is mutilated because it has been abbreviated by an epitomator; Diodorus' account is almost certainly a rewriting of what Ephorus wrote at greater length. Apart from these main sources the passing references of Herodotus and the battered text of a dedication from the Samian Heraeum are of first-class importance.

The main problem of this inquiry is to decide whether there is any independent evidence to support Thucydides' implication that a fleet of 200 ships was totally destroyed and part of a further squadron of fifty ships. The approach to the problem lies through Diodorus. Much of his account could be rhetorical filling. Ephorus was quite capable of describing in broad strokes the first stage of the rebellion; it is not necessary to believe that he owed to another source the driving out of the Persian tax-gatherers or the raising of an army of natives and mercenaries. However, the next stage cannot be pure invention. Artaxerxes sends his uncle Achaemenes with more than 300,000 foot and horse. This force encamps by the Nile, the Egyptians concentrate their forces but wait for the Athenians. The Athenians turn the fighting in Egypt's favour; the Persian survivors take refuge in the White Fort of Memphis. Diodorus' battle is a land battle, which has no place in Thucydides, who merely says that the Athenians and their allies 'sailed from the sea into the Nile, gained control of the river and two thirds of Memphis, and fought against the remaining third, called "the White Fort" '.

Diodorus describes the reinforcements under Megabyzus in much more detail than Thucydides and though his source could have invented the Persian numbers it seems likely that the name of the fleet's commander is borrowed and not invented. The relief of the White Fort, the withdrawal of the Greeks to the island of Prosopitis, and the drying of the channel (that linked two arms of the Nile) are common to Thucydides and Diodorus, but for the final phase Diodorus is more informative than Thucydides. In his account the Egyptians desert the Athenians and surrender first. The Athenians fight heroically, surpassing the heroes of Thermopylae, with the result that the

Persians, anxious to avoid further losses, make a truce by which the Athenians are to leave Egypt in safety. It is unlikely that any significant number of Greeks should have escaped without a truce, but both the desertion of the Egyptians and the truce could have been invented by Ephorus. In Diodorus there is a further complication to which we have already referred (above, p. 452). The Athenians voted a force of 300 triremes (xi. 71. 5) but arrived with 200 (xi. 74. 3), though a Syracusan speaker later refers to the loss of 300 triremes with their crews in Egypt (xiii. 25. 2). There seem to be two sources here; we cannot, however, know whether the 200 ships are independent of Thucydides.

Even if we attribute as much as possible to the rhetoric and inventiveness of Ephorus there are some elements in Diodorus' story that must derive from a source that is independent of Thucydides. Where did Diodorus' source get his material for the initial Persian reaction to the revolt, the sending of a large army to Egypt under the king's uncle Achaemenes? The first source to suspect is Ctesias, and his Persian strategy does in fact resemble the account of Diodorus; but there are differences. The Persian commander is Achaemenides, the king's brother, and his force is 400,000 not 300,000 strong. In the fighting that follows the arrival in Egypt of this force the Athenians play an important part, and in both accounts there is no suggestion that Athenian allies are also in Egypt. But here too there are differences. In Diodorus the Athenians seem to be taking part in a land battle; in Ctesias the Athenians fight in their ships against the Persian fleet. There are also differences in the two versions of the Persian reinforcements under Megabyzus. Ctesias gives Megabyzus 200,000 men and there are 300 ships under Oriscus; in Diodorus also there are 300 ships, but their commander is Artabanus and there are 300,000 men in the army.

There is good reason then to believe that, when Ephorus wrote, Thucydides and Ctesias were not the only sources available for the Egyptian expedition. From some other source Ephorus knew that Achaemenes was the Persian commander who was killed in the first major engagement. He could have found the name in Herodotus (iii. 12. 4 and vii. 7) but Herodotus says that Achaemenes was governor of Egypt at the time and Ephorus would turn more probably to a source that covered the whole Egyptian episode. The natural candidate is Hellanicus who wrote both a *Persica* and an *Atthis*. Thucydides' criticism of Hellanicus' account of the Pentekontaetia is well known: it was brief and the chronology was inaccurate. But Hellanicus was independent of Thucydides and he should have included an account, however brief, of the Egyptian expedition. Had Hellanicus mentioned the early withdrawal of the main part of the Greek fleet, or made the Greek numbers considerably lower than Thucydides, there should have been some clear trace of this in later authors. There is indeed one possible reflection. In a wildly erratic summary of the period Justin (iii. 6. 6), after recording the dismissal of the Athenians from Ithome, says that the Athenians took the tribute reserve from Delos to Athens, and the Spartans, though preoccupied by the helot revolt, sent a Peloponnesian force against Athens. 'The Athenians were then weak as they had sent their fleet to Egypt, and so they were easily defeated in a sea battle. Then, after an interval, when the return of their forces had increased the strength of their fleet and army, they renewed the fighting.' Victory fluctuated, and there was no clear decision. The Spartans returned to reduce the Messenians and negotiated with the Thebans to make war on Athens. 'Faced with this crisis Athens chose two leaders, Pericles a man of outstanding military record and Sophocles writer of tragedies.' From what sources all this confusion is drawn we do not know, but it is highly doubtful whether the note on the fleet's return from Egypt derives from a good source which has otherwise left no traces in Justin. (Justin ix. 1. 3, on Pausanias' occupation of Byzantium, which has been accepted in App. IV, is probably from a different source.)

It remains to discredit Ctesias. His account has won some favour because he gives a number for the Greek fleet which seems historically more probable, and the numbers of Greeks surviving at the end, 6,000, seems too small from a force of some 40,000 men. We cannot, however, salve our consciences by arguing that Ctesias at the Persian court will have had access to Persian sources and, writing to please Persians, would not have been likely to underestimate the number of Persia's enemies. It is quite clear that much of his account is nonsense. His Persian numbers are wildly exaggerated, he does not know the name of the Persian commander at the battle of Papremis, he has no clear appreciation of the Greek position on Prosopitis, he knows nothing of the return to Greece of the Greek survivors through Cyrene. His epitomator has almost certainly made his account less clear than the original but the main mistakes are those of Ctesias. Forty ships in Ctesias is not the number left in Egypt but the number on arrival and they are Athenian, not Greek ships. Ctesias is very unlikely to have known how many were Athenian and how many were supplied by the allies. Forty is too small for the total even of those that were left. Ctesias also gives 6,000 as the number of Greek survivors at the end, and this is more than one would suspect from forty ships after what must have been heavy losses in the defeat at Memphis (they are described by Ctesias (64) as οἱ Ἕλληνες . . . ὅσοι μὴ ἐν τῇ μάχῃ μετὰ Χαριτιμίδου ἀπέθανον). There is a good parallel to Ctesias' under-statement of Greek numbers in the accounts of the battles of the Persian invasion (above, p. 107).

There are further points that need to be considered in Thucydides' account. The Greeks hold out on the island of Prosopitis for eighteen months and it is only by drying the canal between the two arms of the Nile that the Persians overcome them. But the island, Herodotus (ii. 41. 5) tells us, is nine *schoinoi* in circumference, nearly sixty miles. Could the Greeks have defended themselves if they had only forty or fifty ships and were therefore presumably heavily outnumbered by the Persian fleet that had come with Megabyzus. Thucydides also says that after the final disaster on Prosopitis fifty more ships, Athenian and allied, arrived in Egypt, 'knowing nothing of what happened' (Thuc. i. 110. 4: οὐκ εἰδότες τῶν γεγενημένων οὐδέν). It is incredible that they should not have known of the relief of Memphis and the occupation of Prosopitis; during the eighteen months some messages must have got through. What they did not know was that a position which seemed indefinitely safe had been overrun. In that case surely they must have thought that the Greeks controlled the river round Prosopitis, which again implies a large Greek fleet.

APPENDIX 7

Cyprus in the Fifth Century

The reconstruction of relations in the fifth century between the Greeks, particularly the Athenians, and Cyprus offered in the text is not orthodox. It is generally held that after the Ionian revolt Cyprus was virtually cut off from the Greek world, that the expedition of 478 led by Pausanias neither had, nor was intended to have, any enduring effects, and that the Greek operations in Cyprus in the middle of the century had no roots in previous policy. This view is based on the silence of the literary sources and the evidence of archaeology. The silence of the literary sources need not concern us for, as Thucydides emphasized, the only account before his own of the period between the Persian and the Peloponnesian Wars was a meagre outline; and he himself intended no more than an accurate summary. Any reconstruction must, however, be consistent with the archaeological evidence.

The evidence provided by archaeology for the history of Cyprus in the sixth and fifth centuries is abundant, but difficult to assemble and assess. Had the present Antiquities Department been in control when the first enthusiastic rush for Cyprian sanctuaries and cemeteries began towards the end of the nineteenth century, we should know much more; but the rich rewards of the pioneers were reaped by collectors and financiers. A wealth of Cyprian sculpture and pottery found its way into public and private collections in America, England, Germany, and France, but very little was published about the excavations. The splendid Cesnola collection of late archaic sculpture from Cyprus in the Metropolitan Museum of New York is a vivid reminder of this phase;[1] Cesnola was the American consul at Larnaka and used his influence to good effect. He wanted attractive objects for his private collection; others wanted money. In 1886 a consortium of business men financed the exploitation of large cemeteries outside the ancient town of Marium which extended from the archaic period to the Roman. A third of the yield had to be left in Cyprus and found a safe home in the Nicosia Museum; the remainder was auctioned in Paris in 1888 and widely dispersed. Ohnefalsch-Richter, who conducted the excavations, became passionately interested in the history

---

[1] J. L. Myres, *Handbook of the Cesnola Collection of Antiquities* (1914).

of Cyprus, and his book, with the appetizing title of *Kypros, the Bible and Homer*, and a long letter of introduction from Gladstone, gave a very fair account of some of the tombs. A general survey of the cemeteries was also given in 1888 by Hermann.[1] But these accounts, though giving a general impression of the results of the excavation, did not provide the detail that the historian requires. We can still see how many Attic red-figure vases of the early classical period came to the Nicosia Museum from Marium; it would be a very formidable task to trace the distribution of the auction in Paris to national museums and private collections.

The next phase was more systematic and conscientious. The British Museum organized excavations in Paphus, Curium, and Marium, and published accounts of their work.[2] Their methods would not satisfy modern excavators, but the material they found can still be seen in the British Museum and the museum in Nicosia. Meanwhile, Myres, with the help of Richter, had brought order into the Nicosia Museum and published a useful catalogue.[3] In the twentieth century the pace of excavation at first slackened, but interest quickened again in the thirties, and by now an effective Antiquities Department was able to exercise a stricter control over unauthorized digging. Most important of the excavations of this period were those of the Swedish Cyprian Expedition which for the first time introduced modern scientific methods and set an example in the detailed publication of their work.[4] The Swedes, led by E. Gjerstad, attempted by the analysis of stratified levels to establish a framework for the chronology of Cyprian pottery, and they were always concerned with the relevance of their results to the history of the island. The Antiquities Department has also, under two outstanding directors, P. Dikaios and V. Karageorghis, done increasingly valuable work in its own excavations and in recording regularly the island's archaeological news.

The inadequacy of nineteenth-century publications is not the historian's only handicap in studying the archaeological evidence. The excavated sites are not always the sites that have most to offer to the historian. We know considerably more archaeologically about Idalium, which is barely mentioned in the literary sources, than about classical Salamis, which dominates the record. Our archaeological knowledge of Salamis was virtually confined until recently to the Roman, Early

---

[1] P. Hermann, *Das Gräberfeld von Marion* (1888).
[2] A. S. Murray, A. H. Smith, H. B. Walters, *Excavations in Cyprus* (London, 1900); with *JHS* xi (1890), 1–99; xii (1891), 59–198.
[3] J. L. Myres and M. Ohnefalsch Richter, *A Catalogue of the Cyprus Museum* (1899).
[4] *The Swedish Cyprus Expedition* (1927–31) by E. Gjerstad and others (4 vols., 1934–62); henceforward *SCE*.

Christian, and Byzantine periods: considerable light has now been thrown on the earlier history of the city by the excavation of a series of magnificent 'royal' tombs dating from the eighth to the sixth centuries.[1] Meanwhile a French expedition, working in the southern part of the city, has found Rhodian, Ionian, and Attic pottery of the archaic period and 'Attic black glazeware in considerable quantities, showing the importance of the relations of Salamis with Athens after 470'.[2] But this pottery was found out of context and it is doubtful whether Attic black glaze can be dated with sufficient precision to compare the flow before and after 450. What is most needed by the historian of the fifth century is a substantial series of fifth-century tombs which have not been pillaged; it will be a long time before a balanced history of fifth-century Salamis can be written. Soli also should be a key site in reconstructing the relations between the Greeks and Cyprus. One of her rulers was praised by Solon, she held out stubbornly in the Ionian revolt after the disintegration of the Cyprian army in the field, and in Aeschylus' *Persae* she is one of the three Cyprian cities which threw off the Persian yoke as a result of the Greek victory at Salamis in 480.[3] Archaeologically we can see that her craftsmen in the fourth century were still closely following Greek originals in funerary reliefs, at a time when Greek influence on Cyprian sculptors was in eclipse through most of the island, but we know very little indeed about Soli in the fifth century from literary or archaeological sources.

During the sixth century Cyprus was a pawn in the struggle for power that followed the collapse of Assyria. Firmly incorporated in the Assyrian Empire at the end of the eighth century, the island unostentatiously became independent as Assyria disintegrated. In the struggle between Babylon and Egypt for the inheritance Egypt was unable to hold her own by land, and Nebuchadnezzar had little difficulty in securing the submission of Syria, the Phoenician cities, and Judaea. But the fleet of the Saite kings of Egypt could control the eastern Mediterranean, and Amasis annexed Cyprus, probably in the middle of the century. Though the island was an Egyptian dependency for no more than a generation Egyptian styles had a very marked influence on Cyprian sculpture.[4] Before the death of Amasis, however, Cyprus had realized the significance of the Persian Cyrus' dazzling victories. When Cambyses invaded Egypt in 525 Cyprian ships accompanied

---

[1] The first tomb was excavated by Dikaios in 1957. Karageorghis began the systematic exploration of this necropolis in 1962, with spectacular results. V. Karageorghis, *Excavations in the Necropolis of Salamis* (*Salamis*, vol. 3), 1967.

[2] *BCH* xci (1967), 325.

[3] Solon F 8; Hdt. v. 115. 2; Aesch. *Persae* 891–2.

[4] *SCE* iv, pl. 6, pp. 304 f.

him; Cyprus had gone over to Persia without any fighting.[1] But at
first Persian rule rested very lightly on the island. Her cities were still
governed by their own kings and those who had mints continued to
issue their own coins. There is no evidence of Persian influence in
Cyprian architecture or art of the late archaic period, and perhaps
tribute was not systematized until the reign of Darius. The strongest
influence on Cyprus during the last quarter of the sixth century came
not from Persia but from Greece, and its clearest manifestation is seen
in Cyprian sculpture of the period. The Egyptianizing style is discarded and a Cypro-Greek style emerges. Examples from all over the
island that can now be seen in the Cyprus Museum, the Metropolitan
Museum of New York, the British Museum, and the Ashmolean
Museum of Oxford reflect common features and a common style, close
to the Greek archaic but preserving an independent Cypriote in-
gredient.[2] Greek influence on Cyprian sculpture is accompanied by an
increased flow of pottery imports from the Greek world, particularly
from the east Greek states but also in increasing volume from Attica.
The cemeteries of Marium have provided the richest yield both in
quantity and quality, but eastern Greek and Attic imports have been
found in significant quantities at Paphus, Amathus, Curium, and other
sites. The prominence of Marium in the archaeological evidence is not
purely accidental. Though no other comparable group of unexploited
tombs has been found elsewhere, the volume of Greek pottery in
tombs at Marium requires explanation, for Marium seems to have
been insignificant in the Assyrian period. Why should there be so
much Attic black-figure pottery, including a number of elegant Little
Master cups, in a city which the Assyrians did not include among the
seven important kingdoms of the island?[3] The answer is almost certainly the copper in the hills east of the city. Marium lies at the western
end of the copper belt, the nearest port of call for Greek ships intent
on a copper cargo. A mine is still being operated in the district.[4]

The archaeological evidence gives point to the role of Cyprus in the
Ionian revolt. The east Greeks were sufficiently closely associated with
Cyprus to try to make Cyprus an active member of their league and to
send their fleet to aid the Greek cause in Cyprus. In Cyprus there was
a corresponding movement in favour of the Greeks, but beneath the

[1] Herodotus (iii. 19) records but does not date the submission. In Xenophon's
Cyropaedia (vii. 4. 2, viii. 6. 21) Cyprian troops serve under Cyrus even before the
final collapse of Croesus; we would prefer a more reliable authority.

[2] *SCE* iv (2), 109–29 with pls. xi–xvi.

[3] For the quantity of Attic vases see the index of Proveniences in Beazley, *Attic
Red Figure Painters*[2]. Some of the best are described by Beazley in *PBA* xxxiii (1947),
195–244.

[4] For the copper resources of Cyprus see C. Q. Cullis and A. B. Edge, *Report of
the Cupriferous Deposits of Cyprus*, London (Crown Agents), 1927.

surface there were serious divisions. The leader of revolt in Cyprus was Onesilus of Salamis. His ancestor Euelthon had claimed on his coinage to be ruler of all Cyprus and Onesilus had similar ambitions;[1] but he met opposition inside and outside Salamis. He first had to depose his brother Gorgus, who refused to adopt his Greek policy; he then had to attempt to force Amathus to follow him. When the Ionian fleet arrived in Cyprian waters there was apparently a united front behind Onesilus, but in the decisive battle Curium deserted and other contingents followed.[2] In Herodotus' account there is no mention of friction between Phoenicians and Greeks during the revolt in Cyprus. At Salamis it seems that the issue was not between Phoenician and Greek but between appeasers who held discretion to be the better part of valour, and fervent Hellenists who, like the heroic Euagoras, king of Salamis in the fourth century, preferred to fight for freedom, and freedom with a Greek flavour. Nor did Amathus oppose Onesilus because she was dominantly Phoenician; Amathus in her foundation-myth and the names of her kings is a Greek city, and the recently found debris from a destroyed shrine includes a considerable quantity of East Greek and Attic sherds.[3] The Swedes may be right in inferring that there was no traditional hostility between Greeks and Phoenicians in Cyprus until the Persians used the Phoenician minority as a counter against the Greeks after the Ionian revolt.[4]

The decisive victory of the Persian army in Cyprus was followed by a series of mopping-up operations as the cities were individually reduced. Soli alone, according to Herodotus, offered serious resistance, but at Paphus it was necessary to build a siege mound and more than one attempt was made by the garrison to undermine it.[5] We should expect the Persians, influenced by the uprising, to have tightened their hold on the island when the fighting was over; archaeology may indicate two typical measures. Adjoining the town wall of Paphus a substantial building has been excavated which does not seem to be Cyprian in character; the finely fitting blocks of its ashlar walls are thought to reflect the building style of early fifth-century Achaemenid work at Persepolis. This may have been the headquarters of a garrison, not necessarily of Persian nationals, but of troops in Persian pay.[6] Similarly, there was built at about this time on the hill of Vouni, overlooking the plain of Soli, a palace of eastern type which has no close parallel in Cyprus. The position is a strong one and is surrounded by

---

[1] *BMC Cyprus*, lxxxvi–lxxxix. [2] Hdt. v. 104. 3–115. 1.
[3] *BCH* lxxxv (1961), 312–14. [4] *SCE* iv. 2. 477.
[5] *JHS* lxxiv (1954), Arch. Report, 174; F. G. Maier in *Report of the Dept. of Antiquities, Cyprus*, 1967, 31 with 39–42, pls. 8–10. The large number of arrowheads, spearheads, and javelin points in the mound also suggests serious resistance.
[6] J. Schäfer, *Opusc. Athen.* iii (1960), 155–75.

strong fortifications. The Swedish excavators suggest that it was built to dominate Soli, which had offered the most stubborn resistance during the revolt. They also think that it was occupied from Marium, which was now ruled in the Persian interest by non-Greek kings.[1] That Vouni was intended to control and restrict Hellenism in Soli is highly probable; it is more doubtful whether the control of Soli was delegated to Marium, some thirty miles to the west. It is easier to believe in a Persian governor, or a puppet king.

The Cyprian cities sent their contingents to Xerxes' invasion force; they had no practicable alternative. Gorgus, who had opposed the Hellenic policy of Onesilus, was one of the two commanders of the Cyprian contingent, and we hear also in Herodotus of twelve ships from Paphus under the command of Penthylus, eleven of which were lost in a storm.[2] Aeschylus, giving in a resonant chorus of his *Persae* a patriotic roll call of the Greeks who shook off the Persian yoke as a result of the Greek victory at Salamis, includes Paphus, Salamis, and Soli.[3] He has not chosen these cities for the sake of metre, nor because he hoped that they might join the Delian League. It is not unreasonable to believe that they did reassert their Hellenism when they heard of the destruction of the Persian fleet. If this is so, Pausanias was taking his combined Greek force to an island where he could expect support. His intention, we have said, was to encourage the movement for independence among the Cypriote Greeks by a sharp demonstration of power. This must have taken the form of driving out Persian garrisons, which is what Diodorus expressly tells us, though his source may be no more than Ephoran rationalism.[4]

For our present purpose events in Cyprus during the ten years following the expedition of Pausanias are of crucial importance. Was Cyprus immediately abandoned or did the Greeks hope and try to recover the relationship that existed before the Ionian revolt? It is very doubtful indeed whether archaeology will ever be able to isolate such a brief period; the only general conclusion that the present state of the evidence allows is that there was a continuing import of Attic pottery in the first half of the fifth century, but on a much reduced scale. This need not surprise us for before the battle of the Eurymedon Cyprus, or at least part of Cyprus, was a Persian base again.

In 460 or 459 the Athenians led a full levy of the Delian League to Cyprus and for some four years Athenian naval power was dominant in the eastern Mediterranean. The Greek force was soon withdrawn to support the revolt of Inaros, but their successes in Egypt should have encouraged the philhellenic parties in Cyprus. A reaction could be

---

[1] E. Gjerstad, *Corolla Archaeologie* (1932), 145–71; *AJA* xxxvii (1933), 589–98.
[2] Hdt. vii. 98, 195.   [3] Aesch. *Persae* 891–2.   [4] Diod. xi. 44. 2.

expected when the League forces were overwhelmed in Egypt, but when Cimon sailed to Cyprus on his return from ostracism his aim was not merely a demonstration, but the breaking of Phoenician power in the island. He was besieging Citium, the strongest Phoenician city in Cyprus, when he died and before that, according to Diodorus, he had already captured Marium. The importance of Marium we have already seen; Athens was interested in her copper as well as her politics and it is a nice coincidence that the most impressive import from Greece during the fifth century comes from another copper centre. In 1889 Ohnefalsch Richter had the good fortune to find the sanctuary of Apollo at Tamassus still filled with dedications in different states of preservation. Among the ruins were substantial bronze fragments, and with considerable ingenuity Gjerstad has shown convincingly that a bronze head associated with some of these fragments had been purchased some fifty years earlier by the sixth Duke of Devonshire at Smyrna in 1838 or 1839.[1] What has since been known as the Chatsworth head was once the head of a bronze Apollo, slightly larger than life size, standing in the sanctuary of Apollo at Tamassus.

This head has been generally accepted as the work of a Greek sculptor and one of the finest surviving illustrations of the period of transition between late archaic and classical. Gjerstad thought that the sculptor must have come to Cyprus in person to carry out his commission: it is not impossible, though considerably less likely, that the statue was transported from Greece, but in either case such a commission in such a place should be significant. It is therefore interesting to note that Strabo emphasizes the copper-richness of Tamassus;[2] the date becomes important. The generally acceptable limits, I think, would be 470–450; C. Picard prefers 470–460, Gjerstad 460–450.[3] I would like to see in the Tamassus Apollo a reflection of the revival of Hellenism in Cyprus in the first years of the Egyptian revolt.

Cimon's expedition in 451 was intended to bring Cyprus once again within the Greek orbit, but his death led to a more cautious policy. By the Peace of Callias Athens renounced her military ambitions in the eastern Mediterranean and Cyprus was left to fend for herself. One of the effects of the Peace was to increase the eastward flow of Greek trade again, but politically philhellenism was badly shaken. The kings of Marium in the second half of the century have good Greek names and there is an increase in the import of Attic pottery; Cimon's capture of the town may have had more than a

---

[1] E. Gjerstad, *Eranos*, xliii (1945), 236–42. To W.-H. Schuchardt the head is Roman, of the time of Hadrian. The technique is incompatible with such a date; see D. Haynes *Rev. Arch.* 1968, 101–12.

[2] Strabo xiv. 6. 5, 684: μέταλλά τε χαλκοῦ ἐστιν ἄφθονα τὰ ἐν Ταμάσσῳ.

[3] C. Picard, *Manuel*, 2. 1, 122; Gjerstad, op. cit. 236 f.

temporary influence;[1] but Salamis fell on lean days. A Phoenician exile, having first established himself at court, unseated the Teucrid dynasty and seized power for himself. When he met his end in a plot he was succeeded by another Phoenician. Isocrates in his *Euagoras* paints a very gloomy picture of Cyprus at this time. 'The civilization of Salamis was destroyed and the whole island was enslaved to the Great King.'[2]

It was probably in this general context that Citium absorbed the independent Hellenized city of Idalium. King Baalmelek II calls himself in an inscription found at Idalium 'King of Citium and Idalium, son of Azbaal, King of Citium and Idalium, son of Baalmelek (I)'.[3] Gjerstad was convinced by the evidence of the pottery that the western acropolis of Idalium was destroyed *c.* 470 and that this marked the conquest by Azbaal.[4] Numismatists, however, found this date difficult to accept; it allowed too little time for the series of known kings of Idalium and required a considerably earlier date for Azbaal than the coinage evidence seemed to suggest.[5] A. J. Seltman, accepting the earlier date, hoped to solve the problem by suggesting that the coins of Idalium should be attributed to some other minting centre, possibly Paphus.[6] The incidence of 'Idalium coins' in hoards (and particularly the earlier of the two Dali hoards) makes Idalium the more likely minting centre:[7] but, even if the evidence of these coins is found to be irrelevant, there would remain the more serious difficulty of the date of Azbaal. The numismatists' dating of Azbaal in the third quarter of the century was based on coin hoards, and two hoards published in 1969 have strengthened a case that was already strong.[8] The earlier of the two hoards, from Jordan, was sealed *c.* 450 and it includes five coins of Baalmelek I and none of his son. In the second hoard, from Syria, sealed *c.* 425–420, there are two coins of Azbaal and none of his father. In the Celenderis hoard, sealed a little later *c.* 400, there were at least 11 staters of Azbaal.[9] In the hoard that was hidden under a staircase when the palace at Vouni was destroyed *c.* 380 there were 9 coins of Azbaal, 42 of his successor Baalmelek II, and 18 of Demonicus,

---

[1] *BMC Cyprus*, 32 f. Gjerstad, 'Four Kings', *Opusc. Arch.* iv (1946), 21–4. Imports from Marium in the second half of the century include, beside Attic R. F. pottery and black glaze, an attractive Greek grave relief of *c.* 440, Beazley, *AJA* 55 (1951), 333–6 together with *JHS* Arch. Report, 1956, 26 f.; a local grave relief, closely based on Attic, V. Wilson, *RDAC* 1969, 56–63; and (*c.* 400) a very attractive Attic grave relief, Dikaios, *Guide to the Cyprus Museum*[3], p. 141, pl. 20. 4.

[2] Isocr. ix. 19–20.   [3] Rép. d'Epigr. Sém. no. 453.

[4] *SCE* ii. 625; iv. 2. 479 f.n. 5.

[5] G. F. Hill, *The History of Cyprus*, i. 153–5.

[6] A. J. Seltman, *Num. Chron.* 1964, 76–9.

[7] *Num. Chron.* 1871, 1–18.   [8] C. Kraay, *Rev. Num.* x (1969), 181–235.

[9] C. Kraay, *Num. Chron.* 1962, 1–15.

who ruled from 388; the 150 coins of Marium in the hoard all came from the second half of the century.[1] At the earlier end the Larnaka hoard, which was buried shortly after 480, has no coins of Azbaal's father, Baalmelek I.[2] The collective evidence of these hoards against dating the conquest of Idalium by Azbaal as early as 470 is very strong; three Aeginetan tortoises overstruck by Azbaal point the same way.[3] The first Aeginetan tortoises which replaced the turtles were minted after the reduction of Aegina in 457 and before the Peloponnesian War. If we are right in preferring 446–445 as the date for the reopening of the Aeginetan mint it would be difficult to stretch Azbaal's reign back to 470; even if the first issue of tortoises was shortly after 459 the reign would become embarrassingly long.[4] Historically a successful attack on Idalium would suit either date. At 470 it would be part of the Persian reaction which led to the recovery of part at least of Cyprus in the seventies. But the third quarter of the century when philhellenism in Cyprus had lost its Hellenic support would provide an equally appropriate context.

The conquest of Idalium had been preceded by an unsuccessful attack. A bronze tablet inscribed in the Cypriote syllabary, said to have been found on the western acropolis of Idalium, records the rewards given to a Greek doctor and his brothers for help to the wounded 'when the Persians and Citians were besieging Idalium'.[5] When the inscription was set up in the temple of Athena, Idalium had successfully resisted attack. If the fall of Idalium had to be dated in 470 this inscription would mark an early stage in the Persian reaction after 478. It fits, however, equally well in the period which, according to Isocrates, saw the 'barbarization' of the island.

In Salamis Phoenician rule lasted little more than a generation. In 411, or a little earlier, Euagoras who had taken refuge in Cilician Soli and claimed to be of royal Teucrid descent, returned to Salamis and with a mere handful of supporters seized control. According to Isocrates the city was in a sad condition, with no industry, no trade, no harbour.[6] Power could not have been seized and maintained so easily unless philhellenism had strong roots in Salamis, and Euagoras made it clear that he did not stand for a harmony of mixed cultures, but for Hellenism. 'Before the return of Euagoras', says Isocrates, 'the

---

[1] W. Schwabacher, *Opusc. Athen.* iv (1946), 25–45.
[2] Dikaios and Robinson, *Num. Chron.* 1935, 165–90.
[3] *Museum Notes*, vi (1954), 90, correcting *NN and M* xxii (1924), 10; *Num. Chron.* 1960, 34; *Num. Chron.* 1961, 111.
[4] For the Aeginetan mint, see p. 184.
[5] O. Masson, *Inscr. Cypr. Syll.*, p. 135, no. 19; K. Spyridakis, Κυπριακαὶ Σπουδαί, i (1937), 61–3.
[6] Isocr. ix. 29–30.

rulers who were fiercest enemies of the Greeks were thought most of; after his return it was those who seemed most philhellenic.'[1] It was not long before Euagoras made himself known to the Athenian public. He welcomed Andocides in 411 and enabled him to send corn and copper (or bronze) to the Athenian fleet at Samos.[2] A slightly later inscription suggests that he negotiated on Athens' behalf with Tissaphernes, satrap at Sardis, and was honoured with Athenian citizenship.[3] When the Athenian fleet was lost at Aegospotami Conon with his small squadron fled to Cyprus, and Euagoras was largely responsible for winning Persian support for Athens which culminated in the destruction of Spartan sea power at the battle of Cnidus in 394. This, however, was a temporary tactical phase; Euagoras had no wish to remain in the Persian Empire and even when Athens ceased to support him he was prepared to defy all the resources of Persia alone for the cause of Hellenism.

To make the part played by Cyprus in our reconstruction plausible it had to be shown that there were potentially strong elements in Cyprus that wanted Cyprus to be Greek and that there were good reasons why the Greeks of the Aegean should be concerned about Cyprus. The widespread evidence of Greek imported pottery towards the end of the archaic period explains the Greek attempt to hold Cyprus in the Ionian revolt, and there is enough Attic pottery of this period from Marium to indicate specially close relations with Athens. The natural explanation is the copper that was marketed there, and Athens may also have shipped copper from Tamassus at Soli. Athens therefore, apart from the pride of championing Hellenism in the grand crusade against the barbarian, could have had good practical reasons for wanting to protect Greek interests in Cyprus. There was a short period in the fifties when it seemed as if Cyprus had been won for Greece and when Cyprian cities may, with Dorus, Celenderis, and other Greek foundations on the eastern Mediterranean coast, have become tribute-paying allies of Athens. But the disaster in Egypt was a severe warning and the attempt to restore the superiority of the early fifties died with the death of Cimon. But the success of Euagoras shows that Athenian eastern ambitions in the fifth century were not impracticable dreams.

[1] Isocr. ix. 49.

[2] Andoc. ii. 11. In the same speech (20, 21), pleading for his restoration, he implies that he was later, between 411 and 405 (probably in 408 or 407), responsible for the sailing of a substantial convoy of corn ships from Cyprus.

[3] *IG* i². 113. There are references to the Persian King and to Tissaphernes (therefore before 407), but the context is lost.

37–8: Ἀθεναίοις κ]|αὶ βασιλεῖ κα[ὶ τοῖς ἄλλοις χσυμμάχοις

35–6: Ἀθεναίος καὶ βασι]|λέα καὶ τὸς ἄλλ[ος χσυμμάχος

38–9: Τισ]|σαφρένεν.

APPENDIX 8

The Debate on the Peace of Callias

Some of the more important passages are set out and numbered for convenient reference.

T 1. Hdt. vii. 151 : τυχεῖν ἐν Σούσοισι τοῖσι Μεμνονίοισι ἐόντας ἑτέρου πρήγματος εἵνεκα ἀγγέλους Ἀθηναίων, Καλλίην τε τὸν Ἱππονίκου καὶ τοὺς μετὰ τούτου ἀναβάντας, Ἀργείους δὲ τὸν αὐτὸν τοῦτον χρόνον πέμψαντας καὶ τούτους ἐς Σοῦσα ἀγγέλους.

T 2. Hdt. vi. 42. 2 : ταῦτά τε ἠνάγκασε ποιέειν καὶ χώρας σφέων μετρήσας κατὰ παρασάγγας . . . κατὰ δὴ τούτους μετρήσας φόρους ἔταξε ἑκάστοισι, οἳ κατὰ χώρην διατελέουσι ἔχοντες ἐκ τούτου τοῦ χρόνου αἰεὶ ἔτι καὶ ἐς ἐμὲ ὡς ἐτάχθησαν ἐξ Ἀρταφρένεος.

T 3. Thuc. viii. 5. 5 : ἐπήγετο γὰρ καὶ ὁ Τισσαφέρνης τοὺς Πελοποννησίους καὶ ὑπισχνεῖτο τροφὴν παρέξειν· ὑπὸ βασιλέως γὰρ νεωστὶ ἐτύγχανε πεπραγμένος τοὺς ἐκ τῆς ἑαυτοῦ ἀρχῆς φόρους, οὓς δι᾽ Ἀθηναίους ἀπὸ τῶν Ἑλληνίδων πόλεων οὐ δυνάμενος πράσσεσθαι ἐπωφείλησεν.

T 4. Thuc. viii. 56. 4 : Ἰωνίαν τε γὰρ πᾶσαν ἠξίου δίδοσθαι καὶ . . . τέλος ἐν τῇ τρίτῃ ἤδη ξυνόδῳ, δείσας μὴ πάνυ φωραθῇ ἀδύνατος ὤν, ναῦς ἠξίου ἐᾶν βασιλέα ποιεῖσθαι καὶ παραπλεῖν τὴν ἑαυτοῦ γῆν ὅπῃ ἂν καὶ ὅσαις ἂν βούληται.

T 5. Isocr. iv. 120 (380 B.C.) : μάλιστα δ᾽ ἄν τις συνίδοι τὸ μέγεθος τῆς μεταβολῆς, εἰ παραναγνοίη τὰς συνθήκας τάς τ᾽ ἐφ᾽ ἡμῶν γενομένας καὶ τὰς νῦν ἀναγεγραμμένας. τότε μὲν γὰρ ἡμεῖς φανησόμεθα (a) τὴν ἀρχὴν τὴν βασιλέως ὁρίζοντες καὶ (b) τῶν φόρων ἐνίους τάττοντες καὶ (c) κωλύοντες αὐτὸν τῇ θαλάττῃ χρῆσθαι.

| T 6. | *Sea limits* | T 7. | *Land limits* |

(a) Isocr. iv. 118 (380 B.C.) :
εἰς τοσαύτην ταπεινότητα κατεστήσαμεν ὥστε μακρὸν πλοῖον ἐπὶ τάδε Φασήλιδος μὴ καθέλκειν.

(b) Isocr. vii. 80 (357 B.C.) :
οὔτε μακροῖς πλοίοις ἐπι τάδε Φασήλιδος ἔπλεον.

οὔτε στρατοπέδοις ἐντὸς Ἅλυος ποταμοῦ κατέβαινον.

Sea limits | Land limits

(c) Isocr. xii. 59 (339 B.C.):

οὐκ ἐξῆν αὐτοῖς . . . οὔτε μακροῖς
πλοίοις ἐπὶ τάδε πλεῖν Φασήλιδος.

οὔτ' ἐντὸς Ἅλυος πεζῷ στρατοπέδῳ
καταβαίνειν.

(d) Dem. xix. 273 (343 B.C.):

ἐντὸς δὲ Χελιδονίων καὶ Κυανέων
πλοίῳ μακρῷ μὴ πλεῖν.

ἵππου μὲν δρόμον ἡμέρας πεζῇ μὴ
καταβαίνειν.

(e) Lycurg. Leocr. 73 (c. 330 B.C.):

μακρῷ μὲν πλοίῳ μὴ πλεῖν ἐντὸς
Κυανέων καὶ Φασήλιδος.

(f) Diod. xii. 4. 5 (? = Ephorus):

μηδὲ ναῦν μακρὰν πλεῖν ἐντὸς
Φασήλιδος καὶ Κυανέων.

τοὺς δὲ τῶν Περσῶν σατράπας μὴ
καταβαίνειν ἐπὶ θάλατταν κατωτέρω
τριῶν ἡμερῶν ὁδόν.

(g) Plut. Cimon 13. 4:

ἔνδον δὲ Κυανέων καὶ Χελιδονίων
μακρᾷ νηὶ καὶ χαλκεμβόλῳ μὴ
πλέειν.

(h) Aelius Aristides, Panath. 153 (p. 249 Dindorf):

οὐ γὰρ ἐᾷ [sc. ἡ πόλις] πλεῖν εἴσω
Χελιδονέων καὶ Κυανέων.

θαλάττης δ' ἀφέξειν ἴσον πανταχῇ
σταδίους πεντακοσίους.
cf. 169: "οὐδὲν μᾶλλον ἐλᾷς ἄχρι
θαλάττης, ἀλλ' αὐτῆς", φησί, "τῆς
ἵππου δρόμον ἡμέρας τῆς θαλάττης
ἀποσχήσεις."

(i) Aristodemus (FGH 104 F 13, 2):

ἐφ' ᾧ ἐντὸς Κυανέων καὶ Νέσσου
ποταμοῦ καὶ Φασήλιδος, ἥτις ἐστὶν
πόλις Παμφυλίας, καὶ Χελιδονέων
μὴ μακροῖς πλοίοις καταπλέωσι
Πέρσαι.

ἐφ' ᾧ . . . καὶ τριῶν ἡμερῶν ὁδόν,
ἣν ἂν ἵππος ἀνύσῃ διωκόμενος, μὴ
κατίωσιν.

(j) Suda s.v. Κίμων:

ἐκτὸς Κυανέων καὶ Χελιδονέων καὶ
Φασήλιδος (πόλις δὲ αὕτη τῆς
Παμφυλίας) ναῦν Μηδικὴν μὴ
πλεῖν νόμῳ πολέμου.

T 8.(a) Theopompus (FGH 115 F 153): ὅτι . . . καὶ αἱ πρὸς βασιλέα
Δαρεῖον Ἀθηναίων πρὸς Ἕλληνας συνθῆκαι . . . καὶ ὅσα ἄλλα ἡ
Ἀθηναίων πόλις ἀλαζονεύεται καὶ παρακρούεται τοὺς Ἕλληνας.

(b) Id. (F 154) : Harpocr. s.v. Ἀττικοῖς γράμμασιν: Θεόπομπος δ᾽ ἐν τῆι κε´ τῶν Φιλιππικῶν ἐσκευωρῆσθαι λέγει τὰς πρὸς τὸν βάρβαρον συνθήκας, ἃς οὐ τοῖς Ἀττικοῖς γράμμασιν ἐστηλιτεῦσθαι, ἀλλὰ τοῖς τῶν Ἰώνων.

The first two large-scale histories of Greece in England, by Mitford (1795) and Thirlwall (1835), rejected the Peace of Callias without any hesitation. Thirlwall (*Hist. of Gr.* iii. 474 ff.), who was particularly impressed by Dahlmann in Germany (*Forschungen auf dem Gebiete der Geschichte* (1822) i. 1–148), based his case on: (1) The silence of Thucydides. (2) The contradictory statements of the sources concerning the date and terms of the peace. (3) The fact that in the following period the Persian king did not accept the autonomy of the Greek cities in Asia. (4) The criticism of Theopompus that the peace was inscribed in Ionic not Attic letters. 'Any reader, consulting the sources and Harpocration, Ἀττικοῖς γράμμασιν, will realize that Craterus either fabricated or adopted a forgery.' Seven years later Grote boldly took a less fashionable line (*Hist. of Gr.* v. 434 ff.). He accepted the peace as genuine. Isocrates was careless enough for his two references to the Halys line to be ignored. Theopompus' argument from the Ionic script did not disturb him. It was the natural script for a treaty which mainly concerned the Ionian cities (an argument that has been overlooked by many recent critics); alternatively it might have been reinscribed in the fourth century. Grote was not seriously troubled by the silence of Thucydides. The treaty, he thought, did little more than recognize the existing state of things and was not important enough to require a mention by Thucydides. Grote attached considerable importance to Herodotus' reference to Callias' embassy to Susa (T 1). 'It may be advanced as possible that they may have gone with the view to conclude a treaty and yet not have succeeded—this would be straining the limits of possibility beyond what is reasonable.' Perhaps this is a little extreme.

E. Müller (*Rh. Mus.* xiv (1859), 151–3) accepted Grote's conclusions and added a new argument. He was the first to suggest a new meaning for the tribute clause in Isocrates (T 5b). It meant that Persia was allowed to exact tribute from Greek cities not in the League, but she was not to increase their assessments. Most Greek historians, however, of the middle of the nineteenth century continued to believe that the Peace of Callias was an invention of the fourth century. In 1873 Cobet (*Mnem.* i. 97) could say: 'Now all are agreed that the famous peace that was on everybody's lips was forged by the Athenians.' Kocpp, however, in 1893 (*Rh. Mus.* xlviii. 485–511) still found it necessary to argue the case in detail. Most of his arguments had been deployed before, but he added a new point. The συνθήκας to which Isocrates referred were not the terms of the Peace of Callias but Athens' agreements with the members of the League. No one was convinced. In a footnote (loc. cit. 505 n. 1) Koepp drew attention to an inscription that was to introduce a completely new element into the discussion. The stone, preserving a substantial part of a decree honouring a certain Heraclides, had been found on the Acropolis in 1887. Heraclides was honoured for his services to Athens, and these services seemed to be connected with an Athenian embassy to the Persian king and a truce or peace. Foucart, the first editor (*BCH* xii (1888), 163-9), identified this Heraclides with Heraclides of Byzantium who was honoured for his services to Athens in 389 (Dem. xx. 60) and the peace in question with the Peace of Antalcidas. Four years later Köhler (*Hermes*, xxvii (1892) 68-78) showed conclusively that these identifications did not satisfy the epigraphic evidence (see ML p. 203): the decree honoured Heraclides of Clazomenae who was later made an Athenian citizen and nicknamed 'the King'. The peace was with Darius, successor to Artaxerxes, and this new evidence added respectability to Andocides' claim (Andoc. iii. 29) that his uncle Epilycus won for the Athenians the everlasting friendship of the Persian King. Koepp was literally correct in saying that Epilycus' treaty had nothing to do with the Peace of Callias, and that it was not the treaty to which the fourth-century orators so proudly referred, but the firm evidence for a treaty with Darius made a treaty with Artaxerxes much easier to accept.

Within ten years the authenticity of the Peace of Callias had the impressive support of Eduard Meyer, Busolt, and Beloch. Meyer's systematic review (*Forsch.* ii. 71-82) of the evidence and historical implications is still fundamental. To him the treaty was not a formal settlement but a binding statement of intentions. The King undertook not to use force against the members of the League. His forces would not move within a horse's ride from the coast and his fleet would not sail beyond Phaselis in the south and the rocks at the mouth of the Euxine in the north. Meyer, following Müller, interpreted Isocrates' tribute clause to mean that the king accepted a maximum figure for the assessments of some Greek cities, particularly those of Cyprus and the eastern Mediterranean which Athens had to abandon after the Egyptian disaster. Meyer also made the wider point that the peace opened the east again to Greek trade. Thucydides' silence could not be satisfactorily explained, but Meyer regarded the King's demand in 412 to be allowed to bring his ships into the Aegean (T 4) as decisive evidence for a formal agreement. But the clause giving autonomy to all the Greeks was nonsense; the King could never have accepted such humiliation.

Busolt (*Gr. Gesch.* iii (1897), 345-58, with a useful summary of earlier literature) reached the same conclusion but added new points to the debate. He too was primarily influenced by the negotiations with Tissaphernes in 412, and he also thought that the Peace with Darius, which, without the evidence later available, he rightly dated in 423, should be seen as the renewal of an earlier agreement on the accession of a new king. He agreed with Meyer and Müller on the interpretation of the tribute clause in Isocrates and, with Meyer, rejected the autonomy clause on the additional ground that Isocrates would be ignoring what he should have been proudest to acclaim. The exaggeration grew from comparison with the Peace of 386. Busolt took Thuc. viii. 5. 5 (T 3) to imply that the King did not relinquish his claim on the Ionian cities, but did not press for payment until Athens was crippled by the Syracusan disaster. The anti-Greek activities of Pissuthnes at the time of the revolt of Samos and in Colophon at the beginning of the Peloponnesian War were not breaches of the peace, because they were not authorized by the king. Busolt was troubled by the building debate in Plutarch (*Per.* 12), for he saw that in Plutarch's account, when the decision to build the Parthenon was taken, the Greeks were still at war. He therefore felt compelled to date the Peace of Callias after 447. By this dating he raised more problems than he solved, and was not followed by others, but the real difficulty which he exposed was for a long time ignored. After the detailed surveys of Meyer and Busolt even Beloch (*Gr. Gesch.* ii², 177 A 2) could accept the peace without question, and de Sanctis (*Atthis* (1912), 465) regarded the issue as non-controversial.

Scepticism was revived by Walker in the *Cambridge Ancient History* (v (1927), 469–71). He was the first to suggest that Herodotus' reference to Callias' mission to Susa made better sense as an unsuccessful mission early in the reign of Artaxerxes, in 462 or 461, than in 450 or 449, when the Argives would have had no good reason for going to Susa. Walker thought that Thuc. viii. 5. 5 (T 3) was inconsistent with the autonomy clause, that a northern limit for the Persian fleet was not needed, that Phaselis and the Chelidonian Isles were mutually contradictory as limits in the south. At the most there was an informal understanding that the Persian fleet should not enter the Aegean and that the Athenians should not attack the King's dominions. The passage in Thucydides about the king's fleet entering the Aegean (T 4), which convinced Meyer and Busolt that there was a formal agreement, did not convince Walker. Recognized spheres for the two fleets might exist without a formal treaty. By this time it might have been thought that there was nothing new to say; but Wade-Gery gave fresh life to the controversy by a fundamental reassessment of the evidence (*Essays in Greek History*, 201–32).

The treaty with Darius was now brought into the forefront of the discussion. The identification of further names confirmed the dating in

423, and Wade-Gery brought into the open the uncomfortable fact that Darius and not Artaxerxes is the name in the text of Theopompus as it has come down to us: αἱ πρὸς βασιλέα Δαρεῖον Ἀθηναίων πρὸς Ἕλληνας συνθῆκαι. Instead of dismissing the name as a careless mistake, as Jacoby had done, Wade-Gery accepted the text and inferred that the stele which Theopompus attacked contained the treaty with Darius, inscribed in Ionic as was *IG* i². 25 of the same year, after l. 6. This treaty, however, he thought, was in essentials a renewal of the treaty with Artaxerxes. Wade-Gery also found a new explanation for the variation in the recorded terms, which had been a stumbling-block to many. The different land limits were not alternatives but complements. The Halys, which Isocrates alone mentions, was the limit for the royal levy, the three-days-from-the-coast limit referred to the satraps' forces and might be called the Sardis line. For the fleets Wade-Gery suggested a demilitarized zone: 'Kyaneai–Chelidoniai–Phaselis defined the zone into (and beyond) which neither party should send ships of war.' In return for the limitation on Persian land forces Athens was to withdraw all her garrisons from Asia, and the walls of the Ionian cities were to be pulled down. Wade-Gery interpreted Isocrates' tribute clause (T 5*b*) to mean that the Greek cities of Asia were to pay tribute to the king but the assessments were to be the original assessments of Artaphernes. Similar terms are in fact, as Wade-Gery pointed out, offered in the early fourth century by Tithraustes on the King's instructions to Agesilaus (Xen. *Hell.* iii. 4. 25, quoted p. 148 n. 3).

This stimulating study dominated the debate for many years. Wade-Gery's identification of Cyaneae with the southern town known from Hellenistic times had to be abandoned because of the clear indications in Aristides that the peace referred to the well-known rocks at the mouth of the Euxine (J. H. Oliver, *Hist.* vi (1957), 254 f.), and with this change the idea of a demilitarized zone of sea lapsed. Wade-Gery's interpretation of the apparent variants in the land limits is still accepted by Andrewes and Mattingly (*Hist.* x. 16–18; *Hist.* xiv. 277) and has not been decisively refuted. The inference that the Ionian cities of the League had to pay tribute to Persia as well as to Athens was strongly attacked by Gomme (*HCT* i (1945), 334) and others, and was abandoned in *ATL* iii (1950), 275. But however much Wade-Gery's conclusions may be eroded his article will remain basic for its method and imagination.

The fifties were marked by a return to scepticism. The strongest of the attacks was made by D. L. Stockton (*Hist.* viii (1957), 61–73). He pressed the argument from silence more thoroughly than Walker and the nineteenth-century critics. It was not only Herodotus and Thucydides who said nothing; the silence of Lysias in his Funeral

Oration was even more damning, and Plutarch's building debate was crucial. Here, where the mention of a peace was demanded if there was one, the debate in Plutarch presupposed that Athens and her allies were still at war. The King's demand in 412 that his ships should be able to sail in the Aegean, which had recently been accepted by Gomme (*HCT* i. 332) as conclusive evidence for a formal treaty, Stockton explained by the current situation. It was fear of the Athenian fleet rather than the clause of a treaty that kept Phoenician ships out of the Aegean. Stockton's case, however, was considerably weakened by his attempt to eliminate the treaty with Darius in 423. Theopompus' attack, he argued, must have been against the Peace of Callias, and since in his text πρὸς "Ελληνας is meaningless it was not difficult to believe, with Schwartz and Jacoby, that πρὸς Δαρεῖον should also be secluded as a gloss. This is at least arguable, but Stockton's reversion to the identification of Heraclides with the Heraclides of Byzantium, honoured for his services in 389, cannot be accepted. There is no need to repeat the arguments in ML p. 203 (see also Andrewes, *Hist.* x (1961), 3). In this part of his case Stockton has found no support.

Sealey (*Hist.* iii (1954–5), 325–33) and Mattingly (*Hist.* xiv (1965), 273–81) accepted a treaty with Darius in 423. Theopompus saw the stele recording this peace in Ionic and assumed that it was the famous peace about which the orators loved to boast. The tradition knew of only one fifth-century peace. Diod. xii. 26. 2 recalls διττὰς συνθήκας πρὸς τοὺς "Ελληνας: in one (the Peace of Callias) the Greek cities of Asia were autonomous, in the other (the Peace of Antalcidas) they were Persian subjects. Only Andocides boasted of the treaty with Darius, for personal reasons. The suggestion that for the treaty with Darius an Ionic was substituted for an Attic prescript and the terms of the earlier peace in Attic letters retained was dismissed by Sealey; even Theopompus could not have been quite so careless. Mattingly (*Hist.* xiv (1965), 273–81) followed the main lines of Sealey's argument, but added an ingenious explanation of the confusion. What Theopompus saw was the text of the treaty of 423, and the name of the mover of the decree was a Callias, who also proposed the decree of that year concerning the priestess of Athena Nike (ML 71). This Callias was a member of the Boule in 424–423, but not the son of Hipponicus. Of the terms Mattingly accepted the Halys line as the limit of the imperial levy, and a reference in the tribute clause of Isocrates to the eastern cities which Athens had lost as a result of the Egyptian disaster.

A new turn to the argument was provided when the Decree of Themistocles was discovered at Troezen. A lively controversy arose concerning its authenticity and, though opinion was and remains divided, the majority dismissed it as a forgery. One of the most influential contributions to the controversy was a substantial article by Chr. Habicht (*Hermes*, lxxxix (1961), 1–35), in which he showed that a suspicious number of Athenian decrees became known for the first time in the early forties of the fourth century; he suggested that several of them were invented as propaganda, particularly when Athens was attempting to rouse the states of Greece against Philip between the fall of Olynthus in 348 and the Peace of Philocrates in 346. In such a pattern the Peace of Callias fits well and this, Habicht thinks, is when the text which lies behind the orators was invented to be used in company with the decrees of Miltiades and Themistocles and the stern decree against the traitor, Arthmius of Zelea. Habicht was convinced that there was a Peace of Callias, but the stele that Theopompus saw was a forgery. Habicht has opened his net too wide. There is no good reason to suspect the decree against Arthmius (App. 10 (c) p. 508) and the evidence for the peace in Isocrates needs to be seriously considered before such a late forgery is accepted. As has been argued above (p. 136) the language of Isocrates iv. 120 (εἰ παραναγνοίη τὰς συνθήκας τὰς ἐφ' ἡμῶν γενομένας καὶ τὰς νῦν ἀναγεγραμμένας) implies a written or inscribed document already available in 380.

Meanwhile the defence was not unrepresented. Andrewes was sufficiently convinced by the framework of Wade-Gery's study not to argue the case in detail; he was more concerned to explain the silence of Thucydides and he saw a possible clue in the number of omissions about relations with Persia. It was not merely the Peace of Callias and the treaty with Darius that were missing. Hardly less important is Thucydides' failure to record when and why Athens decided to support Amorges against the Persian king. Andrewes suggested that Thucydides may not have realized the importance of Persia until a late stage in the war; he will have died before he had time to fill the gaps. This would be a comforting solution, but it would not explain the omission of the Peace of Callias, if we are right in dating the Pentekontaetia narrative late; and in 425–424 there was too much talk of Persia in the air to be ignored. The parody of the Persian envoy in the *Acharnians* (61–3) at the Lenaea of 425 presupposes that talk about the Persian question was in the air at the time and the arrest of a Persian messenger to Sparta in the autumn should have been a major sensation (Thuc. iv. 50). Nor is it consistent that Thucydides should record the abortive embassy to Susa towards the end of 425 and not mention the successful embassy of 424–423. K. Kraft (*Hermes*, xlii (1964), 158–71) also accepted the peace, but without strengthening the case. His interpretation of Herodotus' statement on the assessment of Artaphernes (T 2) to mean that the principle of assessing on the basis of land was unchanged revives a translation long since discredited. To account for the Phoenician ships that seem to have threatened in the background when Samos revolted in 440 Kraft suggests that Pissuthnes, the satrap of Sardis, commissioned them from one of the Phoenician cities without the king's authority. This is just possible, but as Mattingly emphasizes (*Hist.* xiv (1965), 280) Phoenician ships, without qualification, should mean in Book I what is meant in Book VIII, the Persian fleet. Kraft's most useful contribution was to emphasize again that the clauses restricting Persian movement in the terms of the peace were not concerned with frontiers, but were military definitions, points beyond which the Persians would not bring ships or men. Meiggs (*Harv. Stud.* lxvii (1963), 10–30) argued that the events of the early forties were much easier to understand if they followed a formal peace.

In the increased importance attached to our text of Theopompus which refers to a treaty with Darius not Artaxerxes, the embarrassing addition of πρὸς "Ελληνας has been generally ignored. Only Raubitschek (*Gk. Rom. Byz. Stud.* v (1964), 151–9) has attempted an explanation. He suggests that the treaty with Darius, unlike the treaty negotiated by Callias, was designed to secure help *against* the Greeks. It is difficult to believe that Theopompus would use πρός twice in the same sentence with such different meanings. Nor was Theopompus interested in such niceties. He was attacking the authenticity of a treaty about which the Athenians boasted; πρὸς "Ελληνας should be excluded from the text. Nor should πρὸς Δαρεῖον be regarded as certain. The fourth century (with the exception of Andocides) did not boast about a treaty with Darius. Jacoby, following Stengel, excluded the reference to Darius. They were probably right; the treaty may, like the first Spartan treaty with Persia in 412 (Thuc. viii. 18), have been recorded simply as πρὸς βασιλέα without naming the king.

APPENDIX 9

The Temple of Athena Nike

When Pausanias made his way up to the Acropolis he saw on his right, perched on a high bastion, the temple of Wingless Victory. This had probably by his day become the popular name, concealing the true nature of the cult; for this was Athena Victory, who could not mean to an Athens dominated by Rome what she had meant in the days of freedom. Pausanias climbed up on to the bastion, admired the view, and reminded his readers that it was from this bastion that Aegeus threw himself when Theseus, returning from Crete, forgot to change his sails from black to white.[1] When George Wheler visited Athens in 1667 the temple was still there, remarkably well preserved. In 1685 it was pulled down by the Turks to make way for a battery, but in 1835 Ross, Schaubert, and Hansen were able to find almost all the original blocks and could re-erect the temple practically complete in its original form.

While the identification of the temple has never been in doubt, the date and context of its building have been a subject of continuing controversy. To Ross it was a Cimonian building, linked with the building of the south wall of the Acropolis by Cimon from the spoils of the Eurymedon. The temple commemorated Cimon's victories and illustrated the fighting between Greeks and Persians on the north and south sides of the frieze. For a generation the views of Ross won considerable support, but opposition developed as the sculpture of the frieze of the temple and the balustrade which ran round the bastion were subjected to more systematic attention. 'The free and flowing style of these figures in which no trace of the stiff archaic manner can be perceived proves that the artist had studied the epoch-making sculptures of the Parthenon.' Wolters adopted what at the time seemed a very acceptable compromise. The bastion, he thought, in its present form, was the work of Cimon when he built the south wall of the Acropolis, and there was already on the bastion a sanctuary and cult statue of Nike. Mnesicles, in designing his new Propylaea in 438, originally intended a symmetrical building which could only be secured by encroaching on Nike's sanctuary. Religious forces opposed his policy and the temple, probably built between 437 and the outbreak of war in 431, was their emphatic reply. The outcome of

[1] Paus. i. 22. 4–5.

the struggle could be seen in the drastic curtailment of his south-west wing which was forced on Mnesicles.[1]

Wolters's hypothesis collapsed in part when a block of marble inscribed on both sides with decrees concerning Athena Nike was found in 1897 in a dump of inscriptions that had fallen from the Acropolis.[2] The stone was broken away at the bottom and the dowel holes at the top showed that another stone had once been fitted above it, but the lettering was in excellent condition and the main decisions of what was clearly the first of the two decrees were preserved. A priestess of Athena Nike was to be appointed democratically from all Athenian women by lot, to hold office for life, and her salary, in money and in kind, was laid down. A doorway was to be provided for the sanctuary of Nike and it was to be designed by Callicrates. Next, a temple and a marble altar were to be built and Callicrates was to be the architect. Finally, three members of the Boule were to be appointed to co-operate with Callicrates in submitting designs (of the doorway) to the Boule. Of the mover's name only the ending was clearly preserved, and the letter-forms were the only clue to the date. Kavvadias, the first editor, pointed out that the three-bar sigma was an early sign, but he was careful to note that this was the only early Attic letter-form; his caution has not been generally followed by later scholars, many of whom imply that the dating evidence rests on the letter-forms in general. By 1897 it was already an accepted criterion that the early sigma was not used after 445; Kavvadias suggested a date in the early forties for the decree. Much more of the second decree had been lost, but the opening lines were clear. It was moved by a Callias and its first clause provided for the payment to the priestess by the *kolakretai* of the annual salary stipulated in the first decree. Kavvadias tentatively identified this Callias with the son of Calliades who died when commanding Athenian troops at the siege of Potidaea in 432.

The argument was considerably advanced by the discovery of these two decrees. It was now firmly established that there was a sanctuary of Athena Nike on the bastion before the temple was built. Kavvadias's date, in the early forties, was not questioned, but there remained an embarrassing discrepancy between the date of the decision to build a temple and the apparent date of the sculpture with which the architectural style of the building seemed to conform. The dating of the inscription, however, seemed to receive further support when Körte suggested that the name of the mover of the decree should be restored as [Hipponi]kos, and that the Callias of the second decree was his son.

[1] For a bibliography of the early literature, Judeich, *Topographie*², 219 n. 3, and 220 n. 1.

[2] P. Kavvadias, Ἀρχ. Ἐφ. 1897, 174–94; ML 44, 71.

Hipponikos was the son of the Callias who had negotiated peace with Persia and the temple commemorated, as Ross had originally suggested, the fighting against Persia.[1]

In 1936 further important evidence was added. There were fears for the stability of the bastion and its temple, and once again the temple was taken down. The restoration of the bastion provided for the first time clear evidence for the history of the site.[2] Within its outer case the Mycenaean wall surrounding the bastion still survives, but the original level was some 3 metres lower. At this level two stages in the development of Nike's cult could be seen. Her first altar, broken in pieces, was found with its original inscription in archaic letters of the sixth century.[3] Its successor, uninscribed, was also found, standing in front of a small shrine built of finely finished *poros* blocks.[4] Within this shrine, but on a different axis, was a deposit containing terracotta dedications. It may represent an earlier phase of the cult. The letters of the inscription on the altar cannot be precisely dated and it would be unwise to suggest a closer range than 580–530. Welter, who briefly reported the new evidence, suggested that it might have been associated with the new emphasis given to the Panathenaea in 566. Associating Athena Nike in this way with this festival he suggested that she was more concerned with athletic contests than with battles.[5] If this suggestion, widely accepted, were right the cult will have changed its nature when the temple was built, for both the frieze and the balustrade are concerned with fighting. The new interpretation has been supported by an attempt to identify the cult statue of Athena Nike with the Athena of the Panathenaea prize amphorae,[6] but this identification should be rejected. The cult statue of Athena Nike, as Harpocration tells us, was a wooden image with pomegranate in right hand and helmet in left.[7] It is very doubtful whether there was any change in the basic nature of the cult.

The sixth-century altar was broken in pieces, and that is why a new altar was built. Almost certainly the earlier altar was destroyed at the time of the Persian invasion and the new altar, together with the *poros* shrine, was built after 479, possibly but not necessarily in association with Cimon's building of the south wall of the Acropolis. Before Callicrates' temple was built the level of the bastion was raised by some 4 feet and, since there was a great quantity of marble chippings

---

[1] A. Körte, *Hermes*, xlv (1910), 623–7.

[2] A useful summary by G. Welter, *Arch. Anz.* liv (1939), 1–22.

[3] Welter, 10–12; Raubitschek, *DAA* 329.

[4] Welter, 11 f.; I. T. Hill, *The Ancient City of Athens*, 145. This small shrine (only 2·71 × 1·77 m.) may have been built, or perhaps rebuilt, to shelter a cult statue.

[5] Welter, 12.

[6] Raubitschek, *DAA*, pp. 359–64.   [7] Harpocration, s.v. Νίκη Ἀθηνᾶ.

in the fill, it is reasonably inferred that the bastion must have been raised after, and probably some considerable time after, Mnesicles' Propylaea was started. One further twist to the story was given when West and Dinsmoor reported that the traces which remained of the name of the mover of the decree were incompatible with the restoration [Hippo]nikos; some such name as [Glau]kos was required.[1] It was not apparently noticed at the time that their elimination of Hipponikos, while weakening the association of the temple with the Peace of Callias, weakened also the dating of the decree in the early forties. That date now rests almost exclusively on the three-bar sigma.

The new readings from the top line of the stele led Meritt to examine again the physical aspects of the problem, and in particular the relation between the lower and the upper stones. He emphasized two points: the scarf joint which bound the two stones together was very uncommon and was used to provide the closest possible joint; secondly, the first line of the lower stone began immediately at the top without leaving the vacant space that one might expect. A further feature that had to be explained was the absence of a complete prescript to the surviving decree; before the mover's name there was room for the *epistates*, but not for the secretary, nor for the prytanizing tribe. Meritt concluded that the inscription must have been continuous on the two stones and that the joint came exactly half-way between the bottom line of the top stone and the top line of the lower stone. A full prescript was not needed on the lower stone because it had already been given at the beginning of the upper stone. The decree moved by [Glau]kos was passed at the same meeting of the Assembly as the decree of the upper stone and represented an amendment.[2] The alternative was to suppose that the upper stone carried a relief and that the name of secretary and prytanizing tribe were inscribed on the moulding linking relief with decree. This solution both Dinsmoor and Meritt discarded on the ground that there was no known parallel in the wide range of reliefs crowning fifth-century Attic inscriptions.

A difficult but intriguing question now arose: What was the content of a first decree which could eclipse the importance of building a temple to Athena Nike and yet have some association with it? The answer of Meritt and Wade-Gery was that the first decree provided for the building of a monumental western entrance to the Acropolis in place of the existing Propylaea. The proposal to build a temple to Nike was the move made by conservative forces to ensure that Athena Nike's sanctuary would not suffer from the new building. This was the first move in the long struggle between secular and religious forces which

---

[1] *Hesp.* Suppl. v (1941), 159 n. 337.
[2] Meritt, *Hesp.* x (1941), 307–15.

resulted in a victory for the old order and the drastic curtailment of Mnesicles' ambitious plans.[1]

This is heady stuff and it could explain much that is otherwise puzzling. We are told that there was a violent reaction by the religious forces just before the outbreak of the war which issued in a decree moved by Diopeithes inviting the impeachment of those who disrespected the state cults and taught dangerous doctrines about the heavenly bodies.[2] It is not unreasonable to believe that the conflict between old and new ways of thinking had developed earlier in the forties and thirties. But before we accept this hypothesis we need stronger evidence than this attractive interpretation of the Nike decree, for there are serious difficulties. It is possible that in the early forties, before or soon after the beginning of the Parthenon, the idea was conceived of building a new Propylaea, but it seems to me unlikely that the plan, even if it was already conceived by Pericles and his associates, would have been put before the Assembly some ten years before it was to be carried out. We may also question the very foundation of the hypothesis, that the upper stone contained a decree. Why should a mason, when asked to cut a text which could not have been abnormally long, have used two stones, when a single stele would have sufficed? And if the top stone carried a decree why was the decree on the reverse side of the lower stone not inscribed on the back of the upper stone? Instead it begins some inches below the top of the lower stone. And if the Nike decree was passed at the same meeting of the Assembly as the assumed decree on the upper stone, why was the name of the epistates given? Must we follow Meritt and Dinsmoor in ruling out the alternative explanation, that the upper stone carried a relief and a moulding which linked relief and inscription, and gave the names of secretary and prytanizing tribe?

It must be admitted that no very close parallel can be quoted, but it is no easier to find a parallel for such a joining of two stones for a single inscription. If we discount the nature of the joint there is no serious difficulty. The decree providing regulations for Chalcis after the crushing of its revolt in 446 had a second decree on a separate stone attached at its side and a further stone added above, which almost certainly carried a relief.[3] It is interesting to note that the text of the Chalcis decree begins very much nearer the top of the stone than we would expect, though not quite so near as in the Nike decree. A closer parallel in this respect can be seen in the Eleusis Museum in a stone on which a relief is combined with a decree of 421–420 providing for the bridging of the river Reitas on the way from Athens to Eleusis.[4] The

---

[1] *JHS* lxxxiii (1963), 109 f.   [2] Plut. *Per.* 32. 2; see p. 283.
[3] ML 52.   [4] *IG* i². 81, phot. *AM* xix (1894), pl. 7.

first line of the decree begins immediately under the moulding which links relief and text. I prefer to think that the stone above the Nike decree was used for a relief rather than a decree.[1]

The crucial question still remains: Was there a long interval between the decree ordering the building of a temple to Athena Nike and the actual building of the temple, and if so, why? The approximate date of the temple is no longer in doubt. The sculptures of frieze and balustrade cannot be as early as the forties and the building of the temple almost certainly comes after the abandonment of further work on the Propylaea in 432. A dating during the Archidamian War is now generally preferred.[2] It would satisfy what at first sight seems common sense if the inscription could be moved down to the early twenties, as Mattingly has urged.[3] But the statistical case for the abandonment of the three-bar sigma by 445 is still very strong, and it should be accepted until a satisfactorily proved exception is found. I would also still hold to the association of the temple decree with the Peace of Callias, and another stone may be relevant to the argument. This stone also has inscriptions on front and back which concern the temple of Athena Nike. They were published with very brief discussion in 1923, but have since received very little attention.[4] More than half of the stele is lost, and the surface of the first of the two inscriptions is badly worn. They contain no distinctive letter-forms and it would be dangerous to set narrower limits than 440 to 415. What may be called the second of the two decrees has been interpreted as the final account of expenditure on the temple, but this is no more than a possible interpretation. The first decree seems to be primarily concerned with deciding the design and material for some construction, possibly a doorway, whether it is to be of gold or ivory, and in a passage whose context cannot be precisely restored Athenians and allies seem to be mentioned together. The vital letters justifying the restoration of allies can no longer be securely read on the stone, but the photograph published in 1923 shows that Hiller von Gaetringen was justified in restoring χσυμ[μάχον in line 11 without indicating any doubt about the letters χσ.[5] The conjunction of allies with Athenians in a decree concerning an Athenian temple needs explanation. It would be appropriate if the temple did commemorate the fighting against Persia ended by the Peace of Callias.

[1] See A. Boegehold, *Class. Stud.* presented to B. E. Perry (Urbana, 1969), 175–80, who reaches similar conclusions.
[2] Dinsmoor, *The Architecture of Ancient Greece*² (1950), 185 f.
[3] Mattingly, *Hist.* xi (1961), 169–171; xiv (1965), 278.
[4] A. Pogorelski, *AJA* xxvii (1923), 314–17, Dinsmoor, ibid. 318–21.
[5] *AJA* xxvii. 315.

If inscriptions throw no reliable light on the long interval between the authorization of the temple and its construction it remains to inquire whether any secure inferences can be drawn from the buildings themselves. The final form of the south-west wing of the Propylaea has in fact been the main ground for postulating a continuing conflict between the sponsors of the Propylaea and the sponsors of the temple of Nike. Mnesicles, it is thought, planned a symmetrical building, which could only have been achieved at the expense of Athena Nike. He was continuously frustrated, had to yield step by step, and finally had to resign himself to seeing a new temple of Nike on a raised bastion stealing the limelight from his south-west wing. The wide conflict of views among professional archaeologists and architects concerning design and execution is a stern warning to the amateur, and the problem is made even more complex by the history of publication; many facts have at various times been discovered and have remained unpublished. We shall have more material to work on when Dinsmoor's long-awaited book on the Propylaea is published.

Two facts are abundantly clear from a plan of Mnesicles' Propylaea. In the form in which it was left by him it was a very asymmetrical building, and it was not finished when the work was abandoned. This latter point is even clearer on the ground than in the plan, particularly in the north-east wing. Here a large room was left open to the sky. The socket for the intended roof-beam can still be seen and the sockets for the rafters of the ceiling, but the room was never roofed and the lifting bosses on the walls were not removed. There is similar, but less complete evidence in the south-east wing. Here too a socket for the roof-beam can be seen, rather smaller than the corresponding socket in the north-east wing. No such signs can be seen in the south-west wing which might be expected to balance exactly the north-west wing with its picture gallery. There is, however, evidence which suggests that at one point Mnesicles did not expect the bastion to be raised. When he built his south-west *anta* he did not anticipate the steps that now lead up from the approach to the Propylaea to the bastion and the temple: they were clearly added later. This change in plan does not, however, necessarily reflect a fluctuating conflict between the two interests, and for various reasons I think this unlikely.

Arguments from silence are nearly always dangerous and for the fifth century in particular they cannot carry great weight; but in the Hellenistic period there was considerable interest in the Periclean buildings of the Acropolis, and if there had been a continuing conflict between secular and religious forces, some echo should have survived. It is also difficult to fit the architects into this conflict. Mnesicles presumably was a Periclean in the sense that he was approved by Pericles and his circle, but Callicrates, the architect of the temple of Nike, would be an odd choice to be the architect of the opposition. He was concerned with the Parthenon, he was put in charge of making the Acropolis secure against intruders, and he was the architect for the Middle Wall which was sponsored in the Assembly by Pericles.[1] It looks very much as if both Callicrates and Mnesicles were in sympathy with Pericles. It is also doubtful whether realistic politicians would have agreed to a plan for the Propylaea which meant encroaching on the temenos of Nike. If there was a difference of view I am doubtful whether Mnesicles would have had the support of Periods in wanting to constrict Nike's sanctuary.

If there was no such conflict as has been widely assumed, some other reasons must be found for the long interval that preceded the building of Nike's temple. The beginning may have been delayed because Callicrates was preoccupied with the Parthenon, and because the best skilled labour would be concentrated on the larger temple. It could have been further delayed when Mnesicles was commissioned to build the Propylaea. The final outcome might have been a compromise freely reached between the two architects. Until there is more positive evidence of conflict between Periods and religious conservatives in the forties and thirties, less dramatic causes for the postponement of the building of Nike's temple can be entertained without discredit.[2]

---

[1] Plut. *Per.* 13. 7, *IG* i². 44.   [2] See also Add. p. 597.

Some Controversial Documents

A. THE PLATAEAN OATH

Theopompus (*FGH* 88 F 153) includes among the fabrications of Athenian propaganda for the greater glory of Athens 'the Greek oath which the Athenians say that the Greeks took before the battle of Plataea against the barbarians'; most modern scholars have agreed with him.

Diodorus (xi. 29. 2) records that when the Greeks met at the Isthmus in the spring of 480 they took the following oath: 'I will not set life before liberty, nor will I desert my leaders alive nor dead. I will bury all allied troops who die in the battle, and, if I defeat the barbarians in the war, I will not raze to the ground any of the cities that fought against them, and I will not rebuild any temple that has been burnt and destroyed, but I will let them be and leave them as a memorial of the sacrilege of the barbarians.' Diodorus probably takes his text from Ephorus. It is repeated, with minor changes of wording which do not affect the meaning, by Lycurgus (*Leocr.* 81) later in the fourth century; but Lycurgus adds a clause which is not in Diodorus: 'And all those cities which have chosen the interests of the barbarians I will tithe.' The probable reason why Diodorus does not include this clause is that his source has followed Herodotus (vii. 132), who records the oath to tithe shortly before the battle of Thermopylae.

In 1938 L. Robert published another version of the oath from a stele found at Acharnae (*Études épigraphiques et philologiques*, 307 ff.; for the text see also Tod, *GHI* ii. 204, Daux, *Robinson Studies*, ii. 777 with bibl. 775 n. 1). The inscription is probably earlier than Lycurgus, but not earlier than 360. The Plataean oath was inscribed together with the Ephebic oath on a stele displayed in the temple of Ares to raise morale by reminding demesmen and others of their traditions. In the inscribed text the oath is taken by the Athenians and not by all the allies and there are several minor differences of wording from the literary texts in the early clauses; in the latter part of the decree ere wider discrepancies. Instead of a general tithing clause Thebes alone is concerned and instead of a general clause protecting all the allies three cities are specified: 'I will not raze to the ground Athens, Sparta, nor Plataea nor any other allied city.' There then follow clauses adopted from the Amphictyonic oath which are not in the literary texts. On the other hand there is no reference on the Acharnae stele to the vow not to rebuild the burnt temples, and it is this clause which primarily concerns us. The variations in the text are not difficult to understand. The mention of Thebes, Athens, Sparta, Plataea reflects a time when Athens and Sparta were particularly hostile to Thebes. The temples are not mentioned, because the temples were in fact rebuilt. Nor were the Medizers tithed when the war was over, but in the fourth century her enemies could still look forward with relish to the tithing of Thebes as a long overdue debt (Xen. *Hell.* vi. 3. 20).

The temple clause in the oath has found little favour. It is omitted in the Acharnae inscription, and Isocrates, while mentioning an oath taken by the Ionians not to restore temples destroyed by the Persians (iv. 156), says nothing about an oath taken by Athens and the Greeks of the mainland. Neither of these objections is fatal. The purpose of the stele in the temple of Ares was to encourage bravery and loyalty. It is clear that the text is edited to suit the contemporary purpose, and that purpose would not be in the least advanced by reminding the Athenians that they had broken their oath not to rebuild their temples. As for Isocrates and the Ionian oath there are two possibilities. The mainlanders may deliberately have copied the earlier example of the Ionians, presumably in the Ionian revolt. It is also not impossible that Isocrates' memory was at fault. The positive reasons for accepting the clause are that it explains facts which need explaining and to forge an oath that was deliberately broken presupposes a perversity rare even among forgers. The facts that need explaining are the large number of shrines that were destroyed by the Persians and remained in ruin for a whole generation, and the sudden outburst of rebuilding in the early forties. Why should anyone invent a vow to leave the burnt temples for ever as a memorial of the Persians' impiety when everyone could see that the Parthenon, the temple of Posidon at Sunium, and many others had been rebuilt.

A case for the defence was put forward in 1901 by W. N. Bates (*Harv. Stud.* xii (1901), 321–6), but the evidence at that time was insufficient to make much impression. More weight was added by Dinsmoor in his study of the temple of Hephaestus and Athena, the so-called Theseum, overlooking the Agora (*Hesp.* Suppl. v (1941), 156–60). He dated the beginning of the building to 449 and this was the first of four temples by the same architect, the precursor of the temple of Posidon at Sunium, of Ares at Acharnae, and of Nemesis at Rhamnous. The temples at Sunium and Rhamnous were certainly preceded by earlier temples which were destroyed by the Persians. The evidence for an earlier temple on the site of the Periclean temple of Hephaestus and Athena was not conclusive; there was no evidence for the temple of Ares. Dinsmoor was a firm believer in the authenticity of the Plataean oath. A fuller review of the archaeological evidence confirms his confidence. The old temple on the Acropolis (the Dörpfeld temple) was destroyed and not rebuilt, to be replaced later by the Erechtheum, and it is significant that architectural members of the temple, including cornice blocks, were built into the reconstructed north wall of the Acropolis, near column drums of the earlier Parthenon. This was not due to haste; the careful arrangement of the blocks makes sense only as a memorial of the Persian destruction. The Parthenon that was half built when the Persians came was also destroyed and its successor was not begun until 447. In the Agora the sanctuary of the Twelve Gods, dating from the archonship of the younger Pisistratus in 522–521, remained desolate for more than fifty years and the top of the sill was heavily worn by traffic; it was not until near the end of the century that the area was paved and a new parapet and almost certainly a new altar were erected (M. Crosby, *Hesp.* Suppl. viii (1949), 97–103). The sanctuary of Zeus in the northwest corner of the Agora seems to have remained a ruin on a neglected site until the stoa of Zeus was built *c.* 430 (H. A. Thompson, *Hesp.* vi (1937), 5–77). Apollo had a small apsidal temple built near the middle of the sixth century; it was destroyed by the Persians and not replaced until the fourth century, though a statue by Calamis was set up in the area, possibly before 450 (Thompson, ibid. 77–90). The first temple on the site of the Metröon was also apparently destroyed by the Persians and not rebuilt (Thompson, ibid. 135–40). Outside the city Pausanias mentions the temple of Demeter at Phalerum and the temple of Hera on the road from Phalerum to Athens, whose ruins, it was said, dated back to the Persian invasion (Paus. x. 35. 2).

It has, however, been generally thought that there were exceptions which disproved the rule. The temple that replaced the archaic temple of Athena at Sunium was dated before 450. It was also generally accepted that there was an important Cimonian phase in the sanctuary of the goddesses at Eleusis, and Plutarch tells us, on the evidence of Simonides, that Themistocles rebuilt the Telesterion at Phlya for which his family was responsible and which had been burnt by the Persians (Plut. *Them.* 1. 4). The last of these three apparent exceptions can be disregarded since it was a private and not a state building. The other two exceptions are now no longer secure. Homer Thompson tells me that as a result of his re-examination of the Athena temple at Sunium with W. B. Dinsmoor Jr., taking into account both the material at Sunium and the many members of the building found in the Agora, he is convinced that the temple was begun in the first big wave of Periclean building, but that work was interrupted, as in the Hephaesteum. The Cimonian phase of the Telesterion at Eleusis has been called in question by T. Leslie Shear Jr., in a paper at the annual meeting of the Archaeological Institute of America in 1963. He argued that the so-called Cimonian building was left unfinished because it was really begun (like the earlier Parthenon) in the 480s and was interrupted by the Persians. He now finds no evidence of building activity on the Telesterion between this interruption and the project recorded in the Coroebus inscription (*Eleusiniaka*, i, pp. 173 ff.; Hill, *Sources²*, B. 41).

The long interruption in temple building, when so many had been destroyed, between 480 and 450 needs a special explanation. The Athenian state was not so impoverished in the late seventies and sixties that she could not have afforded to rebuild even Athena's temple on the Acropolis. The Plataean oath provides a satisfactory explanation. (But see Add. p. 597.)

B. THE COVENANT OF PLATAEA

Plutarch in his *Aristides* says that after the battle of Plataea a meeting of the Greek allies was held at which Aristides carried a decree governing future policy. There should be a meeting each year at Plataea of representatives, political and religious (προβούλους καὶ θεωρούς). Every fourth year there should be a Freedom Festival ('Ελευθέρια). The allies should contribute to a common force for the war against the barbarians of 10,000 shields, 1,000 horse, and 100 ships. Finally the Plataeans should be sacrosanct, dedicated to the god, and each year they should sacrifice to the fallen who were buried at Plataea (Plut. *Arist.* 21. 1–2).

This 'Covenant of Plataea' has won very few friends indeed. The most serious objection is that there is no clear reference to it in the two places where it would be most relevant, Thucydides' account of the trial of the Plataeans after their surrender in 427 and Isocrates' *Plataicus* written after the destruction of Plataea in 373. The individual clauses also raise difficulties (most clearly set out in *ATL* iii. 101–4). We hear nothing of annual meetings of representatives in the fifth century. There is no evidence of the Freedom Festival in the fifth or fourth centuries. The character of the force to carry on war against Persia is not well suited to the purpose; there are too few ships and too many hoplites, and the force commanded by Pausanias in 478 bears no resemblance to the proposal. If the Plataeans were declared sacrosanct we should certainly expect them in their defence to emphasize the privilege. The nearest approach to the 'covenant' in Thucydides (iii. 59. 2) is very indefinite: προφερόμενοι ὅρκους οὓς οἱ πατέρες ὑμῶν ὤμοσαν μὴ ἀμνημονεῖν ἱκέται γιγνόμεθα ὑμῶν τῶν πατρῴων τάφων. Plutarch does not disclose his evidence for the decree of Aristides, but

F. Frost (*Class. et Med.* xxii (1961), 186–99) has made a good case for attributing it to local sources, not uninterested in the interests of tourists. Plutarch tells us that there were still in his day meetings of τὸ Ἑλλήνων συνέδριον at Plataea on the day of the battle, and there is evidence of the Freedom Festival in the Hellenistic and Roman periods (Strabo ix. 2. 31 = p. 412, Paus. ix. 2. 6).

In spite of the general scepticism there is much to be said for Larsen's contention (*Harv. Stud.* li (1940), 179) that 'if we did not have an account of the Congress of Plataea, it would almost be necessary to postulate something of the kind'. When the loyal Greeks met at the Isthmus in 480 and when the army assembled for the Plataea campaign the Greeks did not dream of an offensive against Persia. Until the battle of Plataea was decisively won they thought only of the defence of Greece. Pausanias' campaign in 478 presupposes a formal decision to carry on the war, and formal arrangements had to be made for the care of the graves and the dues to the gods. There is probably a genuine core to the 'Covenant of Plataea' but Plutarch's formulation seems to represent a much later attempt to substantiate faded traditions by circumstantial detail.

C. THE ARTHMIUS DECREE

The decree against Arthmius of Zelea was a favourite topic of the orators of the fourth century, for it told a story and pointed a moral. There was once a time when Athens knew how to handle traitors. Remember how they treated Arthmius who brought Persian gold to Greece. Demosthenes gives the first surviving version in his attack on Philocrates in 343 and returns to the theme in his third Philippic in 341. Aeschines follows in 330 when he brings his case against Ctesiphon, and Dinarchus repeats the story.

The decree was inscribed on a bronze stele which was set up on the Acropolis: γράμματα τῶν προγόνων τῶν ὑμετέρων ἀκεῖνοι κατέθεντ᾽ εἰς στήλην χαλκῆν γράψαντες εἰς ἀκρόπολιν (Dem. ix. 41–2); and when Demosthenes continues τί οὖν λέγει τὰ γράμματα; we may safely infer that it could still be read. But though the text was very accessible the orators differ slightly in their wording. From a comparison, however, of the texts we can reconstruct most of the clauses of the decree with a fair degree of accuracy.

In the following analysis Dem. i = Demosthenes ix. 41–3; Dem. ii = Demosthenes xix. 271; Aesch. = Aeschines iii. 258; Din. i = Dinarchus ii. 25, where Dinarchus professes to be repeating the actual words of the decree (γράψαντες διαρρήδην); Din. ii = Dinarchus ii. 24.

I

Dem. i. Ἄρθμιος Πυθώνακτος Ζελείτης ἄτιμος καὶ πολέμιος τοῦ δήμου
τοῦ Ἀθηναίων καὶ τῶν συμμάχων αὐτὸς καὶ γένος.

Dem. ii. Ἄρθμιον τὸν Πυθώνακτος τὸν Ζελείτην ἐχθρὸν εἶναι καὶ πολέμιον τοῦ δήμου τοῦ Ἀθηναίων καὶ τῶν συμμάχων αὐτὸν καὶ
γένος πᾶν.

Aesch. —

Din. i. Ἄρθμιον τὸν Πυθώνακτος τὸν Ζελείτην πολέμιον εἶναι τοῦ δήμου
καὶ τῶν συμμάχων, αὐτὸν καὶ γένος.

Din. ii. —

In this clause πολέμιον is common to all the texts; we can be confident that ἄτιμος and not ἐχθρός was added because Demosthenes
in ix. 44 comments on the use of ἄτιμος which here means not loss
of rights but that the killing of Arthmius will bring no guilt on the
killer.

2

Dem. i and ii. —

Aesch. ἐξεκήρυξαν δ᾽ ἐκ τῆς πόλεως καὶ ἐξ ἁπάσης ἧς ἄρχουσιν
Ἀθηναῖοι.

Din. i. φεύγειν Ἀθήνας.

Din. ii. ἐξήλασαν αὐτὸν ἐξ ἁπάσης τῆς χώρας.

We should perhaps prefer Ἀθήνας to τὴν πόλιν because Dinarchus
claims to be quoting (γράψαντες διαρρήδην).

3

Dem. i. ὅτι τὸν χρυσὸν τὸν ἐκ Μήδων εἰς Πελοπόννησον ἤγαγεν.

Dem. ii. ὅτι τὸν χρυσὸν τὸν ἐκ τῶν βαρβάρων εἰς τοὺς Ἕλληνας ἤγαγεν.

Aesch. κομίσαντα εἰς τὴν Ἑλλάδα τὸ ἐκ Μήδων χρυσίον.

Din. i. ὅτι τὸν ἐκ Μήδων χρυσὸν ἤγαγεν εἰς Πελοπόννησον.

Din. ii. ὅτι φασὶν Ἄρθμιον . . . κομίσαι τὸ χρυσίον ⟨τὸ⟩ ἐκ Μήδων ἐπὶ
διαφθορᾷ τῶν Ἑλλήνων.

There is no doubt that the specific is to be preferred to the general;
Arthmius took his money to the Peloponnese.

An approximate text would be: Ἄρθμιον τὸν Πυθόνακτος τὸν
Ζελείτην ἄτιμον ἔναι καὶ πολέμιον τὸ δέμο τὸ Ἀθηναίον καὶ τὸν χσυνμάχον
αὐτὸν καὶ τὸ γένος αὐτὸ καὶ φεύγεν Ἀθήνας καὶ ὅσες Ἀθεναῖοι ἄρχοσι, ὅτι
τὸν ἐκ Μήδον χρυσὸν ἀπέγαγεν εἰς Πελοπόννεσον.

Aeschines adds a little information which does not seem to have been derived from the inscription. Arthmius, he says, was a *proxenos* of the demos and came to Athens, but was driven out. We cannot control this evidence but there is no good reason to reject it. Aeschines does not expressly say that his visit was on the occasion that he brought Persian gold to the Peloponnese but that is the natural inference from the passage. The orators do not tell us who proposed the decree against Arthmius, nor when it was proposed; Plutarch answers both questions. The proposer was Themistocles and the decree was passed on the eve of Xerxes' invasion (Plut. *Them.* 6. 4: Θεμιστοκλέους γὰρ εἰπόντος καὶ τοῦτον εἰς τοὺς ἀτίμους καὶ παῖδας αὐτοῦ καὶ γένος ἐνέγραψαν). This version is repeated by Aristides (ii, p. 392), but is contradicted by a scholiast on Aristides who says that the author was Cimon, and he gives Craterus as his source. On this point Craterus, who was copying decrees and not following a literary tradition, should be right. We can, however, guess how Themistocles came into the story. Aeschines, after expatiating on the enormity of proposing to confer a gold crown on Demosthenes for an act which in the good old days, as the decree of Arthmius shows, led to outlawry, rounds off his moral with a nice rhetorical flourish (iii. 259): Θεμιστοκλέα δὲ καὶ τοὺς ἐν Μαραθῶνι τελευτήσαντας . . . οὐκ οἴεσθε στενάξειν; 'Will not Themistocles and the dead of Marathon turn in their graves?' It does not require unusual carelessness to associate Themistocles more directly with the decree.

Habicht in his review of fourth-century forgeries includes the Arthmius decree among the inventions of the period immediately following the fall of Olynthus in 348 when Athens was trying to rouse the Greek states against Philip (*Hermes*, lxxxix (1961), 27). It was first used in that year by Demosthenes and Habicht assumes that subsequent orators and writers had nothing but Demosthenes' texts to go on. Craterus in giving Cimon as the author was simply guessing better than Plutarch. Habicht also thinks that the decree outlawed Arthmius from the territory of the allies as well as of Athens in the style of developed imperial decrees which describe the allies as πόλεις ὅσων Ἀθηναῖοι κρατοῦσι. This would point to a date after Cimon's death. Finally Habicht thinks that the story assumes that Zelea was a member of the Delian League at the time, but it appears only once on the pre-war tribute quota lists, in 441–440 (List 14. ii. 38). These arguments do not convince. The inscription could be seen on the Acropolis; if it had been invented in 348 Demosthenes could not have referred it back to the fifth century, nor can we imagine that the state would sponsor the publication of such a document at such a time. It is also clear from the variations listed above that Demosthenes' texts were not the sole source of later references. As for Craterus we know too little about him to deny him the benefit of the doubt. If the text could be read in the late fourth century the simplest explanation is that Craterus could read it less than fifty years later and made Cimon the author because Cimon's name was in the decree. More important is the formulation of outlawry. It is unlikely that Cimon moved a decree with the developed imperial formula; but it is also unlikely that the decree mentioned πόλεις ὅσων Ἀθηναῖοι κρατοῦσι (or ἄρχουσι). Dinarchus' phrase ἐξ ἁπάσης τῆς χώρας should correspond with Aeschines' ἐξ ἁπάσης ἧς ἄρχουσιν Ἀθηναῖοι. The reference is not to the allies but to territory directly controlled by Athens: there is no objection to dating the decree before 450. Nor is Zelea a sign of forgery. There is nothing in the decree which requires Zelea to be in the Delian League, nor is the fact that Arthmius is a *proxenos* of Athens (if fact it is) an indication that Zelea is an ally; all that is required is that Arthmius should be a Greek.

The reference to Athens' allies shows that the decree is later than the establishment of the Delian League. At some time after 477 Arthmius of Zelea, who was probably a *proxenos* of Athens, and certainly lived within easy reach of the Persian satrap at Dascylium, was sent with Persian money to the Peloponnese. The only other reference in the sources to an attempted use of Persian gold in Greece before the Peloponnesian War is in the fifties when Artaxerxes sent Megabazus to Sparta to buy an invasion of Attica and so force the Athenians to leave Egypt (Thuc. i. 109. 2). Arthmius, it has often been suggested, might have accompanied Megabazus. To this view there are decisive objections. Throughout the whole period of the Egyptian expedition Cimon was in exile (above, pp. 422 ff.), nor would Arthmius have come to Athens if his mission was to persuade Sparta to act against Athens, and the decree in that case would probably have cited Sparta specifically rather than the Peloponnese. Demosthenes also makes it clear (ix. 45) that the bribery was not directed against Athens: 'For the Athenians would not have worried if people in the Peloponnese were bought or corrupted, unless they regarded the well-being of all Greece as their concern.' A context has to be found when Cimon is politically active, before 461 or in the short period between his return from ostracism and his death. This second period provides a possible context. The Persians can have known that Athens was building up her fleet and could be expected to try to reverse the balance of power in the eastern Mediterranean; but Persia had much less to fear then than when the Athenians and their allies virtually controlled Egypt. A better context was suggested by Cary (*CQ* xxix (1935), 177–80), who associated Arthmius with the intrigues of Pausanias. It is probable, as has been suggested above (p. 467), that Pausanias while at Colonae did try to interest the satrap at Dascylium in his own ambitions. He could not expect power or sympathy in Sparta, while the constitution remained unchanged, but if the constricting system could be broken Pausanias could become a real king. Arthmius may have taken money to Argos where Themistocles was living since his ostracism. If the main objective was to help Pausanias Arthmius might have called at Athens, where as *proxenos* he must have had connections, to sound the followers of Themistocles. On this hypothesis Arthmius' mission may have been in the early sixties and may have been followed by the recall of Pausanias from Colonae. It is even possible that the Spartans did find that there was a possibility of Pausanias and Themistocles working together.

D. THE CONGRESS DECREE

Plutarch makes it clear that he has inserted his account of the Congress Decree, because it particularly appealed to him as an illustration of Pericles' vision: τοῦτο μὲν οὖν παρεθέμην ἐνδεικνύμενος αὐτοῦ τὸ φρόνημα καὶ τὴν μεγαλοφροσύνην (*Per.* 17. 4). It does not come from the literary sources which he uses for what precedes and what follows, and one passage in particular suggests that Plutarch's source is an inscription. A literary source might have mentioned the sending out of men to carry the invitations to the Congress, but it would not have specified the number nor the age limit; nor should we have expected such a detailed description of the routes to be followed. There is a similar definition of routes in surviving fifth-century decrees, as in the Coinage Decree (ML 45, clause 9), the Clinias Decree (ML 46. 22–8), and in the 425 Assessment Decree (ML 69. 4–6) : in the first Methone Decree the same age limit is specified (ML 65. 16–17). This is the only clause in Plutarch's account that is convincingly epigraphic, but his paraphrase could without difficulty be translated into epigraphic language. It has sometimes been said that the districts to which the envoys are to be sent are similar to the districts of the Athenian empire, but there are significant differences. Rhodes is included by Plutarch in the islands; in the tribute lists the three cities of Rhodes are in the Ionian–Carian district. Byzantium seems to be in the Thracian district and not in the Hellespontine district as in the tribute lists. Euboea is in the island district in the lists, but is here a stepping-stone to Thessaly. As has often been suggested, the list is drawn up in Amphictyonic terms (most recently, *ATL* iii. 105).

As long ago as 1873 Cobet suggested that Plutarch found the Congress Decree in the collection of Craterus (*Mnem.* i (1873), 112–14). Certainly he used this source, not always at second hand (Plut. *Arist.* 26. 4) ; and he knows that some if not all of Pericles' decrees have survived (*Per.* 8. 7). If there was a separate collection of Pericles' decrees this will be the more likely source. The decree is not dated, but it makes good historical sense immediately after the Peace of Callias when Athens needed a new sanction for what was becoming an Athenian Empire. This is the generally accepted context though it is barely consistent with Plutarch's preface: 'When the Lacedaemonians were beginning to be disturbed by the increase of Athenian power' (ἀρχομένων δὲ Λακεδαιμονίων ἄχθεσθαι τῇ αὐξήσει τῶν Ἀθηναίων, 17. 1). This would point to a date before the 'First Peloponnesian War', but after the reforms of Ephialtes, in 461 or possibly 460, and Wilamowitz tentatively accepted this context, seeing a possible reflection in Aeschylus, *Eumenides* 920: ῥυσίβωμον Ἑλλάνων ἄγαλμα δαιμόνων (*Aristoteles und Athen*, ii. 340 n. 15).

The indication of date may be Plutarch's personal assumption or it may have come from the commentary on the inscription. That at any rate is probably the source of his statement that the congress did not meet because of Spartan opposition; for this is qualified by 'as it is said' and is not Plutarch's own inference. But the explanation seems to lack a firm formulation. The decree itself, however, is more important than the reason for its failure, and in the interval between the end of the war with Persia and the beginning of the rebuilding of the temples it makes good historical sense. The temple question will arise from an oath to leave the burnt temples as a memorial of the barbarians' sacrilege (above, pp. 504–7); the sacrifice may have been vowed before the battle of Plataea or as early as 481, and the discussion of the sea will be intended to provide a sanction and funds for the maintenance of a strong Athenian fleet to patrol the seas. Either Athens would become a hegemon of the Greeks rather than of a League with limited objectives or she would have a sanction for maintaining her League as an essential basis for her fleet (Wade-Gery, *Hesp.* xiv (1945), 222–4). The Spartan expedition to take the control of Delphi from Phocis and restore it to the Delphians would be her reaction to the Amphictyonic ambitions of Athens. If we could be certain that the decree was authentic our reconstruction of the mood and measures of the early forties would be considerably strengthened. There are, however, reasonable grounds for doubt.

It is strange that, while the discovery of the Themistocles decree has stirred up a wave of scepticism against fifth-century inscriptions which are known only from literary sources (Habicht, *Hermes*, lxxxix (1961), 1–35), the Congress Decree has for so long remained immune. Its authenticity has now been challenged and the case against it by R. Seager (*Hist.* xviii (1969), 129–40) cannot be lightly dismissed. Seager's main grounds of suspicion concern substance and language: (1) The freedom of the seas was not, he thinks, a theme for diplomatic discussion in the fifth century, nor was it mentioned in the King's Peace (387–386), nor in the decree of Aristoteles, which sets out the objectives of the Athenian Alliance of 377 (Tod, *GHI* ii. 123). It became a topic for debate only when Philip challenged Athens's assumption that the guardianship of the seas was her prerogative, while Philip claimed that 'they should jointly keep under control offenders on the high seas'. (2) τὴν εἰρήνην ἄγωσιν does not mean 'maintain a state of peace' (which would be εἰρήνην ἄγωσιν) but preserve *the* peace, a specific peace. This should be the Peace of Callias, but that was a bilateral treaty between the Persian king and Athens with her allies; it was not a common peace. Moreover the word εἰρήνη was not used in inscriptions for a treaty before 387–386. (3) καὶ μικρὰν πόλιν καὶ μεγάλην would be acceptable in literary prose, but surprisingly rhetorical in an inscription. Similarly κοινοπραγία seems more appropriate to the fourth century, when the idea of a common peace loomed large in politics, than to the fifth. Having assembled the reasons for suspecting the decree, Seager suggests a context in which such a forgery would have an intelligible motive. It may, he suggests, have been invented as political propaganda in the period between the Peace of Philocrates in 346 and the renewal of war between Philip and Athens in 341. Athens had been anxious that the Peace of Philocrates should be extended to all Greek cities who wished to join and this Philip had refused; Athens resented Philip's pretentions to sea power; she also resented his championship of Delphi and dominance over the Amphictyonic Council. The Congress Decree was intended as raw material for the orators who could base Athenian claims in the present on her record in the past.

These arguments are collectively strong but not decisive. The context is not convincing. An attempt that failed when Athens was the strongest power in Greece was not a good advertisement for a revival of the policy when she lacked adequate resources to give weight to her diplomacy. Even the best of orators would not be able to make much capital from a rejected scheme, and if the decree was invented for the benefit of the anti-Macedonian orators why do we hear nothing about it in the orators? The fact that the freedom of the seas is not otherwise discussed in the fifth or early fourth centuries is not an adequate reason for rejecting it in the particular circumstances of the early forties. Athenian sea-power could not be maintained from Athenian resources alone, but the failure of the Greeks generally to respond would provide a better justification for continuing to exact tribute from the allies. Some of the language may seem too rhetorical for a fifth-century decree but there may be fourth-century or Hellenistic colouring in the paraphrase. But the strongest argument in favour of authenticity is the silence of the orators and historians. This could be explained if the decree was not inscribed on stone because it led to nothing. Craterus could then have 'discovered' it in the archives of the Metroon.

I still believe in the authenticity of the decree but not sufficiently firmly to build upon it and, though I find the context advocated by Seager unconvincing, I sometimes think wistfully of the unknown scholar who put speeches of Pericles on the market; they were apparently accepted as genuine in Cicero's day but rejected by the time of Quintilian (above, p. 140). It is not a far cry from realistic speeches to realistic decrees.

E. THE PAPYRUS DECREE

Strasbourg Papyrus Graeca 84: *Anonymus Argentinensis* (*c.* A.D. 100)

I [- - - - - - - - - - - - - - - - - - ὥστε εἶναι τοῖς πρυτάνεσι]

[τοῖς πεντήκοντα καὶ τοῖς προέδροις το]ῖς ἐννέα   First
ἐπιστάτας δύο, καὶ πρόβου   hand

[λοι καὶ συγγραφεῖς ὁπότε δέοι δέκα ἦσα]ν· ἑκάστης γὰρ φυλῆς
ἕνα ἡροῦντ' ἂν

II 3   [ἑκάστοτε "Ὅτι ὠικοδόμησαν τὰ Προπύλαι]α   Second
καὶ τὸν Παρθενῶνα. μετ' ἔτη τρι   hand

[ἄκοντα μάλιστα ταῦτα ὕστερον τῶν Μηδι]κῶν ἤρξαντο οἰκο-
δο[με]ῖν, ἐποι

[ήσαντο δ' ἀπὸ τῶν φόρων εἰπόντος ἐπ' Εὐ]θυδήμου   450–449
Περικλέους γνώμη[ν] εἰς   B.C.

6   [τὰ Παναθήναια ἀνενεγκεῖν τῆι Ἀθηνᾶι] τὰ ἐν δημοσί⟨ωι⟩ ἀπο-
κέιμενα τάλαν

[τα ἅπερ συνηγμένα παρὰ τῶν πόλεων ἦν πε]ντακισχείλια κατὰ
τὴν Ἀριστεί

[δου τάξιν καὶ ἄλλα τρισχείλια ἀναφέρ]ειν εἰς τὴν πόλιν μετ'
ἐκείνο γιγο

9   [μένων τῶν ἔργων· θαλάσσης δ' ὅπως ἂν κρατ]ῶσι, τὴν βουλὴν
τῶν παλαιῶν τριή

[ρων ἐπιμελεῖσθαι ὥστε ὑγιεῖς παραδι]δόναι, καινὰς δ' ἐπιναυ-
πηγεῖν ἑκάσ

III [του ἐνιαυτοῦ πρὸς ταῖς ὑπαρχούσαις δ]έκα "Ὅτι τρισὶν
ἡμέραις ἐβοήθησαν

12   [Εὐβοεῦσιν. τούτοις μὲν παρεγένοντο] Ἀθηναῖοι πολεμου-
μένοις, Θη[β]αίων

IV [δ' ἐκράτησαν βοήθειαν λαβόντες καὶ π]ρὸς τοῦ ῥήτορος τριήρει
ἐπιδρ[ο̄σίμωι] "Ὅτι

[Δεκελικὸς εἴρηται ὁ πόλεμος. τὸν Πελοπ]ονησιακὸν
πόλεμον Δεκελικὸν ἔφη

V 15   [κατὰ μέρος. οὕτω δὲ καὶ Σικελικὸς εἴρητ]αι καὶ Ἀρχιδάμιος
"Ὅτι τῶι πο[λ]έμωι

[παρέστησαν. προδόντος τὰς ναῦς Ἀδειμ]άντου ἡττήθησαν

The text is that of Meritt and Wade-Gery in *Hesp.* xxvi (1957), 164.

In 1901 Bruno Keil, under the intriguing title of *Anonymus Argentinensis*, published a papyrus fragment of unknown origin which had been acquired in Cairo in 1898. The right-hand parts of twenty-six lines with some twenty-five letters were fairly well preserved. There was no objective control of the number of letters missing at the beginning of each line. Estimates have varied from *c*. 20 (Keil) to *c*. 32 (Meritt and Wade-Gery).

In his extensive commentary Keil reached conclusions that could reasonably be regarded as sensational. The document, he thought, corrected current historical assumptions at several points:

1. A commission was appointed in 457–456 to supervise the rebuilding on the Acropolis, and the Parthenon was begun in that year.
2. The League Treasury was moved from Delos to Athens not in 454 but in 450–449.
3. A decision was taken to build 100 new triremes in 449–448.
4. The Athenians helped Euboea against the Thebans between 448 and 445.

According to Keil the text was an epitome of a Hellenistic historian who was well informed.

Few first editions have illustrated more nakedly the danger of going too far too fast. At first Keil's conclusions were widely welcomed, among others by Wilamowitz, Pöhlmann, and Adolph Bauer: six years later they were merely a historical curiosity. Wilcken, in a brilliant article in *Hermes* (xlii (1907), 374–418), though making few changes in Keil's readings, showed that the document was an epitome of an undistinguished commentary on Demosthenes' speech against Androtion. A series of *lemmata*, introduced by "Ὅτι, which paraphrased passages in Demosthenes, were followed by brief historical notes. In ll. 5–8 Wilcken saw a clear reference to a decree of the archonship of Euthydemus (431–430), introduced by Pericles and known from Thucydides ii. 24. 1, which set aside 1,000 talents at the beginning of the Peloponnesian War as an iron reserve. This left 5,000 talents of the reserve to be spent on the war, and the papyrus referred to this sum as collected from the tribute based on Aristides' assessment: another *lemma* referred to the Athenian expedition to Euboea in 357–356. There could have been no greater anticlimax. Wilcken felt that his basic interpretation of the nature of the document would stand, and in this his confidence was fully justified. He also realized that there would be modifications in detail; they have proved to be considerably more important than Wilcken anticipated.

Interest in the papyrus was revived when *ATL* (i. 572), accepting Wilcken's text, suggested very different restorations. The most important was to interpret ll. 3–8 as a commentary on Demosthenes' reference to the building of the Propylaea and Parthenon. Wilcken had identified the Euthydemus of the papyrus with the archon of 431–430 and this made good sense of the 5,000 talents; but it was virtually impossible to relate such a note to the text of Demosthenes. *ATL* reverted to Keil's suggestion that Euthydemus was a mistake for Euthynus, the archon of 450–449, whose name is known from the Miletus inscription D 11 and who is called Euthydemus by Diodorus. The decree was now referred to the decision taken by the Assembly to use the tribute reserve for the rebuilding of Athenian temples, a decree which was implied by the debate in Plut. *Per.* 12 (cf. Wade-Gery, *Hesp.* xiv (1945), 224–6). They also found a second *lemma* in l. 9: *Ὅτι τριήρεις ἔδει ἔχειν εἰς τὴν πόλιν.* In 1957 (*Hesp.* xxvi (1957), 163–97) Meritt and Wade-Gery made a more fundamental review of the document. Only minor changes were made in the readings but the sense was considerably elaborated in new restorations. They now argued for a longer line with 30–2 letters missing from the beginning. The *lemma* concerning triremes was eliminated and ll. 3–11 were all referred to Pericles' decree. This now included the following provisions: (*a*) The tribute reserve of 5,000 talents was to be brought up to the Acropolis and placed in the keeping of Athena. (*b*) A further 3,000 talents was to be brought up to the Acropolis while the building work was going on. (*c*) In order to maintain control over the sea the Boule should ensure that the old triremes were handed over in good condition and that every year they should be responsible for building ten new triremes.

The neatness of these restorations is extremely attractive. The 3,000 talents will be those referred to in the first decree of Callias (ML 58 A. 3). The 5,000+3,000 will be the 8,000 talents referred to in the sources (Diod. xii. 38. 2; Isocr. viii. 126) and the 3,000 will be composed of fifteen annual contributions of 200 talents implied in the second decree of Callias (ML 58 B. 22). Their thesis does not stand or fall with these or similar restorations of the papyrus, but it would be considerably strengthened if the papyrus could be securely claimed in support. There are, however, reasons for hesitation:

1. The new length of line is perhaps not so firmly established as *ATL* would wish. In l. 2 ὅποτε δέοι could be eliminated; in l. 4 the restoration depends on the uncertain last three letters of l. 3 (their previous text ended μετ' ἔτη $\overline{\Lambda\Gamma}$ which gave 33 years from the battle of Salamis, the actual date 447–446 for the beginning of the Parthenon); in ll. 5–6 εἰς | [τὰ Παναθήναια is not very convincing; in l. 7 παρὰ τῶν πόλεων, though it gives good sense, is not needed. Similar queries could be raised on every line.

2. In l. 8 εἰς τὴν πόλιν is unexpected at the date of the papyrus; we should expect εἰς τὴν ἀκρόπολιν, but πόλιν might have been taken from the decree itself.

3. In ll. 8–9 χιψο|[μένων τῶν ἔργων] seems redundant. Some will prefer their earlier version, which introduced a new *lemma*, for there is no logical connection between financial arrangements for the building programme and regulations for ship-building. These cannot surely have been included in the decree, but they are relevant to Demosthenes' emphasis on the fleet.

Considerable doubts about any reference to the 3,000 talents may remain, but the papyrus is still important in adding substance to the building debate in Plutarch, and in giving a total of 5,000 talents to the tribute reserve. We can also believe that the commentator drew directly or indirectly on a genuine decree moved by Pericles which was included in the collection referred to by Plutarch (*Per.* 8. 7). The date, however, should not be regarded as firmly fixed. If the decree itself was dated the archon must have been named Euthynus, but it is unlikely that a decree of 450–449 would in fact have included the archon's name in its prescript (it was more often omitted until 421–420). The source for the date should then be a literary source making the same mistake as Diodorus. But, if this is accepted, the date cannot claim the authority it would have if taken from an inscription. As we can infer from Thucydides' harsh judgement on Hellanicus, the only writer to have touched on the Pentekontaetia (Thuc. i. 97. 2 : βραχέως τε καὶ τοῖς χρόνοις οὐκ ἀκριβῶς ἐπεμνήσθη), and the dates in Diodorus (see App. 2, p. 452), the chronology of the period was not securely established. Pericles' decree must come in the years between the Peace of Callias and the beginning of the Parthenon in 447–446. It could be nearer the beginning of the Parthenon than 450–449.

APPENDIX 11

The Date of the Financial Decrees of Callias

In writing their commentary on the decrees of Callias (ML 58) Lewis and Meiggs felt secure in claiming that 434–433 may be regarded as a firm date. They had read Mattingly's first attack in the *Proceedings of the African Classical Association* (vii (1964), 35–55), but not the much longer restatement of his case in *BCH* xcii (1968), 450–85. Since the date plays a crucial part in my reconstruction of the years of tension before hostilities broke out, Mattingly's reinforced arguments in favour of 422–421 must be met. For the sake of clarity I enclose summaries of his arguments in inverted commas.

1. 'B. 16 requires a special vote of ἄδεια for expenditure beyond 10,000 drachmae from Athena's money. No such vote appears in the treasurers' account of the two payments made for the Athenian ships sent to support Corcyra in the late summer of 433 (ML 61). The first record of such a vote comes in the treasurers' account for 418–417 (ML 77. 15). The phrase [φσεφισαμένο τõ δέμο τèν] ἄδειαν is attached to the second payment of the year, and there are four further instances (ll. 28, 30, 33, 63).'

On any hypothesis this is odd. Why is the sanction recorded for some payments and not for others? Why in particular not for the first?

2. 'There is no evidence for any *eisphora* before 428. When Thucydides says "on that occasion first" (τότε πρῶτον) he means the first ever, not the first of the war (Thuc. iii. 19. 1).'

(a) One cannot in the record of the Pentekontaetia argue from silence, for the preserved record is much too lean. A special levy early in the seventies or even in the fifties would not be surprising. (b) Mattingly, to maintain this argument, has to down-date one of the Hestiaea decrees (*IG* i². 42 with *SEG* x 37), which has generally been placed shortly after the settlement of Athenians in Hestiaea following the crushing of the Euboean revolt in 446. Mattingly overrides the argument from the rounded rho with tail (ᖆ), on the strength of which I would infer a date probably before 438 and certainly before 430 (*JHS* lxxxvi (1966), 92–4). His positive argument in favour of a date near 422–421 is unconvincing. It is based on ll. 23–4 (with Cary's restoration): περὶ] δὲ χρεμάτον ἐσφο[ρᾶς μὲ ἐ]ναι ἐπιφσε|[φίζεν, μὲ τὲν

ἄδειαν φσεφισαμέν]ον ἐὰμ μὲ λειστὸν [hένεκα χ]συλλέφσε|[ος — —.
Mattingly refers to passages in Thucydides that show Athenian concern for piracy in Euboean waters. In the late summer of 431 they
fortified the uninhabited island of Atalante: 'they wanted to prevent
pirates sailing from Opus and other places in Locris and plundering
Euboea (Thuc. ii. 32).' In 426 Nicias, after the battle of Tanagra,
ravaged the coast of Locris (iii. 91. 6). But the risk of piracy in 431 is
no argument against a similar risk in the late forties. Locris had no
love for Athens. She had been controlled by her after the defeat of the
Boeotians at Oenophyta and had won her freedom with the Boeotians
at the battle of Coronea. (c) A third argument has even less weight.
'Since the Old Oligarch does not mention the *eisphora* it had not yet
been used, therefore the decrees must be after 428.' If, however, the
Old Oligarch wrote in 431 or 430 this argument from silence, which
could not be decisive, would be valueless.

3. 'In the auditors' report of 422 one of the payments of 425–424
is described as coming from the Opisthodomus (ML 72 .19–20). This
shows that none of the money paid out in 426–425 had been taken from
the Opisthodomus, whereas B. 23–4 requires all the money of Athena
and the other gods to be kept in the Opisthodomus.'

This anomaly has never been satisfactorily explained. The natural
inference is that only one payment in these years was made from the
Opisthodomus. The inference is unacceptable on either dating of the
Callias Decrees.

4. 'In the catalogue of Athenian resources in 431 (Thuc. ii. 13. 5) the
phrase ἔτι δὲ καὶ τὰ ἐκ τῶν ἄλλων ἱερῶν . . . χρήματα οὐκ ὀλίγα means
the treasures *in* the other temples (in the lower city and Attica),
showing that the treasures of these other temples had not yet been
brought up on to the Acropolis.'

Mattingly rejects the view of *ATL* (iii. 333) that this clause refers to
the temples of Eleusis, Rhamnous, and perhaps others which retained
their treasures because they were adequately protected. His argument
that this cannot be the meaning because the Athenians did not in
fact borrow from Eleusis or Rhamnous is invalid (Pericles included
the gold of the Parthenos in his review (Thuc. ii. 13. 5) though
it was in fact spared); but to the contemporary reader the other
temples would surely be the large class of temples whose treasures
were in fact brought to the Acropolis. I prefer, with Kolbe (*Sitz. Berl.*
1927. 32 = *Thukydides im lichte der Urkunden*, 52 f.) to see a reference to
the treasures that had been concentrated and were tabulated in *IG*
i². 310 by the treasurers of the other gods.

5. 'The use of ἀκρόπολις in B. 5 would be a serious anachronism. As
Thucydides tells us, the earlier name for the Acropolis was πόλις (Thuc.

ii. 15. 6). The first known dated use of ἀκρόπολις in inscriptions is in a decree for the repayment of state debts to Athena in 410 (D. 9); in literature the first reference is in Aristophanes' *Lysistrata* (176), produced in 411, and πόλις is still used in 414 in the *Birds* (832). On this evidence the Decrees of Callias cannot be as early as 434–433.'

There is no adequate statistical basis for a judgement. Mattingly's case carries no weight unless documents can be produced in which πόλις is used where we should expect ἀκρόπολις. For statistical purposes a count of the use of πόλις after 434–433 is valueless unless the context is comparable with that in B. 5; in the standard formula for setting up decrees on the Acropolis πόλις is continuously used into the fourth century (e.g. in 390–389: *IG* ii². 24. 8 στῆσαι ἐμ πό]ληι). In the example in the *Birds*, to which Mattingly attaches considerable importance, archaism would not be out of place: τίς δαὶ καθέξει τῆς πόλεως τὸ Πελαργικόν; the context in the *Lysistrata* has no such associations: καταληψόμεθα γὰρ τὴν ἀκρόπολιν τήμερον. I suspect that if the *Lysistrata* had been written in 434 Aristophanes would have used the same word.

6. 'The use in A of συν for χσυν and the later dative ταμίαις rather than ταμίασι as in B would be anomalous as early as 434/3.'

Here too the statistical approach needs to be handled carefully. The later dative becomes acceptable if the tribute quota lists 25 and 26, which have the later form, are rightly dated by *ATL* in 429 and 428 (as I hold, see App. 13, pp. 531 ff.). The usage of συν and χσυν is much more difficult to explain logically. As Meritt (*Gk. Rom. Byz. Stud.* viii (1967), 131) points out, it is not particularly significant that A has as many as five uses of the later form: this arises merely because A is a longer and much better-preserved inscription than most and the subject requires more compound verbs. Meritt refers to four early tribute lists including the first which have συν, though each list has only one example; συν also appears in the original treaty with Leontini (ML 64, which is generally assumed to be from the forties). There is no steady growth in the popularity of συν. In most inscriptions that have more than one example both forms are used (ML 64, 65, 68, 77, 84, 87, 89) and sometimes for the same word (as συνάρχοντες and χσυνάρχοντες in 77, συνθέκας and χσυνθέκας in 87). In ML 87 and 89, both decrees of 407, the earlier form dominates. This would seem to be a case for the psychologist rather than the statistician.

None of these detailed points which at first sight seem cumulatively impressive will stand up to close scrutiny. But the main reason for being uncompromising is the singular implausibility of Mattingly's reconstruction. No brief summary can do justice to the ingenuity of the argument but the basic conclusions can be fairly stated. Mattingly's view is that in the first half of 422–421 a decree was passed that 3,000 talents should be put in Athena's treasury by the end of the year, and when that had been done, the state should repay its debts to the other gods. Their treasures in cash and kind were still in the temples of Attica and the lower city but a central account was being kept in Athens (cf. *IG* i². 310). The 3,000 talents that were paid to Athena came partly from the tribute of 421 and partly from non-Attic silver and gold that was converted into Attic silver. The debts that were to be repaid to the other gods were not the 821 talents that the state had borrowed between 433 and 422, since the sum set aside for repayment was only 200 talents; they were those which were owing to the temples when their treasures were concentrated on the Acropolis, in 422–421. The two financial Decrees of Callias were carried while Athens was moving towards peace early in 421 and they were moved by Callias, son of Hipponicus, grandson of Callias who had helped Athens to make peace with Persia and later with Sparta.

The context provided by a date early in 421 is not convincing. If the Athenians had left the treasures in their own temples throughout the Archidamian War, why should they have brought them to the Acropolis when they had no fear of further Spartan invasion? Of the various passages in the decrees that suit the earlier period two of the most important must suffice. (*a*) Decree B. 26 ff. requires the treasurers of Athena to count and weigh their treasures; what follows is lost, but inventories of the three divisions of the Parthenon begin in 434–433 (*IG* i². 232). Their beginning should be associated with the Decrees of Callias. (*b*) In *IG* i². 310 there is a partly preserved inventory of the treasures of the other gods, separately listed, and the account is drawn up by the ταμίαι τον ἄλ[λον θεὸν. There is, however, room for not more than seven names, and more probably only five. Mattingly takes this as a sign that this is not the board to be appointed in A, which has the normal strength of ten; and, like Beloch, he believes that the earlier board is referred to in A. 18: παρὰ δὲ τὸν νῦν ταμιὸν καὶ τὸν ἐπισ|τατὸν καὶ τὸν ἱεροποιὸν τὸν ἐν τοῖς ἱιεροῖς, hοὶ νῦν διαχειρίζο-[σι]|ν, ἀναριθμεσάντον καὶ ἀποστεσάσθον τὰ χρέματα ἐναντίον τες βολ[ε̂|ς ἐμ πόλει. To explain the treasurers of *IG* i². 310 Mattingly has to take τὸν νῦν ταμιὸν to be a central board which will be replaced by the board now to be set up. These ταμίαι have been keeping a record through the Archidamian War and *IG* i². 310 is one of their annual accounts; Mattingly also suggests that the ἐπιστάται who come after the ταμίαι in the list of officials may also be a central board. But both these sets of officials, with those that follow, are described as those who διαχειρίζο[σι]ν the treasures; the word suggests contact with the treasures and is quite inapplicable to a central board at Athens who had nothing but their accounts to hand over; and, if there were such a central board of ταμίαι before the decrees of Callias, a central board of ἐπιστάται would be redundant. There should be no doubt that all the officials listed in ll. 18 and 19 are local officials.

But the main weakness of Mattingly's thesis remains what it was before. He has now recognized the difficulty of paying back the debts to the other gods of over 800 talents incurred during the Archidamian War from the total of 200 talents specified in B. 22; that the debts of the Callias decrees were those owing at the time of the transfer to the Acropolis, excluding war debts, is a possible explanation; but he still has not satisfactorily explained how 3,000 talents could have been handed over to Athena by or in 422–421. He proposes two sources: (a) The non-Attic silver and electrum and gold that may have been included in the 6,000-talent reserve of Thuc. ii. 13. 3. This, he thinks, might have been as much as 800 talents. (b) The tribute of 421 estimated at 1,000 talents and perhaps more. There remains still a considerable gap.

That the decrees were moved by Callias, son of Hipponicus, would be chronologically possible in 422–421, but to make him, as Mattingly does, a serious statesman who had great influence in the Boule is going a good deal further than the evidence allows. Mattingly quotes Xenophon's story (*Symposium* viii. 39–42) that Socrates advised Callias to take up politics seriously and to maintain the record of his family in public life. This is not good evidence that Callias did as he was told, and the *Flatterers* of Eupolis, which was probably produced in this year, strongly suggests that he did not. From what we know of him, financial soundness is the last virtue we should expect to find in this son of Hipponicus (above, p. 286). We should remain open-minded on the identification of Callias, but he must be among men prominent in public life in 434–433 and Callias, son of Hipponicus was then too young; Callias son of Calliades seems in the present state of our evidence to be the most likely choice. As a general in 433–432 he would be a suitable man to propose what are evidently emergency measures taken because war seemed imminent.

See also Add. p. 601.

APPENDIX 12

Notes on Tribute Assessments and Payments, 454–431

A. *The first stele* (453–438, Assessment Periods I–IV)

1. *Number of cities*

The reconstruction of the quota lists has provided a firm basis for calculating the number of lines available for each year's list, but in estimating the number of paying states there is a fluctuating margin of error. The number of entries occupying two lines varies considerably from list to list and the number of such entries in the missing part of a list cannot be precisely determined. A bare count of names may also be misleading. Sometimes a single payment covers two cities, and in two cases at least the payments of three cities are recorded under one name. Erythrae is a more serious example; in the second and sixth periods she pays alone for the whole peninsula, but in the third and fourth periods the syntely is broken up and the small settlements are separately listed, providing six names for one. In 446, and to a lesser extent in 449, the separate recording of part payments and complementary payments can also be a distracting factor. In 438, since nothing survives from the final column, no estimate is given.

Number of payments received

Periods I and II		Periods III and IV	
453	140	445	156
452	162	444	158
451	145	443	163
450	157	442	165
449	c. 163	441	173
447	150	440	171
446	c. 162	439	170

	Ionia	Hellespont	Thrace	Caria	Islands	Total
442	31	26	40	45	23	165
441	31	31	41	47	23	173
440	27	33	40	43	23	167
439	28	?30	43	46	23	170

2. *Assessment totals*

Estimates are based on the standard payments during the period of cities that appear in one or more lists. Estimates are added for cities for whom no payments are preserved but who were probably members of the League at the time. For purposes of comparison the assessment total for 454 includes payments for states which may have changed from ship contribution to tribute after 454.

454 498 talents (*ATL* iii. 20–8)
450 432 talents (*ATL* iii. 52–8)
446 417 talents, distributed as follows:

Ionia	Hellespont	Thrace	Caria	Islands
56 T.	82 T.	120 T.	64 T.	95 T.

Very few changes were made in the 443 assessment.

3. *Notes on assessments and payments*

Period I. The most significant feature in the first period is the absence from all fragments of a considerable group of islands. Two explanations have been offered: that they were still contributing ships (*ATL*) or that they withheld their payment as a protest (Nesselhauf, Meiggs. See the discussion above, pp. 118 ff.). The majority of the other absentees from the lists are in Caria; some of them may have paid through neighbours, some may possibly not yet have been incorporated, but the interior of Caria was always to be the least reliable area of the League. Upper Chalcidice was also less firmly held than the coastal cities and the absence of Chedrolus, Othorus, and Serme is probably their reaction to the defeat in Egypt. Financially the only important absentees outside the island district are Acanthus, Potidaea, Iasus, and Mylasa. *ATL* suggest that the first three were still contributing ships (*ATL* iii. 267 f.). It seems to me more probable that Potidaea was influenced by her mother city Corinth, at war with Athens through the fifties, and that Acanthus abstained in sympathy with her mother city Andros. Iasus and Mylasa are both in the group of cities which in the second period seem to follow the lead of Miletus (*ATL* iii. 35), and for part of the first assessment period Miletus was in revolt (above, p. 115).

Period II. Increases. None in Ionia or the Hellespont; in Thrace: Mende with Scione (from 14 to 15 talents); in Caria: Chalcetor, Halicarnassus, Lindus; in the Islands: Dion (on Cenaean promontory). *Reductions.* In Ionia: Cumae, Myus, Oine (on Icarus); none in the Hellespont; in Thrace: Galepsus, Mecyberna, Sermylia, Singus; in Caria: Caryanda, Erine, Idymus, Madnasus, Pedasus, Pelea,

Phaselis, Telandros; in the Islands: Andros, Carystus, Ios, Rhenea, Seriphos, Syros.

The main problems are the 'missing tribute list' and the significance of part payments and complementary payments. A detailed analysis of the evidence is given in *ATL* iii. 28–63. See also above, pp. 153 f., 164–7, and ML 50.

Period III. The reductions are distributed as follows:

Ionia: Colophon, Erythrae, Ephesus, Hairae, Lebedus, Oine (on Icarus), Phocaea.

Hellespont: —

Thrace: Acanthus, Aegae, Aenus, Aphytis, Dicaea (by Abdera), Mecyberna, ?Mende (see p. 528), Phegetus, Sane, Scabla, Stolus, Thyssus, Torone.

Caria: Chalce, Cheronnesus, Cnidus, Erine, Halicarnassus, Idymus, Lindus, Mylasa, Pargasus, Pedies (Lindian).

Islands: —

The evidence for Erine and Idymus is very fitful. Only two payments survive for Erine in the first eight years, 4,130 drachmae in 452 and 3,240 drachmae in 449. In period III there are two payments of 1,000, but the payment of 443 is the last recorded. Idymus pays 1 t. 890 dr. in 452 and 5,200 in 447. Only one payment is preserved in period III, 2,000 drachmae in 444. There is no evidence of payments after the third period, and the restoration of the name in 441 is very uncertain.

It is possible that Carian Astypalaea should be included in the reductions. Her assessment was 2 talents in the first two periods and 1½ talents in the fourth, and 2 again by the sixth. The name is restored against a payment of 2 talents in 443: [Κυλλάνδιοι] is a possible alternative. For Mende see below, B. 3.

In the following there was a reduction either in 446 or 443, and since very few changes can be definitely placed in 443, the majority were probably reduced in 446.

Ionia: Dios Hieron, Miletus.

Hellespont: Alopeconnesus, Dardanus, Limnae, Selymbria, and probably Abydus.

Caria: Camirus, Ialysus, Termerus.

Islands: Chalcis, Eretria.

Only two payments by Abydus are preserved before the fourth period, and both are odd. In 453 the name is restored against a tribute of 4.2260 and in 445 there is a payment of 4.0315. In the fourth period 4 talents is paid regularly, and in 432 there is a payment of 6 talents.

B. *The second stele* (438–431, Assessment Periods V and VI)

1. *Number of cities*

The lists of the fifth and sixth assessment periods are considerably less well preserved than those of the first stele. For 437 only fifteen names survive and the list of 436 is completely missing. For 435 and 434 the approximate number of payments recorded is 156 and 168. In 433 there are some 165 in the district panels and twenty-five small communities, mostly new, in special categories. The lists of 432 and 431 are both well preserved and can usefully be compared.

	Ionia–Caria	Hellespont	Thrace	Islands	Self-assessed	Registered by individuals
432	51[1]	33	39	23	10	?
431	53[1]	27	27	?[2]	5	?[2]

[1] In comparing this figure with other periods it should be noted that Erythrae pays for all six communities on her peninsula.

[2] It is not known how many lines are missing from the bottom of the two columns.

The most significant feature of the comparison is the sharp decline of numbers in the Thracian panel and in the self-assessed (πόλεις αὐταὶ φόρον ταχσάμεναι) in 431. The absentees in Thrace reflect the revolt that broke out in the summer of 432 (above, p. 252). The tribute lost to Athens west of the Strymon is 17 talents together with Potidaea's tribute, normally 6 talents, but raised to 15 talents in or possibly earlier than 432 (see below): Argilus (1,000 dr.), Assera (3,000 dr.), Dicaea (Eretrian colony) (1 t.), Mecyberna (1 t.), Olynthus (2 t.), Phegetus (1,000 dr.), Scabla (3,000 dr.), Scapsa (1,000 dr.), Sermylia (4.3000), Singus (2 t.), Spartolus (3.0500), Stolus (1 t.), Strepsa (1 t.). East of the Strymon there was no tribute from Maronea (10 t.) and Aenus (10 t. in the third and fourth periods, but paying only 4 t. in 435 and absent in 434). All five absentees from the self-assessed are also in the Thracian district together with a sixth, present in 433 but missing in 432.

2. *Assessment totals*

The lists of the fifth period are so poorly preserved that no estimate is attempted. The evidence for the 434 assessment is considerably better, though there are several cities for which we have no evidence. The assessment total was probably *c.* 430 talents.

3. *Notes on assessments and payments*

In thirty-one cases where the tributes of the two periods can be compared without restorations, twenty-seven are unchanged, four changed in 434. The main changes were probably made in 438 and taken over in 434. If the two assessments are taken together there were thirty increases and eight reductions.

Of the tributes which were reduced in 446 at least twelve were restored to their pre-446 level. In Ionia: Colophon, Ephesus, Oene (on Icarus); in the Hellespont: Alopeconnesus and probably Parium; in Thrace: Aegae, Aphytis, Dicaea by Abdera, Mecyberna, Sane, Scabla; in Caria: Cheronnesus, Lindus, and possibly Astypalaea (see under A. 3 above). For Cnidus, Erine, Lebedus, Mylasa, Pargasus, and Phocaea there is no evidence.

Myus, Phaselis, and Syros, reduced in 450, return to their original 454 assessments.

Ten cities have higher assessments than in any of the first four periods: In Ionia: Gryneum, Pygela, Erythrae; in the Hellespont: Byzantium, Lamponeia; in Thrace: Assera, Maronea, Spartolus, Stolus; in Caria Pedies (Lindian).

The payments of the main cities on the peninsula of Pallene are difficult to interpret and they have not been included in the figures for the fifth and sixth assessments. They need to be seen in the light of their earlier tribute history.

	454–450	450–446	445	444	443	442	439	435	434	433	432	431
Potidaea	..	..	..	6	6	6	6	..	6	..	15	abs.
Scione	6	..	6	6	6	6	..	..	15	..	..	4
Mende	8	15	..	..	5	9	5	8	8	8	..	5

In the second period Mende is clearly paying also for Scione. In periods IV and V Scione's assessment is 6 talents, but Mende's payments are irregular, 5 talents in 443 and 438, 9 talents in 442; this latter is probably the assessment, maintaining a combined figure with Scione of 15 talents. In 434 Scione, hitherto consistently assessed at 6 talents, is recorded as paying 15 talents while Mende pays a normal 8 talents, and in 432 Potidaea, hitherto consistently assessed at 6 talents, pays 15 talents and there is no evidence for Mende and Scione. Potidaea's high tribute can be explained by her hostile attitude which led later in 432 to open revolt, but Scione's is much more surprising, especially since at the next assessment in 430, when war had broken out, she was required to pay only 9 talents. *ATL* (iii. 64–5) offer an attractive solution to the problem. Noting that in 434 Scione is listed immediately after Potidaea, they suggest that the cutter has carelessly transposed the figures; the 15 talents should be Potidaea's, and Scione's normal assessment of 6 talents should be restored.

If this explanation is accepted Potidaea's tribute will have been raised to 15 talents either at the assessment of 438 or in the course of the period, perhaps not until 434. This would suggest a longer history to Athenian suspicions of Potidaea, but that is not necessarily inconsistent with Thucydides. The texts as they are inscribed make rather better sense of Potidaea's tribute history, but create a greater difficulty in the isolated high payment of Scione. We prefer the bolder solution of emendation.

The tributes of cities east of the Strymon are also puzzling. Abdera is unaffected, but Maronea, having paid 1½ talents consistently since 453, now has an assessment of 10 talents, while Aenus, after paying 10 talents in the third and fourth periods, has only one payment preserved, 4 talents in 435, and is missing in 434 and 431. It is wiser to say no more than that 'there must be a special explanation'.

c. Assessment comparisons

The table below lists the first and last known pre-war assessments of cities who were required to pay 1 talent or more. Two categories are excluded: (1) Cities whose assessments may have been affected by special circumstances such as a cleruchy settled on their land. (2) Cities who seem to have made no payment after the third period. In the first columns the figures represent the first assessment of 454; where no evidence survives for the first period, the earliest known period in which the assessment is known is added in brackets. In the second column the latest known assessment is added in brackets when there is no evidence for the last pre-war assessment in 434.

IONIA	1	2	THE HELLESPONT	1	2
Clazomenae	1.3000	1.3000 (IV)	Abydos	? 4.3000	6
Cumae	12	9	Arisba	? 2.?	2 (IV)
Ephesus	7.3000	7.3000	Byzantium	15 (II)	18.1800
Myrrhina	1	1	Chalcedon	9 (II)	6
Myus	1.3000	1.3000	Cyzicus	9 (IV)	9
Oine on Icarus	1.2000	1	Dardanus	1.3000	1
Phocaea	3	2 (IV)	Lampsacus	12	12 (IV)
Priene	1	1 (IV)	Parium	1	1
Teos	6	6	Perinthus	10 (II)	10
			Tenedos	4.3000	2.5280

THRACE	1	2	CARIA	1	2
Abdera	15	15	Astypalaea	2	2
Acanthus	3	3	Calydna	1.3000	1.3000
Aenea	3 (III)	3	Camirus	9	6
Aenos	12	10 (IV)	Ceramus	1.3000	1.3000 (IV)
Aphytis	3	3	Chersonese	3	3
Galepsus	1.3000	1000	Cindya	1	1 (IV)
Mecyberna	1 (II)	1	Cnidus	5 (II)	3 (IV)
Mende	8	8	Cos	5 (II)	5
Olynthus	2	2	Halicarnassus	1.4000	1.4000
Peparethus	3	3	Ialysus	10 (II)	6
Samothrace	6	6	Iasus	1 (II)	1
Sane	? 1	1	Latmus	1	1
Scione	6	? 4	Lindus	10 (II)	10

M m

THRACE (cont.):				CARIA (cont.):		
Sermylia	?7.3000	4.3000	Madnasus	2	1
Singus	4	2	Mylasus	1 (II)	5200 (IV)
Strepsa	1	1	Phaselis	6	6
Torone	12 (II)	6	Telandros	1	3000 (IV)
			Termerus	2.3000	3000 (IV)

ISLANDS

	1	2		1	2
Aegina	30	30	Paros	16.1200 (II)	18 (IV)
Ceos	4 (II)	3	Seriphos	2	1
Cythnos	3 (II)	3	Siphnos	3 (II)	3 (V)
Ios	1	3000	Styra	1 (II)	1
Myconos	1.3000	1	Tenos	3 (II)	2

TOTALS

	1	2
Ionia	35.2000	30
Hellespont	68.3000	68.1080
Thrace	88.3000	72.4000
Caria	63.1000	50.3200
Islands	64.2000	62.3000
Grand Total	320.1200	283.5280

The following cities have been omitted from the above table since their assessments may have been affected by special circumstances, known or inferred. Reference is given to discussion in the text. For the convenience of comparison the basic facts or problems are restated, but without reference to sources.

Cleruchies

Andros (250), p. 121: 12 t. in 450, 6 t. in 449 and after. Cleruchy 450.

Naxos (500), p. 121: tribute unchanged from 447. ? Cleruchy 450.

? Carystus, p. 121: 7½ t. in 450, 5 t. from 449. ? Cleruchy 450.

Chersonese (1000), p. 160: 18 t. in first period; incomplete (or in 2 instalments) 449. ? Absent 447. From 446 small communities pay in total c. 2 t. Cleruchy 447.

? Lemnos, pp. 160, 424: 9 t. in first period; 4½ t., first clearly attested 443: probably from 446 or 449. ? Cleruchy 450 or 447.

Revolts

Thasos, pp. 84–6: 3 t. in first two periods, 30 t. from 443, possibly from 445.

Erythrae, pp. 112 ff.: no tribute evidence to compare assessment before and after revolt in the fifties. See also under Colonies.

Colophon, pp. 161 f. : 3 t. in first period, 1½ t. in third period. See also under Colonies.

Miletus, pp. 115 ff.: tribute evidence poor. 10 t. in second period; 5 t. in fourth.

Chalcis, pp. 565–8: ? 5 t. in 447, 3 t. probably from 445. Confiscation of land or Cleruchy.

Eretria, pp. 568–70: ? 6 t. in second period, 3 t. probably from 445. See also under Colonies.

Colonies. All cases are controversial, and cannot be briefly summarized.

? Colophon, pp. 162 f.: Erythrae, pp. 162 f.; Eretria, p. 568.

Special factors

Maronea, p. 249: increased from 1½ to 10, first attested in 435, probably dating from assessment of 438.

Selymbria, p. 249: reduced from 5 t. to 900 dr.; first attested in 434, probably dating from assessment of 438.

Argilus, p. 159: possibly affected by colonies Brea and Amphipolis.

APPENDIX 13

Notes on the Tribute Lists, 430–426

The tribute lists from 453 to 431 were inscribed on two large stelae; those which followed were each inscribed on a separate stele. This considerably increases the problem of dating; between the list of 431 (list 23) and the assessment of 425 (A. 9) no list can be dated with complete certainty but, thanks largely to the work of West and Meritt, the margin of doubt has been very considerably reduced. In the text I have followed without argument the main conclusions of *AFD*, 3–35, with *ATL* iii. 69 f., which may be summarized:

1. The assessment following 434 took place, after the normal interval, in 430, a year of the Great Panathenaea.
2. Two lists survive from this assessment, *IG* i². 218 which they date in 429 (list 25) and *IG* i². 216/17+231, dated 428 (list 26).
3. *IG* i². 214/15 is the list of 428/7 (list 27).
4. This list reflects a new assessment in 428.

This dating of the early war lists represents a substantial change from the earlier conclusions of Meritt and West in *SEG* v (1930). There 216 was thought to precede 218 and to be from 429; 218 was from 427/6 and 214 from the following year, 426/5. Some of the arguments which led to the earlier dating have been revived by Mattingly (*CQ* lv (1961), 154–65) and Nesselhauf preferred to date 216 before 218 (*Untersuchung zur Geschichte der delisch-attischen Symmachie, Klio*, Beiheft xxx (1933), 69–73).

The case for putting 216 and 218 in the same assessment period is very strong indeed:

1. In the seventeen cases where a city's figure is preserved or can with complete confidence be restored in both lists it is the same.
2. In the Hellespontine district some of the cities are listed twice in both lists and the combined totals seem to represent the full payment for the year.
3. The two groups of cities which were first included under separate rubrics in 433 are still listed separately from the main districts, though the formulation of the rubrics is different in these two lists.

The general character of the assessment reflected in these two lists is conservative. Of some sixty known tributes only eleven have been revised, and the five increases are offset by six reductions. In the Hellespontine district Byzantium, who paid a little less than 20 talents in the thirties, now pays nearly 30 talents. Selymbria, whose assessment had been reduced in the thirties from 5 talents to a nominal 900 drachmae, now pays 9 talents, and Daunioteichos, assessed before the war at 1,000 drachmae, now pays 2 t. 4,000 dr. Sigeum alone in the Hellespontine district has her tribute reduced, from 1 talent to 1,000 drachmae. In Thrace Torone's assessment is increased from 6 to 12 talents, but this is a return to the assessment of the second period; Scione, whose normal pre-war payment was 6 talents, now has to pay 9 talents. These increases are balanced by considerable reductions. Abdera's assessment was unchanged before the war at 15 talents which she still paid in 432; in 431, however, her payment was 10 talents and this was her payment in 429. Maronea's assessment had been sharply increased in the thirties from 1½ to 10 talents; she now pays only 3 talents. In 429 Samothrace, who had paid 6 talents continuously before the war, pays only 2 talents, but this might be an incomplete payment. There are also reductions in the assessments of Aenea and Sane. In the islands we have figures for twelve states and they show no changes. For the Ionian–Carian district there is no evidence.

The assessment of 430 shows no sign of financial anxiety. The increases are confined to a few of the richer states and are balanced by reductions elsewhere; the total received was probably no higher than in 432, before fighting had begun. The question which of the two lists is the earlier is better postponed until we have found a date for the next assessment and the answer to this question hinges on the date of *IG* i². 214. Though the surviving fragments give us a miserably small proportion of the complete list, enough survives to show that the assessment on which it is based had a very different character (Meritt, *AFD*, 12–20):

1. In the Hellespontine district, where only six names are preserved, two have not appeared in any earlier lists: Σεριστειχῖται and [Σ]ομβία.
2. In the Ionian district, where thirteen tributes are preserved, four show an increase: Clazomenae now pays 6 talents instead of 1½; Erythrae 12 talents instead of 9; Polichna's assessment rises from 5,000 drachmae to 1½ talents, Gryneum's from 1,000 to 2,000 drachmae. Colophon and Notium make only nominal payments (500 drachmae for 3 talents and 100 drachmae for 2,000 drachmae), but these reflect the Medism of Colophon and the intervention of Persia. The only 'normal' reduction is the 2 talents of Cnidus for her pre-war 3 talents. No payments for any of these cities are preserved from the assessment of 430, but

the pattern of 214 is very different from either of the two lists 216 and 218.

3. The cities that were first listed under separate rubrics in 433 and remained apart from the main district lists seem to have been disbanded in list 214: Besbikos is now in the Hellespontine list and Casos in the Ionian–Carian list. The assessment on which 214 is based seems to be more demanding and later than the assessment represented by 216 and 218. Meritt argued that list 214 was the list of 427 and that it reflects a new assessment in 428. Not all the arguments are equally strong, but an assessment in 428 remains a very probable hypothesis.

(a) The mainland cities opposite Lesbos were taken from Mytilene when her revolt was crushed in 427 (Thuc. iii. 50. 3). In the assessment of 425 these Ἀκταῖαι πόλεις are listed after the Hellespontine district, their natural place. They are not inserted in that place in list 214, which should therefore be before they had been taken over by Athens. They could, however, have been inscribed at a different point in the list, or may not have been formally enrolled until the next assessment.

(b) In 428 Thucydides records a force of money-collecting ships (Thuc. iii. 19. 1). Such squadrons are mentioned only twice elsewhere in the History, in 430 and 425 (Thuc. ii. 69; iv. 75), and we know that those were both assessment years. Gomme had little sympathy with this argument (HCT ii. 202 f. on ii. 69. 1) on the ground that such ships were in regular use, and are only mentioned by Thucydides when some special task was allotted to them. It would not, however, be odd if it were the regular practice to send out rather larger forces of these ships in assessment years.

(c) Thucydides emphasizes the need for increasing revenue in 428 when Mytilene came out in revolt (Thuc. iii. 19. 1), and mentions the eisphora or capital levy raised from the Athenians themselves. It would seem logical that while Athens was taxing her own citizens she should at the same time try to increase the contributions of the allies.

(d) A passage in the assessment decree of 425 insists that in future there shall be a reassessment in every Great Panathenaic year. Strong penalties are laid down for the prytaneis responsible if they fail to carry the business through at the right time. The tone is polemical (A 9; ML 69. 26–33). The inference is that no new assessment was made in 426, the last Great Panathenaic year (see pp. 322 f.).

If 216 and 218 are earlier than 214, and if there was no assessment in 426 we are left to choose between 428 and 427 for the assessment that follows 430. Though the detailed arguments are not compelling the high summer of 428 provides the better context. Thucydides draws attention to the need for more money when a long and expensive siege of Mytilene could be expected; in the high summer of 427, when Mytilene had fallen and the Spartan attempt to relieve the city had failed so miserably, the situation must have seemed considerably less critical.

We may then believe that lists 218 and 216 belong to the years 429 and 428: it remains to decide which comes first. When *SEG* v was published West and Meritt were satisfied that 216 preceded 218, and a little later Nesselhauf came independently to the same conclusion (above, p. 531). Mattingly also prefers this order but offers a completely different pattern of dates and bases his case largely on the Methone decrees (*ATL* ii. D. 3–6; ML 65). The first Methone decree arises from representations made by Methone, which has recently been brought into the empire and already owes money to Athens. The people are to decide forthwith whether they are to assess Methone or whether they should be content with the *aparche* on Methone's assessment at the last Panathenaea (τοῖς προτέροις Παναθηναίοις, D. 3; ML 65. 29–31). The people decide that Methone need pay only the *aparche* (ll. 29–31), and in 216 Methone is listed together with two other Thracian communities under a special rubric: αἴδε τὸν πόλεον αὐτέ[ν] | τὲν ἀπα[ρ]χὲν ἀπέγαγον (26. ii. 51 f.), and there is room for the same rubric with the same cities in list 218 (25. ii. 31 f.). The natural inference is that Methone was making her plea in an assessment year, and 430 has been widely accepted in view of a later passage in the decree (ll. 27–9). The envoys voted by the decree are to tell Perdiccas that if the troops at Potidaea praise him the Athenians will think well of him. The siege of Potidaea began in 432 and ended in the winter of 430/29. The phrase ἐμ Ποτειδ[ά]αι could mean troops either actually inside Potidaea or before Potidaea. In either case the phrase would suit best the assessment of 430.

Mattingly does not accept this conclusion, on the ground that it allows an intolerably long interval between the first and second decrees. In the first decree the Athenians seem to regard matters as urgent. The second decree is firmly dated to the first prytany of 426; if the first decree is as early as any time in the year 430–429 negotiations will have dragged on for three years or more. The first decree requires envoys to make representations to Perdiccas and, if they fail to reconcile him with Methone, they are to ask both parties to send representatives to the Dionysia with powers to take decisions on the matters at issue (D 3. 16–27). In the second decree privileges are conferred on Methone and the Athenians undertake to consider their grievances when the two sets of Athenian envoys, led respectively by Plistias and Leogoras, return and come before the people (D 4. 47–51). Mattingly argues that negotiations with Perdiccas cannot have lasted so long. He would date the first Methone decree in the winter of 427/6 when the Athenians had to decide whether to make an immediate irregular assessment or allow Methone to pay only the *aparche* on the current assessment. Mattingly accepts the point made by *ATL* that the contrast implied in τοῖς προτέροις Παναθηναίοις is between two strictly comparable occasions; in *ATL* this is a contrast between the current Great Panathenaea of 430 and that of 434 (*ATL* iii. 134). On Mattingly's interpretation 'the Assembly would have been anticipating a normal reassessment by only eight months; the coming Great Panathenaea would form the implied balance to the previous Panathenaea, when tribute was last assessed'. This is a strained interpretation but perhaps not impossible. The other main clue to the date is the reference to ἡοι στρατι[ῶται | ἡοι] ἐμ Ποτειδ[ά]αι (l. 27). Mattingly sees in these troops a permanent garrison installed in Potidaea after its capture and the expulsion of its population in the winter of 430/29. He thinks that Potidaea was used as a military base not only in 429 (Thuc. ii. 79. 7) but again probably in 425 (Thuc. iv. 7. 7), and that 'Athens went on to create a complex defence system for the Thraceward area, which was based exclusively on Potidaea' (Mattingly, 161 f.). This surely builds too much on too little. Thucydides' brief account of a minor action in the summer of 425 gives no hint of a strong garrison in Potidaea, nor of a new and complex defence system for the Thraceward area. Simonides, the Athenian general, collected a few Athenians from the garrisons and a number of local allies and took the Mendaean colony of Eion which was betrayed to them. When the Chalcidians and Bottiaeans brought up help Simonides' force was driven out with heavy losses. Nor can any major inferences concerning general defence policies be drawn, as Mattingly would wish, from the Aphytis decree(D. 21), which is concerned solely with the problems of Aphytis. Reference is made to an oath taken by the men of Aphytis to the Athenian settlers in Potidaea and to the Athenian people; this was probably to stiffen the loyalty of Potidaea's neighbour, who may have resented the new settlers. If the Methone decree were referring to a garrison in Potidaea the more likely term would be φρουροί, and if Potidaea had been the centre of a defence system, with a substantial garrison, we should have heard of it at some point in Thucydides' narrative.

Mattingly's interpretation of these two clauses, though not impossible, is very strained; nor is the long interval between the first two Methone decrees difficult to explain. Perdiccas' relations with Athens were notoriously unstable and it is natural that he should continue to resent the Athenian protection of Methone. The four Methone decrees that were inscribed together in 423 are not the only decrees that concerned Methone during these years, for D 4. 50 f. refers to two sets of

Athenian envoys whose return from Perdiccas is expected, and D 3. 16 ff. is concerned with only one: there is no need for either to be identified with the envoys of D 3. The objections to Mattingly's dating and interpretation of the Methone decrees are not perhaps sufficiently decisive if his arguments for redating the tribute lists are in themselves cogent; these must now be briefly examined.

Mattingly accepts 428/7 as a virtually unassailable date for *IG* i². 214 (perhaps in this he is too generous), but he puts 216 before 218 and in a different assessment period: 214 in 428/7; 216 in 427/6; 218 in 426/5. Some of his arguments are attractive: 216 has the same order of districts as 214, but 218 is different; and in 218 the order is the same as in the Assessment Decree of Thudippus from late summer 425. The other main reason for putting 216 before 218 is the new versions of rubrics which first appeared in 433 as πόλες αὐταὶ φόρον ταχσάμεναι and πόλες hὰς hοι ἰδιῶται ἐνέγραφσαν φόρον φέρεν. In 218 they become ταῖσδ[ε ἐταχσαν hοι τάκται | ἐπὶ Κρ[. . .]ο γραμματεύοντος and ταῖσδε h[ε] βολὲ καὶ hοι πεντακόσιοι | καὶ χίλ[ιοι ἔτ]αχσαν. In the list of 216 only two letters (one of which is uncertain) survive from the first rubric and the formula of 218 could be restored, but seven letters of the second rubric can be read and they are very recalcitrant. None of the three restorations suggested in *AFD* 11 has survived criticism, and the restoration proposed in *ATL* ii, though better, is not convincing: [τοῖσδε βο[λὲ [συν τ]ôι | [δικαστερί]ο[ι ἔ]τ[α]- χ[σεν. The omission of the article virtually rules it out; some such restoration as Mattingly's [ταῖσδε πό]λεσ[ιν h]οι | [ἰδιῶται φόρ]ο[ν ἐ]τ[ά]- χ[σαντο (Mattingly, 15 f., n. 6) is preferable. It seems probable that the formulae of 216 were nearer to the pre-war rubrics than the very different formulae of 218. It was a reasonable inference that the rubrics of 218 represented a change of system after 216. One other factor also suggested that the list of 216 was earlier than 218. The record of two small communities, Αἰολῖται and Πλευμês, is an erratic one in the tribute lists. They appear first in 433 among the πόλεις αὐταὶ ταχσά- μεναι. In 432 Αἰολῖται are again listed, but Πλευμês are absent. In 431 both are absent. In 218 they are also both absent but in 216 they are both present. Αἰολῖται certainly and Πλευμês possibly are Bottiaean communities (*ATL* i, Gazeteer, 465, 538 f.) and would naturally be involved in the revolt that was based on Spartolus and Olynthus. If *ATL* dates are accepted these two small states were recovered in 429/8 after a long absence. An improvement in the Athenian position in the area would cause no surprise while an Athenian army was operating on the borders of Macedon or before Potidaea, but we should not expect even this limited success so soon after the decisive defeat of the Athenian forces before Spartolus in the summer of 429 (Thuc. ii. 79).

The arguments supporting the *ATL* dating, however, though un-even, are collectively stronger: (1) List 25. 146: [Πυγε]λὲς hένες ἐπιφορᾶς. It is argued (*AFD* 9) that since the record of ἐπιφορά for a current year is not found on any war-list fragment the institution must have been abandoned at the 430 assessment, and this record of payment for the previous but not the current year must be from 430/29, the first list of the 430 period. This is a probable rather than a certain inference. In the list of 431, which is nearly complete, no ἐπιφορά survives and there is only one instance in the very full list of 432 (22. ii. 26). Had there been on average two a year from 430 to 425 it would not be surprising if no traces survived. (2) In 216. iv. 44–5 *ATL* restore [h]a[ιραι]ἐ[ς | haιρα]ιὲς περυσι[νό] and in 218. i. 43 [haιραι]ὲς hένο (see also Meritt, *DAT* 100). This makes a coherent record for Ionian Haerae, neighbour of Erythrae, if 218 is before 216, but again there are possible alternatives. Mattingly (p. 155) suggests for 218 [Γρυνει]ὲς which is epigraphically sound. (3) Meritt has shown that the prescript of 216 had lines of forty-seven letters which allow the restoration [ἐπὶ τὲς hέκτες καὶ εἰκοστὲς ἀρχὲς] h[ὲι Δα]μιππος Φυλάσιος [ἐγραμμάτευε], dating the list to 429/8. Mattingly offers ὀγδόες in place of hέκτες, making 216 the list of 427/6.

The compelling objection, however, to Mattingly's reconstruction lies in the assessment pattern that he implies. Lists 25 (218) and 26 (216) seem to have very little in common with list 27 (214). The new towns and the tribute increases of this list suggest a very different mood from the conservatism of lists 25 and 26, and the inclusion of some members at least of the pre-war special panels in the normal district lists, as in list 27, must surely be after lists 25 and 26 in which the panels maintain their separate identity. Mattingly also has to infer a new assessment in 426 which is barely consistent with one of the emphasized provisions of the assessment decree of 425 (above, p. 322).

If we accept the *ATL* dating of lists 25 and 26 to 429 and 428 we need to explain why the rubrics in list 26 should be closer to the pre-war pattern than those of list 25. The solution would seem to be that they are expressing the same processes in different ways. The πόλες αὐταὶ ταχσάμεναι initiated negotiations for their assessments (see p. 251), and they were put on the list of the τάκται with whom they negotiated. The communities sponsored by ἰδιόται were not on the list of the τάκται, but the proposals of the individuals who initiated their enrolment had to go through the court and have the final approval of the Boule. Perhaps, as has been suggested (*ATL* iii. 84), their status and tributes were guaranteed against change; this could explain why in the first list of the 430 assessment period reference was made to the Athenian bodies who were responsible in 434. In 428, however, the secretary of the *hellenotamiae* preferred to go back to the more simple pre-war formulae.

APPENDIX 14

Tribute Payments, 453–420

I am grateful to the Oxford University Press and the authors for permission to reproduce, with minor modifications, the record of tribute payments from the revised edition of Hill's *Sources*, with Introduction. I have added columns for the payments in 429, 428, and 420, and for the assessment of 425.

This table is based closely on the Register in *ATL* (vol. i, 216–441, with amendments in vol. ii, 79–83) to which reference should be made for a detailed statement of the evidence. It is intended primarily to give a survey of the changes made by Athens in successive assessments rather than to give precise information for individual years. The states in each district have been arranged in roughly geographical order so that the relation between assessment changes in neighbouring states may be more clearly seen: an alphabetical index, however, is added (p. 560) by means of which any particular state can be quickly found. Assessment periods are divided by thickened lines. For year headings the year in which the tribute was received (normally at the Dionysia in the spring) have been chosen rather than the Attic year.

Nearly all entries in the Quota Lists are incompletely preserved, but it is impossible, without paralysing printer and reader, to indicate in every case the degree of restoration involved. The following principles have been adopted. Where sufficient remains on the stone to make a restoration of the normal tribute highly probable, no mark of restoration is shown. Where a state's assessment is known in a period, the normal tribute is restored for those years in that period in which there is no evidence of the amount paid, unless historical reasons are known which might suggest a different payment. Where, however, there is no evidence from the same period, no figure is restored, unless the state's assessment is the same in the period before and in the period after. So, for example, no figures are restored in the first period (454–450) for states whose quotas are first preserved in 449 or later; on the other hand, a tribute of 3,000 drachmae may reasonably be restored for Caunus in the second and third periods, for which there is no evidence, since a tribute of 3,000 drachmae is well attested for the first and fourth periods.

In restoring states on the basis of correspondence with other lists, even when no direct evidence survives, *ATL* has been followed. In cases where it is impossible to indicate the evidence, even in the rough manner adopted, a question mark is used, and brief notes are given on these entries at the end of each district.

The following abbreviations have been used:

( )   tribute restored.
[ ]   state restored.
[( )]   both tribute and state restored.
X   quota partly extant, showing irregular payment.
abs.   absent from full panel.
?   note at the end of district.

1 states listed at the end of the last column in 447, under the heading M[ετὰ Διονύσια].
2 states paying ἐπιφορά (ATL i. 450–3).
3 states listed as ἄτακτοι (ATL i. 455).
4 states listed under the heading πόλεις αὐταὶ φόρον ταξάμεναι (ATL i. 455–6).
5 states listed under the heading πόλεις ἃς οἱ ἰδιῶται ἐνέγραψαν φόρον φέρειν (ATL i. 455).

The distribution of the cities which Athens claimed to control is shown in a series of maps with explanatory note at the end of the book.

TRIBUTE OF THE ATHENIAN EMPIRE, 453–420 B.C.

For abbreviations see previous page

I. IONIAN DISTRICT

	453	452	451	450	449	448	447	446	445	444	443	442	441
1. Ναπριοι	:	:	1.3000	:	:	:	:	:	⌒	:	:	[(1)]	1
2. Ἀφρος	3⌒	:	:	:	:	:	:	:	:	:	:	:	:
3. Τειχιοῦσσα	:	:	:	:	:	:	:	:	:	:	:	:	:
4. Μιλήσιοι	:	:	(⌒)	:	:	:	:	⌒	⌒	:	:	5	(5)
5. Μύησιοι	:	:	1.3000	:	10⌒	:	:	(1)	:	:	:	(1)	(1)
6. Θερμαῖοι ἐξ Ἰκάρου	(3000)	:	(3000)	3000	1	:	(3000)	3000	:	:	:	[3000]	3000
7. Οἰναῖοι ἐξ Ἰκάρου	1.2000	1.2000	:	1.2000	3000	:	(1)	1	4000	:	(4000)	[(4000)]	4000
8. Πρωνῆς	:	1	:	:	(1)	:	(1)	[(1)]	:	:	:	(1)	[(1)]
9. Μαιάνδριοι	4000	:	(4000)	:	1	:	:	[(1)]	:	4000	:	:	abs.
10. Μαραθήσιοι	:	:	:	:	:	:	:	:	:	:	:	:	3000
11. Πυγελῆς	:	:	:	:	:	:	:	:	:	:	:	[(3000)]	(1)
12. Ἰασθιοι	:	:	:	:	:	:	:	:	(1)	[1000]	(1)	(1)	(1000)
13. Ἐφέσιοι	[7.3000]	7.3000	7.3000	:	(7.3000)	:	:	7.3000	:	:	6	1000	(6)
14. Νοτιῆς	2000	2000	2000	:	2000	:	2000	[2000]	(2000)	:	:	6	2000
15. Διοσερῖται	1000	1000	:	2000	1000	:	1000	[1000]	:	:	:	[(2000)]	500
16. Λεβέδιοι	:	:	:	:	(3)	:	[(3)]	[3]	:	:	:	[(500)]	1
17. Κολοφώνιοι	:	:	3	3 z	:	:	:	:	1.3000	(1.3000)	(6)	[(1)]	1.3000
18. Τήϊοι	3	3	:	(3)	6	:	6	6	6	6	6	[(6)]	6
19. Αἰραῖοι	3	(3)	:	6	(3)⌒	:	[3]	6	1	:	:	[(1)]	1
20. Ἐρυθραῖοι	(1)⌒	3	:	:	8.3300{	:	(9)	8.4000{	:	:	7	[(7)]	[(7)]
21. Βουθειῆς	:	:	:	:	:	:	:	2000	:	:	:	[(1000)]	(1000)
22. Πτελεούσιοι	:	3	:	:	:	:	:	:	:	:	:	[(100)]	(100)
23. Σιδούσιοι	:	:	:	:	:	:	:	:	:	:	:	[(500)]	(500)
24. Πολιχναῖοι	:	:	:	:	:	:	:	:	:	:	4000	(4000)	(4000)
25. Ἐλαιούσιοι	:	:	:	:	:	:	:	:	:	:	100	[(100)]	[(100)]
26. Κλαζομένιοι	(1.3000)	(1.3000)	1.3000	1.3000	(1.3000)	:	1.3000	[(1.3000)]	(1.3000)	(1.3000)	(1.3000)	1.3000	[(1.3000)]
27. Φωκαῖς	:	:	3	3	:	:	(3)	3	1.5250	:	(1.5250)	[(2)]	2
28. Κυμαῖοι	:	:	12	12	:	:	[9]	9	9	:	9	[(9)]	9
29. Μυριναῖοι	:	:	1	1	1	:	[(1)]	1	1	:	(1)	[(1)]	1
30. Γρυνεῖς	:	1000	(1000)	:	:	:	1000	1000	(1000)	:	:	[(1000)]	1000

	420	A9	428	429	431	432	433	434	435	436	437	438	439	440
1. Ναύλοχοι			ı			(1)						[(1)]	1	
2. Λέρος														
3. Τειχιοῦσσα														
4. Μιλήσιοι	10	⊥				⊥								
5. Μυήσιοι		⊥										[(5)]	5	
6. Θερμαῖοι ἐξ Ἰκάρου		⊥			1.3000	(3000)						[(1)]	1	(1)
7. Οἰναῖοι ἐξ Ἰκάρου		⊥			3000	1						[(3000)]	(3000)	(3000)
8. Πριανῆς		⊥	⊥	⊥	(1)						⊥	(4000)	(4000)	
9. Μαιάνδριοι													abs.	abs.
10. Μαραθήσιοι			⊥		2000	2000						[(3000)]	abs.	
11. Πυγελῆς		⊥			1.3000	(1.3000)						[(1)]	1	(1)
12. Ἰσίνδιοι			⊥	⊥	1000	1000						[(1000)]	1000	1000
13. Ἑβρένοι		⊥			7.3000	7.3000						(6)	6	6
14. Νοτιῆς	2000	⊥			2000	(2000)						[(2000)]	2000[4]	[2000]
15. Διοσερῖται	500	⊥				500						[(500)]	500[2]	
16. Λεβέδιοι		⊥			[3]	(3)						[(1)]	1	
17. Κολοφώνιοι	500				(6)	(6)						(1.3000)]	(1.3000)	(1.3000)
18. Τήϊοι				⊥	1	(1)						(6)	6	
19. Αἱραῖοι		⊥	⊥	⊥								(1)	1	
20. Ἐρυθραῖοι				⊥	10.1100	10.1100					[(-)]	(7)	7	
21. Βουθειῆς				⊥							[(-)]	[(1000)]	[1000]	
22. Πτελεούσιοι				⊥							[(-)]	[(100)]	100	
23. Σιδούσιοι		⊥		⊥							[(-)]	[(500)]	[500]	500
24. Πολίχναιοι				⊥							[(-)]	(4000)	4000	4000
25. Ἐλαιούσιοι		⊥		⊥								[(100)]	100	100
26. Κλαζομένιοι				⊥	⊥							(1.3000)	(1.3000)	
27. Φωκαιῆς		⊥										[(2)]	2	
28. Κυμαῖοι		⊥			9	9						(9)[2]	(9)[2]	
29. Μυρριναῖοι		⊥	⊥	⊥	1	1						(1)[2]	(1)[2]	
30. Γρυνειῆς					2000	[2000][2]						[(1000)]	1000	(1000)

I. IONIAN DISTRICT (cont.)

	441	442	443	444	445	446	447	448	449	450	451	452	453
31. Ἐλαῖται	(1000)	[(1000)]	1000	..	1000	..	..	..	..	1000	1000	..	1000
32. Πιταναῖοι	[(1000)]	[(1000)]	(1000)	..	1000	1000	[1000]	..	(1000)	1000	(1000)	1000	(1000)
33. Ἀστυρηνοὶ Μυσοὶ	[(500)]	[(500)]	500	..	..	..	..	..	..	..	..	[500]	..
34. Γαργαρῆς	4660	[(4660)]	..	..	..	[(4500)]	4500	..	..	..	4500	..	..
35. Ἥσσιοι	abs.	abs.	..	..	(1)	[(1)]	[1]	..	1	[(1)]	..	..	1

II. HELLESPONTINE DISTRICT

	441	442	443	444	445	446	447	448	449	450	451	452	453
TROAD													
1. Λαμπώνεια	1000	(1000)	1000	1000	1000	[(1000)]	1000	..	..	(1000)	..	..	1000
2. Τένεδοι	2.5280	(2.5280)	(4.3000)	4.300	..	{ 2.5280 / 3240 / 2160 / 2160 }	X	..	{ 2.5280 / 1.3720 }	..	4.3000	..	..
3. Νέανδρεια	2000	abs.	..	(2000)	2000	[3]	[3]	..	2000	(2000)	2000	..	2000
4. Κεβρῆνοι	abs.	abs.	..	..	..	..	..	..	1.2700	..	..	..	3
5. Σκάψιοι	abs.	abs.	..	..	..	..	..	..	..	..	1	..	..
6. Βηρύσιοι ὑπὸ τῇ Ἴδη	abs.	abs.	..	..	1000	[(1000)]	1000	..	(1000)	..	1000	..	1000
7. Γεντῖνοι	abs.	abs.	500	(500)	500	500	500	..	500	..	500	..	..
8. Ἀξειοί	400	abs.	..	..	..	..	..	..	..	[400]	400	..	..
HELLESPONT, Asiatic shore													
9. Σιγειῆς	1000	1000	..	(1000)	..	1000	760	..	1000	..	..	..	..
10. Δαρδανῆς	1	(1)	(—)	(—)	..	240 / [(1)] / 3240	2760	..	2760	1.3000	..	..	..
11. Ἀβυδηνοί	4	(—)	[(—)]	4.0315	..	(—) / (—)	(—)	..	[(—)]	(—)	..	..	[4.2260]
12. Ἀρισβαῖοι	2	[2]	..	..	..	..	..	..	..	..	..	[2]	..
13. Παλαιπερκώσιοι	[(500)]	500	500	(500)	500	500	500	..	500	500	..	..	..
14. Περκώσιοι	1000	1000	1000	1000	1000	[(1000)]	1000	..	1000	1000	1000	..	..

	440	439	438	437	436	435	434	433	432	431	429	428	A9	420
31. Ἑκαῗται	(1000)	1000	(1000)	:	:	:	:	:	(1000)	1000	⌣⌣	(⌣)	:	:
32. Πιτανῖοι	(1000)	1000²	(1000)²	⌣	:	:	:	:	1000²	:	⌣⌣	:	⌣	:
33. Ἀστυρηνοὶ Μυσοί	:	500²	(500)²	:	:	:	:	:	:	:	: ⌣	:	:	:
34. Γαργαρῆς	:	abs.	(4660)	:	:	:	:	:	:	:	:	:	:	:
35. Ἥσιοι	:	abs.	:	:	:	:	:	:	:	:	:	:	:	:

II. HELLESPONTINE DISTRICT

	440	439	438	437	436	435	434	433	432	431	429	428	A9	420
TROAD														
1. Λαμπώνεια	1000	1000²	:	:	:	:	abs.	(1400)²	1400²	:	1400	:	⌣	:
2. Τενέθιοι	2.5280	[2.5020]	:	:	:	:	(2.5280)	:	2.5280	2.5280	2.5280	2.5280	⌣	:
3. Νεάνδρεια	[2000]	2000	:	:	:	:	abs.	:	[2000]	:	⌣	:	⌣	:
4. Κεβρήνιοι	:	:	:	:	:	:	abs.	:	abs.	:	:	:	⌣	:
5. Σκάψιοι	1	:	:	:	:	:	abs.	:	abs.	:	:	:	⌣	:
6. Βηρύσιοι ὑπὸ τῇ Ἴδῃ	:	:	:	:	:	:	abs.	:	abs.	:	:	:	: ⌣	:
7. Γεντῖνοι	:	:	:	:	:	:	abs.	:	abs.	:	:	:	:	:
8. Αἴξεοι	:	:	:	:	:	:	(400)	:	400	:	400	:	:	:
HELLESPONT, *Asiatic shore*														
9. Σιγειῆς	1000	1000	:	:	:	:	(1000)	:	[(1000)]	1000	1000 [4080]	:	⌣	:
10. Δαρδανῆς	1	1²	:	:	:	:	(1)	: ⌣	1	(1)	1920	(?)	:	:
11. Ἀβυδηνοί	4	4	:	:	:	:	(⌣)	⌣	6	:	5.3260 [2740]	(?)	:	:
12. Ἀρισβαῖοι	2	:	:	:	:	:	abs.	:	abs.	:	(⌣)	:	:	:
13. Παλαιπερκόσιοι	500	500	:	:	:	:	abs.	:	[1500]	}	500	:	⌣	:
14. Περκώσιοι	:	1000	:	:	:	:	abs.	:	:	}	1000	:	⌣	:

II. HELLESPONTINE DISTRICT (cont.)

	441	442	443	444	445	446	447	448	449	450	451	452	453
15. Λαμψακηνοί	12	(12)	(—)			(—) 3600	5200	..	12	12	..	(12)	..
16. Παισηνοί	abs.	abs.	.	(1000)	[1000]	[(1000)]	1000	..	..	1000	1000	..	..
HELLESPONT, *European shore*													
17. Ἀλωπεκοννήσιοι	1000	(1000)	(—)	[(—)]	(—)		..	..	3240	..	(—)	..	18
18. Χερρονήσιοι	1	[(1)]	[(—)]	[(—)]		(—)	..	..	13,4840	..	18	18	
19. Ἀμυραῖοι	500	[(500)]	[(—)]	[(—)]	:(—)	2000	..	..	..	..	..	..	..
20. Ἐλαιούσιοι	[3000]	3000	(3000)	(3000)	(3000)	3000	..	..	..	..	..	..	..
21. Μαδύτιοι	500	[(500)]	(—)	[(—)]	:(—)	..	..	..	..	..	..	..	..
22. Σηστιοι	500	[(500)]	(—)	(—)	(—)	..	..	..	..	..	..	..	..
PROPONTIS, *Asiatic shore*													
23. Παριανοί	2000	(2000)	(—)		(—)			..	..	..	..	1	1
24. Πριαπῆς	500	abs.	..	500	500	500	(500)	..	..	..	500	..	..
25. Ἀρταγυανοί	300	(300)	(300)	(300)	..	[(300)]	300	..	..	..	..	..	..
26. Ζέλεια	abs.	abs.	..	..	..	..	..	..	..	..	..	..	..
27. Κυζικηνοί	9	9	..	..	..	4320	..	..	[(—)]	..	(—)	..	
28. Ἀρτακηνοί	2000	2000	2000	..	(2000)	..	..	..	[(2000)]	..	2000	..	(2000)
29. Προκοννήσιοι	3	3	(—)	..	..	..	..	..	[(—)]	..	(—)	..	..
30. Δασκυλεῖον	abs.	abs.	..	..	..	..	..	..	500	..	(500)	..	500
31. Βρυλλειανοί	abs.	abs.	..	..	..	..	..	..	..	..	..	..	..
32. Κιανοί	1000	abs.	1000	1000	..	1000	..	..	..	..	..	..	1000
33. Καλλιπολῖται	abs.	abs.	..	..	..	..	..	..	..	..	..	..	..
34. Βίσβικος	abs.	abs.	..	..	..	..	..	..	..	..	..	..	2000
35. Μυσοί	abs.	abs.	[1000]	1000	..	..	[1000]	..	..	..	..	..	
36. Ἀρτακηνοί	abs.	abs.	..	1000	..	1000	..	..	1000	..	..	..	1.3000
37. Χαλκηδόνιοι	9	(9)	(9)	9	..	9	9	..	3	..	7,3010	1,3000	..

	420	A9	428	429	431	432	433	434	435	436	437	438	439	440
15. Λαμψακηνοί	:	:	(?)	10.2700 [1.2820]	:	X	:	(—)	:	:	:	:	:	12
16. Παισηνοί	:	↑	:	1000	:	1000	:	(1000)[2]	:	:	:	:	1000	1000
HELLESPONT, European shore														
17. Ἀλωπεκοννήσιοι	:	↑	[80]	[(—)]	[2000]	[2000]	:	2000	:	:	:	:	[1000]	1000
18. Χερρονήσιοι	:	:	1920	1500 +	[(1)]	[1]	:	1	:	:	:	:	1	1
19. Λιμναῖοι	:	:	:	:	(1000)	1000[3]	:	500	:	:	:	:	[(500)]	(500)
20. Ἐλαιούσιοι	:	↑	1080 [1920]	1080 [1920]	[3000]	[3000]	:	3000	:	:	:	:	[(3000)]	(3000)
21. Μαδύτιοι	2000	:	1920 [80]	[80]	[2000]	[2000]	:	2000	:	:	:	:	[500]	500
22. Σήστιοι	:	:	1920 / 1000	1920	[(1000)]	[(1000)]	:	1000	:	:	:	:	[500]	500
PROPONTIS, Asiatic shore														
23. Παριανοί	:	↑	(?)	2100 [3784]	[(1)]	1	:	1	:	:	:	:	2000	(2000)
24. Πριαπῆς	:	↑	:	(500)	:	[(500)]	:	(500)	:	:	:	:	500	500
25. Ἀρταγκαιοί	:	:	300	300	300	(300)	:	(300)	:	:	:	[300]	300	300
26. Ζέλεια	:	:	:	:	:	abs.	:	abs.	:	:	:	:	:	(—)
27. Κυζικηνοί	:	:	8.1680	8.3500 [1920]	9	9	:	(9)	:	:	:	9	:	9
28. Ἀρτακηνοί	:	↑	4320	2000	2000	2000	:	2000	:	:	:	[2000]	:	2000
29. Προκοννήσιοι	:	:	3	3	3	3	:	(3)	:	:	:	:	:	3
30. Δασκύλειον	:	↑	:	500	:	[500]	(500)[2]	abs.	:	:	:	:	:	:
31. Βρυλλειανοί	:	↑	:	3000	(3000)	3000	:	abs.	:	:	:	:	:	:
32. Κιανοί	:	:	:	1000	1000	1000[4]	:	(1000)	:	:	:	:	1000	:
33. Καλλιπολῖται	:	↑	:	1000	[1000][4]	:	1000[4]	abs.	:	:	:	:	:	:
34. Βισβυκος	:	↑	:	(—)	:	abs.	3000[5]	abs.	:	:	:	:	:	:
35. Μυσοί	:	↑	:	:	:	abs.	:	abs.	:	:	:	:	:	:
36. Ἀσηακηνοί	:	:	:	:	:	:	:	abs.	:	:	:	:	:	:
37. Χαλκηδόνιοι	:	:	5.5100 [900]	5.5100 / 900	(6)	6	(6)[2]	(—)	:	:	:	[9]	9	9

N n

II. HELLESPONTINE DISTRICT (cont.)

	453	452	451	450	449	448	447	446	445	444	443	442	441
PROPONTIS, *European shore*													
38. Τυρόδιζα	…	…	…	…	…	…	…	…	…	…	…	abs.	abs.
39. Νεάπολις	…	…	…	…	…	…	…	…	500	500	…	abs.	300
40. Διδυμοτειχῖται	1000	1000	…	…	…	…	1000	(1000)	1000	…	…	(1000)	1000
41. Πέρινθος	…	…	…	…	{3.4930 / 6.1070}	…	[(1000)]	…	…	…	(10)	10	10
42. Δαυνοτειχῖται	…	…	(1)	…	…	…	6	1000	1000	1000 (1)	…	(1000)	1000
43. Σηλυμβριανοί	…	…	(1)	…	[6]	…	…	(6)	…	…	(1)	(5)	5
44. Βυζάντιοι	…	…	…	…	15	…	X	{4.4800 / 3.5840}	…	…	[(—)]	15.4300	15.4300
45. ? Εὐρυμαχῖται	…	…	…	…	…	…	1000	1000	…	…	…	…	abs.

III. THRACEWARD DISTRICT

	453	452	451	450	449	448	447	446	445	444	443	442	441
WEST AND SOUTH OF CHALKIDIKE													
1. Πεταρήθιοι	(3)	…	3	3	…	…	3	[3]	3	…	[3]	3	3
2. Σκαβθιοι	…	…	3	…	[1000]	…	…	…	…	…	…	…	[1000]
3. Ἴκιοι	…	…	…	1500	1500	…	1500	1500	1000	1000	1000	1000	(1500)
4. Αἰσώνιοι	…	…	…	1500	1500	…	[(1500)]	[(1500)]	1500	…	1500	1500	(1500)
5. Μεθωναῖοι	…	…	…	…	…	…	…	…	…	…	…	abs.	:
PALLENE													
6. Ποτειδεᾶται	…	…	…	…	…	…	…	…	[(6)]	6	6	6	(6)
7. Ἀφυταῖοι	…	…	3	3	…	…	3	3	1	1	[1]	1	(1)
8. Νεοπολῖται Μενδαίων ἄποικοι	3000	(3000)	…	3000	(3000)	…	3000	[3000]	3000	(3000)	3000	3000	(3000)
9. Αἰγάντιοι	…	…	…	3000	(3000)	…	3000	3000	2000	2000	2000	2000	(2000)

PROPONTIS, European shore

	440	439	438	437	436	435	434	433	432	431	429	428	A9	420
38. Τυρόδιζα	[300)]	300	[300]	:	:	:	abs.	:	abs.	:	(—)	:	⌣	:
39. Νεάπολις	1000	1000	:	:	:	:	abs.	:	[300]	(1000)	1000	:	⌣	:
40. Διδυμοτειχῖται	1000	1000	:	:	:	:	(1000)	:	1000	(1000)	10	:	⌣	:
41. Πέρινθοι	[10]	:	(10)	:	:	:	(10)	:	10	X	10	:	:	:
42. Δαυνοτειχῖται	1000	1000	:	:	:	:	(1000)	:	1000	(1000)	2.4000 / 9	:	:	2
43. Στηλυμβριανοί	5	:	[5]	:	:	:	900	:	900	(900)	21.4740 / [8.9004½]	:	:	:
44. Βυζάντιοι	[15.0460]	:	:	:	:	:	(—)	:	18.1800	:	:	15.90	:	:
45. ? Εὐρυμαχῖται	:	:	:	:	:	:	abs.	:	abs.	:	:	:	:	:

In 429 and 428 some Hellespontine cities pay their tribute in two instalments. The second payments have a special heading, indicating that they were not sent to Athens, but used to pay troops or crews: [μισθὸν ἐτέ]λεσαν αἰθε....

Note: Εὐρυμαχῖται, district uncertain (*ATL* ii. 85).

III. THRACEWARD DISTRICT

	440	439	438	437	436	435	434	433	432	431	429	428	A9	420
WEST AND SOUTH OF CHALKIDIKE														
1. Πεπαρήθιοι	(3)	:	:	:	:	3	3	(3)	(3)	3	3	:	:	:
2. Σκιάθιοι	(1000)	1000	:	:	:	:	1000	1000	1000	1000	1000	1500	:	:
3. Ἴκιοι	1500	1500	:	1500	:	1500	[1500]	1500	(1500)	1500	1500	1000	:	:
4. Αἰσώνιοι	1500	(1500)	:	:	:	1500³	1500	:	(1000)	1000	:	3	:	:
5. Μεθωναῖοι	..	..	:	:	:	:	abs.	:	:	(3)	:	3	:	:
PALLENE														
6. Ποτειδεᾶται	[6]	6	:	:	:	(6)	6	(—)	15	abs.	:	:	⌣	:
7. Ἀφυταῖοι	1	(1)	:	:	:	:	3	:	:	3	3	3]	⌣	:
8. Νεοπολῖται Μενδαίων ἄποικοι	(3000)	3000	(3000)	:	:	:	3000	3000	3000	3000	3000	(—)	⌣	:
9. Αἰγύπτιοι	2000	(2000)	:	:	:	[3000]	(3000)	:	(3000)	3000	3250	(—)	:	:

III. THRACEWARD DISTRICT (cont.)

	441	442	443	444	445	446	447	448	449	450	451	452	453
10. Θραμβαῖοι	{:6}	1000	1000	1000	1000	:	:	:	:	{6	6	{6	{(6)
11. Σκιωναῖοι	(6)	6	6	6	6	:	:	:	:	8	8	:	:
12. Μενδαῖοι		9	5	:	(⌐)	15	15¹	:	:	:	:	:	:
SITHONE													
13. Σερμυλιῆς	(5)	5	5	5	[5]	{3 (12)	3¹	:	:	5.5500	:	{⌐⌐}	7.4320
14. Γαλαῖοι	:	abs.	:	:	:	4.0560}	:	:	:	:	:	:	(⌐)
15. Τορωναῖοι	(6)	6	6	:	6	:	7.5440	:	:	:	:	:	:
16. Σαρταῖοι	:	abs.	:	2	:	:	:	:	1.5000	4	4	:	X
17. Σίγγιοι	(2)	2	[2]	:	2	(2)	2	:	:	:	:	(⌐)	:
18. Πίλωρος	:	abs.	:	:	:	:	:	:	:	:	:	:	:
ATHOS													
19. Ἀκάνθιοι	(3)	3	3	3	3	{[(1)]	[(2000)]	:	?	:	..	(1)	{2.2000
20. Σαναῖοι	4000	4000	[4000]	(4000)	4000	4000}	1	:	(1)	1	:	:	}
21. Δῖῆς ἀπὸ τοῦ Ἄθω	[1]	1	[1]	:	1	[1]	1500	:	:	2000	:	:	:
22. Ὀλοφύξιοι	[2000]	2000	2000	[2000]	2000	[—]	[(1.3000)]	:	:	4000	4000	⌐	:
23. Θύσσιοι	[1]	1	1	1	1	1.3000	:	:	1.3000	:	:	:	:
24. Κλεωναί	:	abs.	:	:	:	:	:	:	:	:	:	:	:
UPPER CHALKIDIKE													
25. Στρεψαῖοι	(1)	1	1	(1)	1	5	(1)	:	1	(1)	:	:	1
26. Σερμαῖοι	(500)	[500]	500	500	[500]	(500)	500	:	500	:	:	:	:
27. Αἰνεᾶται	(3)⌐	3	3⌐	:⌐	3⌐	[⌐]	[⌐]	:	⌐⌐	⌐	⌐	⌐	4
28. Δικαιοπολῖται Ἐρετριῶν ἄποικοι	⌐	⌐					[⌐]	:					:
29. Τινδαῖοι	:	abs.	:	:	:	:	:	:	:	:	:	:	:
30. Κίθας	:	abs.	:	:	:	:	:	:	:	:	:	:	:
31. Σμίλλα	:	abs.	:	:	:	:	:	:	:	:	:	:	:
32. Γίγωνος	:	abs.	:	:	:	:	:	:	:	:	:	:	:
33. Αἶσα	:	abs.	:	:	:	:	:	:	:	:	:	:	:
34. Αἰολῖται	:	abs.	:	:	:	:	:	:	:	:	:	:	:
35. Πλευμῆς	:	abs.	:	:	:	:	:	:	:	:	:	:	:
36. Σίνος	:	abs.	:	:	:	:	:	:	:	:	:	:	:

	420	A9	428	429	431	432	433	434	435	436	437	438	439	440
10. Θραμβαῖοι			(—)	1085	1000	(1000)		1000	[1000]				(1000)	(1000)
11. Σκιωναῖοι			9	9	4			15					5	(6)⌐
12. Μενδαῖοι			8	8	8		8	8	8		8			⌐
SITHONE														
13. Σερμυλιῆς				abs.	abs.		4·3000	4·3000				(500)	(5)	
14. Γαλαῖοι			abs.	abs.	abs.	3000[4]	3000[4]	[800][3]	(800)					
15. Τορωναῖοι	100		⌐	12	6			(6)					(6)	6
16. Σαρταῖοι				1500	[1500][4]	1500[4]	1500[4]	abs.						
17. Σίγγιοι		⌐		abs.	abs.	1	2	3					2	
18. Πίλωρος			abs.				600[5]	abs.						
ATHOS														
19. Ἀκάνθιοι		⌐	3	3	3	(3)		3						(4000)
20. Σαναῖοι			⌐	1000	[1]	1	1	1	(1)					(1)
21. Διῆς ἀπὸ τοῦ Ἄθω		⌐	⌐	1	1	(1)	(1)	1	(1)				(1)	(2000)
22. Ὀλόφυξιοι			2000	2000	2000	(2000)	(1)	2000	2000					
23. Θύσσιοι			⌐	1	1	1	(1)	1						
24. Κλεωναί			⌐	[500]	abs.	500[6]	500[5]	abs.						
UPPER CHALKIDIKE														
25. Στρεψαῖοι		⌐		abs.	abs.	1	1	1	1				(1)	
26. Σερμαῖοι		⌐		abs.	500	500	500	500					500	⌐
27. Αἰνεᾶται			1	1000	3	(3)	(3)	3	(3)				⌐	⌐
28. Δικαιοπολῖται Ἐρετριῶν ἄποικοι			1		abs.	(1)		1						
29. Τινδαῖοι							3000[6]	abs.						
30. Κίθας								abs.						
31. Σμίλλα								abs.						
32. Γίγωνος								abs.						
33. Αἶσα								abs.						
34. Αἰολῖται		3000	500	abs.	abs.	500[4]	500[4]	abs.						
35. Πλευμῆς			(1000)	abs.	abs.	abs.	1000[4]	abs.						
36. Σῖνος	800		abs.			[1500][5]	1500[4]	abs.						

III. THRACEWARD DISTRICT (cont.)

	453	452	451	450	449	448	447	446	445	444	443	442	441
37. Σπαρτώλιοι	2	2	2	2	:	:	2	[2]	2	2	(2)	2	2
38. Σκαψαῖοι	:	:	1000	1000	1000	:	1000	(1000)	1000	(1000)	1000	1000	[1000]
39. Φαρβήλιοι	1000	:	:	:	1000	:	1000	(1000)	[(1000)]	:	:	1000	[1000]
40. Χεδρώλιοι	:	:	:	:	500	:	500	500	:	:	:	abs.	(700)
41. Ὀθώριοι	:	:	:	:	:	:	[500]	[500]	[(—)]	:	(4000)	?	4000
42. Στώλιοι	:	:	:	:	4000	:	5000	5000	:	4000	:	4000	:
43. Πολιχνῖται παρὰ Στώλιον	:	:	:	:	1	:	[(1)]	1	4000	4000	(4000)	4000	(4000)
44. Μηκυβερναῖοι	2.1880	:	:	:	1600	:	1600¹	(1600)	1000	1000	4000	4000	abs.
45. Φυγήριοι	:	:	:	:	3000	:	3000¹	3000	2000	1000	1000	1000	(4000)
46. Σκαβλαῖοι	:	:	:	2400	2400	:	2400	2400	2400	(2400)	:	[(2000)]	(1000)
47. Ἀσσηρῖται	(2.4000)	(—)	:	:	2	:	:	:	(2)	:	:	(2)	(2000)
48. Ὀλύνθιοι	[1000]	:	:	2400	1000	:	1000	1000	1000	1000	1000	1000	(—)
49. Σταγυρῖται	?	:	:	:	:	:	:	:	:	:	:	1	(2)
50. Ἀργίλιοι	:	:	:	:	:	:	:	:	1	1	1	abs.	[1000]
51. Βεργαῖοι	:	:	2880	:	:	:	:	3240	:	:	:	abs.	(1)
52. ? Μιλτώριοι	:	:	:	:	:	:	:	:	:	:	:	abs.	:
53. ? Πίστασος	:	:	:	:	:	:	:	:	:	:	:	:	:

EAST OF STRYMON

	453	452	451	450	449	448	447	446	445	444	443	442	441
54. Γαλήψιοι	1.3000	(1.3000)	1.3000	:	(1.1200)	:	(1.1200)	1.1200	1.3000	:	:	3000	(3000)
55. Νεάπολις παρ' Ἀντισάραν	1000	:	:	:	1000	:	1000	1000	1000	1000	[(1000)]	1000	:
56. Θάσιοι	3	:	3	3	:	:	(2.2760)	3240	[(—)]	:	30	abs.	:
57. Κιστίριοι	:	:	:	:	:	:	:	:	:	:	:	abs.	:
58. Ἀβδηρῖται	12.5120	:	15	:	15	:	14	1	:	15	:	abs.	(15)
59. Δίκαια παρ' Ἄβδηρα	(3000)	:	3000	3000	3000	:	3000	3000	2000	2000	:	abs.	[(—)]
60. Μαρωνῖται	1.300	1.3000	1.3000	1.3000	1.3000	:	(1.3000)	1.3000	1.3000	1.3000	1.3000	1.3000	(1.3000)
61. Σαμοθρᾷκες	:	(6)	6	6	6	:	(6)	6	[6]	6	6	6	(—)
62. Αἶνιοι	[12]	12	12	:	12	:	(12)	1.2555	[(10)]	10	10	10	[(10)]

	440	439	438	437	436	435	434	433	432	431	429	428	A9	430
37. Σπάρτωλος	(2)	..	(2)	..	..	(2)	2	3.0500	3.0500	abs.	abs.	..	(—)	..
38. Σκαψαῖοι	..	1000	1000	..	..	..	abs.	..	1000	abs.	abs.	abs.	:	..
39. Φαρβήλιοι	(1000)	..	..	..	..	(1000)	1000[3]	500[4]	500[4]	abs.	abs.	abs.	..	..
40. Χεδρώλιοι	..	..	..	..	..	..	500[3]	[1000][4]	1000[4]	abs.	abs.	abs.	..	..
41. Ὀθῶροι	700	..	..	1	..	(700)	700[3]	500[6]	..	..	..	..	..	1000
42. Στώλιοι	(4000)	..	..	..	..	..	abs.	1	..	abs.	..	..	(—)	..
43. Πολιχνῖται παρὰ Στῶλον	..	[4000]	..	(3000)	..	(1)	1	..	..	abs.	abs.	..	[10 DR.]	..
44. Μηκυβερναῖοι	(4000)	..	..	(3000)	..	..	1000	(1)	1	abs.	abs.	..	..	..
45. Φηγήτιοι	1000	..	..	..	..	..	2000	(—)	(—)	abs.	..	..	..	..
46. Σκαβλαῖοι	(2000)	..	..	..	..	3000	3000	3000	1500	abs.	abs.	..	(—)	..
47. Ἀσσηρῖται	..	2	..	..	..	3000	2	3000	3000	abs.	..	..	(—)	..
48. Ὀλύνθιοι	2	..	..	..	..	..	1000[4]	..	[2]	abs.	abs.	..	..	..
49. Σταγυρῖται	1000	(1)	..	1	..	(1000)	abs.	..	..	1000	1000	1000	..	..
50. Ἄργιλοι	(1)	..	..	..	..	..	abs.	..	1000	abs.	1000	1000	..	..
51. Βεργαῖοι	..	..	..	..	..	..	3120	..	3120	3120	..	..	..	..
52. ? Μιλτώριοι	..	..	..	..	..	..	1000[3]	3000[4]	3000[4]	abs.	abs.	abs.	..	..
53. ? Πίστασος	..	..	..	..	..	..	abs.	500[6]	..	..	..	abs.	500	..
EAST OF STRYMON														
54. Γαλήψιοι	..	(3000)	..	..	..	..	abs.	..	..	1000	abs.	1000	..	..
55. Νεάπολις παρ' Ἀντισάραν	..	..	..	..	..	1000	1000	(1000)	1000	1000	abs.	1000	?[60]	..
56. Θάσιοι	..	(30)	..	..	..	..	(30)	30	30	30	30	30	..	..
57. Κυστίριοι	..	..	..	..	..	..	abs.	300[3]	..	abs.	..	..	?[75]	..
58. Ἀβδηρῖται	..	..	..	..	..	(15)	15	..	15	10	10	(—)	?[21+]	..
59. Δίκαια παρ' Ἄβδηρα	(1,3000)	(—)	..	..	..	..	(3000)	(3000)	..	3000	..	..	?[15]	..
60. Μαρωνῖται	(—)	..	..	..	..	10	10	10	(10)	abs.	3	(1)	..	..
61. Σιμοβρύκες	..	4	..	..	..	(6)	6	(6)	(6)	6	2	(1)	..	..
62. Αἶνοι	10	10	..	..	..	4	abs.	..	..	abs.	abs.	..	?[20]	..

Notes: Ἀκάνθιοι (449). There is space for only one numeral in the quota. *ATL* (⊢Ͱ), implying a tribute of 5 talents. (X), a tribute of 10 talents, is formally possible. 'Ἀργίλιοι (453). The reading is clear, X⊡, implying a payment of 10½ talents. *ATL* ii. 79 suggests a cutter's error for ⊢⊡ (a tribute of 1⅓ talents). Μιλτώριοι, Πίστασος. Sites unknown probably in Chalkidike. Ὀθῶροι (442). On the stone Δ⊢Ͱ||||, ? a cutter's error for Δ⊢|||| (as in 440). *ATL* ii. 82.

IV. KARIAN DISTRICT

	453	452	451	450	449	448	447	446	445	444	443	442	441
WESTERN KARIA, coast and islands													
1. Ἄδυμος		(1)		1	1			(1)	(1)	(1)	1	[(1)]	1
2. Βολβαῆς		1030											abs.
3. Πηδασῆς		2		2				1					abs.
4. Ἰασῆς					1			1	(1)	(1)			1
5. Βαργυλιῆς					1000							[(1000)]	1000
6. Μίνδιοι		1000	500	1000	500			4000	[500]	1000	500	[(500)]	[(500)]
7. Πελεᾶται		500	(—)	500	3000		1000	(500)	(3000)	500	(3000)	(3000)	(3000)
8. Καρυανδῆς		4000	1000		3000		500	3000	(500)	(3000)	500	(3000)	3000
9. Καλύδνιοι					500			500				(500)	500
10. Ἀμόργιοι			1.3000	1.3000	(1.3000)			[(1.3000)]		1.3000	[2]	(1.3000)	[(1.3000)]
11. Ἀστυπαλαιῆς		(2)	2				1.3000					1.3000	abs.
12. Κῷοι				(—)	{3.3360 / 1.2640}		(3.3360)	2 } 3.3360 / 2160					
13. Τερμερῆς							[(2)]					(5)	[(5)]
14. Ἁλικαρνάσσιοι	2.3000		2.3000	2.3000	2.3000		(2.3000)	(2.3000)		1.4000	[1.4000]	(3000)	[(3000)]
15. Ἀμυνανδῆς	1.4000	3050	1.4000	1.4000	(2)		(2)	2			3000	[(1.4000)]	1.4000
16. Συαγγελῆς	(—)				1		(1)	(1)	4500	1	[3000]	{[(1)]	[(1)]
17. Οὐρανιῆται		1030		500				1					abs.
18. Μαδνασῆς	2	(—)	2		1			1		(1)		(1)	(1)
19. Δηλμιάνδιοι		1030	1500	1500			[(—)][1]	(—)	(1000)	1000	1000	(1000)	1000
20. Παργασῆς					1000					500	[500]		abs.
21. Κερδμοι	(1.3000)		1.3000	1.3000			(1.3000)	1.3000	[(500)]	(1.3000)		1.3000	[1.3000]
22. Κασωλαβῆς	(2500)	(2500)	(2500)	2500	2500		2500[1]	(2500)					abs.
23. Πλαδασῆς		(2500)		2500	2500		2000	2000				(2000)	2000
WESTERN KARIA, interior													
24. Παρπαριῶται	(1500)			1000	1000		1000	(1000)	1000	1000	1000	[(1000)]	1000
25. Μυδονῆς	(1500)	1500	1500				1500	[(1500)]	1500		1500	[(1500)]	[(1500)]
26. Θασθαρῆς				500			500	(500)			(500)		[500]

[1] footnote

WESTERN KARIA, coast and islands

	420	A9	428	429	431	432	433	434	435	436	437	438	439	440
1. Λάτμιοι	:	:	:	:	1	1	:	:	:	:	:	:	[(1)]	1
2. Βολβαῆς	:	:	:	:	:	:	:	:	:	:	:	:	abs.	abs.
3. Πηδασῆς	:	3000	:	:	1	1	:	:	:	:	:	:	abs.	abs.
4. Ιασῆς	:	:	:	:	:	:	:	:	:	:	:	:	[1]	(1)
5. Βαργυλιῆς	:	1000	:	:	:	:	:	:	:	:	:	:	1000	1000
6. Μύνδιοι	:	:	:	:	500	(3000)	:	:	:	:	:	:	[(500)]	500
7. Πελειᾶται	:	1000	:	:	3000	:	:	:	:	:	:	:	[(3000)]	3000
8. Καρυανδῆς	:	⌣	(=)	⌣	500	1·3000	:	:	:	:	:	:	(500)	abs.
9. Καλύδνιοι	:	⌣	:	:	X	1*	1*	:	:	:	:	:	1·3000	1·3000
10. Αμόργιοι	:	⌣	⌣	:	[1]*	2	:	:	:	:	:	:	abs.	abs.
11. Αστυπαλαιῆς	:	⌣	:	:	(2)	:	:	:	:	:	:	:	1·3000	1·3000
12. Κῷοι	:	:	:	:	3·4465	5	:	:	:	:	:	:	(5)	5
13. Τερμερῆς	:	:	:	:	:	(—)	:	:	:	:	:	:	(3000)	3000
14. Αλικαρνάσσιοι	:	⌣	:	:	1·4000	1·4000	:	:	:	:	:	(1·4000)	1·4000	1·4840
15. Αμυνανδῆς	:	:	:	:	1	1	:	:	:	:	:	:	1	1
16. Συαγγελῆς	:	:	:	:	:	:	:	:	:	:	:	:	abs.	:
17. Ουρανιῆται	:	:	:	:	(1)	:	:	:	:	:	:	:	[(1)]	:
18. Μαδνασῆς	:	:	:	:	:	:	:	:	:	:	:	:	[(1)]	1
19. Απημάνδιοι	:	2000+	:	:	(1)	:	:	:	:	:	:	:	100	100
20. Παργασῆς	:	:	:	:	:	:	:	:	:	:	:	:	abs.	abs.
21. Κερᾶμιοι	:	⌣	:	:	:	:	:	:	:	:	:	:	[(1·3000)]	1·3000
22. Κασωλαβῆς	:	⌣	:	:	:	:	:	:	:	:	:	:	abs.	abs.
23. Πλαδασῆς	:	:	:	:	:	:	:	:	:	:	:	:	2000	abs.

WESTERN KARIA, interior

	420	A9	428	429	431	432	433	434	435	436	437	438	439	440
24. Παρπαριῶται	:	:	:	:	:	:	:	:	:	:	:	:	1000	(1000)
25. Μυδονῆς	:	:	:	:	:	:	:	:	:	:	:	:	[(1500)]	1500
26. Θασθαρῆς	:	:	:	:	:	:	:	:	:	:	:	:	[(500)]	500

IV. KARIAN DISTRICT (cont.)

	441	442	443	444	445	446	447	448	449	450	451	452	453
27. Ναξιᾶται	500	500	(500)	500	:	(500)	500	:	:	⌐	⌐	:	?
28. Αἰωδῆς	abs.	:	..	:	:	:	:	:	:	:	:	:	:
29. Ναρισβαρῆς	[(1000)]	:	(1000)	:	:	1000	1000	:	:	1000	:	:	(1000)
30. Θύδσονος	abs.	:	:	:	:	:	:	:	:	1000	:	:	:
31. Ὑρωμῆς	2500	[(2500)]	:	2500	:	2500	1200	:	[(2500)]	:	:	:	:
32. Ὑμισσῆς	abs.	:	:	:	(5200)	1200	:	:	:	:	:	:	:
33. Χαλκητορῆς	2100	[(2100)]	:	2100	:	(2100)	2100	:	2100	:	:	:	:
34. Μυλασῆς	abs.	[5200]	:	5200	:	1	:	:	1	2000	:	:	:
35. Κοδαπῆς	5200	:	:	:	:	[400]	400	:	(400)	400	:	:	:
36. Κινδυῆς	abs.	(1)	:	:	:	1	:	:	1	:	:	:	:
37. Κᾶρες ὧν Τύμνης ἄρχει	[(1)]	:	:	:	:	:	:	:	:	:	:	:	:
38. Κιλλαρῆς	[(3000)]	:	:	:	:	:	:	:	:	:	:	:	:
39. Ὑθωσῆς	abs.	:	:	3000	:	x	x	:	:	1000	:	:	:
40. Οὐλιαῆς	abs.	:	:	:	:	:	:	:	:	:	:	1030	:

KARIAN CHERSONESE AND ISLANDS

	441	442	443	444	445	446	447	448	449	450	451	452	453
41. Ἰθυμῆς	[(—)]	:	:	:	:	(—)	5200	:	:	⌐	⌐	1.0890	(2)
42. Κυλλάνδιοι	abs.	:	:	:	:	2	2	:	:	2	2	:	:
43. Κυρβασσός	abs.	:	:	:	:	2000	[(2000)]	:	2000	2000	2000	:	2000
44. Κεδρεᾶται ἀπὸ Καρίας	3000	3000	3000	2000	2000	3000	500	:	:	(3000)	3000	:	(3000)
45. Αὐλιᾶται Κᾶρες	500	500	(500)	2000	3000	(500)	:	:	500	500	(500)	500	500
46. Ἐρινῆς	abs.	:	1000	3000	[(500)]	:	:	:	3240	:	:	4130	:
47. Κύδβοι	[3]	3	[3]	:	1000	[5]	5	:	5	⌐	⌐	:	⌐
48. Χῖοι Κᾶρες	abs.	:	:	:	:	2000	2000	:	:	:	:	:	:
49. Χαλκεῆται	2000	2000	[(2000)]	2000	[2000]	3000	[(3000)]	:	3000	3000	:	:	:
50. Βρυκοῦντιοι	abs.	:	:	:	:	500	500	:	:	:	:	:	:
51. Καρπάθιοι	[1000]	:	:	100	:	:	:	:	:	:	:	:	:
52. Ἐτεοκαρπάθιοι ἐκ Καρπάθου	abs.	:	:	:	:	:	:	:	:	:	:	:	:
53. Ἀρκέσσεια	[1000]	1000	:	:	:	1000	[1000]	:	1000	1000	:	:	:
54. Κάσιοι	abs.	:	:	:	:	:	:	:	:	:	:	:	:
55. Οἰᾶται	}	}	:	:	:	(10)	10	:	:	:	(3300)	:	3300
56. Λίνδιοι	6	6	(6)	6	:	2000	(2000)	:	:	:	(8.2700)	:	8.2700
57. Πεδιῆς ἐν Λίνδῳ	[100]	100	:	100	:	10	[(10)]	:	:	:	:	:	:
58. Ἰηλύσιοι	[6]	6	⌐	:	:	9	(9)	:	10	⌐	⌐	:	:
59. Καμειρῆς	[6]	6	⌐	:	:	:	:	:	9	9	(9)	:	[9]
60. Σύμη	abs.	:	:	:	:	:	:	:	:	:	:	:	:

	420	A9	428	429	431	432	433	434	435	436	437	438	439	440
27. Ναξιᾶται					(500)	500							[(500)]	500
28. Ἀλινδῆς													abs.	abs.
29. Ναριοβαρῆς													(1000)	1000
30. Θέϊδωνος		6											abs.	abs.
31. Ὑρομῆς		2+											[2500]	(2500)
32. Ὑμισσῆς													abs.	abs.
33. Χαλκητορῆς		2000											[(2100)]	2100
34. Μυλασῆς													[5200]	5200
35. Κινδυῆς		?4											abs.	abs.
36. Κινθυῆς		(2)											1	abs.
37. Κᾶρες ὧν Τύμνης ἄρχει													3000	(3000)
38. Καλλαρῆς													abs.	abs.
39. Ὑβασσῆς													abs.	abs.
40. Οὐλιᾶδης													abs.	abs.
KARIAN CHERSO- NESE AND ISLANDS														
41. Ἰθυμῆς		⌉⌉+											abs.	abs.
42. Κυλλάνδιοι													abs.	abs.
43. Κυρβασσός		2000+											abs.	abs.
44. Κεδρεᾶται ἀπὸ Καρίας					2000								(3000)	3000
45. Αὐλιᾶται Κᾶρες						500							(500)	500
46. Ἐρινῆς		-		⌉	⌉								abs.	abs.
47. Κινδυα		2+											[(3)]	3
48. Χία Κᾶρες					2000[2]	(2000)							abs.	abs.
49. Χαλκεᾶται		2000+											(2000)	2000
50. Βρυκούντιοι		500											abs.	abs.
51. Καρπάθιοι		⌉			1000								(1000)	1000
52. Ἐτεοκαρπάθιοι ἐκ Καρπάθου				abs.	[1000]4	1000[4]	1000[4]						abs.	1000
53. Ἀρκέσεια					1000								(1000)	1000
54. Κάσιοι				⌉	[1000]4	1000[4]	1000[4]						abs.	abs.
55. Οἰᾶται					10	10							-	abs.
56. Λίνδιοι		⌉			5000	5000							[6]	6
57. Πεδιῆς ἐν Λίνδῳ		⌉			6	6							[100]	100
58. Τηλένιοι		⌉			6	(6)							[(6)]	6
59. Καμειρῆς		⌉											(6)	6
60. Σύμη		3000			[1800]5	[1800]5	1800[5]						abs.	abs.

IV. KARIAN DISTRICT (cont.)

	441	442	443	444	445	446	447	448	449	450	451	452	453
61. Χερρονήσιοι	[(2.4200)]	(2.4200)	2.4200			3	3		3	(3)	3		
62. Πύρνιοι	1000	[(1000)]	1000		[(1000)]	1000	1000		1000	1000	1000		(1000)
63. Καρβασυανδῆς παρὰ Καῦνον	1000	1000	(1000)		[(1000)]	(1000)	1000		1000	1000	1000	1000	
64. Καῦνιοι	[(3000)]	3000	[3000]		[(3000)]	(3000)	(3000)		3000	3000	3000		
65. Πασανδῆς ἀπὸ Καῦνου	3000	3000	[(3000)]		[3000]				3000	3000			
EAST OF KAUNOS													
66. Καλυνδῆς	1	1	(—)										
67. Τηλάνδριοι	[(3000)]	3000	(3000)			(3000)	3000			1			[2000]
68. Κρυῆς ἀπὸ Καρίας	2000	2000	2000		2000	(2000)	2000		2000	2000	2000		1030
69. Ταρβανῆς	[(—)]				1								
70. Τελεμήσσιοι	abs.				10					[(—)]	[(—)]		
71. Λύκιοι	abs.												
72. Φασηλῖται	[3]	3	(3)	(3)		[(3)]	3		3	6	6		6
SITES UNKNOWN													
73. Ἀρλισσοός	abs.			(—)									
74. Κοδαπῆς	abs.			1000						1000	1	(1000)	
75. Πολίχναιοι Κᾶρες	abs.					[1000]	1000			1000			1.0400
76. Σαμβακτύς	abs.												
77. Σίλοι	abs.									1500			
78. Ὑβλισσῆς	abs.					[(—)]	[(—)]		(—)	1060			
79. Ὑλιμῆς	abs.					[(—)]	[(—)]						

	420	A9	428	429	431	432	433	434	435	436	437	438	439	440
61. Χερρονήσιοι		⌐			3	3							[(2.4200)]	2.4200
62. Πίγρμοι						1000							[1000]	1000
63. Καρβασυανδής παρὰ Καῦνον		10			1000	(1000)						(1000)	[1000]	1000
64. Καύνιοι						⌐					⌐		(3000)	[3000]
65. Πασανδής ἀπὸ Καύνου						⌐							(3000)	3000
EAST OF KAUNOS														
66. Καλυνδής		⌐⌐											[(1)]	I
67. Τυμνάνθριοι		⌐				⌐							(3000)	3000
68. Κρυής ἀπὸ Καρίας		1000				[2000]							2000	2000
69. Ταρβανής		⌐											[(—)]	(—⌐)
70. Τελεμήσσιοι		⌐											abs.	abs.
71. Λύκιοι					6	6							abs.	abs.
72. Φασηλῖται													[3]	3
SITES UNKNOWN														
73. Αρλισσός													abs.	abs.
74. Κοδαπής		2000											abs.	abs.
75. Πολιχναῖοι Κᾶρες													abs.	abs.
76. Σαμβακτύς													abs.	abs.
77. Σίλοι													abs.	abs.
78. Ὑβλισσής		2000+											abs.	abs.
79. Ὑλιμής													abs.	abs.

Note. Ναξιᾶται (453). [Ναχσιᾶ]ται Δ[ΓΗΙΙΙΙ].

V. ISLAND DISTRICT

	453	452	451	450	449	448	447	446	445	444	443	442	441
EUBOIA													
1. Καρύστιοι				7.3000	5		5¹	5				5	(5)
2. Στυρῆς					1		(1)	[(1)]			1	(1)	[(1)]
3. Γρυγχῆς				1000	(1000)		1000	(1000)			1000	[1000]	1000
4. Ἐρετριῆς							(6)	(6)				(3)	[3]
5. Χαλκιδῆς							?					(3)	[3]
6. Διακρῆς ἀπὸ Χαλκιδέων								[(—)]				abs.	abs.
7. Ἀθῆναι Διάδες					(2000)		2000	[(2000)]			4000	2000	(2000)
8. Διῆς ἀπὸ Κηραίου					(2000)		2000	2000				(2000)	(2000)
9. Ἑστιαιῆς				1000	(—)		(—)	1000		4000			
WEST AEGEAN													
10. Αἰγινῆται	30	30	30		[26.1200]							(30)	30
11. Κεῖοι				(—)	4		4¹	4		(30)	4	[4]	(4)
12. Καρθαῖοι				2.1500						(4)	3		[(3)]
13. Κύθνιοι				2	3		3¹	[3]			1	[3]	[(1)]
14. Σερίφιοι		1	1		(1)		1	1		(1)	3	[1]	
15. Σίφνιοι												[3]	[(3)]
16. Ἴῆται	1				840		[840]	(3)		(—)		(3000)	[(3003)]
17. Νάξιοι					?		6.4000	(—)	[(—)]	(6,4000)		[6,400]	[(6,400)]
18. Πάριοι					16.1200		[16.1200]	6.4000	[1.3000]			18	(18)
19. Μυκόνιοι			[1.3000]	1.3000			(1.3000)	16.1200		(1.3000)		(1)	(1)
20. Γρυραιῆς				1000	300		300	[(1.3000)]	(1000)			(300)	[(300)]
21. Σύριοι			1500				[(1000)]	300				[(1000)]	1000
22. Τήνιοι					3		3	[1000]		(—)		[2]	[2]
23. Ἄνδριοι				12	6		6	3			6	[6]	(6)
EAST AEGEAN									(6)				
24. Λήμνιοι			9										
25. Ἡφαιστιῆς οἱ ἐν Λήμνῳ		(—)			[3]			2160		(—)	3	(3)	3
26. Μυριναῖοι ἐν Λήμνῳ					[1]			1.4640		(—)	1.3000	(1.3000)	1.3000
27. Ἴμβριοι								(—) 3300	(—)		(—)	(1)	1

	440	439	438	437	436	435	434	433	432	431	429	428	A9	420
EUBOIA														
1. Καρύστιοι	(5)								[(5)]	(5)		[5]	5	
2. Στυρῆς	(1)						(1)		1		[1]	1	2	
3. Γρυγχῆς	(1000)	[1000]							1000	(1000)	3	[1000]	2000	
4. Ἐρετριῆς	(3)	[3]					(3)		3		3		15	
5. Χαλκιδῆς	(3)	[3]					(3)		3			3 ⌐	10	
6. Διακρῆς ἀπὸ Χαλκιδέων	abs.							800[5]	800[5]	[800][5]			2000	
7. Ἀθῆναι Διάδες	(2000)	[2000]					(2000)		2000	[2000]			1	
8. Διῆς ἀπὸ Κηραίου	2000	[2000]							2000	(2000)			(1)	
9. Ἑστιαιῆς														
WEST AEGEAN														
10. Αἰγινῆται	30	[30]									[3]		10	
11. Κεῖοι	4								?					
12. Κορήσιοι	3								3				6 ⌐	
13. Κύθνιοι	1										1	1	9 ⌐	
14. Σερίφιοι	3	[3000]							3				9	
15. Σίφνιοι									1					
16. Ἰῆται	(3000)	[3000]							3		[3]	3000	15	
17. Νάξιοι	6,4000								6,4000				30 ⌐	
18. Πάριοι	18								[(—)]					
19. Μυκόνιοι	1								(1)		1		1000	
20. Ῥηναιῆς	(300)	[300]							300		[300]	1500	1	
21. Σύριοι	(1000)	[1000]							1500		1500	[2]	10	
22. Τήνιοι	2								2		2	(6)	15	
23. Ἄνδριοι	6	[6]							6		6			
EAST AEGEAN														
24. Λήμνιοι														
25. Ἡφαιστιῆς οἱ ἐν Λήμνῳ	3	[(3)]					(3)		[(—)]		(—)		4	2
26. Μυριναῖοι ἐν Λήμνῳ	1.3000	[(1.3000)]					(—)		[(—)]					500
27. Ἴμβριοι	1	[(1)]					[(1)]		[(1)]		[(—)]			1

Notes: Χαλκιδῆς (447). *ATL* Ⴋ; earlier editors Χ. See note on fr. 70, *ATL* i. 36. Νάξιοι (449). *ATL* [ΡΗ⊓ΓΗΙΙΙΙ] [Νάχσο)]. Though the restoration of the name is highly probable, since the entry comes in a long list of island states, we do not restore the quota later normal, since a higher tribute may have been paid before the establishment of the cleruchy on Naxos. The precise date of the cleruchy is not known. Αἰγινῆται (432). The quota, [·] ΗΗΗΗ implies a payment of 14 or 9 talents.

Index to the Tribute Tables

(I have used here—as in Maps 1, 1–vi—the form of transliteration preserved by the authors of *ATL*, and I hope that readers will not be embarrassed by the peaceful coexistence of different conventions within one book.)

Some Problems in Local Histories

Miletus

In the picture we have drawn of the development of Athenian imperialism the years from 454 to 445 are a critical period of general unrest among the allies and determined reaction by Athens. For most of the allies we have to remain content with a vague outline; the story of Miletus we can follow rather more closely. The reconstruction hinges on four separate pieces of evidence: an Athenian decree of 450/49, detailing regulations for Miletus (*ATL* ii D 11); a Milesian decree, undated, providing for the banishment from Miletus of certain men and their families (ML 43); the statement of the Old Oligarch that when the Athenians chose the best men in Miletus, within a short time they revolted and cut down the demos ([Xen.] *Ἀθ. Πολ.* 3. 11); and finally the tribute-quota lists of the first and second assessment periods. (The evidence is more fully set out by Barron in *JHS* lxxxii (1962), 1–2.)

Until recently it was generally inferred from this evidence that the Milesian banishment decree and the Athenian regulations together reflected the recovery of Miletus by Athens. The revolt now ended, in this interpretation, marked the failure of the Milesian oligarchs to co-operate with Athens; as a result Athens intervened and imposed democracy. Closer study of the tribute lists and the Athenian decree has dictated a modification of this reconstruction. From the tribute list of 454/3 it seems probable that Miletus was in revolt but that loyalists in Leros and Teichiussa were paying tribute; Miletus is recorded as paying again in 451 and the natural inference is that Athens recovered the city in the summer of 452 (Meiggs, *JHS* lxiii (1943), 25–7; *ATL* iii. 254). The Athenian decree of 450/49 cannot then mark the original settlement with Miletus after her revolt; it marks a second stage.

The most important provision in the decree is the first, which provides for the sending to Miletus of five officials, variously called τὸς ἄρχοντας τὸς Ἀθεναίον (l. 47) and ℎοι πέντε ℎοι ἄρχοντες (l. 64 and perhaps l. 44). These five men, probably to be elected from the whole people (ll. 4–5), are to consult with Milesian officials (ll. 6–7: συν-[βολεύεν τôι τε αἰσυμνέ|τοι καὶ τ]οῖς προσ[εταίροις - - -), but they are not a temporary commission appointed to solve a particular problem and then return; the references to them in the decree show that they are intended to stay in Miletus. There is also mention of a garrison, φρουροί, though it is not clear whether it is being installed now or has been in occupation since 452 (l. 77: τὸν Μιλ]εσίον ἒ [τὸ]ν φρουρὸν κύριοι ὅ[ντον, from a clause probably defining the authority of the five Athenian officials). If Miletus had become or was now becoming a democracy the Athenian officials would be expected to consult a democratic council. The fact that they are to deal with officials suggests that Miletus is still controlled by oligarchs. There is another possible hint of this in l. 82: -]ντες Μ[ιλέ]σιοι· ἐὰν δὲ σοφρονό[σι - - - - -] δέονται. Sophrosyne was claimed by all but it was more particularly associated with oligarchy. The clause might be saying that if the Milesian oligarchs show the virtues that oligarchs consistently claim, and do not attempt an independent policy, they will find that they can get from Athens what they require (Meiggs, op. cit. 27; ATL iii. 150, 257). If this is right Athens in 450/49 is not satisfied with the settlement of 452; she imposes closer control through resident Athenian officials, but does not yet insist on democracy. What other conditions were imposed on Miletus in 450/49 we shall not know until further fragments of the stele are found, but it is significant that the lines which follow the provision for sending out the five Athenian officials seem to be concerned with military affairs (l. 10: - -] τὸν στρατιο[τί]-δον; l. 11: h]όπλα παρέχεσθαι; l. 13 τέ]τταρας ὀβο[λό]s (rate of pay?); l. 15: Ἀθένα]ζε τοῖς στ[ρα]τιό[τεσι and perhaps l. 8: στρατε]γὸς τὸς Μιλ[εσίον]. It would seem that Athens is imposing on Miletus a specific obligation of providing troops when required.

It remains to date the end of oligarchy in Miletus and the Milesian banishment decree. Meiggs inferred from the tribute lists that the end of the second revolt of Miletus and the change of constitution might have come in 447, for Miletus and her neighbours are almost certainly not included in the tribute list of 447, but they appear at least once, and probably twice in 446 (ATL iii. 35–6). Meiggs accepted the traditional view that the Milesian decree marked the expulsion of the leaders of the revolt when Miletus was first recovered by Athens, in 452. A. J. Earp suggested a later date for the crushing of the second revolt. Pointing out that Miletus does not appear in any of the fragments of the tribute lists of the third assessment period (445–443) and pays 5 talents instead of the earlier 10 talents from 442 onward he inferred that Miletus was in revolt from 446 or 445 to 442 and that the Milesian decree was directed against the oligarchic leaders of the second revolt. When Athens recovered Miletus, a democracy was installed, and the tribute was reduced to encourage recovery (Earp, Phoenix, viii (1954), 142–7).

Barron gave this reconstruction more weight by carrying further arguments used by Glotz in an influential article published in 1906

(*CRAI* 1906, 511–29). Glotz pointed out that the inclusion of descendants in the decree of banishment shows that the crime was treason, and that two of the banished, Alcimus and Cresphontes, had good Neleid names. He interpreted the decree in the light of two fragments from Nicolaus of Damascus (*FGH* 90 F 52, 53), which echoed some of the phrases of the fifth-century decree in a description of the overthrow of the Neleids at the end of the monarchy in Miletus. Glotz suggested that the stele of the banishment decree originally recorded a banishment of the Neleids in the sixth century and that the same stele was used again in the fifth century when the Neleids were again banished. Barron, reviewing the list of Milesian *aisymnetai* and *prosetairoi* from 525/4, preserved in a Hellenistic list (*Milet.* I. iii, no. 122), pointed out that there was a Neleid in office in 450/49 and that Thrason, son of Antileon, who was a *prosetairos* in that year, was *aisymnetes* in 445/4, suggesting continuity in the government of Miletus; moreover the *aisymnetes* of 446/5 was a Pisistratus, a name which also has strong Neleid associations. In Barron's reconstruction Athens tolerated oligarchy in Miletus because the Neleids were of paramount importance in her claim to be the mother city of the Ionian colonies; but in 446, when Euboea and Megara revolted, they turned against her, carried out a purge of the demos, and had to be banished. Barron, like Earp, associated the Milesian banishment decree with the end of the second revolt in 443/2 (Barron, art. cit. 2–6).

This reconstruction is very attractive, but it involves the difficult assumption that Athens, having weathered the acute crisis of 446, having reduced the Euboean rebels and made peace with Sparta, allowed Miletus to defy her for three years. We should therefore consider whether there could be any other plausible explanation of the absence of Miletus from the tribute fragments of the third assessment period. It may be no coincidence that Chalcis and Eretria also are not found on any of the fragments, for they were certainly recovered not later than 445. There may then be a common explanation for all three states; perhaps they were paying off an indemnity before returning to regular tribute payments (cf. the settlement with Thasos in 462 after her revolt, Thuc. i. 101. 3: χρήματά τε ὅσα ἔδει ἀποδοῦναι αὐτίκα ταξάμενοι καὶ τὸ λοιπὸν φέρειν).

We may also doubt whether the evidence justifies belief in a wholesale expulsion of the Neleids. What survives of the banishment decree is on a base which originally carried a stele. The inscription must have begun on the stele itself, an untidy disposition which suggested to Glotz that the stele had already been used for an earlier inscription. It was this that led him to the conclusion that there were two banishments of the Neleids, in the sixth and in the fifth centuries. But Barron is surely right in claiming that the Neleids would not have left a conspicuous memorial of their exile standing for all to see (Barron, p. 3 n. 18). He concludes that 'the decree may be presumed to have been quite long, and in all probability embraced a much greater number of families then the two whose names open our fragment'. Glotz's main argument for inferring an earlier decree is still valid : if there was only one inscription the cutter would normally have organized his text to be contained on the stele, without overflowing on to the base. The evidence of the decree itself also suggests that the number of the banished was small, for the rewards (100 staters) for anyone who kills any of those who are banished by the decree are all to be provided from one man's fortune (ll. 4–5 : ἀπὸ τῶν | [χρημά]των τῶν Νυμ[φαρή]το).

There is one other piece of evidence that favours an earlier date for this Milesian decree. If the state secures any of the guilty he is to be put to death by the *epimenioi* in office at the time. If this were a decree of a democratic Miletus one would have expected the Athenian model to have been followed, with the year divided into *prytanies*. Barron explained the use of *epimenioi* as an invention to avoid *prytaneis*, who could have been confused with the *prytaneis* who were important magistrates in oligarchic Miletus (Barron, op. cit. 4–5). If this were the first known use of ἐπιμήνιοι the view would be attractive, but it is found in an early-fifth-century inscription from Eretria (*IG* xii, suppl. 549; Μεκισστ[ίδ]ος φυλῆς : ἐπιμεν[ι]ούρες. I overlooked this inscription when I read Barron's draft). The apparently small number of the banished, and the implication in ἐπιμήνιοι that the Athenian democratic model had not yet been instituted, suggest that the decree should not be associated with the end of the second revolt. I would also, following Rehm (*Arch. Anz.* 1906, 16), prefer an earlier date for the script. The decree might directly follow the Athenian intervention in 452 ; it might even be earlier.

Euboea

When Euboea revolted successfully from Athens in 411 Thucydides (viii. 96. 2) emphasizes the importance to Athens of the island. In 431 the Athenians had evacuated their sheep and draught animals to Euboea and other off-shore islands, and when Attica was exposed to Peloponnesian invasions Euboea was the nearest important source of food. In the sixth century Athens had been on good terms with Eretria and both sent help to the Ionians in their revolt; but Chalcis had thrown in her lot with the Boeotians and when Cleomenes the Spartan king called on her to help him crush Athens in 506, she responded. The joint operations miscarried : Cleomenes had to withdraw owing to divisions in his ranks, the Boeotians and Chalcidians were separately defeated. According to Herodotus Athens established a cleruchy of 4,000 Athenians on 'the land of the Knights' (Hdt. v. 77. 2), presumably the Lelantine plain, and it may have been these cleruchs who manned the twenty triremes lent by Athens to Chalcis for the battles of Artemisium and Salamis (Hdt. viii. 1. 2 and 46. 2).

There is no specific evidence that the main cities of Euboea were original members of the Delian League, but Euboea had suffered in the Persian invasion and had good reason to support an anti-Persian League. Carystus, however, remained independent. She had no natural links with the centre and north of Euboea, but was cut off by rough hilly ground, and looked more to the Cyclades than to Chalcis and Eretria. Carystus was forcibly reduced by Athens and was made to join the League. It has been suggested above (p. 123) that she may have had to accept a cleruchy in 450 as a result of disaffection in the late fifties. Though Thucydides speaks of the reduction of the whole of Euboea after the revolt of 446 it may be doubted whether Carystus was involved (Thuc. i. 114. 3).

Thucydides, in describing the Athenian settlement when the revolt had been crushed, is explicit only about Hestiaea. The Hestiaeans were expelled and their land was occupied by Athenians, 2,000 in number according to Theopompus (Strabo 445), 1,000 according to Diodorus (xii. 22. 2). With the other cities settlements were negotiated, but the negotiations must have been very one-sided. From the surviving decree (D 17, ML 52) we can see the main terms of the settlement with Chalcis (above, pp. 178 ff.), and since Eretria was required to take the same oath as Chalcis (D 17. 40–4; D 16) the terms imposed on the two cities were probably similar. There remains, however, considerable uncertainty whether cleruchies or colonies were sent to either or both cities. Plutarch (*Per.* 23. 4) says that at Chalcis Pericles expelled the so-called *hippobotai* who were pre-eminent in wealth and standing, but he does not mention cleruchs or colonists. Aelian (*Var. Hist.* vi. 1) is more specific: 'When the Athenians crushed Chalcis they divided the land of the *hippobotai*, as it is called, into 2,000 lots, set aside reservations for Athena in the place called Lelantos, and leased the remainder according to the terms given on the stelae standing by the Royal Stoa.' These two passages may seem to imply the dispatch of Athenian settlers, but if Aelian's text is sound it is barely reconcilable with either cleruchy or colony. The land was confiscated and, apart from the reservation for the gods, was leased, not necessarily only to Athenians: cleruchs and colonists do not lease their land.

The authors of *ATL*, however, believing in a cleruchy at this time, suggest that τὴν δὲ λοιπήν of the manuscripts should be emended to τὸ δὲ λοιπόν; the passage could then mean that only the reservations of the gods were leased, the rest of the land being divided into lots for cleruchs (*ATL* iii. 296). They see a clear reference to these cleruchs in the Chalcis decree (D 17. 52–4: τὸς δ]ὲ χσένος τὸς ἐν Χαλκίδι, ὅσοι οἰκõντες | μὲ τελõσιν Ἀθέναζε), but it is most improbable that Athenians would have called cleruchs or colonists ξένοι (above, p. 180). Andocides in a passage of typical confusion claims that in the golden days of the Peace of Nicias Athens held the Chersonese, Naxos, and more than two-thirds of Euboea (Andoc. iii. 9) and he is echoed carelessly by a scholiast on Aeschines (ii. 175). But Isocrates (iv. 108) makes one of his main defences against the charge of Athenian acquisitiveness their restraint in not occupying Euboea which was nearer and richer than places like Scione and could easily have been taken.

Two other passages have sometimes been brought into the argument. Plutarch in his *Aristides* (27. 2) says that the Athenian demos granted to Lysimachus, son of Aristides, 100 *plethra* of planted land and a daily allowance of 4 drachmae. Demosthenes (xx. 115) is more precise and adds that the land was in Euboea and that the decree authorizing the grant was moved by Alcibiades. One would expect the grant to be made soon after Aristides' death when Lysimachus was young and the mover of the decree will have been the elder Alcibiades. The passage throws no light on what happened in 446/5, but implies that Athens already owned land in Euboea (? confiscated from Carystus) before 450. The other passage comes from Aristophanes' *Wasps* (715 f.): 'Whenever they are frightened of you they offer you Euboea', and a scholiast, using Philochorus (F 130), explains by saying that in the previous year 424/3 there was an expedition against Euboea. But the scholiast may not be right; since the reference to Euboea is followed by a reference to the gift of corn sent by Psammetichus in 445/4 Aristophanes may have in mind the settlement of 446/5, but the language is not sufficiently specific to rule out cleruchy or confiscation.

The evidence is admittedly unsatisfactory; it slightly favours the confiscation of land held by oligarchs but not the dispatch of colony or cleruchy (see also Nesselhauf, *Untersuchungen*, 138; Gomme, *HCT* i. 342–5).

Confiscation of land is suggested by two fragments of a stele which recorded the leasing of land in Chalcis, Eretria, and possibly Posideion. Above the list of leases is a title [*c.* 5]*s* τεμένε. These were plots of land in areas reserved to the gods; we expect Athena's name but there is no room for her before τεμένε (Raubitschek, *Hesp.* xii (1943), 28–33). When Mytilene's land was divided into plots for cleruchs, 300 of the 3,000 were set aside for the gods (Thuc. iii. 50. 2); similarly reservations for the gods are referred to in the decree providing for the colony of Brea (ML 49. 9–11). It does not, however, follow that where there are reservations there will also be a cleruchy or colony. A loss of land by confiscation would help to explain the reduction in the assessment of Chalcis. After the revolt her regular payment is 3 talents (city and figure do not appear together in the fragments until 432, but in 441 and 439 Chalcis may reasonably be restored against an *aparche* of 300 drachmae). Before the revolt the evidence is confined to the single list of 447. Koehler recorded the single figure as X, indicating a tribute of 10 talents; the authors of *ATL*, however, are convinced that 'the discernible cutting on the stone suits ⊓, implying an assessment of 5 talents, and that the left vertical is present on the stone' (*ATL* i. p. 36, fr. 70; phot. p. 37, fig. 46). The reduction then is probably from 5 to 3, not a large reduction, especially when it is remembered that the assessment of 446 was marked by a wide range of concessions.

There is less evidence for Eretria, but there are two further documents that may apply. Hesychius under Ἐρετριακὸς κατάλογος says that a decree was recorded in the archonship of Diphilos (442/1) that the Athenians should choose the sons of the wealthiest citizens as hostages. The decree carried the title 'Eretrian List'. There also survives a statue base which recorded a dedication by a colony, presumably on its dispatch from Athens. Only two letters survive from the name (ἐς Ἐρ - -) and it is formally possible to restore Eresus in Lesbos, Erythrae in Ionia or Eretria (*IG* i². 396, Raubitschek, *DAA* 301). Eresus does not appear in any fifth-century record; Erythrae is proposed in *ATL* (iii. 283 f.) but, as we have seen above (pp. 162 f.), the tribute lists to which appeal is made do not give strong support. There is a reduction in the tribute of Haerae, Erythrae's neighbour, but not in the assessment of Erythrae herself. It is possible that the list of hostages in 442/1 is the sequel to continuing opposition from oligarchs and that at this point Athens sent out a small colony. This would explain the abundance of Athenian white lekythoi from the last third of the century found in Eretria (Beazley, *ARF²* ii. 1226–46; J. Boardman, *BSA* xlvii (1952), 47 n.). There may also be an indication of an Athenian presence in Eretria in Thucydides' narrative of 411. In a sea battle off Eretria in the summer the Athenians were routed by the Peloponnesians and took refuge on land. 'Those who fled to the city of Eretria, thinking it friendly, fared disastrously; those who fled to the fort in the territory of Eretria, which the Athenians held, survived (viii. 95. 6).' There is a clear indication in this passage that there was an Athenian strong-point outside the town of Eretria but in the town's territory. To control the city the key point was the Acropolis; a fort occupied by Athenians outside the city implies that it was protecting either Athenian settlers or land belonging to Athens. This perhaps also helps to explain the inclusion in the accounts of the treasurers of Athena for 410/9 of money spent by an Athenian general at Eretria (ML 84. 17: ἑ|λλενοταμίαις παρεδόθε Προχσένοι Ἀφιδναίοι καὶ συνάρχοσιν στρατεγὸι ἐχς Ἐρετρίας).

No clear light is thrown on events in Eretria by the tribute lists. In only one list before the revolt of 446 does her *aparche* in part survive, in 447; the final numeral was H, but we do not know how many figures preceded it. *ATL* at first restored $HH]H$, a tribute of 3 talents (*ATL* i, List 7. iv. 11; phot. p. 31, fig. 32), but later preferred Ͱ$]H$, 6 talents. Physically it seems unlikely that there were more than three figures (though four would be just possible, since the beginnings of the numerals are not aligned in col. iv as they are in the other columns). Epigraphically 2, 3, 4, 11, 12 talents are all possible and since we have no means of assessing the comparative prosperity of Chalcis and Eretria at this period the pre-revolt tribute of Eretria should remain an open question. The record of Eretrian payments after the revolt is very lean indeed. The name survives, but not the payment, in 442, and the payment, but not the name, in 441. The first unambiguous appearance of both is in 429, showing a payment of 3 talents, and the restoration of the same *aparche* in 442 raises no difficulties.

We hear of further trouble in the year 424/3 when Philochorus records an Athenian expedition against Euboea (*FGH* 328 F 130). Thucydides makes no mention of any such operations during this year, but on such a matter as this Philochorus' evidence should be sound, and the context is very appropriate. In the winter of 425/4 Euboea had not escaped from the extraordinary assessment that followed the spectacular success of Cleon at Pylos. The tribute of Chalcis was increased from 3 to 10 talents and of Eretria from 3 to 15 talents. More important was the crushing defeat of the Athenians by the Boeotians at Delium in the late summer of 424. Euboea had always been sensitive to events in Boeotia. The revolt of 446 was closely linked to the Athenian defeat at Coronea; the battle of Delium must have had repercussions in Euboea. Thucydides' silence and the absence of other evidence rule out major operations. Perhaps a sharp demonstration of strength by Athens was sufficient to restore the situation.

In the assessment of 425 Carystus was specially favoured. Unlike those of Chalkis and Eretria her assessment was not increased; she was still required to pay only 5 talents. This may have been in recognition of her service to Athens, for in the late summer of 425 a Carystian contingent served under Nicias in an attack on Corinth (Thuc. iv. 42. 1). They fought next to the Athenians in the battle line and acquitted themselves well (43. 3–4). Later on 300 Carystians played a significant part with Andrians, Tenians, and Athenian settlers on Aegina in intimidating the democratic Boule of 500 when the 400 dismissed them before the legal date from the Bouleuterion (Thuc. viii. 69. 3). It would be tempting to believe that these Carystians were in fact descended from Athenian cleruchs settled in 450, but though we have seen hints of cleruchies at Andros and Carystus, no source associates Tenos with the policy. Moreover, when Thucydides catalogues the forces at Syracuse, the Carystians are included with the other Euboeans, from Eretria, Chalkis, and Styra, among the subjects of Athens (τῶν ὑπηκόων καὶ φόρου ὑποτελῶν, Thuc. vii. 57. 4).

Thucydides records that not long after the destruction of the Athenian force at Eretria in the summer of 411 the Peloponnesians induced the whole of Euboea to revolt with the exception of Oreus which was occupied by the Athenians themselves (Thuc. viii. 95. 7); but once again one may wonder, as in 446, whether Carystus, geographically cut off, was included in the revolt.

Thasos

Thanks to the fruitful work of French excavators there is more evidence for the history of Thasos in the fifth century than for any other state in the Athenian empire, and Pouilloux's comprehensive publication and analysis of the documents provides an admirable foundation for the historian (J. Pouilloux, *Recherches sur l'Histoire et les Cultes de Thasos*, i, Paris, 1954).

The prosperity of Thasos in the late archaic and early classical periods is well attested by her architecture and sculpture and by the wide distribution of her tetradrachms, especially in Egypt (a list of Egyptian hoards in Pouilloux, 52 n. 1). When Herodotus visited the island the power of Thasos had been broken, but the earlier prosperity was not forgotten. The revenues were derived from mines and from her colonies on the mainland opposite the island. The mainland goldmines of Scaptesyle, according to Herodotus, brought in an annual income of 80 talents, the mines of the island itself rather less. From mines and colonies together the Thasians drew 200 talents, and in the best years 300 (Hdt. vi. 46). Such totals are probably higher than those of contemporary Athens, and the figures may have grown with age, but Thasos was undoubtedly rich and we can accept Herodotus' statement that they paid no dues on their crops. It was on account of her wealth that Histiaeus attacked Thasos when the Ionian revolt was disintegrating; it was the quickest way to collect the resources which he needed to keep his force together. Thasos was saved because the situation in Ionia deteriorated too rapidly; Histiaeus had to return to Lesbos (Hdt. vi. 28).

It was the shock of this raid, Herodotus tells us, that led the Thasians to build warships and strengthen their walls. Her neighbours, however, warned Darius that Thasos was planning revolt and the king ordered the Thasians to pull down their walls and bring their ships to Abdera. It is probable that these neighbours, and particularly Abdera, main rival to Thasos for the trade of western Thrace, were considerably more concerned for their own interests than those of

Persia. Be that as it may, the Thasians complied and when Xerxes invaded they entertained him royally on behalf of their colonies on the mainland; local tradition, which can be relied on to make a good story better, maintained that it had cost them 400 talents (Hdt. vii. 118).

It is doubtful whether the Persian control of Thrace seriously affected the trade of Thasos, but the continued occupation by a Persian governor and garrison of Eion at the mouth of the Strymon could have been a considerable nuisance to Thasian merchantmen and traders. They were probably relieved when the fleet of the Delian League captured the town after a long siege, but the Athenian occupation which resulted was eventually to be more dangerous. There is no reason, however, to believe that the trading interests of Thasos were seriously affected at once. She still controlled her mining interests and colonies on the mainland and her wine had a good name throughout the Aegean world. A fragment of an inscription, probably from the first third of the fifth century, suggests that the government already to a certain extent regulated the wine trade (Pouilloux 37–45). Too little remains to reconstruct the main substance of the regulations, but they concern wine and vinegar, they imply that there was already a standard Thasian amphora, and they end on a strong note: 'concerning wine no citizen nor foreigner may enter under oath a plea of ignorance'. Provision is made for prosecutions against offenders and the prosecutor has to make his deposit with a 300 (παρὰ τριηκοσίοισιν). There is a similar reference to a 300 later in the century when Thasos was ruled by oligarchs, and this has been taken as evidence that before her revolt from Athens in 465 Thasos was controlled by an oligarchy (Pouilloux 43). The inference is probable but not certain (below, p. 574).

Thucydides had no doubt that the reasons for the revolt of Thasos were primarily economic, centring on the control of the Thasian trading colonies on the mainland and the mainland mines which the Thasians operated (Thuc. i. 100. 2 : διενεχθέντας περὶ τῶν ἐν τῇ ἀντιπέρας Θρᾴκῃ ἐμπορίων καὶ τοῦ μετάλλου, ἃ ἐνέμοντο). On surrendering after a long siege the Thasians had to give up their mine and their coastal colonies (Thuc. i. 101. 3). The natural inference is either that the Athenians made the colonies autonomous or that she herself took control of them, as when in 427, having crushed the revolt of Mytilene, she took her mainland dependencies and proceeded to levy tribute from them (Thuc. iii. 50. 3 ; tribute, *ATL* iii. 70). Two of these Thasian colonies are in fact included in the tribute lists, Neapolis and Galepsus; for the remainder there is no evidence. The mine at issue which was taken from Thasos is presumably to be identified with the goldmines of Scaptesyle from which Herodotus says that the Thasians used to get 80 talents a year (Hdt. vi. 46. 3 : ἐκ μέν γε τῶν Σκαπτησύλης τῶν χρυσέων μετάλλων τὸ ἐπίπαν ὀγδώκοντα τάλαντα προσήιε).

Perdrizet (*Klio* LX (1910), 12–21) held that the gold-mining area which Thasos lost could not have passed to Athens. The colonists, whom Athens had sent to occupy the site of Ennea Hodoi, had been destroyed, according to Thucydides, at Drabescus by a united Thracian force. Pedrizet thought that after such a crushing defeat it would have been impossible for Athens to control any mines on the mainland, and he finds support in Herodotus (vii. 112) who, in his description of Xerxes' passage through Thrace, says that Pangaeus is a large and high mountain with gold and silver mines which the Pierians and Odomantians, and more particularly the Satrae, control (μέταλλα τὰ νέμονται Πίερες ...). Herodotus says that the colonists were fighting 'for the gold-mines', and Pedrizet identifies these with the mines of Mount Pangaeus; Drabescus he identifies with the modern Stravic in the Edonian plain, some ten miles from Amphipolis. This identification, however, is barely consistent with Thucydides (i. 100. 3), who says that, when the colonists had got control of Ennea Hodoi, they advanced into the interior and were overwhelmed at Drabescus. The more probable site for Drabescus is the modern Drama, some twenty miles inland from Amphipolis (Leake, *Travels*, iii. 183). The gold-mines for which the colonists were fighting were therefore more probably those which Philip later exploited with so much profit and not the mines nearer the coast on Mount Pangaeus (for the distinction of the two areas see Strabo 331. 34). Herodotus' description of Mount Pangaeus is not firm evidence for conditions on the mainland at the time of his visit to Thasos; as in so much of his description of Xerxes' route he was probably drawing on a geographical source, which by his own day was not entirely up to date. We should accept the natural inference from Thucydides; when the Thasians were required to give up Scaptesyle the Athenians took possession. At the time of the fall of Amphipolis to Brasidas in 424 Thucydides (iv. 108. 1) emphasizes the seriousness of the loss to Athens; the colony sent ship timber to Athens and revenue (χρημάτων προσόδῳ). This revenue probably came from Scaptesyle.

It may be assumed that the surrender of Thasos was accompanied by the establishment of a democracy, though we have no firm evidence until 411 when a democracy was overthrown. The earliest years of the new government must have been very lean, for Thasos had lost the main sources of her wealth, the long struggle against Athens is likely to have exhausted her reserves, and she had to pay an indemnity as well as tribute (Thuc. i. 101. 3, quoted, p. 85). By the mid forties she may have largely recovered. Her indemnity was probably paid off, and though her tribute rises from 3 to 30 talents this higher tribute may represent a smaller total annual payment to Athens. It has indeed been widely maintained that the rise in tribute represents the return of their mainland mining interests or trading colonies, but we prefer to regard 30 talents rather than 3 talents as the normal tribute (above, pp. 85 f.). By now Thasos should have become reconciled to her new status, and relations with Athens were probably much better. It is interesting to find among the magistrates, soon after the mid century, Polygnotus, who had enjoyed the patronage of Cimon and by his monumental paintings had added distinction to buildings for which Cimon was directly or indirectly responsible (above, p. 275). He had been rewarded with Athenian citizenship but spent his later years in his native Thasos. He was followed in office at a short interval by his brother Polydorus (Pouilloux 262, cat. 1, col. 4. 16, 27). Theogenes, son of Timoxenus, was another Thasian who had won a panhellenic reputation, but in a very different field. Theogenes was a famous boxer and pancratist, well known at all the great athletic festivals, who remained undefeated as a boxer for twenty-two years. On his statue base at Delphi he was credited with 1,300 victory crowns (*SIG* 36). He too spent his retirement in Thasos and is said to have played a leading part in local affairs (Dio Chrys. xxxi. 95: ἦν ἀνὴρ οὐδενὸς χείρων περὶ τὰ κοινά). Pouilloux also sees in him an important religious reformer of the cult of Herakles, but he has to lean too heavily on evidence that is very frail (Pouilloux 82 ff. But see P. M. Fraser, *AJA* lxi (1957), 99 f., and Chamoux, *REG* lxxii (1959), 359, though both reviewers are too sceptical about Theogenes' political importance). Theogenes' statue in bronze was set up in the Agora and miracles were later associated with it. A cult grew up after his death and in a recently discovered dedication of the second century A.D. he is a πάτριος θεός. Such men as Theogenes and Polygnotus may have made it easier for the Thasians to adapt themselves to the new relationship with Athens. When Brasidas at the head of a small army in 424 began to make considerable headway in Chalcidice and even captured Amphipolis there is no hint in Thucydides' narrative of trouble in Thasos. It is true that Thucydides, general for the year, was himself based on Thasos, but he commanded a very small fleet of only seven vessels (Thuc. iv. 104. 5). Had anti-Athenian feelings been strong and widespread the Thasians could have made Thucydides' position very uncomfortable, though they knew too much about Athenian sea power to believe that a full-scale revolt was practicable. Thucydides, however, notes that Galepsus, one of the Thasian colonies which paid tribute to Athens, went over to Brasidas after the fall of Amphipolis and that Cleon had to use force to recover it a year later (Thuc. iv. 107. 3; v. 6. 1). Galepsus was followed by Oisyme, another Thasian colony, but the more important Neapolis, now as later, remained loyal to Athens.

During the period of the Thirty Years' Peace and down to the Peace of Nicias the economy of Thasos seems to have depended largely on her wine, and two well-preserved enactments illustrate the importance attached to the wine trade by the state. The first is apparently aimed against speculators and prescribes that no one may purchase grapes on the vine before the beginning of the month Plynterion (c. May), and that all wine must be sold in standard vessels properly sealed. The second ends with a clause that no ship may carry any other wine than Thasian between Athos and a point on the coast to the east which cannot be identified. Two fragments of a rather earlier decree mention καρπόλογοι, presumably officers appointed to collect the dues on crops needed to pay the annual tribute to Athens (Pouilloux 121–34). That relations with Athens during this period were reasonably good is suggested by the reopening of the Thasian mint, which had probably been closed when the Thasians surrendered in 463 (S. E. G. Robinson, *Hesp.* Supp. viii. 333 and 335–6: 'After a break which should coincide with the first revolt there is a resumption from the thirties onwards with pieces reflecting Parthenon style and having a maximum density in the twenties'). If we can infer from such evidence that Thasos had come to accept Athenian control of what had once been her mainland preserve we should probably not regard the substitution of the Attic for the Parian alphabet in public documents from about 430 (Pouilloux 123) as a sign of Athenian pressure.

The developments in the Peloponnesian War, however, introduced new strains. When the tribute of the empire was radically reassessed in 425 the tribute of Thasos was probably doubled to 60 talents. This together with the successes of Brasidas in Chalcidice and at Amphipolis will have strengthened the anti-Athenian elements. By 411 some of these men had been exiled and were waiting for an opportunity to return (Thuc. viii. 64. 4: καὶ γὰρ καὶ φυγὴ αὐτῶν ἔξω ἦν ὑπὸ τῶν Ἀθηναίων παρὰ τοῖς Πελοποννησίοις). Their opportunity came when the Athenians lost the major part of their military and naval forces in Sicily, which gave hope to oligarchs throughout the Aegean. Athens herself caught the infection, and both at Athens and at Samos, their main naval base, oligarchs plotted to take control. When Athenian oligarchs at Samos developed their plans for revolution they hoped to capitalize the general feeling against Athenian democracy by establishing oligarchs in power in the allied cities. Dieitrephes who had been appointed to the Thracian command accordingly dissolved the democracy at Thasos, but this was insufficient for the Thasian oligarchs, moderates as well as extremists. Nothing less than independence would now satisfy them, and in anticipation of Spartan help they restored the fortifications of the city. When the Peloponnesian force, including Thasian exiles and a detachment under a Corinthian commander, arrived revolt was openly declared (Thuc. viii. 64. 3 with *Hellenica Oxyrhynchia* vii. 4).

From the period of the revolt comes a very well-preserved stone
with two decrees inscribed in Parian script, a deliberate nationalist
reaction from the Attic script of recent public documents. The first
decree lays down rewards for anyone who denounces a conspiracy
against Thasos. The second decree, inscribed on the same stone, which
was not originally designed to take it, is concerned with 'any conspiracy in the colonies or any citizen of Thasos or of her colonies
betraying Thasos' (Pouilloux 139; ML 83). Pouilloux argued that
these two decrees came close together, the first in 411 while all was
well but there could be the danger of a democratic reaction, the
second early in 410 when Athens had made a striking recovery, and
Thrasybulus was operating in Thracian waters; this, he thought,
helped to explain why the reward offered to informers dropped from
1,000 staters in the first decree to 200 staters in the second, a sign of
growing financial stringency. New light thrown on the Thasian
calendar now requires a longer interval between the two decrees of
more than a year (Salviat, *BCH* lxxxii (1958), 212–15), but the basic
hypothesis is not seriously affected. These two decrees must surely
come in the period of the revolt of Thasos from 411 to 407, when
Thasos was independent of Athens and ruled by oligarchs. The two
decrees suit the situation very well. The first anticipates a possible
attempt by the demos to regain power from within (cf. the Samian
ἐπανάστασις ὑπὸ τοῦ δήμου τοῖς δυνατοῖς in 412, Thuc. viii. 21); and
before the revolt ended there were Atticizers in exile from Thasos.
After 411 there was more danger to Thasos from the mainland, where
Neapolis had refused to join the revolt. Her loyalty to Athens in this
difficult period is commemorated in two Athenian decrees recorded
on the same stele (ML 89): 'Though besieged by the Thasians and
Peloponnesians they did not despair but carried the war through with
Athens to the end.'

This particular war ended in 407 and the recovery of Thasos is
briefly noted by Diodorus and Xenophon. According to Diodorus
Thrasybulus sailed against the island with fifteen ships, defeated the
Thasian forces, and killed some 200 of them. He then blockaded the
city, forced them to take back the friends of Athens whom they had
exiled, accept a garrison, and return to the Athenian alliance (Diod.
xiii. 72. 1). Xenophon, even briefer, says that Thrasybulus commanded a fleet of thirty ships in Thracian waters with which he
recovered the places that had gone over to Sparta, including Thasos,
which was 'crippled by the fighting, by political strife, and by famine'
(Xen. *Hell.* i. 4. 9). The numbers of ships in Diodorus and Xenophon
are not necessarily inconsistent. Thrasybulus may have commanded
thirty ships but used only fifteen against Thasos. It is more probable that Xenophon is right and Diodorus wrong; fifteen ships seems

too small a force for the reduction of Thasos, however weak her condition.

It would be interesting to follow the political fluctuations in Thasos during the years of revolt, but the evidence is only fitful. When in 411 a strong oligarchy was established in Athens and the most anti-Athenian oligarchs were in power in Thasos, the demos must have felt very helpless; but when Athens disowned extreme oligarchy and the Four Hundred were replaced by the moderate constitution of the Five Thousand the prospect was more open. In the late summer of 411 the Athenian fleet which was dominantly democratic had fought two successful actions in the Hellespont and Thrasybulus was able to sail into Thracian waters in the winter of 411/10. The Athenian revival was not the only shock for the Thasian oligarchs; they also found themselves unable to control their colony Neapolis which remained loyal to Athens. The two Thasian ordinances offering rewards to informers who uncover plots against the government have already been mentioned; there also survives a list of six names of men whose property had been confiscated because they supported Athens (ἐπ' ἁ]ττικισμῶι), four Thasians and two Neapolitans (*IG* xii. 8. 263). The list is dated by local magistrates whose year we do not know, but one of the Thasian names, Apemantus, son of Philon, recurs in an early-fourth-century inscription at Athens. This lists five sons of Apemantus, who had been made *proxenoi* of Athens. Their stele was destroyed when the Thirty ruled Athens, but it was replaced by the restored democracy (*IG* ii². 6 = Tod, *GHI* ii. 98). The confiscations recorded in the Thasian document were carried out κατὰ τὸν ἇδον τῶν τριηκοσίων, by the verdict of the Three Hundred, which recalls the early-fifth-century decree concerning wine and the two decrees offering rewards to informers. These three decrees speak of *a* Three Hundred in a judicial context. The Thasian proscription list speaks of *the* Three Hundred. Though it would be naïve to hold that the article makes no difference it is reasonable to believe that there should be a close connection. The simplest way to relate them is to suggest that in the first three decrees the article is not used because there does not exist a permanent body of 300, but only a general provision for selecting 300 men in certain kinds of cases. When a 300 has been selected its decisions are decisions of *the* 300.

There is a widespread view that Athens temporarily recovered control of Thasos in the winter of 411/10, and this is indeed the natural interpretation of a passage in Xenophon. After their two successes in the Hellespont in the late summer of 411 the Athenian fleet had to disperse to collect money to pay the crews. Early in the summer of 410 the squadrons reassembled in the Hellespont. Theramenes returned with twenty ships from Macedon, Thrasybulus also with twenty

ships from Thasos (Xen. *Hell.* i. 1. 12: Θρασύβουλος εἴκοσιν ἑτέραις ἐκ
Θάσου); they had both collected money. If Thrasybulus brought
money from Thasos itself the natural implication is that he had
recovered the island, or at least been strong enough to make a successful plundering raid. Support has been found for the view that Thasos
now came under Athenian control from an entry in the accounts of
the treasurers of Athena for 409/8 (for the date, W. S. Ferguson,
The Treasurers of Athena, 16–37). During the previous year their predecessors had collected bars of gold from Scaptesyle weighing 300
drachmae. Wade-Gery restored the value in silver as 3,000 drachmae,
and suggested that this could represent the *aparche* from a Thasian
tribute of 30 talents, which had been the island's assessment in the late
forties and thirties (*IG* i². 301. 114–19: [τὸν ἐπετε|ίον ἧὸν [αὐτοὶ
χσυνελέχσα]|μεν φθοῖ[δες χρυσίο Σκαπτ]|εσυλικὸ, [σταθμὸν ἔλκοντ]|ες
HHH, ἀργ[ύριον τούτον γί|γ]νεται X[XX . . . . . . 11 . . . . .). This would
give a gold:silver ratio of 10:1 as compared with 14:1 before the
Peloponnesian War (ML 59, from the Parthenon accounts of 434/3
and 54, the Parthenos accounts). Wade-Gery explained this fall by
the increasing intrusion of gold darics into the Aegean. There is,
however, no other evidence suggesting a rate as low as this and such
other figures as survive are against it; other restorations are possible
in the key passages (W. E. Thompson, *Num. Chron.* iv (1964), 103–23;
cf. D. M. Lewis, *Robinson Essays*, 105–10). It is unlikely that Thasos
had access to the mainland mines while Eion and Neapolis remained
loyal to Athens. Xenophon's ἐκ Θάσου should be interpreted to mean
'from Thasian waters' (Pouilloux 153 f.).

There is a further problem in Xenophon's text for this period.
According to our manuscripts he says that in 409 'as a result of *stasis*
in Thasos the Laconizers and the Spartan harmost Eteonicus were
driven out. Pasippidas the Spartan was accused of joint responsibility
with Tissaphernes' (Xen. *Hell.* i. 1. 32). This text could make political
sense. It was the Spartan custom to establish harmosts in key cities
that came over to them and this not uncommonly proved unsuccessful.
In Chios the Spartan Pedaritus had been allowed by the oligarchs
to act ruthlessly and the result was a growing disillusionment (Thuc.
viii. 38). The expulsion of Eteonicus and the Laconizers could have
meant the renunciation of extreme oligarchy by the moderates, under
pressure from Athens. But though it is tempting to see the dispatch
by Lysander of Eteonicus to the Thraceward area after the collapse of
Athens at Aegospotami (Xen. *Hell.* ii. 2. 5) as confirmation of an earlier
command in Thasos, the prominence of Tissaphernes in the story
would be very difficult to understand. His interest is at once explained
if we accept the clue from Diodorus' account of 403, where Lysander
attacks a city which is called Θάσσων or Θάσον in the manuscripts,

but is in Caria (Diod. xiii. 104. 7). Palmer's emendation to Ἴασον is irresistible and the same emendation makes much better sense of the passage from Xenophon. Iasus in 412 had become the headquarters of Amorges, the Persian rebel with whom Athens was co-operating. Tissaphernes, whose instructions from the king were to kill or capture Amorges, persuaded the Spartans to attack Iasus (Thuc. viii. 28. 2). The attack was successful but Spartan control might well have become unpopular by 409, and by that time Tissaphernes had abandoned Sparta. Before 405 Iasus returned to the Athenian alliance.

APPENDIX 16

Oaths of Allegiance

1. The oath administered to the Islanders after the battle of Mycale probably foreshadows the oath to be administered to the original members of the Delian League.

Hdt. ix. 106. 4: καὶ οὕτω δὴ Σαμίους τε καὶ Χίους καὶ Λεσβίους καὶ τοὺς ἄλλους νησιώτας, οἳ ἔτυχον συστρατευόμενοι τοῖσι Ἕλλησι, ἐς τὸ συμμαχικὸν ἐποιήσαντο, πίστι τε καταλαβόντες καὶ ὁρκίοισι ἐμμενέειν τε καὶ μὴ ἀποστήσεσθαι.

2. There are two descriptions of the administration of the oath when the League of Delos was inaugurated.

(a) Ἀθ. Πολ. 23. 5: διὸ (Ἀριστείδης) καὶ τοὺς ὅρκους ὤμοσεν τοῖς Ἴωσιν ὥστε τὸν αὐτὸν ἐχθρὸν εἶναι καὶ φίλον, ἐφ᾽ οἷς καὶ τοὺς μύδρους ἐν τῷ πελάγει καθεῖσαν.

(b) Plut. Ar. 25. 1: ὁ δ᾽ Ἀριστείδης ὥρκισε μὲν τοὺς Ἕλληνας καὶ ὤμοσεν ὑπὲρ τῶν Ἀθηναίων, μύδρους ἐμβαλὼν ἐπὶ ταῖς ἀραῖς εἰς τὴν θάλατταν.

3. *Erythrae*, ? 453/2. Regulations following a revolt. The stone was copied by Fauvel in the early nineteenth century, but both the stone and the copy are now lost. *CIG* i, addenda 73b, p. 891; *ATL* ii D 10; H. Bengtson, *Staatsverträge*, ii. 134; ML 40.

21 ὀμνύνα[ι δ]ὲ̀ [τά]δε [τὲν] βολέν· βολεύσο hος ἂν [δύ]νο[μ]α[ι] ἄρι̣στ[α κ]-
[αὶ] δικα[ιότα]τα Ἐρυθραίον τôι πλέθει καὶ Ἀθεναίον καὶ τὸν
[χσυ]νμά[χ]ον [κ]αὶ οὐκ [ἀποσ]τέσομαι Ἀθεναίον τô π[λ]έθος οὐδὲ [τ]-
[ὸν] χσυνμάχον τὸν Ἀθεναίον οὔτ᾽ αὐτὸς ἐγὸ ο[ὔ]τ᾽ ἄ[λ]λοι   πε[ί]σομ-
25 [αι οὐ]δ̀᾽ [α]ὐ[τ]ομο[λέ]σ̣[ο] οὔτ᾽ αὐτὸς ἐγὸ οὔτ᾽ ἄλλοι̣ [π]εί[σομαι οὐδέ
π]-
[οτε] τὸν φ[υγά]δον [κατ]αδέχσομαι οὐδ[ὲ] hένα οὔτ᾽ α[ὐ]τὸς ἐγὸ ο̣ὔ̣[τ᾽]
[ἄλλο]ι πείσρμα[ι τὸν ἐς] Μέδος φευγό[ντο]ν ἄνευ τê[ς] βολêς τ[ês]
[Ἀθε]ναίον καὶ τ[ô] δέμο.

Two other fragments concerning Erythrae survive, *IG* i². 11 and 12/13A, and are generally attributed to the lost decree. Some doubt remains (above, p. 421). 12/13A, D 10. 70–3, gives the oath to be sworn by the demos of Erythrae.

[ὀμνύναι δὲ τὸν δῆμον τά]-
δε· οὐκ ἀπο[στέ]σομα[ι] Ἀ[θεναίον τὸ πλέθος οὔτε τὸν χσυνμάχο]-
ν τὸν Ἀθεν[αίο]ν οὔτ' αὐ[τὸς ἐγὸ οὔτ' ἄλλοι πείσομαι, τἐι δὲ γνό]-
[μ]ει τἐ[ι] Ἀθ[ε]ναίον πείσ[ομαι].

4. *Miletus*, 450/49. In the regulations for Miletus there may be a reference to an oath to be administered by the five Athenian commissioners who are being sent out. Lines 73–4: h]ορκό[ντον δ]ὲ hοι πέ[ντε |·····]εοντο[····]ν ἂν ὀμόσε[ι; but these two lines are not followed by any oath formulae.

5. *Colophon*, ? 447/6. D 15, *Staatsverträge* 145; ML 47.

δράσο καὶ ἐ]-
ρô καὶ βολεύσο [ὅ τι ἂν δύνομαι καλὸν καὶ ἀγαθὸν πε]-
ρὶ τὸν δῆμον τ[ὸν Ἀθεναίον ....21..........]
45 [ο]ν καὶ οὐκ ἀποστ[έσομαι τὸ δέμο τὸ Ἀθεναίον οὔτε]
[λ]όγοι οὔτ' ἔργ[οι οὔτ' αὐτὸς ἐγὸ οὔτ' ἄλλοι πείσομαι]
[κ]αὶ φιλέσο τὸ[ν δῆμον τὸν Ἀθεναίον καὶ οὐκ αὐτομο]-
[λ]έσο καὶ δεμο[..............24–6..............οὔτ' α]-
ὑτὸς ἐγὸ οὔτ' ἄ[λλοι πείσομαι - - - - - - - - - - - - - -]
50 μενος πόλιν ο[- ὅρκ]-
ον ἀλεθἐ [τ]αῦτ[α- νὲ τὸν]
[Δ]ία καὶ τὸν Ἀπό[λλο καὶ τὲν Δέμετρα, καὶ εἰ μὲν ταῦτ]-
[α] παραβ⟨α⟩ίνοιμ[ι ἐξόλες εἴεν καὶ αὐτὸς ἐγὸ καὶ τὸ γ]-
[έ]νος τὸ ἐμὸν [ἐς τὸν ἄπαντα χρόνον, εὐορκõντι δὲ εἴε]
55 μοι πο[λ]λὰ καὶ [ἀγαθά].

Lines 44–5 involve the important question whether the allies are included in the oath as by *ATL*: πε]|ρὶ τὸν δῆμον τ[ὸν Ἀθεναίον καὶ περὶ τὸς ξυμμάχος αὐτ]|ôν, or excluded as by Kolbe: πε]|ρὶ τὸν δῆμον τ[ὸν Κολοφονίον καὶ τὸν δῆμον τὸν Ἀθεναί]|ον. Reasons have been given in ML 47 for slightly preferring Kolbe's version (but putting the Athenian demos before the demos of Kolophon. In ll. 49–51 *ATL* probably gives the right sense: οὔτ' ἐς ἄλλην ἀφιστά]|μενος πόλιν ο[ὔτ' αὐτόθι στασιάζον, κατὰ δὲ τὸν ὅρκ]ον ἀλεθἐ [τ]αῦτ[α ἐμπεδόσο ἀδόλος καὶ ἀβλαβôς. For φιλέσο τὸ[ν δῆμον in l. 47 cf. Ar. *Knights* 1341: ὦ Δῆμ', ἐραστής εἰμι σὸς φιλῶ τέ σε.

6. *Chalcis*, 446/5. D 17, *Staatsverträge* 155; ML 52.

(a) Athenian Oath, 3–16:

κατὰ τάδε τὸν hόρκον ὀμόσαι Ἀθεναίον τ-
ὲν βολὲν καὶ τὸς δικαστάς· οὐκ ἐχσελô Χα-

5   λκιδέας ἐχ Χαλκίδος οὐδὲ τὲν πόλιν ἀνά-
στατον ποέσο οὐδὲ ἰδιότεν οὐδένα ἀτιμ-
όσο οὐδὲ φυγῆι ζεμιόσο οὐδὲ χσυλλέφσο-
μαι οὐδὲ ἀποκτενῶ οὐδὲ χρέματα ἀφαιρέ-
σομαι ἀκρίτο οὐδενὸς ἄνευ τῶ δέμο τῶ Ἀθ-
10   εναίον, οὐδ᾽ ἐπιφσεφιῶ κατὰ ἀπροσκλέτο
οὔτε κατὰ τὸ κοινῶ οὔτε κατὰ ἰδιότο οὐδ-
ὲ ἑνός, καὶ πρεσβείαν ἐλθῶσαν προσάχσο
πρὸς βολὲν καὶ δέμον δέκα ἐμερῶν hόταν
πρυτανεύο κατὰ τὸ δυνατόν. ταῦτα δὲ ἐμπ-
15   [ε]δόσο Χαλκιδεῦσιν πειθομένοις τῶι δέ-
[μ]οι τῶι Ἀθεναίον.

(b) Chalcidian Oath, 21–32 :

    κατὰ τάδε Χαλκιδέας ὀμόσαι· οὐκ ἀπο[σ]τέ-
σομαι ἀπὸ τῶ [δ]έμο τῶ Ἀθεναίον οὔτε τέ[χ]ν-
ει οὔτε μεχανῆι οὐδεμιᾶι οὐδ᾽ ἔπει οὐδὲ
ἔργοι οὐδὲ τῶι ἀφισταμένοι πείσομαι, κ-
25   αὶ ἐὰν ἀφιστῆι τις κατερῶ Ἀθεναίοισι, κ-
αὶ τὸν φόρον hυποτελῶ Ἀθεναίοισιν, hὸν
ἂν πείθο Ἀθεναίος, καὶ χσύμμαχος ἔσομα-
ι hοῖος ἂν δύνομαι ἄριστος καὶ δικαιότ-
ατος καὶ τῶι δέμοι τῶι Ἀθεναίον βοεθέσ-
30   ο καὶ ἀμυνῶ, ἐάν τις ἀδικῆι τὸν δεμον τὸν
Ἀθεναίον, καὶ πείσομαι τῶι δέμοι τῶι Ἀθεναίον.

7. *Eretria*, 446/5. D 16; *Staatsverträge* 154. The Chalcis decree implies
that the same oath was required from Eretria as from Chalcis. Lines
40–2 : ἀγαθῆι τύχει τῆι Ἀθεναί|ον ποέσθαι τὸν hόρκον Ἀθεναίος καὶ
Χαλ|κιδέας, καθάπερ Ἐρετριεῦσι ἐφσηφίσατ|ο hο δῆμος hο Ἀθεναίον.
A fragment of the decree for Eretria (*Hesp.* vi (1937), 317–19) can be
restored to correspond exactly.

8. *Samos* 439/8 D 18, *Staatsverträge* 159; ML 56.

(a) Samian Oath, 15–21 :

                                  δρ]-
[άσο καὶ ἐρῶ καὶ βολεύσο τῶι δέμοι τῶι Ἀθενα]-
[ίον hό, τι ἂν δύνομαι καλὸν κ]αὶ ἀ[γ]αθόν, [οὐδὲ ἀ]-
[ποστέσομαι ἀπὸ τῶ δέμο τῶ Ἀ]θεναίον οὔτε λ[ό]-
[γοι οὔτε ἔργοι οὔτε ἀπὸ τὸν] χσυμμάχον τὸν Ἀ-
20   [θεναίον, καὶ πιστὸς ἔσομαι τ]ῶι δέμοι τῶι Ἀθ-
[εναίον.]

In l. 20 πιστὸς ἔσομαι or ἔσομαι πιστός (ATL) is rather more consistent with the friendly tone of the decree than πείσομαι αἰεί (Bengtson).

(b) Athenian Oath, 21–5 :

    Ἀθεναῖος δ' ὀμόσαι· δρ]άσο καὶ ἐρῶ καὶ
    [βολεύσο καλὸν τôι δέμοι τôι] Σαμίον hό τι ἂν
    [δύνομαι καὶ ἐπιμελέσομαι Σα]μίον κατὰ hὰ[.]
    [. . . . . .25 . . . .] Ἀθεναῖον [. .]
25   [. . . . . .26 . . . .] κρατε[. . . .]

Lines 23–6 are restored by ATL: ἐπιμελέσομαι Σα[μίον κατὰ hὰ [h|ομολόγεσαν hοι στρατεγοὶ hοι] Ἀθεναῖον [κα|ὶ hοι ἄρχοντες hοι Σαμίον· Καλλι]κράτε[s εἶπ|ε - - -. Some such restoration is required to account for the list of ten generals which followed.

9. Selymbria, 407; IG i². 115; Staatsverträge 207; ML 87. Selymbria was recovered by the Athenians in 408 and the terms of the settlement made by Alcibiades and the other generals were ratified by the Assembly at Athens when Alcibiades returned to the city in 407. An exchange of oaths is recorded, but the text is not given. Lines 28–31 : ὤμοσαν Ἀθεναῖον οἱ στρατεγοὶ | [καὶ οἱ τριέραρχ]οι καὶ hοι hοπλῖται καὶ εἴ τι|[s ἄλλος Ἀθεναῖον] παρῆν καὶ Σελυμβ[ρ]ιανοὶ π|[ά]ντε[s.

10. Aphytis, ?429. D 21. Aphytis is granted various privileges including the remittance of all tribute except the aparche, but is required to take an oath of loyalty to the Athenians sent out to settle in Potidaea after her surrender in the winter of 430/29, and to the Athenians. Lines 8–10 require the publication on stone of τὸν [δὲ ὅρκον ὃν | [ὤ]μοσαν Ἀφυταῖο[ι τ]οῖς ἐποίκοι[s] τ[οῖς] ἐμ Ποτειδαία[ι καὶ Ἀθηνα|ί]οις. Lines 19 ff. : [τ]όνδε τὸν ὅρ[κον ὤμοσαν] Ἀφυταῖοι [τοῖς ἐμ Ποτειδαίαι· ἐάν τις ἴ|ηι π]ολέμιος [ἐπὶ τὴν πό]λιν τὴν Ἀθη[ναίων ἢ ἐπὶ τὸς ἐποίκος τὸς Ἀ|θηναίων τ]ὸς Ποτείδ]αιαν ἔχοντ[ας, βοηθήσω Ἀθηναίοις κατὰ τὸ δ|υνατὸν καὶ λόγωι κ]αὶ ἔργωι and in l. 24 οὔτε λόγωι ο]ὔτε ἔργωι.

APPENDIX 17

Aristophanes, *Birds* 1021–57

Ἐπίσκοπος, Πισθέταιρος, Ψηφισματοπώλης

1021 Ἐπ. Ποῦ πρόξενοι;

    Πι.   Τίς ὁ Σαρδανάπαλλος οὑτοσί;

    Ἐπ. Ἐπίσκοπος ἥκω δεῦρο τῷ κυάμῳ λαχὼν
          εἰς τὰς Νεφελοκοκκυγίας.

    Πι.   Ἐπίσκοπος;
          Ἔπεμψε δὲ τίς σε δεῦρο;

    Ἐπ.   Φαῦλον βιβλίον
          Τελέου τι.

1025 Πι. Βούλει δῆτα τὸν μισθὸν λαβὼν
          μὴ πράγματ' ἔχειν ἀλλ' ἀπιέναι;

    Ἐπ.   Νὴ τοὺς θεούς.
          Ἐκκλησιάσαι γοῦν ἐδεόμην οἴκοι μένων·
          ἔστιν γὰρ ἃ δι' ἐμοῦ πέπρακται Φαρνάκῃ.

    Πι. Ἄπιθι λαβών· ἔστιν δ' ὁ μισθὸς οὑτοσί.

    Ἐπ. Τουτὶ τί ἦν;

1030 Πι.   Ἐκκλησία περὶ Φαρνάκου.

    Ἐπ. Μαρτύρομαι τυπτόμενος ὢν ἐπίσκοπος.

    Πι. Οὐκ ἀποσοβήσεις; οὐκ ἀποίσεις τὼ κάδω;
          Οὐ δεινά; Καὶ πέμπουσιν ἤδη 'πισκόπους
          εἰς τὴν πόλιν, πρὶν καὶ τεθύσθαι τοῖς θεοῖς;

1035 Ψη. " Ἐὰν δ' ὁ Νεφελοκοκκυγιεὺς τὸν Ἀθηναῖον ἀδικῇ—"

    Πι. Τουτὶ τί ἐστιν αὖ κακόν, τὸ βιβλίον;

    Ψη. Ψηφισματοπώλης εἰμὶ καὶ νόμους νέους
          ἥκω παρ' ὑμᾶς δεῦρο πωλήσων.

    Πι.   Τὸ τί;

1040 Ψη. "Χρῆσθαι Νεφελοκοκκυγιᾶς τοῖς αὐτοῖς μέτροισι
          καὶ σταθμοῖσι καὶ ψηφίσμασι καθάπερ Ὀλοφύξιοι."

    Πι. Σὺ δέ γ' οἷσπερ Ὠτοτύξιοι χρήσει τάχα.

    Ψη. Οὗτος, τί πάσχεις;

    Πι.   Οὐκ ἀποίσεις τοὺς νόμους;

1045   Πικροὺς ἐγώ σοι τήμερον δείξω νόμους.

    Ἐπ. Καλοῦμαι Πισθέταιρον ὕβρεως εἰς τὸν Μουνιχιῶνα
          μῆνα.

    Πι. Ἄληθες, οὗτος; Ἔτι γὰρ ἐνταῦθ' ἦσθα σύ;

Ψη. " Ἐὰν δέ τις ἐξελαύνῃ τοὺς ἄρχοντας καὶ μὴ δέχη-
1050   ται κατὰ τὴν στήλην—"
Πι. Οἴμοι κακοδαίμων, καὶ σὺ γὰρ ἐνταῦθ᾽ ἦσθ᾽ ἔτι;
'Επ. Ἀπολῶ σε καὶ γράψω σε μυρίας δραχμάς—
Πι. Ἐγὼ δὲ σοῦ γε τὼ κάδω διασκεδῶ.
Ψη. Μέμνησ᾽ ὅτε τῆς στήλης κατετίλας ἑσπέρας;
1055 Πι. Αἰβοῖ· λαβέτω τις αὐτόν. Οὗτος, οὐ μενεῖς;
   Ἀπίωμεν ἡμεῖς ὡς τάχιστ᾽ ἐντευθενὶ
   θύσοντες εἴσω τοῖς θεοῖσιν τὸν τράγον.

Enter INSPECTOR

INSPECTOR. Where are our representatives?
PISTHETAIROS. Who's this? Sardanapallos himself?
INSP. I have been appointed, by due process
  Of lottery, to inspect the affairs
  Of Cloudcuckoobury. So here I am.
PISTH. You certainly are. Inspector, eh?
  Who told you to come?
INSP. Oh, someone signed a little scrap of paper.
  Teleas, I think they call him . . .
PISTH. I'll make you an offer. I'll give you
  Something for expenses, and you leave now—
  Save yourself a lot of trouble.
INSP. Marvellous! I really wanted to stay at home
  And go to the big debate. I have some business,
  You know, with Pharnaces.
PISTH. I'll give you what's coming to you, then
  You can go. Ready? . . . Here it is!

(Beats him)

INSP. What's this?
PISTH. The Pharnaces debate!
INSP. Someone be a witness! I'm being beaten,
  And I'm an inspector.
PISTH. Run! Fast! And take your pair of ballot urns
  With you! . . . *(Exit* INSPECTOR*)* Can you stand it?
  They're sending inspectors here already,
  And we've scarcely got our city dedicated
  To the gods . . .

(Enter DECREE-SELLER*)*

D.S. 'If a resident of Cloudcuckoobury
  Commits an offence against an Athenian citizen . . .'
PISTH. What's this piece of rubbish? What's it say?

D.S. Any law you like—dirt cheap. Here—I've got
  All the latest legislation . . . special rate
  For you, sir.
PISTH. Can I have a sample?
D.S. How about . . . 'All citizens of Cloudcuckoobury
  Are to employ the same weights, measures,
  And decrees as the Olophyxians.'?
PISTH. Get ready, you're about to switch
  To the goad standard yourself!

(*Brings out a pointed stick, jabs the* DECREE-SELLER)

D.S. Are you mad?
PISTH. Get your laws out of here. I've got my own laws,
  I passed them today, and they bite!
INSP. (*reappearing on opposite side from departing* D.S.)
  I'll sue you for this! I'll have you for assault!
  Your case'll be up next month.
PISTH. You think so, do you?
  So you've come back then— (*runs at him, driving him off*)
D.S. (*entering at other side: reading aloud*) If the officers
  Are set upon and are not duly received,
  As per decree—
PISTH.   Oh no! Are you back too? (*drives him off*)
INSP. (*reappearing*) I'll ruin you! I'll sue you for a million!
PISTH. (*kicking him*) I'll break your urns and ruin your procedure!
D.S. (*reappearing*) Remember the night you relieved yourself on the
  decree stone?
PISTH. Oh, grab him, someone!   (*Exit* D.S.)
  Hey, come back,
  Come back! Let's get out of here
  And sacrifice the goat to the gods inside.

An *episkopos* is an inspector sent out by Athens, who is concerned
primarily with constitutional and political matters. When Erythrae was
recovered by Athens after a period of revolt a commission of *episkopoi*
was sent out and their duties included the supervision, with the garrison commander, of a new democratic Boule (above, p. 212). Cloudcuckoobury is not yet in the Athenian empire, but it is implied that
Athens assumes control wherever she can.

1021. The inspector first wants to find *proxenoi*, local men who have
undertaken to represent the interests of Athens (above, pp. 215 ff.); he
would rely on them for an up-to-date report on the political situation.
He is elaborately dressed, suggesting eastern luxury, and may have

been intended to represent a well known political figure. For eastern fashions in Athens, cf. *Wasps* 1136 ff.

1022. This line could mean either that he was made an inspector by the lot or that as an inspector he was appointed by lot to this particular mission. The order of words favours the reference of the lot to his mission.

1024–5. The mission resulted from a decree of the Assembly proposed by Teleas. The βιβλίον is the scroll on which the decree was written. If the decree was carried, the proposer would hand over the scroll to the secretary of the Boule who was responsible for the keeping and, where necessary, the publication of records, cf. Tod, *GHI* ii. 97. 21–2: τὸ δὲ βιβλίον | [τοῦ ψηφίσματος παραδοῦναι αὐτ]ῶι τὸγ γραμματέα τῆς βουλῆς αὐτίκα μάλα (403/2 B.C.). Teleas is also mentioned in l. 167, where a scholiast comments that he was a frequent target of comedy as an immoral coward, fickle, and too fond of good food (as in Ar. *Peace* 1008).

1025. The natural inference is that *episkopoi* were paid 'for services rendered' by the cities to which they were sent. I know of no other evidence on the point, but resident Athenian officials seem to have been maintained by the local authorities, D 21. 6–8. There is, throughout Aristophanes, an assumption that anyone who takes office at Athens is primarily interested in the money.

1027–8. The inspector has 'fixed' something with Pharnaces and he would like to be in the Assembly at Athens when Persian business comes up. Pharnaces is presumably the satrap of Dascylium mentioned by Thucydides in ii. 67. 1 and v. 1. The situation in the east was delicate. At some time near the production of the *Birds* Pissuthnes, satrap at Sardis, revolted from the Persian king (above, p. 349). Athens may have supported him; she at any rate supported his bastard son Amorges who carried on the revolt (Thuc. viii. 5. 5). In such a situation relations with the satrap of Dascylium become important.

1032. τὼ κάδω. The two ballot urns which he carried imply that lawcourts on the Athenian model were essential to democracy.

1035. The decree-seller offers three sample decrees. Of these the second is a clear parody of the Coinage Decree discussed above (pp. 167 ff.). It is possible that the other two also reflect decrees that had actually been passed by the Assembly. The first recalls the special procedure and penalties laid down for anyone who killed an Athenian in any city of the empire, a protection that was also extended to favoured *proxenoi* (above, p. 227). This measure, according to our dating, was introduced in the early forties, and was extended later to cases of imprisonment or arrest.

1040. Substantial fragments have been found of the decree banning the minting of silver by the allies and requiring them to use Athenian coins, weights, and measures. The importance attached to the decree is best shown by the addition of a clause to the oath sworn by members of the Boule when they entered office, ML 45 (cl. 12): ἐάν τις κόπτηι νόμισ[μα] ἀργυρίου ἐν ταῖς πό[λεσι κ]αὶ μὴ χρῆται νομ[ίσμασιν τοῖς Ἀθηνα]ίων ἢ σταθμοῖς ἢ μέτ[ροις . . . .: Bergk proposed νομίσμασι for ψηφίσμασι in our text; the change would weaken the joke considerably. Olophyxus was a small place of little economic or political significance on the promontory of Acte in Chalcidice; her pre-war tribute was only 1,000 drachmae. This parody has been one of the main reasons for dating the Coinage Decree in the late twenties or later. Reasons have been given above (pp. 167-72) for preferring a date in the early forties, which might favour a new interpretation of νόμους νέους. Pouilloux has suggested (*Recherches sur l'Histoire et les Cultes de Thasos*, i (1953), 118 n. 3) that if the decree-seller's new laws were in fact old laws the joke would be better. Both the first and the third laws would fit our pattern of the early forties.

1047. The scholiasts are confused and confusing. The pronouncement that Munichion was the month for hearing cases of assault is nonsense, nor is it likely, as another says, that this was the month when foreigners were brought to trial at Athens from the cities. Munichion may have been named as the month following the Dionysia.

1049. τοὺς ἄρχοντας are not the local magistrates but resident Athenian officials in the cities of the empire (above, pp. 213-14). The Coinage Decree and the Clinias Decree show that they were widely spread when these decrees were passed. It is likely that they became one of the most important means of Athenian control when peace had been made with Persia. Though they seem to have been accepted later these officials could have been strongly resented in the immediate aftermath of the peace and a firm decree by Athens against attempts to be rid of them would fit the mood of the early forties.

1054. There must have been a strong temptation to oligarchs as well as dogs to deface or foul decree stones. There may be a recognition of the risk in the regulations laid down for Miletus in 450/49, D 11. 49-50: [· ἐ]ν στέλει [κα]ὶ τοῖς φσεφίσμασ[ι ——|[. .] μὲ διαφθεί[ρεν] μεδὲ κακοτεχν[ἐν—. If such a decree was passed in Athens, it would be essential to have copies published in the cities, as of the Coinage Decree. The stele of this line is presumably such a copy.

SELECT BIBLIOGRAPHY

(I) GENERAL STUDIES

D. W. BRADEEN, 'The Popularity of the Athenian Empire', *Hist.* ix (1960), 257–69.

G. E. M. DE STE CROIX, 'The Character of the Athenian Empire', *Hist.* iii (1954–5), 1–41.

W. KOLBE, 'Die Anfänge der attischen Arché', *Hermes* lxxiii (1938), 249–68.

M. F. MCGREGOR, *Athenian Policy at Home and Abroad* (Semple Lectures), Cincinnati, 1967.

H. B. MATTINGLY, 'The Growth of Athenian Imperialism', *Hist.* xii (1963), 257–73.

—— 'Periclean Imperialism', *Ehrenberg Studies*, 193–224.

R. MEIGGS, 'The Growth of Athenian Imperialism', *JHS* lxiii (1943), 21–34.

—— 'A Note on Athenian Imperialism', *CR* lxiii (1949), 9–12.

—— 'The Crisis of Athenian Imperialism', *Harv. Stud.* lxvii (1963), 1–36.

B. D. MERITT, 'Athens and the Delian League', *The Greek Political Experience*, Studies in honor of W. K. Prentice, Princeton, 1941.

B. D. MERITT, H. T. WADE-GERY, and M. F. MCGREGOR, *The Athenian Tribute Lists*, vol. iii.

H. NESSELHAUF, *Untersuchung zur Geschichte der delisch-attischen Symmachie*, *Klio*, Beiheft 30, 1933.

H. POPP, 'Athens' Relations with the Allies', *Hist.* xviii (1969), 425–43.

T. J. QUINN, 'Thucydides and the Unpopularity of the Athenian Empire', *Hist.* xiii (1964), 257–66.

H. SCHAEFER, 'Die attische Symmachie im zweiten Jahrzehnt ihres Bestehens', *Hermes* lxxi (1936), 129–50.

—— 'Beiträge zur Geschichte der attischen Symmachie', *Hermes* lxxiv (1939), 225–64.

(2) ORGANIZATION AND ADMINISTRATION

J. P. BARRON, 'Religious Propaganda of the Delian League', *JHS* lxxxiv (1964), 35–48.

P. A. BRUNT, 'The Hellenic League against Persia', *Hist.* ii (1953–4), 135–63.

G. E. M. DE STE CROIX, 'Jurisdiction in the Athenian Empire', *CQ* xi (1961), 94–112 and 268–80.

S. K. EDDY, 'Athens' Peacetime Navy in the Age of Pericles', *Gk. Rom. Byz. Stud.* ix (1968), 141–56.

N. G. L. HAMMOND, 'Origins and Nature of the Athenian Alliance', *JHS* lxxxvii (1967), 41–61.

A. R. W. HARRISON, '[Demosthenes] *De Halonneso* 13', *CQ* x (1960), 248–52.

590 SELECT BIBLIOGRAPHY

R. J. Hopper, 'Interstate Juridical Agreements in the Athenian Empire', *JHS* lxiii (1943), 35–51.

H. W. Jackson, 'The Original Purpose of the Delian League', *Hist.* xviii (1969), 12–16.

A. H. M. Jones, 'Two Synods of the Delian and Peloponnesian Leagues', *Proc. Camb. Phil. Soc.* ii (1952–3), 43–6.

A. Kirchoff, 'Der delische Bund im ersten Decennium seines Bestehens', *Hermes* xi (1876), 1–48.

J. A. O. Larsen, 'The Constitution and Original Purpose of the Delian League', *Harv. Stud.* li (1940), 175–213.

H. D. Meyer, 'Vorgeschichte und Begründung des delisch-attischen Seebundes', *Hist.* xii (1963), 405–46.

A. S. Nease, 'Garrisons in the Athenian Empire', *Phoenix* iii (1949), 102–11.

R. Sealey, 'The Origin of the Delian League', *Ehrenberg Studies*, 233–55.

(3) RELATIONS WITH PERSIA

J. Barnes, 'Cimon and the First Athenian Expedition to Cyprus', *Hist.* ii (1953–4), 163–76.

C. W. Fornara, 'Aspects of Pausanias', *Hist.* xv (1966), 257–71.

U. Hausmann, 'Akropolisscherben und Eurymedonkämpfe', *Charites* (ed. J. Schauenburg), Bonn, 1957, pp. 144–51.

M. Lang, 'Scapegoat Pausanias', *Class. Journ.* lxiii (1967), 79–85.

D. M. Lewis, 'The Phoenician Fleet in 411', *Hist.* vii (1958), 392–7.

H. B. Mattingly, 'The Peace of Kallias', *Hist.* xiv (1965), 273–81.

E. Müller, 'Der Cimonische Friede', *Rh. Mus.* xiv (1959), 151–3.

J. H. Oliver, 'The Peace of Kallias and the Pontic Expedition of Pericles', *Hist.* vi (1957), 254–5.

A. E. Raubitschek, 'The Treaties between Persia and Athens', *Gk. Rom. Byz. Stud.* v (1964), 151–9.

—— 'The Peace Policy of Pericles', *AJA* lxx (1966), 37–41.

G. M. A. Richter, 'Greeks in Persia', *AJA* l (1946), 15–30.

P. Salmon, *La Politique égyptienne d'Athènes*, Brussels, 1965.

J. D. Smart, 'Kimon's Capture of Eion', *JHS* lxxxvii (1967), 136–7.

D. Stockton, 'The Peace of Kallias', *Hist.* viii (1959), 61–79.

H. T. Wade-Gery, 'The Peace of Kallias', *Essays in Greek History*, 201–32.

(4) TRIBUTE AND OTHER ECONOMIC ASPECTS

A. D. Amyx, 'The Attic Stelai' (sale records of the property of the Hermokopidai), Part III (vases and containers), *Hesp.* xxvii (1958), 163–307.

A. Böckh, *Die Staatshaushaltung der Athener*, Berlin, 1886.

E. Cavaignac, *Population et capital dans le monde méditerranéen antique*, Strasbourg, 1923.

M. Chambers, 'Four Hundred Sixty Talents', *CP* liii (1958), 26–32.

S. Dow, 'Studies in the Athenian Tribute Lists', *CP* xxxvii (1942), 371–84, and xxxviii (1943), 20–7.

S. K. EDDY, ''Επιφορά in the Tribute Lists', *AJP* lxxxix (1968), 129–43.

—— '460 Talents again', *CP* lxiii (1968), 184–95.

M. I. FINLEY, 'Trade and Politics in the Ancient World', *Second International Congress of Economic History*, vol. i, Paris and The Hague, 1965, pp. 11–35.

A. FRENCH, *The Growth of the Athenian Economy*, London, 1964.

A. H. M. JONES, 'The Economic Basis of the Athenian Democracy', *Athenian Democracy* (Oxford, 1957), pp. 3–20.

F. A. LEPPER, 'Some Rubrics on the Athenian Quota-Lists', *JHS* lxxxii (1962), 25–55.

M. F. McGREGOR, 'The Postscript of the First Attic Quota-List', *Gk. Rom. Byz. Stud.* viii (1967), 103–12.

H. B. MATTINGLY, 'The Athenian Coinage Decree', *Hist.* x (1961), 148–88.

—— 'The Methone Decrees', *CQ* xi (1961), 154–65.

—— 'The Financial Decrees of Kallias', *Proc. Afr. Class. Ass.* vii (1964), 35–55.

—— 'The Date of the Kallias Decrees', *BSA* lxii (1967), 14–17.

—— 'Athenian Finances in the Peloponnesian War', *BCH* xcii (1968), 450–85.

B. D. MERITT, 'Tribute Assessments of the Athenian Empire from 454 to 440 B.C.', *AJA* xxix (1925), 247–71.

—— 'Reconstruction of the Tribute Lists', *AJA* xxxiii (1929), 376–84.

—— *Athenian Financial Documents*, Ann Arbor, 1932.

—— 'The Tribute Assessment of 410 B.C.', *Hesp.* v (1936), 386–9.

—— *Documents on Athenian Tribute*, Cambridge (Mass.), 1937.

—— '*IG* i². 24', *Hesp.* x (1941), 307–15.

—— 'The Early Athenian Tribute Lists', *CP* xxxviii (1943), 223–39.

—— 'Athens and the Amphiktionic League', *AJP* lxxv (1954), 369–76.

—— 'The Top of the First Tribute Stele', *Hesp.* xxxv (1966), 134–40.

—— 'The Second Athenian Assessment Period', *Gk. Rom. Byz. Stud.* viii (1967), 121–32.

B. D. MERITT and A. B. WEST, 'Cleon's Amphipolitan Campaign', *AJA* xxix (1925), 56–69.

—— *The Athenian Assessment of 425 B.C.*, Ann Arbor, 1934.

B. D. MERITT and H. T. WADE-GERY, 'Pylos and the Assessment of Tribute', *AJP* lvii (1936), 377–94.

—— 'Athenian Resources in 449 and 431 B.C.', *Hesp.* xxvi (1957), 163–97.

—— 'The Dating of Documents to the Mid-Fifth Century', *JHS* lxxxii (1962), 67–74, and lxxxiii (1963), 100–17.

B. D. MERITT and M. F. McGREGOR, 'The Athenian Quota List of 421/0', *Phoenix* xxi (1967), 85–6.

B. D. MERITT, H. T. WADE-GERY, and M. F. McGREGOR, *The Athenian Tribute Lists*, 4 vols., Cambridge (Mass.), i, Princeton, ii–iv, 1939–53.

O. MURRAY, "'Ο ΑΡΧΑΙΟΣ ΔΑΣΜΟΣ", *Hist.* xv (1966), 142–56.

H. NESSELHAUF, *Untersuchung zur Geschichte der delisch-attischen Symmachie*, *Klio*, Beiheft 30, 1933.

W. K. PRITCHETT, 'The Attic Stelai', Part II (products and prices), *Hesp.* xxv (1956), 178–317.

—— 'The three-barred sigma at Kos', *BCH* lxxxvii (1963), 20–3.

W. K. Pritchett, 'The Koan Fragment of the Monetary Decree', *BCH* lxxxix (1965), 423–40.

—— 'The Top of the Lapis Primus', *Gk. Rom. Byz. Stud.* vii (1966), 123–9.

—— 'The Location of the Lapis Primus', *Gk. Rom. Byz. Stud.* viii (1967), 113–19.

—— 'The Transfer of the Delian Treasury', *Hist.* xviii (1969), 17–21.

H. T. Wade-Gery, 'The Question of Tribute in 449/8 B.C.', *Hesp.* xiv (1945), 212–19.

A. B. West, 'Aristidean Tribute in the Assessment of 421 B.C.', *AJA* xxix (1925), 135–51.

—— 'The Tribute Lists and the Non-tributary Members of the Delian League', *Am. Hist. Rev.* xxxv (1929–30), 267–75.

A. G. Woodhead, 'The Institution of the Hellenotamiae', *JHS* lxxix (1959), 149–52.

(5) ALLIED CITIES

J. P. Barron, 'Milesian Politics and Athenian Propaganda, *c.* 460–440 B.C.', *JHS* lxxxii (1962), 1–6.

I. B. Brashinsky, *Athens and the Northern Black Sea Area in the 6th to 2nd Centuries B.C.* (in Russian), Moscow, 1963.

J. M. Cook, 'The Problem of Classical Ionia', *Proc. Camb. Phil. Soc.* vii (1961), 9–18.

A. J. Earp, 'Athens and Miletus *c.* 450 B.C.', *Phoenix* viii (1954), 42–7.

L. I. Highby, *The Erythrae Decree*, *Klio*, Beiheft 36, 1936.

R. P. Legon, 'Megara and Mytilene', *Phoenix* xxii (1968), 200–25.

D. M. MacDowell, 'Aigina and the Delian League', *JHS* lxxx (1960), 118–21.

H. B. Mattingly, 'Athens and Euboea', *JHS* lxxxi (1961), 124–32.

—— 'Athens and Aegina', *Hist.* xvi (1967), 1–5.

B. D. Meritt, 'Athens and the Amphiktionic League', *AJP* lxxv (1954), 369–76.

P. Perdrizet, 'Scaptésylé', *Klio* x (1910), 1–27.

H. W. Pleket, 'Thasos and the Popularity of the Athenian Empire', *Hist.* xii (1963), 70–7.

J. Pouilloux, *Recherches sur l'histoire et les cultes de Thasos*, vol. i, Paris, 1954.

T. J. Quinn, 'Political Groups at Chios', *Hist.* xviii (1969), 22–30.

W. P. Wallace, *The Euboean League*, New York, 1956.

(6) INSCRIPTIONS AND MONUMENTS

S. Accame, 'Note storiche su epigrafi attiche del v secolo', *RF* lxxx (1952), 111–36 and 223–45.

A. Boegehold, '*IG* i². 24', *Class. Stud. presented to B. E. Perry*, Urbana, 1969, pp. 175–80.

D. W. Bradeen, 'The Athenian Casualty Lists', *CQ* xix (1969), 145–59.

J. A. Bundgaard, *Mnesicles: a Greek architect at work*, Copenhagen, 1957.

J. Coupry, 'Études d'épigraphie délienne I', *BCH* lxi (1937), 364–79.

F. Courby, *Fouilles de Délos XII. Les Temples d'Apollon*, Paris, 1931.

M. Crosby, 'The Altar of the Twelve Gods', *Hesp.*, Suppl. viii (1949), 97–103.

W. B. Dinsmoor, 'Observations on the Hephaesteion', *Hesp.*, Suppl. v (1941).

—— *The Architecture of Ancient Greece³*, London, 1950.

—— 'Two Monuments on the Acropolis', Χαριστήριον εἰς Ἀναστάσιον κ. Ὀρλάνδον, vol. iv, Athens, 1967–8, pp. 145–55.

F. J. Frost, 'Some Documents in Plutarch's Lives', *Class. et Med.* xxii (1961), 182–94.

Chr. Habicht, 'Falsche Urkunden zur Geschichte Athens im Zeitalter der Perserkriege', *Hermes* lxxxix (1961), 1–35.

C. G. Herington, *Athena Parthenos and Athena Polias*, Manchester, 1955.

L. I. Highby, *The Erythrae Decree, Klio*, Beiheft 36, 1936.

L. H. Jeffery, 'The Battle of Oinoe in the Stoa Poikile', *BSA* lx (1965), 41–57.

W. Judeich, *Topographie von Athen²*, Munich, 1931.

U. Köhler, 'Herakleides der Klazomenier', *Hermes* xxvii (1892), 68–78.

R. Meiggs, 'The Political Implications of the Parthenon', *Greece and Rome* x (1963), Suppl., 36–45.

—— 'The Dating of Fifth-century Attic Inscriptions', *JHS* lxxxvi (1966), 86–98.

R. Meiggs and D. M. Lewis, *A Selection of Greek Historical Inscriptions to the End of the Fifth Century B.C.*, Oxford, 1969.

B. D. Meritt, '*IG* i². 24', *Hesp.* x (1941), 307–15.

—— 'An Athenian Decree (*IG* i². 97)', *Robinson Studies* ii. 298–303.

B. D. Meritt and H. T. Wade-Gery, 'The Dating of Documents to the mid fifth century', *JHS* lxxxii (1962), 67–74, and lxxxiii (1963), 100–17.

W. H. Plommer, 'Three Attic Temples', *JHS* xlv (1950), 66–112.

J. Pouilloux, *La Forteresse de Rhamnous*, Paris, 1954.

C. M. Robertson, *Greek Painting*, Geneva, 1959.

R. Seager, 'The Phaselis Decree', *Hist.* xv (1966), 509f.

—— 'The Congress Decree: some doubts and a hypothesis', *Hist.* xviii (1969), 129–41.

I. M. Shear, 'Kallikrates', *Hesp.* xxxii (1963), 378–424.

H. A. Thompson, 'Buildings on the west side of the Agora', *Hesp.* vi (1937), 1–224.

—— 'The Stoa Poikile', *Hesp.* xix (1950), 327–8.

C. Tiberi, *Mnesicle l'architetto dei Propylei*, Città di Castello, 1964.

R. Vallois, *L'Architecture hellénique et hellénistique à Délos*, vol. i, Paris, 1944.

G. Welter, 'Von Nikepyrgos', *Arch. Anz.* liv (1939), 1–22.

(7) THE LITERARY SOURCES

A. Andrewes, 'The Melian Dialogue and Pericles' Last Speech', *Proc. Camb. Phil. Soc.* vi (1960), 1–10.

—— 'Thucydides and the Persians', *Hist.* x (1961), 1–18.

—— 'The Mytilenaean Debate', *Phoenix* xvi (1962), 64–85.

C. M. Bowra, *Greek Lyric Poetry*², Oxford, 1961.

W. R. Connor, *Theopompus and Fifth Century History*, Cambridge (Mass.), 1968.

K. J. Dover, 'The Chronology of Antiphon's Speeches', *CQ* xliv (1950), 44–60.

J. H. Finley, *Three Essays on Thucydides*, Cambridge (Mass.), 1967.

W. G. Forrest, 'Aristophanes' Acharnians', *Phoenix* xvii (1963), 1–12.

A. W. Gomme, 'Aristophanes and Politics', *CR* lii (1938), 97–109.

—— *A Historical Commentary on Thucydides*, 3 vols. (to v. 24), Oxford, 1945–56.

G. L. Huxley, 'Ion of Chios', *Gk. Rom. Byz. Stud.* vi (1965), 129–46.

F. Jacoby, 'Herodotus', *RE*, Suppl. ii. 205–520.

—— 'Ktesias', *RE* xxxi (1922), 2032–73.

—— 'Some Remarks on Ion of Chios', *CQ* xli (1947), 16–17.

B. Keil, *Anonymus Argentinensis*, Strasbourg, 1901.

W. Kolbe, 'Diodors Wert für die Geschichte der Pentekontaetia', *Hermes* lxxii (1932), 241–69.

A. von Mess, 'Untersuchung über die Arbeitsweise Diodors', *Rh. Mus.* lxi (1906), 244–66.

G. Norwood, 'The *Babylonians* of Aristophanes', *CP* xxv (1930), 1–10.

A. J. Podlecki, 'Simonides: 480', *Hist.* xvii (1968), 257–75.

A. E. Raubitschek, 'Two Notes on Isocrates', *TAPA* lxii (1941), 356–62.

J. de Romilly, *Thucydide et l'impérialisme athénien*, Paris, 1947; trs. P. Thody, Oxford, 1963.

F. Schachermeyer, *Stesimbrotos und seine Schrift über die Staatsmänner*, Vienna, 1965.

E. Schwarz, 'Diodoros', *RE* v (1903), 663–704.

H. Strasburger, 'Thucydides und die politische Selbstdarstellung der Athener', *Hermes* lxxxvi (1958), 17–40.

E. G. Turner, 'ΦΙΛΟΔΙΚΕΙΝ ΔΟΚΟΥΜΕΝ, Thuc. i. 77', *CR* lx (1946), 5–8.

H. D. Westlake, 'Thucydides and the Athenian Disaster in Egypt', *CP* xlv (1950), 209–16.

U. Wilcken, 'Der Anonymus Argentinensis', *Hermes* xlii (1907), 374–418.

(8) MISCELLANEOUS

F. E. Adcock, 'Alcidas ἀργυρολόγος', *Mélanges Glotz*, I, Paris, 1932, pp. 1–6.

A. Amit, *Athens and the Sea*, Brussels, 1965.

J. A. Davison, 'Protagoras, Democritus, and Anaxagoras', *CQ* xlvii (1953), 33–45.

E. Derenne, *Les Procès d'impiété intentés aux philosophes à Athénes au 5ᵉ et au 4ᵉ siècles avant J.-C.*, Liège, 1930.

L. Deubner, *Attische Feste*, Berlin, 1932.

V. Ehrenberg, 'The Foundation of Thurii', *AJP* lxix (1948), 149–70.

W. G. Forrest, 'Themistocles and Argos', *CQ* x (1960), 221–41.

F. J. Frost, 'Pericles and Dracontides', *JHS* lxxxiv (1964), 69–72.

—— 'Pericles and Thucydides, son of Melesias, and Athenian Politics before the War', *Hist.* xiii (1964), 385–99.

—— 'Themistocles' Place in Athenian Politics', *Cal. Stud. Clas. Ant.* i (1968), 105–24.

H. Gallet de Santerre, *Délos primitive et archaïque*, Paris, 1958.

A. W. Gomme, *The Population of Athens in the Fifth and Fourth Centuries*, Oxford, 1933.

A. J. Graham, *Colony and Mother City in Ancient Greece*, Manchester, 1964.

C. Hignett, *A History of the Athenian Constitution*, Oxford, 1952.

A. H. M. Jones, *Athenian Democracy*, Oxford, 1957.

J. A. O. Larsen, 'The Constitution of the Peloponnesian League', *CP* xxviii (1933), 257–76, and xxix (1934), 1–19.

H. W. Parke, 'The Development of the Second Spartan Empire', *JHS* l (1930), 37–50.

G. Prestel, *Die antidemokratische Strömung in Athen zum Tod des Perikles*, Breslau, 1939.

D. W. Reece, 'The Battle of Tanagra', *JHS* lxx (1955), 75–6.

M. Sordi, 'Le Premier Congrès panhellénique et la décadence de l'Amphictionie', *BCH* lxxxi (1957), 61–5.

—— 'La posizione di Delfi e dell'Amphizionia nel decennio tra Tanagra e Coronea', *RF* xxxvi (1958), 48–65.

A. E. Taylor, 'On the Date of the Trial of Anaxagoras', *CQ* xi (1917), 81–7.

H. T. Wade-Gery, 'Thucydides son of Melesias', *Essays*, 239–70.

M. E. White, 'Some Agiad Dates: Pausanias and his sons', *JHS* lxxxiv (1964), 140–52.

A. G. Woodhead, 'The Site of Brea, Thucydides i. 61. 4', *CQ* xlvi (1952), 57–62.

(9) NUMISMATICS

J. P. Barron, *The Silver Coins of Samos*, London, 1966.

—— 'The Fifth-century Diskoboloi of Kos', *Robinson Essays*, 75–89.

B. Fowler, 'Thucydides i. 107–8 and the Tanagra Federal Issues', *Phoenix* xi (1957), 164–70.

P. Gardner, 'Coinage of the Athenian Empire', *JHS* xxxiii (1933), 147–88.

C. M. Kraay and P. R. S. Mooney, 'Two Fifth Century Hoards', *Rev. Num.* x (1969), 181–235.

D. M. Lewis, 'New Evidence for the Gold–Silver Ratio', *Robinson Essays*, 105–10.

J. M. F. May, *Ainos, its History and Coinage, 474–341 B.C.*, Oxford, 1950.

—— *The Coinage of Abdera, 540–345 B.C.* (ed. C. M. Kraay and G. K. Jenkins), London, 1966.

P. Rajo, 'Il cambio di Tartaruga ad Egina', *Riv. Num.* lv (1963), 7–15.

E. S. G. Robinson, 'Persia: Tissaphernes', *Num. Chron.* 1948, 48–55.

—— 'The Athenian Currency Decree', *Hesp.*, Suppl. viii (1949), 324–40.

—— 'A Hoard of Archaic Greek Coins from Anatolia', *Num. Chron.* 1961, 107–17.

C. Seltman, *Greek Coins*[2], London, 1955.

W. E. Thompson, 'Gold and Silver Ratios at Athens', *Num. Chron.* 1964, 103–23.

H. T. Wade-Gery, 'Attic Fifth-century Gold Ratios', *Num. Chron.* 1930, 16–38 with 333 f.

SUPPLEMENTARY BIBLIOGRAPHY
1969–1971

(1) A. ANDREWES and K. J. DOVER, *Gomme's Historical Commentary on Thucydides*, vol. iv (v. 25–vii), Oxford, 1970.

(2) D. ASHERI, 'The Site of Brea', *AJP* xc (1969), 337–40.

(3) D. BLACKMAN, 'The Athenian Navy and Allied Naval Contributions in the Pentecontaetia', *Gk. Rom. Byz. Stud.* x (1969), 179–216.

(4) J. S. BOERSMA, *Athenian Building Policy from 561/0 to 405/4 B.C.*, Groningen, 1970.

(5) H. A. CAHN, *Knidos, die Münzen des sechsten und des fünften Jahrhunderts v. Chr.*, Berlin, 1970.

(6) RHYS CARPENTER, *The Architects of the Parthenon*, London, 1970.

(7) G. L. CAWKELL, 'The Fall of Themistocles', *Essays presented to M. Blaiklock* (ed. B. F. Harris), Auckland, 1971, pp. 39–58.

(8) S. K. EDDY, 'On the Peace of Callias', *CP* lxv (1970), 8–14.

(9) E. ERXLEBEN, 'Das Münzgesetz des delisch-attischen Seebundes', *Archiv für Papyrusforschung* xix (1969), 85–139.

(10) C. W. FORNARA, 'The Date of the Callias Decrees', *Gk. Rom. Byz. Stud.* xi (1970), 185–96.

(11) —— *Herodotus, An Interpretative Essay*, Oxford, 1971.

(12) J. R. GREEN and R. K. SINCLAIR, 'Athenians in Eretria', *Hist.* xix (1970), 515–27.

(13) P. HERMANN, 'Zu den Beziehungen zwischen Athen und Milet im 5. Jahrhundert', *Klio* lii (1970), 163–73.

(14) D. KAGAN, *The Outbreak of the Peloponnesian War*, Ithaca, 1969.

(15) H. B. MATTINGLY, 'Athens and the Western Greeks: c. 500–413 B.C.', *Atti del I Convegno del Centro Internazionale di Studi Numismatici*, Rome, 1969, pp. 201–22.

(16) —— ' "Epigraphically the Twenties are too late" ', *BSA* lxv (1970), 129–49.

(17) LUCY SHOE MERITT, 'The Stoa Poikile', *Hesp.* xxxix (1970), 233–64.

(18) C. L. MURISON, 'The Peace of Callias: its Historical Context', *Phoenix* xxv (1971), 12–31.

(19) R. SEALEY, 'Notes on Tribute-Quota Lists 5, 6, and 7 of the Athenian Empire', *Phoenix* xxiv (1970), 13–28.

(20) C. G. STARR, *Athenian Coinage, 480–449 B.C.*, Oxford, 1970.

(21) W. E. THOMPSON, 'Notes on the Peace of Callias', *CP* lxvi (1971), 29–30.

(22) A. G. WOODHEAD, *Thucydides on the Nature of Power* (Martin Classical Lectures), Cambridge (Mass.), 1970.

The most challenging and enjoyable of these latest contributions is Rhys Carpenter's revolutionary study of the Parthenon (6). By converging arguments from archaeological evidence and architectural styles he has inferred a new Cimonian temple of Athena between the uncompleted temple that the Persians destroyed in 480 and the Periclean Parthenon begun in 447. This 'lost' temple, on the platform built in the eighties, was designed by Callicrates, and the columns had been erected and some of the metopes prepared when Cimon died. On his death Callicrates was dismissed and replaced by Ictinus who, under Pericles' guidance, dismantled what had been built but re-used the columns, spacing them more closely, reduced the metopes to fit the new spacing, and enlarged the platform for a slightly larger temple. The change of political leadership also meant the abandonment of the temple of Athena Nike, a project which had been initiated c. 449 by Cimonians and entrusted to Callicrates, and it was not until Pericles' death that Callicrates could carry out his commission. If this thesis were right my acceptance of the Plataean Oath not to rebuild the temples destroyed by the Persians (App. 10A, pp. 504 ff.) would be barely tenable and my assumption that Callicrates was a Periclean (pp. 502 f.) would have to be discarded. For the historian the main difficulty will be the fact that there is not even a hint of this pre-Periclean temple in the sources. If the Cimonian temple had been carried as far as the metopes and then dismantled some echo should have survived even if only in a scholiast's note on a passage from a lost comedy. When Plutarch said that the Parthenon was built by Callicrates and Ictinus (Plut. *Per.* 13. 7 : τὸν μὲν γὰρ ἑκατόμπεδον Παρθενῶνα Καλλικράτης εἰργάζετο καὶ Ἰκτῖνος) he clearly thought that they worked together on the same building. Nor will the picture of a bitter feud between Cimon and Pericles be widely accepted, though it is not impossible. However, the verdict does not lie with the historian. The basic thesis of a Cimonian precursor of the Parthenon could be right even if the historical framework were misjudged. Nor need the argument from the silence of the surviving sources be quite decisive. We hear very little indeed about the background to building policies; there is nothing, for example, in our sources about the relationship of the Propylaea to the temple of Athena Nike though it is commonly held that the plans reveal a sharp conflict of interests. The ingenious combination of independent arguments from the Parthenon itself is the crux of the matter and only those who are thoroughly familiar with the architecture and sculpture of the period are entitled to judge. I await the verdict of experts to confirm my own doubts.

J. S. Boersma's book (4) also raises new questions about Athenian building policy and I am attracted by his view that the Hephaesteon is the culmination of a Cimonian concentration on the Agora, rather than the beginning of a Periclean programme. I should also have considered more seriously the role of Hippodamus in the Piraeus. It is certain that some basic planning must have been done immediately after the return of the Athenians to Athens in 479, when Themistocles is said to have continued what he began as archon in 493/2 (Thuc. i. 93. 3). The allocation of areas between the navy and commerce may well have been done then, but the naming of the civil Agora after Hippodamus suggests that he was concerned with the later planning of the area behind the ports rather than with a master-plan in the early seventies as Boersma, following Martin, prefers.

The mid-century period remains very controversial. Statistically an article on the Peace of Callias can be expected every two years; three in eighteen months is extravagance. Supporters of the peace need not feel discomfited by C. L. Murison's attack (18). Reviewing the evidence chronologically he concludes that from the first mention by Isocrates in 380 down to Demosthenes' *De Falsa Legatione* in 343 all is vague rhetoric. Murison concludes that terms were invented and published between 352, when Demosthenes is still vague, and 343. This view is inconsistent with the natural meaning of Isocrates iv. 120 which implies that the terms of a fifth-century peace could be *read* as early as 380 and it requires the less natural meaning of φόρων ἐνίους τάττοντας (see above, p. 136). And would Theopompus have attacked the Ionic letters of a stele set up as late as c. 350? Murison also rejects Andocides' evidence for a later treaty with the Persians, but he does not mention the decree of Heraclides, which strongly supports Andocides (above, pp. 134 ff.). On the other hand sceptics may not be convinced by S. K. Eddy's support for the peace (8). Plutarch, after saying that Craterus included a copy of the Peace of Callias in his collection of decrees, proceeds: 'and they say (φασὶ δέ) that this is why the Athenians set up an altar of Peace, and specially honoured Callias who had been their ambassador'. Eddy infers that the evidence for the altar of Peace and the honouring of Callias must derive ultimately from copies of the decrees by which they were authorized. While one forgery might be acceptable, three separate forgeries are too many. Not every one will agree with this interpretation of φασὶ δέ. Eddy also cites the dismantling of Ionian fortifications as proof of the peace, but this could be differently explained (above, p. 150). W. E. Thompson (21) makes two interesting new points. He argues convincingly that Livy's reference to the peace (Livy xxxiii. 20. 1–3) derives from Polybius, who must therefore have thought it genuine: but did Polybius do any independent research? In a second note he makes sense of the Persian King's demand in Thuc. viii. 56. 4 that he should be allowed to build ships by reference to Xenophon, *Hell.* i. 1. 25, where the satrap Pharnabazus urges his Greek allies to build ships from the timber of Ida at Antandros. The debate on the Peace of Callias will continue.

The tribute lists of the second period (450–446) also raise problems that have not yet been satisfactorily solved, and particularly the mystery of the 'missing list'. Sealey (19) accepts Pritchett's thesis that there was a further list on the back of a separate stone crowning the first stele, and rejects the restoration $M[\epsilon\tau\grave{a}\ \Delta\iota o\nu\acute{v}\sigma\iota a]$ as a heading for the last nine names of list 7 (which Sealey numbers 6). There are indeed good reasons for rejecting the restoration, but Sealey's own suggestion that these cities were separately listed in recognition of their outstanding loyalty when their neighbours were disaffected is not more convincing. Mattingly (16) resumes his campaign for redating to the twenties many of the decrees for which a date before 445 has been more widely accepted. I still see no reason to abandon the criterion that the three-barred sigma was obsolete by 445 until the form is found in a later inscription that is explicitly dated. It is not sufficient to show that the twenties provide a good historical context, or even a better historical context; it must also be shown that a date in the forties or fifties is incompatible with the historical context. Mattingly's new argument to support his dating of the Milesian Decree D. 11 in 426/5 depends on his dating of tribute list 25 in 426/5; the objections to that date have been set out above (App. 13, pp. 531 ff.). The case for down-dating the decree recording Athens' alliance with Egesta (*IG* i². 37) is stronger. Mattingly (15) shows that there is no evidence in the literary sources or coins for active Athenian interest in the west before the intervention at Sybaris. This, however, is not inconsistent with an appeal by Egesta in the fifties to the strongest naval power in Greece, and the acceptance by Athens of an alliance in the buoyant mood that followed the reforms of Ephialtes and the first successes in Egypt. If the Egesta inscription, in spite of its three-barred sigma and rounded rho with tail, is to be dated in 421/20 or 418/17 as Mattingly urges, why do the Egestan envoys in Thucydides, when appealing for Athenian help in 415, not even mention their recent alliance?

The epigraphic evidence for the Coinage Decree and the Peace of Clinias is less clear-cut. My dating of the Clinias Decree in 447 is based on an identification of the mover with the father of Alcibiades, and the irregularities reflected in tribute lists 7 and 8. Epigraphically there would be no objection to the thirties, but largely on the strength of the curving upsilons I would still exclude the twenties; nor am I convinced by Mattingly's arguments that the Clinias Decree is later than the Collectors Decree, moved by Cleonymus in 426 (ML 68). The epigraphic argument from the Coinage Decree is again different. Only one of the seven fragments is in Attic script and that may have been cut in Cos rather than Athens. The use of the three-barred sigma in this copy therefore has less force than if it were found in Athens. The other six fragments are in Ionic and the large Olynthus fragment in particular (phot. *ATL* ii pl. 6) seems later than the forties. I now understand also that Russian scholars would date the Odessa fragment late in the fifth century; but we have very few fifth-century Ionic inscriptions which are firmly dated to act as guide. Mattingly's point that the copy on the island of Syme is not likely to have been cut before the incorporation of the island in the Athenian empire, probably in 434/3, favours the later date, though it might reflect an Athenian attempt to reactivate the decree.

The coins themselves still cannot decide the issue, but for the first time the coinage of Athens herself has been brought into the centre of the argument. Hitherto the conservatism of the Athenian mint has discouraged attempts to establish a chronology for the coins of the fifth century, but C. G. Starr (20), after the systematic examination of a very wide sample, has succeeded in devising a defensible classification, dividing the coins between two main periods. The coins of the first period after 480 are distributed between five distinguishable groups, and the very small number of surviving coins suggests that during this period the output of the Athenian mint was very modest until the fifth group. The second period is marked by a massive output of coins which continues the basic patterns of obverse and reverse, but in a simplified and standardized form. In a hoard from the Acropolis there is good evidence for the beginning of the first period in 480, and Starr's criteria for distinguishing his five groups of this period are convincing, but his date for the change is derived from historical argument. He attributes the sharp increase in the output of the Athenian mint to the need for converting foreign currencies in the tribute reserve brought to Athens from Delos in 454 in order to pay in Attic coin for the building programme and the maintenance of the Athenian fleet. The same need, he thinks, determined the issue of the Coinage Decree at the same time, in 449 when peace had been made with Persia. This is an attractive hypothesis, but not decisive evidence for the early date. The re-minting of part of the tribute reserve need not carry with it a ban on allied mints, and part of the increase in output could be attributed to a more intensive exploitation of the Laurium mines.

Meanwhile E. Erxleben (9) has published two parts of a study in depth of the epigraphic, numismatic, and historical aspects of the decree. After an examination of allied coinages mint by mint in rather more detail than Robinson he finds barely any evidence for a break *c.* 450, but considerably more *c.* 465. His conclusion is that the coin evidence gives no clear support either for the early or for the later dating of the decree. His final conclusions are not yet published but the general direction of his argument seems to point against the early forties. The strength of his inferences from the numismatic evidence, however, depends on the dating by style of a very wide range of coins, and here the margin of error is considerable. It should, however, be possible to get firmer evidence from the few states from which sufficient issues survive to provide a basis for classification. J. M. F. May found a break in the coinages of both Aenus and Abdera somewhere near the middle of the century, and now H. A. Cahn, in his detailed study of the coins of Cnidus (5), has found a similar break at roughly the same time. One cannot expect a precise date for these breaks, but we cannot assume a miscalculation of more than twenty years. If these breaks are the result of the Coinage Decree the decree must be considerably earlier than the middle twenties. Historically either date would provide an appropriate context. If the late date proved to be correct it would not seriously modify my conception of the forties as a period of strong imperialism in the teeth of widespread discontent among the allies.

For my reconstruction of the political atmosphere in Greece before the outbreak of the Peloponnesian War I have attached considerable importance to the dating of the financial decrees of Callias in 434/3. Mattingly (15) has restored *IG* i². 300 to support his view that the treasurers of the other gods in *IG* i². 310 are a provisional board and not the standard permanent board provided by decree A, but I hope that the arguments of my Appendix 11 (above, p. 520) remain valid against any date in the twenties. C. W. Fornara (10) has revived Beloch's dating in 418–17, but his basic assumption seems to me unsound. He regards the pre-war dating as incompatible with Thucydides' narrative and the historical situation in 434/3: there could have been no serious talk of evacuating the treasures of the temples of Attica before the open clash with Corinth at the battle of Sybota. In this Fornara minimizes Thucydides' statement that the reason why Athens accepted the alliance with Corcyra was that war seemed inevitable (Thuc. i. 44. 2) and he ignores the Corcyraean claim at Athens that the Lacedaemonians were itching for war (Thuc. i. 33. 3: τοὺς Λακεδαιμονίους φόβῳ τῷ ὑμετέρῳ πολεμησείοντας). There are other difficulties. After 421 we expect public decrees to include the archon's name in their prescript; and, as Kolbe emphasized against Beloch, *IG* i². 370 of 421/20, with its ten treasurers, each named with deme, implies a board of the standard pattern. Fornara dismisses decree B from the argument owing to the very poor state of the text, but the direction to the treasurers of Athena to publish inventories is beyond question and the first inventories date from 433/2.

Miletus, Eretria, and Brea are the subject of shorter studies. Though it seems highly probable that a democracy was installed at Miletus soon after the mid century the first surviving Milesian decree with an Athenian-type prescript was from 380. P. Hermann (13) has now published an inscription, almost certainly from 437/6, with the typical Athenian formulae, a further argument against Mattingly's dating to 426/5 of the Athenian decree laying down regulations for the control of Miletus (D. 11). The detailed review of certain forms of Attic pottery found in Eretria, choes as well as white lekythoi, by J. R. Green and R. K. Sinclair (12), strengthens the view that there was an Athenian settlement at Eretria (above, p. 566). I find less comfort in D. Asheri's argument that the general context of the fragment of Theopompus which refers to Brea favours the location of the Athenian colony in Chalcidice (2), but the reasons for choosing a site near Argilus (p. 159) still seems strong to me.

D. Blackman's article on the navy of the Delian League (3) usefully raises issues which I have passed over too lightly. I also wish I had been able to read Fornara's stimulating interpretation of Herodotus earlier (11). We have much in common and it would be interesting to discuss the divergences.

SELECT INDEX OF CLASSICAL
REFERENCES

INDEX OF INSCRIPTIONS

The numbers in the second column refer to Meiggs and Lewis, *Greek Historical Inscriptions*, unless otherwise stated. D-numbers refer to *The Athenian Tribute Lists*, vol. ii, *SEG* to *Supplementum Epigraphicum Graecum*.

GENERAL INDEX

Abdera, 26, 61, 158, 286; tribute, 526, 529, 532

Abydus, 26; tribute, 526

Acanthus, 52, 211, 334 f., 525, 526

Acarnania, 122, 204

Achaea, 182

Achaemenes, 93, 474

Achaemenides, 474

Acharnae, 155, 504

Acheloion, 227

Acropolis, Athenian, south wall, 66; work suspended in 432 B.C., 201; monumental western entrance, 289; Athenian financial reserves, 289

Actaean cities, 325², 533

Aegae, 526, 528

Aegina, not an original member of the Delian League, 51; war with Athens, 96, 97, 104; subject ally of Athens, 98; concession in Thirty Years Peace, 182–4, 202; Pindar's sympathy, 183, 274; cult of Athena, 296 f.; resumption of coinage, 184; *eikostologos* from, 369; sculptor Onatas, 274; coinage standard, 239, used by Euboean League, 367

Aegospotami, 374

Aenea, 532

Aenus, 61; tribute, 249, 526, 529

Aeolian, 23, 413 f.

Aeschylus, *Persae*, 39, 143; 273

Agis, 353, 354, 365

Agora, Athenian, 96, 277; at Piraeus, 278

Alcibiades (elder), 87, 166, ?567

Alcibiades (younger), disturbs Peace of Nicias, 343; anti-Spartan policy based on Argive alliance, 319, 343 f., 382; Sicilian expedition, 347; advice to Sparta, 354, 359; urges support for Chian revolt, 354; relations with Tissaphernes, 354 f.; feud with demagogues, 373; operations in Hellespont, 368, 371, 372; collects money from Ceramic Gulf, 254; discarded by Athens, 373; and Hegemon of Thasos, 280

Alcidas, 314

Alcimus, 564

Aleuadae, 49

Alexander, Macedonian king, 88, 215

Alopeconnesus, 526, 528

Amathus, 28, 480, 481

Ambracia, 204

Amestris, 436 f.

Amisus, 198

Ammon, 126, 419

Amorges, 134, 349, 494

Amorgos, 250, 251, 353

Amphictyonic League, oath, 505; alliance with Athens, 175, 418 f.

Amphipolis, ?Athenians defeated in 475, 68 f., in 464, 84 f.; Athenian colony, 195; referred to by Antiphon, 241; revenues to Athens, 258; captured by Brasidas, 335 f.; Cleon's failure to recover, 338

Amyrtaeus, 126, 268

Anacreon, 273

Anaea, oligarch refugees at, after Samian revolt, 194; help defeat Athenians in 428, 307; welcome refugees when Mytilene revolts, 348; advise Spartan Alcidas, 314; return to power in Samos, 358

Anaxagoras, relations with Pericles, 283; prosecuted, 304; chronology, 435 f.

Anaxicrates, 127

Anaxilas, 274

Andocides (general), 17, 182

Andocides (orator), 134, 343, 349, 486

Androcles, 317, 373

Andros, Themistocles' exactions, 415; ?an original member of the alliance, 50; cleruchy, 121, 530; ?influence on colonies, 335, 525; tribute, 110¹, 242, 525, 526; troops for Athens, 332, 347; 51, 335, 415

Antagoras, 42

Antalcidas, peace of, 490

Antandrus, taken by Athens from Mytilene in 427, 316; Myt. exiles attempt to seize, 261, 332; helps

NOTE TO MAPS 1 I–VI

These maps are based on the map in *The Athenian Tribute Lists*, which the authors have generously allowed me to use.

A key map (1) shows the division of the empire into districts and separate maps for each district follow (II–VI). The mainland cities (Ἀκταῖαι πόλεις) which were taken by Athens from Mytilene when her revolt was crushed in 427, and which are listed in an appendix in the assessment of 425, are included in the Hellespontine district to which they geographically belong, but the Euxine cities are treated as a separate district. Certain anomalies can be appreciated only in the key map. Lemnos and Imbros, though very much closer to the Hellespontine cities, are included in the Island district. The small island of Anaphe is appropriately listed in the Island district in the assessment list of 425 and the quota list of 417 (for the date see pp. 341 f.), but in 427, her first known appearance, she is included in the Carian district. The island of Nisyros, which is surrounded by Carian cities, is normally in the Ionic district, but is included in the Island district in the assessment of 430.

The tribute tables include only the cities which are known to have paid tribute before the Peloponnesian War. In the district maps the few cities whose first payments are recorded after the outbreak of the war are added. Those whose names are first preserved in the assessment list of 425, though they will not all have actually paid tribute, are italicized.

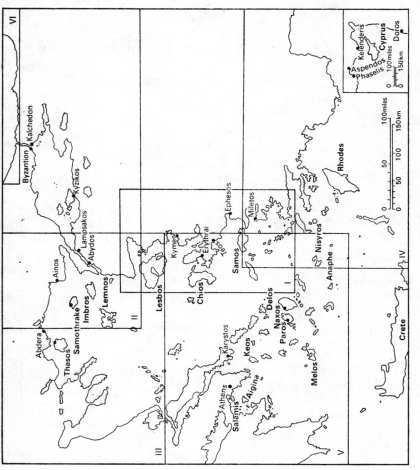

MAP I. THE TRIBUTE DISTRICTS OF THE ATHENIAN EMPIRE

(Key map)

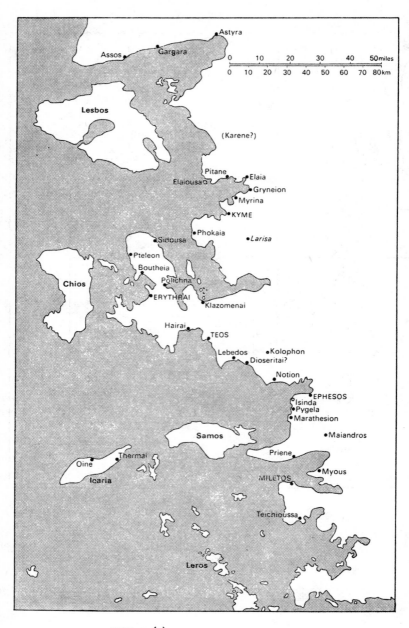

MAP I (I). THE IONIAN DISTRICT

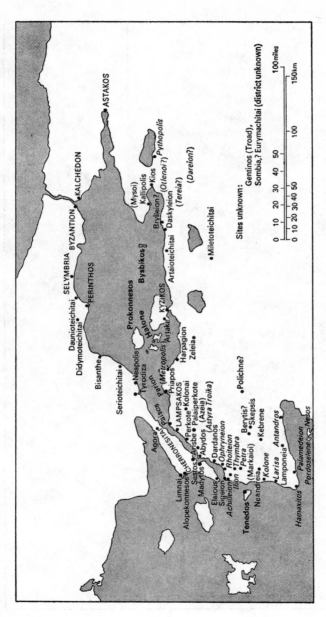

MAP I (II). THE HELLESPONTINE DISTRICT

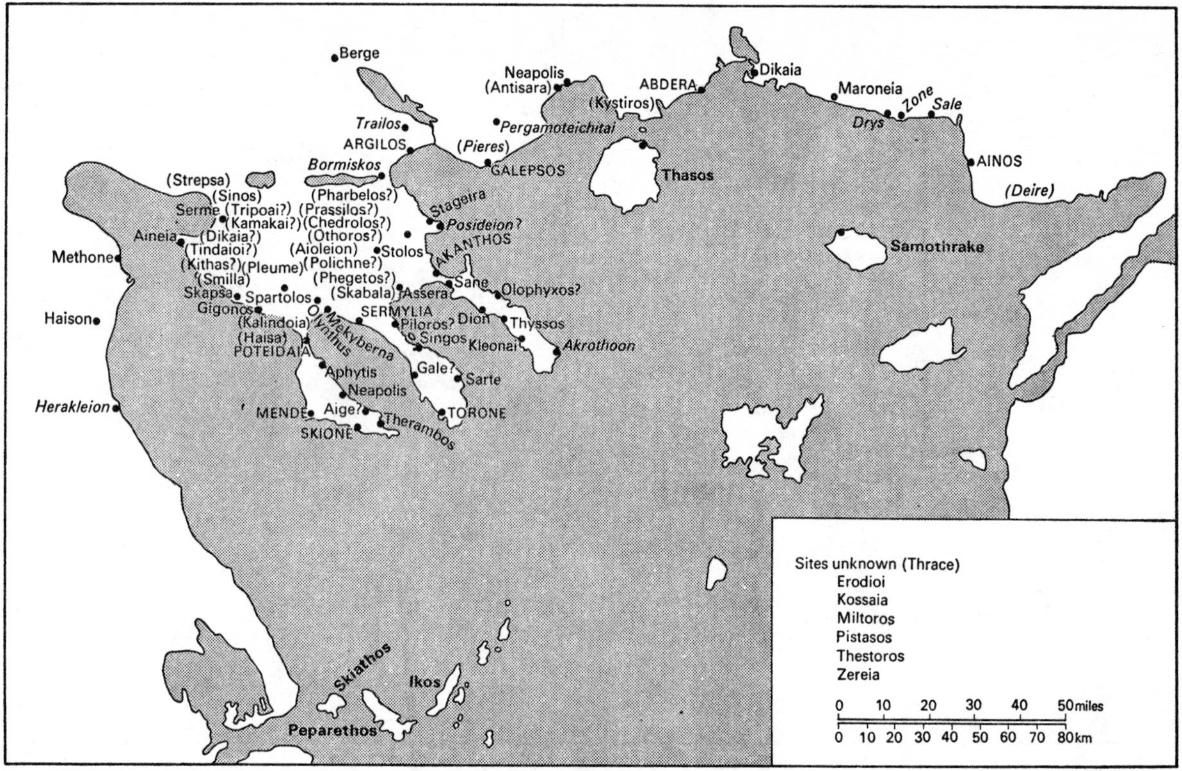

MAP I (III). THE THRACEWARD DISTRICT

Sites unknown (Thrace)
Erodioi
Kossaia
Miltoros
Pistasos
Thestoros
Zereia

0 10 20 30 40 50 miles
0 10 20 30 40 50 60 70 80 km

(Deire)

AINOS

Sale

Zone

Drys

Maroneia

Samothrake

Dikaia

ABDERA

(Kystiros)

Thasos

Neapolis
(Antisara)

(Pergamoteichitai)

(Pieres)

GALEPSOS

Berge

Trailos?

ARGILOS

Bormiskos

Stageira

Posideion?

AKANTHOS

Sane Olophyxos?

Dion Thyssos

Akrothoon

(Pharbelos?)

(Prassilos?)

(Chedrolos?)

(Othoros?)

Stolos

Piloros?

Singos Kleonai

SERMYLIA

Sarte

Gale

(Strepsa)

Serme (Tripoai?)

(Sinos)

(Dikaia?)

(Tindaioi?)

(Karnakai?)

(Ajoleion)

(Polichne?)

(Phegetos?)

(Skabala) Assera

TORONE

Aineia

(Kithas?) (Pleume)

(Smilla)

Skapsa Spartolos

Skabala

Makyberna

Aphytis

Neapolis

Aige? Therambos

Gigonos

(Kalindoia) Olynthus

(Haisa)

POTEIDAIA

MENDE

SKIONE

Methone

Haison

Herakleion

Ikos

Skiathos

Peparethos

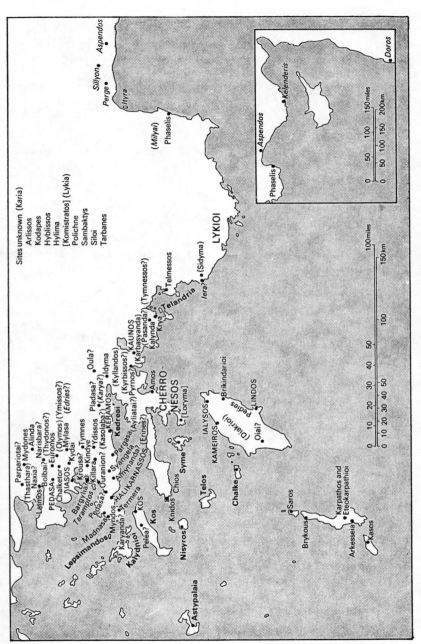

MAP I (IV). THE KARIAN DISTRICT

Sites unknown (Karia)
Arlissos
Kodapes
Hyblissos
Hylima
[Komistratos] (Lykia)
Polichne
Sambaktys
Siloi
Tarbanes

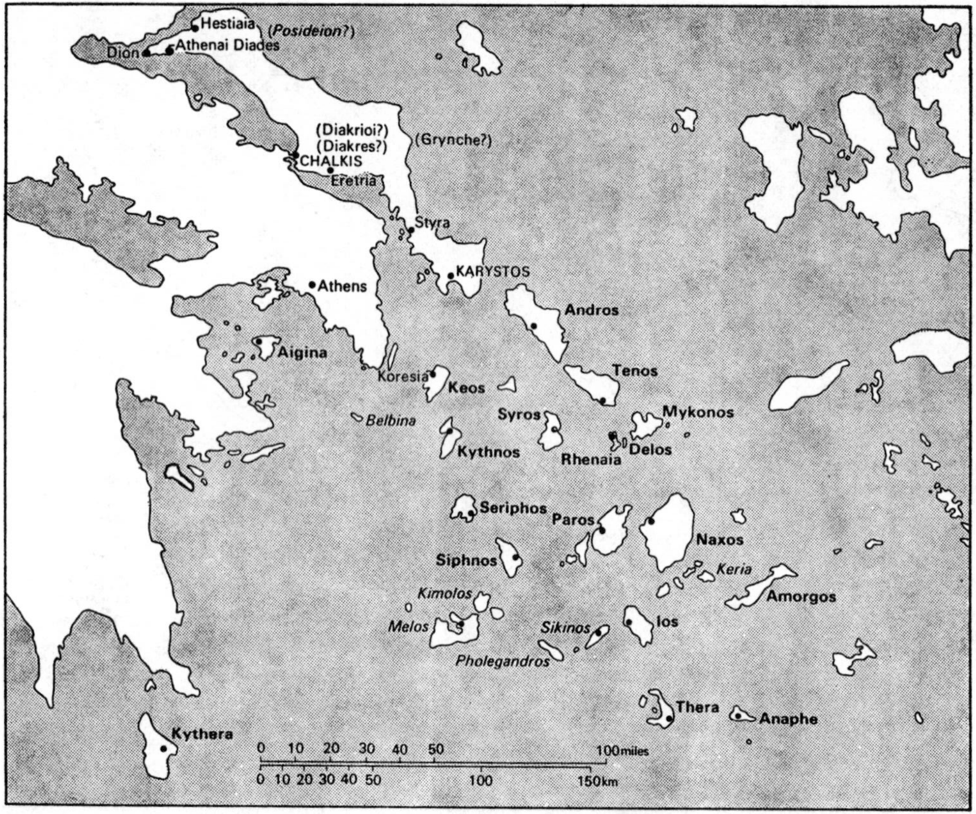

MAP I (v). THE ISLAND DISTRICT

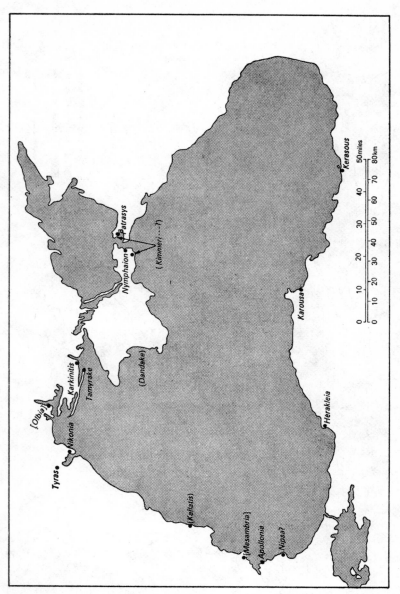

MAP I (VI). THE EUXINE DISTRICT

Kerasous

50 miles
80 km

Karousa

Herakleia

Patrasys

Nymphaion

(Kimneri---?)

(Dandake)

Karkinitis

Tamyrake

[Olbia]

Nikonia

Tyras

[Kallatis]

[Mesambria]

Apollonia

Nipsa?

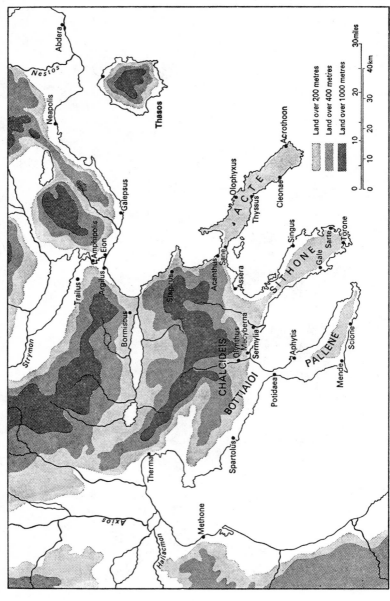

MAP 2. CHALCIDICE AND THE NORTH-EAST

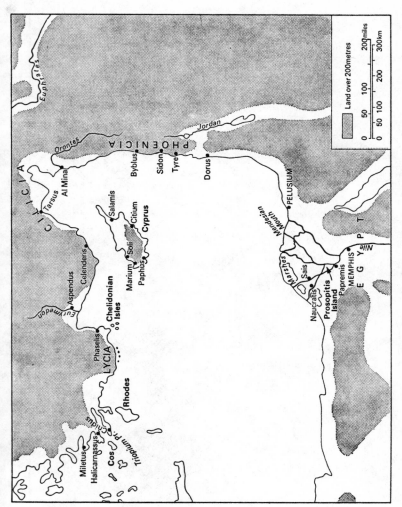

MAP 3. THE EASTERN MEDITERRANEAN

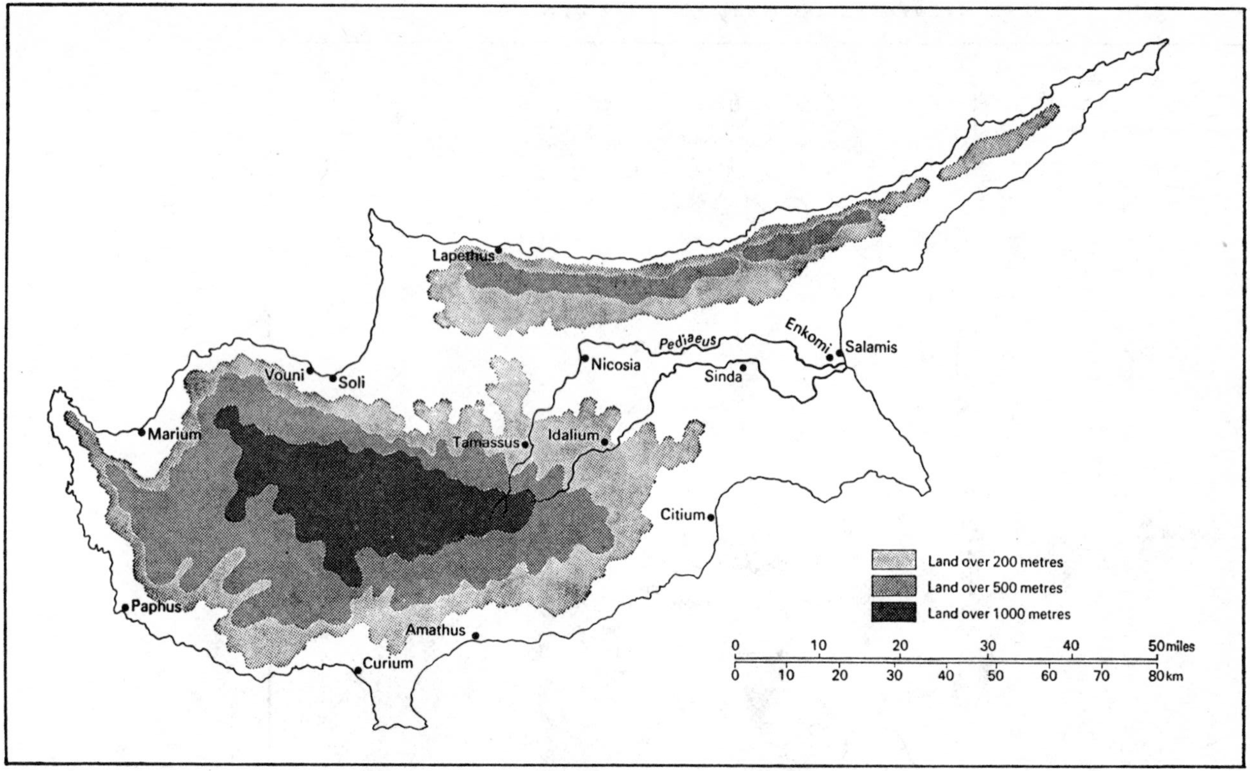
Lapethus
Pediaeus
Enkomi
Salamis
Nicosia
Sinda
Vouni
Soli
Marium
Tamassus
Idalium
Citium
Paphus
Amathus
Curium
Land over 200 metres
Land over 500 metres
Land over 1000 metres
0 10 20 30 40 50 miles
0 10 20 30 40 50 60 70 80 km

MAP 4. CYPRUS